IMPLICIT AND EXPLICIT MENTAL PROCESSES

IMPLICIT AND EXPLICIT MENTAL PROCESSES

Edited by

Kim Kirsner
University of Western Australia

Craig Speelman
Edith Cowan University

Murray Maybery
University of Western Australia

Angela O'Brien-Malone
Murdoch University

Mike Anderson
Colin MacLeod
University of Western Australia

LEA LAWRENCE ERLBAUM ASSOCIATES, PUBLISHERS
1998   Mahwah, New Jersey   London

Lawrence Erlbaum Associates, Inc., Publishers
10 Industrial Avenue
Mahwah, New Jersey 07430

Cover design by Kathryn Houghtaling Lacey

Library of Congress Cataloging-in-Publication-Data

        Implicit and explicit mental processes / edited by Kim Kirsner
    . . . [et al.].
            p. cm.
        Includes bibliographical references and indexes.
        ISBN 0-8058-1359-4 (cloth : alk. paper)
        1. Cognition. 2. Intellect. 3. Human information processing.
    I. Kirsner, Kim.
        BF311.I45   1998
        153—dc 21   97-7356
                                                             CIP

Books published by Lawrence Erlbaum Associates are printed on
acid-free paper, and their bindings are chosen for strength and dura-
bility.

Printed in the United States of America
10   9   8   7   6   5   4   3   2   1

CONTENTS

Part III   Application

Part IV   Synthesis

LIST OF CONTRIBUTORS

Mike Anderson • *University of Western Australia*
James W. Chapman • *Massey University*
John Dunn • *University of Western Australia*
Kevin Durkin • *University of Western Australia*
Melissa Finucane • *University of Western Australia*
Janet Fletcher • *University of Western Australia*
Timothy Griffin • *The University of Sydney*
Kathryn Hird • *Curtin University of Technology*
Kim Kirsner • *University of Western Australia*
Peter Lee • *Murdoch University*
Stephan Lewandowsky • *University of Western Australia*
Colin MacLeod • *University of Western Australia*
Murray Maybery • *University of Western Australia*
Dan Milech • *University of Western Australia*
David L. Morrison • *University of Western Australia*
Drew Nesdale • *Griffith University*
Angela O'Brien-Malone • *Murdoch University*
Clare Roberts • *Curtin University of Technology*
Paul Roberts • *Murdoch University*
Elizabeth M. Rutherford • *University of Western Australia*
Steven Schwartz • *Murdoch University*
Katherine Sofronoff • *University of Queensland*
Craig Speelman • *Edith Cowan University*
William E. Tunmer • *Massey University*
C. D. L. Wynne • *University of Western Australia*

I

INTRODUCTION

1

INTRODUCTION
AND OVERVIEW

Kim Kirsner
University of Western Australia

Craig Speelman
Edith Cowan University

The motivation behind this book was the need for synthesis in the domain of implicit processes. The main questions that sparked the development of this book are as follows: Is there one implicit process or processing principle, or are there many such principles and processes? Are implicit memory, implicit learning, implicit expertise, skill acquisition, and automatic detection simply different facets of one general principle or process, or are they distinct processes performing very different functions? This book has been designed to cast light on this issue.

Because it is impossible to make sense of implicit processes without taking into account their explicit counterparts, consideration also is given to explicit memory, explicit learning, explicit expertise, and controlled processing.

This book is concerned with synthesis. The chapter authors were encouraged to consider principles, processes, and models that stand above a wealth of data collected to evaluate models designed specifically to account for data from a specific paradigm, or even more narrowly, from a specific experimental task (e.g., for lexical decision, fragment completion, and naming in the repetition-priming paradigm). The motivation behind this approach is the proposition that modeling is possible for a much broader data domain, even though there may be some cost where specific tasks are concerned.

By implication, it is our contention that the discipline of psychological science, and cognitive psychology in particular, has been dominated by analysis at the expense of synthesis. Where implicit memory is concerned, for example, this move

3

has produced clear dissociations from explicit memory, but little consideration of the possibility that implicit memory data may reflect the same principle or even the same process as data from the skill acquisition and implicit learning paradigms, and that it could be merged at some abstract information-processing level with other implicit processes. John Anderson's (1982, 1983, 1987, 1993) ACT* model of skill acquisition, for instance, can be generalized to account for many implicit memory effects as well as practice effects (Kirsner & Speelman, 1996).

This first chapter has been designed to provide a foretaste of the breadth of the book. In it we document a series of short sketches, each of which has been included to illustrate some point about implicit processes, or the contrast between explicit and implicit processes. The underlying point that this chapter has been designed to communicate is that implicit processes are not a mere artifact of laboratory research in experimental psychology, but a general property of mind, a universal cognitive feature. The aim of the introduction is to provide an idea of the number and diversity of phenomena that are touched by the contrast between implicit and explicit processes. The chapter is not exhaustive, but it touches nearly every part of the discipline.

SPONTANEOUS TRANSLATION

Consider the case of a 55-year-old patient, B.B. (K. Hird, personal communication, June, 1996). B.B. and his wife were Polish and fluent in that language as well as three others, English, French, and German. B.B. had a deep stroke involving arterial distribution to the left cerebral hemisphere and subcortical regions. The stroke had different effects on his comprehension and production skills. His comprehension of spoken English was unimpaired by the stroke, but his production was severely impaired, and it reflected both word-finding and grammatical difficulties. When asked questions in English, for example, he gave part of his answer in English but occasional words and even phrases were in French, even when he was asked to restrict his responses to English. When asked why he was using French, he denied that he had used French. But, more important for the current argument, when he was specifically asked to translate words and sentences into French, he was unable to do so. Thus, in B.B. we were able to observe spontaneous translation, from English to French, and the inability to translate from English to French under conscious control. B.B. was able to understand instructions given in English directing him to perform specific tasks, including the selective use of English and French, and he could perform many language comprehension tasks. However, when some tasks required an answer in English, he provided part of his answer in French, without awareness and in the absence of any instructions or intention to that effect. Thus, voluntary translation from English to French was impaired by his injury, but involuntary translation from French to English was at least partially intact. Here, then, is a person who has lost control over voluntary translation although his discourse demonstrates that he has retained residual translation skills.

AMNESIA AND MEMORY

B.B. provides an interesting parallel to studies of amnesic patients with Korsakoff's syndrome. When faced with a direct request to recall information about a specific event, Korsakoff patients are usually unable to recall information about that event. That is, they have a failure of "explicit memory." But when they are invited to perform tasks the performance of which will be facilitated by an event, it is evident that the event has influenced performance in some way, for their response is faster or more accurate because of it. That is, their "implicit memory" is intact (see in this volume Dunn, chap. 6; Kirsner, chap. 2). The case of B.B. is slightly different, however. Although he could not translate on request, the underlying ability to translate between languages has been spared to some extent. The difference is that the demonstration of implicit memory and explicit memory requires qualitatively different responses, involving the use of information on the one hand, and knowledge about the original event on the other. The demonstration of spontaneous translation (Perecman, 1984) involves essentially the same response under explicit and implicit conditions, and the only distinction concerns the success or failure of the process that provokes that response. The task can be accomplished under routine or automatic language production conditions, but it fails under deliberate or willful conditions.

Another example of implicit processes involves the Tower of Hanoi (N.J. Cohen, Eichenbaum, Deacedo, & Corkin, 1985). The players in this game are given three small towers or poles, one of which has a set of rings of increasing size placed on it before the start of the game. The task for each player is to move all of the rings from the first tower to the third tower, using all three towers, and ending up with the rings in the same order, but without ever placing a big ring on a small ring. The game can be completed by an expert in a given number of steps, but beginners start with many more steps and gradually approach the optimum sequence used by the expert.

People suffering from amnesia behave in an interesting way when they are invited to play this game. They appear to learn the game just as quickly as people who are not suffering from amnesia. They not only behave as if they understand the rules, but also improve from session to session so that their performance pattern approaches and eventually attains the expert level, when they can complete the task in the smallest possible number of moves. But despite the appearance of normality, when they approach the task each day they talk as if it is a new task that they have not seen before. In other words, by the standards of verbal report they have learned nothing, even when their performance indicates that they are experts. This task falls between implicit memory and implicit learning. Amnesic patients cannot describe their experience with the task, and they cannot identify the features or rules that they used to solve the problem, indicants that are consistent with both implicit learning and implicit memory.

In some respects, then, B.B. and other cases of patients involving a dissociation between conscious and spontaneous translation provide a cleaner example of the distinction between explicit and implicit processes. Where memory is concerned, explicit and implicit retrieval conditions involve distinct tasks and therefore responses. But where translation is concerned the tasks and responses are identical, and the only difference involves the mechanism that triggers or provokes the translation process. The contrast between B.B. and a typical Korsakoff patient provides a useful starting point for this book because it identifies two situations for which the label implicit is appropriate, while hinting at the variety of phenomena that may be included under this umbrella. This book is rich in such contrasts.

CONTRASTS

Another obvious example of the variety of phenomena that have been labeled *implicit* involves the distinction between implicit learning and implicit memory. We already have provided an illustration of the contrast between explicit and implicit memory, involving amnesia. Implicit learning, however, is used to describe a situation where people gradually master new and complex perceptual or conceptual problems despite the fact that they cannot identify the feature or principle on which their new expertise is based (see in this volume O'Brien-Malone & Maybery, chap. 3; Roberts, chap. 7). Implicit learning appears to be different in several other ways from explicit learning. Not only does it occur without conscious awareness, but it is also indifferent to limitations in information-processing capacity and other variables. The contrast between explicit and implicit learning is used, therefore, to refer to the extent to that the student is aware of the stimulus features or qualities that he or she is using to master a particular problem.

Another and closely related contrast is that between implicit learning and the concept of implicit expertise. Whereas the notion of implicit learning is concerned with the extent to which a subject is ever aware of critical stimulus features (O'Brien-Malone & Maybery, chap. 3 of this volume), skilled performance or "implicit expertise" often involves a completely different transformation. As Speelman (chap. 8 of this volume) describes, implicit expertise refers to the situation where people are fully aware of the basis of their expertise during the early stages of skill acquisition, but as fluent performance is approached they become less and less aware of this information until, finally, as a polished performer, they have lost contact with the basis of their expertise entirely. In implicit learning, then, the subject is never aware of the basis of their skill. In expert performance, however, it is often assumed that people start out with a clear idea of the problem, but that, with practice, they may lose contact with the basis of their expertise (see also Speelman & Maybery, chap. 5 of this volume).

The proposition that implicit and explicit processes involve qualitatively differ-ent processes also has shaped much recent memory research. Evidence that amnesia reduces performance on explicit tasks such as recall and recognition memory without impairing performance on implicit memory tasks has been used to support inferences about the structure of memory including, for example, the hypothesis that performance on implicit and explicit memory tasks reflects the operation of distinct memory systems. However, an alternative perspective involves the use of processes rather than systems, and rests on the assumption that amnesia reflects damage to a specific type of retrieval process. As Dunn (chap. 6 of this volume) emphasizes, much debate in this area stems from conflict over the notion of a system, where this could be used with reference to either structural or functional criteria.

PERCEPTUAL PROCESSES

A distinction between explicit and implicit processes also has been made at an even earlier stage of processing, involving perceptual analysis (see MacLeod, chap. 4 of this volume). An experiment described by Marcel (1983a) suggests that semantic information can be extracted from words during brief presentation under conditions where the identity of the word is not known. In one study, he found that response times to test words were influenced by the meaning of a priming word that immediately preceded it, despite the fact that the prime word itself was not recognized. The experimental sequence involved presentation of three stimuli in rapid succession, a prime, a mask (which prevented identification of the prime), and a test word for lexical decision or naming. The implication of this finding is that semantic information about a word may be available, automatically, in the absence of conscious awareness. Thus, the semantic content of a word may become available before the viewer can identify the word, and before conscious processes are involved. A similar observation has been made with respect to processes involved with discourse comprehension (see Speelman, chap. 11 of this volume). The underlying assumption from these observations is that implicit or automatic processes activate all of the representations that might be relevant, after which explicit or conscious processes shape selection of the critical representation.

LEARNING

Whereas explicit and implicit memory concern different ways in which information is retrieved, the terms explicit learning and implicit learning are used to distinguish two ways in which new information is acquired. Explicit learning is used to refer to learning that occurs when people invoke active strategies to discover the rules or principles that underlie some task. Implicit learning, on the other hand, is used to refer to knowledge acquisition that occurs without a deliberate attempt to learn. These learning modes may be distinguished in several ways. Implicit learning, for example, operates outside consciousness, without intent, and with indifference to task demands or work load. Explicit learning, by comparison, depends on intent and conscious processing, and it is assumed to be sensitive to work load. The contrast also involves questions about cognitive development (see Maybery & O'Brien-Malone, chap. 9 of this volume) and neurological insult, the assumption being that implicit learning is relatively indifferent to each of these variables. Maybery and O'Brien-Malone give detailed consideration to the proposition that implicit processes are age-invariant. Their review indicates that there is widespread support for this assumption, in regard to implicit memory, implicit learning, and the application and use of automatic processes. According to O'Brien-Malone and Maybery (chap. 3 of this volume), however, there is no compelling evidence for the conclusion that implicit learning occurs outside of consciousness.

EVOLUTIONARY COGNITION

The proposition that implicit processes are age-invariant has an interesting parallel in evolutionary cognition. Are explicit processes restricted to humans, for example, or, given sufficient care over definitional issues, can explicit learning and memory processes be observed in nonhumans? Wynne (chap. 15 of this volume) demonstrates that, when explicit memory and learning are defined in ways that enable nonhumans to be considered, explicit processes can be inferred from their behavior. According to Wynne, therefore, questions about the relative position of implicit and explicit processes in cognitive evolution must remain open.

Another issue with evolutionary undertones concerns the possible contribution of individual differences to intelligence. According to Anderson (chap. 10 of this volume), traditional psychometric theories of intelligence generally are predicated on the assumption that intelligence is dominated by explicit knowledge and deliberate problem-solving strategies. According to Anderson, intelligence is not synonymous with knowledge, although it is dominated directly or indirectly by higher order strategies. However, Anderson concedes that it is the capability of being conscious that is crucial rather than the role of consciousness or awareness at a particular point in time. Thus, according to this point of view, evidence that a particular component process operates with or without awareness may not be the issue. The central issue concerns the extent to which that process is open to conscious control. Fletcher and Roberts (chap. 20 of this volume) evaluate this view with respect to intellectual disabilities. They explore the possibility that, although intellectual disabilities may be associated with a lack of conscious control in some forms of mental processing, implicit learning could be utilized to build up a repertoire of useful behaviors.

COMMUNICATION

Recent interest in the relationship between explicit and implicit processes has neglected communication to some extent, although this ultimately may provide one of the richest arenas for this issue. The study of reading processes has been an exception, however. Tunmer and Chapman (chap. 21 of this volume), for example, compare two views about the acquisition of reading, one of which focuses on implicit processes throughout skill acquisition, the other of which advocates a two-stage process in which implicit processes are eventually replaced by explicit processes. Speelman (chap. 11 of this volume) is more directly concerned with comprehension skills in the skilled reader. According to Speelman, comprehension is dominated by automatic processes, where these account for our limited awareness of the component processes involved in this skill, and for the importance of data-driven processes. Speelman includes provision for the roles of context and strategic control, however, and the question therefore involves the conditions under which automatic processes provide a sufficient explanation of performance.

The chapter by Hird and Kirsner (chap. 12 of this volume) is concerned with *prosody,* the term used to refer to the suprasegmental aspects of verbal communication. According to Hird and Kirsner, the control of prosody usually involves a mixture of controlled processes driven by communicative intent and "lower" or automatic processes, recruited by specific communicative intentions. Hird and Kirsner acknowledge, however, that the control of prosody may fluctuate from moment to moment as attention is dominated by the propositional as distinct from the pragmatic aspects of communication. Thus, when a propositional challenge is encountered, prosodic control may be restricted to implicit mechanisms, for reception and production. But, when the propositional challenge is reduced, for whatever reason, conscious control may be achieved. Another factor concerns the way in which conscious control processes influence prosody. This could involve direct processes, but the authors favor an alternative approach that emphasizes the role of perceptual targets rather than the detailed control of complex production mechanisms.

The role of prosody in the conveyance of emotions in speech can be illustrated with respect to two famous orators. Although few people would deny that Adolph Hitler exerted what is often referred to as "magnetic control" over his audiences at the Nuremberg rallies and elsewhere, this control usually is explained in generalities that focus on the content of the message rather than the quality with which it was delivered. However, almost any non-German speaker can, when exposed to a tape of his speeches at Nuremberg, appreciate the extraordinary changes in pitch, intensity, and rate that mark the transition from the quiet, intimate tones of his opening remarks to the raw, emotive, almost hysterical outbursts that mark the climax of his delivery.

How were the prosodic changes just described monitored and controlled by Hitler? Were they a simple and indirect product of his attitudes and moods, generated more or less spontaneously without conscious control, or were they the product of extensive practice in oration, used by a person exercising professional care over the acoustic properties that define prosody. And, how were these prosodic changes "read" by Hitler's audience? Did they appreciate and acknowledge the deliberate control of the professional orator, using skills derived from an honorable discipline extending over more than two millennia, or did they respond unconsciously, with feeling and excitement, but without awareness of the oratorical expertise that Hitler was, perhaps arguably, practicing on them?

For a recent and more light-hearted illustration, consider the changing perception of Margaret Thatcher that followed publication of the practice tapes, in which she repeatedly uttered, "enough ... is enough, enough ... is enough, ENOUGH ... IS ENOUGH, **ENOUGH ... IS ENOUGH**," while she mastered the intricacies of control over pitch, intensity, and rate. Would Hitler's audience have reacted differently if they had seen and heard him practicing his prosody before the rally?

The point of this cameo from the history of oratory concerns the production and comprehension of prosody. There are several issues here. First, do speaker decisions about the use of prosody depend on deliberate, conscious, explicit retrieval, or do they depend on automatic, unconscious, implicit retrieval processes? Second, do the decisions themselves involve conscious deliberation about the use of emphasis in, for example, discourse, or are these decisions made automatically? The third issue concerns the nature of prosody, a process that involves changes in perhaps the most implicit or indirect measures of all, that is, in the pitch, amplitude, and duration of spoken language. Similar issues, of course, can be considered with reception: Is it based on automatic, unconscious processes, or does it depend on deliberate and conscious effort on the part of the listener?

EXPERTISE

Questions about implicit and explicit expertise fall on the boundary between learning and memory. One question of general interest to scientists working on all of these topics concerns the extent to which information acquired in one form—under explicit learning conditions for example—can be redescribed and used in other forms, involving implicit tasks for example. One characteristic that is sometimes attributed to experts is that they do not actually understand the basis of their expertise; they can do it, but they cannot say how they do it. This problem can be interpreted in more sympathetic and general terms, however. According to Speelman (chap. 8 of this volume), the inability of experts to describe their expertise stems from the fact that expertise is mode-specific. Thus, just as a bilingual who is fluent in, say, English and French may find that this expertise confers no benefits when they are faced with a comprehension problem involving Chinese, a person who is an expert at cheese tasting may not be able to describe their expertise.

Rumor has it that a leading French cheese producer recently spent millions of francs on development of an expert system to determine the ripeness of Camembert.

The company used the latest knowledge elicitation techniques to identify the type of information being used by the experts. From the experts' responses, they concluded that the critical procedure occurred when the experts squeezed the cheese, and that the crucial variable involved the tension of the surface of the cheese or, possibly, the pressure required to compress the cheese. They subsequently developed automatic procedures for measuring the surface tension of cheese. Their system failed completely, however; the classifications that it made were consistently different from those of the experts. According to the tale, subsequent research demonstrated that the experts actually were using olfactory cues, not surface tension, and that the olfactory information was released when the experts pinched the cheese just enough to break the skin.

The point of this yarn is that it illustrates the distinction between implicit and explicit expertise, another example from the family of contrasts involving implicit and explicit processes. The experts were able to access explicit knowledge about their expertise, and provide verbal reports based on that knowledge. However, the explicit knowledge that they accessed provided false information about the process, despite the fact that they were experts at the task itself. The information that the experts actually were using must have been stored in some form, but it was not "open" to review, despite that, or perhaps because, they had been using the information for years. This type of knowledge often is described as procedural, and contrasted with declarative. But it provides a clear illustration of the contrast between implicit and explicit processes. The obvious nexus between intelligence and knowledge on the one hand, and knowledge and expertise on the other, has produced a predictable focus on knowledge rather than skill in education and training. Perhaps society places a higher value on knowledge than skill, as if it takes more intelligence to acquire knowledge than skill.

Three chapters in this book are concerned with the possible role of implicit processes in skill. Griffin, Schwartz, and Sofronoff (chap. 19) set the scene, claiming that complex procedures used in medical diagnosis are subject to both explicit and implicit processes. Morrison, Lee, and Lawton (chap. 18) consider the distinction between routine and novel operational problems in industrial process control. They claim that conscious processes can impair performance when they are used under routine conditions and, similarly, that automatic processes will impair performance if they are invoked under novel conditions. Milech and Finucane (chap. 17) consider the problems associated with the impact of both individual and normative bias on decision making, and advocate the use of formal models in instruction to enable operators to overcome these difficulties.

SOCIAL, CULTURAL, AND PERSONALITY ISSUES

Other studies suggest that implicit and explicit perceptual processes are differentially sensitive to different types of personality characteristics or disorders. According to MacLeod and Rutherford (chap. 14 of this volume), for example, anxiety has its major impact on automatic or implicit perceptual processes, whereas depression has its impact on explicit processes, subsequent to the influence of conscious or strategic operations. Thus, anxiety acts as a filter, limiting or shaping the type of information that enters consciousness, whereas depression operates through consciousness, controlling the type of information that is selected for more systematic evaluation and reflection.

A growing interest in the role of implicit processes also can be detected in recent research into social and cultural processes. Whereas previous work has focused on the importance of explicit dimensions associated with stereotypes and attitudes, recent research has moved on to less tractable problems associated with implicit bias in stereotypes and attitudes, even at the level of automatic perceptual recognition (Durkin & Nesdale, chap. 13 of this volume).

Questions about the operation of advertising and the mass media have enjoyed a rather different and market-driven history, however (Durkin, chap. 16 of this volume). Whereas the study of cultural and social issues always has been dominated by an explicit or "academic" approach, applied scientists with an interest in advertising and political change have "known" that real change as well as purchasing behavior is subject to more basic or primeval mechanisms.

CONCLUDING REMARKS

Thus far, we have illustrated the distinction between implicit and explicit processing by reference to a broad range of processes or problems. Our initial list includes tasks that involve perception, learning (including its near neighbor, expertise), memory, and translation. This group defines a fundamental family where psychological processes are concerned. How many distinct domains merit consideration in a text of this type? Very few models attempt to encompass all aspects of cognition. The typical approach involves consideration of one domain or even one process, so that models based on restrictions such as this can account for performance on a limited if impressive range of perceptual or memory tasks. But they do not attempt to cover the gamut of behavior. This approach, typical of early stages of scientific enterprise in a domain (Kuhn, 1962), tends to support theoretical division rather than synthesis. It tends to lead to ever finer distinctions even within such narrow areas as perception and memory, where three or four distinct experimental paradigms and theoretical approaches may be identified. The aim of this book is, on the contrary, to treat synthesis as our objective, and to approach this objective by collecting and discussing phenomena that, although they are drawn from diverse areas of psychological science, touch a single issue, concerning the distinction between explicit and implicit processes.

2

IMPLICIT MEMORY

Kim Kirsner
University of Western Australia

Implicit memory is one of the central concepts in this book. Although the term is of recent origin (Graf & Schacter, 1985; Schacter, 1987), the phenomena on which the concept is based have been under consideration from at least the early 1970s, and analogous effects can be detected in earlier paradigms.

This chapter is designed to address three goals. The first of these is introductory. The content of the chapter has been selected so that it can function as an introductory chapter for students and scientists who have not previously come into contact with implicit memory. The chapter, therefore, includes a brief history of repetition priming, that is, of the procedure that gave birth to implicit memory.

The second goal concerns the boundary disputes that have motivated scientists working with repetition priming and implicit memory. The chapter, therefore, includes a brief review of the antecedents of repetition priming in the perception, memory, and skill acquisition traditions, and a review of the distinguishability problems that have engaged cognitive psychologists from each of these and other domains.

The chapter concludes with a preliminary process analysis, illustrating the type of approach that may be required if synthesis is to be achieved in this area. The chapter, therefore, serves as a pointer for the book as a whole. In it, I bring together a number of distinct research traditions, each of which recognized new opportunities in the phenomena and theory associated with repetition priming.

REPETITION PRIMING

The characteristics that have been used to distinguish implicit and explicit processes as distinct from implicit and explicit memory are discussed in a later section. For memory, the main contrast involves the presence or absence of deliberate or conscious recollection (Graf & Schacter, 1985). Where retrieval is based on deliberate or conscious recollection of a specific episode, performance is attributed to explicit memory. But where retrieval does not involve use of these mechanisms, and performance presumably is completed without deliberate, conscious, or willful reference to a specific episode, the evidence of memory is attributed to an implicit process or, more narrowly, implicit memory.

The earliest laboratory demonstrations of implicit memory involved what usually has been referred to as the repetition-priming paradigm. In a typical repetition-priming experiment, subjects are presented with several hundred words in each of two phases. The two phases of the experiment may or may not involve the same task. The lexical decision task often is used in each phase. In the lexical decision task, subjects are presented with letter strings that may or may not constitute genuine English words. The letter strings are presented one by one. The subject's task is to classify each letter string as GENUINE or FALSE, with reference to his or her knowledge of English. Reaction time (RT) is measured for each lexical decision. The critical feature of the experimental design is that the stimuli presented in the second phase are drawn from two sets. The first set consists of NEW stimuli, that is, words and nonwords being presented for the first time in the experiment. The second set consists of OLD stimuli, that is, words and nonwords that actually were presented during the first phase of the experiment.

The critical comparison involves the NEW and OLD word sets. The term *repetition priming* is used to refer to the advantage that almost invariably is observed for the OLD set of words relative to the NEW set of words. The magnitude of this advantage is sensitive to a number of variables; a difference of one hundred milliseconds might be observed for low-frequency words, for example (i.e., words with frequency of occurrence values in natural language of 1 per million), however the difference might be as small as five or ten milliseconds for high-frequency words (i.e., words with frequency values of 100 per million or more). It should be emphasized that subjects typically are given instructions for the lexical decision task prior to each phase of the experiment. It is also possible to implement the experiment as if it involves just one phase. Under these conditions the transition from Phase 1 to Phase 2 is seamless, and the only change involves the introduction of OLD items, and the subjects may or may not be aware of the transition.

In summary, repetition priming refers to the performance advantage enjoyed by OLD words when they are repeated during an experiment. The effect is observed after a single exposure to each word, and, unlike traditional, explicit memory procedures, subjects are not instructed to refer to or use information from the first or study phase of the experiment.

Although the lexical decision task is probably the most popular procedure where repetition priming is concerned, the phenomenon can be observed with virtually any task where speed or accuracy can be measured. Naming, or "confrontation naming" as it is sometimes referred to in clinical contexts, is an even simpler example. The nonwords are omitted. The subjects or patients are presented with a series of words one by one, and instructed to name each word as rapidly as possible. Naming latency—the time from word onset to the beginning of the naming response—is measured, and repetition priming is the difference between naming latency for the OLD and NEW words, a difference that tends to be smaller than that observed for lexical decision.

The effects obtained with the lexical decision and naming generalize to virtually all tasks that involve the identification, recognition, or classification of printed or spoken words or objects. The feature that all of these tasks share is that reference is not made to the initial priming or practice episode: The subject is simply required to name or classify the test stimulus in some way, a task that can be accomplished without reference to the priming episode. For example, qualitatively comparable findings are obtained when the test task involves (a) stimulus identification under degraded viewing or listening conditions (e.g., Murrell & J. Morton, 1974), (b) presentation of letter fragments such as F-AG-E-T for FRAGMENT for stimulus identification (e.g., Tulving, Schacter, & Stark, 1982), and (c) presentation of word stems such as COM— for stimulus identification, as for COMPLETION.

The repetition-priming effect also generalizes to other types of stimuli. For example, repetition-priming effects have been found for pictorial material under (a) threshold exposure conditions (e.g., J. Morton, 1979), (b) picture fragment conditions (Snodgrass, 1989), and (c) normal viewing conditions on an object reality task involving both real and impossible objects (Schacter, L.A. Cooper, Delaney, M.A. Peterson, & Thiran, 1991). Repetition-priming effects also have been observed for larger units of discourse or text. MacKay (1982) and B.A. Levy and Kirsner (1989), for example, found such effects for sentences and 500-word passages of text, respectively.

THE ORIGINS OF REPETITION PRIMING

Thus far, I have described the early repetition-priming studies as if they emerged without precedent from the larger body of cognitive psychology. This is not the case, of course, and questions about domain membership have pervaded much of the subsequent dialogue about repetition priming. Although an understanding of this background may be useful for general purposes, it is particularly important in the present context because it implies that the phenomena and theory of repetition priming were of interest to scientists working in disparate areas of psychological science, the central theme of this book.

Word Recognition

The repetition-priming paradigm and its associated effect have emerged from several research traditions. The first of these involved perception and, more specifically, models of word recognition (e.g., D. Morton & D.E. Broadbent, 1967;

J. Morton, 1979). For scientists working in this area, the effect was explained by reference to models that had been developed to account for word frequency and word bias effects under degraded viewing conditions. These models adopted the language and principles of signal detection theory. Word recognition involved reference to recognition units. Priming reflected changes in sensitivity measures (i.e., d^1) or response criteria (i.e., β). J. Morton (1980), for example, attributed word frequency differences to criteria differences between low- and high-frequency words. However he adopted a more cautious position where repetition-priming or "facilitation" effects are concerned (e.g., Clarke & J. Morton, 1983).

Although Morton's contribution to this area antedated work on amnesia and implicit memory, it may be noted that he specifically excluded meaning from the logogen or word recognition system, and that he argued that consciousness applied only to the products of the logogen system, not the word recognition stage as such (e.g., J. Morton & Patterson, 1980). In one of Morton's later contributions to this area he partitioned repetition-priming effects to allow for both "perceptual" and "episodic" effects (Clarke & J. Morton, 1983). Thus, faced with evidence of cross-modality facilitation, from speech-to-print, rather than compromise the proposition that the logogen system involved abstract representations, he chose to classify the cross-modal repetition priming effects as episodic, as if they belonged to another domain. Thus, according to Morton's last word on the topic, intramodal facilitation involved reference to the logogen system, a system that reflected the operation of word recognition units that behaved like feature detection devices, whereas cross-modal facilitation involved reference to a more traditional, episodic memory system, based on qualitatively different principles. This theme, that two performance components of repetition priming involve a "real" perceptual effect and an artifact of more conscious, deliberate memory for episodes, respectively, runs through much subsequent research and debate.

Repetition-priming effects are relatively, if not absolutely, insensitive to variation in the interval between the priming and test events. For example, Kirsner and M.C. Smith (1974), using a procedure that involved stimulus repetition at selected intervals in a sequence of several hundred words, found only a small reduction in the magnitude of repetition priming beyond that obtained by the presence of a few words between the priming and test trials. D.L. Scarborough, Cortese, and H.S. Scarborough (1977) extended this design, using separate priming and test phases, and found that repetition priming in lexical decision was more or less stable over several hours. Tulving et al. (1982) found that the repetition-priming effect was stable over one week using the fragment completion task.

The first generation of repetition priming studies demonstrated that repetition-priming effects are particularly sensitive to two classes of variables. The first of these involved word frequency, where the magnitude of repetition-priming effects is attenuated for high- relative to low-frequency words under lexical decision conditions (D.L. Scarborough et al., 1977). This effect has been replicated for word identification under degraded viewing conditions (Kirsner, Milech, & Standen, 1983), and for spoken words as well as printed words (Standen, 1988).

The second class of variable that influences the magnitude of repetition priming effects involves changes in stimulus form. Early studies established that changes in lexical form, involving transfer effects in repetition priming from inflections to stems or derivations to stems, for example (e.g., INFLECTION-to-INFLECT), generally reduced the magnitude of priming (Forbach, Stanners & Hochhaus, 1974; Murrell & J. Morton, 1974). Similarly, changes in presentation form from pictures-to-words (Kirsner, Milech, & Stumpfel, 1986; D.L. Scarborough, Gerard, & Cortese, 1979; Winnick & Daniel, 1970), and spoken words-to-printed words (Kirsner et al., 1983; Kirsner & M. Smith, 1974;) generally reduce repetition priming.

In summary, the perceptual tradition was concerned with questions about the temporal and experiential characteristics of representations that supported word recognition, and the possible organization of these representations into modality-specific or modality-independent systems. This generation of research also was concerned with the impact of brain damage on repetition priming, but that interest typically concerned word-finding difficulties and aphasia (e.g., J. Morton & Patterson, 1980) rather than deliberate recollection and amnesia, one of the defining features of research based on amnesia.

Memory: Dissociation

Whereas Morton approached repetition priming from the perspective of perceptual research, Scarborough (D.L. Scarborough et al., 1977), Jacoby (Jacoby & Dallas, 1981), and Tulving (Tulving et al., 1982) approached the phenomenon from a very different point of view. For this group of scientists, the main feature of interest in repetition priming involved the contrasts between the theory and phenomena associated with this paradigm, on the one hand, and more conventional tests of memory on the other. Thus, for all of these authors, the most interesting phenomena involved dissociations between performance on repetition priming and several, more traditional, explicit memory tasks.

Two explicit memory tasks or phenomena merit consideration. They are grouped together because, in each case, the question posed by them can be answered accurately only by reference to specific instances or episodes, that is, by the feature that distinguishes them from implicit memory. The differences between these memory tasks concern the nature of the question posed about the study episode. This can involve reference to the item information (e.g., name the items in the list) or occurrence information (e.g., was APPLE in the list?).

In free recall, for example, subjects typically are asked to provide item information. They are presented with a list of words or other stimuli during a study phase and, then, during a subsequent test phase, they are asked to list the items presented during the study phase. Recognition memory is similar except that subjects are supplied with test items and asked to make occurrence decisions. They are given a mixture of OLD words—words presented during the study phase—and NEW words—words not presented during the study phase—and they are asked to classify each word as OLD or NEW with respect to the study phase. There are, therefore, four possible outcomes, OLD/OLD, an OLD classification for an OLD stimulus; OLD/NEW, an OLD classification for a NEW stimulus; NEW/OLD, a NEW classification for an OLD stimulus; and NEW/NEW, a NEW classification for a NEW stimulus.

In operational terms, the recognition memory task is similar to that used for repetition priming. The study and test phases each involve presentation of single words; the subjects may be instructed to make lexicality decisions during the study phase in each case, and learning or encoding therefore occurs under the same conditions in regard to subject expectations. The only difference involves the test phase, which involves either the same, lexicality task, in repetition priming, or OLD/NEW classification, in the recognition memory task.

Now consider the key difference between the repetition-priming and recognition memory procedures. These occur during the second phase of an experiment. Subjects are given a mixture of NEW and OLD stimuli in each case. But in the recognition memory task they are given specific instructions to classify each stimulus in terms of the OLD/NEW feature. They are given, therefore, a mixture of OLD words (i.e., words from the original list) and NEW words (i.e., words not from the original list), and instructions to classify each stimulus in these terms. Thus, although OLD and NEW words are used in both the repetition-priming and recognition memory tasks, it is only in the latter that subjects are instructed to classify the stimuli on this attribute; in repetition priming both NEW and OLD words should receive a "YES" response in the lexical decision task, indicating that the subject regards them as GENUINE ENGLISH words.

The comparison just described is illustrated in Table 2.1, which summarizes the type of decision required in each task, the type of data that each decision will yield, and the way in which these data are used to explore repetition priming and recognition memory. The critical comparison for implicit memory involves the difference between the OLD and NEW words. The difference, of 100 milliseconds, is typical of the facilitation observed when a word is repeated in an experiment such as that described earlier. It should be noted, of course, that the subject has classified the stimuli in the same way in each case, as "words." *Repetition priming* is the label used to describe the improvement observed for words presented earlier in the experiment (i.e., OLD words) in comparison with words presented for the first time during the test phase (i.e., NEW words).

The critical values for recognition memory do not involve the same sort of comparison. The accuracy values can be combined to give one value that indicates a subject's ability to discriminate between OLD and NEW words. This value, possibly involving the use of signal detection theory to calculate a sensitivity measure (d'), will be high when the levels of "hits" and "correct rejections" are

TABLE 2.1

Stimulus and Response Categories for the Second Phase of an Implicit Memory Task
(Lexical Decision) and an Explicit Memory Task (Recognition Memory).

Repetition Status		Stimulus Categories			
		New		Old	
Lexical Status		Word	Nonword	Word	Nonword
Task Type	Task				
Implicit	Lexical Decision				
	"word"	96/700	NC	98/600	NC
	"nonword"	NC	NC	NC	NC
Explicit	Recognition Memory				
	"new"	80/850	NC	15/850	NC
	"old"	20/800	NC	85/800	NC

Note. The italic values shown in each cell are typical for accuracy (percent correct) and reaction time (msec), respectively, for the conditions concerned. The values not in italics are errors; that is, false alarms (20/800) or errors of omission (15/850). The cells marked NC are not critical for the discussion.

high, and the levels of the "errors of omission" and "false alarms" are low. The second pair of values, of course, can be derived from the first pair. For convenience, and to provide benchmarks for subsequent discussion, I derive implicit and explicit values from Table 2.1. Thus, as described previously, the implicit memory or repetition-priming value is 100 milliseconds, and the recognition memory value is 82.5% correct, a value that should be compared with perfect discrimination (i.e., 100% correct) and chance performance (i.e., 50% correct in the typical experiment where P/old = P/new = 0.5).

The distinction between repetition priming and recognition memory is not based on the mere fact that the effect of experience can be measured in two ways. The two tasks are described in detail in order to characterize the nature of the distinction between tasks that behave in qualitatively different ways. The evidence for dissociation between implicit memory and explicit memory involves reference to several variables. For example, as described earlier, lag effects in repetition priming are either small or absent altogether, whereas lag effects in recognition memory are usually substantial. Unless people are asked to make OLD/NEW judgments almost immediately, the accuracy of their decisions is generally low, and it declines systematically as a function of time (e.g., D.L. Scarborough et al., 1977; Tulving et al., 1982).

Experimental Dissociation. Additional evidence of experimental dissociation involves organizational variables. Experimental treatments that include provision of semantic or alternative bases for the organization of the to-be-remembered material generally enhance performance on explicit memory tasks, whereas they often have little or no influence on implicit memory tasks. This dissociation between explicit and implicit performance even extends to serial position effects, one of the most ubiquitous phenomena in the verbal memory literature. In a recent study, for example, D.M. Brooks (1994) used stem completion and instructed subjects to attempt to complete either (a) all stems, the implicit treatment, or (b) only the stems of words that they could remember from the study list, the explicit treatment. She found a strong primacy effect for the explicit treatment, and attributed the absence of a recency effect to the presence of filler items, material that would have abolished the recency effect. In Brooks' second experiment, however, when words from the end of the list were tested first, both primacy and recency effects were observed under explicit conditions. Brooks found no evidence of a primacy or recency effect under implicit test conditions, and attributed the serial position effects to the use of conscious retrieval processes.

The theoretical interpretation generally advanced to account for this dissociation focuses on retrieval processes. Whereas explicit memory tasks such as recall and recognition memory capitalize on conscious retrieval processes involving experimental or even preexperimental associations, performance on implicit memory tasks depends on reference to the representation of the word or object, an unconscious retrieval process that does not involve the use of interitem association.

A further example of experimental dissociation involves reference to the distinction between automatic processes, such as those involved in reading, and elective processes, such as those involved in word generation, for example, to name the antonym of COLD. Jacoby (1983) found that reading yields more facilitation than generation in implicit memory tasks, whereas reading yields poorer performance on recognition memory tasks than antonym generation. That is, repetition priming following presentation of HOT for reading is greater than that observed following presentation of COLD followed by verbal report by the subject of the antonym of COLD, that is, "hot"; whereas the pattern is reversed under recognition memory conditions. Jacoby interpreted this pattern as a dissociation, and claimed that it involved the operation of distinct memory processes, one of which favored tasks that were subsequently referred to as implicit memory tasks, the other of which involved more elaborative processes and, therefore, explicit memory. Some doubt remains about Jacoby's interpretation of this result, however, as the pattern involves a negative association or correlation rather than a dissociation, an outcome that could be used to support the proposition that one process or mechanism is responsible for the results from each of the implicit and explicit memory tasks.

Neuropsychological Dissociation.   Perhaps the most compelling evidence for the dissociation between implicit and explicit memory involves evidence from amnesic patients and the elderly. Much of the evidence involves laboratory tasks that are substantially removed from the everyday activities of the elderly. However, some tasks involve familiar activities for elderly and memory-impaired people.

Perhaps the most interesting of these involves a reading task developed by Moscovitch, Winocur, and McLachlan (1986). The implicit memory task in their experiments involved a simple sentence-reading problem, where reaction time was the dependent variable. Although age and memory disorder slowed reading time dramatically, from under 20 seconds in the young group to over 40 seconds in the institutionalized and memory-disordered elderly, reading time showed both task and item practice effects for the young, community elderly, institutionalized elderly, and memory-disordered elderly groups. That is, reading time for new material improved significantly for each group from session to session (i.e., task practice), and an additional benefit was observed when the same sentences were involved (i.e., item practice). By comparison, when the subjects were instructed to classify the sentences as OLD or NEW, whereas the young and community elderly groups were able to distinguish the two sets reliably, the memory-disordered elderly could not perform this task reliably.

One additional result merits further comment. Moscovitch et al. (1986) included one experiment that involved recombination of old items from different sets. They found that this treatment reduced or eliminated improvement in reading time, a result that they attributed to changes among interitem connections. Another interpretation is available, however. If the products of sentence analysis are stored as a single record (Kirsner & Dunn, 1985), regardless of linguistic scale (i.e., whether the material involves words or sentences), subsequent cognitive operations involving different components of the original sentences will fail to make contact with a representation at the appropriate level of granularity, and reading will not benefit from the relevant record. The idea underlying this proposition is that cognitive operations leave records that are constrained by task demands and, where these do not match from occasion to occasion, performance will not improve from occasion to occasion. In summary, however, Moscovitch et al.'s study is consistent with a substantial body of research that supports the conclusion that profound memory deficits can coexist with the ability to acquire and use new information on tasks that do not require deliberate or conscious access to that information.

Memory: Association

Source Memory. The explicit memory tasks summarized previously have been used to explore and emphasize qualitative differences between implicit memory and explicit memory. There is evidence that performance on each of these tasks may be dissociated from performance on implicit memory effects such as repetition priming in lexical decision and fragment completion under some if not all conditions. However, the more general claim that performance on all implicit memory tasks is dissociated from performance on explicit memory tasks is difficult to sustain. Consider memory for source, for example. How did you find out about John F. Kennedy's assassination? Did you first learn about it from the radio, television, newspaper, or by word of mouth from a friend? This question is, of course, an explicit memory question, requiring the respondent to reflect on the nature of his or her experience during the initial processing episode. When this type of question is translated into the procedures of the research laboratory, it often emerges in the form of a comparison between binary treatments, as illustrated by the following questions:

Case: Did you read it in upper case or lower case (i.e.,cheese vs. CHEESE)?

Modality: Did you hear it or read it (i.e., "cheese" vs. CHEESE)?

Language: Did you read it in English or French (i.e., CHEESE vs. FROMAGE)?

My colleagues and I have demonstrated in a number of experiments that performance on these explicit memory tasks is negatively associated with the extent of transfer on repetition-priming experiments. Thus, when the explicit memory question involves case, accuracy on the memory question is barely above chance, at approximately 60%, where guessing would give 50% correct. The equivalent values for the modality and language questions are approximately 75% and 90%, respectively. The extent of transfer between treatments, such as those defined by case, modality, and language, depends on many variables including task and word frequency, and it is difficult to define a metric-free measure. One approach that we have adopted involves the use of relative priming: that is, the magnitude of repetition priming observed under cross-treatment conditions (e.g., lexical decision time for printed words following presentation of the same words in spoken form minus lexical decision time for printed words not previously presented during the experiment in any form) expressed as a proportion of the magnitude of repetition priming observed under intratreatment conditions (e.g., lexical decision time for printed words following presentation of the same words in printed form minus lexical decision time for printed words not previously presented during the experiment in any form). Thus, each value is corrected for performance under baseline or "new" word conditions.

Repetition priming is influenced by a number of other variables, however. For example, repetition priming rapidly approaches ceiling conditions for high-frequency words; the measure becomes less reliable under these conditions. The overall pattern is clear, however: Relative priming decreases from approximately 95% for between-case transfer conditions to approximately 50% and 0% for between-modality and between-language conditions, respectively. It should be noted, furthermore, that this association—of decreasing accuracy in source memory and increasing transfer in repetition priming—also has been observed for morphological variables (e.g., Cristoffanini, Kirsner, & Milech, 1986; Downie, Milech, & Kirsner, 1985).

One final caveat is required about this association. The association just reported is not insensitive to the way in which the observer encodes information during the study phase of the experiment. If the learner is deliberately trying to memorize source information, the effect of this explicit learning strategy will mask the effects described previously for the source memory task. In terms of the aforementioned values, then, intentional attribute-encoding strategies will lift source memory to 90% correct or thereabouts, without influencing transfer in repetition priming. Thus, the association is revealed only when the study task is designed to minimize the contribution from intentional learning strategies. The implication of this caveat is that, first, performance on source memory tasks can be influenced by two sources of information, one based on incidental perceptual information, the other on intentional associative information, and, second, when the second of these sources of information is minimized by the use of incidental learning conditions, the association between performance on source memory and transfer under repetition-priming conditions is unmasked. Perhaps the simplest general way to describe this association involves the concept of "confusion."

In summary, although the source memory task is an explicit memory task, which involves deliberate reference to the original study episode, it is not a pure measure based on information from one type of memory. Rather, it is a hybrid task that uses information from at least two types of memory, one based on processing activity activated automatically and nonwillfully during the study event, the other based on elective processes activated willfully in response to task demands during the study event.

QUESTIONS AND ISSUES

Memory Structures Versus Dynamic Processes

One issue that antedated both repetition priming and implicit memory concerned the distinction between stores or structures, on the one hand, and processes, on the other. The distinction is captured explicitly in R.C. Atkinson and Shiffrin's (1968) model of memory. Their model included three memory components: sensory memory, short-term memory, and long-term memory. Voluntary or elective processes also were given several roles, however, one of which concerned the transfer of information from short-term to long-term memory. The structural element in Atkinson and Shiffrin's account attracted criticism from several sources.

One counterargument, advanced by Craik and Lockhart (1972), placed new emphasis on the nature of the processes responsible for the acquisition of new information in memory. For these authors, however, the focus was not on transfer between stores, but on the qualitative impact of different types of encoding operations during the study or learning phase. Thus, deep processing, involving reference to the meaning of the target stimulus, and shallow processing, involving reference to some surface feature of the target stimulus, were central elements in Craik and Lockhart's theory. The central idea in their theory was that memory was facilitated by deep processing. They were referring, of course, to what would now be referred to as explicit memory tasks, including recognition memory and free recall for example. Although concerned with a very different type of mental activity, Craik and Lockhart's argument foreshadowed some of the issues that have emerged in the repetition-priming literature.

Another approach that challenged the value of models involving distinct memory structures was developed by Kolers (e.g., Kolers & Roediger, 1984). Kolers' analysis was developed in parallel with studies involving repetition priming (e.g., Kolers, 1975), however it was based in part on the rich literature of skill acquisition. In one of Kolers' key studies (Kolers, 1975), he found that log reaction time on a reading task was a linear function of log practice, a relationship that has a long history in skill acquisition (e.g., J.R. Anderson, 1982; Rosenbloom & Newell, 1986; Snoddy, 1926) as well as more complex problems involving team as distinct from individual performance (e.g., Argote & Epple, 1990). However, Kolers added one additional point, of relevance to people concerned with memory: that performance was determined by the extent to which the current task or activity involved processes or procedures that had been developed and practiced on some other problem. This is, of course, a restatement of another old chestnut, hitherto discussed under the more applied heading of "transfer-of-training." In its general form, the central idea is that every mental activity lays down a set of traces (Logan, 1988b, 1990), procedures (Kolers & Roediger, 1984), or records (Kirsner & Dunn, 1985; Moscovitch, 1992b), and that these data constitute a resource for future performance and decision making involves a critical change in the direction of memory research.

The idea also has gained currency in object recognition and analysis, where it has been proposed that perceptual operations involve reference to perceptual records—records that may be opened during object analysis, and modified by use (Treisman, 1988).

Systems Revisited

Although the new emphasis on mental operations, and on the impact of those mental operations on traces and records, contributed to a change of focus away from store and transfer models, it also spawned a theoretical solution that retained the distinction between two systems, in one form or another. The distinction has been characterized in a number of ways. At an operational level, for example, the terms *direct* and *indirect* have gained considerable currency (Richardson-Klavehn & Bjork, 1988). Recall is, of course, a direct test of memory, in which subjects are required to report on some earlier experience. Repetition priming in word fragment completion or lexical decision is an indirect test of memory, being indirect in the sense that inferences about memory are based on performance differences between new and repeated items.

Beyond the operational level, two broad approaches can be identified. The first of these harks back to systems, and involves the assumption that dissociations involving explicit and memory tasks reflect their use of different memory systems or subsystems (Schacter, 1993). In its strong form, this view involves reference to distinct neurological systems. In a weaker form, however, the distinction is sometimes identified with different retrieval mechanisms. According to this point of view, explicit memory depends on reference to retrieval processes that involve intentional or conscious recollection of previous experiences, whereas implicit memory does not depend on reference to processes of this type.

The second approach focuses on implicit rather than explicit memory, but analysis of the retrieval mechanism is again to the fore. The critical feature in this approach is that the performance changes that dominate implicit memory data are governed by the concept of reuse or recapitulation, or task-appropriate processing to use Roediger's term (Roediger, Weldon, & Challis, 1989). To cope with the finding that task-appropriate processing effects sometimes are observed in explicit tasks—recognition memory in particular—it is necessary to assume that some of the tasks that have been labeled explicit actually involve or require the use of implicit mechanisms, even if these are only a station on the way to direct memory search. This qualification is not, of course, a problem for either Jacoby or the present author because of our pre-theoretical commitment to task impurity (Dunn & Kirsner, 1988; Jacoby & Kelley, 1992). The interesting feature of these candidate criteria for distinguishing implicit and explicit processes is that although they both involve retrieval mechanisms, they associate these processes with qualitatively different retrieval mechanisms.

The review articles concerned with explicit and implicit memory, and direct and indirect memory tasks generally have focused on evidence of experimental dissociation, from laboratory and clinical studies. They generally have ignored evidence that performance on the two task families are sometimes associated, either positively or negatively. I have described one of these bodies of evidence previously. The proportion of facilitation that occurs under repetition-priming conditions for various types of transformations (e.g., case, modality, and language) generally is associated with memory for source information; that is, increased transfer on implicit memory tasks is generally associated with poorer memory for source, as if performance in the two domains were dominated by one principle, "confusion" being an obvious candidate. The implication of this point is, of course, similar to that made by Jacoby and his colleagues (Jacoby & Kelley, 1992), namely, that it is essential to distinguish between processes and tasks. Two tasks—involving recognition of CHEESE and fromage, for example—activate a process or function that is dominated by the extent to which the two events involve reference to the same representations and processes, and the product of this function is available for use by any decision process, involving source memory or word naming, for example.

Fluency

The idea that performance on cognitive tasks uses information from more than one source or process has a rich history. The importance of this approach is that it stands in contrast to the often implicit assumption that it is possible, given sufficient care, to map specific tasks and processes on a one-to-one basis. Dunn and I discussed the theoretical and empirical implications of this point of view elsewhere (Dunn & Kirsner, 1988) and, more recently, Jacoby and his colleagues (Jacoby & Kelley, 1992) rejected it, and offered a new approach to process analysis.

One of the earliest formal accounts depicting two processes was offered by R.C. Atkinson and Juola (1973). According to their account, performance on the recognition memory task involved the use of information from two sources: first, a fast process that involved reference to item familiarity and, second, a slower process that involved a direct, controlled search through memory. Furthermore, according to Atkinson and Juola, the two processes involved qualitatively different retrieval mechanisms that gave rise to different reaction time distributions. Johnston, Dark, and Jacoby (1985) adopted and then extended this idea. The first point in their argument is that words that are presented for a second time in an experiment can be perceived more readily than words being presented for the first time. Thus far, the point is a redescription of evidence that word recognition occurs at a lower threshold for old words than new words (Jacoby & Dallas, 1981; Kirsner et al., 1983). The additional argument developed by Johnston et al. is that speed or fluency of processing can be used as a cue to facilitate memory decisions. Using a gradual clarification procedure, they found that recognition memory was influenced by both fluency—the time required for identification—and another factor more in keeping with oldness or "discriminability," as if a direct memory search and decision were involved. They also found that the role of fluency was enhanced by the use of nonwords, that is, by use of stimuli for which discriminability would be reduced.

But perhaps the most intriguing of Jacoby's recent studies involved the proposition that fluency changes can be reflected in either performance changes in word recognition, or subjective changes in perception (Jacoby, Allan, J.C. Collins, & Larwill, 1988). Whereas the former involves an increased probability of word recognition at a given signal-to-noise ratio, the latter involves a change in the subjective assessment of the signal-to-noise ratio itself. The results of the experiments described by Jacoby et al. imply that some form of metamorphosis is involved. However, because their findings also indicate that a measure of conscious control or moderation is possible (Whittlesea, Jacoby, & Girard, 1990), strong assumptions about the modularity of this process cannot be sustained. In summary, the results of research involving the concept of fluency indicate that fluent performance may be attributed to either experience or perception.

One elegant consequence of Jacoby's approach to unconscious processes is that it provides a method of studying memory effects where the task requirements do not overtly involve word retrieval processes at all; they involve only questions about the signal-to-noise ratio of a visual or aural mask. Given evidence that extralaboratory practice (i.e., word frequency) and laboratory practice (i.e., repetition priming; Kirsner & Speelman, 1996) produce quantitatively distinct effects on lexical decision time, it would be useful to determine whether or not the impact of these variables on perceived signal-to-noise ratios follows a similar pattern. Put in other words, is the metamorphosis between word recognition and subjective noise touched equally by all forms of practice, or is it specific to repetition priming, a question that has implications for the proposition that extralaboratory and laboratory practice involve qualitatively different processes (Kirsner & Speelman, 1996; B.L. Schwartz & Hashtroudi, 1991)?

Consciousness and Awareness

Given the assumption that all tasks are or can be "impure," it follows that Jacoby's development of a process dissociation technique represents an important advance for research involving implicit memory tasks and, more important, processes (Jacoby & Kelley, 1992; Jacoby, Toth, & Yonelinas, 1993). The central step in the technique developed by Jacoby and his colleagues involves comparisons between performance on treatments that induce cooperation or opposition between what Jacoby and his colleagues referred to as conscious and unconscious processes. Cooperation is assumed when subjects are instructed to complete word stems or fragments by any means. This condition approximates to the normal conditions for these tasks, that is, conditions under which people can use either conscious or unconscious processes, and the scientist cannot determine the origin of specific responses, as implicit or explicit, or conscious or unconscious. Jacoby, Toth, and Yonelinas referred to this as the inclusion condition. Opposition is assumed when subjects are instructed to complete word stems or fragments from words that people judged to be not in the study list, that is, from words that fall outside the set of words that they "know" to be from the list. This step was designed to restrict completions for this treatment to the unprimed or baseline level plus words that were touched only by unconscious processes. Jacoby, Toth, and Yonelinas referred to this as the exclusion condition.

Formally, the conscious contribution to performance is the difference between performance on the inclusion and exclusion conditions. Thus, if the completion rates under inclusion and exclusion conditions are 0.61 and 0.39 respectively, the contribution based on conscious control is 0.22. Then, if it is assumed that the exclusion rate is equal to the unconscious rate multiplied by 1 minus the contribution based on conscious control, it follows that the unconscious contribution is equal to the exclusion rate divided by 1 minus the conscious contribution, and that the unconscious contribution for the aforementioned values is 0.50. As proposed by Jacoby et al. (1993), this analysis parallels the distinction between d^1 and β from signal detection theory. Thus far, the technique has been used to demonstrate selective effects for several variables. For example, Jacoby, Woloshyn, and Kelley

(1989) found that divided attention reduced the impact of conscious control, thereby unmasking the contribution based on unconscious processes, while sparing the unconscious contribution. In a more recent series of studies, Toth, Reingold, and Jacoby (1994), using the procedures outlined earlier, found that the unconscious contribution was indifferent to both depth of processing and self-generation (e.g., name the antonym of COLD), whereas the magnitude of the conscious contribution was sensitive to both of these variables. Conversely, reading had a greater impact on the unconscious contribution than self-generation, an outcome that is consistent with the assumption that the unconscious contribution as measured by Jacoby's technique is largely perceptual in character.

The process-dissociation technique may be challenged on several grounds. One of these was advanced by Joordens and P.R. Merikle (1993), who suggested that the conscious processes could be a subset of unconscious processes, that is, that the relationship between conscious and unconscious processes reflects redundancy rather than independence. It may be noted, however, that Jacoby, Toth, Yonelinas, and Debner (1994) rejected their argument because it relies in part on the pure task assumption.

A second question, raised here, concerns the claimed relationship between the unconscious contribution, as defined and measured by Jacoby and his associates, and unconsciousness, as the term was defined and used by Freud (e.g., Jacoby & Kelley, 1992). According to Jacoby (e.g., Toth et al., 1994; personal communication, November 1993), implicit memory and, more specifically, the unconscious contribution to performance on completion tasks, is dominated by perceptual as distinct from conceptual effects. Schacter, too (e.g., Schacter, 1993), discussing implicit memory tasks, claimed that performance on this family of tasks is virtually or entirely perceptual, and that modality-independent contributions are absent. I am uncomfortable with this point of view for several reasons. The first and most important of these concerns the character of the unconscious world as described by Freud. Far from being restricted to perceptual experience, the Freudian unconscious is dominated, of course, by extraperceptual processes and events, a point that was conceded indirectly by Jacoby and Kelley (1992). The second point contradicts the first. It is that cross-modality effects are the rule rather than the exception on implicit memory tasks, although this is less obvious in completion tasks because these tasks tend to focus on words from high-frequency bands, where cross-modal priming is minimized by the magnitude of practice effects associated with these classes of words.

The Role of Specific Episodes

The idea that the operations that are invoked to solve some perceptual or conceptual problem leave a trace or record is well established (e.g., L. Brooks, 1984; Kirsner & Dunn, 1985; Kolers & Roediger, 1984; Logan, 1988b). However, it has been used in two quite different ways in the implicit memory and word recognition literature. According to one point of view, memory for specific episodes is an artifact in word recognition studies, offering a spurious basis for performance, and compromising inferences that can be made about lexical and other structures. This argument involves, in effect, the problem that motivated development of the process-dissociation technique described earlier. A central goal in this work is to remove that part of performance that can be attributed to conscious retrieval processes, and to unmask genuine unconscious components. It is perhaps no surprise that the process-dissociation technique was developed specifically to cater for performance on tasks where the conscious contribution is more or less transparent, as alert subjects recall material from the study list while they are striving to generate stem completion candidates. Where reaction time tasks are concerned, however, the conscious contribution is anything but transparent. With reaction time in lexical decision and naming tasks in the 500 to 700 millisecond range—far shorter values than would be obtained on recognition memory tasks after a 24-hour delay—the proposition that a substantial proportion of the priming effect nevertheless depends on retrieval of information from or about specific episodes is certainly adventurous. The issue is, however, an empirical one, and development of a process-dissociation technique for reaction time tasks must be a high priority.

According to one point of view, the masked repetition-priming procedure samples the mental lexicon without contamination by episodic information (de Groot & Nas, 1991; K.I. Forster & C. Davis, 1984). The masked repetition-priming paradigm differs from its unmasked cousin in that: (a) the interval between the prime and test stimuli typically involves a few seconds rather than minutes or hours; (b) the sequence of events that precedes presentation of the test stimulus includes rapid presentation of a sequence of words, one of which may be the prime; and (c) the prime is typically presented at a subthreshold duration, although this is in part due to masking effects from the preceding and following stimuli. The masked repetition-priming procedure typically yields different results from the unmasked version. For example, word frequency effects, and the interaction between word frequency and repetition, two effects that dominate unmasked repetition priming, are virtually eliminated under masked repetition-priming conditions.

The masked repetition-priming effects described by Forster and his colleagues also raise an important issue concerning instance-based recognition models. According to K.I. Forster and C. Davis (1984), lexical processes do not depend on reference to specific episodes. Indeed, according to their article, evidence of reference to specific episodes is incompatible with the lexical role. However, because they do not distinguish between conscious and unconscious reference to such information, their position implies that the repetition-priming/implicit memory and recognition memory paradigms should be treated as a single class, based on their use of episodic information. It is not clear, however, how this assumption should be reconciled with the extensive body of neuropsychological evidence that performance on implicit memory tasks is insensitive to amnesia, whereas performance on recognition memory tasks virtually defines the disorder. Put in other words,

Forster's taxonomy ignores the neuropsychological evidence that recognition memory and implicit memory depend on such distinct retrieval processes that they are vulnerable and invulnerable, respectively, to brain damage.

Another approach to this problem was offered by Kahneman and D. Miller (1986). They described a decision-making process that involves reference to information about individual instances, but to a coalition of instances, a solution that enables information from many instances to influence a particular decision even though information about the individual instances cannot be retrieved. Given the semantic and contextual variety of our experiences with individual words, and the sheer scale of that experience given even only 25,000 words per day, the approach developed by Kahneman and Miller enjoys the advantages of the instance-based approach while avoiding the problems associated with the need to recover detailed information about each instance.

According to the second point of view, the proposition that repetition-priming effects are based on retrieval of information from records or traces produced during earlier information-processing events is grasped with enthusiasm. In Logan's case for example (Logan, 1988b, 1990), both practice and repetition-priming effects are attributed to a model that involves access to traces of earlier episodes. This model involves, furthermore, a gradual transition from the use of cognitively expensive algorithms to automatic retrieval of trace information following extended practice. Similarly, Kirsner and Dunn (1985) proposed that each perceptual act produced a perceptual record, and they argued that this record was available for either reuse, when the holder was faced with similar classification problems, or scrutiny, if the task involved an explicit problem, concerning source memory, for example.

The critical difference between these points of view involves the precise form of access that supposedly is involved during the initial retrieval operation. If lexical decision and word identification under degraded viewing or listening conditions follow or depend on conscious recognition that the still unidentified test stimulus is from the initial list, then repetition performance on these tasks is compromised, as it is on stem completion and other tasks of this type. However, if lexical decision and word identification occurs in advance of and independently of conscious recognition that the still unidentified test stimulus is from the initial list, the claim that performance on these tasks is compromised by episodic information is not substantiated. Intuition is not, of course, a criterion; a technique that separates the unconscious and conscious contributions to lexical decision and word identification would be useful.

Skill Acquisition and Repetition Priming

The general proposition that repetition priming and implicit memory involve similar principles to the older tradition of skill acquisition has been widely recognized (Kirsner & Speelman, 1993, 1996; Logan, 1988b, 1990; B.L. Schwartz & Hashtroudi, 1991). Jacoby, too, has compared unconscious processes with automatic processing, a central concept in skill acquisition models (e.g., Toth et al., 1994). The integration of these concepts is, of course, appealing if for no other reason than it would bring two historically disparate strands of research together.

As a starting point to discussion about the equivalence of skill acquisition and repetition-priming effects, it should be noted that they focus on different parameters. In skill acquisition the conventional approach does not always include NEW items at all. Indeed, many classical studies restrict consideration to performance on one stimulus and one task, and they do not provide, therefore, the conditions that are required for measurement of repetition priming. However, even when an experiment involving many practice blocks includes many stimuli, when all of the stimuli are presented during each phase of the experiment, the observed performance changes are influenced, of course, by practice effects involving both the task and the individual items. It is necessary, therefore, to associate separate parameters with task practice and item practice. The obvious way to achieve this goal is to include both NEW (i.e., stimuli presented once only during one practice block) and OLD (i.e., stimuli presented at least once during each practice block) treatments in the experiment. This provides separate measures for task practice—the function relating performance on NEW items for each block to practice—and item practice—the difference between the functions relating performance and practice for NEW and OLD stimuli.

The extent of task practice—practice effects for NEW items—is a contentious issue. In a series of studies, Logan (1988b, 1990) found no evidence of task practice effects in lexical decision. However, although this pattern of results has been replicated under massed practice conditions with the same general task (Kirsner & Pratley, 1996), Speelman and I found substantial task practice effects when practice has been distributed over several days (Kirsner & Speelman, 1996). The picture in regard to pure item practice effects—the difference between the NEW and OLD functions—is also under dispute. For integration involving task and item effects to be achieved, it would be useful to demonstrate that the two functions conform to the power law—the sine qua non of skill acquisition. Logan (1988b, 1990) reported repetition-priming patterns (i.e., differences between NEW and OLD items) that conform to the power law. It may be noted, however, that Logan generally used massed practice conditions that included several presentations of some stimuli during each 3-minute block of trials. When spaced conditions have been used, however, where OLD items are repeated once per day as distinct from several trials per minute, the resulting impact on performance is generally additive, as if repetition priming is a one-shot affair, and indifferent to the power law (Kirsner & Pratley; Kirsner & Speelman, 1996).

Further evidence that integration between skill acquisition and repetition priming may be difficult to confirm was reported by B.L. Schwartz and Hashtroudi (1991). Using a word identification procedure, they found that the two parameters were influenced by different variables, an example of experimental dissociation involving skill acquisition and repetition priming. Schwartz and Hashtroudi also brought together evidence that skill acquisition and repetition priming are subject to neurological dissociation. Whereas patients with Alzheimer's disease show normal and impaired performance on skill acquisition and implicit memory tasks, respectively, patient's with Huntingdon's disease—a subcortical dementia—show normal and impaired performance on implicit memory and skill acquisition tasks, respectively. However, these patterns should be treated with caution as the skill acquisition and implicit memory measures generally were obtained from different tasks, and other variables, therefore, could be involved.

Although Speelman and I (Kirsner & Speelman, 1996) have adopted the proposition that (a) performance on NEW items involves a "skill" acquisition effect, whereas (b) the difference between performance on NEW items and OLD items at a given point on the practice function reflects repetition priming, this point of view should be treated with caution. The problem as we see it is that task as well as item practice effects may be subject to priming. Consider the following provisional process analysis for naming and lexical decision. The key assumption is that processing time for each processing component reflects the power law, and that predictions regarding overall performance therefore must consider the extent of practice experienced by each of the various components, and by the components invoked to solve new stimulus and task problems. The general form of the extended function is described by Equation 1:

$$T = N_{i1}P_{i1}{}^r + N_{i2}P_{i2}{}^r + \ldots + N_{o1}P_{o1}{}^r + N_{o2}P_{o2}{}^r + \ldots + N_{d1}P_{d1}{}^r + N_{d2}P_{d2}{}^r + \ldots$$
$$+ N_{m1}P_{m1}{}^r + N_{m2}P_{m2}{}^r$$

where:

T = Time;
N_i, N_o, N_d, and N_m represent sets of production rules from four hypothetical stages:

> i = a perceptual stage, constrained by stimulus modality,
>
> o = a premotor planning stage, constrained by the requirements of the decision stage (e.g., a phonological code for lexical decision),
>
> d = a decision stage (e.g., for naming or lexical decision)
>
> m = a motor stage (i.e., for response execution);

P = Amount of Practice;
r = Learning Rate.

Equation 1 was developed to explain improvement in all of the processes that intervene between the presentation of a word and the execution of a response to that word. The equation includes a number of power functions, where these are divided into four basic stages. The stage labeled "i" describes improvement in productions responsible for the input or perceptual processing. The "o" stage involves preparation of the code or codes required by the decision stage. Depending on the task, the decision stage might require orthographic, phonological, or gestural codes. The "d" stage represents the execution of productions responsible for the task decision, such as deciding whether the presented letter string is a word or not. The "m" stage represents the execution of the motor programs responsible for the response, for naming or button pressing, for example. Taken together, the "i," "o," "d," and "m" stages constitute an activity record, a concept derived from the notion of a perceptual record (Kirsner & Dunn, 1985), but not restricted to perceptual work. This account is in some respects similar to Logan's (1988b, 1990) instance-based model. However, that is where the similarity ends because, in Logan's account, these stages are not shareable components between processing episodes, as specified by us. In our account, moreover, they are crucial because they account for transfer and priming effects.

Now, when practice effects are expressed in terms of components that involve task and item effects, it is possible that skill acquisition and repetition priming are making separate and qualitatively different contributions to performance, and that these contributions are being made to task as well as item components. Consider, for example, a word recognition model that involves a direct-access process for high-frequency words and an indirect-access model involving grapheme-phoneme conversion for low-frequency words. Efficiency in the second of these processes could be influenced by the presence or absence of low-frequency words in a practice session, a pattern that is suggested by our finding that the rate of improvement on lexical decision for NEW words is sensitive to word frequency. In conclusion then, although we have adopted the proposition that skill acquisition and repetition priming can be associated with practice on NEW items, and the difference between NEW and OLD items, respectively, this is by no means the only possibility; priming might involve a different mechanism from learning, one that is not based on the power law.

One final comment is required concerning the relationship between skill acquisition and awareness. Whereas awareness (or consciousness) has become a central concept in work on implicit memory, requiring development of detailed formal procedures to remove contamination by conscious processes, the idea of removing the contribution from conscious processes from skill acquisition is more or less absurd. When a subject is given repeated exposure to a relatively small set of stimuli on one task, it must be assumed that most or all of the items are eventually available consciously. Are we then to assume that skill acquisition and the power law reflect growth in the contribution from conscious processes? But this proposition raises an intriguing paradox because most models and general accounts of skill acquisition (e.g., J.R. Anderson, 1982; Fitts, 1964; Logan, 1990) include the assumption that practice actually reduces the connection between conscious processes and performance.

PARADIGMS

Context and Reality

Thus far, the bulk of work involving implicit memory has been based on laboratory studies involving word or object recognition or classification and, more significantly, situations where the role of context has been attenuated or removed entirely. However, because listening, reading, writing, and speaking rarely are required by adults working within their lingual limits, models based on decontextualized performance have limited appeal. Implicit memory has been, therefore, open to the claim that most of the critical work is based on performance obtained under decontextualized and, therefore, unrealistic conditions. Two points merit detailed consideration.

The first point concerns the difference between practice functions involving laboratory and extralaboratory experience. Word frequency tables are based, of course, on extralaboratory experience. The values typically are based on frequency counts obtained from newspapers and many other printed documents. They are restricted, therefore, to reading. But they nevertheless provide relatively realistic counts for performance in that modality. Several studies indicate that reaction time on naming and lexical decision tasks typically follow the power law; that is, log reaction time is a linear function of log word frequency where the word frequency values are derived from word frequency tables such as that prepared by Kucera and Francis (1967). In a single study (Kirsner & Speelman, 1996), however, although the results confirmed the proposition that the power law provides a good fit for the relationship between lexical decision and extralaboratory practice (i.e., word frequency), and a better fit than the exponential, the results showed that the slope of the function relating lexical decision to laboratory practice was 100 to 1,000 times steeper than the function based on extra-laboratory practice, while itself conforming to the power law to a considerable extent. This result suggests that even if the two processes reflect the same mathematical function, their sensitivity to practice is so different that generalization between the two domains must be problematical. It could be explained, for example, if it is assumed that reading under normal conditions rarely involves analysis of individual words. Another possible explanation is that, unlike most laboratory experiments (cf. J.V. Bainbridge, Lewandowsky, & Kirsner, 1993; Masson & Freedman, 1990), reading induces people to select semantically precise interpretations of each word. The implication of this argument is that practice effects are restricted to representations that are defined semantically as well as morphologically and orthographically, a restriction that is immaterial when words are presented in isolation because the citation sense is activated but critical when words are presented in context, and only one meaning or referent is activated. Regardless of the preferred explanation—and several others are available—the results suggest that the gulf between laboratory and realistic or contextualized research may be far from trivial.

Further evidence that the consequences of normal communication produce a remarkably detailed record for continuing use by speakers involves analysis of word duration. Studies involving a series of procedural and narrative descriptions have demonstrated that not only do people shorten word duration when they repeat a word (Fowler, 1989; Fowler & Housum, 1987), they actually restrict word shortening to occasions that involve the same referent, and increase word duration to repetitions that involve a different referent (C. Robertson & Kirsner, 1996). Robertson and Kirsner also found that this effect was indifferent to the lag between first and second use, over 20 words or seconds, or longer. Clearly, then, these data suggest that we preserve and use a detailed record of what we have said for many seconds, otherwise we would be unable to moderate word duration to facilitate communicative intent during conversation.

Cognitive Evolution

The critical question that guided preparation for this book concerns the role of implicit processes in learning, memory, and other aspects of human performance. Implicit processes have been used in many ways, however. A short list includes the following distinctions: implicit and explicit memory (Schacter, 1987), implicit and explicit learning (Reber, 1989a), automatic and controlled processing (Schneider & Shiffrin, 1977), and declarative and procedural memory. This list, of course, does not do justice to the full range of tasks that have been developed under these headings. Implicit memory alone has been used to refer to repetition-priming effects in lexical decision, word identification, picture naming, fragment completion, stem completion, and a number of related tasks.

A central issue concerns the viability of all of these distinctions. Do each of these distinctions, paradigms, and tasks reflect the operation of unique processes, or do they all reflect the operation of one underlying process or, more cautiously perhaps, one design principle? The problem is given further significance by the availability of other cognitive models with obvious claims to participation in this debate. For example, many of the phenomena identified by implicit memory scientists also may be observed in the skill acquisition paradigm, or inferred from models developed for that domain (Kirsner & Speelman, 1996). The position that we wish to advance in this book is that, although each of the paradigms and tasks identified in the preceding summary must have at least one unique process, for they are after all different tasks, they all involve the operation of a single overarching process or, more cautiously, a single design principle.

One argument for the proposition that a single process or design principle is involved involves an extension of an argument developed by scientists concerned with the evolution of cognition. According to Sterrer (1992) and Wuketitis (1986), for example, each organism consists of a hypothesis or a set of hypotheses about its environment. These hypotheses are subject to continuous evaluation and selection on the basis of predictive performance, and modified by adaptation to provide a better fit. More specifically, the organism, as hypothesis, must consist of (a) predictions, where these consist of internalized information about the relationship between objects and events; (b) machinery to take advantage of these predictions; and (c) energy to operate the machinery and to provide a safety margin to deal with events that are unpredictable in principle.

The critical feature that must be added to this account is that the cognitive machinery developed for the acquisition, representation, recognition, and use of predictive information must achieve something approaching a complete set of capabilities for all of these domains before it can derive benefit from their individual availability. Thus, it is of no value to an organism if it can only acquire and represent predictive information; if adaptive benefit is to be obtained the organism must be able to recognize examples under confrontation conditions or detect their occurrence in complex situations. This, then, is the heart of the argument. Although it does not mean necessarily that acquisition, representation, and retrieval involve the same process, it does mean that perhaps the more specialized machinery designed to meet each of these functions must use commensurate data. Thus, at least some part of the system must be designed according to a single, unifying principle. These components, therefore, must constitute a system—in the sense that the parts cannot operate without the whole—or else adaptive value will not be realized.

The general implication of the foregoing argument is that research in the area under consideration must develop methods that unify as well as methods that divide. The major inferential procedures in this area focus on procedures that divide—experimental and neuropsychological dissociation in particular. New inferential steps must be developed that will confirm the proposition that performance on two otherwise disparate tasks reflects the operation of one unifying process or principle.

3

IMPLICIT LEARNING

Angela O'Brien-Malone
Murray Maybery
University of Western Australia

DEFINITION AND CHARACTERISTICS

Implicit learning has been characterized as an unconscious process by which knowledge is acquired without a deliberate attempt to learn. Its converse, explicit learning, occurs when there is active engagement in conscious strategies to discover the rules underlying a task. Other purported characteristics of implicit learning are that it is unselective, storing all contingencies between stimulus variables, and that it is not capacity limited. By contrast, explicit learning utilizes only those variables selectively maintained in a limited-capacity working memory (Berry & D.E. Broadbent, 1988; D.E. Broadbent, 1989; Hayes & D.E. Broadbent, 1988). It also has been argued (Reber, 1992) that implicit learning predates the evolution of explicit learning; consequently, implicit compared to explicit learning should be more robust to neuropsychological insult. These aspects of implicit learning form the focus of this chapter. Other aspects of implicit learning that Reber derived from his position on evolution, but that are not examined here, include the suggestion that implicit learning should have a narrower population variance, and emerge earlier in the child and be less related to age, than explicit learning (see chap. 9 of this volume for further discussion of developmental issues in implicit learning), and that implicit learning should be independent of IQ, and exhibit interspecies commonalities.

CLASSES OF EVIDENCE

Empirical evidence for implicit learning typically is based on a design that contains two measures, one purported to reflect predominantly implicit processes, the other predominantly explicit processes. The two measures can be different indices addressed to the same learning episode; for example, it could be argued that a reaction time (RT) index reflects implicit learning, whereas a questionnaire index reflects explicit learning. Alternatively, the two measures could be the same index, but gathered from two tasks or two conditions; for example, accuracy could be recorded for learning under conditions presumed to promote implicit processing, and for learning under conditions presumed to promote explicit processing. The prototypical design also contains one or more independent variables, which can be either experimental (e.g., level of exposure to a set of rules) or individual-difference (e.g., amnesic vs. intact memory) in kind. The critical evidence is either a *single dissociation*, where one measure and not the other is affected by an independent variable, or a *double dissociation*, where the two measures are differentially affected by the manipulation of two independent variables, or affected in opposite ways by the same independent variable.

An example of the single dissociation form of evidence is Lewicki, T. Hill, and Bizot's (1988) demonstration of shortened RTs for locating a target when its position was determined by complex rules, coupled with an inability to describe any of the rules in a subsequent interview. That is, exposure to the rule-governed stimuli affected the RT measure, which was argued to be sensitive to knowledge acquired unconsciously, but did not affect the interview measure, which was argued to reflect knowledge acquired consciously.

An example of the use of a double dissociation argument is Berry and D.E. Broadbent's (1984) demonstration that instruction and practice had differential effects on system control and questionnaire measures of knowledge of an interactive system. Practice improved system control but not questionnaire performance, whereas instruction improved questionnaire performance but not system control.

There are two criticisms of the single dissociation form of evidence. The first relates to the problem of guaranteeing the exhaustiveness of the instrument used to assess conscious knowledge (Perruchet, Gallego, & Savy, 1990; Reingold & P.M. Merikle, 1990; Shanks & St. John, 1994). Many of the tasks purported to be implicitly learned embody complex rules. Therefore, it is possible some level of mastery can be achieved by employing other, perhaps simpler, correlated rules. Thus any exhaustive assessment of conscious knowledge must be receptive to all the correlated rules that could be entertained, as well as to the veridical rules, a position that is difficult to establish.

The other criticism relates to a possible difference in the sensitivity of measures; it could be that the measure purported to reflect conscious awareness is less sensitive to acquired knowledge than is the measure purported to reflect implicit learning (Shanks & St. John, 1994). Some empirical refutations of implicit learning have used more sensitive indices of knowledge (e.g., Dulany, Carlson, & Dewey, 1984). However, in reply, proponents of implicit learning have argued that these indices are not exclusive, that is, that they are affected by both conscious and unconscious knowledge (e.g., Reber, Allen, & Regan, 1985; Reingold & P.M.

Merikle, 1990). The central problem is that although some have specified what the measure of conscious knowledge should have in common with the measure of implicit knowledge (e.g., common retrieval cues, according to Shanks & St. John, 1994), no one has been able to clearly specify just how the measure of conscious knowledge should differ from the implicit measure.

Another complication is that implicit learning theorists adopt different positions on the conscious access issue. Some theorists (e.g., Lewicki, T. Hill, & Czyzewska, 1992) have argued for a *no-access position*, that is, that implicit learning processes lay down knowledge that is unavailable to conscious access. However, other theorists (e.g., Hasher & Zacks, 1979, 1984; Reber, 1989a) adopt the weaker view that knowledge acquired via implicit processes may be accessed consciously. This *possible-access position* is contrasted with the *no-access position* at various points in this chapter.

In terms of the *correlated rules* and *sensitivity* criticisms described previously, double dissociations are somewhat impervious to at least the sensitivity criticism, because both measures are affected by at least one variable. However, although being evidence often interpreted as indicative of the existence of two systems (but see Dunn & Kirsner, 1988), finding a double dissociation does not in itself confirm the conscious versus unconscious nature of the hypothesized systems.

TASK DOMAINS

In this section we describe the three types of task that have predominated in the literature on implicit learning: artificial grammar tasks, interactive tasks, and serial pattern learning tasks. Simple covariation tasks also have been used in implicit learning research, primarily to explore developmental issues; hence they are discussed in chapter 9 of this volume

Artificial Grammars

The modern notion of implicit learning was introduced in a series of articles by Reber (e.g., 1967, 1969, 1976). The paradigm he developed has been used extensively in the literature[1] and is based on artificial grammars, one of which is depicted in Fig. 3.1. Directional constraints on movement through the grammar are imposed, with each movement from one point in the grammar to the next generating a letter, and lawful movement through the model from an input to an output point generating a grammatical letter string. Different grammatical strings can be generated by taking different paths through the model.

---

[1]Articles illustrative of the use of the artificial grammar task include Cleeremans and J.L. McClelland (1991), Servan-Schreiber and J.R. Anderson (1990), Vokey and L.R. Brooks (1992), and Whittlesea and Dorken (1993).

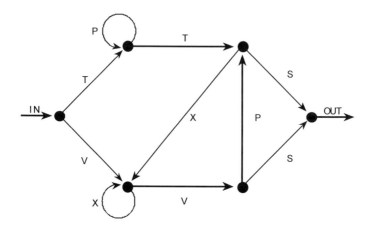

FIG. 3.1. Example of an artificial grammar. Letter strings such as TPTS, TPPTXVPS, and VVPXXVS are grammatical; VXS, TPTPS and VXXVPXT are ungrammatical. From Reber (1967, p. 856, Figure 1). Copyright © 1967 by Academic Press Inc. Reproduced by permission.

Under Reber's paradigm, subjects in implicit learning conditions are exposed to grammatical letter strings in a study phase during which they are not informed of the existence of the grammatical rules. Their exposure to the strings in this phase does not emphasize the rule-governed nature of the stimuli. They may be asked, for example, simply to memorize the strings (Reber, 1967, 1969, 1976). Typically, the study phase is followed by a test phase in which subjects are told that the studied strings conformed to a set of rules, and are asked to discriminate grammatical strings from ungrammatical strings (i.e., letter strings that cannot be lawfully generated from the grammar).

Interactive Tasks

Introduced by D.E. Broadbent (1977; Broadbent & Aston, 1978), dynamic interactive tasks also have been used extensively in the literature.[2] In these tasks, the subject typically attempts to move a system toward target outputs through manipulating inputs. For example, in Broadbent's (1977; D.E. Broadbent, FitzGerald, & M.H.P. Broadbent, 1986) transportation task, the subject manipulates the frequency of the bus service and the car-parking fee in trying to settle the system onto specified levels of bus usage and car-parking patronage. In another task, the subject interacts with a computer person called Clegg (Berry & D.E. Broadbent, 1984). The subject

_____

[2]Articles illustrative of the use of interactive tasks include Berry and D.E. Broadbent (1984), Sanderson (1989), and Stanley, R.C. Matthews, Buss, and Kotler-Cope (1989).

selects one of 12 levels of friendliness (e.g., *very rude*, *loving*) with the aim of moving Clegg's response to a target intermediate point, say *friendly*.

In the interactive tasks expected to elicit implicit learning, the subject's input does not determine the system's output in any simple manner, because the equations governing the system either are complex or counterintuitive, or involve nonsalient variables or random perturbations. For example, Clegg's response is determined by the equation:

$$\text{Response} = 2(\text{Input}) - \text{Response}_{\text{previous trial}} + \text{Random}$$

Thus, the equation is moderately complex for a rule-abstraction task, there is random perturbation (-1, 0, or 1 is added), and Clegg's behavior conflicts with a popular "balance-scale" schema for modifying friendliness (Maybery & O'Brien-Malone, 1996). With interactive tasks, learning typically is assessed by some index of performance accuracy. Conscious knowledge typically is assessed using a questionnaire-administered postsystem-interaction.

Serial Pattern Learning

Two forms of serial pattern task, one introduced by Nissen and Bullemer (1987), the other by Lewicki and his associates (Lewicki, Czyzewska, & Hoffman, 1987; Lewicki et al., 1988), have been used in a number of studies.[3] In the form of task introduced by Nissen and Bullemer, a sequence is instantiated over a number of items, often a 10-place sequence over four items, where the items might be locations on a computer screen. For example, numbering the screen locations 1 through 4, the sequence might be 4231324321. The subject is exposed to a number of repetitions of the sequence through the appearance of an indicator at the various screen locations. The subject's task is to respond by pressing a key corresponding to the location in which the indicator shows. The task is presented as a choice-RT task, with the subject not told that a sequence exists. Learning is evinced by declining RTs over the sequenced trials (where the extent of the decrease is greater than that found on randomly ordered trials). Conscious knowledge is assessed post RT task by asking the subject either to predict the next occurrence of the indicator over a set of sequence-governed trials, or to report whatever they can of the sequence.

Lewicki's task (Lewicki et al., 1987, 1988) is similar in that it is presented as a choice-RT task, learning is assessed by declining RTs across rule-governed trials, and the same prediction and verbal-report methods can be employed in assessing conscious knowledge. However, Lewicki's task involves a set of short sequences, and each sequence is interrupted by uninformative "noise" trials. More specifically, Lewicki et al. (1987) exposed their subjects to a series of "simple" trials in each of which a stimulus occurred in a quadrant of the computer screen. The subjects' task was to identify the quadrant as quickly and as accurately as possible. After six of

---

[3]Articles illustrative of the use of serial pattern tasks include Lewicki et al. (1987), Nissen and Bullemer (1987), and Perruchet and Amorim (1992).

these trials, a further trial occurred in which the to-be-located stimulus occurred on-screen with distractors. Once again, the subjects' task was to indicate the quadrant in which the target stimulus was located. The quadrant in which the target occurred in these trials-with-distractors was determined, under one of 24 rules, by its position in four of the preceding six simple trials (simple trials 1, 3, 4, and 6), whereas on the remaining simple trials (2 and 5) the stimulus location was randomized.

PURPORTED CHARACTERISTICS
OF IMPLICIT LEARNING

In this section we review work from the three task domains. The review is organized under four purported characteristics of implicit learning: that it operates outside consciousness, without intent, without capacity limitation, and that it is robust to neuropsychological disorders that undermine explicit processing.

Without Consciousness

The concept of *consciousness* is not a unitary one. Natsoulas (1978) identified at least seven different meanings of the term. In these circumstances it is reasonable to ask what implicit learning theorists mean when they use the terms *conscious* and *unconscious*. Reber (1992) defined what he meant by consciousness as "the capacity to play a causal role in the inner workings of oneself" (p. 113). This definition is consistent with his earlier (1989a) description of implicit learning as an unconscious process of knowledge acquisition that operates in the "absence of conscious, reflective strategies to learn" (p. 219). Baars (1992) pointed out that in taking this definition Reber is presupposing conscious wakefulness and perceptual consciousness, and, Baars noted, other terms that have been used to describe this form of consciousness are monitoring, reflective, overt, and declarative. It is this concept of consciousness that underpins the discussion in this and following sections of this chapter.

Central to the discussion in this section is the distinction, mooted earlier, between the *no-access* and *possible-access* positions. Under both positions, the implicit system acquires knowledge unconsciously; that is, there is no conscious awareness of the learning process and the learner has no intent to learn. The difference between the two views is that under the no-access position (e.g., Lewicki et al., 1992) implicitly acquired knowledge remains closed to consciousness, whereas under the possible-access position (e.g., Reber, 1989a) implicitly acquired knowledge is not held to be necessarily unconscious. The important point is that evaluations of conscious access to knowledge after the learning incident is completed (e.g., as with a posttask questionnaire) can be used to test the no-access, but not the possible-ac-cess, position.

Another point that should be raised here regarding the no-access and possible access positions is that a test of the accessible status of implicitly acquired knowledge is a test of the conscious–unconscious status of the *learning process* only under the no-access position (and then only given an acceptance of the assumption that *only* unconscious processes can lay down unconscious knowledge). The possible-access position, in the absence of a means of interrogating the learning process *itself*, does not yield a testable position with regard to the consciousness, or otherwise, of the acquisition process. Thus, under the possible-access position, the argument for the unconscious nature of implicit learning depends critically on two things: (a) the (almost pretheoretical) assumption that learning that occurs under conditions in which the subjects do not intend to learn is, necessarily, unconscious, and (b) that, in the experimental paradigms used to investigate implicit learning, an unintended-learning condition is successfully instantiated.

We return to the possible-access position in the following section on intention. In this section we review the evidence on the unconscious status of implicitly acquired knowledge, that is, the evidence relevant to the no-access position.

Artificial Grammars. The most general claim to have emerged from this literature is that subjects who have been simply exposed to grammatical exemplars are later able to discriminate grammatical from ungrammatical exemplars and that this learning is implicitly acquired (R.C. Mathews et al.,1989; Reber, 1967, 1976, 1989a; Reber & Allen, 1978; Reber, Kassin, S.M. Lewis, & Cantor, 1980; Reber & S.M. Lewis, 1977). There is convincing evidence that learning under the exposure conditions used by Reber and various colleagues does occur. Subjects who are informed prior to the study phase of the existence of the rules, and are encouraged to discover them, do no better at making later judgments of grammaticality than subjects who study the strings without that information (in fact they sometimes do worse), and both groups of subjects perform the categorization task to above-chance levels (Abrams & Reber, 1988; Dulany et al., 1984; Perruchet & Pacteau, 1990; Reber, 1976; Reber et al., 1980). Reber (1989a) argued that implicitly acquired knowledge is not completely unconscious, but that the aspects of the implicit database that are explicable do not reflect the total sum of implicit learning on a task. Thus he held the possible-access position on conscious access.

Other researchers, notably critics of implicit learning research, have evaluated the no-access position in their consideration of the data yielded by the artificial grammar paradigm. Dulany et al. (1984) asked their subjects to identify on paper which segments of the test strings indicated grammaticality or nongrammaticality. Subjects' performances in this identification task predicted the accuracy of their grammaticality judgments with no residual. On this basis Dulany et al. argued that learning of artificial grammars is not unconscious. Instead, they suggested that what subjects learn is a number of microrules that correspond to the actual grammar with varying degrees of accuracy, and that these rules are conscious and reportable. Perruchet and Pacteau (1990, 1991) identified these microrules with knowledge of permissible bigrams. Perruchet and Pacteau (1990) showed that, after the effect of knowledge of permissible leading letters of grammatical strings had been removed, memorizing bigrams in the study phase led to accuracy in grammaticality judgments comparable to that which followed memorizing complete letter strings. They also showed that, following study, subjects succeeded in categorizing bigrams to an extent that could underpin the typical level of success on the complete-string grammaticality task. In response to Dulany et al., Reber et al. (1985) made the point that subjects may be able to identify the critical segments of the grammatical or ungrammatical strings using implicitly acquired knowledge; that is, they question whether the identification task necessarily reflects consciously acquired knowledge.

Reber very often has collected free reports from his subjects regarding their categorization of letter strings as being grammatical or ungrammatical (e.g., Abrams & Reber, 1988; Allen & Reber, 1980; Reber & Allen, 1978; Reber & Lewis, 1977). He has claimed, on the basis of these reports, that subjects have some ability to verbalize their knowledge of the grammar, but that their implicit knowledge exceeds the knowledge they can consciously access. Unfortunately, no formal analyses of these verbal reports have ever been published. However, Dienes, D. Broadbent, and Berry (1991) collected free reports from their subjects, and did publish the results of a formal analysis of them.

Dienes et al. (1991) explored their subjects' knowledge of the grammar by requiring them to perform, post study, the usual grammaticality judgment task and to give a free report of the rules they used in making these judgments. In addition, the subjects performed a sequential letter detection test that indexed the subjects' knowledge of permissible bigrams and positions. In this test the subjects were shown fragments of letter strings and were required to say, for each letter contained in the grammar, whether that letter could be a possible next letter. They found that subjects acquired accessible knowledge of acceptable bigrams, and bigram positions (as evident on the sequential letter detection test), which could account for their ability to categorize letter strings as grammatical or ungrammatical. However, they also found that the rules these subjects generated in free report were not adequate to account for this categorization performance.

Thus several studies indicate that knowledge of permissible leading letters and permissible bigrams underpins artificial grammar learning. Also, subjects can identify which particular segments of complete strings contribute to their grammatical judgments. Nevertheless, their free reports do not contain enough information to support their level of accuracy in grammatical judgments. Obviously, an impediment to a definitive conclusion is the absence of an agreed-upon index of conscious access. However, the no-access position appears untenable in respect of artificial grammar learning, because even free reports convey some valid knowledge of the grammar.

Interactive Tasks.   The conclusion of many researchers using these tasks to explore implicit learning has been that subjects exposed to these systems show dissociations between acquired system control and verbal knowledge of the system (e.g., Berry & D.E. Broadbent, 1984; D.E. Broadbent et al., 1986). Early evidence suggesting a system control-verbal knowledge dissociation can be found in an article by D.E. Broadbent and Aston (1978). The system they used was based on multiple equations, some of which exhibited lags between inputs and their effects upon output variables. The results suggested that gains in verbal knowledge made by subjects were unrelated to their ability to control the lagged aspects of the system. Other early articles, for instance, D.E. Broadbent (1977) and Shepherd, E.C. Marshall, Turner, and Duncan (1977), found similar patterns of dissociation.

Articles by Berry and D.E. Broadbent (1984) and D.E. Broadbent et al. (1986) further investigated the relationship between the ability to control a system, and verbal knowledge of that system. In both of these articles, dissociations between verbal knowledge and system control are reported. Important to note, Berry and Broadbent found evidence of a double dissociation, with instruction improving postexposure verbal knowledge but not system control, whereas practice improved system control but not verbal knowledge. Furthermore, they found no evidence that ability to control the system, and verbal knowledge, were positively associated for subjects exposed to their task. Similar results have been found in other articles, for instance, Berry and D.E. Broadbent (1987a, 1988).

These studies suggest that the ability to control complex interactive systems may be dissociated from awareness of the rules governing the systems. However, the observation of dissociations, whether single or double, although being consistent with the possible-access position, is not, in principle, sufficient to satisfy the no-access position and so evince the unconscious nature of the learning process. It is, for instance, as Shanks and St. John (1994) noted, possible to account for double dissociations of the type observed by Berry and D.E. Broadbent (1984) by postulating two conscious systems that encode different types of knowledge. To satisfy the no-access position, observations of *no* verbal access to the database would be required.

Sanderson (1989) reported evidence of associations between task performance and verbal knowledge measures. In addition she argued that, because subjects must overcome prior inaccurate mental models that they initially apply to the task, more sensitive measures of verbal knowledge would consider changes in mental models (rather than simply accuracy in stating the rule). Using this approach, she showed that the verbal reports generated by subjects changed with exposure to an interactive task. Furthermore, albeit at considerably greater levels of practice than had been used by previous researchers who had found dissociations (D.E. Broadbent et al., 1986), she found associations between verbal knowledge and task performance. However, Maybery and O'Brien-Malone (1996) found significant correlations between task control and verbal knowledge even for participants with just 20 trials of experience with the Clegg task. We also showed that provision of a simple heuristic effected significant improvements in both system control and verbal knowledge even at very low levels of practice.

This evidence does not support the no-access position on verbal access, however, as for artificial grammars, the possible-access position may still be sustainable.

Serial Pattern Learning.   A number of researchers have reported that when subjects are exposed to serial-pattern-learning tasks they learn the pattern without apparently having access to the corresponding verbal knowledge. These claims have been made using both the Nissen and Bullemer task, and the Lewicki task.

Several articles have shown that, using the Nissen and Bullemer serial RT task, subjects show decreases in RT attributable to learning the sequence (Hartman, Knopman, & Nissen, 1989; Nissen & Bullemer, 1987). Analyses of the subjects' verbal reports (and sometimes their performance on a prediction task), subsequent to their exposure to the sequence in the RT task, usually yield a subgroup of subjects who do not show better than chance ability to identify the sequence. This subgroup of subjects nevertheless shows the pattern of decreases in RT described earlier (e.g., Hartman et al., 1989).

One difficulty inherent in these data is that the decreases in RT shown by these subjects are not as extreme as those shown by subjects having better than chance reporting of the sequence. Thus, one possible interpretation of this evidence is that the measure of conscious access was insufficiently sensitive to detect low levels of knowledge.

Lewicki et al. (1988) tested nine subjects on the matrix-scanning task. Subjects received a large number of exposures to the covariation before being transferred to a different rule. Their RT to location of the target showed a decline until transfer, when RT increased. Although this pattern of RTs indicated that some learning of the covariation had been achieved, in postexperimental interviews none of the subjects appeared to have any knowledge of the covariation. Perhaps the most telling point in this study is that the subjects were all academics from a university psychology department, and all knew that the investigators' area of research was implicit learning. Similar results have been reported by Lewicki et al. (1987) and Stadler (1989).

However, critics of this research have pointed out that the matrix-scanning task is vulnerable to the criticism of correlated hypotheses. Perruchet et al. (1990) demonstrated that Lewicki et al.'s (1988) results could be accounted for by the relative frequencies of occurrence of the movements of the target from one quadrant to another across trials. It follows, therefore, that Lewicki et al.'s assessment of their subjects' verbal knowledge, which was based on their set of complex ordering rules, was flawed. Furthermore, Perruchet et al. found that subjects, when asked to perform a prediction task, revealed accessible knowledge regarding the relative frequency of occurrence of these movements. These authors noted that this does not mean that the knowledge held by the subjects necessarily was acquired by a conscious process, however, their data stand against the no-access position.

Summary.   There would seem to be little evidence supporting the no-access position from the experimental paradigms generally in use in the implicit learning literature. (For a more exhaustive coverage of the evidence against the no-access position, see Shanks & St. John, 1994.) In one sense this conclusion is unsurprising for, as Holyoak and Spellman (1993) noted, it is "difficult to show conclusively that knowledge is inaccessible to consciousness, because the methodology for assessing access to implicit knowledge is inevitably open to challenge" (p. 282).

Thus, the claim for the unconscious quality of implicit learning hinges upon the possible-access position. As was noted previously, under this position the argument for the unconscious nature of implicit learning depends critically on two things, the assumption that unintentional learning is unconscious, and that implicit learning paradigms successfully instantiate an unintended-learning condition.

Without Intention

The idea that implicit learning should proceed in the absence of the intention of the learner to learn the regularity of interest is central to the implicit status of this learning. Widespread theoretical support for this position can be found in the literature. For instance, as noted in the last section, Reber (1989a) defined implicit learning as an unconscious knowledge-acquisition process that occurs "in the absence of conscious, reflective strategies to learn" (p. 219). Hayes and D.E. Broadbent (1988) pointed to Hasher and Zacks' (1984) concept of the automatic encoding of frequency information, for which one of the criteria is that it proceeds independently of intention. Berry (1993; Berry & Dienes, 1993) has argued that implicit learning is associated with incidental learning conditions, and that the learner acquires knowledge without necessarily having an intent to do so. Similar definitional positions can be found in Holyoak and Spellman (1993), Perruchet and Pacteau (1991), and others. They also can be found in related literatures; for instance, Holender (1986), in discussing the unconscious semantic activation literature, wrote: "It is fundamental that an indicator of awareness must be intentional" (p. 51), and, in the context of implicit memory, Schacter, J. Bowers, and Booker (1989) equated conscious recollection with "intentional, voluntary, or deliberate recollection" (p. 48).

This point raises a problem inherent in the implicit learning paradigms currently in use. Subjects in all of the experimental paradigms used in the literature are clearly consciously and deliberately engaged in doing *something*. The critical issue is that the subjects are not consciously and deliberately *attempting to learn the particular stimulus regularity*. Yet, in each of the three major approaches used in the domain, subjects are exposed to the regularity of interest in such a way that if they knew the regularity they would be better able to perform the task in which they *are instructed to engage.*

Artificial Grammars.   For instance, in the artificial grammar task subjects generally are instructed to memorize strings of letters. These letter strings are presented to the subjects one at a time. During a presentation the subject must attempt to remember the string and, once it has been removed, to reproduce it. Thus, the subject's goal in performing the artificial grammar task is memorization, and one strategy that could be employed to aid memorization of strings of meaningless letters is to look for regularities in those strings. (That subjects do develop mnemonic strategies during the study phase of the artificial grammar task has been acknowledged by Reber, 1989a; Reber, Walkenfeld, & Hernstadt, 1991.)

Interactive Tasks.   Similarly, in the interactive tasks devised by Berry and Broadbent, subjects are asked to control the interactive system. Of course, effective control of the system demands sensitivity to the regularity that governs the system. Therefore, inasmuch as the subjects are attempting to comply with the instructions they have been given, they must be deliberately attempting to learn the regularity.

Serial Pattern Learning.   In the serial-pattern-learning tasks, subjects are asked to perform under RT conditions. Here the subject's goal is to perform at their fastest while maintaining accuracy. The information that would allow subjects to maximize their achievement of this goal would be knowledge of the actual regularity inherent in the task.

O'Brien-Malone and Maybery (1994) reported having exposed subjects to the Nissen and Bullemer sequence under genuinely incidental conditions. The sequence was instantiated over four colors, and was presented to the subjects via a series of words, where each word was printed on-screen in one of the four colors. The subject's task was to count particular features of the letters in each word. Thus the dimension of the stimuli on which the regularity was instantiated (the colors of the words) was irrelevant to the task the subject was asked to do. When subsequently asked to perform a color-matching task under RT conditions, subjects showed no advantage from this prior incidental exposure.

So, in each of the three major methodological paradigms, inasmuch as subjects do engage in deliberate cognitive activity directed at performing as per the instructions they receive, then the solution they are attempting to learn is, at least in part, the regularity itself. Furthermore, there is some evidence that exposure under genuinely incidental conditions, at least in the case of the Nissen and Bullemer sequence task, does not yield evidence of learning.

Summary.   The present methodologies do not rule out the possibility that subjects may acquire knowledge without an intention to learn. However, they do not provide a strong instantiation of an unintended-learning condition. Further research using methodologies that do not lead to subjects possibly adopting an intended processing of the stimulus regularity is needed. Exposing the subjects to the stimuli in such a way that they must encode the dimension of the stimulus on which the regularity is instantiated, while they are engaged in completing a task for which this regularity is completely irrelevant, would seem to be a useful research strategy.

Without Capacity Limitation

It is debatable whether evidence relevant to the question of the relationship between attention and implicit processes can directly inform the issue of the consciousness or unconsciousness of the learning process. Some authors have assumed an equivalence between processes requiring attention and conscious processes (e.g., G. Mandler, 1975; Posner & C.R.R. Snyder, 1975), whereas others have argued against such a simple assumption (e.g., Kihlstrom, 1987). Nevertheless, many domains within psychology that are relevant to implicit learning, and to this book, have given particular importance to the resource requirements of processing (e.g., Hasher & Zacks, 1984, and Shiffrin & Schneider, 1977, have different conceptions of automatic processing, but both assume little or no attentional resources are consumed by these processes). Furthermore, some implicit learning theorists (D.E. Broadbent, 1989; Dienes et al., 1991; Hayes & D.E. Broadbent, 1988) have argued that implicit learning should be invulnerable to manipulations of cognitive resources. In this section, we review the evidence on the status of implicit learning with regard to cognitive capacity.

Artificial Grammars. Dienes et al. (1991, Experiment 2) exposed subjects to the artificial grammar task under dual versus single task conditions. In addition, they manipulated, between subjects, the order of priority of the two tasks. Subjects in the dual-task condition were required to generate random numbers at 2-second intervals while being exposed to the grammatical exemplars in the study phase. Post study the subjects categorized letter strings as being either grammatical or ungrammatical, gave a free report of the rules they had used in the categorization task, and performed the sequential letter detection task. Dienes et al. found that the priority manipulation had no effect on either classification performance, free report, or performance on the sequential letter detection task, although the priority manipulation did affect random number generation. However, all measures of knowledge showed an impact due to the presence of the dual task. Dienes et al. interpreted their results as indicating that some specific resource required for grammar learning is taken up by the random number generation task in an "all-or-none" (p. 883) fashion, and they speculated that one possibility is that random number generation occupies the articulatory loop.

Interactive Tasks. Hayes and D.E. Broadbent (1988) examined implicit and explicit learning using two versions of an interactive task: one where the output was determined by the current input (this was expected to be learned selectively, or explicitly), and one where the output was determined by the previous input (this was expected to be learned unselectively, or implicitly). Subjects exposed to the different versions of the task yielded quite different learning and transfer data. In the explicit version, subjects quickly mastered the task, they were able to describe the algorithm accurately, and their relearning of a transformed relationship was rapid. However, under dual task conditions, their ability to learn the new relationship was decreased, indicating that this form of learning was vulnerable in circumstances of capacity limitation. Initial learning was slower on the implicit version (relative to the explicit version) and was not accompanied by verbal knowledge, and learning of the transformed implicit relationship was also slow. However, learning of the transformed implicit relationship was *enhanced* under secondary task conditions. On the basis of this double dissociation, Hayes and Broadbent concluded that implicit learning was differentiated from explicit learning in not utilizing conscious working memory and in not being subject to its resource limitations.

In another study by Porter (1986, cited in D.E. Broadbent, 1989), subjects were exposed to a computer game in which they had to try to achieve two goals. The game consisted of moving a whale around a computer screen on which there were a number of obstacles (icebergs). The two goals were to eat plankton and to avoid being harpooned by Eskimos. What Porter found was that although subjects showed an improvement in performance on both these tasks, they had good verbal knowledge only of how to achieve the goal of eating plankton, but not of how to avoid being harpooned. Furthermore, the addition of various secondary tasks impacted markedly on eating plankton, and marginally, or not at all, on avoidance of being harpooned. Thus Porter's results are congruent with those of Hayes and Broadbent.

However, Green and Shanks (1993) attempted unsuccessfully to replicate Hayes and D.E. Broadbent's (1988) results. They were able to find some evidence supportive of one half of Hayes and Broadbent's double dissociation: Green and Shanks' subjects showed poorer learning of a transformed relationship in the implicit version compared to subjects exposed to the explicit version. But of the critical second half of the double dissociation—that the subjects exposed to the implicit version of the task should show better learning of a transformed relationship under dual-task conditions than the subjects exposed to the explicit version of the task—they found no evidence. In fact they found the reverse: Subjects exposed to the implicit version of the task showed a greater impact of the secondary task upon their learning of the transformed relationship than did subjects who received the explicit version. Green and Shanks argued that their results are congruent with an explanation based on differences in task difficulty. Furthermore, Maybery and O'Brien-Malone (1996) found, with the Clegg task, that both task control and verbal knowledge were detrimentally affected by a concurrent task.

Serial Pattern Learning.   The role of attentional processes in the serial-pattern-learning paradigm is not simple. Nissen and Bullemer (1987) found that the addition of a secondary task to their sequential learning task impacted highly on the subjects' learning, on both measures of RT and accuracy of sequence generation. Furthermore, Hartman et al. (1989) found that subjects who did not report awareness of the sequence showed *no* learning of it (on the RT measure) when it was instantiated in words that the subject had to read—a highly automated activity (i.e., when the sequence was instantiated as: MUSIC, RULER, LADY, OCEAN, LADY, RULER, MUSIC, LADY, RULER, OCEAN). However, they found that subjects who reported no awareness of the sequence nevertheless *did* show some learning of it when it was instantiated in words that the subjects were required to categorize—a less highly automated activity. Thus a strong case can be made that some involvement of attention is necessary for subjects to learn the sequence used throughout many of the serial-pattern-learning articles. However, there are some difficulties in interpreting this result for the general case.

A. Cohen, Ivry, and Keele (1990) examined the effect that the structure of a sequence has upon subjects' learning of it under dual-task conditions. They argued that sequences can be considered to be of two classes: those having at least one unique association between two constituent items, and those in which there are no unique associations. They found that sequences having a unique association could be learned under dual-task conditions, and that varying dual-task difficulty did not produce a differential impact on the amount of learning of the sequence. On the other hand, a sequence that had no unique associations within its constituent items appeared to be unable to be learned under dual-task conditions. Cohen et al. hypothesized that there are two learning systems by which sequences can be learned: an associative mechanism by which sequences with some unique constituent item pairings are learned, and a hierarchical mechanism by which sequences without unique associations between constituent items are learned.

In a later article, Curran and Keele (1993) examined this hypothesis. They argued that their data supported the existence of two independent mechanisms for sequence learning, only one of which requires attention. Furthermore, they claimed that these mechanisms operate independently, in parallel, without intermechanism feedback, and that the sequential information acquired by each of these mechanisms is represented in qualitatively different ways. The Nissen and Bullemer (1987) sequence contains no unique associations between constituent items, and Curran and Keele contended that learning on this sequence—whether with or without awareness—required attention, and could be distinguished from the nonattentional learning mechanism that they postulated.

Summary.   The argument that implicit learning is invulnerable to the influence of concurrent tasks that demand attentional or working-memory resources receives, at best, equivocal support across the three major paradigms. A more specific argument—that sequences involving a unique association can be learned outside the influence of concurrent demands—is supported, but deserves more intensive research.

Robustness of Implicit Learning

Reber (1992) argued that cognitive systems appearing earlier in the course of evolution should show greater robustness to neuropsychological insult when compared to more recently evolved systems. In particular, he argued that implicit learning should be robust in the face of disorders that undermine explicit processing. Several articles are pertinent to this claim.

Artificial Grammars.   Abrams and Reber (1988) compared a diverse group of psychiatric inpatients (schizophrenics, depressives, alcoholics) with an undergraduate sample using the artificial grammar paradigm. The two groups performed comparably on grammaticality test judgments, consistent with intact implicit learning in the psychiatric group. Furthermore, a second experiment showed that a similar diverse group of inpatients performed at chance level on a concept-learning task intended to elicit explicit learning.

Knowlton, Ramus, and Squire (1992; see also Knowlton & Squire, 1994) also used the artificial grammar paradigm and compared amnesic and normal subjects on their ability to perform the grammaticality categorization task, and on their recognition and judgments of similarity of exemplars. The control and amnesic groups were not significantly different in accuracy of grammaticality judgments; however, the controls outperformed the amnesiacs for both recognition and similarity judgments. Knowlton et al. concluded that "classification learning can proceed normally without intact explicit memory" (p. 176). A similar conclusion could be drawn from the Abrams and Reber (1988) article.

However, there are reasons for a more cautious conclusion than that drawn by Knowlton et al. (1992). It is possible that the amnesiacs actually acquired knowledge of the grammar using explicit processes, but subsequently forgot the learning incident (the amnesiacs' performance on the recognition and similarity tests was above chance). Similarly, although the Abrams and Reber (1988) article suggests that the inpatient group showed a decrement in explicit processing relative to the control group, it is possible that the inpatients suffered selective (as opposed to global) decrements in explicit processing. Thus, these articles, although supporting the robustness of artificial grammar learning in amnesiacs, do not provide compelling evidence for the implicit characterization of that learning.

Another aspect of the robustness of implicitly acquired knowledge is that of its robustness to decay over time. Allen and Reber (1980) examined the knowledge of artificial grammars subjects retained after a 2-year period. They examined the subjects' ability to correctly categorize strings as grammatical or ungrammatical where knowledge of the grammars originally had been acquired under two different learning procedures, namely paired associate learning and observational learning. They found that although knowledge acquired under both forms of learning had decreased with time, subjects in both groups still were performing at levels that were significantly above chance. However, some information that subjects did appear to have acquired explicitly in the original data, namely initial letter constraints, appeared to have been lost. Furthermore, the patterns of errors in categorization that occurred in the original data, and that distinguished paired associate from observational learning, were still intact. Thus, this article suggests that some forms of learning produce knowledge that is more robust to decay than that acquired by explicit learning processes.

Serial Pattern Learning.   Nissen and Bullemer (1987) compared the performances, on their sequence-learning task, of a small group ($n = 6$) of elderly subjects exhibiting memory disorders associated with Korsakoff's syndrome, and a group of elderly control subjects. Although the Korsakoff patients showed longer RTs on the task than did the controls, they nevertheless showed the typical pattern of reducing RTs with increasing exposure. However, when questioned about the existence of a repeating sequence, *all* of the control subjects, and *none* of the Korsakoff patients, reported noticing a sequence. Similar results were found by Knopman and Nissen (1987) using a considerably larger sample ($n = 28$) of Alzheimer's patients and a group of elderly control subjects.

In addition, Nissen, Knopman, and Schacter (1987) examined evidence from a normal population under conditions of drug-induced amnesia. They found that subjects who had been injected with scopolamine showed dramatically reduced ability to recall word lists, yet, although they were slower in their responses than the control subjects, they still exhibited the typical reduction in RTs with exposure to the sequence. The scopolamine-affected subjects also showed significantly less ability to generate the sequence than did the controls.

However, work by Knopman (1991) suggests that the notion of a clean map from impaired and preserved learning in amnesiacs on to explicit and implicit should be regarded with caution. Over a series of experiments, Knopman examined the performance of normal subjects under conditions of drug-induced amnesia. Subjects were tested under one of two drug conditions—lorazepam or scopolamine—and on one of two versions of the sequence-learning task. Subjects were exposed either to the usual variant of the sequence (which required motor responses) or to an instantiation of the sequence that required verbal responses. The effects of type of drug administered on sequence learning depended on which instantiation of the sequence the subject received. Learning on the verbal sequence showed an impact under both the administration of scopalamine or lorazepam, whereas lorazepam did not affect subjects' learning on the usual instantiation of the sequence. Thus, Knopman's results, when combined with those of Nissen et al. (1987), indicate that under amnesia induced by the administration of either scopalamine or lorazepam, subjects can learn the usual instantiation of the sequence, but cannot learn a verbal instantiation.

Interactive Tasks.   To date, the question of the robustness of implicit learning to neuropsychological insult has not been investigated using this paradigm.

Summary. Few studies have been conducted using implicit learning paradigms and populations showing neuropsychological deficits. However, the results of the studies to date support Reber's robustness claim. Other work, not using the implicit learning paradigms examined in this chapter, has demonstrated the robustness of some learning to disorders such as amnesia. There is, for instance, evidence for intact skill acquisition and repetition priming in amnesiacs (N.J. Cohen, 1984; Schacter, McAndrews, & Moscovitch, 1988). The performance of amnesiacs on the Nissen and Bullemer sequence-learning task has been discussed in this wider literature as indicating implicit retention on a skill-learning task (Schacter et al., 1988). Of course, the interesting thing about this implicit learning task is that similar performance to that observed in amnesiacs (i.e., RT decrements unaccompanied by awareness of the sequence) also is seen in some normal subjects. Although the current studies using implicit learning paradigms do not provide conclusive evidence of the unconscious quality of implicit learning, they are supportive of it, and they do provide evidence for the robustness of implicit learning in neuropsychologically disordered populations.

CONCLUSION

In this chapter we have focused on the question of the unconscious status of implicit learning. Our examination of this issue has been based on two theoretical positions with respect to the relationship between the learning (acquisition) process and the knowledge that is acquired. First, the no-access position is that the implicit learning process is unconscious and lays down knowledge that is not available to conscious access. Second, the possible-access position is that the implicit learning process is unconscious and lays down knowledge that may be accessed consciously. Because implicit learning consistently has been shown to yield some accessible knowledge when a variety of measures, usually employing forced choice procedures, have been used, the conclusion must be that the no-access position cannot be sustained. Thus the claim that implicit learning is unconscious must rest upon the possible-access position. However, this position does not necessarily predict different effects upon interrogation of an explicitly, as opposed to implicitly, acquired knowledge base. We have argued that, in the implicit learning literature, consciousness is equated with intentional involvement in the learning process. Thus, the testability of the possible-access position hinges on instantiating an unintended-learning condition. However, because the paradigmatic tasks are not constructed in such a way as to instantiate genuinely unintentional learning, a defense of this position is still outstanding.

In addition to the evidence regarding the accessibility of the knowledge base, and the unintentional nature of implicit learning, we examined two other claims that may bear on its purported unconscious nature. These were that implicit learning is invulnerable to the manipulation of attentional resources, and that it is robust to neuropsychological insult. The evidence regarding the first of these claims is equivocal. However, the hypothesis deserves further research, particularly with respect to sequence learning. To date only a few studies have been conducted using implicit learning paradigms in populations showing neuropsychological deficits, but the results of those studies are encouraging. Thus although the no-access position has been refuted, the possible-access position remains a viable hypothesis.

ACKNOWLEDGMENTS

Angela O'Brien-Malone can now be contacted at the Department of Psychology, Murdoch University, Murdoch 6150, Western Australia.

4

IMPLICIT PERCEPTION: PERCEPTUAL PROCESSING WITHOUT AWARENESS

Colin MacLeod
University of Western Australia

The idea that certain cognitive processes may operate without conscious awareness is not new. In an extensive review of early philosophical writings, spanning the period A.D. 130 to 1800, Whyte (1978) provided convincing evidence that an acceptance of nonconscious mental operations was widespread well before the origins of contemporary psychology. Paradoxically perhaps, the advent of experimental psychology within the latter half of the nineteenth century served to stifle, rather than to stimulate, endeavors to understand the nature of nonconscious information processing. The reliance placed by early psychological researchers, such as James (1890) and Wundt (1888), on the use of the introspective method to collect the data on which their theories of cognitive processes were constructed, simply placed nonconscious cognition beyond the scope of accepted scientific enquiry.

Nevertheless, the refinement of psychological theories concerned with the role of nonconscious processing continued during this period within the domain of psychiatry, stimulated principally by psychoanalytically oriented scholars (e.g., Freud, 1912; Jung, 1916). These psychoanalytic theories typically construed the unconscious as a system characterized by a distinctive psychological content (e.g., instincts, motivation, and repressed memories), and governed by a distinctive set of psychological processes (e.g., the pleasure principle and defence mechanisms). According to this position, therefore, it was held not only that complex information processing could occur without awareness, but also that the rules controlling such nonconscious processing differ qualitatively from those that underpin conscious cognition. Despite their theoretical elegance, however, psychoanalytic approaches were compromised by a reliance on controversial assessment techniques that required highly idiosyncratic subjective interpretations of data yielded through a variety of introspective techniques. Concerns over the validity of such data precluded widespread acceptance of this approach by experimental psychologists, who progressively developed increasing reservations about the use of introspection to study cognitive processing.

The advent of behaviorism offered a convenient means of sidestepping the problematic issue of consciousness and, in the early decades of the century, this became the dominant approach adopted within experimental psychology (Watson, 1914, 1924). By restricting the focus of psychological investigation exclusively to the observed relationships between environmental manipulations and behavioral consequences, the behaviorists avoided any need to speculate about subjects' levels of awareness for intervening cognitive processes. By the mid-1950s, however, it was becoming clear that models based solely on stimulus–response contingencies were unable to account for many aspects of behavior, including not only high-level functions like language (Chomsky, 1959), but even simple patterns of choice reaction times (e.g., Crossman, 1953; Hyman, 1953). Concurrently, the development of information technology was providing a wealth of processing metaphors from which theorists were able to construct increasingly precise information-processing models of human cognition. Ultimately, this led to the reintroduction of mentalism into experimental psychology, and to the development of the information-processing paradigm (D.E. Broadbent, 1958; G.A. Miller, Galanter, & Pribram, 1960). Before long, the resulting new generation of cognitive theorists were rediscovering the old hypothetical dichotomy between conscious and nonconscious aspects of the cognitive system. Since this time, there has been a major resurgence of interest in this distinction which has continued to strengthen throughout recent years (cf. N. Block, 1995; Dennet, 1991; Kihlstrom, 1993).

One focal point for much of this renewed interest in nonconscious processing has lain within the area of perception, and theorists have held differing opinions concerning the degree to which stimuli, presented outside of subjects' conscious awareness, undergo full perceptual processing. Although the issue is still contentious, considerable evidence now has been produced to support the view that stimuli not only may receive high-level structural analysis, but also may access their semantic representations and exert a detectable effect on experience and behavior, all without subjects becoming conscious of their presence (cf. D.M. Merikle & Reingold, 1992). In this present overview, three lines of evidence for this position are critically reviewed, each differing in terms of the techniques employed to restrict conscious awareness of stimuli. The first section considers experiments that have manipulated attention, and have demonstrated semantic processing of unattended stimuli that subjects are unable to report having consciously perceived. The next section reviews studies that have employed faint or brief exposure conditions to eliminate conscious perception of stimuli, yet have produced findings to indicate that semantic processing of these stimuli nevertheless takes place. A third section briefly outlines experiments that have been carried out on subjects who show restricted conscious awareness as a result of biological factors, such as neurological lesions or general anaesthesia, but who display an ability to perceptually process stimuli that they cannot consciously apprehend. It can be seen that these three domains of research have yielded substantial converging support for the occurrence of perception without awareness. Furthermore, as is outlined in a fourth section, there is evidence to suggest that the processing rules that govern nonconscious perception may indeed differ qualitatively from those controlling the processing of information that individuals can consciously perceive.

EVIDENCE OF PERCEPTION WHEN AWARENESS IS RESTRICTED BY ATTENTIONAL MANIPULATIONS

It is an everyday experience that our subjective awareness of external stimuli can be modified by directing the allocation of our attentional resources. Allocating attention toward any particular source of information increases our awareness of stimuli presented from this source, while also decreasing our level of awareness for stimuli presented outside this focus of attention. However, the fact that unattended stimuli typically are poorly represented within awareness need not imply that such stimuli do not undergo extensive perceptual processing. In order to investigate the cognitive fate of unattended stimuli, many researchers have employed experimental paradigms requiring that subjects must attend selectively to one source of information, while ignoring information simultaneously presented through a different source, and have assessed the degree to which these unattended stimuli undergo cognitive processing. One of the best known examples of this methodology is the dichotic listening task, introduced by Cherry (1953), which requires subjects to monitor information presented to one ear while ignoring information presented simultaneously to the other ear. More recently, similar techniques have been developed within the visual domain, usually requiring subjects to process stimulus words presented within the foveal region of the visual field while ignoring words that are presented simultaneously within the parafoveal region (e.g., Bradshaw, 1974). Although researchers agree that such selective attention tasks often greatly impair subjects' abilities to report the identity of the unattended stimuli, a variety of evidence suggests that these unattended stimuli nevertheless may undergo substantial perceptual processing.

In his early highly influential model of attentional selectivity, D.E. Broadbent (1958) proposed that different sources of information are encoded concurrently via multiple channels within the cognitive system. According to this account, the contents of these multiple channels simultaneously are perceptually processed only to a structural level of analysis and, on the basis of this structural analysis alone, the content of some channels, but not others, proceed to a limited-capacity central processor. Broadbent's model contends that only then does the central processor carry out semantic analysis, which is restricted to this selected subset of the total available information. It is the content of this limited-capacity system, which has been selected on the basis of its structural characteristics to receive semantic analysis, that corresponds to the content of conscious awareness according to this theory. Despite its simplicity, Broadbent's account not only posits that perceptual processing does occur prior to awareness, but also construes the nonconscious processing system as being organized in a qualitatively different manner from that which handles the processing of those stimuli that a perceiver is consciously aware of. Specifically, according to Broadbent, nonconscious processing is carried out by a large-capacity system, within which multiple sources of information are analyzed in parallel. In contrast, conscious experience is considered to be the product of a limited-capacity system that operates only on a small subset of selected information at any given time.

D.E. Broadbent's (1958) model proposes that the perceptual processing carried out on an unattended stimulus is restricted to the structural analysis of this information. However, considerable evidence instead suggests that unattended information may be processed to a semantic level of analysis. Some of this evidence is anecdotal. For example, most people will have experienced the common "cocktail party" effect, when in a noisy social gathering one finds that a previously unattended conversation suddenly intrudes upon our awareness when the topic changes to a matter of personal relevance. Assuming that this effect is genuine, then it is difficult to explain how it could occur unless the unattended conversation had been undergoing some degree of semantic analysis, to monitor for topic relevance. The validity of the phenomenon has been supported by the common experimental finding, initially reported by Moray (1959), that subjects do indeed tend to selectively perceive their own name when it is presented to the unattended ear during a dichotic listing task. Of course, it is possible to account for Moray's finding without suggesting that nonconscious semantic processing of an unattended message takes place, simply by proposing that the unique structural properties of one's own name might be sufficient to ensure that this information gains access to consciousness. However, it is less easy to dismiss Treisman's (1960) more powerful evidence that unattended information does indeed receive semantic analysis during a dichotic listening task.

Treisman (1960) simultaneously presented subjects with two sections of quite different text, one to each ear, and required them to repeat aloud (or "shadow") only that message presented to one attended ear. When the messages presented to each ear unexpectedly were switched, partway through the task, Treisman observed that her subjects tended to respond by erroneously switching to shadowing the other ear (to which the meaningful continuation of the previously attended text now was presented). Treisman, and other researchers who have replicated this robust effect, pointed out that such a switch in shadowing behavior could not occur unless the information presented to the unattended ear was undergoing some degree of semantic analysis. Otherwise, subjects could not appreciate that the message presented to this unattended ear continued the meaning of the originally attended text. Findings of this nature led J.A. Deutsch and J. Deutsch (1963) to conclude that perceptual processing can extend beyond structural analysis, to the level of semantic access, without this requiring conscious awareness of the stimuli being processed. Indeed, according to Deutsch and Deutsch's theoretical formulation, all the information that impinges on the senses is fully processed for meaning, and the selection mechanism that determines the limited content of awareness is guided by the outcome of this semantic analysis.

In keeping with D.E. Broadbent's (1958) earlier account, the model of perceptual processing put forward by J.A. Deutsch and D. Deutsch (1963) not only proposes the existence of nonconscious stimulus processing, but also contends that such processing differs qualitatively from that which occurs within awareness. Like Broadbent, Deutsch and Deutsch argued that multiple channels of stimulus information can be processed in parallel within the nonconscious system, which is unconstrained by the capacity limitations that characterize the conscious processing system. Unlike Broadbent, however, Deutsch and Deutsch did not consider that nonconscious information processing is restricted to the structural level of analysis but, instead, contended that extensive semantic analysis also takes place without any phenomenal awareness of stimulus content.

Since this seminal research, a great deal of additional evidence has accrued from a wide range of later attentional studies to provide further support for the claim that stimuli can be processed semantically without perceptual awareness (e.g., J.L. Lewis, 1970; Philpott & Wilding, 1979; Treisman, Squire, & Green, 1974; Underwood, 1976). The dichotic listening paradigm has continued to yield much of the relevant data, with researchers frequently reporting that the meaning of information presented to the unattended ear can influence conscious experience. For example, MacKay (1973) found that the interpretation of homophones presented to the attended ear can be systematically constrained by the simultaneous presentation to the other ear of a word related to only one meaning of the homophone. Also, it has been demonstrated that when galvanomic skin responses (GSRs) are conditioned to certain semantic categories of stimuli, then these GSRs can be elicited when category exemplars are presented to the unattended ear using a dichotic listening procedure. Furthermore, such effects persist even when subjects are quite unable to report the meanings of the unattended stimulus words, and when these words represent new category exemplars that were not used with the initial conditioning procedure (e.g., Corteen & Dunn, 1974; Corteen & Wood, 1972; P.M. Forster & Govier, 1978; Govier & Pitts, 1982; J.N. von Wright, K. Anderson, & Stenman, 1975). Such findings suggest that unattended stimuli, which subjects are unable to report perceiving, not only undergo semantic analysis but also are categorized, and serve to evoke emotional responses based on previous learning experiences, all without their identity being consciously apprehended.

Similar findings have been produced using a visual analogue of the dichotic listening procedure, in which subjects have been required to allocate attention to stimuli presented within the foveal region of the visual field, while ignoring information simultaneously presented at distances varying between 1° and 5° of visual angle from the fovea. For example, in a study employing this procedure, Bradshaw (1974) observed that the meaning subjects imposed upon an ambiguous homograph presented to the foveal region was constrained when unambiguous words, related to either possible meaning, were presented to the parafoveal area. The fact that subjects were unable to report the identities of these parafoveal words led Bradshaw to conclude that semantic analysis of parafoveal stimuli proceeds without requiring that these stimuli become represented within consciousness. Consistent with this conclusion have been the findings of other researchers, who have reported that the meanings of unreportable parafoveal words can both facilitate and impair the processing of stimuli presented within the foveal region. Thus, when Underwood, Whitefield, and Winfield (1982) recorded the speed with which their subjects could access the identity of foveal words, they found that this was increased when semantically related words were simultaneously presented to the parafoveal region. Conversely, Kahneman and Chajczyk (1983) reported a parafoveal replication of the well-known Stroop effect (Stroop, 1938), in which the speed with which subjects were able to name the colors in which foveal stimuli were presented was impaired when the names of incongruent colors simultaneously were exposed parafoveally. In each of these studies, the effects indicated that the meanings of the parafoveal stimuli must have been accessed, yet subjects demonstrated an inability to report the content of this unattended information. Once again, this suggests that perceptual processing can continue to the level of semantic analysis, without this being accompanied by any conscious awareness of stimulus identity.

Despite the consistency of such findings, many theorists dispute the capability of attentional studies to sustain the conclusion that semantic processing can take place in the absence of stimulus awareness. Such critics argue that subjects performing these attentional tasks may become momentarily aware of the unattended information during stimulus presentation, due to brief periods of attentional switching. Even though these conscious experiences of the unattended stimuli may be too fleeting to enable their subsequent report, it is possible that the semantic processing of such stimuli might be mediated by such transitory episodes of awareness (e.g., P.A. Merikle, 1982). Some researchers have failed to find support for this argument when they have sought evidence for momentary awareness of unattended stimulus identity, by unexpectedly interrupting subjects during stimulus presentation and asking them to immediately report the unattended information (e.g., Bargh, 1982). However, in other studies it has been observed that subjects can indeed report the identity of unattended stimuli, though only for a brief period of time following their presentation. For example, Glucksberg and C.N.J. Cohen (1970) found that such stimuli could be reported at delays approaching 5 seconds, whereas Klapp and Lee (1974) demonstrated that some subjects could identify unattended stimuli following delays of up to 10 seconds. Such findings appear to confirm the argument that reduced attention to a stimulus need not always serve to entirely eliminate awareness of stimulus content. Furthermore, when procedural modifications have been applied to the dichotic listening procedure, designed with the intention of reducing the likelihood that subjects may become momentarily aware of unattended stimulus information, then it sometimes has been found that those effects taken as evidence of nonconscious semantic analysis fail to replicate. For example, Newstead and Dennis (1979) observed that in the dichotic listening procedure employed by MacKay (1973) the unattended words occurred infrequently, and they argued that the emergence of these words from a background of silence may have induced a brief switch of attention toward them. These researchers amended Mackay's procedure by embedding the critical unattended words, which coincided with the presentation of attended homophones, within a continuous stream of unattended words in order to minimize the probability of such attentional switching. Under such conditions, Newstead and Dennis were unable to replicate MacKay's earlier finding that the meanings of words appearing in the unattended ear biased the interpretation of homophones simultaneously presented to the attended ear. On the basis of this demonstration, they concluded that the semantic processing of supposedly unattended stimulus words in MacKay's original study may not have occurred nonconsciously, but rather may have been mediated by a transitory awareness of these stimuli resulting from momentary switches in attentional allocation.

In an influential review of the literature, Holender (1986) convincingly argued that this possibility of momentary awareness for supposedly unattended stimuli never can be excluded in attentional studies of this sort. Because of this, he contended, demonstrations that information that subjects have been instructed to ignore nevertheless undergoes semantic analysis cannot constitute adequate evidence that semantic analysis occurs without stimuli being consciously represented. Holender argued that such claims can be sustained only if awareness of experimental stimuli is precluded by the characteristics of stimulus displays themselves, rather than by requiring subjects to voluntarily maintain a pattern of resource allocation style when processing the information that is presented. That is, using Holender's terminology, subjects' awareness of stimuli must be experimentally restricted by *data limitations* rather than by *resource limitations*, before it would be legitimate to conclude that these stimuli could not have been processed consciously. A wide range of studies have indeed manipulated stimulus awareness in this manner, usually by restricting the intensity or duration of exposure. Considerable support for the proposal that nonconscious perception proceeds to the level of semantic analysis has been forthcoming from many of the experiments that have adopted this more rigorous approach, and this literature now is reviewed in some detail.

EVIDENCE OF PERCEPTION WHEN AWARENESS
IS RESTRICTED BY EXPOSURE MANIPULATIONS

The proposal that conscious experience can be influenced by the presentation of stimuli that, because of their low intensity or brief duration, do not become consciously represented, has received considerable scrutiny throughout the history of experimental psychology (e.g., Baker, 1937; D.E. Broadbent & Gregory, 1967; Coover, 1917; Dixon, 1968, 1971, 1981; G. Gordon, 1967; J G. Miller, 1939; Sidis, 1898; Stroh, Shaw, & Washbourne, 1908; A. Williams, 1938). The earliest such studies most often manipulated stimulus intensity, and commonly yielded findings to suggest that structural processing was evident even when stimulus intensity was too low to enable subjects to report stimulus presence. For example, Dunlap (1900) presented subjects with a version of the Muller–Lyer illusion in which the critical arrow lines, terminating the central straight lines, were drawn extremely faintly. Despite their reported inability to consciously perceive these arrow lines, subjects' perception of the central lines were influenced by their presence, as evidenced by their judgments concerning the relative lengths of these central stimuli. Subsequent researchers have criticized Dunlap's methodology, contending that his measures of awareness were inadequate, and served to discourage subjects from reporting the faint arrow lines, even if these could have been consciously detected (e.g., Titchener & Pyle, 1907; Trimble & Eriksen, 1966). However, his conclusion, that the structural processing of stimuli can occur even when exposure conditions prevent their conscious representation, now has been supported by researchers using quite different experimental methodologies.

For example, when stimulus information has been presented tachistoscopically, at exposure durations too short to permit subjects to report its presence, it often has been observed that the structural properties of this information still can contribute to the occurrence of visual illusions (e.g., Bressler, 1931; Gellatly, 1980; Walker & Myer, 1978). Additional evidence that the perceptual processing of stimulus structure does not require awareness of stimulus presence has been forthcoming from research that has investigated the "mere exposure" effect on the rated likeability of meaningless stimuli. It is a well-established finding that subjective preferences are increased for stimuli that have been exposed previously, whether these are meaningless figures (e.g., Fink, Monahan, & Kaplowitz, 1989), colors (e.g., Franchina, 1991), or any number of other classes of visual stimuli (cf. Bornstein, 1989). Many experiments now have demonstrated that this increased preference for previously exposed stimuli continues to be displayed even when these earlier exposures have been so brief that subjects have shown chance performance rates on tasks requiring them to discriminate the identities of the stimuli being exposed (e.g., Bornstein, 1987; Kunst-Wilson & Zajonc, 1980; Seamon, Brody, & Kauff, 1983). The apparent structural processing of stimuli that fall outside the limits of conscious perception does not appear restricted to the visual modality. Martin, Hawryluk, and Guse (1974) reported having successfully conditioned GSRs to high-frequency tones, above the auditory spectrum that subjects were able to report perceiving consciously. Also, it has been reported that faint olfactory stimuli, which subjects report being unable to consciously detect, can serve to influence a range of cognitive and affective judgments (e.g., Cowley, A.L. Johnson, & Brooksbanck, 1977; Kirk-Smith, Booth, Carroll, & D. Davies, 1978).

Although the aforementioned findings, from those studies that have restricted awareness through the use of stimulus exposure manipulations, do suggest that nonconscious perceptual processing may indeed occur, they permit the possibility that this may be restricted to the low-level structural analysis of stimulus information. However, evidence also has been produced to indicate that the elimination of stimulus awareness through such data limitation procedures need not prevent semantic processing. One of the earliest bodies of literature to sustain this claim concerned the phenomenon known as "perceptual defense." Bruner and Postman (1947) were among the first to demonstrate that, when taboo words and neutral words are tachistoscopically exposed for progressively longer intervals until subjects can accurately report their identity, the exposure durations required to permit identification of the taboo words tend to be significantly longer than the exposure durations required to identify the neutral words. The numerous replications of this finding, reviewed by Erdelyi (1984), have led to the argument that subjects must identify the meanings of the words prior to becoming aware of them, in order for these meanings to affect perceptual thresholds in this way. Such an account has not gone uncriticized, although the most compelling criticisms have not been well supported by subsequent research. Therefore, although early critics suggested that the perceptual defense effect was likely to reflect frequency differences between the taboo words and the neutral words (e.g., Howes, 1954; Howie, 1952), later studies that have more carefully matched stimulus frequencies have continued to find that taboo words require longer exposures than neutral control words before subjects can accurately report their identity (e.g., L.H. Levy, 1958; Sales & Haber, 1968). The alternative argument also has been put forward that the perceptual defense effect reflects a simple response bias that operates after awareness of stimulus content as been attained. Specifically, some theorists have suggested that, although subjects may become equally aware of the identity of taboo and neutral words at the same exposure durations, they may be less willing to emit the taboo words as responses until some increased exposure duration makes them absolutely certain that this is required (e.g., Eriksen, 1963; Minard, 1965). However, later experiments, using appropriate statistical techniques to eliminate the influence of possible response biases, have confirmed that subjects do genuinely display a reduced ability to consciously discriminate the identity of emotionally negative words at exposure durations that permit them to accurately identify matched emotionally neutral words (e.g., Bootzin & Stephens, 1967; D.E. Broadbent & Gregory, 1967). Clearly, such findings invite the conclusion that the affective tone of stimulus words can be discriminated under exposure conditions that do not permit their conscious identification, implying that perceptual processing to the level of semantic analysis can occur in the absence of awareness.

Support for the hypothesis that semantic representations of briefly, or faintly, exposed words can be activated without any conscious awareness has not been restricted to studies investigating the perceptual defense phenomenon. It has been reported that the semantic content of stimuli that subjects claim to be unable to consciously detect, due to the brevity or low intensity of their presentations, systematically influences measures such as dream content (e.g., Fisher, 1960), and mental imagery (e.g., Henley & Dixon, 1974; Mykel & Daves, 1979). Also, in keeping with findings reported by MacKay (1973) and Bradshaw (1974) from their studies of dichotic listening and parafoveal vision, researchers have found that stimuli rendered nonconscious through such exposure manipulations can affect the interpretations of ambiguous stimuli being processed consciously (e.g., Allison, 1963; M.J. Goldstein & Barthol, 1960; G.J.W. Smith, Spence, & Klein, 1959). For example, it has been observed that subjects' judgments concerning the emotional expressions conveyed by simple line drawn faces, of indeterminate emotional status, tend to be biased by the affective tone of simultaneously presented emotional descriptor words, exposed at brief durations precluding their conscious identification (e.g., Henley, 1975; Sackeim, Packer, & Gur, 1977; Somekh & Wilding, 1973). Similar effects also have been observed on more complex judgment tasks. Thus, when Bargh and Pietromonaco (1982) employed brief exposures, which they claimed did not permit conscious awareness, to present subjects with single words related to hostility during a vigilance task, they observed that these subjects subsequently rated a target person as significantly more hostile. In a replication and extension of this study, Erdley and D'Agostino (1988) found that brief exposure of words related to honesty in the initial vigilance task resulted in subjects judging the target person to be more honest, whereas brief exposure of words related to meanness resulted in them judging the target person to be more mean, despite the fact that these subjects were quite unable to identify the briefly presented words on a subsequent recognition task. Such findings have led researchers to conclude that stimulus information presented outside of awareness is indeed processed for meaning, with the semantic structures activated as a result of this processing playing a role in guiding interpretation and judgment.

However, even when stimuli are presented so briefly that subjects report being unaware of their identity, it remains possible that some degree of conscious awareness for such stimuli is experienced. Studies that assess awareness only by asking subjects to identify briefly exposed stimuli may underestimate true levels of awareness, given that subjects' responses may reflect their low levels of confidence rather than the complete absence of conscious perception. Holender (1986) formalized this criticism in some detail, arguing that reducing stimulus exposure duration might reduce subjects' certainty concerning the accuracy of their perceptual experience, before it eliminates their awareness of this perceptual experience. When confidence falls below some threshold level, subjects may choose to report that they do not know what was presented, even though their conscious perceptual experience may still accurately represent stimulus identity. If this is so, then the evidence obtained to indicate the semantic processing of stimuli that subjects report being unable to identify need not imply that such semantic processing is not mediated by conscious awareness of these stimuli. As Holender pointed out, the methodological implications of this criticism are straightforward. Absence of awareness should not be inferred solely on the basis of subjects' claims concerning their conscious experience. Rather, subjects must be required to make a forced-choice discrimination concerning the presence or identity of the stimulus. Only if they show chance levels of performance on such forced-choice discrimination tasks (i.e., in signal detection terms, display a d' of zero when performing this discrimination) can it be concluded that subjects are unaware of the stimuli. Holender acknowledged that one particular method of precluding stimulus awareness has convincingly met this criterion. The method is known as backward pattern masking and, in recent years, this exposure manipulation has been one of most common techniues employed to investigate nonconscious processing.

The backward masking approach involves presenting stimuli for durations that, although very brief, normally would permit conscious perception. However, a second stimulus, or "mask," then promptly is exposed within this same location, and this serves to eliminate awareness of the initial stimulus. The efficacy of this procedure depends on the type of mask and the temporal characteristics of the presentation (cf. Neisser, 1963, 1967). When the mask consists of a homogeneous bright field, with an energy content substantially higher than that of the original stimulus, then conscious awareness of the initial stimulus is most severely restricted when the mask is exposed simultaneously with this original stimulus (Eriksen & J.F. Collins, 1964, 1965). Commonly termed *energy masking*, this effect appears to occur peripherally, being observed only when both the initial stimulus and the mask are presented to the same eye (Turvey, 1973). Although there is little evidence to indicate that the semantic content of the initial stimulus is activated under energy-masking conditions, this is not the case when an alternative type of procedure, known as pattern masking, is employed. Pattern masking involves presenting a random pattern, usually consisting of fragments of the initial stimulus features, rather than a homogeneous bright field, after the initial stimulus has been briefly exposed. The degree to which this pattern-masking procedure restricts conscious awareness of the initial stimulus increases as the stimulus onset asynchrony (SOA) between this stimulus and the mask is extended to somewhere between 20 and 50 milliseconds. Further increases to this SOA then serve to attenuate the degree to which the pattern mask reduces awareness of the prior stimulus. Given that a pattern mask presented to one eye can prevent awareness of an initial stimulus presented to the other eye, it is evident that the pattern-masking effect operates centrally (Turvey, 1973). Many researchers now have provided compelling evidence that, even when backward pattern masking effectively eliminates awareness of stimuli, as indicated by chance performance on forced-choice discriminative judgment tasks concerning the presence or absence of such stimuli, semantic analysis of the masked stimuli nevertheless can occur (e.g., D.G. Allport, 1977; Kemp-Wheeler & A.B. Hill, 1987; Marcel, 1978, 1980, 1983b; Marcel, Katz, & M. Smith, 1974).

For example, Kemp-Wheeler and A.B. Hill (1987) demonstrated that, although their subjects could not accurately determine whether or not pattern-masked emotional words were appearing on a visual display unit (VDU) screen, they nevertheless reported changes in their subjective emotional states that were consistent with the affective tones of these masked words. Also, it has been demonstrated that the well-established Stroop effect (Stroop, 1938) can be observed under backward masking conditions. Marcel (1983b) presented subjects with colored patches on a VDU screen, and required them to name the color of each patch. Congruent and incongruent color names were exposed across these patches using a backward masking procedure, and subjects showed no ability to report the identities of these word stimuli on a forced-choice discrimination task. Nevertheless, Marcel observed that the color-naming latencies for the patches were significantly increased when the incongruent, rather than the congruent, color words were briefly exposed, indicating that the meanings of these words had been accessed, despite subjects' inability to consciously apprehend their identity.

Robust lexical priming effects, characterized by reductions in decision latencies concerning target words immediately following the presentation of semantically related prime words (cf. Meyer, Schvaneveldt, & Ruddy, 1972; Schvaneveldt & Meyer, 1973), also have been observed when these prime words have been rendered undetectable through the use of a pattern-masking procedure. Some researchers have convincingly demonstrated such priming effects on lexical decision tasks, which require subjects to identify the lexical status of the target words (e.g., Fowler, Wolford, Slade, & Tassinary, 1981; Kemp-Wheeler & A.B. Hill, 1988). For example, on each study within a series of four experiments that used both dichoptic and binocular pattern-masking procedures to eliminate awareness, Kemp-Wheeler and Hill observed that their subjects were faster to accurately respond to letter strings that were legitimate words, when these had been preceded 500 milliseconds earlier by a masked word related to their meanings. Across the four experiments, these researchers had taken great pains to ensure that their subjects had been unable to discriminate the presence of the primes, using a forced-choice procedure that required subjects to guess whether or not a prime word had been present on every trial, and employing very conservative criteria to eliminate those few individuals who showed accuracy levels that differed from chance. In another carefully designed series of three experiments, Greenwald, Klinger, and Liu (1989) included a large number of detection trials to assess the efficacy of their masking procedure, and used signal detection measures to verify that their subjects could not discriminate the presence of pattern-masked prime words. However, these subjects displayed a significant speeding of their decisions concerning the affective valence of target words, when these targets were preceded by prime words that matched their emotional valence. Several other experiments using backward masking to eliminate subjects' awareness hve provided additional evidence to indicate that the meanings of primes presented outside awareness influence the processing of target stimuli (e.g., K. Forster, Booker, Schacter, & C. Davis, 1990; Hines, Czerwinski, Sawyers, & Dwyer, 1986). Collectively, such priming studies offer very firm support for the hypothesis that stimuli that do not enter awareness nevertheless can be processed to a semantic level of analysis.

Additional strong support for this hypothesis has come from a particularly elegant methodology introduced by Marcel (1983b). In this experiment, Marcel employed a backward pattern-masking procedure, within which words were exposed on 50% of trials, whereas on the remaining trials no word was presented. On each trial, subjects were required to make one of three forced-choice discrimination judgments. One discrimination task required them to decide whether or not a word had appeared at all (i.e., presence–absence judgment); another involved presenting them with two subsequent words and having them decide which was structurally most similar to the word that might have been presented initially (i.e., structural judgment); whereas a third discrimination also involved presenting two words subsequently, but required that subjects decide which was most similar in meaning to the word that may have been presented prior to the mask (i.e., semantic judgment). Early in the experimental test session, SOA between the initial word (or initial blank field) and the pattern mask was sufficiently long to permit accurate performance on all three discrimination tasks. However, Marcel gradually reduced this SOA during the course of the test session, and observed how this impaired performance across the different types of discrimination. Although this progressive reduction of SOA ultimately eliminated accuracy across all three discrimination tasks, subjects' performance declined to chance levels first on the presence–absence judgment task. Further reductions in SOA were required before subjects' performance on the structural judgment task also declined to the level predicted by chance alone. Even at this SOA, however, which did not permit subjects to make accurate decisions concerning either the presence of a stimulus, or its structural properties, above-chance performance continued to be observed on the semantic judgment task, indicating that subjects were able to access the semantic attributes of these undetectable masked stimuli.

Therefore, a broad range of experiments have employed a diverse variety of exposure manipulations not only to erase subjects' self-reported awareness of stimulus content, but also to eliminate subjects' abilities to detect the presence of stimuli as assessed by forced-choice judgment tasks. Yet, despite the efficacy of these exposure techniques in eliminating awareness of stimulus presence, a great many researchers have obtained powerful evidence to indicate that stimuli presented in such ways nevertheless undergo considerable perceptual processing. Such studies have obtained findings to suggest that such perceptual processing is not restricted to the structural analyses of these stimuli, but continues to the level of semantic access. Still more evidence that perceptual processing takes place in the absence of awareness has been provided by experiments in which subjective awareness has varied as a result of biological factors. This third source of empirical support for the occurrence of perception without awareness now is considered.

EVIDENCE OF PERCEPTION WHEN AWARENESS IS RESTRICTED BY BIOLOGICAL FACTORS

A range of biological factors can eliminate the conscious perception of stimuli presented under exposure conditions that normally would permit stimulus awareness. Some studies suggest that, despite their impact upon phenomenal experience, such biological factors nevertheless may permit structural processing of the information that subjects cannot report perceiving. Often the biological factors that affect awareness represent pathological conditions that compromise the perceptual system in some way. Some such conditions are fairly trivial, such as color blindness. Ruddock and Waterfield (1978) found that a colored pattern comprised of red and green elements sharing equivalent luminance, which their red-green color-blind subjects reported being unable to consciously perceive, nevertheless contributed to the depth perception experienced by these subjects when presented as part of a stereoscopic array. More commonly, the pathology results from localized lesions within regions of the visual cortex, which destroy perceptual experience within specific areas of the visual field. Despite the phenomenal experience of total blindness within these visual sectors, an extensive body of literature now has developed to indicate that subjects retain an ability to make above-chance discriminative judgments concerning stimuli appearing within such regions, a capacity that has become known as *blindsight* (cf. Farah, 1994; Gazzaniga, Fendrich, & Wessinger, 1994; Weiskrantz, 1993).

Early evidence for the existence of blindsight came largely from demonstrations that cortically blind individuals, usually suffering damage to the striate cortex of the occipital lobe, often appeared able to localize stimuli presented within the "blind" regions of their visual fields. Initially, this capacity to localize such stimuli was inferred on the basis of eye movements (e.g., Poppel, Held, & Frost, 1973), but subsequent research found that subjects could accurately point toward the location of such stimuli, even while adamantly insisting that they could not possibly perform this pointing task because of their blindness (e.g., M.G. Sanders, Warrington, J. Marshall, & Weiskrantz, 1974). The validity of this much replicated effect was called into question by Campion, Latto, and Smith (1983), who argued that such accurate discriminative ability might result from scattered light reaching intact areas of the visual field, enabling subjects to make accurate judgments (although perhaps unknowingly) on the basis of their conscious perceptual experiences. However, when more sophisticated methodologies have been employed to control luminance conditions in ways that eliminate the possibility of light scatter, many subjects continue to show the ability to localize stimuli presented within scomata (e.g., Zihl & Werth, 1984). Furthermore, more detailed investigations suggest that the amount of information that can be extracted from stimuli presented within blind fields extends well beyond spatial location. When Marcel (1982) forced cortically blind subjects to grasp for objects presented within their blind hemifields, he found that they adjusted their hands in advance according to the shape, size, and location of these objects, despite reporting no visual awareness of what they were reaching for. Evidence from forced-choice discrimination tasks also has accumulated to indicate that such individuals are sensitive to the motional direction and orientation of objects presented within their blind hemifields, despite reporting no phenomenal visual experience, and despite failing to reveal the most rudimentary visual capacity under normal opthalmic assessment (cf. Cowey & Stoerig, 1992; Milner, 1992).

Though less well documented, there is some evidence to suggest that neurological damage can eliminate conscious awareness of stimuli, without preventing the perceptual processing of such stimuli, within other sensory systems too. For example, Paillard, Michel, and Stelmach (1983) reported a tactical analogue of blindsight in a woman experiencing hemi-anesthesia as a result of a lesion within the sensorimotor cortex. Though this patient reported experiencing no perceptual sensation whatsoever when she was touched on her left hand, she demonstrated high levels of accuracy when forced to guess the locations of such tactile stimulation. Clearly, these demonstrations that accurate stimulus discrimination, sometimes of a complex nature, can continue even when the neural regions supposedly enabling conscious representation of such stimulus information are destroyed, strongly suggest that perceptual processing can occur outside awareness. Nevertheless, it should be recognized that such studies provide evidence only of structural stimulus processing under such conditions. In contrast, however, when one considers the growing number of studies that have assessed perceptual processing when conscious awareness has been more grossly eliminated, through the use of general anesthesia, it is possible to find evidence that both structural and semantic processing of stimulus information continues to take place.

Given that the principal purpose of general anesthesia is to produce the global elimination of conscious experience, it is not surprising that surgical patients who have been exposed to auditory stimulus information while rendered unconscious through anesthesia typically report no awareness of this exposure, and display an inability to later recall what was presented (e.g., Cork, Kihlstrom, & Schacter, 1993; Villemure, Ploudre, Lussier, & Normandin, 1993). Nevertheless, several researchers have demonstrated that such stimulus presentations can exert an impact upon a variety of subsequent measures, suggesting that the stimuli must have been processed despite subjects' lack of consciousness (cf. Andrade, 1995; Caseley-Rondi, P.M. Merikle, & K.S. Bowers, 1994). Thus, although their subjects insisted that they had no memory for the stimuli that had been presented during the general anesthesia, K. Millar and Watkinson (1983) found that they selected these presented words more frequently on a subsequent forced-choice recognition task. Some investigators also have reported that words presented to anaesthetized subjects are later produced with disproportionate frequency on a category exemplar generation task (e.g., Jelicic, de Roode, Bovill, & Bonke, 1992; Roorda-Hrdlickova, Wolters, Bonke, & Phaf, 1990). Other researchers have exposed word pairs to unconscious surgical patients, and have found this to increase the likelihood of these individuals responding with the second word when the first member of a pair is provided as the cue in a word association task (e.g., Kihlstrom, Schacter, Cork, Hurt, & Behr, 1990). Additionally, the commonly observed increase in the likeability of stimuli which have previously been presented has been reported for nonsense words exposed under general anesthesia (e.g., R.I. Block, Ghoneim, Sum Ping, & Ali, 1991).

Although such findings strongly suggest that unconscious surgical patients do perceptually process auditory stimuli, they do not require the conclusion that such processing extends beyond structural analysis. However, there also is evidence to indicate that patients under general anesthesia can access the meanings of auditory messages. For example, it has been observed that the presentation of statements containing new factual information to anaesthetized subjects can improve these individuals' subsequent performance on a general knowledge test that requires them to employ this information (e.g., Goldmann, 1986; Jelicic et al., 1992). Furthermore, when anaesthetized subjects have been given instructions to touch their ears, nose, or chin during the postoperative period, several researchers have found that these behaviors then occur with increased frequency following the recovery of consciousness (e.g., Bennett, Davis, & Giannini, 1985; Goldmann, Shah, & Helden, 1987). Clearly, such observations require the conclusion that auditory stimuli, exposed to unconscious patients under general anesthesia, can be processed deeply enough to access its semantic content.

Therefore, as has been the case when awareness has been restricted either by attentional manipulations or exposure manipulations, those experiments that have considered restrictions of awareness resulting from biological factors also have provided substantial support for the hypothesis that perception can proceed to the level of semantic analysis, without this requiring conscious awareness of stimulus content.

DISSOCIATIONS BETWEEN CONSCIOUS AND NONCONSCIOUS PERCEPTUAL PROCESSING

Clearly, the definitive dissociation between conscious and nonconscious perception lies in the restriction of stimulus awareness to the former class of perceptual event. However, for differing reasons, a number of researchers have drawn attention to the potential importance of establishing whether these classes of perception are characterized by other types of dissociations also. Some, such as Shevrin and Dickman (1980), have been motivated principally by theoretical considerations. Shevrin and Dickman distinguished two postulates concerning the psychological unconscious, discriminating a "weak postulate" from a "strong postulate." The weak postulate holds simply that nonconscious processes do occur, and operate outside awareness in ways that can influence conscious experience and behavior. The strong postulate adds the corollary that the rules governing nonconscious processing differ qualitatively from those that underpin conscious processing. Thus, according to Shevrin and Dickman's position, it is necessary to search for qualitative dissociations between conscious and nonconscious perception, in order to establish whether the distinction between these two forms of perception provides support for the weak or the strong postulate concerning unconscious cognition. In contrast, other researchers have advocated the search for additional dissociations on the basis of methodological considerations. For example, Holender (1986) argued that whenever evidence for nonconscious perception comes from the observation of effects, under conditions designed to restrict stimulus awareness, that simply represent equivalent or attenuated versions of effects commonly observed when stimulus awareness is permitted, then it remains possible that these may be mediated by partial or transient awareness of the stimulus information. However, he pointed out that if the effects observed under conditions designed to eliminate conscious perception were found to differ qualitatively from those observed when awareness f stimuli is permitted, then this would suggest that these effects cannot represent the result of limited residual awareness. A similar position was taken by Reingold and P.M. Merikle (1988), who proposed that a strong criterion for nonconscious perception would require the existence of effects that occur more powerfully when stimulus awareness is eliminated, than when such awareness is permitted.

A number of studies have reported dissociations that meet Reingold and P.M. Merikle's (1988) strong criterion for nonconscious perception. For example, Dagenbach, Carr, and Wilhemsen (1989) examined the magnitudes of semantic priming effects demonstrated on a lexical decision task when target words were preceded by pattern-masked primes. As the SOA between the primes and the masks were systematically reduced, so subjects' abilities to consciously identify these primes gradually fell to chance, despite the fact that significant priming effects continued to be displayed when such masked primes were semantically related to the target words. Although these variations in SOA did modify the magnitude of this semantic priming effect, the nature of this modification differed according to whether or not the presentation condition permitted awareness of these primes. When prime awareness was possible, reducing this SOA served to reduce the priming effect. In contrast, when prime awareness was no longer possible, reducing this SOA instead served to increase the priming effect. Additional evidence that semantic priming effects can strengthen under conditions that preclude conscious awareness of primes was provided more recently by Klinger and Greenwald (1995). These researchers required subjects to perform a simple judgment task concerning target words, which were preceded by related or unrelated prime words. Awareness of these prime words was manipulated using a binocular pattern-masking procedure, and subjects' abilities to detect such primes were calculated using a signal detection analysis. Klinger and Greenwald not only found evidence of significant semantic priming effects under exposure conditions that precluded accurate detection of the primes, but also observed that these priming effects were greatest for those subjects who showed the least ability to detect the prime presentations. This pattern of findings fully satisfies Reingold and Merikle's strong criterion for accepting that nonconscious perceptual processing does indeed proceed to the level of semantic analysis.

Still stronger support for this position has been provided by demonstrations that certain priming effects not only are strengthened when primes are exposed in ways that eliminate awareness of their presence, but occur exclusively under such exposure conditions (e.g., Bonanno & Stillings, 1986; Bornstein & D'Agostino, 1992; Jacoby & Whitehouse, 1989). Jacoby and Whitehouse, for instance, reported an illusion of memory that can be induced by the presentation of word stimuli under conditions designed to prevent awareness of their identity, but that fails to appear when these stimuli are presented in a manner that permits their conscious perception. Specifically, these researchers presented subjects with a long list of words that they attempted to memorize, then gave them a recognition memory task. In this recognition memory task, old and new words were exposed individually on a VDU, and subjects were required to decide whether or not each item had been included in the initial list. On some trials, immediately prior to a new word being presented for recognition judgment, this same word was flashed briefly on the screen and backward masked. The duration of this brief exposure was either sufficiently long to permit stimulus awareness, as evidenced by subsequent report of stimulus identity (i.e., 200 ms in one experiment and 600 ms in another), or too short for such awareness to occur (50 ms in one experiment and 16 ms in other). Under the latter exposure condition, it was found that this brief prior exposure of the new word led to a significant increase in subjects' tendencies to falsely claim that this item had appeared in the initial test list. Jacoby and Whitehouse attributed this effect to the increased sense of familiarity induced by the nonconscious processing of the word, immediately prior to its presentation in the recognition judgment task. In contrast, consistent with their expectations, they found no evidence that the brief exposure increased the false recognition of new words under the exposure conditions that permitted stimulus identification. Indeed, the brief prior exposure of the words under these conditions served to significantly decrease the likelihood of subjects falsely recognizing these new words as members of the initial list, perhaps because any feelings of familiarity were likely to be attributed to the brief prior exposures that subjects were aware of seeing.

Demonstrations of such dissociations, involving the restriction of certain priming effects to exposure conditions that eliminate subjects' abilities to identify prime stimuli, meet the stringent evidential criteria for nonconscious perception recommended by Reingold and D.M. Merikle (1988). However, they still provide support only for Shevrin and Dickman's (1980) weak postulate concerning the psychological unconscious. That is, although such findings represent powerful evidence that nonconscious perception does indeed take place, they do not require the conclusion that perception without awareness necessarily follows different rules from those that govern conscious perception. However, Marcel (1980) reported a lexical priming study, also employing a backward pattern-masking procedure, which does offer support for Shevrin and Dickman's strong postulate, according to which nonconscious perception should be characterized by quite distinct laws of organization. In this experiment, subjects were presented with a lexical decision task in which the target word was preceded by a sequence consisting of two prime words. The prime word immediately prior to the target word was a homograph, and it was possible that one meaning of this homograph could be related semantically to the target word. The word presented prior to this ambiguous prime always was related to only one meaning of the homograph, and thus could serve to constrain the interpretation of this ambiguous prime stimulus by cuing only one of its possible meanings. When no backward masking procedure was employed to eliminate awareness of either prime word, then subjects showed facilitated lexical decisions for the target words only when these were related to the meanings of the preceding homograph primes that had been cued by the immediately prior primes, as in the sequence HAND-PALM-WRIST. No such priming effects were observed when the final target words were related to the alternative meanings of the homograph primes, as in the sequence HAND-PALM-TREE. Thus, it appeared that only the cued meaning of the homographs was activated when these primes were presented in a manner that permitted their conscious identification. However, when Marcel introduced a backward masking procedure to eliminate conscious awareness of the homograph primes, he found a rather different pattern of priming effects. Specifically, under such exposure conditions, lexical decisions were facilitated for target words related to either meaning of the homographs, regardless of the initial cue words that were presented. On the basis of this observation, Marcel concluded that the nonconscious perceptual system is not limited by the capacity constraints associated with the conscious perceptual system, and so the parallel processing of multiple meanings can be sustained when perception occurs outside awareness. According to Marcel, such parallel processing of alternative meanings is no longer possible when perceptual representations enter awareness, because of the severe capacity limitations that characterize the conscious processing system, and so single meanings of stimuli must be selected for representation within awareness.

Clearly, Marcel's (1980) conclusion that nonconscious perception is governed by a large-capacity system capable of processing multiple sources of information in parallel, whereas conscious perception is mediated by a system marked by severe capacity limitations, is consistent with Shevrin and Dickman's (1980) strong postulate concerning the psychological unconscious. Furthermore, it is a conclusion that has been sustained by subsequent research. For example, in a particularly elegant recent series of experiments, Debner and Jacoby (1994) constructed independent indices of conscious and nonconscious perceptual processing by employing a variant of the process dissociation procedure introduced earlier by Jacoby and his colleagues to distinguish conscious and nonconscious memory functioning (e.g., Jacoby, 1991; Jacoby et al., 1993). Each trial first briefly presented a word followed by a pattern mask, under a range of possible SOA conditions. Immediately after this pattern-masked word was presented, subjects were shown a word stem, which they were required to complete according to either of two possible instruction conditions. The instruction on some trials was to complete the stem to make the word that had just been briefly exposed (i.e., inclusion instruction), whereas on other trials this instruction was to complete the stem to make any word other than that which had just been briefly exposed (i.e., exclusion instruction). Following the standard process dissociation rationale, Debner and Jacoby then mathematically extracted an index of the degree to which subjects demonstrated conscious perceptual processing of the masked words (labeled C)[1] and an independent index of the degree to which they demonstrated nonconscious perceptual processing of these stimuli (labeled U).[2] Across all four experiments, significant values were yielded on both the U and C indices, providing clear evidence that both nonconscious perceptual processing and conscious perceptual processing took place across the trials. Of most relevance to the current considerations, however, were the final three experiments in the series, which each required subjects to perform this perceptual task either alone, or in the presence of a capacity-consuming secondary task involving the simultaneous summation of numbers. Across these experiments, Debner and Jacoby observed that the reduction of processing capacity resulting

---

[1] C = probability of completing stem with prime word in inclusion condition—probability of completing stem with prime word in exclusion condition.

[2] U = probability of completing stems with prime words in the exclusion condition / (1–C).

from the simultaneous performance of this secondary counting task was associated with a significant decline in the index of conscious perceptual processing, but with no change in the index of nonconscious perceptual processing. This pattern of findings is fully consistent with Marcel's (1980) proposal that conscious perception is mediated by a limited-capacity processing system, whereas nonconscious perception is governed by a processing system that is not characterized by such capacity constraints.

In conclusion, the range of dissociations that have been observed when contrasting tasks and measures designed to assess nonconscious perception against those assumed to assess conscious perception, not only attest to the validity of the distinction between these two modes of perception, but also suggest that they may be mediated by quite different cognitive systems. As such, although these findings do lend further support to Shevrin and Dickman's (1980) weak postulate that nonconscious processing does indeed take place, they also provide good evidence for their strong postulate, according to which nonconcious processing is governed by qualitatively different principles from those that control conscious processing.

SUMMARY AND CONCLUSION

This chapter has reviewed a wide range of studies that have attempted to empirically evaluate the hypothesis that stimuli can be processed perceptually in the absence of conscious awareness. Although acknowledging the methodological criticisms that have been directed against particular experimental paradigms, it is difficult to avoid the conclusion that an impressive degree of converging support for this hypothesis now exists. Not only does it appear that perceptual analyses of structure can proceed without awareness of stimuli, but also there is good evidence that stimuli can activate their semantic representations without subjects being consciously aware of their identity, or even their presence.

Furthermore, the overall pattern of findings suggests the need not only to recognize the existence of a dichotomy between conscious and nonconscious perceptual processing, but also to seriously entertain the possibility that this dichotomy might distinguish two qualitatively different processing systems, each characterized by quite different laws of organization. When perceptual processing occurs outside awareness, then it appears to be unrestricted by obvious capacity limitations, and it would seem that each stimulus input simultaneously can activate multiple internal representations in parallel. In contrast, conscious perceptual processing is characterized by pronounced capacity limitations and, perhaps as a result of this restriction, it appears that only one internal representation of a stimulus input can, at any given point in time, form part of conscious perceptual experience.

Thus, it seems likely that the presence or absence of phenomenal awareness may represent only one of the distinguishing features associated with a more fundamental dichotomy that exists between two basic modes of perception. One mode appears to be best characterized as an unlimited-capacity system that embodies a parallel processing architecture and functions without requiring conscious mediation. The other mode seems better construed as a limited-capacity system permitting only serial processing, and its operation corresponds closely to phenomenal experience. Elsewhere in this text, evidence is reviewed to suggest that very similar qualitative distinctions have emerged when researchers have contrasted the properties of learning with and without awareness, and when performance on tasks assessing conscious and nonconscious memory has been compared. Such similarities suggest the possibility that the distinction reviewed in this chapter, between conscious and nonconscious perception, may represent only one manifestation of a more fundamental dichotomy between conscious and nonconscious cognition, which holds across all aspects of information processing. If so, then it is clear that a mature cognitive science not only must accommodate this distinction within structural accounts of the cognitive system, but also must take steps to advance our understanding of the psychological functions served by the existence of these two alternative modes of processing.

5

AUTOMATICITY
AND SKILL ACQUISITION

Craig Speelman
Edith Cowan University

Murray Maybery
University of Western Australia

Perceiving being an act, it is, like all other things that we do, performed more easily with each repetition of the act. To perceive an entirely new word or other combination of strokes requires considerable time, close attention, and it is likely to be imperfectly done, just as when we attempt some new combination of movements, some new trick in the gymnasium or new "serve" at tennis. In either case, repetition progressively frees the mind from attention to details, makes facile the total act, shortens the time, and reduces the extent to which consciousness must concern itself with the process. (Huey, 1908/1968, p. 104)

In describing cognitive processes, a distinction frequently is made between automatic and controlled processes. This distinction is as common as the one made between implicit and explicit processes, and shares many features with this distinction. For example, automatic processes, like implicit learning processes (see chap. 3 in this volume), typically are characterized as proceeding without conscious awareness, without intent, and with minimal allocation of attentional resources. In contrast, controlled processes, like explicit learning processes, typically are described as implicating conscious awareness and intent, and as making demands on attentional resources.

There appear to be two main types of automatic processes. One type begins as a controlled process, and through extensive practice, becomes automatic (e.g., the process whereby a red traffic light leads to a stop response). This type of automatic process is the focus of Schneider and Shiffrin's (1977) theory of automatic and controlled processes. The other type is at no stage controlled and in fact may be built into the human-information processing system (e.g., recognizing particular frequencies of light as different colors). This second type of automatic process is the focus of Hasher and Zacks' (1979) theory of automatic and effortful processes. The current chapter concentrates on the former type of automatic process, and focuses on the various means by which a process can become automatic. Chapter 9 of this book provides an in-depth treatment of the alternative, "hardwired" automatic process described by Hasher and Zacks.

There also appear to be at least two ways in which cognitive processes can become automatic in the sense that conscious awareness is not required for their operation. One way is via implicit learning, as described in chapter 3. In this form of learning, the knowledge is below awareness at all stages of practice. In contrast, in the second method of developing automatic processing, knowledge is initially explicit. This form of acquisition is the major focus of this chapter. Before acquisition is considered, however, the major distinguishing features of automatic and controlled processes are described.

THE NATURE OF AUTOMATIC
AND CONTROLLED PROCESSES

We begin this section by describing Schneider and Shiffrin's (1977; Shiffrin & Schneider, 1977) distinction between automatic and controlled processes. There are obvious parallels between this distinction and Posner and Snyder's (1975) distinction between automatic and conscious modes of processing. Note in particular that Posner and Snyder described an automatic process as occurring "without intention, without giving rise to any conscious awareness, and without producing interference with other ongoing mental activity" (p. 56). Our intention is not to devalue the importance of Posner and Snyder's earlier work; it is simply convenient for us to focus on Schneider and Shiffrin's work, in that they addressed more directly the acquisition of expertise in describing the transition from controlled to automatic processing.

The framework in which Schneider and Shiffrin (1977; Shiffrin & Schneider, 1977), developed the distinction between automatic and controlled processes is one in which information processing consists of the activation of sequences of memory nodes. Controlled processing is when there is willful allocation of attention to achieve the activation of what may be a novel sequence of memory nodes. The flexibility provided by controlled processing is offset by its serial and capacity-limited nature. Automatic processing, by contrast, is when external or internal stimulus conditions trigger the activation of a sequence of memory nodes, and the sequence unfolds without willful direction and with minimal dependence on attentional resources. An automatic process develops only after extensive practice in which a particular eliciting stimulus configuration invariably requires a particular process-

ing sequence. That is, the automatic mode of processing is restricted to well-practiced regular routines. One advantage of automatic processing is that a sequence of
nodes can be activated with minimal allocation of attention. However, disadvan-
tages are that the sequence is difficult to suppress when the eliciting conditions are
present, and it is not easily modified.

One example of automatic processing is the Stroop phenomenon (Posner &
Snyder, 1975; Shiffrin & Schneider, 1977), where the task is to identify the ink
colors of printed words. The central result is that performance is adversely affected
when the words are color names that are not in correspondence with the ink colors;
for example, the names might be RED, BLUE, and YELLOW, printed in yellow,
red, and blue ink, respectively. One explanation for this phenomenon is that the
process of reading print for meaning is so well practiced that it runs off automatically when the appropriate stimulus conditions are present. That is, although the
subject has the intention to identify the colors of print, she or he cannot suppress
the reading of the words. It is this obligatory aspect to the reading of words for
meaning that has led it to be identified as an example of automatic processing.
Skilled driving provides other examples purported to reflect automatic processes,
such as the acts of braking and changing gears. These actions are dictated by the
stimulus conditions (e.g., a red light, an incline), and seem to require no deliberate
conscious initiation, at least at the level of these subcomponents of the driving
activity. Also, their stereotypic nature is frustratingly evident when the driver shifts
to a car with a different configuration of pedals or gears (e.g., one with transposed
positions for the fifth and reverse gears).

Much of the research addressed to the automatic-controlled dichotomy has
employed the visual-search paradigm in which the participant is asked to search
displays for target items (Schneider & Fisk, 1982; Schneider & Shiffrin, 1977;
Shiffrin & Schneider, 1977). Target and distractor items are usually digits, letters, or
words. For example, the participant might be searching for either of two targets, a G
or an X, in displays that contain four letters or digits. The number of items in the
target set and the number of items in the visual display can be manipulated
independently. A critical additional manipulation is whether items appear with
consistency as targets or distractors (consistent mapping), or whether they shift status
(variable mapping) across trials. Thus, for consistent mapping (CM), digits might
always serve as targets and letters as distractors, whereas for variable mapping (VM),
digits and letters might exchange target-distractor roles across trials.

The CM versus VM manipulation is critical because Shiffrin and Schneider
claimed that extensive practice shifts the balance of processing under CM from
controlled to automatic, whereas processing remains predominantly controlled
under VM (Schneider, Dumais, & Shiffrin, 1984; Schneider & Shiffrin, 1977;
Shiffrin & Schneider, 1977). Accordingly, several differences that emerge in CM
and VM performance following extensive practice are attributed to automatic and
controlled processing, respectively. First, search is completed much more quickly

and accurately under CM conditions than under VM conditions (Schneider & Shiffrin, 1977; Shiffrin & Schneider, 1977), consistent with the characterization of automatic processing as fast, error-free, and effortless, and controlled processing as slow, error-prone, and effortful. Second, whereas VM performance deteriorates with an increase in either the size of the target set or the size of the visual display, these effects are either absent or minimal for CM (Schneider & Shiffrin, 1977; Shiffrin & Schneider, 1977). These results are linked to how automatic processing is potentially parallel in operation, whereas controlled processing is limited to the serial processing of inputs (Schneider et al., 1984). Third, imposition of a concurrent task substantially impairs practiced VM performance but has an insubstantial effect on practiced CM performance (Schneider & Fisk, 1982). These outcomes are identified with the dependence of controlled processes on central attentional or working-memory resources, in contrast to the independence of automatic processes in respect of those resources. Fourth, changing the target set (an integral part of VM) causes pronounced negative transfer for CM (Shiffrin & Schneider, 1977). This result is identified with the stereotypic nature of automatic processes, which contrasts with the flexible character of controlled processes. Finally, subjects report that they subvocally rehearse the target set in conditions expected to elicit controlled search, but that they do not engage in this rehearsal in conditions expected to elicit automatic search (Shiffrin & Schneider, 1977). These anecdotal reports are consistent with the idea that conscious awareness is implicated in controlled processing, but need not be involved in automatic processing.

In sum, automatic processes are said to be fast, accurate, and effortless, on the one hand, but obligatory, ballistic, and stereotypic on the other hand. It also is claimed that automatic processes can proceed without intent, without conscious awareness, with minimal allocation of central attentional or working-memory resources, and in parallel. The reader is referred to Bargh (1992b), Logan and Cowan (1984), J.G. Phillips and Hughes (1988), Schneider et al. (1984), Schneider and Shiffrin (1977), and Shiffrin and Schneider (1977) for detailed discussions of these characteristics.

Schneider and Shiffrin's automatic-controlled dichotomy has been the subject of two significant lines of attack. The first addresses the inappropriateness of a simple dichotomy (e.g., Bargh, 1992b; J.G. Phillips & Hughes, 1988). The essence of this criticism is that the central characteristics attributed to automatic processes—lack of awareness, control, intention, and attentional-demand—do not inevitably co-occur. That is, processes can be identified that have some, but not all, of these characteristics. For example, Bargh argued that Stroop interference, although occurring without, or even in spite of intent, nevertheless requires the allocation of some spatial attention. Similarly, Phillips and Hughes argued that, whereas response *execution* is said to demand less attention than response *preparation*, the former can be more affected than the latter by a manipulation of conscious awareness. The alternative to the automatic-controlled dichotomy view is that processes can be differentiated on a number of somewhat independent dimensions, such as the levels of conscious awareness, attentional demand, intent, and control (Bargh, 1992b; J.G. Phillips & Hughes, 1988).

After considering the diverse phenomenon to which the term automatic has been applied, Bargh (1989) argued that they do share one characteristic, a ballistic feature: that once an automatic process is initiated, it must run to completion. Bargh (1992b) took this feature as characteristic of the general class of automatic processes, and specified subtypes distinguished in terms of the preconditions for activation of the processes. For example, a *preconscious process* is activated solely by relevant stimulus conditions; that is, it is not conditional on a particular intent, on any substantial allocation of attention, nor on conscious awareness. This is the archetypal automatic process. Another of Bargh's (1992b) subtypes is *goal-dependent automatic processes*, for which the preconditions are the relevant stimulus conditions, as for preconscious processes, but in addition, the existence of a particular intent. Most of the examples of skilled performance examined in this chapter fall under this latter subtype—there must be some intent to engage in a particular activity (e.g., driving) if an automatic process (e.g., braking in response to a red light) is to be observed. Nevertheless, our approach is compatible with Bargh's general conceptualization in which automatic processes are described in terms of their eliciting preconditions.

The second line of attack on Schneider and Shiffrin's theory of automatic and controlled processes concerns the absence of a description of the mechanisms underpinning the transition from controlled to automatic processing. The rest of this chapter focuses on mechanisms proposed in explanation of this transition.

THE ACQUISITION OF AUTOMATICITY

Shiffrin and Schneider's characterization of the differences between automatic and controlled processing, and the circumstances under which each will be observed has been a significant influence on research in this field. However, lacking in this characterization is a mechanism whereby controlled processes can become automatic. Shiffrin and Schneider discussed the role of practice and the type of practice necessary but not how practice has the effects it does. In other words, Shiffrin and Schneider did not address the question of how practice leads to the characteristics of automaticity identified earlier. In recent years a number of theories of skill acquisition have emerged that do posit some mechanisms for the acquisition of automaticity. Broadly speaking, these theories fall into two categories. One type involves a procedural account, where procedures for performing tasks are refined and strengthened with practice. The other type of theory involves a memory account, where performance is determined by memory retrieval, and this process becomes faster and more efficient with practice. These different theories are not necessarily mutually exclusive, and indeed many forms of expertise probably can be explained only by recourse to both types of theory, or at least a theory that combines the two approaches (Staszewski, 1988). Examples of both types of theory are described later. However, two features of skill acquisition that all theories attempt to account for—the three phases of skill acquisition and the power law of practice—are be described first.

THE THREE PHASES OF SKILL ACQUISITION

Fitts (1964) suggested that there are three phases involved in the acquisition of skill. Fitts termed the early phase the *cognitive stage*. This stage lasts for only a few trials while the subject comes to terms with instructions and develops performance strategies. According to Fitts, these strategies develop from general "sets" and strategies developed from previously learned tasks. Knowledge is explicit and typically rule-based, and performance is slow and error-prone. This stage involves strong demands on cognitive-attentional resources. Refinement of the performance strategy comes in the intermediate phase—the *associative stage*. Features of the previously learned strategies that are appropriate to the new situation are strengthened on the basis of feedback, whereas inappropriate features are weakened. This process forms new associations between specific stimulus cues and appropriate responses. In the end phase—the *autonomous stage*—the components of the performance strategy slowly become more autonomous so that they are less subject to cognitive control or external interference. As a result, skilled performance of the task requires increasingly less processing, which means that more processing resources can be used for other activities. During this phase, skills continue to become faster and more efficient although the rate of improvement slows with practice.

The three phases of skill acquisition feature in the framework of Shiffrin and Schneider (1977; Schneider & Shiffrin, 1977). In this framework the qualitative differences in performance associated with the three phases are said to result from a gradual shift from controlled processing to automatic processing. Performance in the first phase is attributed to controlled processing. Performance in the second phase involves a mixture of controlled and automatic processing, and the third phase is associated mainly with automatic processing.

Fitts (1964) provided no theoretical accounts of the processes he identified in the three phases, although he did point out where he thought existing theories were useful in this scheme. For instance, the selection of previously learned general sets and strategies for incorporation into new strategies draws on Crossman's (1959) general probability learning model. In this model, subjects are presumed to possess a repertoire of methods for performing a task. Each method is selected at random and the probability of its subsequent selection is dependent on its performance speed—the faster ones being more likely to be selected. This process predicts the typical power function speed-up found in skill acquisition (e.g., Newell & Rosen-bloom, 1981). However, other features of Fitts' description of skill development are not specified to the same extent. Fitts' account lacks a clear process description of how performance strategies are refined through the various stages of skill development. A description of the processes involved in skill acquisition is necessary to be able to understand how automaticity might result. However, it should be noted that there does exist strong evidence for the existence of three qualitatively different phases during skill acquisition (e.g., Ackerman, 1988).

Ackerman (1988) demonstrated that skill acquisition is associated with different types of abilities at different stages of practice. These stages correspond to the three phases of skill acquisition identified by Fitts. According to Ackerman, initial performance on a task is highly correlated with general cognitive-intellectual ability. That is, superior performance on a task is associated with higher general intelligence. Ackerman suggested that this was because general intellectual abilities determine the development of performance strategies early in practice. However, as practice continues, and performance strategies become gradually fixed, the second phase of skill acquisition is entered and performance level is predicted less by general abilities. Instead, Ackerman found that performance in this phase is best predicted by perceptual-speed ability, an ability that reflects "the speed with which (simple) cognitive test items can be completed" (p. 290). The reason for this is that procedures and strategies are being refined and compiled during this phase, and so individual differences in the speed of this process should be associated with the speed with which basic cognitive processes can be executed. Eventually, however, as cognitive processes improve toward asymptote, perceptual-speed ability no longer predicts task performance. At this stage, performance has entered the third phase of skill acquisition. Ackerman found that performance in this phase was best predicted by psychomotor ability. According to Ackerman, by this stage of practice, most cognitive skills will have been refined and strengthened almost as far as possible. Individual differences in task performance will be best accounted for then by individual differences in speed and accuracy of motor responding, as measured by such tasks as simple reaction time, rotary pursuit, and tapping speed.

Ackerman's (1988) work provides further support for the existence of three qualitatively different phases of skill acquisition. However, it does not provide any further insight to the nature of the processes underlying these phases. This was not Ackerman's aim. He did suggest, however, that his theory of the relationship between these phases and various psychological abilities is entirely consistent with the ACT* theory of skill acquisition proposed by J.R. Anderson (1982, 1983, 1987) and described later.

THE POWER LAW OF PRACTICE

Skills that are acquired in the three-phase manner typically result in performance improvements described by the power law of practice. For example, consider a task such as simple arithmetic (Speelman & Kirsner, 1996) that involves subjects performing equations such as the following:

SOLIDS = 10

LIME = 15

(SOLIDS x LIME)/2 = ?

In a typical skill acquisition study, subjects are given hundreds or even thousands of trials; feedback is given after each trial (i.e., "correct" or "incorrect"), and reaction time and accuracy are recorded. Speelman and Kirsner (1996) demonstrated that practice with the arithmetic task, where values for SOLIDS and LIME change with each trial, leads to an improvement in performance that can be described well by a power function. Figure 5.1 depicts the results from 250 trials of the arithmetic task for 12 subjects. As shown in Fig. 5.1a, reaction time (RT) improves dramatically during the early stages of practice, but the rate of improvement decreases gradually throughout the experiment until, after 150 trials or more, performance is hardly declining at all, although improvement is never entirely eliminated. Figure 5.1b shows the same results on log-log coordinates, where it is evident from the straight-line fit to the data that the rate of improvement is consistent throughout the experiment, a sure indication that improvement can be described by a power function (Newell & Rosenbloom, 1981). This illustration of the power law of learning has been reported many times, for tasks as simple as rolling a cigar (Crossman, 1959), to tasks as complex as fault diagnosis in electronic

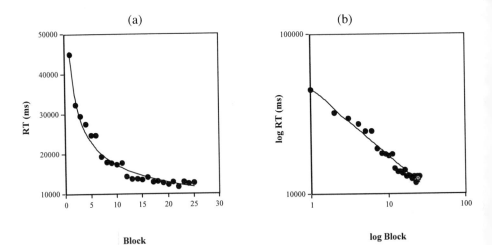

FIG. 5.1. Practice data for 12 subjects performing simple mathematical calculations. Figure 5.1a is plotted on linear-linear axes and Fig. 5.1b is plotted on log-log axes. The lines in both figures represent the best-fit power function of the form $RT = NP^c$ ($RT = 45,400.235\ P^{-0.422}$, $r^2 = 0.996$, rmsd = 1,208 ms).

circuits (Carlson, Sullivan & Schneider, 1989). Application of the power law, moreover, is not restricted to one type or class of operation; it has been observed for motor learning tasks (e.g., positioning a cursor on a screen monitor with a mouse—Card, English, & Burr, 1978), perceptual-motor tasks (e.g., mirror drawing—Snyder & Pronko, 1952), perceptual learning tasks (e.g., scanning pages of text for visual targets—Neisser, Novick, & Lazar, 1963), and cognitive tasks with relatively little perceptual or motor content (e.g., alphabet arithmetic—Logan, 1992a; writing books—Ohlsson, 1992). And finally, although it raises questions of generality that go beyond the aims of this book, the power law provides a satisfactory fit to the rates of improvement observed for the engineering products of groups of people working together as a team, as if the law applies to corporate as well as individual cognition (Argote & Epple, 1990).

PROCEDURAL THEORIES OF SKILL ACQUISITION

Anderson's ACT* Theory

A comprehensive account of skill acquisition is provided by John Anderson's ACT* theory (J.R. Anderson, 1982, 1983, 1987). The three phases described by Fitts (1964) feature in ACT* also, although the processes involved in each phase are detailed to a greater extent. According to ACT* the first phase (cognitive phase) involves the acquisition of explicit knowledge. Knowledge of this type is typically in the form of declarative rules concerning a particular domain. For example, a novice in the radiological field may remember being told by an expert radiologist that a particular set of X-ray features are indicative of a particular disorder. The memory of this advice is declarative knowledge. The second phase of skill acquisition (associative phase) involves the compilation of declarative knowledge into procedural knowledge. In ACT* this is described as the acquisition of production rules: rules that associate particular stimulus conditions with appropriate actions (e.g., if X-ray contains Feature A, Feature F, and Feature M, then consider Diagnosis X). Acquisition of this type of knowledge corresponds to a drop-out of verbal rehearsal of instructions and the associated reduction of working-memory load, resulting in smooth and accurate performance. The final phase of skill acquisition (autonomous phase) involves a strengthening process that enables fast, reliable execution of productions. Performance at this stage of practice usually proceeds without thought, and may appear automatic, given sufficient practice.

According to ACT*, there are two ways in which skill acquisition can result in automatic performance. The first is associated with the compilation of declarative knowledge into procedural knowledge. This process actually involves two other processes: proceduralization and composition. Proceduralization refers to the process whereby declarative knowledge is converted into productions. This process leads to knowledge that is, if not automatic in the way defined previously, is certainly of a form that is difficult to describe verbally. In fact, by definition, productions cannot be reported on verbally (J.R. Anderson, 1982). Productions only alter the contents of working memory. In ACT* only the contents of working memory can be reported, not the processes that led to their creation. Thus, if someone was asked to report on their procedural knowledge, at best they could only describe the successive contents of their working memory, and therefore reconstruct what must have taken place during performance. As a result, protocols can only be an approximation to the nature of procedural knowledge. Hence, once knowledge has been proceduralized, it is no longer as accessible to verbal report as it was when in declarative form.

The other process involved in compilation is composition. Composition describes the process whereby several productions are collapsed into a single production. These productions must occur in a sequence and share the same overall goal. The new production now does the work of the sequence, but in fewer steps. For example, consider the following set of productions for solving for x in an algebraic expression of the form a = x + c:

IF	goal is to solve for x in equation of the form a = x + c	
THEN	set as subgoal to isolate x on RHS of equation.	**(1)**

IF	goal is to isolate x on RHS of equation	
THEN	set as subgoal to eliminate c from RHS of equation.	**(2)**

IF	goal is to eliminate c from RHS of equation	
THEN	add -c to both sides of equation.	**(3)**

IF	goal is to solve for x in equation	
	and x has been isolated on RHS of equation	
THEN	LHS of equation is solution for x.	**(4)**

After executing these rules a number of times, composition will result in collapsing Productions 2 and 3 into:

IF	goal is to isolate x on RHS of equation	
THEN	add -c to both sides of equation.	**(5)**

With further practice, Productions 1, 5, and 4 will be composed to the more sophisticated:

IF	goal is to solve for x in equation of the form a = x + c	
THEN	subtract c from a and result is solution.	**(6)**

Thus several productions have been composed into one production that performs the same task but in only one step.

The important point to note about composition is that the reduction in the number of production rules means that a task now is performed in fewer discrete steps. As a result the contents of working memory are not updated as often throughout the task and so cannot act as a clue to how the task was performed. This explains why some experts are unable to verbally describe their expert strategies. Knowledge about performance strategies initially may be explicit, or at least reconstructable from the intermediate products of performance (i.e., the contents of working memory). However, with practice, this knowledge is no longer accessible to verbal report because it has been transformed into the condition and action statements of production rules. Only the initial conditions and final products of performance appear in working memory, and so only these are available to report (see Speelman's chapter on implicit expertise, chap. 8 of this volume).

In addition to the contributions compilation makes to the efficiency of skilled performance, it also leads to speed-up in performance. That is, compiled productions perform tasks in fewer steps than uncompiled productions. If each processing step is associated with a unit of time, then this translates into time savings. But the speed-up associated with compilation is not sufficient to explain the vast amount of speed-up that characterizes skill acquisition. Hence ACT* includes a further characteristic of skill acquisition—strengthening. The strength of a production determines how rapidly it applies, and production rules accumulate strength as they successfully apply.

Combination of compilation and strengthening accounts for the classic power-functions that characterize learning curves. ACT* formalizes this as follows:

$$T = X + N\,P^c \text{ where}$$

	T	= task performance time
	X	= performance time at asymptote
	N	= initial # of productions
	P	= practice
	X + N	= time on trial 1
	c	= rate of learning, $c < 0$
		= f + g
	f	= the fraction by which the # of steps is reduced by composition
	g	= related to memory decay.

J.R. Anderson (1992) claimed that the ACT* theory can account for most of the commonly described features of automaticity. For example, the following is an ACT* account, taken from J.R. Anderson (1992), of some of the most frequently cited features of automaticity associated with the Sternberg-like visual search task described earlier. In particular this account explains the effects of CM and VM practice.

In the visual search task, and its close analogue the memory search task, subjects are told that a digit will appear on a computer screen. They are instructed to say "yes" if the digit is in a given set, say {2, 4, 7}, which is present on the screen in the visual search task, or has been committed to memory in the memory search task. According to J.R. Anderson (1992), in order to perform this task subjects are required to recognize when a digit appears on the screen, and to set the subgoals of classifying the digit and saying the appropriate response. Anderson proposed that, in the initial stages of practice, subjects would develop productions like the following to perform the task:

IF   the goal is to categorize a stimulus in location X
        and n1 is in location X
THEN   set as subgoals to determine the category of n1   (7)
        and to say the category name of n1.

IF   the goal is to determine the category of n1
        and n1 is in set Y
THEN   n1 is in category Y.   (8)

IF   the goal is to say the category name of n1
        and n1 is in category Y
        and R is the response for Y
THEN   say R.   (9)

However, with practice, Anderson claimed that subjects eventually will develop productions of the form:

IF   the goal is to categorize a stimulus on the screen
        and 4 is on the screen
THEN   say *yes*.   (10)

The process whereby Productions 7, 8, and 9 are transformed into Production 10 is another example of compilation—what originally took three steps to achieve is now achieved in one step. With further practice, Production 10 will be strengthened and so will be executed very quickly. Other productions will be developed that are specific to the other elements of the target set. That is, eventually specific productions are developed to classify each item in a target set. Furthermore, regardless of the size of the target set, with sufficient practice there will be a specific production for each item in the set. In this way, set-size effects disappear with practice because each item in a target set is classified by a compiled and strengthened production. This then accounts for the disappearance of set-size effects with CM practice: CM practice enables the development of specific productions for each item of a target set.

However, with VM practice, the items in the target set change from trial to trial. In this case, there is no opportunity to develop specific productions for each item. Thus subjects have to rely on more general productions, such as the following:

IF   the goal is to categorize a stimulus on the screen
        and n1 is on the screen
        and n1 is in the target set
THEN say *yes*.   (11)

Given that this production is more complicated than Production 10, its execution will be slower than the more simple production (J.R. Anderson, 1992). Furthermore, because Production 11 includes a condition that involves verifying whether a number is in the target set (i.e., n1 is in the target set), the time to match this condition will be affected by the size of the target set. Thus, according to this account, VM practice confers little opportunity for learning and should show a set-size effect.

The ACT* account of the effects of CM and VM practice can provide an explanation for a result reported by Czerwinski, Lightfoot, and Shiffrin (1992). They demonstrated that VM practice can produce near-automatic processing, if the amount of practice is increased. CM practice usually results in much more experience with individual items than is the case with VM conditions. However, Czerwinski et al. showed that if the amount of experience with particular items is equated across conditions, then VM practice results in performance close to that of CM conditions. According to the ACT* account, this result is due to the development of specific productions for particular items in the modified version of VM practice.

In summary, Anderson's ACT* theory suggests that many features of automaticity result from the compilation of declarative knowledge into procedural knowledge. With practice this compilation leads to very efficient and fast productions that are not accessible to verbal description. Thus, according to this view much of the implicit nature of some forms of expertise may result from the automatic application of knowledge that was previously explicit. An alternative view proposes that many features of automaticity result from the effects of practice on memory retrieval processes. Two forms of this view are discussed in the next section.

MEMORY THEORIES OF SKILL ACQUISITION

Logan's Instance Theory

Many of the changes accompanying the development of automaticity are linked to diminished demands on attentional resources. Logan (1988a, 1988b) argued that this approach to theory does not add to the explanation of automaticity. Logan claimed that the account does not describe a mechanism whereby resource demand is reduced. In contrast, Logan proposed that the achievement of automaticity with skill acquisition is not associated with a gradual reduction in demands on attentional resources. In fact, Logan's explanation is not even based on the concept of limited cognitive resources. Instead, he proposed a memory-based explanation where automaticity is achieved through a transition from algorithmic computation (early in practice) to single-step memory retrieval (late in practice). (Note that a similar transition was described by Siegler, 1988, and forms the centerpiece of his theory of cognitive development—see chap. 9 of this volume) Performance early in practice relies on the execution of an algorithm developed through conscious deliberation. Each time the algorithm is executed successfully the solution is remembered. In fact, Logan proposed that the whole processing episode is represented in memory. This representation is termed an instance. Eventually, performance on the task will result either from execution of the algorithm, or from retrieval of past solutions stored as instances. Acquisition of skilled performance is seen as a race between algorithm execution and the direct retrieval of a past solution. Whichever of these two is fastest controls performance. As the number of instances increases with practice, the probability increases of retrieving an instance in less time than it takes to execute an algorithm. Finally, automatic performance results when performance relies solely on stored instances, that is, when direct retrieval of a past solution is always faster than the execution of a general algorithm. This explanation of how practice results in faster performance can provide an account of the power law (Logan, 1988b).

The instance theory's explanation of common features of automaticity follows directly from its description of the processes involved in skill acquisition. For instance, consider again the visual-search task. According to the instance theory, in the initial stages of CM practice, subjects perform the task on the basis of a general algorithm that involves a search of the target set for the probe item. This general algorithm could perform this task in a manner similar to that described by Productions 7, 8, and 9, or even Production 11. Although performance is under the control of this general algorithm, subjects store instances of pairings of particular stimuli (e.g., digits in the target set, and digits not in the target set) with particular responses (e.g., "yes" and "no"). Eventually the number of these instances is sufficient for their retrieval times to be faster than the execution of the algorithm. As a result, performance comes to be controlled by instance retrieval alone, and therefore becomes automatic. Set size initially should affect performance time because performance is under the control of the general algorithm and this involves a serial search of the target set. Eventually, however, as specific instances are retrieved for specific stimulus–response pairs, set size would cease to affect performance time.

The effects of VM practice on performance in the visual-search task also can be accounted for by the instance theory. According to this account, the nature of VM practice means that specific pairings of stimuli and responses are not repeated sufficiently for large numbers of specific instances to be stored in memory. Thus retrieval of these instances, on average, will not be faster than the performance of a general algorithm. As a result, performance will show little improvement with practice, and performance time will be affected by set size. However, according to this account, if the amount of VM practice is increased so that the amount of practice of specific stimulus–response pairings is equivalent to that provided by CM practice, then automaticity should be observed. The instance theory, therefore, can predict the results of Czerwinski et al. (1992).

Skilled Memory

Another account of expert performance relates many of the automatic features of expertise to highly efficient memory retrieval processes. Unlike Logan's theory, which describes automaticity as resulting from the retrieval of memory instances from an ever-increasing distribution of instances, skilled memory theory (Chase & Ericsson, 1982; Ericsson & Staszewski, 1989; Staszewski, 1988) claims that many of the features of automaticity result from a highly specialized long-term memory coupled with extremely efficient retrieval mechanisms. In other words, whereas the instance theory views expert performance as almost a by-product of the representation of a large amount of information in memory, skilled memory theory ascribes expert memory performance to changes in the way information is represented in and retrieved from long-term memory. This theory is not proposed as a comprehensive account of skill acquisition. However, the claim is that many of the extraordinary feats exhibited by some types of experts could result only from a highly developed memory system.

The most frequently cited example of the superior memory abilities of experts comes from the early studies of chess masters by de Groot (1966, 1978). In one set of experiments, chess players of varying skill levels were presented with chess boards of midgame configurations (i.e., configurations of chess pieces that could be expected in the middle of a game). After a 5-second exposure, the masters were able to reconstruct the board configurations from memory almost perfectly. However, there was a sharp drop-off in this ability for players below the master level.

Another example of the role of skilled memory in expert performance comes from Staszewski's (1988) work with mental calculators. Staszewski trained two subjects to perform multiplication calculations such as $23 \times 37,864$, without the aid of electronic calculators or pen and paper. After many hours of training, these two subjects were able to reduce their solution times for such problems from more than 120 seconds to around 30 seconds. Anyone who attempts this task can appreciate how remarkable this feat is. The task is a difficult one because the multiplicands and intermediate results must be remembered while the computations are performed. To be able to perform these operations accurately, and so swiftly, demonstrates that these mental calculators possess exceptional memory processes. Similar memory skills have been observed in a wide range of domains, including bridge (Charness, 1979), go (Reitman, 1976), electronics (Egan & B.J. Schwartz, 1979), computer programming (McKeithen, Reitman, Rueter, & Hirtle, 1981), baseball

(Chiesi, Spilich, & Voss, 1979), soccer (P.E. Morris, Tweedy, & Gruneberg, 1985), dance, basketball, and hockey (Allard & Starkes, 1991), and restaurant waiters (Ericsson & Staszewski, 1989).

The skilled memory theory of Chase and Ericsson (1982) proposes that experts develop exceptional memory abilities with practice. According to this theory, skilled memory can be characterized by three principles.

The first principle is referred to as the meaningful encoding principle. This refers to the way in which experts process information in their domain of specialization and the memory benefits this brings. According to this principle, experts use their extensive prior knowledge to process information in familiar tasks in meaningful ways. This then leads to more elaborate and accessible memory representations than those formed by novices. Experts' specialized knowledge enables the organization of information into meaningful chunks that are automatically accessed and retrieved. This chunking ability enables experts to circumvent the usual capacity limitations of short-term memory (i.e., short-term memory is capable of holding up to 7 ± 2 items of information; G.A. Miller, 1956). For example, if someone is presented briefly with the following letters:

A L T M F U O E R

and then asked to recall them, they might have difficulty recalling all of the letters, particularly in the correct order. However, if the letters were rearranged into the following order:

F O R M U L A T E

there would be much less difficulty associated with recalling the letters in order. According to the meaningful encoding principle, experts make use of this feature of memory to increase their working-memory capacity. By processing information in terms of their extensive knowledge base, large amounts of information (e.g., nine letters in the preceding example) can be represented as smaller amounts of information (e.g., one word in this example). Thus, rather than short-term memory (STM) capacity being increased, experts engage the resources of long-term memory (LTM) to make better use of STM.

Evidence for this meaningful encoding principle comes from the study of chess masters. As mentioned previously, masters are able to remember mid-game configurations in a glance. This suggests that, when processing chess configurations, masters appear to exceed the STM limitations of 7 ± 2 units of information. Chase and H.A. Simon (1973) suggested that masters process chess configurations in meaningful chunks, and just as in other examples of the effects of chunking, this would appear to result in an increase in the capacity of STM.

Chase and H.A. Simon (1973) investigated this proposal with two methods: de Groot's (1996, 1978) memory recall task (described earlier), and a perception task.

The perception task was similar to the memory task except subjects were able to view the original configuration of pieces while reconstructing this configuration on another board. In both tasks, Chase and Simon noticed that subjects placed pieces on the board in short bursts. In the memory task, subjects would place a number of pieces on the board and then pause, apparently considering the next group of pieces to position. In the perception task, similar behavior was observed; however, during the pauses subjects looked at the original configuration. Chase and Simon also noted that there was a limit on the number of groups of pieces, or chunks, recalled by subjects; this limit was the usual 7 ± 2 limit of STM. This limit was the same for all subjects, regardless of player ability. However, the average chunk size increased with skill level. For beginners, on average, each chunk contained 2.4 pieces. The chunk size for Class A players (intermediate between beginner and master) was 2.6 pieces, and for masters, 3.8 pieces. Further analysis revealed that, in novices, pieces within chunks were related by superficial visual features, such as color and spatial proximity. However, in masters, pieces within chunks were related mainly by chess functions, such as defense or attack configurations and identity of type of piece. Thus, chess players appear to process chess configurations in chunks. Masters are able to process configurations in terms of bigger, more meaningful chunks, and so have better memory.

Further evidence that these chunks are meaningful, especially for masters, comes from another famous result of the original de Groot (1966, 1978) studies. In the memory task, when subjects were shown random configurations of chess pieces instead of midgame configurations, the memory performance of the masters was just as poor as that of the beginners. Presumably then, with this type of material, masters are unable to make use of their extensive knowledge of chess configurations and their meaning. As a result, they cannot encode the random configurations in any particularly meaningful way and so suffer the same STM constraints as chess novices. Similar effects have been observed with number mnemonists: Their exceptional memory skills for numbers are not exhibited with letters (Ericsson & Staszewski, 1989). Thus, the superior memory of experts appears to result from their processing familiar material in meaningful chunks.

The second principle of skilled memory theory is the retrieval structure principle. According to this principle, experts make use of memory structures to keep track of serial order and/or intermediate results of processing. These can take many forms, but are usually abstract and hierarchical. Their nature reflects experts' sensitivity to the types of constraints present in frequently encountered problems. For instance, expert mental calculators make use of organized data structures that enable efficient encoding, representation, and retrieval of digit strings during computation (Ericsson & Staszewski, 1989). These structures help overcome the memory load associated with remembering multiplicands and intermediate results. Other experts use different types of structures that reflect different purposes. Some number mnemonists use elaborate versions of the method of loci to store large numbers of digits in prescribed orders (Ericsson & Staszewski, 1989). A waiter studied by Ericsson and Polson (1988) recoded dinner orders into wordlike acronyms (e.g., for salad dressings, Blue cheese, Oil-and-vinegar, Oil-and-vinegar, Thousand island = BOOT). In this way, information about seating position could be retained with information about dinner order. The advantage of these retrieval structures is that, when processing familiar material, experts can access and utilize their extensive knowledge and keep track of important information, such as serial order, or intermediate results.

The third principle of skilled memory theory is the speed-up principle. This principle states that, with practice, retrieval from LTM becomes faster, eventually approaching the speed with which information is retrieved from STM. Evidence that retrieval times from LTM are reduced with practice has been reported with mental calculators (Staszewski, 1988) and waiters and chess players (Ericsson & Staszewski, 1989). There is even some evidence that this speed-up is consistent with the power law of practice (Staszewski, 1988).

In summary, skilled memory theory accounts for the exceptional memory skills of some experts by proposing that experts use their extensive knowledge to process information in terms of meaningful chunks. This enables experts to encode, process, and retain a greater amount of information than would normally be possible within the limits of STM. Experts also use retrieval structures that organize the information being encoded and processed. These structures facilitate the retention of information that is important for efficient performance, such as serial order. Finally, experts have practiced the retrieval of specific types of information from LTM to the extent that it is as fast as retrieving information from STM. Together these three principles lead to memory performance that has the characteristics of a STM with an expanded capacity, but in fact is the result of a highly efficient LTM.

Skilled memory theory provides explanations for several characteristics of automaticity. First, much of the rapid performance of many experts can be attributed to highly efficient retrieval from a LTM full of domain-specific information. For example, chess masters can encode a board full of pieces in 5 seconds. Their chunking ability enables them to recode a large amount of information into a smaller set, and their extensive practice has meant this process is fast. Thus, masters can look at midgame configurations and immediately "see" meaningful configurations, much the same as normal readers can look at a page of letters and see words.

A second feature of automaticity accounted for by skilled memory theory is its mandatory nature. Chess masters and mental calculation experts appear to encode familiar information in LTM incidentally while they perform particular tasks. When chess masters are asked to suggest the next move from a configuration of pieces, they recall as much information about the configuration in a surprise recall as when they are warned of the recall in advance (Lane & L. Robertson, 1979). Mental calculators can distinguish between old and new problems with at least 80%

accuracy (Staszewski, 1988). So, when an expert encounters familiar material, it would appear that a trace is automatically left in LTM.

A third feature of automatic performance that can be attributed to skilled memory is resistance to capacity competition. Experts in many domains exhibit resistance to working-memory capacity constraints. Tasks that apparently involve a heavy memory load are executed with ease by experts. According to skilled memory theory, this is because experts' memory for familiar material is so fast and efficient that there is little competition for cognitive resources with other forms of cognitive processing. For example, Staszewski's (1988) study of two mental calculators involved two forms of problem presentation: oral and visual. The oral condition involves a heavier memory load than the visual condition because the calculators have to remember both multiplicands, and intermediate results, while performing the computations. Initially, this additional memory load was indicated by longer solution times in the oral condition. However, with extensive practice, the differences between the oral and visual conditions disappeared. Hence the calculators were able to develop memory skills that alleviated the additional load imposed by oral presentation. Ericsson and Staszewski (1989) described the performance of a chess player who was just below the level of master. This player could suggest moves in blindfold chess faster than he could do if he saw the board. The additional memory load associated with remembering the entire configuration of pieces on the board obviously did not trouble this player. Thus, some of the resistance to capacity competition in automatic performance may be attributed to skilled memory.

CONCLUSION

In this chapter, a number of theories of skill acquisition have been described. The main aim was to consider the various accounts of the mechanisms underlying the transformation of controlled processing into automatic processing. Anderson's ACT* theory was presented as an example of a theory that described skill acquisition as mainly a process of refining and strengthening procedures for performing tasks (see Newell, 1989, for a description of an alternate theory of this type—SOAR). The description of Logan's instance theory and the skilled memory theory of Chase, Ericsson, and Staszewski demonstrated that many features of the development of automatic performance can be accounted for by the effects of practice on memory retrieval processes.

To a large degree, Logan's position, and that of skilled memory, sit comfortably with Anderson's ACT* theory. Although the two types of theory propose different mechanisms whereby performance gets faster with practice, they both lead to similar predictions. For example, both Logan and Anderson proposed that, whereas performance early in practice will be deliberate and possibly accompanied by a reportable algorithm, with consistent practice performance will rely on a single-step process. In other words, skilled performance is characterized as the initiation of certain responses by particular stimulus conditions.[1] Certainly, in many different domains this has been claimed to be the essence of expert performance (see chap. 8 of this volume). For example, chess masters often have been reported as having the ability to glance at a chessboard midgame and find that particular configurations of the pieces immediately suggest sequences of moves (e.g., Charness, 1991). Physicists "see" physical principles in problem descriptions and these then lead to solution strategies (Larkin, McDermott, D.P. Simon, & H.A. Simon, 1980). Radiologists detect features in X-ray slides that initiate strategies for reaching a diagnosis (Lesgold et al., 1988). It is this type of skill that often is identified as the fast, effortless, and automatic feature of expertise. It also is considered extraordinary by the layperson because the nature of the ability that leads to this type of performance is usually inscrutable, by both the observer and the performer. According to the ACT*, instance, and skilled memory theories, however, this ability is simply a result of many years of consistent practice at a particular task. Experts' extraordinary abilities are seen as less a result of being blessed with mysterious talents and more a result of hard work.

---

[1]For this reason Logan (1992b) actually referred to the ACT* theory and the instance theory as memory-based explanations of automaticity. That is, automatic performance is characterized as the retrieval of a specific solution from memory in response to particular stimulus conditions.

6

IMPLICIT MEMORY AND AMNESIA

John Dunn
University of Western Australia

The study of human amnesia has profoundly affected theories of memory function. In particular, it provides dramatic evidence for major distinctions between different kinds of memory and, as many theorists suggest, for the existence of multiple memory systems. The primary datum offered by the study of amnesic subjects is the demonstration that while being severely impaired on some kinds of memory tests, amnesics perform normally on other kinds of memory tests. This dissociation provides a cogent underpinning to the distinction between implicit and explicit memory, a distinction that corresponds, broadly speaking, to the kinds of memory tasks amnesics can and cannot do.

Implicit and explicit memory are distinguished by the extent to which cues and instructions require subjects to consciously recollect information from prior relevant study episodes (Graf & Gallie, 1992; Graf & Schacter, 1985; Schacter, 1992b). Explicit memory tasks require conscious recollection of the to-be-remembered material; implicit memory tasks do not. It is now well established that amnesics are impaired on explicit memory tasks such as recall and recognition but often are unimpaired on implicit memory tasks. The aim of the present chapter is to examine the distinction between these two forms of memory in relation to studies of amnesia. The study of amnesia is important to students of memory for two reasons. First, it represents a profound disorder of memory that requires explanation in its own right. Second, the pattern of spared and impaired functions found in amnesia will be relevant to theories of normal human memory. Any theory of memory, as well as accounting for experimental results found with normal subjects, also must be able to account for the patterns of results found with memory-impaired subjects (Schacter, 1992b).

WHAT IS AMNESIA?

Amnesia is literally the absence of memory. It suggests a memory so deficient that no information can be retained. However, such a literal interpretation cannot be maintained. In practice, two difficulties emerge in the characterization of amnesia as the simple *absence* of memory.

First, it is rarely the case that memory is completely eradicated. Although, as a kind of shorthand, amnesic subjects are talked about as if their performance on criterion memory tasks is at zero, this is almost never the case. Amnesia represents a severe *relative* impairment of memory—amnesic subjects always will show some residual memory function, no matter how small.

The second difficulty in applying the term *amnesia* is that the detection of memory impairment depends on the way memory is measured. This point forms the theme for much of the present volume as well as forming the main focus of this chapter. Briefly, it turns out that subjects who have pronounced difficulty in remembering information when tested explicitly may be normal when tested implicitly. It should be noted that this kind of dissociation is not restricted to only implicit and explicit forms of memory. Dissociations produced by brain damage also may be found for pairs of explicit memory tasks (Parkin, Dunn, Lee, O'Hara, & Nussbaum, 1993) and pairs of implicit memory tasks (Butters, Heindel, & Salmon, 1990).

With the aforementioned qualifications in mind, an amnesic patient, as conventionally understood, is an individual who is markedly impaired on the following simple test. Some material, usually a set of words, is presented that in quantity exceeds the subject's immediate memory span (usually five to nine unrelated items). The subject inspects the stimuli and is instructed to try to remember as much of it as possible. Following inspection, or study, of the material, the subject's attention is redirected for a short period (as little as 20–30 seconds). One way of distracting subjects is simply to talk to them. The subject is then asked to recall as much of the studied material as they can. Being amnesic implies poor performance on this test. It says nothing in principle about performance on other tests of memory or other unrelated functions.

PRESERVED LEARNING IN AMNESIA

Amnesics show preserved learning on some kinds of tasks, which may be thought of as testing memory "implicitly." Demonstrations of preserved learning effects in amnesia fall into two broad classes. The first of these concerns the acquisition or improvement of a particular skill, where amnesic subjects improve their performance on a task as a result of the cumulative effects of simple repetition or practice. This improvement may occur even without explicit recollection of the practice episodes. The second class of preserved learning in amnesia concerns item-specific priming effects, where repetition of a particular stimulus leads to a change in the processing of that or a related stimulus. These two classes are discussed separately for three reasons. First, they often have been investigated using different research paradigms that tend to focus on different theoretical questions. Second, it has been suggested that the two kinds of task involve different processing requirements (Moscovitch, 1992a), and third, there is evidence that the two kinds of task are empirically dissociable (Butters et al., 1990).

Procedural Learning

As mentioned earlier, there is considerable evidence that amnesics are able to acquire and master new skills. The range of such skills is informative. Early investigations showed that amnesic subjects acquired perceptuomotor skills such as mirror tracing, bimanual tracking, and rotary pursuit at normal rates (for reviews, see N.J. Cohen & Eichenbaum, 1993; Parkin, 1982, 1988). In these tasks, subjects are confronted with an apparatus over which they must acquire predictive control. The behavior of these systems (e.g., the spinning disk in rotary pursuit) is ordered and, in principle, predictable. In order to master the task, subjects need to learn the underlying rule-based behavior of the system, and to acquire expertise at the motoric components that reflect this rule, although the fact that the task has a significant motor component is neither necessary nor sufficient to show preserved learning.

Later studies revealed the importance of rules in determining preserved learning by amnesics. In an important early study, N.J. Cohen and Squire (1980) demonstrated intact perceptual learning in amnesic subjects. In this study, subjects were required to read sets of three mirror-reversed words. Both amnesic and control subjects benefited from practice. Over trials, some word triples were repeated exactly, whereas others were presented only once. Amnesics and controls were not different in the rate at which they learned to read nonrepeated triples, demonstrating the acquisition of a novel reading skill that was unrelated to any particular stimulus. However, control subjects learned to read repeated triples at a faster rate than amnesics, suggesting that controls were able to make greater use of their explicit memory to recognize repeated words and to short-circuit the need to laboriously read each word at a time. Amnesic subjects, impaired in their ability to recognize repeated words, failed to receive this benefit.

In the case of reading mirror-reversed words, it is possible that subjects are learning a general rule for reflecting words or letters. It appears that as long as a correct response can be determined from the application of such a rule, amnesics are able to learn at normal rates. This applies even to complex cognitive rules such as that required to solve the Tower of Hanoi task (N.J. Cohen et al., 1985), generating sequences of numbers according to an arithmetic algorithm (Kinsbourne & Wood, 1975), learning to assemble jigsaw puzzles (D.N. Brooks & Baddeley, 1976), and mastering Berry and D.E. Broadbent's (1984) "sugar production" and "computer person" implicit learning tasks (Squire & Frambach, 1990). In each of these cases, a correct response is determined by the conjunction of the current situation and an internalized rule or tactic. For example, in the study conducted by Kinsbourne and Wood, their amnesic patient learned to generate a Fibonacci number sequence. This is a numerical series in which the next number is calculated by adding together the previous two. The correct output is therefore a function of (a) the current situation (the last two numbers generated) and (b) the rule (add them together). The Tower of Hanoi and implicit learning tasks admit to a similar analysis (N.J. Cohen & Eichenbaum, 1993). It should be pointed out that the rule does not have to be explicitly available to the subject, and usually is not. Few normal subjects are able to articulate the rules governing implicit learning tasks such as the "computer person" (O'Brien-Malone & Maybery, chap. 3 of this volume), and the amnesic patient H.M., when confronted with the Tower of Hanoi, was unable to state anything about how to solve it despite the fact that he had acquired considerable skill at this task over previous practice sessions. Furthermore, H.M. denied any explicit recollection of having undergone such practice (N.J. Cohen et al., 1985).

It is suggested that amnesics are able to learn tasks that are rule governed. These are tasks for which the appropriate behavior is not arbitrarily related to the current situation but rather can be derived from that situation through the application of the rule. An apparent exception to this description is the serial reaction time studied by Nissen and her colleagues (Nissen, 1992; Nissen & Bullemer, 1987; Nissen, Willingham, & Hartman, 1989). In this task, subjects press one of four keys in response to lights that flash on and off in one of four locations. Unknown to subjects, the sequence of lights is repeated after every 10 trials. With practice, response time decreases and Nissen et al. showed that amnesics learned at the same rate as normal controls. Interestingly, subjects were learning something about the particular 10-trial sequence, because any gains in response time were abolished when the pattern was replaced by a random alternation.

The reaction time task is interesting because although the sequence of stimuli is rule governed, it is not of the sort that allows general prediction. It is simply an arbitrary sequence of locations. If amnesics can learn such a sequence, as they appear to do, it suggests that they can acquire new associative information. That is, they have learned to predict (implicitly at least) the next stimulus from the previous stimulus or stimuli based solely on individual associations between these stimuli. Nissen et al. (1989) also examined learning of a 10-point maze by the same subjects. The maze shares formal similarities with the serial reaction time task. Both consist of a sequence of choice points at which a decision of what to do next is made. In the case of the reaction time task, the subject waits until a command is given—the implicitly predicted stimulus appears and the appropriate response is made. In the case of maze learning, the subject must explicitly generate the next response. Consistent with previous attempts to teach amnesics to navigate mazes, the amnesics studied by Nissen et al. failed to learn at anything like the same rate as the normal controls. Previously, it had been shown that amnesics can learn only simple mazes in which the number of choice points is less than or equal to their span of immediate memory (Parkin, 1982).

Why are amnesics able to learn the serial reaction time task, but not the maze-learning task? Nissen et al. (1989) suggested that the crucial difference concerned the fact that response generation was implicit in the serial reaction time task and explicit in the maze-learning task. The same or similar knowledge is being acquired in the two cases but, for some reason, can be expressed only implicitly. As mentioned earlier, if this is so, then amnesics are capable of learning arbitrary associations between stimuli. This is an important point, as previous investigations of procedural learning in amnesia suggest that amnesics are acquiring the general rule that determines the behavior of the system under consideration. In a later section, the evidence that amnesics can acquire arbitrary associations, even when tested implicitly, is reviewed. Although this evidence is not yet fully conclusive, it strongly indicates that such learning by amnesics is severely impaired. Thus, normal learning of the serial reaction time task is an unusual and potentially important observation. But is there an alternative explanation?

One of the difficulties in drawing conclusions from the kinds of task that amnesics *cannot* do, is that they may fail at those tasks for reasons unrelated to their memory difficulties. For example, Korsakoff amnesics (a favorite study population) have a variety of additional impairments relating to perception and to problem solving (Parkin & Leng, 1993). Whereas success at a particular task suggests that performance on that task does not depend on the memory processes that are impaired in amnesia, the opposite is not necessarily true. Failure on a task does not necessarily mean that performance depends on the same impaired memory processes. That being said, it is intriguing to consider why amnesics may be able to learn the sequential reaction time task but not an equivalently complex maze. Nissen et al. (1989) suggested that the crucial difference lay in the extent to which the reaction time task constrained response selection. However, the results admit to an alternative explanation, one that makes use of the fact that amnesics can learn short sequences that can be contained within their span of immediate memory. Improved performance on the sequential reaction time task may not be due to subjects acquiring knowledge about the entire sequence. Rather, they may be learning something about the internal relationships of the sequence that could be summarized in terms of a small set of "rules." For example, in contrast to a random sequence, immediate repetitions of the same stimulus never occur in the serial reaction time task. Similarly, repetitions across an intervening stimulus were also relatively unlikely. By abstracting these partial rules, subjects may improve their response times in the absence of any ability to be able to generate the next response in the sequence. If this explanation is valid, then amnesics' capacity to improve on the serial reaction time task may be understood within the framework that they can acquire novel procedures or rules, but not arbitrary associations.

The acquisition of procedural skills at a normal rate by even severely amnesic subjects is a remarkable phenomenon. It represents one of two theoretically significant dissociations of performance found in amnesia (the second is discussed next). Attempts to account for this dissociation are discussed later.

Item-Specific Priming

Item-specific or repetition-priming effects refer to a facilitation or change in the processing of a stimulus as a result of its prior presentation. Typically, experiments demonstrating this effect consist of study phase in which a set of items are presented, followed by a test phase in which these items and a set of new items are presented for subjects to respond to in some way. In a variant of this procedure, first and second stimulus presentations are interleaved continuously over a single test phase (e.g., B. Gordon, 1988). A variety of tasks have been used to assess priming. These include perceptual identification, lexical decision, word stem completion, word fragment completion, picture fragment completion, and object decision tasks, to name a few. They are all examples of *implicit memory* tasks. That is, they show the effects of prior exposure to stimulus material in the absence of conscious or explicit recollection of that event. For example, in a stem completion task, subjects are asked to complete three-letter strings to form English words. Thus, when presented with REA——, subjects may choose to generate *reach, reason, real,* or *readjudication*! Priming occurs when the probability of choosing a particular word to complete the stem is increased by its prior exposure in the study phase.

A crucial feature of repetition priming, which separates it from procedural learning, is that it is specific to the item that is presented at study. Although it is possible that subjects, as a result of acquiring either some facility with the experimental task or some familiarity with the setting, may perform more proficiently in the test phase than in the study phase, this general facilitation is independent of priming effects,which pertain to a particular stimulus. Prior presentation of an item benefits the processing of that item over and above any general benefit that may accrue to any other item.

Item-specific priming has attracted considerable research interest because it is functionally dissociable from measures of *explicit memory*. A number of variables have been found to selectively affect either priming or explicit memory. Generally, manipulations that encourage conceptual or elaborative processing of stimuli at study strongly affect explicit memory but appear to have little or no effect on priming. In contrast, variables that change the physical characteristics of the stimulus between study and test have large effects on the amount of priming observed but have little or no effect on explicit memory (for reviews, see Richardson-Klavehn & Bjork, 1988; Schacter, Chiu, & Ochsner, 1993). Such dissociations have been interpreted by some theorists as indicating that repetition priming does not depend on the memory processes that support explicit memory. In order to test this idea, researchers have turned to studies of amnesia. If priming and explicit memory are independent, then priming ought to be unaffected by amnesia.

Priming in Amnesia. It is ironic that whereas researchers of normal memory in the 1980s turned to studies of amnesia in order to investigate the relationship between priming and explicit memory, one of the first demonstrations of repetition priming occurred using amnesic patients. Warrington and Weiskrantz (1974) showed that amnesics' ability to identify fragmented pictures benefited from prior exposure to these pictures despite their greatly impaired explicit memory for the material. Since that time, numerous studies have shown intact repetition priming in amnesic patients (for reviews, see Schacter & Graf, 1986; Shimamura, 1986). Much of this work has examined priming of printed words. More recently, Schacter and his coworkers have extended the basic result to other domains, demonstrating intact priming in amnesics for line drawings of three-dimensional objects (Schacter, L.A. Cooper, & Treadwell, 1993) and for spoken words (Schacter, Church, & Treadwell, 1994).

Investigations of priming in amnesia complement studies of normal subjects. Priming appears to depend on different memory processes to those that subserve explicit memory tests such as recall and recognition. The prior presentation of an item alters the way it is processed in amnesics in the same way as in normals, but in the former case with the absence of any conscious recollection of the item having been presented before. This represents a fundamental datum that theories of memory need to address and to explain. Before turning to a consideration of such theories, additional results (some of which are less clear-cut and hence more controversial) concerning priming in amnesia need to be examined.

Dissociation With Procedural Learning. Amnesic subjects demonstrate a dissociation between explicit memory, for which they are severely impaired, and procedural learning and item-specific priming, for which they have been shown to be normal. One straightforward interpretation of this is that there are two memory systems or processes, one supporting explicit memory and the other supporting implicit memory, at least as indexed by procedural learning and item-specific priming. Prior to the late 1980s, this appeared to be a satisfactory explanation, at least as a first approximation. Since that date, however, an increasing number of studies have shown that various implicit memory tasks are dissociable from each other in both normal (Roediger, Srinivas, & Weldon, 1989) and brain-damaged populations (Heindel, Butters, & Salmon, 1988; Keane, Gabrieli, Fennema, Growdon, & Corkin, 1991; Salmon, Shimamura, Butters, & S. Smith, 1988; for a review, see Butters et al., 1990). In several of these studies, item-specific priming, using a stem completion task, was found to be impaired in patients with Alzheimer's disease. Alzheimer's disease is a progressive dementing illness that affects intellectual functioning. Such patients often have memory impairments to the same degree as amnesic patients. In addition, Salmon et al. (1988) compared Alzheimer's disease patients, amnesic patients, and patients with Huntington's disease on the stem completion task. Huntington's disease is a progressive neurological disorder that primarily affects central motor functioning but that, eventually, induces a generalized dementia. The Huntington's patients, unlike the Alzheimer's patients, were found to have normal levels of priming. One way of interpreting these results, is to suppose that patients with Alzheimer's disease are more seriously impaired on all memory tests. However, Heindel et al. (1988) found that amnesic patients, Alzheimer's disease patients, and normal controls learned a procedural task (pursuit rotor) at the same rate and significantly better than did the Huntington's disease patients. Thus, Alzheimer's disease patients appear to be impaired on item-specific priming (measured by stem completion) and normal on procedural learning (measured by pursuit-rotor). In contrast, Huntington's disease patients show normal repetition priming effects but are impaired on procedural learning.

Conceptual Priming.   Item-specific or repetition priming occurs when a stimulus is repeated either exactly or in some kind of physically altered state. In word completion, only the first three letters are repeated. In perceptual identification under stimulus-limited conditions, a word is flashed briefly on a screen followed by a patterned mask. In each case, the target word is identifiably processed in some way at test. Recently, attention has been directed to a procedure known as *conceptual priming*. This is the name given to a range of tasks in which conceptual rather than perceptual analysis is facilitated. In one such task, subjects are asked to generate a word that renders a difficult to interpret sentence meaningful. For example, the subject might see the sentence, "The haystack was important because the cloth ripped," which makes little sense until the word *parachute* is suggested. Conceptual priming on this task occurs when subjects are re-presented with sentences and there is an increase in the probability of generating the disambiguating word. It may be regarded as conceptual, as opposed to perceptual priming, because a change in the perceptual processing of the sentence is unlikely in itself to help subjects to generate the appropriate word. The relevant change in processing must occur at a conceptual or semantic level.

The existence of conceptual priming in amnesics would be another demonstration of preserved learning, this time at a semantic rather than at a perceptual level. It also may indicate a capacity to form new associations (see later), between the sentence and disambiguating word. In order to investigate this possibility, McAndrews, Glisky, and Schacter (1987) gave the aforementioned task to a group of amnesics and found priming lasting for up to 1 week, despite impaired ability to recognize the sentences as having been previously presented. However, the amount of priming was less than that found for normal controls and, in addition, Cermak, Blackford, M. O'Connor, and Bleich (1988) failed to find a similar effect in their severely amnesic patient S.S. The possibility exists, therefore, that the effect found by McAndrews et al. may have been due to contamination from explicit memory processes.

Learning of New Information

In a standard item-specific priming experiment, the stimulus material consists of known and familiar words. Priming by amnesics can be attributed, therefore, to some kind of activation of preexisting representations of this material in memory (R. Diamond & Rozin, 1984). The "memory" revealed by repetition priming can be viewed as analogous to sensitization in a conditioning paradigm rather than having a truly associative character. It would be of considerable interest, therefore, to know whether amnesics are capable of genuine new learning or the instantiation of novel representations or associations.

It is fair to say that the question of new learning in amnesia is presently quite controversial (for an excellent review, see J. Bowers & Schacter, 1993). There is confusion and disagreement over basic findings and considerable debate concerning the appropriate interpretation of confirmed results. Nevertheless, it is instructive to examine the issue and to identify some of the areas of broad agreement.

Priming of Novel Visual Stimuli. The most direct demonstration of implicit memory for new information would be to show priming for nonwords. These are pronounceable letter-strings such as *brem* or *kilp* that are presumed to have no prior representation in memory. If amnesics can show priming of nonwords then it would be shown that they can instantiate new material in memory. The difficulty with this strategy is that priming of nonwords is difficult to demonstrate in normals. Early results using primarily lexical decision tasks typically failed to show any facilitative effect of prior study of nonwords (e.g., D.L. Scarborough et al., 1977). In part this may be attributed to the response demands of lexical decision tasks where words and nonwords are assigned to different responses. Later studies, using word identification tasks in which words and nonwords can be treated identically, were more successful in demonstrating reliable priming effects for nonwords (e.g., Salasoo, Shiffrin, & Feustel, 1985). A similar pattern of initial null findings followed by reliable demonstration of nonword priming occurred in studies using amnesic subjects (Cermak, Talbot, Chandler, & Wolbarst, 1985; R. Diamond & Rozin, 1984; B. Gordon, 1988; Haist, Musen, & Squire, 1991). It is now clear that amnesics and normal controls reveal equivalent priming effects for nonwords, although these are usually less in magnitude than those obtained for words. In a continuous variant of this procedure, Musen and Squire (1991) asked amnesics and controls to read a list of five nonwords 20 times over. Reading time decreased at the same rate in both groups. This effect was also material-specific, because reading time did not decrease for a list of 100 unique words or nonwords. Thus, amnesics can be shown to benefit from the prior presentation of new information in the form of nonwords.

In contrast to the difficulty found in demonstrating priming effects for nonwords, it turned out to be easier to demonstrate priming in amnesics for novel visual objects. Schacter, L.A. Cooper, Tharan, and Rubens (1991) demonstrated priming for novel stimuli in amnesics using their *object-decision task*. In this task, line drawings of three-dimensional block objects are presented for study. In this phase, subjects inspect the figure and decide on its principal axis of orientation—whether it seems to face to the left or to the right. Following this, a test phase occurs in which the previously studied material and similar but nonstudied material are presented for a brief duration. This time, subjects are asked to decide whether the object is possible or impossible. Half the "objects" are impossible. That is, there is no real three-dimensional object that corresponds to the line drawing. The basic result in this paradigm is that subjects are more accurate in deciding that studied objects are possible compared to nonstudied objects. No difference is found for impossible objects. Schacter et al. demonstrated a similar robust priming effect for amnesics. It is conceivable, however, that this result could have depended on some explicit memory for the studied patterns. On a subsequent recognition memory test, amnesic subjects, although impaired relative to normals on their explicit memory for presented patterns, still performed substantially above chance. The possible contamination of implicit memory performance by explicit memory was not a problem in a similar study conducted by Gabrieli, Milberg, Keane, and Corkin (1990). In this case, priming of novel two-dimensional line drawings was demonstrated in the severely amnesic patient H.M. Subsequent recognition memory of studied patterns was at chance for the amnesic patient, whereas priming was *greater* than in the normal controls.

The previous results support the view that amnesics reveal implicit memory for novel visual stimuli where these are either letter strings or line drawings. The theoretical significance of this is discussed later, but for now it is worth pointing out that this ability can be explained in terms of the acquisition of pattern analyzing *procedures*. On this view, priming of novel patterns represents an adjustment of the visual processing system to the perceptual analysis of these stimuli. The critical point is that a geometric pattern, line drawing, or letter string, is processed as a single perceptual unit. This is in contrast to the situation in which different stimuli are arbitrarily related as, for example, in a paired-associate learning task. Because much of explicit memory appears to be based on just these kinds of associations, it is of interest to know whether amnesics can show implicit memory for novel associations. This issue was investigated in a series of studies by Graf and Schacter (1985; Schacter & Graf, 1989), the results of which have been equivocal (for a summary, see Bowers & Schacter, 1993).

Acquisition of New Semantic Knowledge.   There have been a number of studies that attempt to show that amnesics are able to acquire new semantic knowledge. It has been known for some time that amnesics are able to generate highly associated response words to given target words. For example, given the word *hot*, amnesics, like normals, are likely to respond with the word *cold* and to use this information to facilitate the learning of such pairs (Cutting, 1978). This is taken to mean that amnesics' existing semantic memory system (in which context-independent associations are presumed to be stored) is normal and largely intact. The crucial question is whether they are capable of adding new associations to this memory. The indications from studies of implicit memory for new associations would seem to suggest that they are not. However, it appears that with sufficient practice, new associations can be acquired. Using the method of *vanishing cues*, Glisky and Schacter (1988) demonstrated the acquisition of computer responses in a severely amnesic patient. In this procedure, a stimulus and the first n letters of a response word are presented together. When the response is correctly completed, n is decremented by one and the procedure repeated. Glisky and Schacter were able to show that their amnesic patient was able to learn to produce the correct response word after n had reduced to zero. Similarly, Tulving, Hayman, and Macdonald (1991) showed that their amnesic subject, K.C., was able to generate the correct response word following training on sentence frames of the form "Medicine cured HICCUP" accompanied by tangentially relevant pictures. In contrast, Gabrieli, N.J. Cohen, and Corkin (1988) failed in their attempt to teach H.M. the meanings of a set of unusual and archaic English words. Even after extensive training on the set of words, H.M. was unable to match even one word with its meaning.

It is difficult to know what to make of these mixed findings. Sorting them out is especially important because, as we see later, whether amnesics are capable of acquiring new semantic knowledge turns out to have considerable theoretical importance. One thing is clear though, if amnesics do acquire semantic knowledge they do so at an abnormally slow rate. The success achieved by Glisky and Schacter (1988) and by Tulving et al. (1991) came only after long and extended practice. Because it is likely that even the most severely affected amnesic patient maintains some residual capacity to acquire new information, these results simply may reflect that when given sufficient time, opportunity, incentive, and favorable conditions, a considerable amount of learning is possible. The theoretical significance of this fact is not clear. It should be borne in mind that procedural learning and item-specific priming in amnesia attracts theoretical interest because they are virtually intact. The acquisition of new semantic knowledge does not appear to belong in this category.

THEORETICAL APPROACHES

The previous sections offer a selective overview of what is currently known about the learning and memory capacities of amnesic patients with particular reference to investigations of implicit memory. Little or no attention has been paid to other, equally important issues, for which studies of amnesia have been and are relevant. These would include the aetiology of amnesia, its relation to brain structure, its typology, and the relationship between amnesia in humans and learning and memory in animals. For a discussion of these and other issues see N.J. Cohen and Eichenbaum (1993) and Parkin (1992).

By far, the dominant aim of most studies of learning in amnesia has been to demonstrate a dissociation between implicit and explicit memory. The basic story that emerges is that despite profound impairment in explicit memory, amnesics show the effects of prior learning on a number of different kinds of task. All of these tasks can be classified as implicit memory tasks and can be further subdivided into tasks that demonstrate procedural learning and tasks that demonstrate item-specific priming. There is unequivocal evidence that amnesics are capable of learning on both kinds of task.

Table 6.1 presents a summary of the kinds of task reviewed earlier organized in terms of the nature of amnesic performance. The fundamental amnesic impairment is in explicit long-term memory. There is also evidence of impaired learning in semantic memory. In contrast, the evidence also clearly shows that amnesics are capable of normal procedural learning and priming of words, nonwords, and novel visual patterns. In addition, although less certain, existing evidence suggests that amnesics also are impaired on priming for new associations and for conceptual priming effects.

What does this pattern of data mean? In particular, does the pattern of impairments manifested in amnesia tell us anything important about the normal working of memory? For most theorists, the answer is yes. It is felt that studies of amnesia reveal facts about memory that would be considerably less apparent if investigations were limited to intact memory systems. Such theorists account for the pattern of amnesic deficits by postulating the existence of *multiple memory systems.* According to this view, memory is organized into two or more largely independent "systems" that are differentially involved in implicit and explicit memory tasks. Amnesics are impaired on only one system, that which subserves explicit memory. Debate among these theorists primarily concerns the number and nature of these systems. However, this is not the only possible approach to the data. Before considering the multiple memory approach in more detail, an alternative theoretical perspective warrants attention.

Processing View

In contrast to the multiple memory system approach, some theorists have argued that existing data can be adequately accommodated by a unitary memory system that is accessed by a variety of different processes. This view has been most closely associated with Jacoby (1991), Roediger and his colleagues (Roediger, 1990a; Roediger, Rajaram, & Srinivas, 1990; Roediger, Srinivas, & Weldon, 1989), and Graf and his colleagues (Graf & Gallie, 1992; Graf & Ryan, 1990). On this view, the observed dissociations between different memory tasks do not require the postulation of novel memory "systems" but instead can be accounted for by differences in the way in which information is processed within a single memory system. The fundamental principle of this approach is that the degree to which information is accessed depends on the similarity between the processing opera-

TABLE 6.1

Classification of Tasks According to Comparative Performance of Amnesic Subjects

Normal	Impaired	Uncertain
Immediate explicit memory	Explicit (long-term) memory	
Procedural learning	Acquisition of new semantic knowledge	
Priming of words		Priming of new associations
Priming of nonwords		Conceptual priming
Priming of novel visual patterns		

tions engaged in at study and the processes engaged in at retrieval—a principle referred to as *transfer-appropriate processing*. In general, tests that induce one kind of processing will be dissociable from tests that induce another. In particular, a distinction is drawn between *data-driven processing* that is largely automatic and focuses upon the perceptual characteristics of a stimulus, and *conceptually driven processing* that is optional, under conscious control, and focuses on the meaningfulness of the stimulus and its association with information already in memory. Tasks that invite largely data-driven processing on the part of the subject will be dissociable from tasks that invite largely conceptually driven processing. To a great extent, implicit memory tasks tend to be data-driven whereas explicit memory tasks are conceptually driven, although it is possible to construct conceptually driven implicit memory tasks and to show that they are also dissociable from other implicit memory tasks (Roediger, Srinivas, & Weldon, 1989).

The processing view represents a major theoretical counterpoint to the multiple memory systems view and also seems to account for much of the data from studies of normal memory. It raises a number of issues concerning the interpretation of dissociations and what it means to talk of a memory system. These questions are examined later. However, the processing view suffers from two serious limitations. The first is conceptual. It is usually not possible to specify the kinds of processing that a given test of memory will require. Consequently, before examining performance on that test, it does not appear to be possible to predict the effect of any experimental manipulation. This leads to the charge of circularity (Nelson, 1994). The second limitation of this view is that it does not seem to be able to offer a compelling account of why long-term explicit memory is selectively impaired in amnesia. An obvious suggestion from the theory would be that amnesics are deficient in conceptually driven processing, yet there is little or no evidence that this is the case. Amnesics are fully able to process language, have intact intellectual skills, and are able to elaborate the meaning of verbal material. It is possible that although amnesics engage in such processing, its effects are disconnected from memory. However, if conceptually driven and data-driven processing are simply different ways of instantiating information into a unitary memory system, it is difficult to account for why there should exist a class of patients in which one of these types of processing simply has stopped working. For this reason, most researchers who have studied memory in amnesia have opted for some form of a multiple memory system view.

Multiple Memory System View

According to the multiple memory systems view, the primary dissociations observed in studies of amnesia imply the existence of a nonunitary memory system. On this view, the task of the theorist is to determine from the patterns of impaired and unimpaired performance of amnesic and other brain-damaged subjects, the number and nature of these memory systems. What is exactly meant by the term *system* in this context is currently the subject of some debate and is discussed in more detail below. For present purposes, it is sufficient to think of a memory system as a functionally and possibly neuroanatomically distinct processing system that contributes to performance on tasks ordinarily thought of as tests of memory.

Perceptual Representation System.   One of the first attempts to account for the effect of amnesia on implicit and explicit memory, was in terms of the distinction between episodic and semantic memory (Schacter & Tulving, 1983; Tulving, 1985). However, it is now clear that repetition-priming effects observed in amnesia cannot easily be accommodated within this framework, prompting Schacter and Tulving (Schacter, 1990, 1992a; Tulving & Schacter, 1990) to propose that priming reflects the operation of a *perceptual representation system* (PRS) that is distinct from both of these memory systems. The PRS is itself decomposable into a number of domain-specific subsystems or modules that nevertheless share a common function or processing principle. These are a visual word form system involved in the analysis of words presented visually, an auditory word form system involved in the analysis of words presented auditorally, and a structural description system involved in the analysis of spatial objects (Schacter, 1992a). All of these subsystems are concerned with computing a *structural description* of a given stimulus, conceptualized as a relatively abstract but domain-specific representation of the perceptual, but not semantic, content of a stimulus. Similar characterizations of a *perceptual record* of analysis have been proposed by others including Kirsner and Dunn (1985) and Moscovitch (1992a). The PRS is automatically engaged during perceptual analysis and is "tunable" to the particular stimuli that have been presented, leading to a selective adaptation that determines repetition-priming effects.

The PRS account incorporates an *activation view* of priming, identified by Schacter (1987) as one of three possible approaches to understanding repetition-priming effects (the others being the processing and multiple memory systems views). This view originated with the logogen theory initially proposed by J. Morton (1969) in the context of word recognition. Central to this approach is the idea that perceptual processing, up to but not including the formation of semantic and associative links, is modifiable by experience and hence is reflected nonconsciously through implicit memory. For this reason, the PRS theory represents the confluence of a set of similar ideas concerning word and object recognition that have been discussed by many researchers for some time. This being said, there are two areas where the theory is currently challenged. These concern its generality as an account of all implicit memory effects and details concerning its true domain-specificity and independence from semantic memory.

Concerning the generality of the PRS account, although it provides a good explanation of item-specific priming effects, it does not readily account for the acquisition of procedural skills nor, directly, for the instantiation of new information (i.e., nonwords). In the case of normal acquisition of procedural skills, it is not clear whether this represents the operation of yet another memory system or whether all implicit memory effects can be subsumed within a single PRS-style framework.

Concerning the details of its operation, there is some recent evidence for an effect of semantic context on repetition priming (J.V. Bainbridge et al., 1993). In the study by Bainbridge et al., context-specific priming of homophones was found. If one meaning of a word is suggested by its context, such as *river*-BANK, then no repetition-priming effects are observed if the word is presented again in a different context, such as *money*-BANK. This effect is reminiscent of implicit memory for new associations, and may be similarly accounted for in terms of explicit memory involvement. However, the possibility remains open that semantic context may mediate the perceptual analysis of stimuli.

Lastly, the perceptual representation system is viewed as containing a number of domain-specific subsystems, identified according to both input modality (visual, auditory) and mode (verbal, pictorial). The existence of significant priming across both modality (Kirsner et al., 1983) and mode (Kirsner et al., 1986) draws into question the idea that these are fully independent subsystems. At the very least, the theory will need to be elaborated and extended in the light of these data.

Procedural Versus Declarative Memory.   Presently, the most articulated and general proposal to account for the amnesic dissociations within the multiple memory systems view is the distinction between *procedural* and *declarative* memory (Cohen, 1984; Cohen & Eichenbaum, 1993; Cohen & Squire, 1980; Squire, 1992). As initially described, procedural memory was concerned with the acquisition of perceptuomotor and cognitive skills. Declarative memory was seen as a separate system concerned with memory for explicit facts and events, information that can be brought to mind and "declared." Thus declarative memory subsumes semantic and episodic memory as subsystems. In contrast to this form of memory, procedural memory can be manifested only by the specific activities or procedures that it subserves. For example, suppose as a child you learned to ride a bicycle. Declarative memory would consist of your knowledge that you once could ride a bicycle and some, at least, of the specific learning experiences you had as you acquired this skill. Procedural memory for bicycle riding would consist of the myriad of abilities required for successful control of the vehicle and could be assessed directly only by getting on a bicycle and trying to ride it.

Recently, the distinction between procedural and declarative memory has been elaborated differently by N.J. Cohen and Eichenbaum (1993) and Squire (1992). In light of the fact that different implicit memory tasks can be dissociated from each other, Squire has argued that procedural memory does not correspond to a single integrated system in the brain, but is rather an umbrella term, similar to implicit memory, that refers to a number of separate subsystems each subsuming a different function, such as skill acquisition, item-specific priming, and other forms of learning such as classical conditioning and habituation. In contrast, Cohen and Eichenbaum maintained that whereas procedural memory is composed of a number of different subsystems (of which the PRS may be regarded as one), there is sufficient commonality in their rules of operation to properly regard them as constituting parts of a single system.

N.J. Cohen and Eichenbaum (1993) also have elaborated to a greater extent the nature of declarative memory. This, they argued, is an integrated system that represents the output of cortical processors concerned with functional descriptions of perceptually distinct objects and events encountered during learning. Declarative memory serves to relate these descriptions to each other and to the various affective and behavioral responses produced by them. The point stressed by Cohen and Eichenbaum is that the formation of flexible, and in their words, promiscuous, connections between stimuli is the province only of declarative memory. No other memory system serves this function. From this view comes a clear prediction. If amnesia can be characterized as an impairment in declarative memory, then amnesics will be selectively unable to learn associations between perceptually distinct items. Thus, episodic memory is impaired because this requires an association between an item and its spatio-temporal context. Semantic memory is impaired because this usually requires an association between two different items (e.g., a word and its meaning). On the other hand, characteristics of existing or new perceptual categories can be acquired. Thus, item-specific priming and nonword priming are intact while implicit memory for new associations should not be found (as such associations can reflect only the operation of declarative memory). If amnesics can be shown to acquire interitem associations in a normal manner, then the present proposal would need to be rejected or substantially modified.

The procedural/declarative proposal has two positive features. As well as accounting for the data reasonably well, it is founded on a process description that renders it falsifiable in principle. In addition, it is marked by its generality. The theory has been articulated in such a way as to make sense of functional dissociations observed in studies of amnesia and studies of normal memory, as well as analogous results of lesion studies in the animal domain. Consideration of the latter are beyond the scope of the present article, but serve to strengthen the theory by extending its explanatory scope.

One or More Memory Systems?

At present, the primary data offered by studies of human amnesia concern functional dissociations between tasks. Amnesics are impaired on some tasks and intact on others. The major theoretical division between the processing view and the multiple memory system view concerns the correct interpretation of these dissociations and the appropriate use of the term "memory system." These issues currently are being debated and it is likely that they will continue to be debated, no matter what the fate of the various theories outlined earlier. For this reason, it is useful to examine these issues in a little more detail.

Roediger and his colleagues (e.g., Roediger et al., 1990), argued that although task dissociations are consistent with the existence of separate memory systems, they also can be accommodated within a processing framework. That is, different processes operating within a unitary memory system are also capable of producing dissociations between tasks. This view is undoubtedly correct (for a similar argument, see Dunn & Kirsner, 1988). Furthermore, theorists ought to employ Occam's Razor and posit the existence of multiple memory systems only when a more parsimonious processing account has been shown to be inadequate. A second point, raised by Dunn and Kirsner and recently emphasized by Jacoby (1991), is that a dissociation between two tasks may tell us little about the underlying processes or memory systems involved, because of the possibly complex relationships between the processes and tasks concerned. This especially becomes an issue when, as is presently the case, two or three memory systems are thought to subserve performance on a large number of tasks. The kinds of dissociations or other intertask relationships that might be expected under these conditions is simply not known. Interpretation then can become a minefield in which dissociations that conform to theoretical expectations are highlighted whereas those that seem to indicate fractionation of a favored memory system are selectively ignored. For example, it has been known for some time that recall can be dissociated from recognition, yet little interest has been directed to whether this indicates the existence of multiple explicit memory systems.

What Is a Memory System?   What does it mean to say that something constitutes a memory system? Surprisingly, despite the widespread use of this term, there is currently little agreement concerning its status. It may be that it is a feature of the scientific paradigm in which neuroscientists and neuropsychologists work that "system" is invoked as a natural means of explaining the selective impairments of memory in amnesia. In fact, investigations of amnesia often are construed as attempts to discover the nature of the damaged memory system. Yet the term has not received an agreed definition.

In an influential article, Sherry and Schacter (1987) attempted to lay the groundwork for a consideration of what might be meant by a memory system. They compared criteria based on anatomical or structural separation with criteria based on functional incompatibility and different rules of operation. They argued that domain-specific modules that handle different classes of stimuli in similar ways for the same end should be viewed as part of a single processing system even if they are also neuroanatomically distinct. Thus, functional criteria are paramount. These ideas appear to guide Schacter's description of the PRS as composed of functionally similar subsystems and Cohen and Eichenbaum's description of procedural memory.

More recently, Schacter and Tulving (1994) proposed three criteria for postulating distinct memory systems. First, a system should enable a person to perform a large number of tasks of a particular class or type, independently of the specific informational contents of the task. Thus, episodic memory constitutes a system because it enables subjects to remember particular autobiographical events irrespective of the content of those experiences. Second, a system should be describable in terms of a list of its attributes, functionality, and rules of operation and the ways in which it relates to other systems, memory, perceptual, or otherwise. Third, multiple systems should be postulated only when there is good reason for believing that a unitary system is insufficient. Schacter and Tulving argued that this occurs when there is a set of *converging dissociations* that appear to contrast one class of tasks with another. This, they suggested, overcomes the criticism that if every dissociation is taken seriously, the number of memory systems would proliferate without bound.

It is clear that further work is required to refine and develop the concept of a memory system so that researchers will be able to recognize one during their daily work. It is a difficult concept to get right because the term *system,* in everyday language, is based on both structural *and* functional criteria. Thus, a transportation system in a country is identified in terms of both its function, delivering goods from one place to another, and the fact that it is composed of structurally characteristic components such as roads, railways, vehicles, and so on. Similarly, anatomists can talk about the circulatory system of the body partly because it is composed of such structurally distinct components as blood, blood vessels, and a heart. In practice, another structurally separate system, the nervous system, is also intimately involved in the *function* of the circulatory system—moving blood around the body. The rate at which the heart pumps, the width of blood vessels, and even properties of the blood itself are all affected by signals transmitted through the nervous system. It is a moot question whether we would make the same distinctions between these two systems if they were anatomically indistinguishable.

CONCLUSION

Far from appearing to be an indivisible and monolithic entity, memory appears to manifest itself in a variety of different ways. Studies of amnesia over the last 20 years have revealed a rich source of information concerning the function of human memory. Increasingly, theories of human memory are being tested and evaluated in relation to the patterns of deficits found in amnesia. Theories based on the study of both normal and impaired memory function represent the current "state of the art" concerning our understanding of human memory. Despite vigorous debate over methods, concepts, and interpretation, there has been a gratifying convergence of thinking about the nature of memory that suggests that real progress has been and continues to be made.

7

IMPLICIT KNOWLEDGE AND CONNECTIONISM: WHAT IS THE CONNECTION?

Paul Roberts
Murdoch University

In this chapter I attempt to elucidate the phenomenon of implicit learning by discussing the nature of implicit knowledge. In so doing I make a distinction between two senses in which so-called implicit knowledge could be said to be implicit. Research concerned with implicit learning typically has construed implicit knowledge as unreportable knowledge. However, within this framework there are two possibilities. First, implicit knowledge might be implicit in the sense that it is knowledge that is unreportable for some reason, despite being explicitly represented. Second, implicit knowledge might be implicit in the sense that it is knowledge that is not merely unreportable, but knowledge that also is represented implicitly. The relevant literature has not clearly distinguished between these two possibilities, either conceptually or empirically. In the experimental study of implicit learning, attention has been focused largely on whether the knowledge in question is available for verbal report, with less concern for the underlying representational format of that knowledge. In contrast, the enterprise of modeling implicit learning has been concerned to construct models that learn without explicitly representing what they learn. As a result, it is unclear how the phenomenon of implicit knowledge should be conceived. Is it simply an unreportable form of the reportable knowledge that subjects display, not qualitatively different in format from reportable knowledge, or is it qualitatively different in format to reportable knowledge? The latter possibility appears theoretically more tractable, because if

119

so-called implicit knowledge is qualitatively different to reportable knowledge, in the sense of not being explicitly represented, then this may explain the lack of reportability of the knowledge that is represented. However, if implicit knowledge is explicitly represented, despite being unreportable, then it is difficult to explain why such knowledge should be unreportable. Furthermore, knowing that unreportable knowledg is implicitly represented severely constrains the kind of processes and models that can be postulated to account for the phenomenon of implicit knowledge and implicit learning.

Connectionism has been construed by a number of authors as a useful paradigm for developing models of implicit learning because it appears to implement this theoretically tractable conception of implicit knowledge (see e.g., Cleeremans, 1993; Dienes, 1992; Kushner, Cleeremans, & Reber, 1991; Roberts & C. MacLeod, 1995a). If it is the case that all implicit learning is implicit in the "not explicitly represented" sense implied by connectionist models, then connectionism may well be a useful integrative framework for understanding implicit learning. However, because it is not clear in which sense implicit learning is implicit, it is not clear whether a connectionist model of a particular implicit learning process is appropriate. Distinguishing between the two senses of implicit, I suggest, results in conceptual clarity when talking about implicit knowledge and provides a theoretical handle with which to begin to investigate the nature of implicit learning.

TWO SENSES OF IMPLICIT

The term *implicit*, as it is used in the literature, generally has been employed to refer to processes that are not conscious. For example, Reber (1989a), in his review of implicit learning, said that "Implicit knowledge results from the induction of an abstract representation of the structure that the stimulus environment displays, and this knowledge is acquired in the absence of conscious, reflective strategies to learn" (p. 219). Conventionally, then, implicit learning is essentially unconscious learning. Implicit learning generally is diagnosed when subjects are unable to report what they have learned. Of course, there are many reasons why acquired knowledge may be unreportable, and hence appear to be unconscious. For example, the reported knowledge, although functional, may not conform to the experimenters' expectations, leading to the erroneous conclusion that the subject is confabulating, and hence that they are unaware of what they have learned (see e.g., Perruchet & Pacteau, 1990). However, such methodological problems can be addressed by careful experimental design. Therefore, despite such problems, researchers have made the reasonable assumption that (in appropriately designed experiments) poor verbal report indicates lack of awareness of what has been learned. Thus, implicit knowledge is generally operationalized as unreportable knowledge.

Despite the general adherence to this conception of implicit knowledge in the implicit learning literature, there is another, and more specific sense in which knowledge can be said to be implicit. In order to distinguish it from the generic, "merely unconscious," sense of implicit I refer to this second sense of implicit as *representational implicitness*. Dennett (1983) has advocated that we should say "that information is represented explicitly in a system if and only if there actually exists in the functionally relevant place in the system a physically structured object, a formula or string or tokening of some members of a system (or 'language') of elements for which there is a semantics of interpretation, and a provision (a mechanism of some sort) for reading or parsing the formula" (p.216). And, that we should say that, "for information to be represented implicitly, we shall mean that it is implied logically by something that is stored explicitly" (p. 216). Thus, if knowledge is representationally explicit, some search process can potentially recover that knowledge because it exists as a discrete object that can be "found." By contrast, knowledge that is representationally implicit cannot literally be recovered because it does not exist as a discrete object that can be found. Rather, representationally implicit knowledge only exists as a logical consequence of knowledge that is explicitly represented and hence can only be inferred, not directly recovered. This property of implicitly represented knowledge may provide the basis for an explanation of why some knowledge that people demonstrably possess nevertheless cannot be reported.

Perhaps the easiest way to grasp the notion of representational implicitness is to consider a simple knowledge acquisition system that works by storing veridical copies of exemplars or instances of a particular class. Assume that if this system is told that a particular exemplar is a member of a class then that exemplar is stored under the class label. Let us say that the system's task is to learn to identify exemplars of a concept defined by the conjunction of two critical features. The final representation of the concept that is possessed by this system would consist of the total pool of exemplars it had encountered. What is explicit in such a representation is each exemplar that the system has been exposed to, and hence the features that particular exemplars possess. What is implicit in such a representation is the rule ("f1 and f2") that is implied by the exemplars that are stored. Despite the fact that there is no explicitly represented rule in sight in such a scheme, this kind of representation can support rather good generalization to previously unseen exemplars (L. Brooks, 1978; Hintzman, 1986).

The notion of representational implicitness naturally explains the phenomenon of implicit knowledge. Clearly, if knowledge is represented implicitly then it is not directly recoverable. Thus, the conceptual representation in the previous example, which consists of stored exemplars, will not easily support a verbal report of the underlying conceptual rule. In order to infer the rule from such a representation, one would have to generate a hypothesis about the nature of the concept and test this "in the head." This undoubtably would be difficult and hence would be unlikely to lead to an accurate report of the conceptual rule implicit in the representation. The point, then, is that representational implicitness naturally explains the unreportability of knowledge. One cannot easily report knowledge that is implicitly represented because it is not directly recoverable. By contrast, if unreportable knowledge is representationally explicit, then it is unclear how one should go about explaining that lack of reportability. If it is true that unreportable knowledge is representationally explicit, then the question becomes one of why knowledge that is directly recoverable is not reportable. Of course, it is possible to design a model of implicit learning that relies on explicit representation and yet yields unreportable knowledge. However, this comes at the cost of a principled connection between the nature of the learning mechanism and the unreportability of what is learned. When a model of implicit learning relies on implicit representation then such a principled connection is maintained. When a model of implicit learning relies on explicit representation then rather ad hoc hypotheses about why that knowledge is unreportable need to be formulated. Thus, the most tractable explanatory framework is one that identifies unreportable knowledge with representational implicitness. Indeed, all the models that have been proposed as potential candidates for a model of implicit learning exploit the notion of implicit representation for explaining the existence of functional but unreportable knowledge. In what follows several such approaches to implicit learning are briefly canvassed.

Several authors have suggested instance storage models of implicit learning. For example, Hayes and D.E. Broadbent (1988) suggested that implicit learning, which they call u-mode (unselective-mode) learning, may proceed by unconsciously storing information about responses to particular situations. Stanley et al. (1989) suggested that, in explicit learning tasks, subjects acquire an explicit mental model of the task that can be verbally reported. However, in implicit learning tasks, Stanley et al. suggested that subjects rely on what they called memory-based processing. Memory-based processing is simply the reliance on the memory for particular task-relevant events in the absence of an explicit mental model of the task. As noted previously, a representation that consists of stored instances is unlikely to provide an adequate basis for reporting the conceptual structure of the task and hence is likely to lead to poor verbal report, and consequently, the attribution that the knowledge is unconscious.

Another approach to implicit learning that results in knowledge representations where information is implicit was suggested by Kellogg and Bourne (1989). They posited that learning can proceed either strategically or automatically. Whereas strategic learning is said to proceed by the testing of explicit hypotheses, automatic learning is said to proceed by the automatic storage of a feature frequency distribution in long-term memory. Essentially, they proposed an independent cue model where the relative frequency of occurrence of features in examples of a class and nonexamples of a class determines the cue validity of a feature. So, features that occur frequently in examples, but infrequently in nonexamples, have a high cue validity because they can be employed to discriminate examples from nonexamples reliably. Note that, unlike an exemplar model, such a model does not result in a representation preserving information about the structure of individual exemplars.

Rather, it abstracts feature frequency information from exemplars. In this kind of a model the critical features are representationally explicit. What is representationally implicit is the rule describing the class of objects that the system identifies. Specifically, what is representationally implicit is the knowledge about the relationship between the critical features. Although a representation in this model explicitly represents the critical features, it does not specify how they are related. For example, two features could be critical, but could be related either conjunctively (f1 AND f2) or disjunctively (f1 OR f2). The only difference between these two cases is that the criterion for considering a stimulus an example would have to be set differently. In the first case, two features must be present to provide a sufficient weight of evidence for a positive response, whereas in the second case only one feature need be present to provide a sufficient weight of evidence for a positive response. Because this information is not represented explicitly it cannot be directly recovered. Again, this is likely to lead to knowledge that is difficult to report and consequently the attribution that the knowledge is unconscious.

Recently, connectionist models also have been employed to model implicit learning (Cleeremans, 1993; Dienes, 1992; Kushner et al., 1991). Because of the increasing popularity and importance of connectionist models in psychology and cognitive science generally, the following section provides a brief overview of the nature of connectionist models before turning to the motivation behind the adoption of a connectionist framework for modeling implicit learning.

CONNECTIONISM AND IMPLICIT KNOWLEDGE

Connectionist models utilize the interaction between large numbers of simple units, which have excitatory and inhibitory relations to each other, in order to process information (see e.g., Rumelhart, Hinton, & J.L. McClelland, 1986). They are driven by frequency of co-occurrence to build associative connections between features and category labels. However, connectionist models do not simply utilize associative strengthening to implement an independent cue approach to learning, in the manner of the model described earlier. Rather, the processing of cues is highly interactive in connectionist models (Whittlesea, 1989). Indeed, the rise of interest in connectionist modeling may be seen to some extent as having been driven by empirical results in psychology that highlighted the ubiquity of interactive processing in human cognition. J.L. McClelland, Rumelhart, and Hinton (1986) referred to this aspect of human cognition as the ability to satisfy multiple simultaneous constraints. An example of this, provided by McClelland et al., is the interdependence of syntax and semantics. In the syntactically equivalent sentences:

I saw the grand canyon flying to New York.

I saw the sheep grazing in the field.

"flying to New York" and "grazing in the field" do not perform the same grammatical role, as purely syntactic considerations would suggest. Rather, preexisting semantic knowledge constrains interpretation of the syntax. The point that McClelland et al. made is that there are numerous examples of this sort to be found in human cognition, suggesting that different kinds of information are processed in a highly interactive manner and in mutually constraining ways that allow processing "problems" to be "solved."

These kind of effects are rather easily and naturally modeled by connectionist architectures, as are a number of other related effects that are features of human cognition. The following properties of connectionist models were considered significant by J.L. McClelland et al. (1986) because they mirror critical properties of human cognition:

1. They are good at disambiguating inputs with multiple interpretations.
2. They exhibit emergent rulelike behavior without explicitly representing rules or hypotheses.
3. They exhibit content addressable memory, allowing retrieval to be cued by any attribute of the to-be-retrieved representation.
4. They exhibit graceful degradation. This means that incorrect or missing input information will not have a completely disastrous effect on processing. Rather, performance will degrade gradually as a function of the proportion of incorrect or missing input information.
5. They exhibit default assignment. This means that unknown properties of inputs will be assigned as a function of their similarity to those inputs where the property is known.
6. They exhibit spontaneous generalisation. This means that typical values of properties of particular classes of inputs are retrieved automatically.

The critical property that has made connectionist architectures appear to be such good candidates for modeling implicit processes is the fact that they can represent knowledge implicitly (cf. Dienes, 1992; Kushner et al., 1991).[1] That is, they can function in a rulelike manner without the need for the explicit representation of rules. Thus, researchers who model implicit processes in connectionist architectures are subscribing to the representationally implicit conception of implicit knowledge. Clearly, then, connectionist models explain the unreportability of acquired knowledge in implicit learning in the same way as the previously discussed models: Acquired knowledge is difficult to report because it cannot be directly recovered. At least on one account, however, knowledge acquired by a connectionist system is much more radically representationally implicit than in the previously discussed models. It is to this conception of connectionist representation that we now turn.

---

[1]It also may be the case that some or all of the other listed properties of connectionist models are selectively characteristic of implicit processes. Currently the literature has little to say on these issues.

The nature of representation in connectionist architectures was discussed in detail by Fodor and Pylyshyn (1988). Fodor and Pylyshyn contrasted representation in connectionist architectures with representation in classical architectures. Classical models are based on the familiar assumption that cognition consists of symbol manipulation. Elements (symbols) are placed in different relations to produce expressions that represent states of affairs. This often is achieved by explicitly represented rules, something that is impossible in connectionist models.

The critical property of classical architecture that distinguishes it from connectionist architecture, according to Fodor and Pylyshyn (1988), is the combinatorial structure of its representations. In classical architectures, representations are constituted by structurally atomic parts that are combined to form more complex structures. Of particular importance is that within these complex structures the atomic parts retain their identity. This allows the processes that operate on classical representations to be sensitive to their structure. For example, in a classical system the complex "P&Q" is represented by the concatenation of the "P" symbol and the "Q" symbol. This has the effect of allowing the rest of the system to read the constituents of the expression from the representation of the complex. Thus, the constituent structure of the representation P&Q is representationally explicit.

According to Fodor and Pylyshyn (1988), constituent structure in connectionist representations is not representationally explicit. Because the processing mechanism in connectionist systems is association, states of affairs can only be related probabilistically, but not structurally. So, although the complex representation "P&Q" might happen to be associated with its constituents, "P" and "Q," this association is not mandatory in a connectionist system. In a classical system, however, such an association is mandatory, because "P" and "Q" are literal structural constituents of "P&Q." In Fodor and Pylyshyn's terms, the data structures of connectionist architectures are atomic. Thus, even complex states of affairs that are logically related to simpler representations are represented as undifferentiated atoms. The representation of the complex P&Q is simply a node (or pattern of activation distributed across nodes) that becomes active when P is the case in conjunction with Q being the case. There is no way the rest of the system can read the constituents of the expression from the activity of that node. This point can be appreciated by considering an example provided by Fodor (1986). Consider the two networks in Fig. 7.1, with the nodes representing the propositions with which they are labeled. It is important to realize that these labels are just that; they have no meaning for the system. The labels simply indicate the conditions that activate that node.

Node 2 in these networks reads the situation with respect to Nodes 3 and 4 to determine its response. Node 2 becomes active in Net A in response to a different state of affairs to that which causes Node 2 in Net B to become active. In Net A, Node 2 becomes active if EITHER Node 3 or 4 becomes active, whereas in Net B Node 2 becomes active if BOTH Node 3 and 4 are active. However, a further node in the system, Node 1, which becomes active when Node 2 is active, has no access

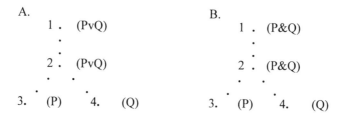

FIG. 7.1. Two networks, representing a disjunction (A) and a conjunction (B). From Fodor (1986). Copyright © 1986 by The University of Arizona Press. Reprinted with permission.

to information about the state of affairs that caused Node 2 to become active. That is, it cannot distinguish between the case in which only one of Nodes 3 or 4 is active and the case in which both of Nodes 3 and 4 are active. From the point of view of Node 1, in each network, the world has the same structure; that is, Node 2 is either on or off. Such processing characteristics seem to preclude the system ever knowing what it is doing. In short, such processing characteristics result in knowledge representations where constituent structure is representationally implicit.

DISTINGUISHING BETWEEN THE
TWO SENSES OF IMPLICIT

It is important to recognize that although connectionist models, and representational implicitness generally, may explain how one can possess knowledge without being able to report that knowledge, it is not clear that so-called implicit knowledge is in fact representationally implicit. It is theoretically possible for knowledge to be explicitly represented but unavailable for report. This could happen because the relevant, explicitly represented knowledge might be contained within a processing module that was not transparent to conscious inspection, although such knowledge might be recoverable by nonconscious processes (cf. Chomsky, 1980).

Implicit learning research has employed procedures (verbal report) that, although suggesting that people are unaware of possessing some item of knowledge, fail to distinguish between the case where that knowledge is explicitly represented and the case where that knowledge is implicitly represented. It seems important to establish what the nature of representation in implicit learning is like because this dictates the kind of explanation of implicit knowledge that must be sought, and dramatically constrains the kinds of models that are plausible models of implicit learning. For example, if it is the case that implicit learning results in the explicit representation of constituent structure (of which subjects are unaware) then connectionism is clearly an inappropriate architecture for modeling implicit learning.

Indeed, under these circumstances, any model that relied on representational implicitness as the explanatory principle underlying the poor verbal report that is characteristic of implicit learning would be suspect. Under these circumstances, one would have to appeal to rather different explanatory principles, principles that seem much less theoretically tractable than that of representational implicitness. Therefore, it seems important to attempt to establish whether, in fact, implicit learning results in knowledge that is characterized by representational implicitness or whether it results in representationally explicit, but unconscious knowledge.

How then should we go about distinguishing between these two kinds of implicitness? Fodor and Pylyshyn (1988) discussed what can be construed as a critical test for discriminating between atomic and classical representations. I refer to this as *decompositional inference*. Consider learning to discriminate exemplars of a concept, defined by the conjunction of two features P and Q. Although atomic representation would be sufficient to enable the accurate discrimination of exemplars and nonexemplars, it would not permit the inference that exemplars contain P, and that exemplars contain Q. Indeed, any operation requiring the decomposition of the representation of "P&Q" into its constituents would fail. This follows from the fact that if structural constituents are not represented explicitly then they will not be able to be recovered by any process.

If Fodor and Pylyshyn (1988) were correct, we should be able to distinguish between those representations where constituent structure is representationally implicit and those representations where constituent structure is representationally explicit, by employing this decompositional inference test. Thus, this test offers the potential for determining whether constituent structure is representationally implicit, or whether it is representationally explicit, albeit unavailable to conscious processes. Recently, Roberts and C. MacLeod (1995b) employed this decompositional inference test in an attempt to distinguish between the two kinds of implicitness. They trained people to discriminate exemplars of two concepts, each defined by the conjunction of two features. One of these concepts was trained under conditions that favored implicit (unreportable) learning whereas the other was trained under conditions that favored explicit (reportable) learning. Subjects then engaged in a decompositional inference task that required them to recover the structural constituents of the concepts that they had learned. The critical features consisted of a particular color and a particular shape. Therefore, the decompositional inference test consisted of presenting subjects with partial stimuli that contained no color information but could contain the critical shape feature, and asking them to indicate whether these partial stimuli COULD be examples of the concept. Thus, subjects were forced to recover the structural constituents of the concepts they had learned in order to perform accurately on this task. The results demonstrated that the decompositional inferencing performance associated with the concept that had been learned implicitly was significantly less accurate than the decompositional inferencing performance associated with the concept that had been learned explicitly. This result is consistent with the notion that, for the conceptual knowledge acquired in the implicit learning condition in this task, constituent structure was representationally implicit.

The reader will have noticed, however, that the decompositional inferencing task just described requires a very deliberate and conscious attempt by the subject to recover the structural constituents of the concepts that have been learned. Thus, the reduced ability of subjects to decompose representations that have been acquired implicitly may be a result of the fact that these representations are not available to conscious processes, rather than a result of the structural properties of the representations themselves. This highlights a general problem that is likely to be encountered in attempting to distinguish empirically between the two senses of implicit knowledge. If implicitly acquired knowledge appears to be unrecoverable, then this may not necessarily be a result of the representational implicitness of that knowledge; it may simply reflect the inability of a particular test to detect recovery. Unless one knows that a particular test definitely will be sensitive to recovery, if recovery is possible, a disturbing uncertainty prevails.

This is, of course, not a problem if one can find a test that is sensitive to the recovery of unreportable knowledge. More recently, Roberts and C. MacLeod (submitted) found that knowledge of constituent structure that is unreportable and that is not recoverable by the decompositional inferencing task described previously, is recoverable within a priming paradigm. Specifically, the name of the concept that was learned implicitly facilitated processing of the structural constituents of that concept. That is, the name of a concept learned implicitly primed the structural constituents of that concept. This implies that the structural constituents of the concept that was learned implicitly were activated by the concept name, and in that sense recovered. Thus, at least in this experiment, it would be incorrect to explain subjects' poor verbal report by appealing to the representational implicitness of the knowledge they had acquired. Rather, this experiment suggests that implicitly acquired knowledge is explicitly represented, but is not available to conscious processes.

Is there any other evidence in the literature that knowledge that subjects are unable to report is nevertheless explicitly represented? The only relevant evidence seems to come from studies of the implicit learning of artificial grammars. In this task subjects are presented with strings of letters that are generated by a complex artificial (finite state) grammar. In the training phase, subjects typically are required to memorize a set of grammatical strings, with no suggestion that the strings are structured or related in any way. In a test phase, subjects are informed of the existence of rules determining the structure of the strings and must attempt to discriminate between grammatical strings and strings that violate the rules of the grammar. Typically, although subjects are unable to report the rules of the grammar (e.g., Reber, 1967) they are above chance at discriminating grammatical strings. On the basis of these kinds of findings, Reber (see Reber, 1989a, for a review of these studies) has suggested that artificial grammar learning occurs implicitly and results in abstract knowledge of which subjects are largely unaware.

Despite the fact that subjects usually cannot report the rules of the grammar they have learned, Dulany et al. (1984) found that when subjects were asked to indicate the parts of strings that made them grammatical or ungrammatical their responses accounted entirely for their grammaticality judgements. This suggests that subjects can recover information about critical letter transitions and hence that this information is not representationally implicit. Furthermore, in a task that is similar to the decompositional inferencing task described previously, Dienes et al. (1991) found that subjects were able to predict, with a significant level of accuracy, which letter came next when they were presented with the stem of a grammatical string and required to make a forced choice. However, subjects were not accurate when asked to freely report features that would discriminate grammatical strings. These results seem to imply that, although subjects are unaware of the transition rules contributing to the grammaticality of strings, they are able to recover these rules under certain conditions (e.g., when making a forced choice).

Further support for this conclusion is evident in a study by Reber (1969). He investigated the effect of initially training subjects on a particular artificial grammar and then subsequently training them on a grammar where the surface structure was different to that of the initially learned grammar (i.e., different letters were systematically substituted for the originally trained letters), but the underlying abstract structure of the grammar was the same. Subjects were just as good at learning to discriminate grammatical strings derived from this new letter set as they were at relearning the initially trained grammar, suggesting that subjects had access to the abstract rules of the grammar and that these could be applied to the new letter set. Presumably, these abstract rules are about valid sequential relationships between variables because they are available for transfer to a new set of letters that obey the same sequencing rules. This implies that the information about valid sequential relationships is directly recoverable and hence representationally explicit.

A ubiquitous problem associated with interpreting these kinds of results is whether the transfer might not be explicable in terms of conscious knowledge. Such an interpretation of the study by Reber (1969) may be ruled out by the results of a study by R.C. Mathews et al. (1989). In this study, when subjects were switched to learning a grammar with a different letter set, but the same underlying abstract structure as the one they initially had been trained on, they evidenced essentially no interruption in their learning curves. This seems to suggest that the critical sequential relationship knowledge was unconsciously applied to the new letter set without the need for intervention by conscious processes. If conscious processes had been involved in this transfer, one would expect an initial drop in performance on the subsequently trained grammar as subjects consciously and effortfully deciphered the mapping of the new letters onto the transition relationships. Thus, it seems rather unlikely from these results that the recovery of sequential relationship information can be attributed to conscious knowledge on the part of subjects. Hence, the correct conclusion seems to be that subjects possess explicitly represented, but unconscious, knowledge of the sequential relationships defining artificial grammars.

CONCLUDING REMARKS

In the preceding discussion I have attempted to highlight a constellation of related issues that need to be addressed in order to gain a theoretical handle on the nature of implicit knowledge and implicit learning. It was pointed out that the term implicit has been used somewhat ambiguously in the literature to date. On the one hand, researchers have typically used the term to mean simply unreportable, whereas on the other hand, models of implicit processes have traded on the notion of representational implicitness in order to explain the unreportability of implicitly acquired knowledge. Despite this identification of unreportable knowledge with representational implicitness, there has been little attempt to empirically test the assumption that unreportable knowledge is representationally implicit. Indeed, the experiments cited in the previous section suggest that, at least sometimes, knowledge that subjects cannot report is representationally explicit. Such findings have profound consequences for how implicit knowledge and implicit learning are conceptualized. The concept of representational implicitness seems to provide a theoretically tractable account of why knowledge that can be utilized nevertheless should be unavailable for verbal report. However, if knowledge that is unreportable turns out to be explicitly represented, then the concept of representational implicitness does not provide an appropriate explanatory framework for implicit knowledge and implicit learning. It follows from this that models that implement representational implicitness are not appropriate or complete models of implicit learning.

These considerations suggest that a priority for those researchers interested in understanding implicit learning should be to investigate whether the knowledge that is unreportable in implicit learning is also representationally implicit. Two steps seem to be important in following this prescription. First, precisely which aspect of subjects' knowledge is unreportable should be identified; that is, is it the critical attributes that are unreportable, or is it the relationship between those attributes that is unreportable, or is it both? Second, having established exactly what subjects are unable to report, an appropriate test of the representational implicitness of that knowledge should be devised.

The form that this test should take is not necessarily transparent. For example, in the Dienes et al. (1991) study cited earlier, subjects were able to predict with a high level of accuracy which letter came next when presented with the stem of a grammatical string. This seems to suggest that subjects can decompose their implicitly acquired knowledge representations to recover information about letter transitions, even though they are unaware that they possess this information. However, it would be a mistake to take this as evidence that subjects possessed an explicit representation of the structure of the grammar that could be decomposed. This is because positive evidence of recovery does not imply decomposition if there is a way in which recovery may be achieved without literal, structural decomposition of the relevant representation. Consider the following argument for why predictions about letter transitions in artificial grammars would be expected to be accurate even if such information is not explicitly represented.

An artificial grammar is clearly a concept created through a family resemblance structure (R.C. Mathews et al., 1989). Family resemblance structures have the property that features are correlated with, but not defining of the concept. In addition, features also are correlated with each other. Hence, with frequent presentation, co-occurring features will become associated with each other and with the concept. Thus, although the representation of the letter transition rules may be implicit, stems of grammatical strings will tend to activate a valid letter to fill the next position in the string. This would allow subjects to perform the stem completion task employed by Dienes et al. (1991) and the task employed by Dulany et al. (1984), despite being unable to decompose their representation of the transition rules of the grammar. Quite clearly then, a simple connectionist model, which stores covariations implicitly, could produce this effect, simply by learning the correlations between pairs of letters. In the experiment by Roberts and C. MacLeod (submitted) cited earlier, any correlational "clues" that would have supported such a strategy were specifically excluded. Nevertheless, evidence of representational explicitness was still obtained.

Interestingly, there appears to be a way of diagnosing representational implicitness in existing paradigms that circumvents the problem of correlational cuing. When attempting to assess representational implicitness in existing tasks, where the potential for such cuing exists, probably the best way around this problem is to rely on the transfer of abstract relational knowledge as the test of representational explicitness, as in the studies by Reber (1969) and R.C. Mathews et al. (1989) cited previously. This strategy is indicated because abstract relational knowledge is, by definition, independent of the attributes over which it is defined. Thus, even if spurious correlational cuing occurs in a particular task, if the relevant relational information is represented implicitly then direct recovery of that information is impossible. Consequently, the transfer of abstract relational knowledge, such as valid sequences in artificial grammars, should be severely impaired if that information is represented implicitly.

Because of the ability of tests of the transfer of abstract relational knowledge to unambiguously diagnose representational implicitness, it seems likely that the transfer of abstract relational knowledge will become increasingly important in the investigation of implicit learning. Indeed, a number of researchers recently have begun moving in this direction. In a further unpublished study, Roberts and C.

MacLeod (submitted) found that knowledge of conjunctive and disjunctive relations transferred to different sets of features despite the fact that this knowledge was acquired implicitly. And Lewicki et al. (1992) alluded to an unpublished study that also appears to suggest the explicit representation of abstract relational knowledge that is unconscious. Using their matrix-scanning procedure (see Lewicki et al., 1988), they found evidence for the transfer of a covariation between letters to a task where the covariation was between numbers.

It appears then, that when tests of representational implicitness are applied to implicit learning tasks, there is some evidence that the knowledge of how to perform these tasks is explicitly represented. This conclusion tends to undermine the legitimacy of modeling implicit learning in ways that exploit representational implicitness. Of course, not all unreportable knowledge resulting from implicit learning may be representationally explicit. The point is that we currently do not know with any certainty whether representational implicitness is an appropriate characterization of so-called implicit knowledge. If it is not, and all unreportable knowledge turns out to be representationally explicit, then we will have to look to rather different kinds of explanations for the existence of such knowledge. If the concept of representational implicitness is raised from the status of an assumption, to that of an hypothesis to be tested, we at least have the potential for discriminating between the alternative explanations of implicit knowledge.

II
THEORY

8

IMPLICIT EXPERTISE: DO WE EXPECT TOO MUCH FROM OUR EXPERTS?

Craig Speelman
Edith Cowan University

Writing about music is like dancing about architecture.

—Elvis Costello

A common definition of an expert is someone who knows all the answers in his or her field of specialization. This definition has been extended somewhat in modern cognitive psychology as experts and their special skills have come under close examination. Although a precise and universal definition of what constitutes expertise is not available (Salthouse, 1991; Sloboda, 1991), it would seem that most psychologists agree that the performance of experts is usually superior to that of novices, where superior can mean faster, more accurate, more efficient, with less resources, and various combinations of these. Psychologists also agree that this superior performance often results from the different methods by which experts process, represent, and approach tasks in their domain compared to novices. Thus, experts perform better because they possess superior skills.

Experts in many fields are highly valued. Their superior performance sets them apart, not only from novices, but from those of more intermediate levels of skill and experience. Thus, the specialist radiologist is seen as possessing skills not available in all those who inspect X-ray slides. The physics professor is considered to have reached the peak of present-day physics knowledge. But it is not only for their performance abilities that experts are prized. The possibility that they will pass on some of their expertise often is considered as valuable as the expertise itself. As a result, many hours are spent in universities, hospitals, trade schools, workshops, and various other training venues, with experts attempting to pass on their knowledge and skills to novices. More recently, attempts have been made to develop so-called "expert systems," computers designed to make decisions like experts.

Although expertise has been successfully acquired by novices for centuries, there is a major bottleneck in the process of experts imparting their expertise to others. This concerns the difference between what experts say they do and what they actually do. The reason for this discrepancy is not that experts are, consciously or unconsciously, attempting to conceal their secrets. On the contrary, it would appear that experts are often unaware of the nature of their secrets. They actually do not know how they do what they do. Furthermore, they are usually unaware of this gap in their knowledge as well. Often then, experts will instruct novices in their domain in methods that are not actually expert methods, but are methods that experts have developed as reasonable hypotheses for what they themselves must be doing.

Some forms of expertise, then, are tacit or implicit (P.E. Johnson, 1983; Sloboda, 1991). The superior performance of experts suggests they possess something that novices do not. However, their attempts to describe the nature of this expertise reveals that it is not readily accessible to conscious awareness.

This chapter is concerned with the nature of this implicit expertise and methods by which it may be acquired. The chapter also includes discussion of the possibility that the implicit nature of some expertise is simply the result of attempting to access knowledge in a manner inappropriate for that form of expertise. The implications of this for instruction and the development of expert systems also are considered.

THE NATURE OF IMPLICIT EXPERTISE

The terms *implicit expertise* and *implicit knowledge* have been used to refer to a particular type of skill. This type of skill is elusive, and difficult to define in operational terms precisely because it is implicit. It involves skill or knowledge that experts possess despite the fact that they cannot describe it in verbal terms. Their skill or knowledge is inferred from their performance on some diagnostic or process control task, even when they cannot describe the rules or procedures that they are using to solve the problem. P.E. Johnson (1983) referred to this characteristic as the paradox of expertise: "As individuals master more and more knowledge in order to do a task efficiently as well as accurately, they also lose awareness of what they know. The very knowledge we wish to represent in a computer program as well as the knowledge we wish to teach others, often turns out to be knowledge that individuals are least able to talk about" (p. 79).

An obvious everyday example involves bicycle riding. Virtually everyone in the normal population can ride a bicycle, yet virtually none of us can put into words anything of scientific value about the physical forces that in some sense must be mastered if we are to balance and move the machine. In this perhaps extreme case, the quantitative descriptions of the skill belong in a different realm from the skill itself, and it would be difficult for even a physicist to master the task given information concerning the nature and magnitude of the physical forces to be balanced. The skills required for bicycle riding can be described in another way, involving control of gross movements of the limbs and torso, however, this, too, offers little value to the novice; the gulf between verbal description and physical control is too great. Even advice such as "the faster the forward motion, the easier it is to balance" is of little benefit to the novice, especially one fearful of falling off the bicycle. Thus, regardless of the type of description used, they provide a poor basis for acquisition of this form of expertise. Trial and error with a bicycle is generally assumed to be more valuable.

Other areas of expertise that have been examined more systematically reveal the same type of implicit knowledge. Hatano (1988) reported that abacus experts, although extremely swift and accurate in their calculations, could not explain the meaning of the steps of abacus operation. Saxe and Gearhart (1990) described the training of Brazilian straw weavers and noted that expertise and knowledge verbalizability were uncorrelated—the expert trainers provided instruction in the form of demonstrations rather than verbal tuition. Annett (1986) showed that the ability to perform a motor skill, such as tying a shoelace, is independent of the ability to describe the action.

In some areas of expertise, there is a dissociation between what experts say they do and what they actually do. Thus, although their expertise is implicit, experts sometimes feel they can provide a verbal description of their knowledge. Furthermore, this description typically bears only a superficial relationship to the expertise. An example of this was provided by Holyoak (1991). He described some unpublished research by Lundell where subjects were given extensive practice at providing diagnoses of the state of a power plant. At the end of practice subjects were accurate on 75% of trials. Lundell then interviewed subjects about how they performed their diagnoses and from these interviews extracted rules to reflect each subject's knowledge. These rules then were compared with the subjects on a new set of diagnosis problems. The rules were only correct on 55% of trials, whereas the subjects continued to be accurate on 75% of trials. Furthermore, the rules derived for one subject were no better at predicting that subject's performance than rules derived for other subjects.

Some experts are aware of the dissociation between their expertise and their description of their expertise. P.E. Johnson (1983) noted that a medical colleague of his taught a method of diagnosis to his medical students that appeared to differ from the method he actually used. When Johnson brought this discrepancy to the attention of his colleague, his colleague claimed that he did not know how he arrived at diagnoses and yet he was required to teach his students how to reach diagnoses. As a result he taught methods that appeared plausible to him and hoped these would suffice. Johnson labeled this type of reasoning reconstructive and claimed that it was exhibited by practitioners in many fields of expertise. In some areas, however, experts are not aware that a discrepancy exists between what they think they do and what they do, believing that the information they supply regarding their methods is accurate (Berry, 1987).

There are a number of features of implicit expertise that may contribute to its implicit nature. Three of these features are considered here. The first concerns the methodological difficulties associated with experts providing verbal descriptions of their expertise. The second concerns the manner in which implicit expertise is acquired. The third concerns the manner in which expert knowledge is mentally represented. Although these issues are considered here in separate sections, it is obvious that they are fundamentally related.

METHODOLOGICAL PROBLEMS

The most straightforward methods by which experts have been required to give verbal accounts of their knowledge are questionnaires and interviews. These methods require experts to describe the processes involved in their performance and typically occur after a task has been completed and sometimes away from the task situation altogether. The major problem with these methods is that experts are being asked to verbalize about their skills away from the environments in which they are normally applied. Their expertise may be context-sensitive, and so will not be accessed in the interview situation (L. Bainbridge, 1977; P.E. Johnson, 1983). Thus, experts will have to rely on reconstructive reasoning to provide explanations for their behavior (P.E. Johnson, 1983).

In order to overcome the shortcomings of questionnaires and interviews, many investigators have obtained verbal protocols from experts. With this method, experts are required to talk aloud while they perform a task. The aim of this approach is to obtain a more "online" record of the processes occurring during performance (Berry, 1987). The assumption is that by having experts report on their thinking during performance, rather than following performance, more accurate information about the nature of their thought processes will be obtained. Unfortunately there are many reasons to doubt the validity of this assumption (Nisbett & T.D. Wilson, 1977) and many features of the protocol-gathering process that restrict the validity of the obtained reports (L. Bainbridge, 1977; Berry, 1987). A number of these, summarized from Bainbridge and Berry, are listed below:

1. Protocols are incomplete: They provide information about expert knowledge, but not the full range of knowledge. That is, they cannot indicate the limits of an expert's knowledge. For instance, what is not mentioned is not necessarily what is not known.
2. Experts often cannot verbalize as fast as they can reason, and so they may leave out steps in their reasoning process, or leave out things that seem "obvious" to them.

3. Experts may not mention all of the information attended to during perform-ance. This can lead to unexplained behavior.
4. Providing a protocol may not be possible if the task itself involves some form of verbal communication.
5. Experts need experience at thinking aloud to provide effective protocols. Giving a running commentary often can be a demanding secondary task. As a result, mental capacity may be limited for the task of interest and so performance of this task could be affected. Performance may be less efficient, or the method by which the task is performed may be altered (see following).
6. Having to provide a commentary during performance changes the task situation and so may affect the way in which the task is performed. Experts may become self-conscious and this could affect their method of operation. For instance, if multiple methods exist they may opt for the one most easily described. This may involve adopting a beginner's method, or the officially sanctioned method, because these are more likely to be represented in a verbal form.

Some commentators doubt the usefulness of all forms of verbal data, suggesting that they "provide, at best, information about what subjects are thinking about, but little direct information about how they are thinking (i.e., about the underlying information processing)" (Rouse & N.M. Morris, 1986, p. 352). Furthermore, there is even suggestion that because subjects providing verbal data are sensitive to the demand characteristics of the data-gathering situation (Adair, 1973), they are simply providing what they think the inquirer wants rather than information about the processes underlying their performance (D.A. Norman, 1987; Rouse & N.M. Morris, 1986).

ACQUISITION

There appear to be at least two ways in which implicit knowledge can be acquired. One way is via implicit learning; the other is via skill acquisition.

In implicit learning, knowledge is implicit at all stages of practice. A large number of studies have demonstrated that subjects can learn to perform complex tasks and yet be unable to describe accurately the knowledge underlying their performance (for a detailed discussion of this type of learning, see chap. 3 of this volume). For example, Reber (1967, 1976) had subjects learn to classify letter strings as gram-matical or not with respect to an artificial grammar. With experience, subjects came to perform this task accurately. However, they were not able to articulate the structure of the grammar that led them to their classifications. Broadbent and his colleagues have demonstrated similar dissociations between implicit and explicit knowledge in the learning of complex systems (Berry & D.E. Broadbent, 1984, 1987a; D.E. Broadbent et al., 1986). Subjects learned to operate fictional systems responsible for the control of sugar production and relations with a union in a factory, a city's transport network, and a country's economy. In all cases, subjects were required to achieve target output values by manipulating input values for particular parameters. Each system was based on a small number of equations that related input parameters to output parameters. Through experience with each system, the subjects were eventually able to achieve their targets regularly. However, they were not able to describe the relationships between the input and output parameters of each system. There is some suggestion that this form of unconscious learning (Lewicki, 1986) may underlie much of the superior pattern recognition skills exhibited by experts in some fields (Bransford, Franks, Vye, & Sherwood, 1989), where experts apparently see things differently than novices (Chase & H.A. Simon, 1973; Chi, Feltovich, & Glaser, 1981; Lesgold, 1988; Myles-Worsley, Johnston, & Simons, 1988; Schoenfeld & Herrmann, 1982) and often are not aware of this difference between their perception and that of novices (Bransford et al., 1989).

In contrast to implicit learning, with the second method of acquiring implicit expertise, knowledge is initially explicit. According to Fitts (1964), there are three phases involved in this method of acquisition (see chap. 5 of this volume). In the first phase performance is slow and deliberate, and the knowledge underlying performance can be verbally articulated. With practice, however, performance becomes much faster and fluent, until the third phase where performance is automatic, and the ability to describe the processes involved in performance has been lost.

J.R. Anderson (1982) proposed the ACT* theory as an account of the qualitative changes in performance that occur during the three phases of skill acquisition. According to this theory, there are two ways in which the three-stage method of skill acquisition can result in implicit expertise. The first is associated with the compilation of declarative knowledge into procedural knowledge. Composition comprises part of this process and describes the phenomenon whereby several processing steps, or productions, are collapsed into a single production. These productions must occur in a sequence and share the same overall goal. The new production now does the work of the sequence, but in fewer steps. For example, consider the following set of production rules that might be developed for solving algebra equations:

IF   goal is to solve for x in equation of the form $a = bx + c$
THEN set as subgoal to isolate x on RHS of equation.   (1)

IF   goal is to isolate x on RHS of equation
THEN set as subgoals to eliminate c from RHS of equation and then to   (2)
        eliminate b from RHS of equation.

IF   goal is to eliminate c from RHS of equation
THEN add -c to both sides of equation.   (3)

IF   goal is to eliminate b from RHS of equation
THEN   divide both sides of equation by b.   **(4)**

IF   goal is to solve for x in equation and x has been isolated on
            RHS of equation
THEN   LHS of equation is solution for x.   **(5)**

After executing these rules a number of times, composition will result in collapsing Productions 2, 3, and 4 into:

IF   goal is to isolate x on RHS of equation
THEN   add -c to both sides of equation and then divide both sides of   **(6)**
            equation by b.

With further practice, Productions 1, 6, and 5 will be composed to the more sophisticated:

IF   goal is to solve for x in equation of the form $a = bx + c$
THEN   subtract c from a and divide result by b and result is solution.   **(7)**

Algebra "experts" recognize this immediately and may no longer consider the intermediate steps. This becomes obvious when the algebra expert attempts to tutor a novice, and wonders why they persist in trying to solve a problem in such a roundabout manner. Thus, explicit knowledge can become implicit as composition supersedes the original detailed knowledge with more efficient knowledge. Although the original knowledge is not replaced, it is not used often and eventually fades in memory, making accessibility difficult. The more efficient productions are used more often and become the basis of skilled behavior.

The speed and efficiency of performance is increased through compilation. However, skill acquisition usually is characterized by a greater speed-up than can be accounted for by compilation alone. Hence, a further characteristic of skill acquisition described by ACT* is strengthening. The strength of a production determines how rapidly it applies, and production rules accumulate strength as they successfully apply. So skill is characterized by very quick, automatic performance.

The combination of the composition and strengthening mechanisms during skill acquisition can account for the "paradox of expertise" (P.E. Johnson, 1983). This describes implicit expertise that has been acquired from knowledge that was originally explicit. As more and more knowledge is acquired while mastering a task, experts appear to lose awareness of what they actually know. According to ACT*, this is because experts have compiled their knowledge into efficient production rules that no longer resemble the original declarative knowledge. Thus, accessing this procedural knowledge is unlikely to be informative. Furthermore, because of strengthening, this procedural knowledge typically is executed in an automatic fashion. As a result, performance may be so fast as to be beyond the limits of awareness, that is, too fast for the performer to report. Therefore, expertise resulting from composition and strengthening may be implicit because its essential elements (i.e., the processing steps involved in performance) either never enter awareness or are too fast to be noticed.

Logan's (1988b) instance theory (see chap. 5 of this volume) also provides an account of why some aspects of expertise are explicit to begin with but become implicit with practice. According to Logan, initial performance on a task is controlled by a general algorithm. Each time the task is performed an instance is stored in memory, reflecting the initial conditions of the task and the solution attempted. With continued experience of the task, performance will be controlled by execution of the algorithm or by a single-step retrieval of a past solution from memory. Which of these processes controls performance will be determined by a race—the fastest process wins. In the initial stages of practice, this race will be won by the algorithm on most occasions. However, as the number of instances in memory increases, a distribution of retrieval times will result. The effect of this is that the probability of retrieving an instance from memory in less time than it takes to execute the algorithm will increase as the number of instances increase. Thus, with increased practice, performance will be more likely to result from the retrieval of instances from memory.

The process whereby algorithmic processing gives way to instance retrieval can provide an account of how skill acquisition can result in the loss of explicit knowledge. Because automatic performance is said to be due to a single-step retrieval of information from memory, this means that "there are no intervening steps or stages upon which to introspect" (Logan, 1988a, p. 587). Hence, the knowledge that is represented as an instance will be inaccessible to consciousness.

Although the theories of Anderson and Logan propose different mechanisms underlying the acquisition of skill, they both lead to similar predictions. For example, both theories propose that performance early in practice will be deliberate and possibly accompanied by a reportable algorithm. With consistent practice, however, performance will rely on a single-step process. As a result, information regarding the methods used during performance will be unavailable to awareness.

In summary, the skill acquisition theories of Anderson and Logan characterize expert performance as the initiation of certain responses by particular stimulus conditions. Certainly in many different domains this has been claimed to be the essence of expert performance. For example, chess masters often have been reported as having the ability to glance at a chess board midgame and find that particular configurations of the pieces immediately suggest sequences of moves (e.g., Charness, 1991). Physicists "see" physical principles in problem descriptions and these then lead to solution strategies (Larkin et al., 1980). Radiologists detect features in X-ray slides that initiate strategies for reaching a diagnosis (Lesgold, Glaser, Rubinson, Klopfer, Feltovich & Wang, 1988). It is this type of skill that often is identified as the fast, effortless, and automatic feature of expertise. It also is considered extraordinary by the layperson because the nature of the ability that leads to this type of performance is usually inscrutable, by both the observer and the performer. According to the theories of Anderson and Logan, however, this ability is simply a result of many years of consistent practice at a particular task. Experts' extraordinary abilities are seen as less a result of being blessed with mysterious talents and more a result of hard work (see Ericcson, Krampe, & Tesch-Römer, 1993). Hatano (1988; Hatano & Inagaki, 1986) even went so far as to describe this form of expertise as "routine." He suggested that it results from performing the same task many hundreds of times, "simply to get things done" (1988, p. 266). According to Hatano, routine expertise is only useful as long as the task remains the same, because it is not flexible in the face of changes to task conditions.

The preceding should not be construed as an attempt to dispel the mystique of experts. Rather it should be viewed as an attempt to reveal the generality of expertise, an extraordinary feature of ordinary human cognition. Consider the "talent" exhibited by the competent reader in extracting meaning from words on a page. As the reader's eyes are cast across a page of text, particular stimuli (i.e., words, phrases, sentences) automatically initiate particular responses (i.e., meaning). The processes involved in comprehending text, and language in general, are easily as complex, if not more so, than any involved in playing chess, no matter what standard of players are involved. However, extending the implicit learning theories of Reber and Broadbent and the skill acquisition theories of Anderson and Logan into language leads to similar sorts of predictions as can be derived for other areas of expertise. Namely, with extended practice, performance becomes fast, effortless, and automatic and seemingly inaccessible to introspection.

REPRESENTATION

Experts often are reported as perceiving features of their domain of expertise in ways fundamentally different to that of novices. Experts are said to "see" different things than novices (Charness, 1989). Although this feature of expertise may be related to the acquisition of skill as described in the previous section (e.g., Lesgold, 1984), some researchers view this difference in perception as an indication that experts and novices possess different mental models of the domain (e.g., Rouse & N.M. Morris, 1986). The two views are not necessarily incompatible: At present it is difficult to determine their compatibility because no theories have attempted to describe the process whereby skill acquisition leads to a change in the mental model of a task. Furthermore, the relationship between the representation of procedural skill developed through practice (e.g., production rules) and representations that embody someone's view of a domain (e.g., mental models) has never been clearly articulated (J.R. Wilson & Rutherford, 1989; although see Hatano, 1988; Hatano & Inagaki, 1986; Patel & Groen, 1991). It may be possible to unite the two approaches to skilled performance in the future. However, for the moment it is sufficient to consider how the mental model approach can illuminate other features of implicit expertise.

As suggested in the previous section, some forms of expertise are implicit because they involve knowledge that has been compiled. The original explicit knowledge is now in a form that is inaccessible to introspection. An alternative explanation for implicit expertise is that experts' mental models of their domain represent knowledge in a form that is difficult to verbalize, such as a spatial mental model, or a pictorial mental model (Rouse & N.M. Morris, 1986). The difference between the two accounts is a subtle one. In the first account, compiled knowledge is inaccessible because the type of knowledge that would provide a useful account of performance (e.g., intermediate steps) does not exist. In the second account, knowledge is represented in a form that is incompatible with verbalization. Thus, the form in which knowledge is represented is suggested to affect the manner in which it can be addressed.

The concept of a mental model is a vague one involving many definitions (e.g., Gentner & Stevens, 1983; Johnson-Laird, 1983; Rouse & N.M. Morris, 1986; Yates, 1985). In general, a mental model is described as an internal representation of some aspect of the world, whether real or fictional, that is isomorphic to the world and so can be used to explain, predict, and simulate events in the world. Mental models often are described as representations of real-world entities that can be "run" to simulate the behavior of these entities (de Kleer & J.S. Brown, 1983; Greeno, 1989; D.A. Norman, 1987; J.R. Wilson & Rutherford, 1989), even to the extent that predictions can be generated beyond a person's experience with the entities (Hatano & Inagaki, 1986).

Mental models have different forms depending on their domain of application and their required function. The fact that experts and novices view particular domains differently suggests that they possess different mental models of these domains. In order to comprehend experts' superior performance it would seem necessary to capture their unique mental models. Unfortunately, this is not a straightforward exercise (Berry, 1987; Rouse & N.M. Morris, 1986) as many experts are often unable to verbalize their models (N.M. Morris & Rouse, 1985; Saxe & Gearhart, 1990; Van Heusden, 1980; Whitfield & Jackson, 1982; Wickens, 1984). To some extent the vague nature of definitions of mental models may contribute to this difficulty in extracting mental models from experts. However, there is evidence to suggest that the nature of some experts' mental models simply may be incompatible to verbalization in much the same way as it is not possible to use a compact disc player to extract information from a vinyl record. Saxe and Gearhart (1990) claimed that expert Brazilian straw weavers are unable to verbalize their weaving methods because their skill is represented in a sensorimotor form. R.J. Phillips (1978) suggested that the reason most people are poor on tests of face recall is that we lack a sufficient vocabulary for communicating information about faces. Gammack and R. Young (1985) assumed the incompatibility of some forms of knowledge to verbalization as the basis for their recommendations of the most effective means of accessing expert knowledge. For example, they suggested that memory probe techniques should be used to elicit knowledge of facts, whereas sorting tasks should be used to assess classificatory knowledge.

Rouse and N.M. Morris (1986) suggested that verbalizing a mental model will be difficult when it represents spatial, pictorial, and imagelike information. In contrast, verbalization should be easier when the mental model represents verbal or symbolic information. They went on to claim that experts often possess "conceptually abstract, pattern-oriented mental models" (p. 356), which contributes to the difficulty in accessing these models via verbalization methods. It is possible, however, that some expert mental models are accessible to verbalization. Rouse and N.M. Morris (1986) and Sanderson (1989) reported that explanatory mental models appear to be more verbalizable. Explanatory mental models represent causal relationships between variables and events and their use by experts therefore may involve explicit manipulation. That is, experts explicitly manipulate features of their models when performing tasks in their specialist domain. As a result, verbalizing may be a natural feature of the expert's performance, and so verbalizing about their mental model will be easier (Rouse & N.M. Morris, 1986). Evidence for this was provided by Sanderson, who manipulated the necessity to develop explanatory mental models in learning to control a complex system. One group of subjects was provided with a graphical aid to control the system. The aim of this manipulation was to discourage subjects from developing an explanatory mental model of the system. Subjects in this condition showed improved performance with practice but were unable to verbalize correctly about the task. In contrast, another group of subjects were encouraged to develop a mental model that explicitly represented relationships between system variables. These subjects demonstrated an increased ability to verbalize about the system. Furthermore, in contrast to many studies that demonstrate that increased learning leads to decreased verbalization, Sanderson's study demonstrated that when subjects develop an explanatory mental model, both performance and verbalization improve with practice. Thus, some mental models are easier to describe verbally than others and the reason for this appears to be related to the purpose of the mental models.

The proposal that some types of mental models facilitate verbalization more than others was supported by Hatano (1988; Hatano & Inagaki, 1986), who claimed that the ability to verbalize knowledge represented in a mental model is the defining characteristic of adaptive expertise. Hatano suggested that there are two forms of expertise: routine and adaptive. Routine expertise arises from a great deal of practice in a domain where the task does not change. As described in the previous section, this type of expertise is brittle when task conditions are altered, and usually is accompanied by an inability to describe the underlying knowledge. In contrast, adaptive expertise develops through experience with a domain where the nature of the task changes often. Adaptive experts usually are motivated to understand causal relationships within the domain, and are prepared to experiment and discuss their knowledge with others in order to develop a deeper conceptual understanding. According to Hatano, it is this deep conceptual knowledge that gives adaptive experts their greater flexibility compared to routine experts when task changes occur. Furthermore, the process whereby adaptive expertise is acquired—in particular, the regular interrogation, expression, and manipulation of knowledge—creates a mental model of the domain that is easily verbalized. That is, the knowledge underlying adaptive expertise is represented in a form that is compatible with verbalization because it is normally used for that or similar purposes.

In summary, implicit expertise may result from the representation of knowledge in forms that are incompatible to verbal description. Some expert knowledge is represented as spatial or pictorial mental models that are difficult to describe in verbal form, whereas some other expert knowledge is represented in representations that are more amenable to verbalization, such as propositional representations of causal relationships. What determines the way in which expert knowledge is represented appears to be related to the purposes for which the knowledge is used.

ONE PRINCIPLE

There appear to be at least three methods by which knowledge can become inaccessible to verbalization: (a) through implicit learning; (b) through processes of compilation, such as those described by Anderson and Logan; and (c) through developing a particular type of conceptualization of a task, represented as a mental model. It is possible to view all of these methods as different expressions of one principle: Experts will be best at doing that which they are expert at doing. Although this may appear to be a trivial generalization, it actually goes a long way to accounting for why we often do not observe experts performing particular feats, such as verbalization, and why it may be unreasonable for us to expect them to be able to do so. It also accounts for some of the methodological difficulties associated with interrogating experts about their skills.

Experts are not good at doing everything in their particular domains (Camerer & E.J. Johnson, 1991). For example, expert radiologists are very good at recognizing X-ray slides of abnormalities. In this task they show recognition skills similar to that which we all exhibit with face recognition. However, these experts are poor at recognizing X-rays depicting normal features, poorer even than complete novices (Myles-Worsley et al., 1988). This result may appear surprising. However, consideration of what an expert radiologist does in order to become expert renders this result not only unsurprising but expected. A typical radiologist views many X-rays every day, usually without spending a great deal of time with each one. The radiologist's job is to detect abnormalities quickly. As a by-product of this skill, the radiologist needs to be able to identify quickly X-rays that are normal so that he or she can avoid wasting time examining such slides. Therefore, when faced with a normal X-ray, the expert radiologist can be expected to scan the slide quickly, determine that it is normal, and then cease processing it for further details. In contrast, it can be expected that the expert will detect abnormal X-rays quickly and process these in greater detail in order to diagnose the abnormality. It is straight-forward to see how a combination of these two strategies leads to the observed recognition results (for a similar interpretation of these results, see Vicente, 1992).

The important point to note here is that experts normally do not master every feature of their specialist domains. Thus, the verbalization of expert knowledge will only be possible where verbalization is, or is close to, a major feature of expert performance. The major feature of expert Brazilian straw weavers is their ability to weave various patterns. They have the ability to provide instruction in these tech-niques but it is only in the form of physical demonstrations (Saxe & Gearhart, 1990). Because verbalizing the techniques is not a major feature of their skill, they have never developed the ability to describe these techniques. In contrast, experts who routinely question their knowledge to reach a deeper understanding, and attempt to describe it to others, should possess the ability to verbalize their expertise because that is part of the process by which their expertise was acquired (Hatano, 1988).

In conclusion, although implicit expertise may result from different modes of acquisition, its implicit characteristic may be a result of one principle. Knowledge acquired in a particular fashion will be most useful when it is accessed in a similar manner. This principle has been expressed in various forms many times before (e.g., Bransford et al., 1989; Kolers & Roediger, 1984; Singley & J.R. Anderson, 1989; Willingham, Nissen, & Bullemer, 1989). Its importance with respect to expertise concerns the fact that different domains of expertise appear to result in different forms of knowledge. Holyoak (1991) suggested that this is because experts adapt to the inherent constraints within their domains. Thus, the nature of expertise is determined to a large extent by the nature of the domain. As a result, techniques for accessing expert knowledge should be tailored to particular forms of expertise. Many of the difficulties associated with attempting to develop expert systems from an expert's verbal protocols (Berry, 1987; Rouse & N.M. Morris, 1986) may be due to violations of this principle. Knowledge and mode of access to that knowledge appear not to be independent. Asking an expert to exhibit his or her expertise in a manner dissimilar to his or her normal mode of expression will make the expert appear less than expert. Asking a pilot to describe the essential elements of a flying maneuver when the maneuver normally is performed behind the controls of a plane may be just as farcical as an author being asked to "rewrite" a novel by drawing pictures. Certainly, a more accurate picture of an expert's knowledge could be achieved by constructing techniques for accessing that knowledge that are closer to the expert's normal mode of access.

9

IMPLICIT AND AUTOMATIC PROCESSES IN COGNITIVE DEVELOPMENT

Murray Maybery
Angela O'Brien-Malone
University of Western Australia

One impetus to the investigation of implicit and automatic processes in cognitive development has been theoretical extensions from work in adult cognition. In particular, Hasher and Zacks (1979) proposed that some encoding processes, similar in characteristics to the automatic processes described by Shiffrin and Schneider (see chap. 5 of this volume), are innate and, therefore, operate efficiently from an early age. A similar claim was made by Reber (1992) in arguing that implicit learning processes predate explicit learning processes in evolution, and so the former, but not the latter, should be invariant of ontogenetic development. Another related possibility concerns age-invariant implicit memory contrasting with age-sensitive explicit memory. These proposals have fostered three somewhat independent areas of empirical developmental work, which we review later in the chapter.

A second major impetus to the investigation of implicit and automatic processes in cognitive development has been Piagetian theory. The developmental stages described by Piaget are ordered not only according to increasing structural complexity of the systems supporting cognition, but also according to increasing conscious access to those systems. Thus the sensorimotor stage is characterized by the absence of reflective thought, the preoperational and concrete-operational stages by increasing conscious access to thoughts, and the formal-operational stage by the ability to make thought the object of itself (Piaget, 1950). The process by which behavior comes under conscious control, which Piaget labeled *cognizance*, became the focus of some of his later work (e.g., Piaget, 1976). This process refers to the transition from *automatic sensorimotor regulation* to *active conscious regulation*. When an action sequence is under automatic sensorimotor regulation, the child is conscious of the goal toward which the sequence is directed, and the outcome of its enaction (i.e., whether the goal is achieved or not), but is not conscious of the components of the sequence. Later, when the sequence comes under active conscious regulation, the child is aware of and can control the individual actions of the sequence. This provides flexibility because the components of the sequence can then be combined in different orders, or with components of other sequences, to achieve alternative goals. Building on Piaget's substantial start is Karmiloff-Smith's (1992, 1994) theory of *representational redescription,* according to which representations initially *implicit* in form may subsequently be redescribed to an *explicit* form. This redescription provides benefits based on accessing the components of explicit representations akin to the benefits that Piaget described for the transition from automatic sensorimotor regulation to active conscious regulation. Karmiloff-Smith's theory is considered in detail later in the chapter.

We also review Case's (1985, 1992, 1995) theory of cognitive development and associated empirical work. This is of interest here because one of the mechanisms Case proposed to explain transitions in children's cognition is that processes increase in efficiency, and thereby make reducing demands on a central pool of information-processing resources. This idea is allied to the resources view of automaticity (Shiffrin & Schneider, 1977; see also chap. 5 of this volume). Finally, Siegler's theoretical work on children's skill acquisition (Siegler & Jenkins, 1989; Siegler & Shipley, 1995; Siegler & Shrager, 1984) is reviewed, then compared with Logan's (1988b) *instance* theory of automaticity (chap. 5 of this volume).

Given the dearth of comparative reviews of these areas of developmental work, we conclude the chapter with some points of communality and others of contrast. We argue that current theory—which allows for the initial formation of either implicit or explicit representations, and the translation of one to the other—must be extended to specify the mechanisms responsible for establishing and utilizing either form of representation, and for translating one to the other.

IMPLICIT LEARNING

In the first three sections, we review the areas of developmental work where interest has centered on whether a particular class of implicit or automatic processes operates efficiently from early in life, and therefore shows little ontogenetic variation. In this section we consider implicit learning processes.

The extensive work on implicit learning was reviewed in chapter 3. There we argued that implicit learning has been characterized as operating without conscious awareness and without intent, and to be data-driven in that the information available to the system is not in any way selected. By contrast, explicit learning has been said to operate within conscious awareness and with intent, and to use only a restricted selection of the available information.

Pertinent to the current chapter is Reber's (1992) adoption of arguments based on evolution in elaborating the distinction between implicit and explicit learning. He argued that the implicit or unconscious system developed earlier in evolution than did the explicit or conscious system. He further argued that earlier-evolving systems are more invariant and resilient than later-evolving systems. Therefore, compared to explicit processes, implicit processes should be stable across individuals and across the life span (i.e., invariant of IQ and age), and be more robust to psychological or neurological disorder. Evidence bearing on the question of robustness to neuropsychological disorder was reviewed in chapter 3. The research pertaining to the claimed life-span invariance of implicit learning is reviewed later, but first we reflect on the circumstances said to be conducive to implicit learning, the capabilities attributed to the implicit learning system, and the consequences Reber's position would have for developmental theory were it to be true.

Implicit learning supposedly occurs in circumstances when the relationships to be learned are too complex to be handled by the limited-capacity explicit system, or when the relevant information is not salient, and therefore is not selected for processing by the explicit system. For instance, in the interactive tasks introduced by D.E. Broadbent, the participant is asked to provide inputs to a system, such as a model economy, with the aim of achieving certain outputs. The relationships between inputs and outputs are either complex or counterintuitive. Nevertheless, with practice, adults develop reasonable control of these systems, and it has been claimed that this control is mediated by implicit learning (see chap. 3 of this volume).

The implicit system therefore is ascribed remarkable capabilities: It can, independent of the learner's conscious intent, abstract extremely complex rules even when they might be instantiated in stimuli that are not salient. If these capabilities are available from an early age and remain intact across the life span, as Reber (1992) claimed, then the implications for developmental theory would be profound. Although it has long been recognized that children may know more than they can tell, it is not widely accepted that complex learning can proceed independent of conscious awareness and of the intention to learn. Further, few developmentalists would accept that young children are capable of learning rules as complex as any that can be learned by adults.

Despite its significance, the evidence bearing on Reber's (1992) age-invariance claim is thin. Only a handful of studies using implicit-learning paradigms have examined performance as a function of age. First, in the literature on aging, three studies have compared samples of younger and older adults. Myers and Conner (1992) asked 16- to 19-year-olds and 30- to 59-year-olds to control one of Berry and D.E. Broadbent's (1984) interactive tasks. The two groups performed at equivalent levels in learning to control the system, however the younger participants outperformed the older participants on a verbal-knowledge questionnaire designed to assess explicit or conscious knowledge of the system. Similar results were reported by D.V. Howard and J.H. Howard (1989, 1992), who compared more extreme samples of younger and older adults on Nissen and Bullemer's (1987) sequence-learning task. In each of the three experiments reported in the Howard and Howard papers, the reaction time data showed equivalent levels of learning in the two samples. However, performance on a prediction task, which was argued to reflect conscious knowledge of the sequence, always favored the younger groups. Therefore, the consistent conclusion from these studies is that younger and older adults are comparable on indices argued to reflect implicit learning, however the younger adults are superior on indices argued to require conscious access to the acquired knowledge.

Thus, Reber's (1992) age-invariance claim is supported in comparisons of younger and older adults, because performance in two of the implicit learning paradigms was shown to not deteriorate with senescence. But what of the other end of the life span? First, several studies reported in Lewicki (1986) had the restricted aim of demonstrating implicit learning in children from a single age group. Lewicki's approach is exemplified by Experiment 5.2, where a task using simple covariations was employed. Five-year-old children were presented with matrices of 16 pictures, divided into four quadrants. In the learning phase, each matrix was brought from behind and placed in front of the child, the cover was removed, and the child simply pointed to a particular picture (a house). Two stimulus features were critical. One was the color of the matrix cover (red or blue), which covaried with the house positioned in the left or right half of the matrix. The second feature was the side of approach of the experimenter (left or right), which covaried with the house positioned in the upper or lower half of the matrix. In the subsequent test phase, lifting the cover on a matrix showed "windows" covering the 16 pictures and the child was asked to guess where the house was located. The critical data were that the children's guesses showed evidence of them using the color-of-cover and side-of-approach cues to predict the correct quadrant for the house. However, according to Lewicki, the children could not verbally report the relevant covariations that led to their successful performance.

Finally, in a more extensive study, Maybery, Taylor, and O'Brien-Malone (1995) used Lewicki's implicit task as well as an explicit task in a direct test of Reber's age-invariance and IQ-invariance claims. Low-, medium-, and high-IQ subgroups were selected for each of two age groups, 5- to 7-year-olds and 10- to 12-year-olds. The IQ-invariance claim was supported in that there was no effect of IQ on implicit learning performance, but there was an IQ effect on explicit learning performance.

However, the age-invariance claim was not supported because the older children outperformed the younger children in implicit learning as well as in explicit learning. Interestingly, age appeared to moderate the modest correlation found between implicit and explicit learning performance ($r = 0.33$), for when age was controlled, the correlation was rendered nonsignificant ($r = 0.09$). Mayberry et al. argued that the implicit and explicit tasks may tap dissociable abilities that are associated only because each improves across childhood, an argument reinforced by the results from tests of verbal knowledge that followed the learning tasks: The children accurately reported the cues that mediated explicit learning, but had no insight into the cues that mediated implicit learning.

Thus, the available evidence, limited as it is, provides support for Reber's (1992) assertion that implicit learning capabilities remain intact with senescence, whereas explicit learning capabilities deteriorate. The complementary assertion that implicit learning capabilities are fully developed early in life and show minimal improvements across childhood compared to explicit learning capabilities, has not been supported in the only directly relevant published study.

INNATE AUTOMATIC PROCESSES

Hasher and Zacks (1979, 1984) proposed that encoding processes fall on a continuum from *automatic* to *effortful*. The contrast between automatic and effortful processes is similar to that described by Shiffrin and Schneider between automatic and controlled processes (see chap. 5 of this volume). Under both formulations, automatic processes require minimal attentional resources, can be initiated without awareness or intent, and are difficult to inhibit, whereas effortful or controlled processes display the contrasting characteristics.

However, Hasher and Zacks, although acknowledging that automatic processes can be acquired through practice (chap. 5), proposed that some automatic processes are innate. These innate automatic processes allow us to "orient to the routine flow of events in our environment" (Hasher & Zacks, 1979, p. 360) and, accordingly, encode three forms of information—spatial location, event frequency, and temporal order. Being *hard-wired* or innate in origin, these functions "should be widely shared and minimally influenced by differences in age, culture, education, early experience, and intelligence" (Hasher & Zacks, 1979, p. 360). Finally, the innate automatic processes were said to subserve their functions in an optimal way. Therefore, the registration of information on spatial location, event frequency, and temporal order should be as efficient under incidental as under intentional instructions, and should not improve with strategy-instruction or practice.

Thus, the innate automatic processes described by Hasher and Zacks (1979, 1984) are very similar to the implicit learning processes posited by Reber and others, in both operating characteristics and the proposed invariance in relation to variables such as age and intelligence. The two formulations differ in several ways, however. First, the implicit learning processes are argued to be pervasive in the information they encode, whereas Hasher and Zacks identified the innate automatic processes with only specific classes of information (e.g., spatial location). Second, it is claimed that knowledge acquired through implicit processes need not be available to consciousness (chap. 3 of this volume), whereas information garnered by innate automatic processes is available to consciousness (Hasher & Zacks, 1979). And third, implicit learning need not be optimal; it might be outstripped by explicit learning, particularly when only a few salient variables are relevant to the task at hand. In contrast, the innate automatic processes are said to provide optimal encoding.

Interestingly, several studies have reported that the functions identified with the innate automatic processes—memory for spatial location, event frequency, and temporal order—are fulfilled better under intentional rather than incidental instructions (R.L. Greene, 1984; Naveh-Benjamin, 1987, 1990; Naveh-Benjamin & Jonides, 1986; Sanders, Gonzalez, Murphy, Liddle, & Vitina, 1987; Sanders, Wise, Liddle, & Murphy, 1990; Sanders, Zembar, Liddle, Gonzalez, & Wise, 1989). Based on their results, Sanders and his coworkers argued that innate automatic processes do not necessarily provide optimal encoding, a position that is close to that held by the implicit learning theorists.

Critical to this chapter is Hasher and Zacks' (1979) claim concerning the age-invariance of the hypothesized innate automatic processes. Consistent with the claim, several studies have found no age effects on the processing of frequency information in primary-school children (D. Goldstein, Hasher, & Stein, 1983; Hasher & Zacks, 1979), nor when comparing children to adults (Hasher & Chromiak, 1977; M.K. Johnson, Raye, Hasher, & Chromiak, 1979). There is even evidence that infants encode frequency information (Antell & Keating, 1983; Starkey & R.G. Cooper, 1980) and spatial-location information (Kail & Siegal, 1977; Wertheimer, 1961). However, the literature also contains reports of significant age effects in frequency encoding (M.E. Mathews & Fozard, 1970; Naveh-Benjamin, 1987, 1990; J.M. von Wright, 1973) and spatial-location encoding (Acredelo, Pick, & Olsen, 1975; J.M. Mandler, Seegmiller, & Day, 1977; Schulman, 1973).

Therefore, the evidence is equivocal regarding the claim of Hasher and Zacks (1979) that frequency and spatial-location encoding processes are innate and automatic, and therefore do not show age effects. Nevertheless, taking the studies cited in the previous paragraph collectively, a reasonable conclusion is that the effect size for age in relation to memory for frequency and spatial location is substantially less than it is in relation to memory tasks expected to tap effortful encoding processes (e.g., tasks such as digit span, see Siegler, 1991). Thus, there is some force to the claim that automatic processes, which allow us to "orient to the routine flow of events in our environment" (Hasher & Zacks, 1979, p. 360), operate efficiently from a young age.

IMPLICIT MEMORY[1]

In the adult literature, implicit memory is said to be observed when a prior exposure to a stimulus facilitates later performance of a task, in the absence of reference to this prior exposure. Thus, implicit memory may operate without the conscious awareness of the subject. Conversely, explicit memory is observed in circumstances where the subject necessarily refers to this prior exposure in completion of the task, and, therefore, requires the conscious awareness of the subject. Conscious awareness, in this sense, is born of the task instructions that refer to the prior exposure and require the subjects to have the intention of retrieving information from that event (see Richardson-Klavehn & Bjork, 1988, for a discussion of issues inherent in the definition of implicit and explicit memory). This approach can reasonably be used to study implicit and explicit memory in adults, but has obvious problems when the subjects are infants or young children.

A considerable body of work investigating memory in infants and children exists. A critical issue is: What aspect of memory can be said to be the subject of these investigations? Although much of the work in older children can be classified as investigations of explicit memory (see Naito & Komatsu, 1993, for a limited discussion of this point), the research involving infants is less easily interpreted.

In an article addressing this issue, Schacter and Moscovitch (1984) argued that the most useful conceptualization of infant performance on memory tasks is in terms of two different forms of memory, termed the *early* and *late systems*. In this conceptualization, the early system is available to the infant almost from birth, and is unconscious or procedural. The late system, available from approximately 8 months of age, is conscious, or episodic. This position is not inconsistent with that of Piaget and Inhelder (1968/1973) who made a distinction between memory in the broad sense—including, for example, the reproduction of habits and the acquisition of skills—and memory in the strict sense—the conscious recollection of specific personal events. Similarly, J.M. Mandler (1984, 1988) argued that infant memory performance reflects two types of memory: primitive recognition, or the ability to recognize familiarity without necessarily being consciously aware of that familiarity, and recall, which allows conscious access to the conceptual system.

At first glance it seems possible that these distinctions may map on to the implicit/explicit distinction used in the adult literature. However, this relationship remains contentious, largely due to the lack of research using equivalent tasks for infant and adult subjects. In light of this, a recent article by McKee and Squire (1993) assumes particular importance. These authors compared the performance of adult amnesic patients, in whom explicit memory is damaged but implicit memory is intact, with that of normal adults on the visual paired-comparison task. This task

---

[1]Space prevents our giving a detailed coverage of the literature dealing with changes in implicit memory over the life span. Our comments here are selective and focus on the developmental period. More extensive reviews can be found in Graf (1990), and in chapters by Light and La Voie, Mitchell, Naito, and Komatsu, and Parkin, in Graf and Masson (1993).

involves exposing the subject to a stimulus, and, after some retention interval, exposing the subject concurrently to the original stimulus and a novel stimulus. The measure of interest is the amount of time spent looking at the novel, compared to the familiar, stimulus. This task has been used extensively in infant research, and infants' performance on this task has been argued to reflect the early form of memory (Schacter & Moscovitch, 1984). If performance on the visual paired-comparison task was spared in amnesiacs it would indicate that the brain systems used in explicit memory were not implicated in the performance of this task. McKee and Squire found that the amnesiacs exhibited a decrement in performance relative to the normal subjects.

This result, however, does not necessarily imply that the explicit system underpins performance of this task by infants. The evidence suggests that, by 5 months of age, infants' performance on novelty preference tasks is robust to length of the retention interval, even under study to test intervals of up to 24 or 48 hours (see, e.g., Fagan, 1990; Schacter & Moscovitch, 1984). However, McKee and Squire's (1993, Experiment 2a) data show an effect of duration of retention interval, with decrements in performance being observed at a retention interval of only 1 hour. One speculation is that infants and amnesic adults use different forms of memory to perform this task. At any rate, no simple interpretation of the infant literature would appear possible at this time.

Only a small number of articles have used experimental paradigms from the adult literature to investigate implicit memory in older children. (See chap. 2 of this volume for a discussion of the experimental paradigms used to investigate implicit memory in adults.) These articles have been reviewed in detail by several commentators (e.g., Graf, 1990; D.B. Mitchell, 1993; Naito & Komatsu, 1993), and there appears to be a consensus in their interpretation. Because we have no new points to add to this discussion, our comments are brief.

It is well established that explicit memory in children improves with age (Bjorklund & Bjorklund, 1985; Naito & Komatsu, 1993; Siegler, 1991). Older children outperform younger children on tasks requiring more processing resources, or more efficient use of resources; on tasks requiring the use of mnemonic strategies; and on tasks assessing metamemory.

However, the story with implicit memory is quite different. When implicit memory paradigms are used to investigate memory in children, developmental differences are typically not observed. These comparisons, which usually are based on the magnitude of priming effects, have been made between children as young as 3 years with older children and adults (Graf, 1990; D.B. Mitchell, 1993; Naito & Komatsu, 1993). A number of different paradigms have been used in these investigations, for instance, picture completion (Parkin & Streete, 1988) and word-fragment completion (Naito, 1990), and various dependent measures have been employed, for instance, naming latency (Carroll, Byrne, & Kirsner, 1985), and word production (Greenbaum & Graf, 1989).

In summary, although the interpretation of research concerned with memory in infants remains problematic, the investigation of implicit and explicit memory in older children has yielded consistent results: Explicit memory shows substantial improvements with age; implicit memory does not.

REPRESENTATIONAL REDESCRIPTION

Theorists such as Hasher and Zacks (1979, 1984), Lewicki (1986), and Reber (1992), who posit automatic or implicit encoding processes, devote much more space to the characterization of these processes than to their controlled or explicit counterparts. Indeed, given the power sometimes ascribed to implicit processes (see, e.g., Lewicki, 1986), one wonders just what additional adaptive function explicit processes could serve. This gap in theorizing is filled by Karmiloff-Smith's (1992, 1994) developmental model, where the emphasis is on the redescription of knowledge to explicit forms after initial success in a domain has been achieved under the service of implicit representations. The advantage provided by this redescription is that explicit representations can be analyzed into components, reconfigured to provide solutions to novel problems, and adapted to other domains through processes such as analogy. This section reviews Karmiloff-Smith's *representational redescription* model.

Karmiloff-Smith (1992) elaborated Piaget's argument that, with experience, the child's mental representations become increasingly open to conscious reflection. She argued that experience in a subdomain (e.g., drawing a person) leads first to implicit representations. Although these representations enable behavioral mastery (e.g., a reasonable depiction of a person), the processes they subserve have many of the characteristics of Shiffrin and Schneider's automatic processes (chap. 5 of this volume): They are elicited only under restricted stimulus conditions (i.e., they are bound to the subdomain in which they develop), and are stereotypic (e.g., the child cannot easily interpolate an addition to the draw-a-person routine). This latter characteristic applies because implicit representations are procedural in form and sequentially specified (Karmiloff-Smith, 1992). Two additional characteristics are that implicit representations are stored independently of each other, and each is bracketed; that is, its component parts cannot be accessed. Foreshadowed by Piaget (1976), these characteristics preclude the decomposition and recomposition of the skills that form the child's initial mastery of a domain.

One illustration of the restrictions imposed by this form of representation is provided by our observation of a 4.5-year-old girl, E.M., who was attempting to assemble some alphabet blocks, working from Z backward. Her representation of the alphabet appeared to be limited to the entire forward sequence. This meant that to place each block, E.M. had to rehearse the sequence from letter A through to the last letter she had placed. Much to her frustration, the obligatory nature of the rehearsal process meant that she often overshot the last letter placed (e.g., she would find herself rehearsing U V W when trying to place the letter before T). Interestingly, her response to this, in restarting her rehearsal, was often to rehearse much more slowly, an approach that frequently met with success. This is reminiscent of Piaget's (1976) analysis of children's conscious awareness of the order in which they moved their hands and knees when crawling. Some children initially unable to correctly report the order, were able to do so after they were told to either quicken or slow their crawl.

After behavioral mastery is achieved, the implicit representations can be *redescribed* into explicit forms. Not all of the details of the implicit representations are retained through the redescription process, however the simpler explicit representations can be reflected upon, broken into their constituents, and interrelated. They therefore enable processing that is flexible and productive, much like the controlled processing described by Shiffrin and Schneider (chap. 5 of this volume). Taking one of Karmiloff-Smith's examples, explicit representations would allow modifications to a child's person-drawing routine, for instance, interpolating the drawing of an extra head when instructed to draw an impossible person. Another illustration comes from E.M. who, at age 5.5 years, showed flexibility in working with the number sequence. For example, she was observed to spontaneously say "2, 4, 6—they are fair numbers" (i.e., numbers that would allow equal shares), and a week or so later she began to count collections of objects by two, rather than employ the regular counting sequence. To us this illustrates the interchange between knowledge of the counting sequence and knowledge of cardinal value, and modification of the former under the constraints of the latter. This modification is possible only if the counting sequence is represented in a way that enables access to its constituents.

Although the redescription of implicit to explicit representations is at the heart of Karmiloff-Smith's (1992, 1994) model, there are several ancillary features. First, the impetus to redescription is that the implicit representations in a subdomain become stabilized after behavioral mastery is achieved through practice. This means that the initial development of implicit representations and their redescription to explicit representations is expected to occur at different rates in different subdomains, reflecting the child's pattern of experiences. Thus, Karmiloff-Smith has abandoned Piaget's stages in that development is not seen as synchronous across subdomains.

Second, different levels of explicit representation are described. At the first level, E1, the representations are open to analysis and are manipulable, but are "not available to conscious access and verbal report" (Karmiloff-Smith, 1994, p. 701). At Level E2, the representations are consciously accessible, but may not be available to verbal report (e.g., as with a visuospatial image). Finally, at Level E3, the representations are available in a code that permits verbal report.

A third ancillary feature is that the success of a child's behavior in a domain can show a nonmonotonic progression, with performance temporarily showing a deterioration after the acquisition of explicit representations. The explicit representations available immediately after redescription may not be optimal, and may be overzealously applied (e.g., the "ed" suffix may be overgeneralized for past tense); only later will the explicit representations be amended to reflect the complexity of the environment (e.g., exceptions will be appended to the "ed" past-tense rule).

The final ancillary feature is that Karmiloff-Smith (1992, 1994) allowed for a process of *proceduralization,* which is the reverse of the redescription process. That is, whereas the redescription process provides for the transfer of initially implicit information to explicit forms, the process of proceduralization (or in the extreme, *modularization)* results in knowledge becoming "more encapsulated and less accessible" (Karmiloff-Smith, 1994, p. 699). This process of proceduralization is quite similar in description to the transition from controlled to automatic processing discussed at length in chapter 5.

Empirical evidence consistent with the representational-redescription process was reviewed extensively in Karmiloff-Smith (1986, 1992). Here we illustrate the nature of this evidence by recounting her description of developments in the skill of block balancing. Karmiloff-Smith and Inhelder (1974; see Karmiloff-Smith, 1986) asked children aged 4 to 9 years to balance a number of different blocks across a narrow bar. Some of the blocks were conventional (Type A), some had a visible weight stuck on one end (Type B), and others had lead concealed in one end (Type C). Each Type A block balanced at its midpoint, whereas the balance point for each Type B and Type C block was toward its weighted end. The youngest children of the sample succeeded in balancing all blocks, but their behavior was interpreted as reflecting implicit representations: "They simply moved the block back and forth along the bar, via data-driven processes, using the proprioceptive feedback of the direction of falling of the block, until they succeeded in balancing it" (Karmiloff-Smith, 1986, p. 181). Surprisingly, children in the midrange of the sample (6 to 8 years) could balance only the conventional (Type A) blocks. For each irregular (Type B or Type C) block, they placed the block at its geometric center on the bar, and when it failed to balance, declared it to be a block that could not be balanced. Karmiloff-Smith (1986) argued that these children were dominated by a simple explicit rule that had been abstracted from their block-balancing experiences, namely, that blocks balance at their geometric center. Finally, the oldest children in the sample balanced all three types of blocks, but did so in a way that differentiated them from the youngest children. They initially tried the midpoints of the blocks, then, where necessary, used proprioceptive feedback to find the appropriate balance point. Also, their behavior was systematic and showed planning in that they chose successive blocks that were similar in appearance, and used information on where the previous block had balanced in initially placing the current block on the bar. Karmiloff-Smith (1986) argued that the child was "now in control of the coordination between external information and the explicitly represented internal theory guiding the external behavior" (p. 182).

The block-balancing study is representative of the numerous studies that Karmiloff-Smith (1986, 1992) has reviewed from diverse domains (including language, mathematics, physics, and drawing) and age groups (infancy through to adolescence). However, limited research addressed to the representational redescription process has been conducted outside Karmiloff-Smith's laboratory. One reason for this could be that the theory is not presented in a rigorous form that enables predictions to be generated. Presentation is at the level of a framework rather than a theory. Some crucial definitions are not operationalized, for example, a domain is "the set of representations sustaining a specific area of knowledge" (Karmiloff-Smith, 1994, p. 696). More important, the theory is unconstrained. For example, it does not specify under what conditions the opposing processes of proceduralization (explicit to implicit) and representational redescription (implicit to explicit) operate. Nor does it provide a means for predicting the behavioral consequences of either process; for instance, the redescription of implicit to explicit representations may or may not yield the U-shaped pattern of behavioral mastery described previously for the block-balancing task.

SKILL ACQUISITION AND
THE DEVELOPMENT OF AUTOMATICITY

The process of proceduralization described by Karmiloff-Smith is not developed in any detail—it is offered as an alternative to Fodor's (1983) view that modules are innate, but is not elaborated beyond that point. Earlier we noted that the proceduralization process is similar in description to the transition from controlled to automatic processing (chap. 5), and in this section we review two theories that ascribe a role in cognitive development to mechanisms analogous to those proposed in the literature on adult acquisition of automaticity.

In chapter 5, Speelman and Maybery describe several theoretical approaches to understanding skill acquisition and automaticity, two of which are relevant here. Under the resources position (Shiffrin & Schneider, 1977), practice in a domain shifts processing along a continuum from controlled to automatic. Controlled processes make substantial demands on a pool of central attentional resources. Although these resources can be shared among processes, they are finite in quantity, and place a limit on the number of controlled processes that can run concurrently. Automatic processes are said to make minimal demands on this pool of attentional resources. Therefore many more automatic than controlled processes can run concurrently without interference.

The second approach reviewed by Speelman and Maybery is Logan's (1988b) *instance* theory of automaticity. Logan argued that initial performance relies on an algorithm that computes answers to problems. Each successful application of the algorithm is represented as a problem-specific instance in memory. When a particular problem is repeated, it can be solved through either the application of the algorithm or the retrieval of an instance from memory. These processes race against each other. As practice unfolds, the ensemble of instances builds for each problem, and the probability increases that an instance will be retrieved before the algorithm computes an answer. Thus, with practice, performance comes to depend more on memory retrieval and less on algorithmic computation.

In this section, we review two theories of cognitive development. First we consider a particular application of the resources view in Case's (1985) theory. Then we review Siegler and Shrager's (1984) *distributions of associations* theory, which shares several of the features of Logan's instance theory of automaticity.

Processing Efficiency

Case (1985, 1992), like some other developmental theorists (e.g., M. Chapman & Lindenberger, 1989; Halford, 1982, 1993), argued that children's thought is limited by the capacity of a pool of central information-processing resources. However, the novelty of Case's position is that the size of this pool remains constant with age.[2] Nevertheless, it can support more complex thought in older children, because processes become more efficient (i.e., move toward the automatic end of the automatic-controlled continuum) with age. According to Case (1985, 1992, 1995), all processes benefit from an increase in efficiency attributable to the maturation of the nervous system. Further improvements may result from the development of conceptual structures, and from increases in the efficiency of specific processes as a function of practice. However, there is an upper limit to the possible extent of conceptual and practice-based improvements. This limit is determined by the child's current level of maturational development (Case, 1995). Thus, older children process information more efficiently as the result of maturation, practice, and conceptual development. This increased efficiency enables the concurrent implementation of more processing and storage functions, which can subserve increasingly complex thought.

Case's proposal is attractive for two reasons. First, it can explain the development of the complexity of children's reasoning without appealing to an increase in the capacity of their processing resources. Second, the proposal provides a neat explanation not only for developments in reasoning, but also for increases in short-term memory. This is because Case's (1985) proposal includes the idea that a common pool of processing resources subserves both storing and operating on information (in more conventional terms, retaining and processing information). Thus the child's total processing space (TPS) is divided between operating space (OS) and short-term storage space (STSS). That is:

---

[2]There is insufficient space to summarize the full theory that Case (1985) presented. In particular, we do not consider his distinction between attentional capacity, which is argued to increase with age, and information-processing capacity, which is argued to remain constant with age. We are especially interested in his arguments concerning information-processing capacity, because these arguments relate to theories of adult skill acquisition.

TPS = OS + STSS

Increases in short-term memory are explained in terms of increases in the efficiency of processes such as encoding. This increased efficiency means that there is reduced demand for operating space, which leaves more of the total space free for short-term storage. The gains in STSS through increases in operating efficiency contribute not only to increases in short-term memory, but also to increases in the complexity of the child's thought in areas as diverse as problem solving, storytelling, and drawing. This is because STSS is used to hold the goal hierarchies (executive control structures) that regulate thought. The larger the STSS, the more elaborate the goal hierarchy that can be assembled, and the more complex the thought that is enabled.

Case (1985, 1992) gathered together a large database to support his claim that there is a developmental increase in the complexity of the strategies that children enact across a diverse range of tasks. These strategies are analyzed as to the goal hierarchies they entail, and these analyses provide indirect support for the view that STSS increases with age, as a result of increases in processing efficiency.

However, more direct evidence for Case's STSS-OS resource trade-off position came from Case, Kurland, and Goldberg (1982) using the counting span task. Each trial of this task uses a series of cards, each containing randomly dispersed green and yellow dots. The task is to count the green dots on each card, then, on the completion of counting, to recall the count totals for all cards in the set. The number of cards in the set increased across trials, and counting span is the maximum number of cards for which the count totals can be retained. Case et al. argued that counting span should reflect the STSS-OS trade-off because the counting process should draw on OS, whereas concurrently retaining the count totals should draw on STSS. More efficient counting should mean a reduced demand on OS, an increased STSS, and therefore a larger counting span. Older children should count more efficiently and therefore have larger spans. The efficiency of counting was assessed directly by timing children to count 50 dots spread across 10 cards, with speed emphasized. The central results supporting the trade-off position were (a) consistent increases in both counting span and speed of counting with age (kindergarten to Grade 6), and (b) a substantial correlation between the two measures ($r = .71$) which remained significant when age was partialed out. Thus, the Case et al. study appeared to offer direct evidence supporting the STSS-OS resource trade-off position.

However, a recent study by Halford, Maybery, O'Hare, and P. Grant (1994) questions Case's trade-off position while leaving intact the more general position that processes increase in efficiency across childhood. Halford et al.'s experiments used an adaptation of the card-counting task in which (a) a memory preload was presented, (b) the child engaged in some form of processing such as counting, and (c) recall of the preload was attempted. The advantage of this procedure is that storage and processing demands can be manipulated independently—the size of the preload can be varied, as can the difficulty of the intervening processing (e.g., counting forward vs. backward). Several predictions follow from Case's STSS-OS trade-off view. First, because the intervening processing should be performed more efficiently by older children, fewer resources should be siphoned off to OS, therefore more STSS should be left for retaining the preload. Consequently, less of the preload should be lost by older compared to younger children. Further, retention of the preload should be adversely affected if a more demanding processing task (e.g., counting backward rather than forward) is imposed, but this change should affect the older children less than the younger children, because the increase in OS demand with the change in processing task should be less for the older children. Finally, the extent of loss of preload information should be inversely related to a measure of processing efficiency, such as counting speed.

Halford et al. (1994) could not find support for any of these predictions. They concluded that different pools of resources appear to serve short-term retention and processing. Nevertheless, Halford et al. reported substantial correlations between different measures of processing efficiency, such as counting speed and rehearsal speed, correlations that were mediated by age. Therefore, processing efficiency does appear to increase significantly across the primary-school years. One question left unanswered is whether this increase in processing efficiency is domain-independent, and perhaps the product of maturation of the nervous system, or domain-specific and the product of practice. We return to this question after reviewing Siegler's work, which attributes much of cognitive development to domain-specific practice.

Skill Acquisition

As noted earlier, the distributions-of-associations (DoA) model of children's skill acquisition (Siegler & Shrager, 1984; see also Siegler, 1989; Siegler & Jenkins, 1989; Siegler & Shipley, 1995) has many features in common with Logan's (1988b) instance theory. These common features are elucidated after the DoA model is described. The section concludes with a summary of a recent extension to the DoA model.

According to the DoA model, a child unpracticed in a particular domain relies initially on a backup strategy (an algorithm). For example, in solving addition problems, the child might count out each addend on his or her fingers, then count the total (the *count-all* strategy described by Siegler & Jenkins, 1989). As the child practices in the domain, familiar problems can come to be solved by an alternative means, direct retrieval of an answer. Retrieval is based on a distribution of associations that is particular to the problem under solution. Figure 9.1 (taken from Siegler & Jenkins, 1989) shows two hypothetical distributions of associations, one for the more highly practiced 2 + 1 problem (top panel), the other for the less well-practiced 3 + 5 problem (bottom panel). Each distribution reflects the learning that has accrued from the previous solutions to the problem in question. Each time

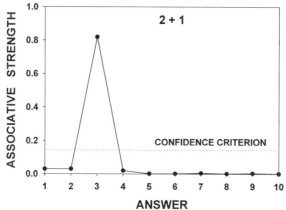

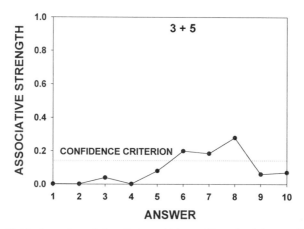

FIG. 9.1. Distributions of associations for two addition problems, 2 + 1 (top panel) and 3 + 5 (bottom panel). From Siegler and Jenkins (1989, Figure 2.2, p. 31). Copyright © 1989 by Lawrence Erlbaum Associates. Adapted by permission.

an answer is generated for a problem, that answer gains in associative strength. The distribution for the 2 + 1 problem in Fig. 9.1 has a peak at the correct answer 3, whereas the distribution for the 3 + 5 problem is flatter, with a less pronounced association for the correct answer 8. These differences essentially reflect the more extended practice for 2 + 1.

Siegler argued that a child in the intermediate stages of practice on a particular problem can derive an answer through two alternative means, sometimes direct retrieval, sometimes application of an algorithm (Siegler, 1989; Siegler & Jenkins, 1989; Siegler & Shipley, 1995; Siegler & Shrager, 1984). The process responsible for this mix is as follows. When confronted with a problem such as 3 + 5, the child first attempts retrieval. The probability that a particular answer will be retrieved is the ratio of its associative strength to the sum of the strengths for all answers (for the answer 6, the ratio might be 0.2/0.8 = 0.25). If a retrieved answer has an associative strength greater than the child's confidence criterion (0.15 in Fig. 9.1), then that answer is reported. If the retrieved answer has a strength below the criterion (e.g., as for the answer 5), the child may reattempt retrieval. However, after a fixed number of failures to retrieve an answer above criterion, the child resorts to a backup strategy (e.g., the count-all strategy). Well-practiced problems like 2 + 1 have peaked distributions that result in a high proportion of responses based on retrieval; less well-practiced problems like 3 + 5 have flat distributions that result in a high proportion of responses based on a backup strategy.

Siegler has assembled extensive evidence in support of the DoA model. The model has been applied to the development of children's addition, subtraction, multiplication, spelling, word identification, and time telling (for reviews, see Siegler, 1989; Siegler & Jenkins, 1989; Siegler & Shipley, 1995). As well as providing accounts of general performance trends, Siegler also has addressed the detailed trial-to-trial performances of children displaying a variety of strategies. For example, Siegler (1987) collected reaction time (RT), accuracy, and verbal-report data from 5- to 7-year-old children as they solved simple addition problems. Several methods of answering were observed, including retrieval, and backup strategies such as the count-all strategy described earlier, and the min strategy where the child counts on from the larger addend (e.g., for 3 + 5, the child counts 5, 6, 7, 8). On trials where the count-all strategy had been reported, the best predictor of the differences across problems in RT and accuracy was the sum of the two addends. On trials where the min strategy had been reported, the best predictor was the size of the smaller addend. These data support Siegler's contention that qualitatively different solutions are applied, even by the same child on repetitions of the same problem.

The DoA model provides an account of the development of a skill that approximates Logan's instance theory account. In both cases, novice performance is based on computing an answer (with an algorithm or a backup strategy). As practice proceeds, records are stored of the solutions to particular problems (instances or associations). As these records accumulate, solutions increasingly are achieved through retrieving rather than computing an answer.

The major difference between the two proposals is that for Siegler, retrieval and backup strategies run in series, whereas for Logan, they run in parallel. More specifically, for Siegler and Shrager's DoA model, the child first attempts retrieval, and then implements an algorithm only if retrieval fails to deliver an answer with an associative value above the confidence criterion. For Logan's model, instance retrieval and the algorithm run concurrently, with the answer provided by the faster process.

Compton and Logan (1991) presented evidence bearing on this issue when they compared Logan's instance model (*race model* in Compton and Logan) with a serial model in accounting for performance changes as adults practiced alphabet–arithmetic problems (e.g., A + 2 = C, G + 6 = M). The critical feature of performance was that the variance in solution times decreased with practice in accord with a power function. A power function is predicted by the instance model, but not by the serial model that Compton and Logan evaluated.

However, as Compton and Logan (1991) acknowledged, the particular serial model they considered is simpler than the DoA model. Indeed, we have shown with simulations that a more elaborate version of the serial model (one where associative strength approaches asymptote according to a negatively accelerating function) can generate a practice function for the variance in solution times not unlike the function observed by Compton and Logan.

Further, Siegler and Shipley (1995) reported several features of children's strategy use that are not easily accommodated by the instance model; these include: (a) use of multiple strategies, for example, the min and count-all strategies as well as retrieval, by a single child in a single session; (b) the tendency to favor certain strategies on certain problems, for example, to favor the min strategy on problems like 2 + 9 where there is a large difference in the addends; (c) improvement with practice in the speed and accuracy of execution of each strategy; and (d) qualitative differences in individual performance, reflecting, for example, differences in willingness to rely on retrieved answers. To use the racing analogy, more than two horses run, there are horses for courses, horses improve each time out, and punters have favorite horses.

A model proposed by Siegler and Shipley (1995)—the adaptive strategy choice model (ASCM)—can accommodate these features of children's strategy use. ASCM retains the basic features of the Siegler and Shrager (1984) model, such as distributions of associations, but contains more sophisticated strategy-selection mechanisms. Strategies, including retrieval, compete for application based on their histories of performance (a) across all problems, (b) for problems sharing features with the current problem, and (c) for previous occurrences of the current problem. This means that strategy selection is both more flexible (e.g., retrieval is not inevitably attempted) and more intelligent (e.g., novel problems are tackled with strategies that were effective on problems with shared features).

Thus, ASCM, the most recent model proposed by Siegler, probably can account for more phenomena than Logan's instance model. However, the central feature differentiating the models, serial versus parallel application of strategies, remains contentious. Nevertheless, for present purposes it is the features that are common to the two models that are more important. The models share the assumption that skill acquisition consists of a transition from the application of an algorithm early in practice to the reliance on direct retrieval of answers late in practice. Thus, skill acquisition is domain-specific and reflects the accrual of knowledge.

CONCLUDING OBSERVATIONS

Several of the elements of Karmiloff-Smith's (1992, 1994) framework correspond to concepts from the adult cognition literature. Behavior governed by implicit representations has the stimulus-driven and stereotypic characteristics associated with automatic processes, and its constituents are closed to analysis, as has been claimed for implicit learning in the adult literature (see chap. 7 of this volume). Also, behavior governed by explicit representations is top–down, flexible, and open to analysis, as has been said of controlled processes and explicit learning processes in the adult literature. Further, Karmiloff-Smith allowed for *proceduralization*—roughly, the change from explicitly controlled to implicitly controlled behavior—which is analogous to the shift from controlled to automatic processing in Shiffrin and Schneider's (1977) formulation. The novelty of Karmiloff-Smith's position is that she postulated the reverse change, that is, *representational redescription*, under which implicit representations are redescribed to explicit forms. What then is the status of these proposals with reference to the work reviewed in this chapter, and where should developmental theory and research head next?

Implicit Encoding Processes

The emphasis in Karmiloff-Smith's (1992, 1994) work is in characterizing the implicit representations, which underpin initial success in a domain, and the explicit representations into which they can be redescribed. Because she did not specify in any detail the encoding processes that establish the initial implicit representations, then at first blush it would seem that her work is complemented by proposals like those advanced by Hasher and Zacks (1979) and Reber (1992). That is, the innate automatic processes or implicit learning processes postulated by the latter authors could provide the initial implicit representations.

The problem with this synthesis is that, according to Hasher and Zacks (1979) and Reber (1992), a basic set of encoding processes operate invariant of ontogenetic development and domain (e.g., frequencies are encoded automatically, no matter whether they apply to words, objects, or faces). In contrast, Karmiloff-Smith (1992, 1994) claimed that initial learning is subject to domain-specific constraints. These constraints operate through the preferential encoding of certain classes of stimuli and through restrictions on the computations that can be performed on those inputs. This idea was developed in detail by Gallistel, A.L. Brown, Carey, Gelman, and Keil (1991), who argued that human infants, like the young of other species, are predisposed to attend to certain classes of stimuli. They also argued that there is considerable adaptive value in an organism being sensitive to different classes of stimuli at different stages in its development.

The difficulty in evaluating whether implicit encoding processes are subject to age- and domain-specific predispositions is that the form of the purported predispositions has not been enunciated. Therefore, it is difficult to set up empirical tests that could disconfirm the predispositions view. This is perhaps why research has been restricted primarily to studies concerning the age-invariance of implicit learning, implicit memory, and innate automatic processes.

Although the outcomes are equivocal in each of these research areas, the broad conclusion in each case is that the effect size for age for the implicit or automatic process is substantially smaller than it is for the contrasting explicit or effortful process. This provides some support for the view that implicit encoding processes are functional from an early age, and show little variation across the life span. However, developmental work in the area of implicit learning is sparse. Also, the developmental literature addressed to the innate automatic processes would benefit from a meta-analysis. The emphasis in this analysis should be on the effect size for age, calculated separately for intentional and incidental study conditions, because the latter may better reflect the contribution of automatic processes independent of effortful processes.

Representational Redescription and Explicit Processes

Karmiloff-Smith (1992) provided detailed descriptions of advances in several domains that are consistent with the transition from implicit to explicit representations (see Piaget, 1976, for similar observations). One aspect of her theory that is underspecified, however, is the mechanism through which the explicit representations are abstracted. There is speculation as to possible neural-network architectures that could provide the redescription (Karmiloff-Smith, 1992, 1994), but these are diverse and untested.

One particular issue is whether the redescription is driven entirely from the bottom up, with the explicit representation simply reflecting the most salient structure of the implicit representation (this seems to be Karmiloff-Smith's position), or whether the redescription is driven at least partly from the top down. The latter possibility would allow for an interrogation of implicit representations guided by explicit goals. So, for example, when asked to describe what part of the action in throwing a boomerang is similar to that of throwing a cricket ball, the boomerang-throwing routine might be accessed with reference to whether maximum force is applied; however, if asked to compare boomerang throwing with frisbee throwing, access might be made with reference to whether spin is imparted. Whether access to the implicit representation is possible might depend on whether performance has stabilized, as Karmiloff-Smith argued, but what is abstracted from the representation when access is made may depend on the goal that motivates access. Thus, the explicit representations formed would reflect the joint influence of the goals that motivated their generation and the structure inherent in the implicit representations they were abstracted from.

Another issue concerns the constraints that might apply to the processes that operate on explicit representations. One of the few domain-general maturational changes that Karmiloff-Smith (1994) came close to conceding is that at around age 1.5 years the child is first capable of "holding two representations simultaneously in mind and representing hypothetical events in general" (p. 702). Although different in detail, Halford (1982, 1993) has presented a comprehensive account of developmental changes in the complexity of the representations that the child can apprehend. Halford's theory also provides a mechanism, structure mapping, through which representations can be interrelated either within or across domains. The contrasting lack of specification of constraints and mechanisms in Karmiloff-Smith's treatment of the processes operating on explicit representations contributes to its characterization as a framework rather than a testable theory.

Proceduralization and Mechanisms of Developmental Change

In an earlier section we noted that the proceduralization process described by Karmiloff-Smith (1992, 1994) is similar in description to the transition from controlled to automatic processing. This led us to consider two approaches to automatization, one based on resource demands, the other on memory retrieval. First we evaluated two of Case's (1985) claims: (a) that, with age, processes become more efficient and make reduced demands on resources (i.e., move toward the automatic end of the automatic-controlled continuum); and (b) there is a trade-off between processing and short-term retention because both draw on a common pool of resources. The available evidence is consistent with the first claim, but inconsistent with the second. Next, we considered Siegler's view that skill acquisition consists of a transition from application of an algorithm early in practice to reliance on direct retrieval of answers late in practice (Siegler, 1989; Siegler & Jenkins, 1989; Siegler & Shrager, 1984). Clearly, some developmental changes are the result of an increasing reliance on memory retrieval, particularly for the areas such as mathematics and reading that Siegler has targeted.

The qualitative change in performance described by Siegler should proceed at a rate determined by the child's accumulation of domain-specific practice. However, it is also possible, as Case (1985, 1995) argued, that general improvements in processing efficiency overlay any particular domain-specific changes. One source of improvement in processing efficiency could be neurological changes such as the myelination of axons, which continues into the teenage years (Case, 1985, 1995; Dempster, 1992). According to Dempster, "myelinated axons seem to propagate impulses more rapidly and with less energy...and are less susceptible to abnormal transmission from fiber to fiber" (p. 50). (Dempster discussed other potentially relevant neurological changes to the prefrontal cortex in childhood and old age, and both Dempster and Case described correspondences between patterns of neurological change and patterns of cognitive development.)

Evidence consistent with systemwide life-span changes in processing efficiency has been gathered by Kail and by Hale (for recent reviews, see Cerella & Hale,

1994; Kail, 1993). This evidence comes from speeded tasks such as choice RT, mental rotation, and picture naming. One basic technique in this research is to plot the reaction times for a target age group, say 10-year-olds, against those for a reference group of young adults. Each point represents the means for the two groups for one of several conditions or tasks. Typically, the points in this Brinley plot fall on a straight line, reflecting the fact that the RTs for the target group can be derived from the RTs for the reference group by multiplying by a constant (around 1.4 for 10-year-olds). Furthermore, changes in the constant across childhood conform to a negative exponential function, whereas changes across middle- and old-age conform to a positive exponential function (Cerella & Hale, 1994; Kail, 1993). The conclusion from this evidence is that there are domain-independent increases in processing efficiency through childhood, which are mirrored by decrements in middle and late adult life. One intriguing avenue for future research would be to apply the multiple-task multiple-age-group design from this literature to speeded tasks that purportedly tap implicit processes (e.g., priming tasks). This would address whether there are age-related changes in the efficiency of implicit processes that concord with those summarized earlier.

We hope we have left the impression that the current theoretical proposals relating to the role of implicit or automatic processes in cognitive development are too unconstrained. Proposals allow for implicit and explicit representations and the translation of one to the other (through redescription or proceduralization). The way ahead must be in specifying the mechanisms responsible for establishing and utilizing either form of representation, and for translating one to the other. There are some recent attempts to provide this specification. For example, Dienes and Fahey (1995) promoted the storage of specific instances in a look-up table as the mechanism underpinning implicit learning, and, as indicated earlier, Halford (1982, 1993) provided a rigorous description of a structure-mapping mechanism that could be applied to the problem of how explicit representations are interrelated.

ACKNOWLEDGMENTS

Angela O'Brien-Malone is now at Murdoch University. We thank Janet Briggs, Kim Kirsner, and Craig Speelman for their very helpful comments on early drafts.

10

INDIVIDUAL DIFFERENCES IN INTELLIGENCE

Mike Anderson
University of Western Australia

What influence, if any, has the distinction between implicit and explicit processing had on conceptions of intelligence? In this area, the distinction has been, itself, implicit. There are at least two reasons for this. The first is that it is only relatively recently that intelligence has been viewed in information-processing terms (see Hunt, 1980; Sternberg, 1983) and it is within the information-processing framework that the distinction has been important. The second reason is historical. The study of intelligence was that part of psychology that dealt with human rationality, logic, and problem solving—in other words the application of our conscious, rational faculties in the pursuit of *knowledge*. Consequently, the essence of intelligence usually is regarded as the possession of some kind of explicit representation. Implicit knowing (getting it right without knowing why) simply would not be regarded as intelligent knowing. I return to the distinction between intelligent and unintelligent knowing in a later section.

The lack of explicit theorizing about implicit processing in mainstream theories of intelligence has led me to pursue a particular strategy for this chapter. First, I outline the major theories of individual differences in intelligence and attempt to see where they stand as far as the implicit/explicit distinction is concerned. Second, I discuss what little research there is on the relationship between implicit processing and IQ. Third, I explore the relationship between intelligence and knowledge and subsequently recast the question in terms of a particular individual differences theory that uses an information-processing framework (my own). Finally, I consider a case study, that of idiots savants, where the relationship between explicit knowledge and what we consider to be intelligence is most obviously contrasted.

THE PSYCHOMETRIC APPROACH TO INTELLIGENCE

For the better part of a century the psychological quality "intelligence" has been measured using the ubiquitous intelligence test. As every undergraduate knows (or should!) the origins of the intelligence test can be traced back to Alfred Binet, as can the impetus for the derivation of the intelligence quotient (IQ) by William Stern.

Binet believed that tests of intelligence should be tests of the higher mental faculties including: memory, imagination, mental imagery, attention, comprehension and perceptual skill in spatial relations. Consequently, Binet devised "tests" of these faculties by asking subjects what they knew (by definition requiring explicit knowledge) and to solve particular kinds of problems that required conscious thought. In short, the higher mental faculties as characteriZed by Binet appeared to be distinguished from lower mental faculties, in that they are closely allied to conscious thought and knowledge. Although Binet set the scene for the development of intelligence tests and, indeed, the seminal work of Piaget on the development of intelligence, his conception of intelligence stood in contrast to the school of thought originating with Francis Galton and developed by Charles Spearman. What became known as the London school, held that individual differences in intelligence result from variations in low-level properties of the human nervous system. Such differences give rise to the phenomenon Spearman (1904) called general intelligence or g. However, even Spearman conceded that Binet's tests were the best, albeit indirect, measure of the attribute we call intelligence. Following Binet, standard intelligence test batteries such as the Wechsler Adult Intelligence Scale (WAIS) largely ask subjects what they know or alternatively to solve novel test problems. For many, then, intelligence and knowledge are synonymous (Ceci, 1990; Howe 1990). That is to say, intelligent people are characterized by knowing more, for example that Goethe wrote Faust.

Although it is clear that much of the knowledge sampled by intelligence tests could be characterized as explicit, it is unclear whether many aspects of the problem solving involved in, for example, Raven's Matrices (J.R. Raven, Court, & J. Raven, 1987) are available to introspection. Judging by at least one empirical investigation, the complexity of the mental operations involved in solving Matrices problems is sufficient to make this unlikely (Carpenter, Just, & Shell, 1990). Indeed, these researchers had to engage in a great deal of experimentation to attempt to discover what mental processes were involved—a redundant task had their subjects known exactly what it was they were doing when attempting such problems. I return later to the issue of whether intelligence can be regarded, in any case, as synonymous with knowledge.

The major psychometric debate over the nature of individual differences in intelligence was that between Spearman (1904, 1927) and Thurstone (1938), a debate that still has a modern counterpart (see M. Anderson, 1992b; H.J. Eysenck, 1988; H. Gardner 1983; Jensen 1982). The debate focused on whether individual differences are best characterized as differences in a general ability, or *g* (Spearman) or differences in multiple independent abilities (Thurstone). Spearman conceived of his general ability as being due to individual differences in levels of mental energy fueling particular "cognitive engines." The more mental juice we have the more intelligent we are. Whether Spearman thought intelligence was an implicit or an explicit psychological function is barely an intelligible question in this context. Arthur Jensen, perhaps the foremost contemporary *g* theorist, has defined a mental ability as "some particular, conscious, voluntary behavioural act that can be assessed as meeting (or failing to meet) some clearly defined standard" (Jensen & Weng, 1994, p. 236). Intelligence or general mental ability manifests itself in explicit knowledge or particular mental skills. However, individual differences in intelligence according to Spearman and Jensen are *caused by* a processing parameter outwith an individual's awareness. Similarly, it is unlikely that the question of whether intelligence is a property of implicit or explicit processing would be intelligible to Thurstone. Although his Primary Mental Abilities (viz. verbal, word fluency, number spatial visualisation, rote memory, inductive reasoning, deductive reasoning, and perceptual speed) have a flavor of conscious processing about their operation, it is a moot point whether the source of individual differences in these abilities is itself a property of a conscious process.

Broadly, then, the psychometric approach to intelligence is agnostic about the relative contribution of explicit and implicit processing to intelligence test performance. Some measures of intelligence are based on explicit knowledge but even here it could be argued, by Spearman at least, that the process underlying these differences in explicit knowledge is itself implicit. As is the case for many of the psychological areas presented in this book, the distinction between explicit and implicit processing becomes more intelligible when the distinction can be viewed from theoretical perspectives that themselves are couched within an information-processing framework.

INFORMATION-PROCESSING
THEORIES OF INTELLIGENCE

The application of a cognitive or information-processing framework to theories of individual differences in intelligence did not come about until the late 1970s. Two basic research strategies have been used to attempt to determine empirically where in the information-processing system the major source of individual differences lies.

The *cognitive correlates* approach of Hunt and colleagues (Hunt, 1980; Hunt, Lenneborg, & J. Lewis, 1975) sought to correlate performance on various information-processing tasks, hypothesized to measure different processes, with performance on psychometric tests. Most of Hunt's research concentrated on measuring aspects of verbal information processing with tests of verbal intelligence but others attempted to pursue the same strategy for spatial abilities (Pellegrino & Kail, 1982).

Hunt (1980) considered that the source of individual differences could be located at different levels in the information-processing system. The most basic level he called information-free mechanisms, the next level is the structure and content of the knowledge base, and the final level is strategies for accessing knowledge to solve particular problems. In terms of levels it could be argued that the higher levels are more likely to be accessible to awareness or part of explicit processing, and Hunt claimed empirical evidence for the idea that it is in these processes that the greatest source of intelligence-related differences is to be found.

Sternberg (1983, 1984) used a different research approach, known as *cognitive components*, but came to much the same conclusion. Instead of correlating performance on information-processing tasks with psychometric test performance, Sternberg's componential research attempted to identify the information-processing components involved in solving particular intelligence test problems. The components and their properties are derived by fitting information-processing models with different parameters to reaction time data.

Sternberg (1984) claimed to identify three levels of cognitive components and called this his *triarchic theory* of intelligence. The most basic level he called *performance components*, which are the information-processing mechanisms evoked by particular problem-solving tasks. For example, in solving analogies such as *Nurse is to Doctor as Lawyer is to?*, Sternberg has identified empirically different stages of processing such as *encoding* stimulus information and *mapping* correspondences between the terms in the analogy. In the theory, each stage of processing is the province of a different performance component and the process of solving a problem means, in effect, instantiating a particular sequence of performance components. Sternberg reported consistent individual differences in the operation of performance components. Of course, to solve a particular problem the solver must generate a sequence of operations that is likely to result in a successful solution. To make this possible two other kinds of information-processing components are required. Intelligent problem solving requires a knowledge base that is continually updated and a means of recognizing the relevance of information in the knowledge base for current problem solving. The components responsible for this Sternberg called *knowledge acquisition* components. Finally, *metacomponents* are responsible for selecting a particular sequence of performance components to achieve a particular task goal (strategies) and monitoring feedback on progress. Performance components, knowledge acquisition components, and metacomponents operate in concert, but there is a hierarchy that runs from simple to complex and, perhaps, from implicit to explicit. Sternberg argued that his data show that it is primarily individual differences in metacomponent functioning that underlie individual differences in intelligent problem solving.

Both Hunt and Sternberg recognized sources of individual differences at different levels in the information-processing system. Although they have not been overly concerned with the implicit explicit distinction, they concurred that it is in the level most likely to be part of explicit problem solving that the major differences lie.

IMPLICIT PROCESSING, MENTAL RETARDATION, AND IQ

So far we have seen that the distinction between implicit and explicit processing has not been a major concern in the study of individual differences in intelligence. However, theorists interested in implicit processing have become interested in intelligence (Reber, 1989a; Reber et al., 1991). The principal claim is that performance on tasks that require explicit information processing for their solution (e.g., series completion tasks) are related to IQ, with higher IQ subjects performing better. Performance on tasks that are learned using implicit processing (e.g., artificial grammars) is unrelated to IQ differences. The reader should turn to the chapter 3, in this volume, by O'Brien-Malone and Maybery, for a full description of this research. Reber's (1992) thesis is that implicit learning is supported by unconscious inductive systems that are evolutionarily older than the explicit learning systems. It is the explicit learning system that is related to individual differences in intelligence as measured by IQ tests. However, somewhat remarkably, Reber (1992) argued that if "true" intelligence involves the ability to profit from one's experiences with a complex environment then implicit cognitive processes may turn out to be the best measure of "true" intelligence. This is a bizarre speculation because implicit processes are largely unrelated to any individual differences associated with age or IQ and are even robust in the face of brain damage. Reber's speculation is a classic case of using the term intelligence in two senses. One use refers to individual differences within the human species and the other refers to adaptation of the species. I argue later that these alternative referents map onto computationally distinct cognitive mechanisms.

In research on the deficiencies of problem solving associated with cultural familial mental retardation, the dominant view is that it is the conscious or strategic aspects of problem solving that are most affected by lower IQ. For example, Brown and colleagues (A.L. Brown, 1974; Campione, A.L. Brown, & Ferrara, 1982) have claimed that whereas basic processes may function less well in people with lower IQs, they have more difficulty in utilizing problem-solving strategies or generalizing knowledge gained in specific situations to novel situations. So, again, it is not only that there may be deficiencies in the speed or efficiency with which basic processes are carried out (although some researchers might deny even this; see Belmont & D.W. Mitchell, 1987), but the major deficits may be in the way in which component processes are selected, organized, and monitored. In this view mental retardation is a deficiency in the ability to utilize explicit knowledge (from instruction) in domains other than the one in which it was learned. This results in lack of insight, failures of "learning to learn," lack of transfer of training and the failure to develop general executive or metacognitive skills. (See chap. 20 in this volume for an extensive review of this literature). Consistent with this hypothesis is the view of Spitz (1982, 1986) that it is tasks that require "thinking," as opposed to, for example, the recall of facts, that are most affected in the mentally retarded.

The complementary position in research on the nature of mental retardation is that information processing that does not constitute conscious thought processes is not deficient in the mentally retarded. This view has some supporting evidence. For example, following the work of Hasher and Zacks (1984) "automatic" processes involved in incidental recall of frequency of occurrence seem to be unaffected by lowered IQ (Ellis, Palmer, & Reeves, 1988).

The picture painted so far in this chapter is one of peripheral interest in the question of whether implicit or explicit processing is related to individual differences in intelligence. In part this is due to the lack of consensus of how individual differences in intelligence might best be *understood*, as opposed to described, in information-processing terms. In turn this is due, in no small measure, to the varying levels of description applied to the referents of the term intelligence (see H.J. Eysenck, 1988, for a discussion). Nevertheless, the issues that I have identified that are pertinent to the question may be listed as follows:

1. Is intelligence synonymous with knowledge and if so is this in the main explicit or implicit knowledge?
2. Are differences in intelligence associated with differences in basic information-processing components or with differences in higher order strategic processes?
3. Is intelligence associated only with conscious thought and not at all with evolutionarily older implicit knowledge acquisition mechanisms?

To attempt to answer these questions I present a brief outline of a theory (my own!) that allows us to address each issue and then attempt an answer to each question from the perspective of that theory.

KNOWLEDGE, THINKING, AND INTELLIGENCE

That more intelligent people know more is uncontentious. However, that there is more to intelligence than knowing is disputed by some (Ceci, 1990; Howe, 1990; Howe & J. Smith, 1988). Jensen (1984), somewhat disparagingly, referred to this belief as the "specificity doctrine," the belief that intelligence is nothing other than a ragbag of bits and pieces of knowledge. Advocates of the specificity doctrine also tend to believe that variations in knowledge (and, therefore, intelligence) are experientially driven. If this view of intelligence were to be taken seriously, then a consideration of the relationship between implicit processing and intelligence would melt into the chapter by O'Brien-Malone and Maybery on implicit learning, simply because individual differences would be due to nothing other than variations on the exogenous factors that influence implicit and explicit learning. However, this view should not be taken seriously.

For extensive discussion and subsequent refutation of the specificity doctrine see M. Anderson (1992a) Jensen (1984), Nettelbeck (1990), and Sternberg (1988). These researchers have dismissed the view that knowledge and intelligence are synonymous. They argued that intelligence is an endogenous information-processing capacity underlying knowledge acquisition. Most would agree that this capacity is, in all probability, highly heritable (Bouchard, Lykken, McGue, Segal, & Tellegen, 1990). Some of the strongest evidence in favor of intelligence being a property of information processing is the finding that performance on virtually knowledge-free information-processing tasks is correlated with knowledge-rich intelligence test performance. In particular, it is claimed that speed of information processing is correlated with IQ. Such evidence comes from two main tasks, the reaction time measures used by Jensen and the inspection time task pioneered by Nettelbeck (1982, 1987; Nettelbeck & Lally, 1976).

SPEED OF PROCESSING AND IQ

Jensen and colleagues (Jensen 1980, 1982; Jensen & Munro, 1979) have shown that choice reaction time is correlated with differences in IQ. The apparatus used by Jensen presents the subjects with a semicircle of eight stimulus lights, each with a response button situated immediately below. Subjects are presented with a very simple task. When one of the stimulus lights is illuminated, they move their finger from a "home" button to press the response button below that light. By varying the number of lights that are used, the information load of the task can be changed (Hick, 1952). The task allows independent measures of the duration of decision processes (DT = decision time), which is taken to be the time from the onset of the stimulus light to the lifting of the finger off the home button, and motoric processes (MT = movement time), the time between lifting the finger off the home button and pressing the button below the stimulus light. Decision times increase with the information load of the task in a way well described by Hick's law, namely a linear increase with $\log_2$ of the number of alternatives (typically from two to eight lights, equivalent to one and three "bits" of information).

The main findings using this task are:

1. Decision times correlate with IQ but movement times do not (Jensen & Munro, 1979).
2. The slope of the linear function relating information load to decision times is correlated with IQ—higher IQ subjects have shallower slopes; that is, they

process each bit of information in a shorter time (Jenkinson, 1983; Jensen & Munro, 1979)

3. The correlation between IQ and decision time increases as the information load of the task increases; that is, the more information that has to be processed, the greater the difference between high- and low-IQ subjects (Jenkinson, 1983; Jensen & Munro, 1979; G.A. Smith & Stanley, 1983). Jensen has concluded that the principal cause of individual differences in intelligence is variations in rates of neural processing, a view consistent with that of Spearman, but clearly at odds with that of Sternberg and Hunt.

It is not surprising that Jensen's conclusions have not gone unchallenged given that they rest on contentious assumptions about the underlying processes involved in reaction time performance (Longstreth, 1984, 1986; Rabbitt, 1985). Yet, data from another task with different performance requirements lend some support to the view that speed of information processing may be the ontogenetic basis of individual differences in intelligence.

In a typical inspection time task, a subject is required to make a perceptual discrimination (usually, which of two lines is the longer) at different exposure durations of the stimulus. The exposure duration of the stimulus is varied by employing a backward mask to prevent further stimulus processing. The crucial distinguishing feature of this task compared with the reaction time task described earlier is that there is no requirement for speed of response. Speed of processing is estimated from the psychophysical function relating accuracy to exposure duration of the stimulus. At exposures as short as 500 milliseconds, all subjects, even the mentally retarded, perform with high levels of accuracy. However, as exposure duration decreases so does accuracy and lower IQ subjects require longer exposure durations than higher IQ subjects for a given level of accuracy. Inspection time (IT) can be calculated for each subject (traditionally the exposure duration necessary to maintain 97.5% accuracy) and correlated with IQ. Average inspection time is around 120 milliseconds (line length discriminations at 97.5% accuracy) and the population correlation with IQ is estimated at around 0.5 (Kranzler & Jensen, 1989; Nettelbeck, 1987). In other words, 25% of the variance in measured intelligence may be due to differences in speed of information processing.

The relationship between simple measures of speed of processing, which appear to be knowledge-free, and knowledge-rich intelligence test performance belies the belief that intelligence and knowledge are synonymous (M. Anderson, 1992a). However, there is clearly a principled relationship between intelligence and knowledge (because higher IQ people know more). What these data imply is that faster speed of processing allows the development of a larger and more complex knowledge base and supports a greater complexity of problem-solving ability. Before we consider this relationship in more detail, another phenomenon should be addressed that is more directly relevant to the issue of intelligence and implicit processing.

INTELLIGENCE AND MODULARITY

The idea that cognitive functions are organized in a modular fashion in the brain is one of the major current concerns of cognitive science (Fodor, 1983; Shallice, 1988). Briefly, the modularity thesis holds that complex cognitive functions are subserved by hard-wired, fast, mandatory, and informationally encapsulated processing modules (Fodor, 1983). Modular bases have been proposed for a diversity of cognitive functions, including visual perception (Marr, 1982), language acquisition (Chomsky, 1986), and many aspects of speech perception (see Massaro, 1989). Further, modular damage has been implicated in cases of prosopagnosia, where there is an inability to recognize faces (see Newcombe & A.W. Young, 1989); deep dyslexics, where the "meaning" of words is mistaken in a bizarre fashion (J.C. Marshall & Newcombe, 1966; J. Morton & Patterson, 1980); visual agnosics, for whom the recognition of everyday objects becomes extremely difficult (G.W. Humphreys & Riddoch, 1987); and autism (Baron-Cohen, Leslie, & Frith, 1985; Leslie, 1991). In addition, it seems likely that many of the phenomena of psychological functioning regarded by developmental psychologists as central to the development of intelligence, such as causality (Leslie, 1986), the object concept (Baillargeon & Graber, 1987; Spelke, 1987), and theory of mind (Leslie, 1987), may be supported by processing modules.

If we consider the list of functions of putative modular processes in the light of what we know about intelligence test performance, a striking feature emerges. None of these functions would be tested by standard tests of intelligence simply because they show almost no individual differences that are related to individual differences measured by intelligence tests. In other words, modular processes are independent of measured intelligence, although they do contribute to intellectual development (M. Anderson, 1992a). Therefore, not all knowledge, or for that matter information processing, is related to individual differences in intelligence. It seems that only knowledge acquired through thought is related to individual differences in intelligence. This sweeping statement can be justified by a more detailed consideration of an information-processing theory of intelligence that allows us to capture the distinctions between thought and information processing.

THE THEORY OF
THE MINIMAL COGNITIVE ARCHITECTURE

The theory of the minimal cognitive architecture (M. Anderson, 1992b) outlined in Fig. 10.1, allows for two routes to knowledge acquisition, which, roughly, cleaves individual differences in intelligence from cognitive development. Individual differences in intelligence are attributed to variations in speed of processing and developmental changes in cognitive competence to the maturation of modular functions.

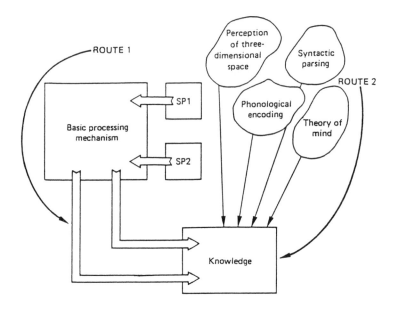

FIG. 10.1. Two routes to knowledge. Route 1 knowledge is acquired by thinking. Route 2 knowledge is given directly by modules that mature at different times in development. From M. Anderson (1992b, Figure 6.1). Copyright © 1992 by Blackwell Publishers. Reprinted with permission.

Route 1 Knowledge Acquisition (Thought): Knowledge That Is Acquired by the Implementation of an Algorithm Generated by a Specific Processor. Problem-solving algorithms generated by two specific processors, one specialized for verbal representations and the other for spatial, are implemented by a *basic processing mechanism*, which varies in its speed of processing. The higher the speed of the basic processing mechanism the more complex the algorithms that can be implemented. The speed of this mechanism can be estimated by measures such as inspection time. When an algorithm generated by a specific processor is implemented we can be said to be *thinking*, the process by which most knowledge is acquired. The basic processing mechanism represents a knowledge-free, biological constraint on thought. Variation in the speed of the basic processing mechanism is the primary cause of *individual differences* in intelligence.

Route 2 Knowledge Acquisition: Knowledge That Is Directly Given by Dedicated Modules. Modules are dedicated, computationally complex, mechanisms whose function is to provide us with evolutionarily prescribed information that could not be furnished by general-purpose problem solvers, that is, by the specific processors. The computations of modules are not constrained by the speed of the basic processing mechanism and they are, therefore, unrelated to individual differences in intelligence. The maturation of modules is the primary cause of cognitive development and affords, in effect, new cognitive competences. Therefore, individual differences in intelligence and cognitive development are caused by different and unrelated cognitive mechanisms.

The reader is referred to M. Anderson (1992b) for a detailed justification of the theory, but at least one major distinction (that between thought and knowledge) is held in common with a psychometrically based theory of individual differences—the theory of fluid and crystallized intelligence (Cattell, 1963). Briefly, fluid g is measured by tasks that require thought and reasoning and was considered by Cattell to be the biological basis of intelligence. Crystallized g, on the other hand, is considered to be the conversion of fluid ability into stored knowledge. Although crystallized g will be correlated with fluid g it is subject to other influences as well, including variations in experience and motivation.

THE RELATIONSHIP BETWEEN IMPLICIT PROCESSING AND THE MINIMAL COGNITIVE ARCHITECTURE

The manifestation of intelligence is found in thought processes and thought processes are constrained by the speed of the basic processing mechanism. Thus, in agreement with Spearman, the primary cause of individual differences in intelligence is a processing parameter that can be nothing other than implicit. However, because the manifestation of intelligence is thought, many intelligent processes can, at least in principle, be considered as explicit. Modular processes, on the other hand, which are unrelated to intelligence, are implicit processes *par excellence*. It is not possible to be aware of modular processing, only its products, for example, seeing the world, recognizing a face, understanding a sentence. Although these are considered to be "hard-wired" examples of modules, the theory argues that it is possible to develop modules (non-thought-based processing) through extensive practice. The resulting "automatic" processing should then be independent of intelligence.

One conjecture of the theory that is particularly related to the implicit/explicit question is that the thought/module distinction may map onto quite different computational implementations. Thought, which is constrained by the speed of the basic processing mechanism and therefore related to individual differences in intelligence, is slow, serial, and symbolic. Modules, by contrast, are fast, parallel, and may be network based.

IDIOTS SAVANTS

The existence of idiots savants are a challenge for most theories of intelligence. I now discuss two examples of savant abilities that highlight the possible overlap between implicit/explicit distinction and conceptions of intelligence.

Idiots savants are individuals who can perform remarkable cognitive feats, despite their very low measured intelligence. Examples are calculating what day of the week any calendar date falls on (Hermelin & N. O'Connor, 1986; Howe & J. Smith, 1988; N. O'Connor & Hermelin, 1984), high musical ability (Hermelin, N. O'Connor, Lee, & Treffert, 1989; Sloboda, Hermelin, & O'Connor, 1985), artistic talent (Hermelin & N. O'Connor, 1990; N. O'Connor & Hermelin, 1990), the ability to learn foreign languages (N. O'Connor & Hermelin, 1991), and the ability to factorize numbers (Hermelin & N. O'Connor, 1990; Horowitz, Kestenbaum, Person, & Jarvik, 1965). In this final section I discuss the abilities of two kinds of calculators, calendrical and prime number, because of the possible contrasting way their abilities may be related to intelligence given the likely processing basis of their ability.

The most extensively studied groups of savants are the calendrical calculators (CCs). They can answer questions such as: "What day of the week was the 24th of July 1955?"; "In what years between 1955 and 1995 does the 19th December fall on a Sunday?"; "What day of the week will the 19th of March, 2010 be?" Their talent is remarkable given both their IQ and the level of their ability. N. O'Connor and Hermelin (1984) discussed three possible bases for CC ability: rote memory, expertise with formulae, and knowledge of rules and regularities in the calendar.

On the face of it, an extensive rote memory for dates is ruled out by the fact that most CCs are highly accurate for days in the future for which no known calendars exist. In addition, N. O'Connor and Hermelin (1984) pointed out that extensive long-term memory is normally associated with higher levels of general intelligence—the very thing these individuals do not possess.

Almost all researchers agree that CCs are not using any of the known formulae for calculating dates (see, e.g., Spitz, 1994, for a discussion of the algorithms discovered by Lewis Carrol). This is because the basic arithmetic calculations required by these formulae have been shown to be outside the competence of most CCs. Further, these formulae can be used to calculate days from dates but not to answer questions that CCs can, such as name dates on which specific days (e.g., the second Saturday in March) will fall.

One hypothesis with some experimental support is that CCs make use of knowledge of rules and regularities of the calendar (Hermelin & N. O'Connor, 1986; N. O'Connor & Hermelin, 1984; A.M. Rosen, 1981). Examples of such rules are date/day mapping repeats every 28 years; certain months (e.g., April and July in nonleap years) share the same date/day mapping; in nonleap years the current date will fall on the following day the next year. It could be that if CCs know such facts (explicit knowledge) then they could be used to work out dates from say a detailed knowledge of the day/date mapping in the current year. There is little doubt that some CCs know some or all of these rules, because they have been explicitly stated by these subjects (N. O'Connor & Hermelin, 1984; A.M. Rosen, 1981; R.L. Young & Nettelbeck, in press). But is this knowledge the basis of their ability?

N. O'Connor and Hermelin (1984) studied eight CCs with IQs ranging between 47 and 88. Their basic technique was to measure the response times to produce days when presented with dates. The dates used all bore some systematic relationship to rules of the calendar. For example, could the subjects make use of the 28-year rule and the fact that the date/day mapping was repeated in certain months? It turns out that subjects take longer to respond the further the date is from the current year (either forward or backward) but years that fell 28 years from the year of testing were disproportionately fast, thereby supporting this hypothesis. Further, this group of CCs did show facilitation when dates were repeated for months with the same date/day mapping. This evidence is consistent with the idea that the use of such knowledge is central to their ability. However, R.L. Young and Nettelbeck (1994), in a study of three CCs found little evidence for the use of such knowledge (rules and regularities) in performance. They suggested that the performance of their subjects is based on their detailed knowledge of perpetual calendars. Such devices take advantage of the fact that there are only 14 basic templates for date/day mappings. Particularly telling is the finding that the accuracy of day identification was closely tied to the years spanned by the particular perpetual calendars in their possession. So perhaps it is the case that some CCs with higher IQs can abstract knowledge of the calendar, but it is not likely that this knowledge is the basis of their ability. If it is not then what is?

Norris (1990) conjectured that calendrical calculation may be based on a pattern association mechanism commonly used in connectionist architectures. Norris demonstrated using simulations that a multilayered network after extensive training was capable of recognizing days from dates, even for dates in the future and for dates with which it had not been trained. In such a network there is no explicit representation of rules and regularities, performance being based on repeated exposure to particular calendars with passive generalization to any novel date presented. Interestingly, R.L. Young and Nettelbeck (1994) reported that their subjects were slow to learn associations in a memory task, *but* their delayed recall of material was vastly superior to that predicted either by their rate of learning or by their intelligence. We are left, then, with an image of individuals with a great interest in calendars (for reason or reasons unknown) whose detailed knowledge of specific calendars is represented in a connectionist memory system that allows CCs to produce answers when presented with dates. Calculation or rules are not used in this production. If this is so, then their ability is an implicit ability and, consequently, not at odds with their intelligence. In terms of the minimal cognitive architecture outlined previously, CCs perform this feat using a modular process that is independent of their intelligence. But is this so for all kinds of savant calculators?

Hermelin and N. O'Connor (1990) investigated the calculating ability of an autistic young man, M.A., of very low measured intelligence who is able to factorize numbers, that is, to reduce composite numbers (nonprimes) to their prime divisors. M.A. has a nonverbal IQ of 67 and virtually no speech or communication (his verbal

IQ is unscorable). His performance when factorizing numbers was remarkable; he accurately factored 70% of the numbers greater than 10,000 in an average time of 38.2 seconds (compared with 40% accuracy and average time of 48 seconds in a mathematically trained control subject). In a subsequent study where reaction times to primes and nonprimes were measured, Anderson, O'Connor, and Hermelin (in press) showed that M.A. performs this feat by implementing a strategy that involves genuine calculation.

The Greek astronomer and mathematician, Eratosthenes (3rd century B.C.) discovered an algorithm for determining whether or not a number is prime. Any target number should be divided by all the prime numbers less than or equal to the square route of the target number. If a target number cannot be divided without a remainder then it is prime. For example, if the target number were 67 then it would be divided by the primes 2, 3, 5, 7, none of which do so without a remainder, whereupon we can be sure it is a prime number. By a careful analysis of M.A.'s response times and by comparing his performance to that of mathematics students who reported using this strategy and with computer simulations of this strategy, Anderson et al. concluded that this was the strategy that M.A. uses.

In the current context this result is important. It shows that the ability relies on calculation and not on memory. That there is no pattern to the series of primes makes it impossible, in any case, to recognize previously unseen primes by generalizing from the body of already seen primes. In contrast with the CCs discussed earlier, M.A. seems to be using a complex rule that requires calculating abilities comparable to that of mathematics students. In short, in terms of the theory of the minimal cognitive architecture outlined previously, M.A.'s performance requires thought and as such requires "intelligence" for its implementation. Consistent with this are the additional facts that M.A.'s speed of processing as measured by an inspection time task is in the above-average range (M. Anderson, 1992b) and that in contrast to his general psychometric profile, M.A.'s performance on Raven's Progressive Matrices is equivalent to that of someone with an IQ of at least 128. Again, we have consistency. M.A.'s performance suggests rule-based strategies that can be explicitly represented and require (in some sense) intelligence—and at least in terms of speed of processing he can be said to possess the necessary "intelligence."

CONCLUSION

Psychometric theories of intelligence have little to say about the implicit/explicit distinction, but the nature of intelligence tests themselves acknowledge the importance of explicit knowledge and problem-solving strategies. More modern information-processing theories such as those of Hunt and Sternberg again tend to associate intelligence with explicit knowledge and strategies. Consistent with this view, Reber (1989a) claimed that implicit processes are unrelated to individual differences in IQ, and Hasher and Zacks (1984) claimed this for automatic processes.

With the aid of the theory of the minimal cognitive architecture (M. Anderson, 1992b) we can now answer the three pivotal questions concerning intelligence and implicit processing given earlier:

1. Is intelligence synonymous with knowledge and if so is this in the main explicit or implicit knowledge? Intelligence is not synonymous with knowledge, but knowledge that is associated with intelligence can be made explicit (having been acquired through thought processes), whereas implicit knowledge is not associated with intelligence (being acquired through modules).
2. Are differences in intelligence associated with differences in basic information-processing components or with differences in higher order strategic processes? Intelligence is associated with both, although the latter depend on the former.
3. Is intelligence associated only with conscious thought and not at all with evolutionarily older implicit knowledge acquisition mechanisms? Yes, with the caveat that although the thought process does not have to be conscious, it has the capability of being so.

11

THE AUTOMATICITY OF DISCOURSE COMPREHENSION

Craig Speelman
Edith Cowan University

To what extent are the processes that underlie discourse comprehension open to inspection during their operation? Certainly nothing is revealed when we try to follow the process whereby marks on a page are translated into meaning. Such attempts can even interfere with comprehension. Intuition and careful reflection reveal little as well, as is attested to by the existence of a vast research literature describing scientific attempts to uncover the nature of comprehension processes. This might suggest that discourse comprehension is a completely automatic process, with no conscious control or awareness. The extent to which this is the case is the topic of this chapter.

The comprehension of discourse is a complicated process. The entire process from signal perception to final comprehension involves many subprocesses, the study of which comprises most of modern cognitive psychology. These subprocesses include the perception of speech sounds and letters, syntactic parsing, determining the meanings of individual words, making connections between concepts in different sentences, and making inferences about information not explicitly stated. At each point along this path, processes can be identified that apparently run completely without awareness. For instance, when we read a text, it is not obvious how we make sense of the marks on the page. Somehow we are able to interpret these marks and combine them into something meaningful; first into words, then phrases and sentences, and finally into a plausible interpretation of what the writer had in mind at the time of writing the text. What is extraordinary about this achievement is that it is executed completely without awareness of the many different processes that result in this final interpretation. For example, it is not a necessary feature of comprehension to be aware of the processing that is involved in determining whether an oval-shaped character on the page is the letter *o*, or a zero, or part of the letter *a*. Nor is it obvious how context helps us to disambiguate the meaning of *bank* as a money institution or the side of a river while we are doing so. Instead the meaning of discourse appears to pop into our head virtually as we see or hear it, apparently with very little effort on our part except that associated with paying attention to the signal. This chapter reviews some of the subprocesses that underlie the apparently magical process of discourse comprehension, the means by which their presence has been revealed, and the extent to which these processes can be said to proceed automatically or are under some form of strategic control.

IMPLICIT AND EXPLICIT PROCESSES
IN DISCOURSE COMPREHENSION

The research literature on discourse comprehension virtually ignores the distinction between implicit and explicit processes. The fact that, until recently (e.g., McKoon & Ratcliff, 1992), there has been little consideration of whether a discourse comprehension process was automatic or controlled reveals that the general issue of awareness has been considered almost irrelevant. The concept of memory being implicitly or explicitly addressed during comprehension is not considered. Whether comprehension involves any implicit or explicit learning is not discussed, although implicit learning is often suggested as a means by which grammatical knowledge is acquired (e.g., Reber et al., 1980). The notion that discourse comprehension is opaque to introspection because it is a form of implicit expertise is rarely discussed. To do so would require consideration of the acquisition of such a skill and in the discourse processes literature this is not considered either (although see Tunmer & Chapman, chap. 21 of this volume). Comprehension is studied as if it is a static system not subject to the effects of experience. As is discussed later, however, to consider discourse comprehension as an acquired skill may be a useful means of revealing its nature. The terms *implicit* and *explicit* are most often used only in the context of whether information has been explicitly stated in discourse or whether it is implied and therefore should be inferred during comprehension. Thus, because of the history of research in this area, it is difficult to consider directly how comprehension might be viewed with respect to an implicit/explicit processes distinction. As a result, this chapter reviews some of the research on discourse comprehension with the aim of determining the degree to which some of the processes involved in comprehension can be viewed as automatic processes, or processes that involve some degree of strategic control.

Two different types of discourse processes are examined to determine the extent to which they can be considered automatic. The first type of process is concerned with the basic structure of sentences, such as the syntactic structure and the lexical constituents. These processes are discussed with respect to the controversial issue of whether they represent modular processes, which encompasses the automatic/strategic issue. The second type of discourse process is concerned with inferences beyond the individual word level. These inferences typically are required during comprehension in order to fill the gaps between what is said and what is meant. The issue discussed here concerns whether these inferences are made automatically or whether they are under strategic control.

MODULAR PROCESSES IN
DISCOURSE COMPREHENSION

Running through the automatic versus strategic nature of comprehension is an associated issue concerning the modularity of language processes. A number of theorists (e.g., see Garfield, 1987) claim that various processes involved in comprehension are modular in the Fodorian sense (Fodor, 1983). This means that the processes are informationally encapsulated and mandatory. The thrust of this claim, then, is that these processes are only capable of processing particular types of information, are not affected by other processes, and once initiated, will proceed automatically to completion. Evaluating whether language processes possess these features is thus important in determining whether language modules exist. However, these features are the same as those identified by Shiffrin and Schneider (1977; Schneider & Shiffrin, 1977) as defining automatic processes. Thus, evaluating whether language processes are modular is equivalent in many respects to determining whether they are automatic.

Are Language Processes Informationally Encapsulated?

A module is said to be informationally encapsulated when it can process one particular type of information but is unable to process other forms of information. In other words, information flows in one direction through a system of modules: A module will receive and operate on its particular type of information, and then pass on the information in its processed form to be operated on by another module. Thus modules operate autonomously of other modules. For example, in the language system syntactic processes are considered autonomous from semantic processes in the sense that semantic information cannot impact on syntactic processes. However, these modules are considered hierarchical so that higher level processes (e.g., semantic) receive and operate on information from lower level processes (e.g., syntactic).

Proponents of the modular view claim that the syntactic module processes discourse with respect to a number of syntactic rules. In most circumstances these rules perform satisfactorily, resulting in correctly parsed phrases and sentences. However, in some situations these rules return an inappropriate parse that leads to a temporary break in the flow of comprehension. Such disruptions in comprehension are considered favorable to the existence of a syntactic module. Typical demonstrations of disruptions in comprehension use "garden-path" sentences, so called because the early part of the sentence suggests to readers a phrase structure parsing that turns out to be inappropriate at some later point in the sentence. For example, consider the following sentences:

The defendant examined by the lawyer turned out to be unreliable.   **(1)**

The evidence examined by the lawyer turned out to be unreliable.   **(2)**

The initial part of Sentence 1 is temporarily ambiguous up to "by." "The defendant examined" could mean the defendant was doing the examining, or it could mean that the defendant had been examined by some other agent. The most common interpretation is the former. Proponents of the modular view claim that the reason for this bias is that the syntactic module uses the minimal attachment principle as one of its parsing rules (Clifton & Ferreira, 1987). This principle states that each new item in a sentence will be interpreted so as to minimize the number of new syntactic phrase nodes required at that point in the sentence. Thus, "examined" is interpreted to be part of a verb-phrase involving "the defendant," rather than as a reduced relative verb that leads to the expectation of an agent being specified later in the sentence. Although this principle leads to an incorrect parse in this instance, most of the time it generates the correct solution.

The crux of the modular argument with respect to sentences like 1 and 2 concerns the extent to which information other than syntactic information encroaches on the parsing process. If the syntactic parsing process is modular it should be informationally encapsulated, and therefore only sensitive to syntactic information. In that case, readers should be equally likely to be led "down the garden path" in Sentences 1 and 2 because they share the same syntactic structure. If, on the other hand, there is no syntactic module, then readers should be affected by the additional information present in these sentences. In Sentence 1, "defendant" is an animate noun and so can both "examine" and "be examined by." Thus, the nature of this noun could not be used as a cue to the correct parse. In contrast, in Sentence 2 "evidence" is an inanimate noun and therefore cannot "examine." This pragmatic information could be used as a cue in the parsing process. The modular view, however, states that the syntactic module cannot process such pragmatic information, and so will process both sentences according to the same principle, resulting in equivalent disruptions to reading.

Ferreira and Clifton (1986) investigated whether subjects' reading of sentences like 1 and 2 is affected by pragmatic factors. On the basis of eye movement data, they found that reading was disrupted at the phrase "by the lawyer" in both sentences. This disruption was associated with subjects finding it necessary to reparse the sentence after they realized that the original parse was inappropriate. Ferreira and Clifton reported that this disruption occurred to an equal extent in both sentences.

They claimed that this result demonstrates that syntactic processes are insensitive to pragmatic information, which supports the autonomous nature of syntactic processes. Others have reported similar results and conclusions (Frazier, 1987; Perfetti, Beverly, Bell, Rodgers, & Faux, 1987; Rayner, Carlson, & Frazier, 1983).

Doubt exists as to whether sentences such as 1 and 2 are suitable for testing the autonomy of syntactic processes. Crain and Steedman (1985) claimed that these sentences in isolation are unnatural. In natural discourse, nouns being referred to for the first time, and of which the comprehender is not already aware, normally are introduced with an indefinite article (e.g., *a*) rather than the definite article (i.e., *the*). This is a linguistic device that conforms to what H.H. Clark and Haviland (1977) referred to as the "given/new principle" of communication: Entities that are new to the discourse are referred to differently to those that are old or given. In the view of Crain and Steedman, Sentences 1 and 2 do not carry as much contextual information as they could if they were embedded in natural discourse. Such discourse would introduce the "defendant" and "evidence" entities prior to Sentences 1 and 2 such that referring to them with the definite article in these sentences would not violate the given/new principle. The reader then would know what defendant or evidence the writer was referring to in these sentences. Furthermore, according to Crain and Steedman, this information would contribute to the pragmatic information already available in these sentences. If syntactic processing can be affected by information other than syntactic, then embedding garden-path sentences in discourse in this way should increase the likelihood of detecting contextual effects.

Altmann (1987; Altmann & Steedman, 1988) has examined reading times of garden-path sentences in natural discourse and obtained results that suggest syntactic decisions are not made in isolation of pragmatic and contextual information. A number of others also have reported results consistent with the suggestion that context can override syntactic parsing preferences (Britt, Perfetti, Garrod, & Rayner, 1992; Rayner, Garrod, & Perfetti, 1992). These results suggest that the set of processes responsible for syntactic analyses of discourse are not informationally encapsulated and therefore may not constitute a module. However, this issue is still controversial. Some researchers continue to report no effects of context on parsing and others report the opposite. Some attempt to reconcile these differences by suggesting that they are related to the particular methodology used, such as eye movements or reading times (e.g., Rayner et al., 1992), whereas others consider the types of discourse materials used may be responsible (e.g., Britt et al., 1992).

Another set of results may be illuminating with respect to the elusiveness of context effects. Just and Carpenter (1992) reported that subjects were able to make use of pragmatic information in syntactic decisions in sentences like 1 and 2, only if they possessed a large working-memory capacity. Subjects' capacity was assessed by performance on the Reading Span test (Daneman & Carpenter, 1980). Just and Carpenter found that subjects with a high reading span were less likely to be led down the garden path in sentences like 2 than low-span subjects. According to Just and Carpenter, high-span subjects possess a greater working-memory capacity and therefore have a greater ability to consider pragmatic information when making syntactic decisions. Just and Carpenter concluded that this result demonstrates that typical garden-path effects are not the result of an informationally encapsulated syntactic module. Instead, they claimed, the syntactic encapsulation often exhibited by subjects is due to a capacity constraint.

At the very least, the results referred to here demonstrate that contextual and pragmatic information can affect parsing but may not do so in all situations. This, of course, weakens the claim for a syntactic module, and therefore the possibility that syntactic processing is automatic. It also raises the question of how processes can appear to be both modular in some situations and nonmodular in others. This question is considered at the end of this section. However, Just and Carpenter's (1992) claims that some modularlike behavior may result from capacity constraints is an interesting form of explanation, where processes possess modular characteristics for reasons other than they are modular. Another hypothesis of this sort is considered later.

Are Language Processes Mandatory?

Another defining feature of modules is they are mandatory. That is, once a module receives information that corresponds to its specific requirements, this information will be processed automatically. For example, if the lexical module receives "bank" in discourse, it will automatically process it as the word *bank* by generating all of its possible meanings for higher level modules to process. This generation of multiple meanings for words is considered "dumb" in that it is insensitive to the comprehender's current goals or the current context. Thus even though the discourse may be concerned with financial institutions, in response to "bank" the lexical module will generate both "place where money is deposited" and "ground at edge of body of water" (Carpenter & Just, 1989; Frazier, 1987). A number of studies have reported results consistent with this suggestion (e.g., Kintsch & Mross, 1985; Swinney, Onifer, Prather, & Hirschkowitz, 1979). However, other studies have failed to observe the activation of multiple meanings for ambiguous words (e.g., Duffy, R. Morris, & Rayner, 1988; Foss & Ross, 1983; Tabossi, 1988a), or even the activation of various aspects of the meaning of unambiguous words (i.e., gold is both yellow and malleable; Tabossi, 1988b). This conflict in results may be associated with the delay between presentation of a word and testing for activation of multiple meanings (Tabossi, 1988a). There are some reports that irrelevant meanings are activated for as little as 300 milliseconds (Seidenberg, Tanenhaus, Leiman, & Bienkowski, 1982; Swinney, 1979), whereas intended meanings remain active for at least 1 second, and even longer if it is reinforced by subsequent information (Carpenter & Just, 1989). Alternatively, the conflict may result from the use of different materials in different studies. Tabossi (1988a) suggested that some studies that failed to demonstrate context effects used materials that, despite providing a context in which ambiguous words could be interpreted, were not sufficiently constraining for disambiguation. Thus an overall view of this research does not support the hypothesis that accessing a word's meaning from the lexicon is automatic in the sense that all meanings are accessed simultaneously. Furthermore, other results have been reported that conflict with any suggestion that this process is mandatory.

Fodor (1983) claimed that we cannot avoid processing linguistic input as language, that once activated, language processes are mandatory. But what does this mean with respect to lexical processes? Does it mean that, as suggested previously, every time an ambiguous word is presented, no matter what the context, all of its meanings are activated? Two pieces of evidence suggest otherwise. The first concerns the finding that semantic priming is attenuated when words are processed nonsemantically, such as counting the number of syllables in a word (Parkin, 1979; M.C. Smith, Theodor, & Franklin, 1983). Thus, all meanings of a word are not necessarily activated automatically on presentation of the word. Furthermore, there appear to be situations where words can be processed in a manner isolated from their meaning. The second piece of evidence against mandatory lexical processing concerns the second presentation of an ambiguous word in discourse. Foss and Speer (1991) proposed that when an ambiguous word is first encountered in discourse all meanings of the word are activated. Context does not have an immediate effect on disambiguating the meaning of the word. However, in passages where such words were encountered a second time, Foss and Speer were unable to find any evidence for the activation of multiple meanings. Instead, they claimed that the only information to be activated by such words is associated with the entity set up in the ongoing discourse model to represent the word. That is, after the ambiguous word is encountered, the intended meaning is eventually selected on the basis of information in the passage. This meaning is represented in the reader's discourse model along with other relevant information associated with that word in the passage. When this word is subsequently encountered in the discourse, it is the intended meaning plus associated discourse information that is activated. Thus, the information activated in this situation is context-dependent.

As was noted with respect to the modular nature of syntactic processes, lexical processes apparently possess modular characteristics in some situations only. It is not the case that all meanings of a polysemous word are activated automatically on presentation of the word. Sometimes the context within which the presentation occurs can affect what is activated. Again, as with syntactic processes, it is necessary to consider how lexical processes can appear both modular and nonmodular.

Summary and Conclusions on Modularity

The modular conception of language processes is controversial but is important with respect to the automatic/strategic issue. For example, evidence that lower level processes can be affected by higher level information (e.g., context effects in syntactic parsing; Britt et al., 1992) calls into question the modular nature of language processes, and therefore suggests that apparently automatic processes can be strategically controlled. Thus, evidence of this kind suggests that many language processes that appear to be modular may, in some circumstances, be open to strategic control and therefore may not be modular in the strict sense. Such phenomena raise the question of how processes can be appear to be both modular and nonmodular. As suggested earlier, the nature of such processes may be revealed by considering their development. For instance, language processes may acquire their modular aspect with experience in a manner akin to the development of domain-specific skills as described by Anderson's ACT* theory (J.R. Anderson, 1983; see Speelman & Maybery, chap. 5 of this volume). In other words, the large amounts of experience adults have had comprehending language has led to the development of an overlearned skill, which is automatic in a lot of respects, but has been developed to be flexible in response to the nature of the problem.

INFERENCES DURING COMPREHENSION:
AUTOMATIC OR STRATEGIC?

In order to comprehend discourse, we must perform a substantial amount of processing on the input signal. The meaning of an utterance is rarely a simple function of the combination of the meanings of individual words. Rather, words and their meanings are merely the initial input to a complicated process. This process involves listeners and readers performing many forms of inference in order to fill the gaps inherent in discourse. Such gaps are a reflection of the efficiency of language in conveying information: Speakers/writers and their listeners/readers share similar knowledge about what does and does not need to be said. When constructing a message, we take into account this shared knowledge and shape the message to provide pointers to which knowledge is necessary for comprehension of the new information that is being stated. Listeners and readers will need to detect those cues in order to fill in the gaps between what is said or written, and what is meant. Consider the following example:

We checked the picnic supplies.

The beer was warm.

As mentioned earlier in this chapter, when a concept is referred to in discourse by the use of the definite article *the* it usually means that the concept has been introduced earlier in the discourse. However, in this example, "the beer" is encountered in the second sentence without beer being mentioned previously. We are not surprised by the introduction of a term with the definite article in this situation, though, because in the context of "picnic supplies" beer is a predictable entity. When "the beer" is encountered, we infer that this refers to a constituent of "the picnic supplies." Thus, although beer was not explicitly referred to as part of the picnic supplies, our knowledge of picnics enabled us to draw this inference, which further enabled us to realize the connection between the two sentences.

There is nothing controversial about the observation that inferences form a major part of comprehension. Certainly there are many situations where it would be impossible to comprehend sentences on the basis of the words and their individual meanings alone. However, what is not clear about these inferences is the extent to which they are performed automatically. Some inferences are so complicated and yet are performed so quickly and effortlessly, that it seems unlikely they could involve any form of strategic control without serious disruption to the flow of comprehension. One type of inference that is commonly performed during comprehension is considered in this section in terms of whether it is routinely performed automatically or whether there is room for strategic control.

Anaphoric Reference

One of the simplest forms of inference made during comprehension is that involved in realizing that various noun phrases refer to the same entity. For example, consider the following passage:

Susan walked passed a park on the way to the shops.

She marveled at the color of the leaves on the trees.

The process of determining that the person referred to as "she" in the second sentence is the same person referred to as "Susan" in the first sentence appears to be a trivial one. The process often is seen as an extension of the processes that determine the meanings of individual words: The majority of words refer to concepts that are new in the context of discourse, whereas anaphors refer to concepts that have already been invoked. Most of the time, we seem unaware of having to make such inferences during comprehension, and rarely are we required to think about who or what an anaphor, such as "she," might refer to. Does this lack of awareness of the processes involved in anaphoric reference indicate that they are automatic? Certainly the apparent unconscious nature of these processes has suggested to some that resolution of anaphora is automatic in the sense that encountering some form of anaphor automatically will lead to identification of its referent earlier in the discourse (see S.B. Greene, McKoon, & Ratcliff, 1992).

If the resolution of anaphoric reference is an automatic process, then the process should be characterized by other features in addition to being unavailable to conscious awareness. For example, the identification of a referent should be almost immediate. Certainly anaphoric reference is considered an online process where readers and listeners are attempting to integrate new information as it is encountered (Garrod & Sanford, 1977). Many studies have demonstrated resolution times of the order of 800 milliseconds (e.g., Dell, McKoon, & Ratcliff, 1983; Speelman & Kirsner, 1990). Furthermore, if the process is automatic, encountering an anaphor should result in an obligatory identification of the appropriate referent. That is, the process is stimulus-driven and involuntary. This suggests that the ease of resolution should be unaffected by factors associated with the structure of discourse. So, the physical distance (e.g., the number of words, phrases, clauses, or sentences) between an anaphor and its referent should not affect resolution ease and this typically is found (Oakhill, Garnham, & Vonk, 1989). However, resolution ease is affected by a number of other features of discourse structure, such as sentence voice (Speelman & Kirsner, 1990), the nature of the verb relating potential antecedents (Oakhill et al., 1989), and the grammatical position in which the antecedent of an anaphor appears in the discourse (Oakhill et al., 1989).

The conflicting evidence as to the obligatory nature of anaphoric reference should lead to the conclusion that the resolution process is not automatic. However, it is possible that the factors affecting the ease of resolution of anaphoric reference, in fact, are affecting the accessibility of antecedents in discourse memory. Consider the fact that whenever anaphoric reference is examined experimentally, responses to antecedents are examined as a function of the presence or absence of some anaphoric reference to them. These responses are collected after presentation of the anaphor and typically involve subjects being required to produce the appropriate antecedent or recognize that a test word was part of the preceding discourse, where the test word could be the antecedent of the anaphor. As a result of these testing procedures, responses to the antecedents may reflect features of the resolution process, but they may also reflect characteristics of the discourse representation of the antecedents (Speelman & Kirsner, 1990). Thus, from such results, it is difficult to draw any conclusions about the automaticity of the resolution process.

S.B. Greene et al. (1992) regarded some types of anaphoric reference as involving automatic identification of a unique referent. They suggested that experiments, such as those reported by Dell et al. (1983), demonstrate evidence of this automatic process. In these experiments subjects read brief passages (see Table 11.1) and then were required to make recognition judgments on test words presented at the end of each passage. The test words were presented at some point during the last sentence. This sentence contained an anaphor (e.g., the criminal) that referred to an entity encountered earlier in the passage (e.g., a burglar). The test word was either the word describing this entity (burglar) or a word that was mentioned in the same proposition as the initial mention of the referent (garage). Dell et al. reported that when test words followed anaphors, recognition of referents was facilitated compared to when testing followed a control phrase (e.g., "A cat" in place of "The criminal"). Furthermore, recognition of the associates of referents also was facilitated following anaphoric reference. Dell et al. concluded that encountering an anaphor leads to the activation of its antecedent in the discourse, increasing the accessibility of referents in the representation of the discourse. This increased accessibility facilitates the recognition of referents when they are used as test words. Furthermore, Dell et al. suggested that an anaphoric reference actually involves the activation of the representation of the proposition relating the referent to its associate, thus increasing the accessibility of the associates as well. Greene et al. considered that this increase in the accessibilities of concepts following anaphoric reference reflects an automatic process of activation.

Despite the existence of results of the type reported by Dell et al. (1983), S.B. Greene et al. (1992) claimed that resolution of anaphoric reference is not always automatic. They described situations where the identification of one unique referent does not always occur. For example, consider the passage in Table 11.2. If resolution of anaphoric reference is automatic, encountering "she" in the third sentence of this passage would result in an increase in the accessibility of its referent (Mary) in the discourse representation, resulting in facilitated recognition for this word compared to the nonreferent (John). However, Greene et al. reported that, in passages like the one presented in Table 11.2, neither referents nor nonreferents were facilitated by the presence of an anaphor. Thus no unique referent is identified in response to the anaphor. This result means that anaphors do not always activate their referents and so undermines any claim that the resolution of anaphoric reference is automatic.

There is a major difference between the passages used in S.B. Greene et al.'s (1992) study and the types of passages used in previous work that has demonstrated results consistent with automatic resolution of anaphoric reference. In most of the previous work, it can be argued that the referent to the anaphor is part of the focus of attention of the discourse. In normal discourse, entities that comprise this focus are more likely to be referred to later, and so are foregrounded in memory to increase their accessibility to subsequent reference (S.B. Greene et al., 1992; Morrow, 1985). In the passages used by Greene et al., there are two entities in the focus of attention

TABLE 11.1

An Example of the Passages Used in the Study by Dell, McKoon, and Ratcliff (1983)

Test Words: burglar (referent of anaphor)
                garage (associate of referent)
A burglar surveyed the garage set back from the street. Several milk bottles were piled at the curb. The banker and her husband were on vacation. The criminal slipped away from the streetlamp.

TABLE 11.2

An Example of the Passages Used in the Study by S. B. Greene, McKoon, and Ratcliff (1992)

Test Words: Mary (referent)
                John (nonreferent)
Mar y and John were doing the dishes after dinner. One of them was washing while the other dried. Mary accidentally scratched John with a knife and then she dropped it on the counter.

(see Table 11.2). Despite the obvious gender cues, Greene et al.'s results indicate that the accessibilities of both entities were unaffected by the encounter with the anaphor. This suggests that both entities are potential referents. According to Greene et al., the differences in passages and associated results suggests that anaphor resolution is not automatic in the sense that a unique referent is always identified immediately on encountering an anaphor. However, they argued that the process is automatic in that the proposition containing the anaphor is connected immediately to whatever is in the current focus of attention of discourse. Depending on the goals of the reader, or the demands of the situation, the reader may proceed with strategic processing to determine what, if anything, in the current focus is suitable as a referent.

This model accounts well for the fact that ease of identification of referents can be affected by grammatical position, the nature of the verb relating potential antecedents, and context (Oakhill et al., 1989). All of these factors have effects on the extent to which an entity is perceived to be part of the discourse focus (S.B. Greene et al., 1992). Thus if an entity is not part of the current focus then reference to it may be difficult to resolve (Speelman & Kirsner, 1990).

In summary, the unique identification of a referent following an anaphor appears to be an automatic process in some situations but not in others. This suggests a question similar to one considered earlier with respect to syntactic and lexical processes: How can processes appear to be both automatic and nonautomatic? Again the answer may lie in consideration of the development of such processes. S.B. Greene et al. (1992) made the point that many of the experiments that demonstrate nonautomatic resolution of anaphoric reference typically use abnormal forms of discourse. They argued that anaphoric reference is used most often in situations where there is one concept in the current discourse focus (e.g., see Table 11.1). Thus listeners and readers would have considerable experience at resolving anaphoric reference in such situations. Such situations, where the anaphor is attached to whatever concept is in the current focus, can be described as involving consistent mapping between stimulus and response. This type of situation is associated most often with the potential to develop automatic processing (Schneider & Shriffin, 1977; Shiffrin & Schneider, 1977). The extensive practice listeners and readers receive with these types of anaphoric reference may explain the apparent automatic nature of the processing. In contrast, situations that involve more than one potential referent in the current focus (e.g., see Table 11.2), or that feature anaphors that refer to concepts outside of the current focus, are less typical forms of discourse. Thus readers and listeners will not have much practice dealing with this form of discourse. Furthermore, the experience they have will involve varied mappings between stimuli and responses (i.e., each situation will not always result in the same solution). This is because the resolution process may require substantial inference to determine which entity is the appropriate referent. Practice with tasks involving varied mappings is much less likely to lead to automatic processing than with tasks involving consistent mappings (Schneider & Shriffin, 1977; Shiffrin & Schneider, 1977). Hence resolution of anaphoric reference in these types of situations will not be automatic. Therefore, a skill acquisition model of anaphoric reference can account for the apparent automatic and nonautomatic nature of the process.

CONCLUSIONS

Comprehension possesses three features that suggest it involves mainly automatic processes: (a) Much of comprehension takes place outside of awareness, (b) many comprehension processes are unaffected by context and so appear to be mandatory and data-driven, and (c) most of the comprehension process is very fast. That is, processing during comprehension appears to occur in real time, as the stimuli (i.e., words) are encountered. The major conclusion of this chapter, however, is that, despite these three features, many comprehension processes are not automatic. A number of processes were discussed that appear automatic in some contexts. However, in other situations these same processes appear open to strategic control or the influence of contextual factors. How such processes could appear to be both automatic and nonautomatic was considered from a skill acquisition perspective. This perspective proposes that discourse comprehension is a complex skill that we develop with extensive practice. The justification for this proposal relies on the fact that skilled behavior can be both automatic and flexible, depending on the situation. Skills that are acquired and executed in consistent environments typically result in automatic performance. However, when skills are acquired and executed in environments where conditions are not consistent, performance is more likely to require strategic control. As was described in this chapter, discourse comprehension appears automatic in situations that involve or suggest consistent mappings between discourse and interpretation. Examples include stereotypical forms of discourse that comprise common language usage, such as the use of anaphors to refer only to entities that are in the current focus of attention. Comprehension does not involve automatic processes when the mappings between discourse and interpretation are atypical. Such mappings often require context-specific inference (e.g., "The ham sandwich at Table 5 would like some dessert"). Therefore, comprehension is a good example of skilled behavior because it involves automatic processes when the situation requires routine performance, but is flexible when the situation is less stereotypical (see Speelman, chap. 8 of this volume). The important point to note here is that, as with all skills, the processing context determines which particular subprocesses of comprehension can be applied, and so determines when performance will appear automatic or controlled.

The proposal that discourse comprehension is a skill that involves both automatic and controlled processes accords well with other current views of comprehension. For example, Just and Carpenter (1992) have demonstrated that the efficiency of many processes in comprehension is determined by the working-memory capacity of readers. Just and Carpenter imposed extrinsic memory loads on their subjects during comprehension and found that various processes involved in comprehension collapsed or were adversely affected in both speed and accuracy, as a function of the subjects' memory span. If a subject's span was large then the effect was small or nonexistent, whereas when the span was small, the effect was large. A commonly cited feature of automatic processing is an insensitivity to the effects of extrinsic processing loads (Schneider & Shriffin, 1977; Shiffrin & Schneider, 1977). Thus, Just and Carpenter's results suggest that although many comprehension processes may appear automatic in their normal context, it is only when they are required to compete for resources with other processes that their lack of automaticity is evident. Furthermore, Just and Carpenter speculated that the extent to which discourse processes are automatic, and therefore affected by extrinsic processing loads, could be determined by the level of practice experienced by these processes. In a related vein, Yekovich, Walker, Ogle, and Thompson (1990) suggested that the capacity of a reader to draw inferences during comprehension is associated with the reader's level of knowledge of the text domain. Texts in specialist domains will automatically activate domain-specific knowledge in the expert. According to Yekovich et al., this leads to automatic inferences in some contexts and can release resources to enable further inferences (see also Morrow, Leirer, & Altieri, 1992). In this way, domain-specific expertise can compensate for low verbal ability in determining a reader's capacity to draw inferences during discourse comprehension.

To propose that discourse comprehension is a complex skill that develops with practice and that reflects experience in its limitations should not be a surprising claim. After all, the ability of children to comprehend and produce speech improves with age, and is a direct result of experience (i.e., children raised in English-speaking households learn to speak English). We cannot read prior to formal instruction, but we can after substantial effort and practice. However, the impression fostered by a great deal of research in this area is that comprehension is a reflection of the operations of fixed cognitive structures, automata that process restricted types of information and are unaffected by outside influences. Too much of the psycholinguistic literature ignores the fact that comprehension is a process that develops throughout life rather than a process that is fixed at some point in life. As has been demonstrated in this chapter, consideration of the development of processes involved in comprehension can lead to insights as to their nature.

12

CONTROL PROCESSES
IN PROSODY

Kathryn Hird
Curtin University of Technology

Kim Kirsner
University of Western Australia

This chapter is concerned with *prosody*. The term is usually used with reference to the suprasegmental properties of verbal communication. Terms such as *speech melody*, *intonation*, *speech rhythm*, *tone of voice*, and *stress* are also used to refer to these properties. Prosody involves variation in the acoustic properties of the speech signal that does not contribute to phonemic differentiation.

Three types of prosody merit consideration. The first, linguistic prosody, marks temporal boundaries between linguistic units, and it therefore contributes to segmental analysis. The second, pragmatic prosody, is used under conversational conditions to indicate turn taking, given/new distinctions, and other forms of communicative intent. The third, emotional prosody, identifies emotional states such as sadness and happiness. Both pragmatic and emotional prosody apply to suprasegmental analysis, the former at a macrostructural level, the latter at an even broader level involving the discourse as a whole.

The central argument in this chapter is that although prosody is subject to conscious control under exceptional conditions, it usually is used without awareness during language comprehension and production. Thus, although many of its functions are executed automatically, without cognitive cost, they are not "veiled."

Research involving prosody is fragmented. One tradition has focused on the relationship between fundamental frequency and linguistic boundaries, involving tone units and lexical stress for instance (Ladd, 1988). Another tradition has focused on physiological performance, concerning the relationship between the respiratory system and the acoustic signal (Lieberman, 1967). Yet another tradition has focused on the acoustic properties of speech, without reference to linguistic or pragmatic issues ('t Hart & R. Cohen, 1973). In broad terms, these traditions approach speech on a "bottom–up" or "data-driven" as distinct from "top–down" or "conceptually driven" basis. As yet, little consideration has been given to the cognitive factors that must anticipate and direct the selection and use of prosodic processes, or to the central issue behind this chapter—the more specific role of explicit and implicit processes in the control of prosody in speech production. This chapter has been drafted, therefore, to provide a platform for the application of ideas about explicit and implicit processes, and the operational concomitants of this contrast, to prosody.

The chapter includes a functional definition of prosody, a brief review of its physiology and physics, and a description of the relationship between these parameters. The chapter also includes a frame of reference describing (a) the way in which different types of prosody moderate the speech signal, (b) the relationship between the various types of prosody, and (c) the nature of the control processes that govern prosody, including a provisional description of the more specific roles of explicit and implicit processes.

DEFINITION, CLASSIFICATION, AND MEASUREMENT

Linguistic Prosody

According to Monrad-Krohn's (1947) classifications, linguistic prosody refers to those aspects of the acoustic signal that permit the listener to distinguish temporal boundaries. This classification includes syllable, word, phrase, clause, and sentence boundaries. The rhythm of spoken language also is coded in the language-specific patterns of stressed and unstressed syllables (Ladd, 1983). Not only are these rhythmic patterns involved in determining segment boundaries but the perception of these patterns is also crucial for some semantic distinctions. For example, con'tent and content' refer to different concepts. Con'tent refers to material inside a container or vessel. Content' refers to an emotional state. In written communication this distinction could be made only via contextual support.

The function of linguistic prosody is to flag segmental boundaries within the continuous acoustic signal. This is achieved by modulation of the relationship between the duration, intensity, and frequency throughout the vowels in utterance segments as well as the relative duration of pauses between phonemes and breath groups (Farnetani, Torsello, & Cosi, 1988).

Knowledge of the rules governing the use of linguistic prosody within a language permits the listener to identify lexical and morphological units. This information is essential for the perception of syllable, word, phrase, sentence, and boundaries around semantic units. The ability to identify boundaries is particularly useful when decoding low-frequency words, unfamiliar morphological combinations, or when the speech signal is degraded by background noise (Wingfield, Lombardi, & Sokol, 1984).

Without knowledge of the rules governing the segmentation of the acoustic signal, nonnative and novice language users, as well as those people with some forms of aphasia (Caramazza, 1984; Levelt, 1989; Luria, 1973), perceive connected speech as a continuous stream of sounds.

The manner in which native language users acquire expertise in the use of linguistic prosody is becoming a topic of considerable interest in the literature. There is evidence to suggest that infants as young as 6 months of age already have acquired knowledge about the prosodic rules of their native language (De Boysson-Bardies, Sagart, & Durand, 1984; Hirsh-Pasek et al., 1987; Jusczyk, Cutler, & Redanz, 1993; Mehler et al., 1988).

The ability to segment the acoustic signal may not be restricted to the implicit domain, however. As competent language users, adults are able to imitate different sounds, copy accents, and exaggerate production of the segmental boundaries. Consider, for example, accounts of "motherese," where parents exaggerate prosodic features of speech in order to enhance their infants' comprehension. Comedians such as John Cleese make their living out of portraying caricatures of others and exaggerating their speaking styles.

Is it necessary, however, to have conscious control over the parameters involved in the production of linguistic prosody in order to achieve these segmental deviations? As an alternative, for example, control could be achieved by a matching process in which speakers shape production to match auditory templates rather than by conscious manipulation of the components of the speech production mechanism.

Pragmatic Prosody

Pragmatic prosody refers to the adjustments in the acoustic signal that are interpreted in the context of a complete message rather than segment-by-segment modifications. It is therefore concerned with larger segments of the acoustic signal than those analysed for linguistic purposes. The acoustic signal corresponding to sentence boundaries (Ladd, 1988), breath groups (Lieberman, Katz, Jongman, Zimmerman, & M. Miller, 1985), or performance structures (Gee & Grosjean, 1983) has received considerable attention.

It is sometimes claimed that pragmatic prosody transmits information pertaining to the deep or implied message (Umeda, 1981). For example, listeners identify sarcasm when there is a complete mismatch between the prosodic message and the propositional message that is transmitted simultaneously. Communication of emphasis, given/new distinctions, interrogative/declarative distinctions, turn taking, and some forms of humor depend on the integration of information transmitted through both the propositional and prosodic components of spoken language.

Two assumptions have been adopted about the relationship between the segmental and suprasegmental aspects of communication. The first of these is that they involve independent channels. Thorsen (1983), for example, developed a model of prosody in which it is assumed that the prosodic pattern is defined by a separate process, and that prosody is added once the structure of the segmental message has been formulated. The alternative assumption is that the processes responsible for the propositional and pragmatic aspects of communication interact during an early stage of planning, when conditional and nonlinear integration occurs (Ladd & Cutler, 1983).

It is important to consider the proposition that pragmatic prosody is not simply carrying information that is largely redundant (Menn & Boyce, 1982), or simply coloring the propositional message, as is reported by some authors (e.g., Hauser & Fowler, 1992).

Emotional Prosody

Some authors ignore the distinction between pragmatic and emotional prosody. The distinction cannot be ignored for two reasons, however. First, their communicative functions are logically distinct. Second, whereas pragmatic prosody typically is defined with reference to specific macrostructural units, where this may comprise one syllable or many sentences, emotional prosody may be defined for a complete dialogue, lasting minutes or even hours.

The label *emotional prosody* may be misleading. The feature that arguably defines the examples of emotional prosody is that they are all moderated by the activity of the autonomic nervous system. Emotional prosody refers to the manner in which the speaker's emotional status is communicated through voice quality. It can be differentiated from pragmatic prosody in two ways. First, emotional prosody is difficult to control or modify at will and, second, emotional prosody may be indifferent to variables such as race, culture, and education (Frick, 1985; Ladd, Silverman, Tolkmitt, Bergmann, & Scherer, 1985; Scherer, 1986; Scherer, Ladd, & Silverman, 1984).

Scherer (1986) suggested that emotional prosody occurs in response to arousal or depression of general body functions. For example, if the body is preparing for fight or flight, the basic biological functions of the respiratory and laryngeal musculature take precedence to speech. When an individual attempts to control the effect of emotion on the body, the result is compromised voice quality and speech production giving way to the highly recognizable nervous, aggressive, or depressed tone of voice and speech style (Frick, 1985).

It should be noted that the preceding examples involve both reception and production issues. Thus, for a complete understanding of the given/new differentiation, for example, it is not sufficient to describe the processes that underpin prosodic variation during language production. It is also necessary to provide a description of the processes used by the listener to extract and use that information (Farnetani et al., 1988).

Overview

The four types of prosody have proved difficult to distinguish by acoustic methods. Prosodic variation normally carries all types of information concurrently. Definition of the way in which each communicative function is represented in the signal therefore becomes a difficult task (van Wijk, 1987). Furthermore, although prosodic and propositional information must be integrated by the receiver to establish the affective, emotional, and linguistic status of the message, the information-processing stage at which this occurs is unknown (Ladd & Cutler, 1983). However, development of a model describing the relationship between each type of prosody and the critical acoustic parameters, is crucial to the production of intelligible, synthesized speech for speech recognition systems as well as speech rehabilitation programs. The balance of this chapter is concerned primarily with pragmatic prosody. This bias was dictated by its central role in communication (Collier, 1990), and by our pretheoretical expectation that the most interesting questions about the role of explicit and implicit processes in prosody concern pragmatic function. It should not be inferred, however, that the authors regard questions about the contribution of explicit and implicit processes to the other types of prosody as unimportant.

METHODOLOGICAL ISSUES

Acoustic Measurement and Perceptual Salience

Prosody describes variations in the acoustic characteristics of voice. Voice is a complex and periodic sound wave. Acoustic analysis of voice, therefore, involves measurement of the frequency, intensity, and duration of the acoustic signal.

Early studies involving acoustic analysis of prosody typically reported changes in the average fundamental frequency throughout the utterance. The apparent perceptual salience of pitch in spoken language encouraged researchers to believe that most information was carried in the fundamental frequency of the acoustic signal (A. Cohen, Collier, & 't Hart, 1982). In addition, it was important to select only one of the acoustic parameters for analysis as the process is, or was, very time consuming.

Recent research has demonstrated that it may be necessary to extract information concerning the relationship between the acoustic parameters. Scherer (1986), for example, suggested that emotion may be transmitted through subtle variations in the patterns of energy distribution throughout the acoustic signal. The complexity of the analytic problem emerges in other ways. For example, differences between read and spontaneous speech (House, Rowe, & Standen, 1987), characterization of dysprosody following right hemisphere brain damage (Bryan, 1989; Ryalls & Behrens, 1988), and gender differences (Frick, 1985; Scherer, 1986) are in some instances apparent only when the standard deviation of frequency is analyzed or the spectral patterns are compared. To date there has been no clear mapping between changes in fundamental frequency and various emotions (i.e., happiness, sadness, anger), despite the fact that listeners usually can identify these emotions in conversation.

The relationship between the frequency and intensity of an acoustic signal also has been the topic of discussion. Many studies have demonstrated that there is a direct correlation between the two parameters and, therefore, they omit reference to intensity as it is thought to be redundant. The relationship between frequency and intensity in speech is not direct in all contexts, however, and the features that specify this diversion have not yet been identified (J.E. Atkinson, 1978; Pierrehumbert, 1979).

In summary, it is evident that improved access to software for acoustic analysis and increased speed of performing the task of acoustic analysis has led to changes in our understanding of the manner in which prosody is coded in the acoustic signal. Further research is required to develop understanding of the mapping relationships between variations in the acoustic signal, the role of perceptual salience, and communicative intent.

Measurement Units

The status of measurement units in the analysis of the acoustic signal has attracted considerable attention. The issue discussed previously, concerning the relationship between intonational contours and propositional elements, has focused on features of the acoustic signal such as intensity and frequency peaks, intensity and frequency troughs, fundamental frequency, variation of fundamental frequency, and duration of segments, clauses, sentences, pauses, and junctures (A. Cohen et al., 1982; Ladd, 1988; Vaissiere, 1983). Based largely on perceptual judgment, individual features have been selected as critical prosodic parameters in communication on the basis of their perceptual saliency. Emphasis, for example, is thought to be indicated by a rapid increase in the frequency of the stressed syllable of the key word (e.g., "I said *no!*"); and turn completion is thought to be signaled by an increase in duration of the vowel of the stressed syllable of the final word in an utterance (e.g., "That's about all I have to say right now...") (Farnetani et al., 1988).

It is our contention that this approach is predicated on the interesting but challengeable pretheoretical assumption that the problems of speech analysis will be solved by a bottom–up analysis, that is, by analysis of the acoustic signal in the absence of a process or cognitive model of communication. The message initially is segmented into linguistic units such syllables, words, phrases, clauses, and sentences. The aim of acoustic analysis then is to identify modulations that systematically correspond to these linguistic units and their perceptual boundaries. The top–down approach, by contrast, is not concerned with linguistic segmentation of the prosodic contour, but more broadly, with communicative intent and how this is reflected in modulation of the prosodic contour (Hauser & Fowler, 1992; Umeda, 1981).

The bottom–up and top–down approaches to the analysis of prosody are not necessarily mutually exclusive. The compound nature of the prosodic signal permits the listener to detect a number of different types of information simultaneously. That is, a listener may be able to detect syllable, word, phrase, and sentence boundaries of a verbal language only if they know the prosodic rules that mark these boundaries in the continuous acoustic signal. At the same time, the listener is also able to detect the mood of the speaker and the pragmatic intent of the speaker's message by applying the associated prosodic rules that govern communication of this information. The manner in which the listener decodes the various types of information must depend, therefore, on subtle modulations and novel interactions of the three acoustic parameters of intensity, frequency, and rate. Research investigating the effect of damage at specific sites within the brain on the ability to process complex acoustic signals allows conjecture on the way in which listeners may decode prosody in spontaneous speech.

THEORETICAL ISSUES

Early articles on prosody were motivated by diverse theoretical issues. Each discipline adopted its own research paradigm and methodology, making integration exceptionally difficult. For example, researchers involved in psychoacoustics focused on analytic technique (A. Cohen et al., 1982) and researchers involved in psycholinguistics focused on the relationship between acoustic and linguistic structure (Ladd, 1983). Neurologists and speech pathologists, motivated by acquired communication impairments in neurologically impaired patients, focused on issues concerning the lateralization of prosodic control (Ross, 1981; Ross, Edmondson, Seibert, & Homan, 1988). More recently, cognitive scientists have focused on the role of prosody in memory (Speer, Crowder & Thomas, 1993) as well as synthesized speech and speech recognition systems (S. Young, 1990).

The Relationship Between the Pragmatic and Propositional Channels

Perhaps the most important question concerns the form of the relationship between prosodic and propositional language processes. Suppose, for convenience, that prosodic and propositional information occupy separate channels. Is the information transmitted on these channels perfectly correlated, partially correlated, or independent? Put in other words, does prosody provide redundant, complementary, or independent information?

Ladd and Cutler (1983) advanced the idea that prosody is integral to the propositional message. The basic idea is that there is just one primary language processor, that this processor is responsible for defining the prosodic as well as propositional messages, and that the "two" messages are, therefore, complementary, if they are not actually identical. Ladd and Cutler also suggested that prosody is processed "online," an idea that has attracted considerable attention (e.g., Ladd, 1983).

The idea that the two channels are less than perfectly correlated has received much support from theoreticians. Halliday (1967) and Bolinger (1978), for example, suggested that intonational prominence is related to the communicative value of the parts of the message. According to Bolinger, each utterance includes two messages. The first message is in the words and involves the actual details of the topic. The second message is embedded in the speaker's prosody, and provides a further comment on the topic. It includes, for example, information about the relative importance of different parts of the message.

A stronger claim concerning the independence of prosody has been advanced by Menn and Boyce (1982). Based on detailed acoustic analysis of spontaneous conversation between parent–child dyads, they suggested that prosodic information may be "noncongruent" as distinct from "parallel" with the propositional message.

The dual-channel approach also has been supported in the psycholinguistic literature. This support is based on the nonverbal character of prosody and indirect evidence that it is used to impart a separate message. Vaissiere (1983) proposed that prosody is processed *in parallel* to the propositional message, and that it serves to embellish the critical message encoded in semantic and syntactic structure.

Menn and Boyce (1982) acknowledged that prosody could occur with or without awareness. They were interested in dialogue and, more particularly, the extent to which successive utterances involved correlated changes in pitch, for both intra- and interspeaker utterances. They concluded that pitch changes reflect or signal discourse structure, and that pitch and "text" (i.e., propositional language) sometimes convey different information. The intraspeaker findings have no implications for the present argument, however; evidence that pitch changes involving inter- speaker utterances are correlated suggests that prosody may be carried from speaker to speaker implicitly, without awareness.

Lieberman (1967) approached this problem from a physiological perspective. According to Lieberman, the basic prosodic unit spans a breath unit, and syntactic structures have developed to accommodate this physiological process. The prosodic units, therefore, are closely tied to both syntactic structures and breath units. This point of view has an interesting developmental corollary however. If prosody is used communicatively *prior* to the acquisition of propositional language, the traditional relationship between the propositional and prosodic functions must be modified or even reversed, with prosody being critical, if it is not preeminent. Braine recognized this problem in an early article (Braine, 1963), and proposed that prosodic structures provide building blocks for information units in communica- tion, a position that actually reverses the relationship between prosody and propo- sitional language. This idea has received renewed interest in developmental language research (Gerken, Jusczyk, & Mandel, 1994; Weismer & Hesketh, 1993).

The relationship between prosody and propositional language also has phyloge-netic implications. Braine's (1963) proposal that prosodic structures provide build-ing blocks for information units in communication is supported by recent evidence obtained by Hauser and Fowler (1992). Hauser and Fowler analyzed the calls of vervet monkeys. Using acoustic analysis, they found that declination of fundamen-tal frequency (observed over coherent units of an utterance in human speech) also may be observed in nonhuman primates. Hauser and Fowler suggested that this aspect of prosody reflects a natural function of the vocal tract, and that it plays an important role in communication for this reason. That is, the natural fall in fundamental frequency across a breath unit simply reflects the reduction in sub-glottal pressure as air is gradually expended by communicators, of all species.

Gerken et al. (1994) also addressed the bootstrapping account of language development, that is, the idea that the structure of language is learned by responding to the correlation between syntactic boundaries and prosodic changes. This idea does not have full support, however, as there is evidence demonstrating that prosodic changes do not map directly onto syntactic boundaries. Prosodic changes were shown to be independent of syntactic structure and reflect prosodic units referred to as phonological phrases (Gerken et al., 1994). These authors demon-strated that language learners needed to carry out active inferential processes across sentence boundaries and use other information in order to determine accurate syntactic representation.

If propositional and prosodic information use separate or even independent channels, it is possible that they are governed by different principles or organiza-tion and representation. This question identifies two very different approaches to research in this area. Under the derivative assumption, where prosody is a mere extension of the propositional system (e.g., Ladd, 1983), the analysis of prosody is constrained by the rules of syntax and semantics. Research predicated on the alternative assumption, that prosody is not a subordinate function, recently has been addressed in the cognitive literature. Speer et al. (1993) investigated the representation of the prosodic element of spoken language in an auditory memory task. They were interested in the relationship in memory between the verbal elements and the melodic or prosodic elements. They used a paradigm originally developed to test memory for the words and tunes of songs. Speer et al. proposed that there were three storage possibilities: (a) independent storage of the compo-nents, (b) holistic storage where the two components are thoroughly connected in perception and memory, and (c) integrated storage. Research into the memory of words and tunes of songs supported the integration theory where the two elements were related in memory and that one component was better recognized in the presence of the other.

In a series of three experiments, Speer et al. (1993) reported evidence to support the idea that prosody was an important and integral part of the ability to remember spoken information. They found that memory for prosody was good when it was used to disambiguate the syntactic form of an otherwise ambiguous sentence as well as when it was invoked to communicate subtle information. The idea that lexical or syntactic codes support prosodic information was not supported. Speer et al. found that prosody was maintained in memory even for strings of nonsense words, and the authors rejected the idea that prosodic information is redundant. They suggested instead that prosody is an integral part of memory representation.

Developmental Issues

Several questions about the contribution of prosody to the acquisition of communication skills in children merit detailed consideration. First, does prosodic skill precede propositional skill developmentally? Second, are the critical developmental features of prosody innate? Third, if prosodic skill does precede propositional skill, is it a prerequisite for the acquisition of effective communication; for the selection and control of communicative intent, for example? Fourth, are prosodic skills acquired explicitly, with conscious awareness, or implicitly, without conscious awareness? Fifth, as it is difficult to isolate exclusively prosodic contours in adult communication, is it possible to overcome this problem by studying the way in which prosody is used in the prelinguistic infant, that is, when it is his or her sole means of vocal communication?

Infants become successful communicators long before they are proficient in their use of propositional language forms. For example, infants can communicate a variety of emotions and moods before they utter their first word. A combination of gesture, prosody, and babble represents consistent communicative codes shared by the child and its caregiver (Owens, 1992). Single-word utterances in conjunction with a variety of prosodic contours also can be shown to encompass a variety of speech acts. That is, the infant is capable of initiating vocal discourse, turn taking, and terminating interaction without propositional language skills. Within that discourse, the infant is also able to communicate questions, commands, and statements without use of linguistic structures (Owens, 1992).

Some researchers have claimed that adult intonation plays a critical role in the way in which children acquire adult communication skills (e.g., Braine, 1963). Other workers have argued that the key elements of prosody are innate, and that they emerge according to a biological program during infancy. Lieberman (1967), for instance, claimed that the presence of basic synchronization between laryngeal muscles and the chest muscles leads to the production of the basic intonation contour for language.

Evidence to support the notion that prosodic rules may be learned and are essential for the development of propositional language skills comes from the analysis of early language models provided to infants by caregivers. Research has shown that caregiver speech contains prosodic cues that are exaggerated and synchronized with the propositional structure of language. This is in contrast to adult speech directed toward other adult speakers (Gerken et al., 1994).

In summary, infants are sophisticated in the use of some forms of prosody for communicative purposes long before they become proficient with the propositional rules of their native language. Less is known about the second question identified earlier, however, and it is possible that developmental changes in prosody reflect both maturational and modeling processes.

Relatively little has been published about the remaining questions, concerning the role of prosody in the acquisition of communicative skill, the way in which prosodic functions are integrated, or the relative contribution of explicit and implicit processes to the acquisition of prosody. Observation, and the available evidence, suggest, however, that prosodic skills may be acquired and exercised implicitly, before explicit acquisition and control strategies are recognized and mastered (Hirsh-Pasek et al., 1987).

Hemispheric Specialization

Three obvious questions merit consideration. First, are prosodic processes lateralized (Ryalls & Behrens, 1988)? Second, if prosodic processes are lateralized, does the pattern follow that observed for propositional language (Ross, 1981)? Third, if prosodic processes are lateralized, do the observed patterns have any implications for the nature of the underlying control processes, in regard to the nonconscious/conscious distinction for example?

It is interesting to note that the communicative value of prosody was identified only as a consequence of Monrad-Krohn's (1947) relatively recent reports about patients with disrupted prosody or "dysprosody." This suggests that prosodic information in normal verbal communication may be processed nonconsciously. It is only when listeners do not obtain information that they need for interpretation that they are aware of its routine role in communication. The implications of this argument are directly relevant to the central issue in this chapter; namely, whether prosody involves conscious or nonconscious control processes?

Early clinical studies suggested that the left hemisphere was, in most cases, the dominant hemisphere, and that it was generally responsible for propositional language functions. The left hemisphere typically was treated by Gazzaniga and other early authors as the seat of conscious awareness (e.g., Gazzaniga, 1989; Luria, 1973). These early studies also assumed that the left and right hemispheres involved distinct information-processing styles. In particular, the left hemisphere was characterized as "sequential" and "analytic," whereas the right hemisphere was characterized as "parallel" and "holistic."

The right or nondominant hemisphere was thought to lay a less significant role in language and thought. Hughlings Jackson (1879), for example, although he did not use the term *prosody* specifically, suggested that mechanisms involved in communicating "affective language" could be represented in the right as well as the left hemisphere. He was probably the first scientist to implicate the right or nonconscious cerebral hemisphere in language processes. Jackson was also the first person to raise questions about the control of prosody.

More recently, Ross (1981) suggested that neural organization for affective prosody is localized in the right hemisphere, and that it mirrors the functional organization of propositional speech and language processes in the left hemisphere. That is, there are specialized areas for reception and motor control processes. This model has been the source of considerable debate in the literature (e.g., Ryalls & Behrens, 1988). Robin, Tranel, and Damasio (1990) and Shapiro and Danly (1985), for example, suggested that lateralization of the processes involved in prosodic processing depends on the way in which task demands are interpreted by the speaker. There is, however, considerable agreement that the nondominant hemisphere is specialized for at least some prosodic control processes (Ryalls & Behrens, 1988). For instance, perceptual and acoustic studies of prosody in subjects with right cerebral hemisphere damage demonstrate that lesions in this part of the brain lead to significant changes in the ability to communicate emotional and affective suprasegmental information (Shapiro & Danly, 1985; Tompkins & Mateer, 1985; van Lancker & Sidtis, 1992).

Analysis of prosody in subjects with left hemisphere lesions also reveal prosodic disturbance, but of a markedly different nature. Dysprosody associated with the dysarthrias (Darley, Aronson, & J. Brown, 1975) or verbal dyspraxia (Boss, 1984; Kent & Rosenbeck 1982), for example, reflects disruption in the use of prosody to mark segmental boundaries, whereas this is preserved in subjects with right cerebral hemisphere lesions.

Sidtis and Volpe (1988) conducted a study involving a comparison between subjects who suffered a single cerebrovascular accident in the distribution of either the left or right middle cerebral artery, on their ability to discriminate complex-pitch and speech stimuli presented dichotically. The purpose of this study was to determine if speech stimuli were processed differently than complex sounds even though they are both acoustically complex signals. Results revealed a dissociation between processes involved in auditory processing of speech versus complex-pitch signals. The left hemisphere damaged group was impaired in their ability to discriminate speech but not complex-pitch stimuli whereas the reverse was true for the right hemisphere group. That is, the right hemisphere damaged group had difficulty in dichotic complex-pitch discrimination but not dichotic speech discrimination. Sidtis and Volpe concluded that their data supported the notion of complementary cerebral organization for complex-pitch and speech discrimination but it also supported the idea that following focal damage the two hemispheres respond differently. They further reported that their results reflect asymmetries in cerebral organization for these tasks and not simply asymmetries in the auditory periphery or brainstem.

The available evidence is consistent with the idea that prosodic processes are lateralized, and that the pattern of their lateralization is different from the pattern generally observed for verbal skills. There is some suggestion, furthermore, that the right hemisphere is the dominant hemisphere where prosodic processes are concerned. If it is further assumed that the right hemisphere is responsible for nonconscious processes, a position that has been widely accepted although rarely demonstrated (cf. Gazzaniga, 1989), the possible association between prosody and nonconscious processes is clear.

In summary, the results of these studies support the idea that each cerebral hemisphere is specialized for a particular type of signal analysis, where this depends on the temporal, spectral, and speech characteristics of the signal. The detailed patterns of specialization are consistent with the idea that the right hemisphere is involved in interpretation of pragmatic and emotional prosody where this is characterized by global excursions of fundamental frequency and complex spectral patterns throughout the complete utterance. The results also support the idea that the left hemisphere is involved in processing rapid temporal changes typical of propositional prosody and that this information is required for interpretation of voice onset, formant frequency, and vowel duration for example.

In conclusion, it is suggested that the left and right cerebral hemispheres are specialized for the analysis of specific stimulus dimensions, and that, because each dimension plays a different role in, say, pragmatic prosody and the propositional aspects of communication, lateralized damage will yield asymmetric patterns of impairment. Thus, prosody per se may not be lateralized, but right hemisphere damage will yield more impairment to pragmatic prosody because it depends on low-level processes that are themselves lateralized.

The Mapping Problem

Although analysis of the functional and acoustic domains associated with prosody yields apparently neat lists of categories and dimensions, respectively, attempts to design a table describing the mapping relationship between these domains have not been successful (Thorsen, 1983). The reasons for this are as follows. First, information about all of the functional categories and subcategories is transmitted simultaneously in the acoustic signal (Ladd, 1983; Speer et al., 1993). Second, some prosodic cues may be redundant. Wingfield et al. (1984), for example, found that subjects switched to duration or amplitude to preserve comprehension when pitch perception was impaired, at high presentation rates, although they were more likely to attend to pitch at normal presentation rates. Third, the state of each parameter in the signal may be relevant to more than one functional category or subcategory (Farnetani et al., 1988). For example, information about duration may be used to (a) identify unit boundaries and (b) differentiate *given* from *new* information (Farnetani et al., 1988). Fourth, differentiation of some or all of the emotional categories may depend on information about all of the acoustic parameters (Frick, 1985; Scherer, 1986). Fifth, technical limitations generally have limited researchers to one acoustic parameter, although the problem probably demands simultaneous analysis of all acoustic parameters, including spectral analysis (Frick, 1985;

Scherer, 1986). Finally, it is possible that the final product is guided by conditional or nonlinear processes, such that the feature selected to impart information about one communication variable may depend on the current status of the set of features used for emotional, pragmatic, and linguistic prosody. Thus, if duration is "in use" to specify old–new status, change in some other pragmatic variable will be restricted to intensity or fundamental frequency, whereas, if duration is "free" it could be used to mark change in this variable. In conclusion, the search for the invariant features of prosody may be based on a false premise.

In summary, it is difficult to specify rules describing the relationship between the functional categories and acoustic parameters of prosody. The mapping function appears to involve flexible, context-sensitive rules that change from situation to situation if not occasion to occasion (Scherer, 1986).

Relationship Between Emotional, Pragmatic, and Linguistic Prosody, and the Subsystems Responsible for the Control of Speech

Figure 12.1 depicts the various ways in which emotional, pragmatic, and linguistic prosody are represented in spoken communication. This schema is a provisional description of the processes responsible for the simultaneous representation of the prosodic and propositional aspects of verbal communication in the acoustic signal. Four levels are included in the figure. A heterarchical rather than hierarchical relationship is assumed to exist between the processes involved at each of the levels. The first level includes the control processes for emotional, pragmatic, and linguistic prosody. The second level consists of the motor command subsystems required for the control of the physiology of respiration, phonation, and articulation. The function of the second level determines the constantly changing shape of the aerodynamic cavity at the third level. The fourth level represents the output of the interleaving function of Levels 1 to 3, that is, the acoustic representation of speech. Specification of a single entity—the aerodynamic cavity—at the third level reflects our assumption that respiration, phonation, and articulation produce interdependent effects in a closed system (Gracco, 1990).

The figure also depicts the mapping relationships between the control processes and the motor command subsystems responsible for respiration, phonation, and articulation, and the effectors that influence the shape of the aerodynamic cavity. As shown in the figure, the various sources of prosodic influence operate unevenly on the motor command subsystems. Whereas emotional prosody influences all three subsystems, linguistic prosody influences only phonation and articulation, and pragmatic prosody selectively influences phonation.

The spatial organization of the control level is determined by the temporal status of each source of prosodic variation relative to the segmental structure of propositional language. Emotional prosody typically is maintained for long periods, and changed gradually, without direct contingencies involving propositional language.

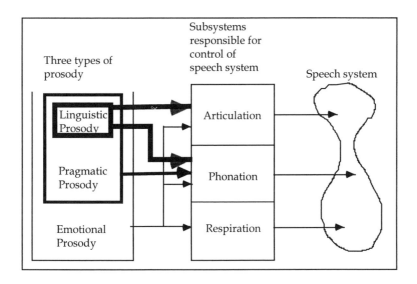

FIG. 12.1. Prosody: Function, components, and organization.

As emotional prosody is both suprasegmental and continuous, it is given the outside position in the model. Linguistic prosody involves juncture. It is discontinuous and segmental, and, therefore, it is given the inside position in the model. Pragmatic prosody may be applied to a variety of linguistic units, ranging from a simple utterance such as "OK" to much larger units involving several hundred words, such as a description of a holiday for example. Pragmatic prosody is therefore supraseg-mental, but, because it can change abruptly to attract attention to changes in communicative intent, it is discontinuous rather than continuous. Pragmatic pros-ody is located between linguistic and emotional prosody in the model. The figure also acknowledges the distinction between trait and state influences on emotional prosody. This distinction is predicated on the assumption that, as with variables such as anxiety and depression (MacLeod, chap. 14 of this volume), day-to-day variation can be observed among people who are chronically sensitive to or chronically insensitive to stress, for example. It is not suggested however that trait and state differences involve different mechanisms.

The difference between this description and a model of prosodic control that reflects a bottom–up perspective is that this description allows for the inde-pendent representation of control processes required for each type of prosody. The bottom–up model of prosodic control suggests that the overarching intona-tion contour is the product of the compilation of changes that occur at the level of a tone unit (A. Cohen et al., 1982; Ladd, 1988). Support for the alternative position that pragmatic prosody is controlled by processes separate to those that are involved in the control of linguistic prosody was reported by Speer et al. (1993). They demonstrated that the propositional content of speech was stored and retrieved separately from the intonation contour. Further support for the notion that pragmatic prosody and linguistic prosody are controlled by separate processes is found in the clinical literature. Subjects with right cerebral hemisphere damage demonstrate intact control for linguistic prosody as reflected by their completely intelligible speech samples whereas their ability to use and understand pragmatic prosody is impaired (Hird & Kirsner, 1993; Ryalls & Behrens, 1988).

This model provides a framework for discussing the relative impact of explicit and implicit processes on prosody, while honoring the assumption that these functions are encoded in, and decoded from, the same signal.

Pragmatic Prosody—Controlled or Automatic?

The central question concerns the level and form of control of pragmatic prosody. We assume, for convenience, that emotional prosody is governed by factors outside the realm of deliberate or conscious control mechanisms. This is not to suggest that emotional prosody is invulnerable to retraining; only that it is not generally subject to conscious online control during conversation. Linguistic prosody can be set aside as well, our assumption being that it is determined by practice and feedback, so that selection of the lexical entries for the noun and adverbial forms of a word such as content (i.e., con'tent vs. content') automatically recruits the inflection that is appropriate to a specific sense, an assumption that parallels selective access to the various meanings of homographs (J.V. Bainbridge et al., 1993). A similar caveat may be applied to the control of linguistic prosody. Online monitoring would be cognitively expensive, and could be implemented only at the expense of some other process, semantic planning being the obvious example. It may be assumed, however, that explicit processes could be used to shape the use of stress, although the extent to which such training would generalize to untrained forms in adult speakers is unclear.

The distinction between explicit and implicit processes may be considered with reference to several aspects of pragmatic prosody, although the distinction between controlled and automatic processes offers a better benchmark for some purposes. The first of these concerns acquisition. Although acquisition is not our primary concern in this chapter, it is safe to assume that many key elements of pragmatic prosody are acquired implicitly, during and possibly before propositional language. Certainly, the prevalence of prosodic "errors" in otherwise fluent second-language speakers is consistent with the assumption that prosodic contours act as building blocks for propositional language. Thus, the pragmatic building blocks or templates are the first to be installed, and the hardest to unravel and reshape for second-language purposes. Indeed, the extent to which new pragmatic prosody can be acquired under anything other than immersion conditions—where it is possible to accumulate sufficient evidence for automatic processing—is unclear.

The distinction between explicit and implicit processes is directly relevant to the online control of prosody during conversation. However, before considering this issue, it is necessary to make a further distinction, between the shaping of pragmatic skills on the one hand, and online control of pragmatic prosody on the other. Under training conditions, it is surely possible for people—public speakers in particular—to develop and refine specific prosodic skills. A short list of the skills that may be open to conscious shaping during "training" probably includes processes that shape the aerodynamic cavity—respiration, phonation, and articulation—as well as more specific communicative targets such as resetting of fundamental frequency, resetting of amplitude, rate of articulation, and more general speech devices that are used to disguise meaning or induce humor by establishing conflicting messages on the prosodic and propositional channels.

Where routine conversation is concerned, it is our hypothesis that pragmatic prosody depends on a mixture of controlled and automatic processes. Controlled processes, involving conscious planning and review, will be required to define communicative intent, and prepare a discourse plan. But, below that, the processes that set and manage specific prosody are recruited automatically, as a product of decisions about communicative intent. Thus, the detailed instantiation of a given intent, as it flows through the production system depicted in Fig. 12.1, is assumed to be outside the conscious control of the speaker under normal conversational conditions. It is our further suggestion, however, that speakers, as well as listeners, can monitor their own prosody, and provide error correction, in ways that parallel selection and order errors (Cutler, 1982). This hypothesis relies on two further assumptions. The first of these is that prosodic control is too complex, and involves too many microcontrol mechanisms to support conscious online control. It is a production parallel of the argument developed by Hayes and D.E. Broadbent (1988), that selective learning (i.e., S-mode learning) can be supported only where the number of categories is small and the nature of the S-R mappings simple. When the number of categories is large, and the S-R mappings complex, skill acquisition is restricted to the unselective learning (i.e., U-mode learning).

The second question concerns the retrieval of background knowledge and scenarios for the formation of production plans from long-term memory. According to J.O. Greene and Cappelli (1986), retrieval occurs automatically, at no cost, whereas preparation of a serial production plan for discourse involves a cognitively expensive process. But this view assumes that all retrieval occurs automatically, a conclusion that suggests that conversation should be unimpaired in amnesia, a conclusion that is at odds with Korsakoff's (1955) initial description of that condition, although there is a dearth of recent evidence on this point.

Apart from a comment by Collier (1990) that prosody is processed unconsciously by speakers, there is little reference in the literature to the issue of whether the control processes for prosody are implicit or explicit, controlled or automatic. This may be due in part to a large body of literature that supports the notion that prosody is secondary in significance to the propositional message and that its communicative function is merely to embellish the ideas already coded in at the segmental level. Further insights into prosody, therefore, will not improve our understanding of speech processing. An alternative explanation for the apparent lack of discussion surrounding this topic is that as prosody is processed implicitly, it has been taken for granted, and researchers have focused on those aspects of verbal communication that are subject to conscious control processes.

Consideration of a model of control of pragmatic prosody that includes top-down processing permits research to address a number of questions. Are all aspects of prosodic control processed implicitly? Is it possible to describe a highly complex system that has sufficient flexibility in its control mechanisms to permit the majority of its functions to be under implicit control and therefore cognitively very cheap, while still permitting some of its functions to be controlled explicitly for specific communicative purposes on some occasions, even if it is cognitively very expensive? What would be the advantage of such a system? These issues take on increasing importance when considering the theoretical underpinnings of rehabilitation programmes for people who have acquired neurogenic communication disorders. Although some communication disorders are a consequence of impairment in the control of prosody others involve disorder in the use of the propositional aspect of the communication. Regardless of what type of communication disorder, rehabilitation programs are dependent on improved understanding of the relationship between the control processes for all aspects of communication and how this knowledge influences the type of retraining that can be offered to ensure successful outcomes.

In summary, we propose that the control of prosody usually involves a mixture of controlled processes driven by communicative intent and "lower" or automatic processes, recruited by specific communicative intentions. It is suggested, furthermore, that where communication involves reference to old information or knowledge, that information may be retrieved by either implicit or explicit memory processes. It must be acknowledged, however, that prosody can be brought into focus by a shift in intention—from the textual to the pragmatic content of the message—and it then may be subject to conscious influence, during either reception or production. Finally, although we have given little consideration to the issue in this chapter, it is suggested that if the pragmatic information involves invariants, these operate above the level of the aerodynamic cavity, and they therefore will not be detected in the acoustic representation. Rather, because they operate on an analog system with an infinite number of states, their specific manifestation in the speech signal will vary from context to context.

13

STEREOTYPES AND ATTITUDES: IMPLICIT AND EXPLICIT PROCESSES

Drew Nesdale
Griffith University

Kevin Durkin
University of Western Australia

Human beings are social animals and, as such, process enormous amounts of social information daily. This information can be explicit or implicit, and the processes involved may be conscious or unconscious. Some of the relevant information may be drawn top–down from memory (e.g., previously acquired representations about the attributes of different types of people), and some may be inferred or constructed (e.g., in the course of appraising a new person or situation). Some of the information may be descriptive and factual (e.g., members of that ethnic group have a different skin color to me) and some may be evaluative and affective (e.g., I prefer my group).

Social psychologists studying these kinds of phenomena (especially, stereotypes and attitudes) thus are confronted with processes very closely related to those investigated by students of implicit cognitive processes, as illustrated in several other chapters in this book. Social information is particularly interesting in terms of the interaction of conscious and unconscious processes because of the simultaneous involvement of both categorization and affective orientation. As we see later, each of these processes might occur either consciously or unconsciously, and their valences might be congruent or otherwise.

This chapter aims to show how our understanding of stereotypes and attitudes has profited from attention to processes that may be activated automatically and, often, without awareness. Although both stereotypes and attitudes have been part of the mainstream of theory and research in social psychology since the 1920s, our discussion also gives particular attention to the largely neglected issue of the relationship that might exist between stereotypes and attitudes. After briefly reviewing the prevailing conceptions of "stereotype" and "attitude," we outline four possible relationships between attitudes and stereotypes that have been suggested and discuss a variety of perspectives on how these relationships might be acquired and changed. These include, first, that group attitudes (prejudice) are an inevitable consequence of stereotypes; second, that a stereotype is simply the cognitive accompaniment of a group attitude; third, that a stereotype is the cognitive component of an attitude; and fourth, that stereotypes and attitudes are independent processes that might, or might not, be consistent in apparent valence.

Based on this review, it is proposed that recent evidence favors the latter position and that much of the divergence in viewpoints can be attributed to the mainly explicit measures of attitudes and stereotypes that traditionally have been utilized by researchers. Indeed, as is shown, the recent literature suggests that both constructs necessitate the use of implicit as well as explicit measures. That is, there is accumulating evidence that social group categories (e.g., male, female; Black, White) may be activated automatically and without awareness and, in turn, automatically activate affect and cognitions (stereotypes) associated with the group category. The possibility that attitudes and stereotypes are implicit and independent processes has considerable theoretical and empirical significance and, of course, has important implications for change strategies.

STEREOTYPES

Stereotypes are generalizations held by groups of people about the attributes and behavior of other groups of people (R.G. Gardner, 1973; Tajfel & Forgas, 1981; D.M. Taylor & Lalonde, 1987). Most social psychologists regard stereotypes as an inevitable outcome of adaptive cognitive processes, whereby individuals seek to simplify and organize the abundance of information potentially available in a diverse and complex social environment (cf. Dovidio & Gaertner, 1993; Tajfel & Forgas, 1981).

Several points should be noted about the nature of stereotypes as defined here. First, the attributes comprising any given stereotype may encompass various dimensions, including personality traits, social roles, and physical characteristics (Deaux & Kite, 1985). Second, the stereotype refers to the attributes that are *believed* to be possessed by the group members rather than attributes that are *known* to be possessed by group members (D.M. Taylor & Lalonde, 1987). That is, an important feature of a stereotype is that it is a selective cognitive construct. As such, it may influence both the *perception* of members of a social group (rendering those attributes that are congruent with the stereotype highly salient, others less so) and the *prediction* of their likely behavior.

Third, the attributes comprising the stereotype of a group are those that are believed to be most typical of that group (R.G. Gardner, 1973). This view contrasts with the differentiation approach, according to which stereotypes are comprised of traits that differentiate one group (e.g., males) from another (e.g., females; Biernat, 1990). The point here is that although the two sets of attributes (i.e., those that are typical vs. those that differentiate) might show considerable overlap, this is not necessarily the case. As has been pointed out elsewhere (Ashmore, Del Boca, & Wohler, 1986), the attributes that are considered to be most typical of each gender are not necessarily believed to differentiate strongly between the genders.

Finally, and important to note, stereotypes are *shared* beliefs (Durkin, 1987; Tajfel & Forgas, 1981). This conception contrasts with those writers who appear to view a stereotype as the attributes that an *individual* ascribes to a group (e.g., Ashmore & Del Boca, 1981; Biernat, 1990). The important point is that stereotypes *matter* to the parties concerned, because they reflect and help to maintain aspects of the relative social standing of those groups (Tajfel & Forgas, 1981). For this reason, we might expect the cognitive processes of stereotyping to be intimately linked to the affective processes.

ATTITUDES

An *attitude* is defined for our present purposes as "affect for or against a psychological object" (Thurstone, 1931; but see Fishbein & Ajzen, 1975; Fiske & S.E. Taylor, 1991; Zanna & Rempel, 1988, for fuller discussions of the difficulties of defining attitude). That is, attitudes are viewed here as consisting of unidimensional evaluative judgments (usually measured on scales such as liking, favorability, and pleasantness). As earlier, the attitudes of particular relevance are those that are held in relation to social groups (e.g., men, women, Blacks, Whites, Serbians, Protestants). Such intergroup attitudes encompass prejudice, typically taken to be the negative feelings toward the members of particular social groups (G.W. Allport, 1954).

THE INTERACTION BETWEEN
STEREOTYPES AND ATTITUDES

Although the preceding discussion suggests that stereotypes and attitudes are distinctively different entities in that "stereotype" refers to a set of beliefs about a social group, whereas (group) attitude refers to an affective or evaluative orientation or judgment toward a group (e.g., D.M. Taylor & Lalonde, 1987), there has been a common and long-held assumption that the two entities are closely related, if not in a state of dependency. Most recently, this view has been of particular significance to stereotype researchers who have argued that both affect and cognition may be necessary to explain the effects of stereotypes (see Fiske, 1981, 1982; Fiske & Pavelchak, 1986; Hamilton, 1981; Higgins, Kuiper, & Olson, 1981; S.E. Taylor, 1981). According to Fiske (1982), for example, "...affect is the very reason stereotypes matter" (p. 55).

Indeed, at one level, the view that stereotypes and attitudes are not independent seems difficult to dispute, given the essential nature of stereotypes. That is, whereas a stereotype is a set of beliefs or cognitions about the attributes characteristic of the members of a particular group, the attributes themselves consist of traits and behaviors that very frequently are suffused with evaluative connotations. For example, a particular stereotype might include the attributes of lazy, music-loving, dirty, sensual, stupid, and so on. Given that beliefs and affect are thus seemingly inextricably intertwined in a stereotype, the question that follows is: How can there be anything other than a consistent and dependent relationship between stereotypes and attitudes?

Although there appears to be a *prima facie* case for there being a close relationship between stereotypes and attitudes, there are actually at least three versions of this position. One view (i.e., *stereotype primacy*) is that group attitudes (prejudice) are an inevitable consequence of stereotyping (e.g., Billig, 1985; Ehrlich, 1973). The basic argument "is that as long as stereotypes exist, prejudice will follow" (Devine, 1989, p. 5). Implicit in this position is the view that the negative affect associated with the content of the stereotype effectively comprises or underwrites the prejudice.

Although the automatic mechanism posited to underlie this process is taken up later in this chapter, suffice it to say at this stage that there is agreement that stereotypes do not necessarily contain only negative items, let alone only items that are evaluatively consistent (e.g., Greenwald & Banaji, 1993; T. Hickey, L. Hickey & Kalish, 1968; Nesdale, 1987). Further, it ignores the possibility that group attitudes may be acquired before the related stereotype. Indeed, research has shown that ethnic attitudes or prejudices are acquired by children prior to ethnic stereotypes (e.g., Aboud, 1988; Blake & Dennis, 1943; Brigham, 1974; Kirby & R.C. Gardner, 1973).

A second view (i.e., *attitude primacy*) is that stereotypes are merely cognitive accompaniments of the affect that is felt toward the members of a particular social group. According to G.W. Allport (1954), for example, "Stereotypes are not identical with prejudice. They are primarily rationalisers. They adapt to the prevailing temper of prejudice or the needs of the situation....They wax and wane with the intensity and direction of prejudice" (p. 204).

Consistent with this view is the evidence noted previously that ethnic attitudes or prejudices are acquired by children prior to ethnic stereotypes, and that intergroup prejudice is typically (but not necessarily) accompanied by a matching stereotype (e.g., Wrightsman & Deaux, 1981). However, as noted earlier there is also evidence that stereotypes do not necessarily contain only items that are evaluatively consistent, whereas other writers have tended to stress the distinctive, yet related, contributions of stereotypes and affect (e.g., Eagly & Mladinic, 1989) and, elsewhere, their autonomy and independence (e.g., Dovidio & Gaertner, 1993; R.C. Gardner, 1973; S.E. Taylor & Falcone, 1982).

One variant of the former view (i.e., *stereotype and attitude primacy*) draws on the tri-component view of attitudes (e.g., Katz & Stotland, 1959; Krech & Crutchfield, 1948). According to this position, an attitude is comprised of three components: cognitive (belief), affective (feeling, evaluation), and conative (i.e., action tendency or disposition). In an analogous way, stereotypes have been conceptualized by some writers to be the cognitive component of an attitude toward an outgroup, with the attitude also comprising affective and conative components (e.g., Eagly & Mladinic, 1989; Secord & Backman, 1974).

This version of the stereotype-affect relationship, however, suffers from the same problems that have troubled attempts to define and measure attitudes over many years (see McGuire, 1968). For example, what is to be the relationship between the components and the overarching attitude or evaluation, as well as that among the components? Although some researchers have operationally equated the affective component with the general attitude or evaluation (e.g., R. Norman, 1975; Rosenberg, 1956), others have argued that the general attitude is formed from some combination of the affective and cognitive components (e.g., Petty & Cacioppo, 1986; Zanna & Rempel, 1988). And, although the tri-component conceptualization calls for three components that are distinct yet related, researchers over the years have found this structure to be difficult to demonstrate (McGuire, 1968). As a result, although some researchers have persisted with attempts at validating the tri-component view (e.g., Bagozzi, 1978; Breckler, 1984; Kothandapani, 1971), many now simply equate attitudes with an affective or evaluative response, which is conceptually and operationally distinct from a belief or cognitive response (e.g., Fishbein & Ajzen, 1975).

In sum, although the preceding discussion has considered three versions of the commonly held view that stereotypes and attitudes are closely related, if not dependent, entities, support for the general position is clearly not unambiguous. Moreover, other researchers have reported findings that actually point to the independence of stereotypes and affect (e.g., R.G. Gardner, 1973; L.A. Jackson & Sullivan, 1988; S.E. Taylor & Falcone, 1982).

Accordingly, the fourth approach we consider is that the relationship between stereotypes and affect is actually not one of dependence but, instead, the two are independent processes (i.e., *independent stereotypes and attitudes*). Evidence for this position has been provided in a series of studies by Gardner and his colleagues (R.C. Gardner, 1973; R.C. Gardner, D.M. Taylor, & Feenstra, 1970; R.C. Gardner, Wonnacott, & D.M. Taylor, 1968; Kirby & R.C. Gardner, 1973) on the intercultural attitudes and stereotypes of English and French-Canadians. The consistent finding from these studies is that endorsement of a group stereotype can be independent of attitudes or affect toward that group. The research suggest that stereotypes and attitudes are not equivalent concepts; they cannot be used interchangeably.

Other studies (e.g., Nesdale & McLaughlin, 1987; S.E. Taylor & Falcone, 1982) have addressed the extent to which affect-laden judgments (e.g., evaluations, causal attributions) are correlated with seemingly related stereotype-driven cognitive responses (e.g., recall for stereotype consistent versus inconsistent information). For example, S.E. Taylor and Falcone examined the relationship between the extent to which male and female university students categorized information heard in a discussion as male- versus female-presented, and the extent to which they favored male versus female speakers. Consistent with the previous findings, the two responses were found to be unrelated.

However, although these and other similar findings (e.g., L.A. Jackson & Sullivan, 1988; Sigelman, Carr, & Begley, 1986) are consistent with the conclusion that stereotypes and attitudes are independent, it needs to be recognized that the great majority of research studies over the years on stereotypes and attitudes have employed direct or explicit measures, typically involving some type of self-report on a formal scale (e.g., Thurstone or Likert scales, in Edwards, 1957) or informal scale. Under these circumstances, subjects have been aware that their beliefs (i.e., stereotypes) and/or attitudes relating to particular social groups are the focus of interest.

The obvious problem with these methods, and of particular relevance to the present discussion, is that there is no protection against artifactual findings; that is, subjects might construct their responses to best meet the perceived objectives of the experimenter (Orne, 1962) and/or to present themselves in the most socially desirable light (Cook & Selltiz, 1964). In short, the evidence that stereotypes and attitudes are independent might simply reflect, for example, an understanding on the part of subjects that it is acceptable to know a stereotype (because it is socially shared), but that it is socially undesirable to display prejudice.

These considerations emphasize the need for more indirect or implicit measures in stereotype and attitude research—measures that neither inform the subject of what is being assessed nor request self-report concerning it. And, responding to this need, the past decade has seen the emergence of a series of studies on stereotypes and attitudes that have employed indirect rather than direct measures.

Important to note, whereas "most social psychologists since the 1930s have assumed that attitudes, and to a lesser extent stereotypes, operate in a conscious mode" (Greenwald & Banaji, 1993, p. 2), the increasing adoption of indirect measures by current researchers also reflects an emerging articulation between research in cognitive psychology on implicit memory and research on social cognition (Devine, 1989; Dovidio, N. Evans, & Tyler, 1986; Greenwald & Banaji, 1993). Specifically, researchers in social cognition have begun to examine the extent to which stereotypes and attitudes are implicit versus explicit. Clearly, evidence that one or both of stereotypes and attitudes involves implicit processes has important implications for their relationship as well as for other cognitive processes and behavior.

IMPLICIT STEREOTYPES

One of the earliest studies to address this issue, using an indirect technique from cognitive psychology, was conducted by Gaertner and McLaughlin (1983). Using a lexical decision paradigm, these researchers found that White subjects responded faster to *White*-positive than to *Black*-positive word pairs (e.g., *White*-ambitious vs. *Black*-ambitious) although there was no response difference to *White*-negative versus *Black*-negative word pairs (e.g., *White*-stupid vs. *Black*-lazy).

However, in this study neither the White nor Black stereotype had been independently assessed, and stereotypic association and affect were confounded in the traits used (e.g., "ambition" is stereotypically associated with Whites and is evaluatively positive). Dovidio et al. (1986) subsequently employed a priming paradigm to examine separately the effects of stereotype and affect on how people process stereotypic information about Blacks and Whites. Subjects first were presented with a prime (*Black* or *White*) followed by a target (a positive or negative trait from the Black or White stereotype) and were asked to judge if the target "could ever be true" or was "always false."

The results indicated that the *Black* and *White* primes significantly facilitated responses to traits stereotypically attributed to each group. In addition, positive traits were more strongly associated with *Whites* than *Blacks*, whereas negative traits were more strongly linked with *Blacks* than *Whites*. However, because subjects had up to 2 seconds to respond to a target following a prime, there remains the possibility that subjects might have managed their responses. Dovidio et al. (1986) sought to dismiss this possibility on the grounds that their response times were consistent with other "nonsensitive" categorization results (e.g., Rosch, 1978). Moreover, they reported that there was no evidence of subject sensitivity in their reaction times to *Black* primes or to negative *Black* traits.

In a further study, Devine (1989) assessed the automatic activation of the Black stereotype using a more acceptable attentionless processing paradigm (Bargh & Pietromonaco, 1982). The primes were presented parafoveally and were followed immediately with a pattern mask. The primes were labels for the social category *Blacks* (e.g., Blacks, negroes, niggers) or were stereotypic associates (e.g., poor, lazy, athletic), or were neutral words. High- and low-prejudice subjects were required to indicate the location of each presented word on a screen. In a separate task, the subjects subsequently were required to evaluate a series of ambiguously hostile behaviors by a race-unspecified target on a set of scales, six of which measured the extent to which stereotype-congruent (i.e., hostility rated) interpretations of the target's behavior were made. As predicted, Devine found that both high- and low-prejudice subjects inflated the stereotype-related judgments of the target's behavior. Devine interpreted these results as demonstrating that the automatically activated stereotype influenced the interpretation of ambiguous stereotype-congruent behaviours performed by a race-unspecified target and that this effect occurred even in low-prejudice subjects.

However, although this study appears to have identified automatic, unconscious processes in stereotyping, one cautionary note still needs be expressed. Contrary to Devine's (1989) conclusion, it is possible that the stereotypic trait words simply primed hostility information rather than the Black stereotype (Greenwald & Banaji, 1993; Locke, C. MacLeod, & I. Walker, 1994).

Setting this caution aside, the findings from these and other studies on gender (e.g., Banaji, Hardin, & Rothman, in press; Greenwald & Banaji, 1993) have contributed to several writers concluding that stereotypes may be automatically activated, without conscious awareness, in the presence of social group labels or trait terms stereotypically associated with a social group (Fiske, 1992; Greenwald & Banaji, 1993; Hamilton & Sherman, 1993).

However, the position is not clear cut. It is important to note, for example, that Gilbert and Hixon (1991) also have reported evidence suggesting that the automaticity of stereotype activation may be impeded and that, given activation, their application also may be inhibited. In the first phase of Gilbert and Hixon's study, subjects performed a word fragment completion test in which some of the words were stereotypically associated with Asians, while being exposed to either a White or an Asian female assistant. Half of the subjects completed the task under an additional cognitive load (a rehearsal task). In a second phase, subjects formed an impression of the assistant as she described her life with, again, half the subjects also being required to undertake an additional visual task. The results indicated that cognitively unloaded subjects in the first phase made more stereotypic completions than cognitively loaded subjects. In the second phase, only subjects who were cognitively unloaded in the first phase but cognitively loaded in the second phase made more stereotypic ratings of the Asian versus the White assistant.

Based on these findings, Gilbert and Hixon (1991) concluded that the automatic activation of stereotypes is not unconditional; at the least, people must have adequate processing resources for activation to occur. In contrast, once activated, the application of stereotypes may be influenced by other considerations such that they are more likely to be applied when conscious deliberation becomes difficult. When deliberation is possible, application may be inhibited for reasons of social desirability and/or because individuation of the target becomes possible.

At least three observations can be made concerning Gilbert and Hixon's (1991) study and conclusions. First, given that most subjects could accurately recall the race of the assistant in the first phase of the experiment, it is certainly arguable whether the procedure of "merely exposing" subjects to the assistant's race actually engaged implicit stereotyping. Second, Gilbert and Hixon's procedure did not provide for the possibility of the automatic application of the stereotypes during the second phase of the experiment. Third, and most important, Gilbert and Hixon's results, in the light of other discussions (e.g., Brewer, 1989; Fiske & Neuberg, 1990), emphasize the importance of viewing "stereotypic activation" as being comprised of two processes that might be termed *category activation* and *stereotype engagement*, which may differ in their potential for automaticity. The former, category activation, refers to the process whereby a particular social category or attribute (e.g., skin color, gender) becomes salient to a perceiver whereas the latter, stereotype engagement, refers to the subsequent process of eliciting the set of traits associated with the activated category.

Indeed, a full description of the operation of stereotypes also would appear to call for the addition of *stereotype application* as the logical third phase in the stereotyping process. In this phase, the fully prompted stereotype either does, or does not, impact on subsequent processes (e.g., impression formation, judgments).

THE STEREOTYPING PROCESS

Considering stereotyping as a three-phase process, the question to be answered is whether each phase can be accomplished implicitly and/or explicitly. Might it be, for example, that social categories may be automatically activated, but stereotypes may not be automatically engaged? Although there appears to be more agreement on some of these issues than others, the research to date is not definitive.

Both Brewer (1989) and Fiske (1992; Fiske & Neuberg, 1990), for example, argued for the automaticity of what we have termed *category activation* as the initial and highest priority response of perceivers in social interaction. Brewer, for example, claimed that:

> The mere presentation of a stimulus person activates certain classification processes...that occur automatically and without conscious intent....Whenever a novel social object is encountered, an initial identification stage is postulated to precede any conscious, goal driven information processing...[and this] process is one of "placing" the individual social object along well-established stimulus dimensions such as gender, age, and skin colour. (pp. 5–6)

Compared with category activation, there is less consensus about the automaticity of *stereotype engagement*. For example, Fiske (1992; Fiske & Neuberg, 1990) claimed that activation of a category automatically engages the associated set of traits. Moreover, in accepting that people cannot control stereotype engagement, Fiske's model also appears to allow for automaticity in what we have termed *stereotype application* to processes such as impression formation and person memory (Fiske & Neuberg, 1990). However, Fiske considered such category-based processes to be the default option that can subsequently be controlled and overridden by motivational considerations (e.g., outcome dependency, self-presentation) that prompt greater attention to specific attributes and give rise to individuated rather than category-based responses (Fiske & Neuberg, 1990).

In contrast, Brewer's (1989) model, although specifying automaticity in *category activation*, appears to call for controlled rather than automatic processing in stereotype *engagement* and *application*. In brief, following category activation which "...is automatic in the sense of being stimulus controlled and not attentionally mediated" (p. 6), processing ceases if the other person is perceived to be incompatible or irrelevant to the perceiver's current needs or goals. If the other person *is* considered to be relevant, controlled processes are instigated either in engaging an iterative process of fitting the other person to as closely matching a category or subtype as possible, or in producing a personalized, data-driven impression. Thus, according to this model, both stereotype engagement and application would appear to be explicit, controlled processes.

Viewed in the light of these models and research, Gilbert and Hixon's (1991) claim that "the activation of racial stereotypes is not an unconditionally automatic consequence of exposure to a person" (p. 515) actually appears to refer to the inhibition of stereotype engagement, following category activation, as a result of reduced cognitive processing capacity.

However, it needs be emphasized that the extent to which each of the processes of category activation, stereotype engagement, and stereotype application are automatic, and the conditions that potentiate automatic versus controlled processes at each stage, largely remain to be assessed. No studies appear to have provided unequivocal evidence of the automatic engagement of stereotypes following the automatic activation of social categories, and the conditions under which such stereotypes may or may not be automatically applied.

IMPLICIT ATTITUDES

Several researchers have also recently addressed the possibility that attitudes to social groups may be activated automatically and without awareness.

Perdue and Gurtman (1990), for example, employed a masked priming paradigm to examine the automaticity of attitudes to the aged, a group that has long been the object of prejudice in Western society. In this study, following the brief and undetectable presentation of the prime *old* (or *young*), which subsequently was masked, subjects were presented with a strongly positive or negative trait and asked to indicate whether the trait was a generally "good" or "bad" attribute for someone to possess. The results indicated that the prime *old* facilitated negative more than positive descriptors, whereas the reverse occurred for the prime *young*. Thus, even when the primes were outside conscious awareness and the attitude activation was irrelevant to the judgment task, the attitude objects, *old* or *young*, significantly influenced the judgment task, generating negative and positive attitudes, respectively.

Using the same masked priming paradigm, Perdue, Dovidio, Gurtman, and Tyler (1990) subsequently examined the automatic activation of ingroup and outgroup attitudes in response to the ingroup primes of *we*, *us,* and *ours*, and the outgroup primes of *they*, *them*, and *theirs*. Consistent with the previous study, the ingroup primes facilitated positive more than negative traits whereas the reverse occurred for outgroup primes. In a similar study, Dovidio (1990) found that White subjects responded more quickly to very positive characteristics following a *White* than a *Black* masked prime, and more quickly to very negative characteristics following a *Black* than a *White* masked prime.

In sum, recent studies on attitudes to groups suggest that the latter can be activated automatically and without awareness, that is, that these are implicit group attitudes. More specifically, as with stereotypes, it seems possible to consider the attitude process as comprising three phases: *category activation, attitude engagement* (i.e., the attachment of an affective valence to an activated category, and *attitude application* (i.e., the impact of an activated group attitude on other processes such as memory, impressions, etc.). Considered in these terms, it would appear that the automatic engagement of group attitudes following category activation has been demonstrated more unequivocally than has the automatic engagement of stereotypes following category activation. Somewhat similarly, however, the automaticity of application of group attitudes, like implicit stereotypes, is less clear cut.

Finally, bearing in mind Gilbert and Hixon's (1991) findings, it might be speculated that given that an attitude is presumably less (cognitively) complicated, hence less demanding of processing resources, the engagement of an attitude versus a stereotype following category activation would be faster and less likely to be inhibited by processing constraints. This view, of course, is consistent with that proposed by Zajonc (1980).

RELATIONSHIP BETWEEN STEREOTYPES AND ATTITUDES

Assuming for the moment that both stereotypes and attitudes may be activated automatically and without awareness, what are the implications for the stereotype-attitude relationship? To return to the broad distinction between dependent and independent relationships that was raised at the outset of this chapter, it could be argued that the more recent evidence actually substantiates the dependence position. For example, it could be argued that because both stereotypes and attitudes may be automatically activated, and that the traits comprising stereotypes are typically suffused with affective connotations, it is plausible that attitudes are consistent with stereotypes, with one, perhaps, simply being temporally prior in activation. According to this position, evidence of stereotype-attitude inconsistency would simply reflect the inhibition of one of the two automatically activated processes at the point of application or expression.

Devine's (1989) model of the stereotype-prejudice relationship accords with this approach. Briefly, this model posits that a stereotype, having a long history of activation in a shared culture, becomes a well-learned set of associations that is automatically activated by a category member. At the same time, the associated group attitude or prejudice also is activated for it simply reflects the affective tone of the stereotype. In contrast, the development of personal beliefs (presumably also incorporating affect) that conflict with the stereotype are necessarily newer structures that require controlled processes that are intentional and involve the active attention of the individual.

On this basis, the model predicts that persons with high prejudice will be those whose personal beliefs match those of the group stereotype, whereas those with little or no prejudice will be those who have decided that the stereotype is personally inappropriate as a basis for evaluation and behavior. In the presence of a group member, the latter engage in the intentional inhibition of the automatically activated stereotype and prejudice as well as activate the newer personal belief structure.

However, as has been noted previously, the claim that an attitude (prejudice) is an inevitable consequence of stereotyping (i.e., that the activation of a stereotype underwrites or presupposes the activation of an attitude matched in affective tone) remains to be substantiated. Indeed, in addition to the evidence produced by direct measures that stereotypes and attitudes may be unrelated and autonomous (e.g., R.C. Gardner et al., 1970), there is also evidence for the independence of stereotypes and attitudes from more indirect measures. Recall that Dovidio et al. (1986) found that the *White* prime facilitated White versus Black stereotype traits, whereas the reverse occurred following the *Black* prime. In addition, however, the results also revealed that the *White* prime facilitated positive versus negative traits, whereas the reverse occurred following the *Black* prime. Based on these results, the researchers argued that "evaluative associations as well as cognitive representations are linked to social categorisation...and that both can independently affect how information is encoded, organised and retrieved" (Dovidio et al., 1986, pp. 33–34). Subsequent research essentially confirmed these findings (Dovidio, N. Evans, & Tyler, 1988).

These results provide fuel for an independence position in which evidence of stereotype-attitude inconsistency need not necessarily reflect inhibition at the point of application. Moreover, the attitude automatically activated in relation to a category label need not reflect the affective tone of (the elements of) the stereotype. Because automaticity depends on extended practice, it simply may be the case that a person learns a culturally/shared social stereotype, and also develops his or her personal attitude that may be inconsistent with the affective tone of the stereotype, but yet may be automatically activated by the category label.

Fiske (1981, 1982; Fiske & Pavelchak, 1986) developed a model that, to an extent, fits with this approach, although it does not explicitly encompass (or exclude) the possibility that stereotypes and attitudes are automatically activated. However, given her recent writings, referred to previously (i.e., Fiske, 1992; Fiske & Neuberg, 1990), it is clear that her model could be modified to encompass automaticity.

In brief, this model holds that each social category or group label has associated with it both the set of attributes comprising the stereotype as well as an "affective tag" (i.e., attitude) that comprises the evaluative value attached to that social group (i.e., good, liked, favorable vs. bad, disliked, unfavorable). This overall category affective tag may result from several sources, including "an initial weighted averaging of the lower level affective tags (i.e., the affective values associated with the individual attributes comprising the stereotype set);...from a conditioned response to the category label; or it could come from socialisation—for example, someone else stating that a certain category is good or bad—" (Fiske & Pavelchak, 1986, p. 172). Although the overall affective tag may be acquired in one of these several ways, once the tag is established, it becomes independent of the affective tags of the individual attributes. And, once the category label is activated, the affect associated with the label is also activated. That is, the affective response is category based rather than piecemeal (i.e., based on affect tagged to the individual attributes) and, indeed, is considered to be instigated prior to any stereotype-driven cognitive response (cf. Zajonc, 1980, 1984). Thus, this model allows for an individual to know a group stereotype, yet to have associated with the group label an attitude that either does or does not match the affect associated with the attributes in the shared stereotype.

Although, as noted earlier, the model does not especially encompass the automatic activation of stereotypes and attitudes, Fiske and Pavelchak (1986) did allow, for example, that "category-based affect is presumed to be an efficient (i.e., rapid and effortless) mode of affective response" (p. 174) and that "category-based affective processing should occur whenever categorisation occurs, regardless of the conditions that elicited category-based responses" (p. 181). Notwithstanding these observations, the thrust of the model would appear to lend itself easily to the incorporation of automatic activation of stereotypes and attitudes. Once accomplished, the revised model would allow for *both* consistent and inconsistent relationships between stereotypes and attitudes. In addition, although both processes would be automatic in the sense of being uncontrolled and beyond awareness, it nevertheless would predict an even faster affective than stereotypic activation because the former involves only one versus several tags to the category label. Finally, the model would not exclude the possibility that, once activated, the application of stereotype and/or attitude may be inhibited by other processes (cf. Gilbert & Hixson, 1991). To date, however, aside from providing support for the notion that an affective response is category based rather than piecemeal (see Fiske & Pavelchak, 1986), much of the model remains to be assessed.

CONCLUSIONS

Stereotypes and attitudes have important implications for social behavior, interpersonal judgments, group relations, and the distribution of resources and opportunities within a society. For these reasons, they have long been prominent among the topics of social psychological enquiry. However, until recently, research has focused on the relatively explicit dimensions of these phenomena, examining the nature and pervasiveness of stereotypes, the strength and pervasiveness of attitudes, and the modification of these often very problematic aspects of human relations. Recent developments at the points of intersection of social and cognitive psychology have prompted new interests in the still more subtle but arguably more fundamental processes whereby stereotypes and attitudes are evoked and engaged. The evidence reviewed in this chapter suggests that the two processes are independent, though interacting and certainly of mutual significance.

Several researchers have argued that stereotypes can be brought into play automatically by exposure to a stimulus person belonging to the stereotyped social category. Knowledge and activation of the stereotype is not dependent on a prejudicial attitude toward the target; studies have shown that even nonprejudiced individuals tend to be well aware of the stereotype, and that social information processing can be facilitated by stereotype-relevant primes even when presented out of consciousness. Other researchers have shown similarly that attitudes can be tapped in implicit processes, with subjects' responses to affectively biased terms being facilitated by prior exposure to affectively weighted attitude objects.

Although research into these issues is still at a relatively early stage, studying them offers important perspectives on the structures and influences of cognitive categorization, and asserts the relevance of a vital component of human cognition that sometimes is overlooked in mainstream cognitive psychology, and even in social psychology, namely affect. At an important practical level, fuller understanding of how these processes operate, and their possible independence, has important implications for attempts to explain and to mitigate the undesirable consequences of stereotypes and social prejudices. If implicit and explicit processes are independent, it is possible for individuals to maintain or change to a nonprejudiced outlook yet still sustain underlying information that is prejudicial to the target of their social judgments.

14

AUTOMATIC
AND STRATEGIC
COGNITIVE BIASES IN
ANXIETY AND DEPRESSION

Colin MacLeod
Elizabeth M. Rutherford
University of Western Australia

It long has been recognized that individuals suffering from emotional disorders commonly experience pronounced elevations of negative ideation. In clinical depression, for example, thoughts concerning hopelessness and low self-esteem tend to predominate (Beck, 1967; Eaves & Rush, 1984), whereas clinically anxious patients frequently report thoughts concerning personal vulnerability and the anticipation of harm (Beck, Laude, & Bohnert, 1974; Hibbert, 1984). Recent conceptual accounts of emotional pathology (e.g., Beck, 1976; Beck, Emery, & Greenberg, 1986) place particular emphasis on such patterns of thinking not only as markers of clinical disorders, but also as potential causes of these clinical conditions. If this is so, then in order to understand the aetiology of emotional pathology, it becomes necessary to identify the cognitive basis of the abnormal thinking patterns that underpin such clinical conditions. This realization has catalyzed a great deal of recent research into the association between emotional vulnerability and idiosyncratic patterns of selective cognition (cf. C. MacLeod & A. Mathews, 1991; A. Mathews & MacLeod, 1994; J.M. Williams, Watts, C. MacLeod, & A. Mathews, 1988).

Some of the most influential theoretical positions have attributed the unusually negative thought contents associated with the emotional disorders to low-level selective processing biases that operate within the cognitive systems of individuals with high levels of vulnerability to anxiety or to depression (e.g., Beck & D.A. Clark, 1988; Bower, 1981, 1983). These cognitive biases are assumed to favor the selective processing of emotionally negative information. Although they ultimately serve to increase the representation of such negative information within conscious experience, most theorists propose that the biases themselves operate quite automatically, in the sense that they occur without volition and operate outside of conscious awareness. According to such accounts, therefore, the thoughts experienced by individuals who are high in vulnerability to anxiety or depression are systematically distorted by cognitive biases that operate "behind the veil," automatically exerting an implicit influence on subjective experience without either intention or awareness.

In this chapter we first briefly review two such influential accounts. Although they differ in important details, each predicts the presence of such pervasive automatic processing biases in clinically anxious and depressed patients. We then critically review the burgeoning experimental literature that has developed from the empirical evaluation of these predictions concerning the patterns of selective encoding and retrieval shown by anxious and by depressed individuals. Throughout this review, we not only report the types of processing biases that have been observed, but also consider the evidence to indicate that these biases operate automatically within the cognitive system. On the basis of this critical appraisal, we argue that vulnerability to anxiety and vulnerability to depression are characterized by quite different patterns of processing selectivity. Furthermore, the claim is developed that, whereas those processing biases associated with anxiety vulnerability do indeed appear to operate automatically, those associated with vulnerability to depression seem more likely to reflect the application of controlled cognitive strategies. We finish the chapter by discussing the theoretical and applied implications of the discrepant patterns of automatic and strategic cognitive biases associated with vulnerability to anxiety and depression.

TWO COGNITIVE ACCOUNTS OF EMOTIONAL VULNERABILITY

The association between cognition and emotion has been of considerable interest both to clinical researchers such as Aaron Beck, who have been motivated primarily by a desire to better understand the cognitive factors that may underlie emotional pathology, and to cognitive-experimental researchers such as Gordon Bower, who have been motivated more by the recognition that our understanding of fundamental cognitive mechanisms can be enriched by the study of individual differences. Despite the independence of their origins, and the substantial differences in the cognitive mechanisms implicated within each theoretical model, these two accounts share a remarkable similarity in terms of the predictions that they generate.

Beck's Schema Model

Beck and his colleagues (Beck, 1976; Beck & D.A. Clark, 1988; Beck et al., 1986) have drawn on the construct of schemata (Bartlett, 1932) to formulate their cognitive model of emotional vulnerability. They construed a schema as a proto-typical representation within long-term memory, developed to accommodate the regularities inherent in different classes of situations or events. Schemata normally remain latent within the cognitive system but, once activated, they play an active role in guiding information processing. According to schema theorists, such acti-vation commonly is triggered by a partial match between environmental input and the contents of a schema. Although the influence of schemata will be entirely adaptive under most circumstances, Beck argued that certain types of schematic structures can operate to distort information processing in ways that increase the likelihood of emotional pathology.

Specifically, Beck implicated two hypothetical classes of maladaptive schemata in the mediation of emotional pathology. The first, which he termed the *depresso-genic schema*, can develop as a result of early experiences involving loss or failure, and incorporates a prototypical representation of such situations. When individuals possessing such a schema subsequently encounter the types of minor loss or failure events that precipitate a mild dysphoric mood state, then the depressogenic schema can become active. Beck termed the second type of maladaptive schema the *danger schema,* and he considered that this corresponds to a prototypical representation of situations involving the threat of personal danger. Developed to accommodate early experiences concerning risk and hazard, the danger schema remains latent until subsequently activated by minor threat events that slightly elevate state anxiety. Once active, these cognitive structures then operate to distort cognitive processing in ways that favor the automatic encoding and retrieval of information concerning loss and failure in the case of depressogenic schema, or threat-related information in the case of danger schemata. These cognitive distortions lead to the intensifica-tion and maintenance of the negative mood state, thus further activating the maladaptive schema. According to Beck, these schema-driven biases proceed quite automatically, being mediated by neither intention nor conscious awareness.

Bower's Network Model

Bower's account of the association between cognition and emotion represents an extension of his earlier network model of human memory (J.R. Anderson & Bower, 1973). In keeping with other network conceptualizations of the memory system (e.g., A.M. Collins & Loftus, 1975; A.M. Collins & Quillian, 1969), Bower assumed that information is stored as nodes within a memory net, and that information is accessed by activating the appropriate node beyond some threshold level. Over time, nodes that commonly are activated simultaneously come to develop shared associative connections, resulting in the emergence of cognitive priming effects. Specifically, when any node is activated then this activation automatically spreads through the associative connections to partially activate, or "prime," connected nodes also, which therefore become easier to access.

In extending this model of human memory, Bower simply introduced the assumption that each distinct emotional state is represented as a node within the memory system, which becomes activated whenever that emotional state is experienced (Bower, 1981; Bower & P.R. Cohen, 1982). Over time, such emotion nodes will come to develop associative connections with other nodes that commonly are activated simultaneously with them, which will tend to be those with emotionally congruent content. Once this network structure has developed then, whenever an emotional state activates the corresponding emotion node, this activation automatically will spread through the memory network to prime other nodes containing emotionally congruent information, which thus will become more available to a wide variety of cognitive processes including encoding and retrieval.

Although such mood-congruent processing effects should be shown by everyone, Bower's account leads to the prediction that they should be most pronounced in those individuals who have developed unusually strong associative connections between any particular emotion node and other emotionally congruent nodes in memory. Thus, Bower's model predicts that the degree to which any particular mood state serves to elicit an emotion-congruent processing bias should be greatest in individuals with a high level of trait vulnerability to that emotion. Bower pointed out that these cognitive biases should proceed quite automatically, being mediated by neither intention nor awareness.

Although they differ in terms of assumed mechanisms, the theoretical accounts offered by Beck and by Bower thus converge on a very similar set of predictions. They each predicted that cognitive biases favoring the processing of emotionally congruent information should be evidenced, in both anxiety and depression, across encoding and retrieval operations. They each also predicted that such effects should be triggered by anxious or depressed mood state, but should be most evident in individuals with a high level of trait vulnerability for that emotion. Finally, they each predicted that these biases should operate quite automatically, in the sense that they should occur without volition and should not require conscious mediation.

SELECTIVE INFORMATION PROCESSING
IN ANXIOUS AND DEPRESSED SUBJECTS

In this central section, we evaluate the support that has been provided for Beck's and Bower's predictions by research that has contrasted the patterns of selective processing demonstrated on emotionally valenced stimulus materials by subjects differing in levels of anxiety and depression. Studies that have investigated encoding and memory are reviewed in turn and, for each cognitive operation, we separately consider the patterns of findings associated with anxiety and with depression. Throughout this review, we endeavor not only to determine whether the predicted emotion-congruent processing biases do occur, but also to establish whether these effects do indeed operate automatically within the cognitive system.

Selective Encoding in Anxious Individuals

A number of studies have presented clinical anxiety patients with emotionally toned target words under conditions that make their detection difficult, and have found support for the prediction that such individuals will show an increased ability to detect the more emotionally threatening stimuli. For example, it has been found that when fear relevant words are presented to the unattended ear during a dichotic listening task, these are detected more reliably by agoraphobics, social phobics, and obsessional patients than by normal control subjects (e.g., Burgess et al., 1981; Foa & McNally, 1986). There is evidence to suggest that this enhanced detection of threat stimuli can indeed be triggered by anxious mood state. Thus, Foa and McNally found that the enhanced detection of threat targets was eliminated in their obsessional subjects after this anxiety disorder had been successfully treated, whereas Parkinson and Rachman (1981) found that normal mothers temporarily experiencing high levels of state anxiety, because their children were about to undergo surgery, also showed enhanced auditory detection of threat words embedded in white noise. Furthermore, there is evidence to suggest that trait anxiety too may play a role. For example, A. Byrne and M.W. Eysenck (1995) found that normal subjects with high levels of trait anxiety were faster than those with low levels of trait anxiety to detect an angry target face within a stimulus array of 12 faces in a photographic display, regardless of whether or not they underwent an anxiety mood induction manipulation.

However, this kind of emotional target detection paradigm suffers from a number of methodological limitations. For one thing, it is impossible to distinguish an encoding bias from a response bias using this type of experimental approach. Subjects who more rapidly report the presence of threat stimuli during such an active search procedure either may have encoded such stimuli more efficiently, or else may simply demonstrate a biased pattern of guesses under uncertainty, resulting in an increased likelihood of endorsing the presence of threat stimuli. Another limitation of the detection paradigm, particularly pertinent in the current context, concerns its incapacity to distinguish automatic from strategic cognitive processes. Given that subjects are explicitly instructed to detect threat stimuli in these experiments, any increased ability to do so could reflect a more effective strategic capacity to intentionally scan for threat, rather than an automatic bias that operates, without volition, to favor the encoding of threat stimuli.

Studies that do not suffer from the methodological limitations outlined earlier also have found evidence to suggest that anxious individuals orient attention towards threat-related information. C. MacLeod, A. Mathews, and Tata (1986) presented generalized anxiety patients and nonanxious control subjects with pairs of words (one emotionally threatening, and one emotionally neutral) in an upper and lower screen location on a VDU monitor. Subjects were required simply to read the upper word aloud, and to press a hand-held button whenever they detected a small dot probe, which could appear with equal frequency in the proximity of either word. These researchers reasoned that detection should be fastest for probes presented within attended areas of the screen, and so any attentional bias toward threat words should result in reduced detection latencies for probes occurring in the spatial vicinity of the threat member of each word pair. MacLeod et al. found that their clinically anxious patients showed a significant reduction in detection latencies for the probes presented in the proximity of threat words, relative to those appearing in the proximity of neutral words, suggesting that these individuals did indeed orient encoding resources toward the threat-related stimuli. In contrast, the nonanxious control subjects showed a marginally significant increase in detection latencies for probes in the area of threat relative to those in the vicinity of neutral words, suggesting the possibility that nonanxious individuals may selectively orient encoding resources away from threat-related stimuli.

Considerable subsequent research employing this dot probe paradigm to assess selective attention repeatedly has confirmed that clinically anxious patients detect probes in the vicinity of threat with disproportionate speed, particularly when such threat stimuli are related to those patients' principal domains of concerns (e.g., Mogg, A. Mathews, & M. Eysenck, 1992; Tata, Leibowitz, Prunty, Cameron, & Pickering, 1996). Some of this clinical research also has endeavored to assess the validity of Beck's and Bower's expectations concerning the degree to which this effect is mediated by state and trait anxiety. The results have not always been clear cut. For example, Mogg et al. (1992) contrasted the pattern of probe detection latencies shown by a population of recovered anxiety patients against those shown by current anxiety patients and never-anxious control subjects, with the assumption that recovery modifies mood state without changing an individual's trait vulnerability. The current patients showed a significant speeding to probes in the vicinity of threat words, which was not shown by the never-anxious control subjects. However, the recovered patient group showed a profile of detection latencies that fell intermediate to the patterns shown by the other two groups, and that differed significantly from neither. Hence, it was difficult to draw conclusions about the relative involvement of state and trait anxiety in the mediation of this anxiety-linked effect. However, data collected from nonclinical populations have tended to strongly support the prediction that state anxiety will elicit an attentional bias toward threat, and will do so to the greatest degree in those subjects with a high trait vulnerability to anxiety. Consistent with this position, D.E. Broadbent and M. Broadbent (1988) found that the magnitude of speeding to detect probes in the vicinity of threat was best predicted by the *product* of state and trait anxiety scores. Even more direct evidence is provided by a study reported by C. MacLeod and A. Mathews (1988), in which high- and low-trait anxious students were tested using the dot probe task on two occasions, early in the semester when state anxiety was low, and during the week before major examinations when state anxiety was elevated. When state anxiety was low, the patterns of probe detection latencies did not differ between the high- and low-trait subjects. However, as state anxiety levels increased, the high-trait subjects developed a significant selective speeding of detection latencies for probes near words related to examination threat (e.g., failure) relative to those near neutral words. In contrast, low-trait subjects responded to elevated state anxiety by showing a tendency toward selective slowing of detection latencies to probes in the vicinity of threat stimuli, relative to those in the vicinity of neutral stimuli.

Thus, data from probe detection tasks strongly support the contention not only that anxiety is associated with an encoding bias favoring threat stimuli, but also indicate that this represents a latent characteristic of high-trait anxious subjects that is elicited by elevated levels of state anxiety. This type of paradigm does not suffer from the methodological limitations of the emotional target detection task described earlier. Additionally, because the task does not explicitly instruct subjects to seek out emotionally valenced targets, it seems likely that the anxiety-linked attentional bias observed within this paradigm may indeed represent an automatic cognitive process rather than the increased efficiency of a volitional process. However, even stronger evidence for the automaticity of this anxiety-linked encoding bias has been forthcoming from studies that have instructed subjects to make intentional efforts to actively *avoid* the encoding of the critical stimulus information.

Those studies that have investigated the selective processing of information that subjects have been explicitly instructed to ignore commonly have employed interference measures to assess preferential encoding (cf. C. MacLeod, 1990, 1991, 1993). This methodology involves presenting subjects with some central task that they are required to perform, while simultaneously ignoring distracter stimuli. A sensitive measure of performance on the central task is recorded, and the degree to which subjects are able to ignore different classes of distracter stimuli is inferred from the extent to which the presence of these distracters interferes with performance on the central task.

One of most commonly employed interference methodologies within this field of research represents a variant of the Stroop color-naming task (Stroop, 1935). In this version of the task, subjects are presented with words of differing emotional tones, which appear in different ink colors, and are required to name the ink colors as rapidly as possible while simply ignoring the distracting word content. Many researchers have demonstrated that anxious individuals commonly demonstrate disproportionately long color-naming latencies on emotionally threatening stimulus words, suggesting a selective inability to ignore the content of such words. Such heightened color-naming interference on threatening stimuli now has been reported across a very wide range of clinical anxiety disorders, including generalized anxiety disorder (e.g., A. Mathews & C. MacLeod, 1985), social phobia (e.g.,

Hope, Rapee, Heimberg, & Dombeck, 1990), spider phobia (e.g., Watts, Trezise, & Sharrock, 1986), panic disorder (e.g., Ehlers, Margraf, S. Davies, & Roth, 1988), obsessive compulsive disorder (e.g., Lavy, van Oppen, & van den Hout, 1994), and posttraumatic stress disorder (PTSD; e.g., Cassiday, McNally, & Zeitlin, 1992). Commonly, the magnitude of the anxiety-linked interference effect has been found to be particularly great on those specific threat words that are most closely related to the anxiety patients' principal domains of personal concern (e.g., A. Mathews & C. MacLeod, 1985; Mogg, A. Mathews, & Weinman, 1989). For example, Lundh and Ost (1996) found their social phobic patients showed greatest interference on words related to social threat, whereas McNally, Riemann, and Kim (1990) found their panic disorder patients showed greatest interference on words related to physical threat.

Beck's and Bower's theoretical accounts also predict that selective encoding of emotionally threatening information will be triggered by elevated state anxiety, although to the greatest degree in high-trait anxious individuals. Research findings from the color-naming interference paradigm have tended to be consistent with this position. Certainly, as anxious mood state wanes in these clinical patients, then the magnitude of the color-naming interference shown on emotionally threatening words also tends to decline (e.g., A. Mathews, Mogg, Kentish, & M. Eysenck, 1995; Mogg, Bradley, N. Millar, & White, 1995). To test the prediction that state anxiety should elicit the most pronounced encoding biases in those subjects reporting the highest levels of anxiety vulnerability, some studies have examined the cognitive consequences of elevating this mood state within the normal population (C. MacLeod & Rutherford, 1992; Richards, French, W. Johnson, Naparstek, & J. Williams, 1992). For example, MacLeod and Rutherford tested groups of high- and low-trait anxious students as state anxiety changed as a function of proximity to major examinations. In the high-trait anxious group alone, the elevation of state anxiety was associated with a significant increase in the magnitude of the threat interference effect shown on the color-naming task, suggesting that only these subjects responded to state anxiety by showing a selective increase in the encoding of threatening information. Indeed, low-trait anxious subjects tended to display reductions in the magnitude of threat interference as their level of state anxiety increased, suggesting the possibility that such individuals may selectively avoid encoding threatening information as they become more state anxious.

Interference tasks, of the type reviewed previously, also have yielded further evidence to support the claim that this anxiety-linked encoding bias represents an automatic, rather than a strategic, cognitive phenomenon. Perhaps the strongest evidence that the anxiety-linked encoding bias operates at an automatic level of processing has been produced by variants of the interference task that have endeavored to restrict subjects' conscious awareness of the emotional stimulus information. Even under circumstances where subjects are unable to report the identity of distracter stimuli, individuals who are characterized by a high vulnerability to anxiety continue to demonstrate increased interference on a central task when threat-related distracters are presented simultaneously with performance. In an early demonstration of selective interference from unreportable emotional stimuli, A. Mathews and C. MacLeod (1986) required generalized anxiety patients and nonanxious controls to perform a central simple reaction time task, while carrying out a dichotic listening task involving the shadowing of a neutral message presented to an attended ear, and the ignoring of emotionally valenced distracter words presented to the unattended ear. The clinically anxious patients alone displayed a selective slowing of responses on the central reaction time task when threat-related, rather than emotionally neutral, distracter stimuli were presented simultaneously to the unattended ear.

More recent criticisms of the dichotic listening procedure, as a means of presenting stimuli outside of awareness, have led to the increased use of backward masking as the preferred method of eliminating conscious awareness of verbal stimuli (cf. Holender, 1986). Backward masking involves the brief visual presentation of stimulus words, usually for exposure durations of 20 milliseconds or less, swiftly followed by the presentation to the same location of a "mask" consisting of rotated and inverted letter fragments (cf. Turvey, 1973). Under such exposure conditions, subjects typically are unable to identify the presence of the initially presented word. Yet many studies have provided evidence to indicate that this word nevertheless does undergo semantic processing (e.g., Greenwald et al., 1989; P.M. Merikle & Reingold, 1990). To assess the automaticity of the selective encoding bias that appears to characterize anxiety vulnerability, C. MacLeod and Rutherford (1992) presented their high- and low-trait anxious students, experiencing elevated state anxiety due to impending exams, with 20-millisecond exposures to colored threatening and nonthreatening stimulus words, each of which immediately was replaced by a pattern mask that appeared in the same color. Although subjects were quite unable to determine whether or not a word had appeared under such exposure conditions, the high-trait anxious individuals still took disproportionately longer to name the color of the display when a threat word, rather than a neutral word had been exposed. Using this same procedure to eliminate awareness of word content, C. MacLeod and Hagan (1992) found that, in a sample of normal women undergoing a routine medical procedure, both trait anxiety and state anxiety correlated significantly with the magnitude of the color-naming interference effect shown on masked threat word trials relative to masked neutral word trials. More recently, researchers employing variants of the masked color-naming task have confirmed that generalized aniety disorder patients also continue to show increased color-naming interference on trials that present threatening words, rather than nonthreatening words, even when the use of backward masking makes it impossible to report the presence of these words (e.g., Bradley, Mogg, N. Millar, & White, 1995; Mogg, Bradley, R. Williams, & A. Mathews, 1993). On the basis of such findings, it seems appropriate to conclude that the selective processing of threat stimuli content, demonstrated by both clinically anxious patients and by high-trait anxious normals under stress, does indeed operate quite automatically, taking place not only without volition, but also occurring prior to conscious awareness of stimulus content.

However, it is possible that strategic processes also may play a critical role in the mediation of anxiety-linked encoding biases. Indeed, it has even been argued that the critical cognitive distinction between high-trait anxious normal individuals, and clinically anxious patients, may lie in the differential use of cognitive strategies to modify the emotional impact of encoding biases that operate at an automatic level within the cognitive system (e.g., C. MacLeod, 1991). Studies such as those of Mogg et al. (1995) and Bradley et al. (1995) have revealed that clinically anxious patients display equivalent patterns of elevated color-naming interference on threat words under both masked and exposure conditions. This not only suggests that the threat-encoding bias shown by these clinical patients is initiated prior to conscious awareness of the emotional stimuli, but also indicates that this bias continues to operate once these stimuli become consciously available. In contrast, normal subjects high in trait anxiety typically display a threat interference effect only under conditions that prevent stimulus awareness. For example, the significant correlation between the threat interference effect and anxiety observed by C. MacLeod and Hagan (1992), under a masked exposure condition, were entirely eliminated when these same stimuli were presented under an unmasked exposure condition. Likewise, the elevation of the threat interference effect displayed by the high-trait anxious subjects, under the masked exposure condition within C. MacLeod and Rutherford's (1992) color-naming study, did not occur when these same stimuli were displayed in an unmasked exposure condition. Therefore, it is tempting to speculate that the similar patterns of selective encoding shown by clinically anxious patients and high-trait anxious normals at an automatic level of processing might account for their shared high levels of anxiety vulnerability, but that the capacity to strategically suppress such encoding selectivity, which is exhibited by normal subjects alone, may prevent this automatic encoding bias from eliciting the severe emotional disturbance characteristic of anxiety pathology.

In summary, therefore, there is a wealth of evidence from a wide variety of experimental paradigms to support the prediction, generated by both Beck's and Bower's models, that anxious individuals should display a selective encoding advantage for emotionally threatening information. As predicted by these models, this encoding bias, which is particularly pronounced on those threat stimuli of greatest personal relevance and which is pervasive across a broad spectrum of clinical anxiety disorders, can be elicited by elevations in state anxiety, but only in high-trait anxious individuals. Furthermore, this anxiety-linked encoding bias appears to operate at an automatic level within the cognitive system. As such, it occurs without volition, persisting even when subjects actively endeavor to avoid encoding the emotional stimuli, and proceeds without conscious mediation, being displayed even when the emotional stimuli are presented outside of awareness.

Although both clinically anxious patients and high-trait normal subjects under stress demonstrate this encoding bias at an automatic level of processing, it seems possible that the nonclinical subjects may possess an ability to strategically suppress the encoding bias under circumstances that permit the engagement of controlled processing. If one assumes that the selective encoding of threatening stimuli can contribute toward the intensification of anxious mood state, then it can be argued that the inability to strategically suppress this automatic encoding bias may account for the inordinate severity of emotional pathology observed in clinically anxious patients.

Selective Encoding in Depressive Individuals

Despite their differences, the models of emotion and cognition proposed by Beck and by Bower each hold that the patterns of preferential processing shown on threat-related stimuli by anxious subjects should be mirrored by equivalent patterns of preferential processing on depressogenic stimuli in depressed subjects. However, though a number of researchers have argued in support of such a negative encoding bias in depressed individuals, the evidence for this hypothetical effect is considerably less compelling in depression research than is the case with anxiety.

D.M. Clark, Teasdale, D.E. Broadbent, and M. Martin (1983), and Challis and Krane (1988) both employed lexical decision tasks and mood induction techniques to test the prediction that elevated levels of depression should be associated with a selective reduction in the time taken to confirm the lexical status of negative stimulus words, relative to either neutral or positive control words. However, neither was able to find any support for the contention that depressed individuals should more readily encode depressogenic stimuli. To address the possibility that clinically depressed patients may show a trait-linked encoding advantage for negative stimuli that cannot be elicited in normal individuals simply by the induction of depressed mood state, C. MacLeod, Tata, and A. Mathews (1987) tested clinically depressed individuals on a lexical decision task. Once again, however, the depressed subjects revealed no sign of speeded lexical decision latencies on negative words relative to either neutral or positive words, compared to the nondepressed controls. This finding suggests that clinical depression is not associated with an encoding advantage for emotionally negative information.

Attentional probe studies similarly have failed to find a depression-linked selective encoding advantage for emotionally negative information (Gotlib, McLachlan, & A.N. Katz, 1988; C. MacLeod et al., 1986; McCabe & Gotlib, 1995). For example, MacLeod et al. included a group of clinical depressives within their original probe detection study, and found that such individuals showed no differential detection latencies for those probes presented in the vicinity of negative words and those presented in the vicinity of neutral words.

Experiments that have employed the color-naming interference task described earlier, to address the prediction that depressed individuals will display increased color-naming latencies on emotionally negative words, have produced more mixed findings. In an early study using this paradigm, Gotlib and McCann (1984) observed that college students reporting naturally elevated depression, unlike those who reported low depression, did indeed show selective slowing to color name emotionally negative words relative to neutral words. However, as this experiment did not assess students' anxiety levels, it is possible that the increased color-naming interference shown by these subjects on negative words may have reflected their elevated levels of anxiety, rather than their high levels of depression. Typically, it is questionnaire measures of state or trait anxiety, rather than depression, that correlate significantly with the magnitude of color-naming interference shown on emotionally negative words (e.g., A. Mathews & C. MacLeod, 1985; Mogg et al., 1989; J.M.G. Williams & K. Broadbent, 1986). Research on clinically depressed patients has failed to reveal convincing support for the hypothesis that these individuals will demonstrate heightened cooler-naming interference on emotionally negative words (Bradley et al., 1995; Mogg et al., 1993).

To summarize, therefore, despite the wealth of evidence that individuals with heightened vulnerability to anxiety are characterized by an automatic encoding bias favoring negative information, there is little convincing evidence to indicate that such an encoding bias operates, at either an automatic or a strategic level of processing, in individuals with heightened depression. This apparent dissociation between the cognitive correlates of anxiety and depression represents a problem for the models put forward by Beck and by Bower, and we return to this problem later in the chapter.

Selective Memory in Anxious Individuals

Given the striking evidence that, for anxious individuals, an automatic encoding bias operates to favor the processing of threatening information, it may come as some surprise to discover how little support has been forthcoming, from conventional recall and recognition paradigms, to sustain Bower's and Beck's parallel hypothesis that anxious individuals should display a memory advantage for such threat-related information (cf. C. MacLeod & A. Mathews, 1991; A. Mathews & C. MacLeod, 1994). The occasional findings to support the presence of such an effect typically either emerge from studies vulnerable to methodological criticism, or else fail to replicate.

It does appear to be the case that clinically anxious individuals may show a disproportionate ability to retrieve negative events from autobiographical memory (Burke & A. Mathews, 1992; McNally, Lasko, Macklin, & Pitman, 1995; McNally, Litz, Prassas, Shin, & Weathers, 1994). However, it is unnecessary to attribute such differences to biased memory retrieval, given the strong likelihood that the anxiety-disordered patients in these studies may simply have experienced a greater number of aversive events than the control subjects.

Those experiments that have circumvented this problem, by examining the retrieval of emotional stimuli encoded in the laboratory, have tended not to find evidence of an anxiety-linked bias on conventional memory tasks (e.g., A. Mathews & C. MacLeod, 1985; Mogg et al., 1989). For example, after Mogg, A. Mathews, and Weinman (1987) had presented generalized anxiety patients and control subjects with threatening and nonthreatening words in an incidental encoding task, the patients showed no enhanced ability to recall the threatening items in an unexpected memory test. A similar failure to obtain an anxiety-linked memory advantage for threat-related information has been reported across a wide range of anxiety disorders including spider phobia (Watts et al., 1986) and social phobia (e.g., Rapee, McCallum, Melville, Ravenscroft, & Rodney, 1994; Sanz, 1996).

Although some researchers examining phobic patients claim to have found that these individuals show a recall advantage for threatening information, these studies suffer from serious methodological limitations. For example, Nunn, Stevenson, and Whalan (1984) reported that their agoraphobic patients displayed better recall than their control subjects for words related to their agoraphobic concerns, such as *cinema* or *travel*, whereas Rusted and Dighton (1991) reported that their spider phobics showed better recall than their control subjects for spider-related words. However, because such phobic stimuli would have been threatening only for the phobic groups, these studies provide no opportunity to contrast selective memory for threat across the anxious and nonanxious groups. Furthermore, subsequent research often has failed to replicate the findings obtained in these experiments (e.g., Pickles & van den Broek, 1988).

Research investigating the memorial correlates of state and trait anxiety within the normal population consistently has failed to support the prediction that anxious individuals should display better recall of threat-related information (Dalgleish, 1994; Foa, McNally, & Murdock, 1989). For example, when Dalgleish followed a spelling task, given to high- and low-trait anxious subjects, with an unexpected memory test, he found that the high-trait subjects displayed no better recall for threatening words than was shown by the low-trait anxious individuals.

Therefore, it has proven consistently difficult to find convincing experimental support for the prediction that elevated anxiety should be associated with a memory advantage for emotionally threatening information. However, it should be noted that performance on both recall and recognition memory tasks commonly is affected not only by low-level cognitive operations that proceed automatically, but also by a rich and varied collection of retrieval heuristics, many of which can be strategically implemented under volitional control. Across the past decade, it has become common to distinguish explicit memory tasks, on which performance can readily be influenced by volitional strategies and mediated by conscious recollection, from implicit memory tasks, on which performance appears resistant to volitional strategy manipulation and that typically occurs without awareness (cf. Richardson-Klavehn & Bjork, 1988; Roediger, 1990a; Schacter, 1987, 1989). Some researchers have argued that, if it is the case that individuals with heightened vulnerability to anxiety are characterized by a memory bias that operates only at an automatic cognitive level, then it is plausible that this bias may best be detected on implicit memory tasks, rather than on explicit memory tasks such as recall or recognition (e.g., J.M.G. Williams et al., 1988).

Recent research that has contrasted anxious individuals' implicit and explicit memory for emotional stimulus materials, has provided considerable support for this proposal (e.g., Amir, McNally, Riemann, & Clements, 1996; C. MacLeod & McLaughlin, 1995; Mathews, Mogg, May, & M.W. Eysenck, 1989). Following a simple encoding procedure, MacLeod and McLaughlin used a recognition task to assess explicit memory, and a word identification task to assess implicit memory (with the word appearing on screen for a brief exposure duration, precalibrated to permit approximately 50% accuracy). Implicit memory was expressed as the increased identification accuracy demonstrated on those words that had been exposed in the encoding phase, relative to matched words that had not been presented earlier. MacLeod and McLaughlin found that their generalized anxiety patients and control subjects displayed equivalent recognition memory for the threat words and the neutral words. However, their anxiety patients displayed greater implicit memory than the control subjects for the threat words, and less implicit memory for the neutral words.

It remains to be seen whether research on nonclinical populations can determine the degree to which this anxiety-linked implicit memory advantage for threat-related information represents a characteristic of high trait vulnerability to anxiety in nonclinical subjects. At present, results are mixed, with some researchers reporting enhanced implicit memory for threatening stimuli in high-trait anxious normals (e.g., Richards & French, 1991), but others failing to replicate this finding in nonclinical subjects (e.g., Nugent & Mineka, 1994). Nevertheless, the overall pattern of findings clearly invites the conclusion that even extreme levels of anxiety are not associated with any mnemonic advantage for emotionally negative information on explicit memory tasks, which assess the strategic retrieval of conscious memories through volitional search processes. However, an anxiety-linked memorial advantage for negative information appears evident on implicit memory tasks, which assess the automatic functioning of memory processes that operate outside awareness and without volitional control.

Selective Memory in Depressed Individuals

Once again, the effects that have been observed by researchers working on depression stand in direct contrast to the findings more commonly obtained with anxious subjects. Despite the apparent absence of an anxiety-linked recall bias, a voluminous literature now attests to the existence of a robust recall bias in depressed individuals, operating to favor the retrieval of negative information (cf. Blaney, 1986; M.H. Johnson & Magaro, 1987; J.M.G. Williams et al. 1988).

Many of the early memory studies were carried out on clinically depressed patients, and investigated the recall of emotional events from autobiographical memory using the same cuing procedures as have been employed by researchers studying anxiety. Although D.A. Clark and Teasdale (1982) and J.M.G. Williams and K. Broadbent (1986) have shown that clinical depressives recall more emotionally negative events than do control subjects, the point has already been made that autobiographical memory effects need not implicate retrieval operations. Indeed, it is quite possible that depressed patients may have experienced an inordinate number of recent negative events, and so simply have more negative memories available to report.

Nevertheless, even when emotionally valenced stimulus materials are encoded within the laboratory, it still is the case that clinically depressed individuals display a relative recall advantage for the more negative stimuli. Derry and Kuiper (1981) presented clinically depressed patients and nondepressed control subjects with a self-rating task, in which they were exposed to positive and negative trait adjectives and required to decide whether or not each term was self-descriptive. Following this encoding procedure, an unexpected memory test was given, in which all subjects were instructed to recall as many trait adjectives as possible from the initial rating task. Derry and Kuiper found that the depressed patients, when compared to the control subjects, showed a relative recall advantage for the more negative trait adjectives. Using variants on this task, many other research studies now have replicated this recall advantage, in clinical depressives, for negative trait words exposed in a self-referent encoding task (e.g., Bradley & A. Mathews, 1983, 1988; A. Mathews & Bradley, 1983).

Additional compelling evidence against the possibility that depression-linked recall biases may represent differential encoding, rather than differential retrieval, comes from the many studies that have demonstrated that the degree to which subjects demonstrate facilitated recall of emotionally negative information varies with fluctuations in level of depressed mood state. Thus, for example, when D.A. Clark and Teasdale (1982) cued retrieval from long-term autobiographical memory at different times of the day, they found that diurnal variations in their clinical patients' levels of depression predicted the likelihood of a negative recall bias being displayed. Given that the actual contents of long-term autobiographical memory must have remained constant across the day, Clark and Teasdale's observation strongly suggests that variations in depression were associated with changes in memory retrieval operations. Also, it indicates that depressed mood state, and not only trait vulnerability to depression, must play a role in mediating the observed negative recall bias.

Two additional sources of evidence lend further support to the proposal that mood state contributes to the mediation of this depression-linked memory bias. First, it has been found that the recall advantage for emotionally negative information shown by untreated clinical depressives is eliminated when their depressed mood state is alleviated through clinical therapy (e.g., Dobson & Shaw, 1987; Slife, Miura, Thompson, Shapiro, & Gallagher, 1984). Second, it has been demonstrated that the induction of depressed mood state in a group of normal subjects can serve to increase the degree to which these individuals display a recall advantage for negative information (e.g., Sutton, Teasdale, & D.E. Broadbent, 1988; Teasdale & M.L. Russell, 1983). Although this finding, that depressed mood state can elicit a recall advantage for depression-congruent information, is fully consistent with the models of emotion and cognition developed by Beck and by Bower, these models each predict that elevations in depressed affect should elicit the most pronounced recall biases in those individuals who are most vulnerable to depression. A few studies have provided data that are consistent with this prediction.

For example, Teasdale and Dent (1987) employed a mood induction procedure to elevate level of depressed mood state in two groups of subjects. Subjects in one group were known to have a heightened vulnerability to depression, having recovered from a previous diagnosis of clinical depression, whereas the subjects in the other group had no particular vulnerability to this emotion. Both before and after the mood induction manipulation, subjects were given a memory task that assessed their ability to recall negative and positive information. The mood induction procedure elevated depression to an equivalent degree in both groups, and this elicited a general recall advantage for negative information. However, the magnitude of the negative recall bias elicited by the depression induction was disproportionately great in the group with the heightened vulnerability to depression. Findings have been similar from experiments that have induced depressed mood state in subjects scoring high and low on the personality dimension of neuroticism (Bradley, Mogg, Galbraith, & Perrett, 1993). Clearly, therefore, the pattern of findings from those studies that have endeavored to dissociate the involvement of state and trait variables in the mediation of depression-linked recall biases have been consistent with the models proposed by Beck and by Bower.

However, whereas the models of Beck and of Bower construe such patterns of selective memory as automatic cognitive biases, certain observations suggest the alternative possibility that the negative memory biases displayed by depressed individuals may represent strategic effects. For example, McDowell (1984) was able to demonstrate that depressed patients only exhibit better than normal recall of emotionally negative stimulus words if they have initially encoded "mixed" stimulus lists containing both pleasant and unpleasant items. When presented with negative or positive words alone, then depressed patients subsequently showed no enhanced recall for the former class of stimuli. McDowell argued that the negative recall bias shown by depressives arises because of the ways in which these individuals allocate processing resources from a limited-capacity system, thus implicating strategic cognitive processes in the mediation of the depression-linked memory bias. Additional evidence that the selective memory bias shown by depressed subjects may not operate automatically, is provided by the observation that manipulations that influence subjects' intentions during stimulus processing can eliminate the occurrence of this recall effect. For example, several of those studies that have obtained a depression-linked recall advantage for negative trait adjectives, following an encoding task requiring subjects to judge whether each word describes themselves, have failed to find any evidence of such a recall bias when subjects have been required to judge whether these terms describe some other individual (e.g., Bradley & A. Mathews, 1983, 1988; Derry & Kuiper, 1981). The fact that the manipulation of intention can so easily remove the depression-linked recall bias appears inconsistent with the view that this effect operates automatically, which would place it outside the influence of volitional control.

We have made the distinction earlier between explicit memory tasks, such as recall or recognition, where performance appears to be influenced by strategic factors, and implicit memory, where performance more directly reflects automatic processes. Therefore, if it is the case that the negative recall bias displayed by depressives is mediated by strategic processing, then it would be expected that this bias should be less evident on tasks assessing implicit memory than has proven to be the case on tasks assessing explicit memory. To test this prediction, Denny and R.R. Hunt (1992) exposed clinically depressed patients and nondepressed control subjects to emotionally negative and emotionally positive stimulus words, in a self-referent encoding task, then unexpectedly assessed their memory for these stimuli using tests of both explicit and implicit memory. In the recall procedure these researchers employed to measure explicit memory, they found that the depressed patients were able to recollect significantly more negative words than positive words, whereas the control subjects demonstrated the reverse pattern of selective retrieval. However, when Denny and Hunt measured implicit memory, by assessing the degree to which initial exposure to stimulus words increased the degree to which these items were generated on a word fragment completion task, they observed no depression-linked memory bias. Both groups of subjects showed equivalent performance across negative and positive words. Denny and Hunt concluded that depression is associated with no enhanced implicit memory for emotionally negative information. Virtually identical findings have been reported by Watkins, A. Mathews, Williamson, and Fuller (1992), who also used explicit and implicit memory tasks to compare the patterns of selective memory shown by clinical depressives and normal control subjects. Therefore, it appears that the depression-linked memory advantage for negative information is restricted to those memory tasks that explicitly require subjects to engge search strategies in order to intentionally conduct a search of memory.

In conclusion, there is little doubt that depression is associated with facilitated memory for emotionally negative information. As predicted by the models developed by Beck and by Bower, this negative memory bias is elicited by elevated levels of depressed mood state, with this occurring to the greatest degree in those subjects who have a high level of vulnerability to depression. However, because the memory bias seems only to occur when subjects process stimulus information with certain intentions, only when positive and negative items are presented in a mixed format that taxes processing capacity, and only on explicit memory tasks, it seems likely that this depression-linked memory bias may represent a strategic rather than an automatic cognitive bias.

THEORETICAL AND APPLIED IMPLICATIONS

Although this overview of the literature provides only an introduction to the wealth of research that has investigated the cognitive underpinnings of emotional vulnerability over the past decade, it serves adequately to indicate that the patterns of processing associated with anxiety appear to differ fundamentally from those associated with depression. Individuals with heightened vulnerability to anxiety show an increased tendency, especially when state anxiety is elevated, to selectively encode the more negative elements of their environment, even when they endeavor to avoid encoding such materials, and when they are unaware that such stimuli are present. They also show enhanced implicit memory for emotionally negative information, but display no such bias on intentional memory tasks such as recall. The overall pattern of findings provides compelling support for the hypothesis that the cognitive biases associated with anxiety vulnerability function at an automatic level of processing, occurring without volition and operating outside of conscious awareness. In contrast, individuals vulnerable to depression do not appear to demonstrate a selective encoding advantage for negative stimuli, and show no implicit memory advantage for negative information. However, depressed individuals do show a very robust explicit memory advantage, which operates to systematically favor the recall of emotionally negative information on tasks that require the intentional scrutiny of memory. The evidence suggests, therefore, that the memory bias associated with vulnerability to depression may function at a strategic level of processing, reflecting the volitional application of consciously mediated search heuristics. This striking dissociation between the patterns of cognitive bias associated with anxiety, and with depression, has important theoretical and applied implications, which we conclude by considering.

The theoretical models of emotion and cognition developed by Beck and by Bower both predict that the profiles of cognitive biases associated with anxiety, and with depression, should essentially be equivalent. These models demand that in both anxiety and depression such processing selectivity for depressogenic or danger-related information should occur quite automatically, and should be evident on tasks that assess encoding and memory. Thus, the striking dissimilarities observed between the patterns of selective processing associated with anxiety and with depression serve to refute the validity of these early accounts. Indeed, this dissociation seems inconsistent with *any* theoretical account of emotion that conceptualizes the cognitive basis of different emotions such as anxiety and depression in terms of some common processing mechanism. Instead it offers support for the views of theorists, such as Oatley and Johnson-Laird (1987), who have argued that, because each basic emotion will have evolved to facilitate the execution of those specific types of cognitive functions most appropriate to the particular circumstances that elicit this emotion, then each emotion will likely be associated with a unique mode of information processing. This realization has led to the development of more refined models, which now commonly delineate the alternative classes of processing mechanisms likely to be implicated in the cognitive mediation of different emotional conditions (e.g., Barnard & Teasdale, 1991; A.K. Johnson & Multhaup, 1992; Williams et al., 1988).

For example, Williams et al. (1988) have attempted to accommodate the observed discrepancies between the cognitive biases displayed by anxious and depressed individuals by drawing upon the distinction made by Graf and G. Mandler (1984) between two processes that can act on mental representations. Specifically, Graf and G. Mandler delineated the process of *integration* from that of *elaboration*. These researchers construed integration as an automatic cognitive operation that proceeds without volition to temporarily strengthen the internal structure of a mental representation. A highly integrated representation is rendered more available in the sense that activation of any part will more reliably and more rapidly activate the whole, meaning that such representations will be more readily accessed when only some of their features have been fully processed. In contrast, Graf and Mandler conceptualized elaboration as a strategic process, which operates under conscious control to develop and strengthen connections between mental representations. Highly elaborated representations will be retrieved more readily through intentional memory search as a result of these enriched associative connections.

Williams et al. (1988) proposed that individuals with an elevated vulnerability to anxiety may be characterized by a heightened tendency, elicited by anxious mood state, to demonstrate increased integrative processing of mental representations for emotionally negative information. In contrast, they proposed that individuals with an elevated vulnerability to depression may be characterized by a heightened tendency, elicited by depressed mood state, to demonstrate increased elaborative processing of such negative mental representations. Such an account explains why anxious subjects show an automatic increase in the accessibility of negative mental representations when cued with their features in perceptual tasks and implicit memory tasks, whereas depressed subjects show only a strategic enhancement of their ability to intentionally retrieve such negative representations during explicit memory search tasks. C. MacLeod and McLaughlin (1995) have pointed out that these particular biases may have developed because of their evolutionary value under the circumstances that commonly elicit depression and anxiety. Given that depression tends to be elicited when important plans already have led to loss or failure, it may be most adaptive to respond cognitively to this emotion by strengthening associative connections between disparate mental representations of other losses and failures, and consciously reflecting on any rules that can be extracted from their similarities to guide future behavior in ways that minimize the risks of repetition. However, given that anxiety is more likely to be elicited when an individual faces imminent personal danger from some external threat, the more adaptive cognitive response to this emotion may be to strengthen the internal structure of one's mental representations of threatening information, in order that such representations will more rapidly be accessed in response to minimum stimulus information, indicating the presence of an external threat.

Whether or not Williams et al.'s (1988) account proves capable of withstanding rigorous empirical scrutiny, it is clear that the differential involvement of automatic and strategic processes in the mediation of the discrepant patterns of cognitive bias associated with anxiety and depression can be handled only by theoretical models that distinguish not only these two emotions, but also these two modes of information processing. Furthermore, the delineation of the distinctive cognitive biases associated with anxiety and depression may have practical implications that stretch beyond an immediate impact on theoretical accounts of emotion and cognition. These practical implications will depend, in part, on the assumed causal nature of the association between emotional vulnerability and selective information processing. There are two possibilities, each of which are considered in turn.

The most conservative position would be to attribute no causal status to the selective processing biases reported in this review. All this position requires us to accept is the presence of certain cognitive "markers" of each emotion. Individuals vulnerable to anxiety show, especially when state anxious, increased automatic encoding of negative information and enhanced implicit memory for negative information. Individuals vulnerable to depression show, especially when experiencing state depression, enhanced explicit memory for negative information. These cognitive markers provide clinical researchers with the potential to develop cognitive techniques that may prove capable of assessing emotional vulnerability more sensitively, and more objectively, than traditional self-report measures. For example, by assessing the degree to which individuals display particular selective processing biases, it may be possible to obtain a more precise index of their anxiety vulnerability than is forthcoming from more conventional questionnaire indices of trait anxiety. Recent support for this possibility has been provided by C. MacLeod and Hagan (1992), who used a masked and unmasked color-naming interference task to initially assess the automatic and strategic encoding biases shown by a population of women stressed by a minor cervical examination. The subset of women who subsequently received a diagnosis of cervical pathology completed a rating scale, some weeks afterwards, to indicate the degree to which this later traumatic event had induced dysphoria. Conventional questionnaire measures of emotional vulnerability, taken on the initial test session, proved incapable of predicting the levels of dysphoria elicited by the subsequent diagnosis. However,

MacLeod and Hagan found that the individual differences in the degree of slowing to color name threat words, relative to nonthreat words, under the masked exposure condition, powerfully predicted the intensity of this later dysphoric reaction to the subsequent diagnosis of pathology. In a more recent study using a similar experimental design, C. MacLeod and Ng (1997) compared the capacity of the color-naming interference task, and questionnaire measures of emotional vulnerability, to predict the later emotional reactions of high school graduates traveling overseas to commence tertiary education. Individual differences in the degree to which subjects slowed to color name threat words not only predicted the magnitude of their state anxiety elevations on their arrival in the host country, but did so better than any of the conventional questionnaire measures.

If one entertains the hypothesis that the patterns of selective information processing associated with vulnerability to anxiety, and to depression, may contribute causally to the development and maintenance of such emotional vulnerability, then additional applied possibilities can be identified. This position leads to the prediction that emotional vulnerability may be attenuated by directly manipulating particular patterns of selective processing. Although numerous cognitive therapies now have been developed for the treatment of emotional disorders, these approaches presently tend to focus rather generally on challenging the maladaptive beliefs that often characterize these conditions (cf. Meichenbaum, 1995). As yet, cognitive therapies have not been designed to precisely target those specific processing biases known to be associated with each type of emotional vulnerability. The present review suggests that cognitive therapy for depression may be most effective if this were to employ techniques designed to therapeutically manipulate patterns of selective recall, whereas cognitive therapy for anxiety would more appropriately employ techniques designed to modify patterns of selective encoding. Furthermore, the observation that cognitive biases underpinning anxiety and depression may be differentially mediated by automatic and strategic processes also could have important practical implications for the most appropriate design of these cognitive therapies. For depressed patients, it is possible that cognitive therapy may best proceed simply by providing explicit instructions to patients concerning the use of alternative memory search strategies. In contrast, it may be more appropriate to provide anxiety patients with repeated exposure to highly structured training sessions, designed to shape alternative patterns of automatic encoding selectivity through extended practice on cognitive tasks that reward alternative patterns of selective encoding, such as the attentional avoidance of threatening stimuli.

For the present, such clinical applications remain at an early stage of development. However, it seems clear that recent advances to our understanding of the cognitive biases underpinning vulnerability to anxiety, and to depression, have brought our discipline to the brink of a fruitful new collaboration between the clinical practitioner and the cognitive researcher. As this partnership develops and matures, we can look forward to developing a more sophisticated appreciation of the ways in which emotional vulnerability is mediated by the cognitive biases that operate both before, and behind, the veil of consciousness.

ACKNOWLEDGMENTS

Preparation of this chapter was partially supported by Australian Research Council Grant 337088 to Colin MacLeod.

15

A NATURAL HISTORY OF EXPLICIT LEARNING AND MEMORY

C.D.L. Wynne
University of Western Australia

If a lion could talk, we could not understand him.
—Wittengenstein (1958, p. 223)

Give me orange me give eat orange me eat orange give me eat orange give me you
(Longest utterance of Nim, a chimp)
—Terrace, Petitto, R.J. Sanders, and Bever (1979, p. 895)

Natural history is a term that conjures up images of 19th-century explorers bringing back stuffed specimens, and naming mountains after their monarchs and benefactors, an escapade that perhaps served its purpose in its time, but that surely, I fear I hear the reader asking, has been thoroughly superseded by the end of the 20th century. However, the comparative analysis of cognition is a very young science—very few journeys have yet been made and whole dark continents await our exploration. Natural history is very much the appropriate form of analysis at our present state of ignorance.

Why should we care about the distribution of a cognitive trait through the animal kingdom? I see at least three major reasons. First, our understanding of ourselves as human beings is intimately linked to our sense of our intellectual uniqueness. Any evidence on the question of cognitive commonalties between ourselves and other species would directly address our understanding of what it means to be human beings. Second, although our knowledge of the physical world has taken great strides in the last three centuries, our knowledge of the psychological worlds of our fellow species remains at a very low level. Third, and of most practical importance, any advances in our understanding of how animal and human cognition are related would have significant practical consequences for the study of the functions of the brain/mind system. Much basic research on brain and mind is carried out on nonhuman species for practical and ethical reasons. Our ability to use animal models to understand dysfunctions of the human brain/mind system (such as drug addiction, brain damage after stroke, neurological syndromes such as Alzheimer's disease, Korsakoff's syndrome, schizophrenia, etc.) is therefore limited by our lack of understanding of commonalities in the brains and minds of humans and other animals. Where the comparative study of brains is theoretically quite straightforward (although often of fiendish technical difficulty), the comparative study of minds is at a much more primitive stage, and therefore acts as a brake on these studies.

A fully fledged evolutionary analysis of cognition is difficult for several reasons. First, there is no (or very little) fossil record of any behavioral trait. Thus, it is difficult or impossible to extrapolate the evolution of a trait from observations of its distribution in extant populations because we cannot distinguish common ancestry from convergent evolution. Second, there is always the possibility that, despite all the plausible stories of the adaptive value of cognitive abilities, there has been no selection for cognitive prowess—this ability may have developed as an epiphenomenon of increasing brain size (selected for some other reason). Third, we know that evolution by natural selection is only interested in reproductive advantage, yet we have no way of measuring the reproductive advantage of cognition.

For all these reasons, I have chosen the somewhat archaic designation natural history to make clear that my ambitions, for the present at least, do not go beyond defining and assessing the distribution of an ability.

But what is this thing "explicit learning and memory"? The distinction between implicit and explicit processes in learning and memory has been drawn in other chapters in the present volume (Dunn; Kirsner; O'Brien-Malone & Maybery) and elsewhere (e.g., Graf & Schacter, 1985; Reber, 1992; Schacter, 1987). Unfortunately, many of these dichotomies prove of little use once we leave the familiar shores of human psychology.

PROBLEMS OF DEFINITION

In attempting to understand explicit learning and memory, the problems do not lie in finding definitions of learning and memory that can be applied to nonhumans, but in the definition of *explicit*. Explicit learning and memory are defined in several different ways in the literature, not all of which apply even to the standard tasks used to assess this ability in intact human subjects.

Definition 1: Conscious Awareness and Intent

The most prevalent definitions of explicit learning and memory consider conscious awareness of the material learned and conscious intention to learn to be the defining characteristics of this form of learning. This distinguishes explicit learning from implicit learning, which is characterized by the absence of an intention to learn, and the lack of conscious awareness of what has been learned (Holyoak & Spellman, 1993; Reber, 1992; Schacter, 1987; see also O'Brien-Malone & Maybery, chap. 3 of this volume).

This definition is problematic for attempts to map a natural history of explicit learning and memory.

First, it is not itself a final definition, but rather appeals to another set of definitions—definitions of consciousness. Reber (1992) defined consciousness as "the capacity to play a causal role in the inner workings of oneself" (p. 113). This definition sounds seductive as a description of my own consciousness, however, none of the standard tasks used to demonstrate explicit learning and memory (assessed elsewhere in this volume by O'Brien-Malone & Maybery) could be said to have demonstrated consciousness in this sense. Indeed it is difficult to imagine how such an ability could ever be demonstrated empirically. If we were confronted with a subject whose capacity for conscious awareness were in question, what tests could be performed to assess whether it has consciousness of this type?

Second, it implies that the distinction between implicit and explicit learning and memory relies on negative evidence—on the failure of a subject to consciously report what it knows. Reber (1992) called this the "problem of experimental indeterminacy" (p. 107). In any situation where a subject is believed to be performing implicitly, without explicit knowledge, this demonstration depends on guaranteeing the exhaustiveness of whatever instrument is being used to assess the contents of consciousness. The failure to consciously report knowledge may be a consequence of the manner of interrogating consciousness. Certainly, different procedures differ in the degree of conscious awareness they uncover in otherwise similar situations (see Reber, 1989a; see also O'Brien-Malone & Maybery, chap. 3 of this volume).

These problems are intensified by the fact that some theorists (e.g., Hasher & Zacks, 1979, 1984) allow information gained unconsciously (implicitly) to subsequently become available to consciousness. This means that the ability to consciously report learned material does not necessarily imply that the material was learned explicitly.

A long time ago, Thorndike (1911) commented on the negative influence on comparative psychology of an emphasis on conscious report: "So long as introspection was lauded as the chief method of psychology, a psychologist would tend to expect too little from mere studies, from the outside, of creatures who could not report their inner experiences to him in the manner to which he was accustomed." (p. 3). In fact, however, the operational definition of consciousness implied by the empirical studies of explicit learning and memory is really quite simple—namely the ability to report to the experimenter what has been learned. A comparative analysis of *this* ability is not as difficult as it might at first appear. As we see later the ability to report on one's own behavior is remarkably widespread in the animal kingdom. The assessment of this ability is the first subsection in the body of this chapter.

Definition 2: "One-shot" Learning and the Memorization of Arbitrary Associations

Not all definitions of explicit learning cause problems for comparative studies. Explicit learning has been stated to be the learning of arbitrary facts and associations in a single (or limited number) of trials (Holyoak & Spellman, 1993). Conversely, implicit learning typically requires multiple presentations of material to be learned, and shows a gradual acquisition function, rather than the step function of explicit learning (Schacter et al., 1993).

Clearly there is nothing in this definition that precludes studies on nonhuman subjects. This, therefore, forms the second subsection in the body of this chapter.

Definition 3: Flexible Representations

Explicit learning is considered to result in more flexible representations of knowledge than is implicit learning (Holyoak & Spellman, 1993). Whereas implicit knowledge is generally limited to the domain in which the original learning episode took place, explicit knowledge is not so domain-limited and is more widely generalizable. Implicit memory is "brittle" in that it is impaired by any change in the original problem situation. A range of tasks using spatial stimuli have demonstrated rich representations in nonhuman subjects. I review spatial learning and memory in the third subsection of the body of this chapter.

Definition 4: Hippocampal Amnesia

The distinction between implicit and explicit learning and memory has repeatedly been identified with the amnesic syndrome observed after damage to the hippocampal system (Graf & Schacter, 1985; Reber, 1992).

People with damage to the hippocampal formation rapidly forget newly acquired sensory and cognitive information—typically within seconds to minutes. The best known human case, H.M., has a severe, largely anterograde amnesia. He is unable to explicitly remember any events subsequent to the operation in which his hippocampal formation was bilaterally ablated. Some limited forms of memory are spared, however. H. M. and similar amnesiacs acquire and retain perceptual and motor skills and some limited forms of cognitive information about as well as normals (N.J. Cohen & Squire, 1980; Corkin, 1968; Warrington & Weiskrantz, 1968B). However, even on those tasks where memory sparing is observed, these subjects are unable to verbally report their past experience and express no familiarity with the task materials when presented with them. H. M., for example, has been successfully trained on the Tower of Hanoi problem. This task involves three pegs and five discs. At the start of the task the disks are arranged in decreasing order of size on the left-most peg. The subject's task is to rearrange the disks in the same order on the right-most peg in the smallest number of moves, subject to the constraints that he or she may move only one disk at a time, and that a larger disk must never be placed on top of a smaller one. This task is moderately difficult (the optimal solution requires 31 moves), and normal subjects show a gradual reduction in the number of moves they make as they are repeatedly tested. H. M. and other amnesic subjects also show a progressive improvement on the task with repeated testing (N.J. Cohen et al., 1985). The remarkable thing about H. M.'s performance improvement is that he could not explicitly remember (verbally report) having ever seen the task before, and had no insight into his task-solution strategy.

This pattern of memory damage, where verbally reported (conscious) memories are lost, but nonverbal memory is spared, shows substantial overlap with the dichotomy between explicit and implicit memory. The identification of the implicit/explicit distinction with the functions of the hippocampal formation has two very substantial advantages for our purposes. First, there is broad agreement on the types of memory function subsumed by the hippocampal formation, and these are all operationally defined in terms of experimental tests, many of which can be performed on nonhuman subjects. Second, with this anatomical marker we can speculate more widely about the prevalence of explicit learning and memory than would be possible on the basis of the few species that have had their learning and memory abilities tested. The study of the distribution of brain structure was well underway in the last century, and it is clear that a structure considered homologous to the mammalian hippocampus is observed throughout the vertebrates, including birds (Bullock, Orkand, & Grinnell, 1977). Thus we have a prima facie reason to believe that explicit learning and memory might be at least as widespread. The question of hippocampal involvement in nonhuman explicit learning and memory does not form a subsection of its own, but is considered throughout the body of this chapter.

THE NATURAL HISTORY OF
EXPLICIT LEARNING AND MEMORY

We now have a chart for our voyage. We now set out to assess the distribution of explicit learning and memory, which we can recognize by four signs: (a) report of knowledge to conspecifics or experimenter, (b) "one-shot" or rapid learning of arbitrary material, (c) rich multidimensional associations in the spatial domain, and

(d) the influence of hippocampal damage on learning and memory. The first three of these signs are considered next under separate subheadings. The question of the influence of the hippocampal formation is considered within each subheading.

Report

The productivity, semanticity, grammar, and sheer vocabulary of human language remain well ahead of anything that has ever been found in or taught to another species. Terrace et al. (1979) reported the results of training a chimpanzee to communicate with sign language for the deaf. After more than 18 months of training, Nim's longest utterance was "Give me orange me give eat orange me eat orange give me eat orange give me you" (Terrace et al., 1979, p. 895); and his mean length of utterance remained around 1.5 words.

However, our interest in report lies solely in identifying nonhuman cases of explicit learning and memory. We are not interested in the complexity of the report, but in the sheer fact of it. In assessing whether a patient with brain damage is suffering any impairment of the explicit learning/memory system, it would be quite irrelevant if we discovered that this subject had suffered damage to speech production and/or comprehension areas and was no longer able to express him or herself clearly. All that is important is whether or not he or she were able to report in some way the results of learning experiences.

Bees.   A particularly dramatic and well-known example of report in a very modest being is that of the waggle dance of the honeybee, discovered by von Frisch (1967). The brain of the bee is less than one cubic millimeter in volume and contains only 950,000 neurons (Menzel, 1990). Notwithstanding these limitations, foraging bees report to hive-mates the position of a food source and its distance from the hive. This is achieved by means of a dance in a figure-of-eight form on the vertical wall of the hive. The rate of the dance indicates the distance from the hive of the food source (the faster the dance, the closer the food source). The angle to the vertical of the central part of the figure of eight indicates the angle between the sun and the food source, as seen at that point in time from the hive. If the bee's return journey to the hive has been sufficiently lengthy that the sun's position has changed, it will correct the vertical angle of the waggle dance to provide accurate sun bearing information for the sun's new position.

The information communicated in the waggle dance may also be the result of a single learning experience—thereby also fulfilling the definition of explicit learning as being one-shot learning of arbitrary information.

Pigeons.   Though there is no evidence that pigeons spontaneously report information to each other, there is a seam of research showing that they can readily be trained to report to an experimenter about some aspect of their behavior.

Pigeons have been trained to report on the number or pattern of pecks they have just emitted. These experiments involve two phases. Shimp (1981), for example, first trained pigeons in a Skinner box to peck either quickly or slowly onto a central response key. This they readily learned to do. From time to time two side keys were lit up, one red and one green. A peck on the green side key was rewarded if the previous response sequence on the center key had consisted of fast responses, whereas the pigeon had to peck on the red side key to get reward if the previous center-key response sequence had consisted of slow responses. With training, the subjects learned to report what kind of response sequence (fast or slow) they had just produced, demonstrating the ability to report on their own past behavior.

In a subsequent study, Shimp (1982) trained pigeons to produce runs of different numbers of responses. The pigeons made either a short run of responses, or a long run. As in the earlier experiment, the subjects occasionally would be interrupted by two choice keys, red and green. As before, they had to respond to green if they had made a short run of responses, or red for a longer run. Once again, the pigeons were successful in learning to do this. Both these cases are clear examples of explicit learning in the senses of report of material learned, and the learning of arbitrary associations. These cases, however, cannot be considered one-shot or rapid learning.

Parrots.   Pepperberg (1981, 1983, 1990) has trained an African grey parrot (Alex) to use more than 40 verbal labels and combine these in meaningful, multiword utterances. Alex's use of words is literally verbal, because, exploiting this species' ability to mimic sounds, he has been trained to speak the words out loud. Pepperberg used a Model-Rival technique in which the parrot had to compete with a "rival" (a human confederate of the experimenter) for the experimenter's attention. This rival also modeled correct responses that Alex learned to emulate. Alex is able to name objects, and describe how many he has been presented, as well as their qualities such as shape or color, and whether two items are the same or different.

This ability to name and describe items is clearly report, and also qualifies as explicit learning on the grounds of the arbitrariness of the material learned and the speed of learning.

Summary.   This brief review indicates that there is plentiful evidence among nonhuman species for explicit learning in the sense of the ability to report knowledge to others. A wide range of social animals can communicate information to conspecifics. I chose to discuss honeybees because their nervous system is so much simpler than one might expect for such an advanced ability, but other obvious examples include primates, dogs, and dolphins. Whereas the waggle dance of the bee is a spontaneous, apparently preprogrammed behavior, some other species have been trained experimentally to give reports of their experiences. I have not here gone into the various ape-language projects. Their limited successes are quite well known (e.g., Wallman, 1992). Less well known is that parrots and even pigeons have also been trained to report on their behavior.

Given the association mentioned previously, between explicit learning and memory and an intact hippocampal formation, it is interesting that little effort has been made to analyze the anatomical substrates of the ability to report in the aforementioned cases. Neither apes, rats, pigeons, or parrots have been studied from this viewpoint. The only species where the ability to communicate has been localized in the brain is the honeybee—which has a brain so small that no hippocampal formation is recognized.

One-Shot Learning and the Memorization of Arbitrary Associations

Amnesic subjects such as H. M. are severely impaired in the ability to memorize arbitrary pieces of information. For example, H. M. fails on tests where he must select an item out of an array that matches (i.e., is identical to) one he was shown as recently as 5 seconds earlier (Sidman, Stoddard, & Mohr, 1968). This ability to recognize material as familiar after a single presentation is a feature of explicit memory. Conversely, gradual learning of motor skills and habits, gradual learning about reinforcers (classical and operant conditioning), and gradual changes in responsiveness to repeated stimulation (habituation and sensitization) are forms of implicit learning and are generally spared in amnesic patients.

Many of the examples of report in nonhuman subjects reviewed earlier also indicated the ability to learn arbitrary material rapidly. Several other tasks have been studied in nonhumans providing a broad range of evidence for the distribution of one-shot learning and the memorization of arbitrary information.

Delayed Nonmatching to Sample and Other Forms of Recognition Memory. Recognition memory is the ability to respond differentially to a stimulus due to its having been presented before. If a subject can respond in the desired way on the basis of a single prior presentation, then we have a strong case of explicit memorization in the sense of learning that is one-shot, and of arbitrary information.

On a delayed nonmatching to sample task a subject first is shown a sample stimulus. This then is removed for some period of time before two comparison stimuli are presented. One of these will be the same as the sample stimulus, the other different. Correct choice is defined as selection of the item different from the original sample stimulus. An important point here is whether the same stimuli are repeatedly used on different trials. When stimuli are reused across trials the (slight) possibility exists that some kind of implicit learning of patterns of reward relationships may take place. More convincing evidence for explicit memorization is provided by studies using "trial-unique" stimuli, that is stimuli that only appear in one trial each. When trial-unique stimuli are used, the memorization on each trial can only be one-shot and hence explicit in form.

In studies on primates with trial-unique stimuli, a single object is first presented as a sample stimulus—the subject displaces it to obtain reward. After a delay, the sample stimulus is presented again in a different position, this time along with a novel stimulus—the subject has to displace the novel item to obtain food reward. Progressively longer delays between sample and comparison stimuli are tested to measure the duration of memory. Whereas this task is learned by normal monkeys at delays of up to a few minutes, subjects with hippocampal lesions perform very poorly at delays over 8 seconds (Zola-Morgan, Squire, & Mishkin, 1982).

Similar conclusions about the explicit memorization abilities of monkeys and the dependence of these abilities on an intact hippocampal formation can be drawn from a simple study by Phillips and R.R. Mishkin (1984). Monkeys were given food under an object, and then exposed to a delay before being given a choice between that item and another, novel item. Subjects with a lesioned hippocampal formation, unlike intact subjects, were unable to remember for more than a few seconds which of the two choice objects had just been baited.

Rats have been trained on delayed nonmatching to sample in a variety of ways. They have been trained with conventional objects as cues (Mumby, Pinel, & Wood, 1990; Rothblat & Kromer, 1991), in a Y-maze with visually and tactically distinct arms as cues (Aggleton, 1985; Gaffan, 1972; Rafaelle & Olton, 1988), or using the spatial position of the sample as a cue (Olton, Becker & Handleman, 1979; G.J. Thomas & Gash, 1988). In all these versions the cues were reused repeatedly. Otto and Eichenbaum (1992) used 16 different odors as cues in the two arms of a Y-maze. In this way they were able to test trial-unique stimuli. Just as in humans and primates, normal rats learned the task well. Subjects with lesions to the hippocampal formation were normal at short delays, but impaired at longer delays. Even lesioned subjects could remember what to do (run down the maze, choose a stimulus, etc.), but just like amnesic humans in recognition memory tasks, they simply forgot what sample stimulus had been presented.

Probably the largest literature on delayed nonmatching to sample in nonhumans concerns pigeons. The standard apparatus for testing pigeons is a three-key Skinner box. At the start of a trial, the center key is illuminated with white light. After this stimulus has been pecked a number of times (to ensure the subject is attending to the correct response key), the sample stimulus appears on this key. Once this sample stimulus has been pecked a few times it disappears and is followed by a delay before the two side keys are illuminated. One side key contains the sample stimulus, the other an alternative nonmatching stimulus. D.S. Grant (1976) demonstrated above-chance performance at delays up to 60 seconds if the sample stimulus was presented for at least 4 seconds. A.A. Wright, Cook, Rivera, Sands, and Delius (1988) showed that pigeons can perform well on this task with trial-unique stimuli.

Though the literature on matching to sample in pigeons is very extensive (see Roitblat, 1993, for a recent review), there do not appear to have been any studies on the involvement of the hippocampal formation in these performances. The only relevant study used an older form of delayed recognition task (the Konorski pair comparison). On this task, the subject is presented two stimuli in succession. Its task is to respond (on two response keys) whether or not the stimuli were identical. Delays can be imposed between the presentation of the stimuli and the opportunity to respond. Sahgal (1984) found that normal pigeons showed good performance at delays up to 10 seconds, but pigeons with lesions to the hippocampal formation faired badly at any delays over 1 second.

Delayed matching to sample has been demonstrated in the dolphin, both in the auditory (Roitblat, Penner, & Nachtigall, 1990) and visual systems (Herman, Hovancik, Gory, & Bradshaw, 1989), and in a combined visual/auditory task (Forestell & Herman, 1988). Performance remained highly accurate at delays of up to 80 seconds (Herman et al., 1989). There do not appear to have been any dolphin studies with trial-unique stimuli.

Goldfish also have been tested on delayed matching to sample. Steinert, Fallon, and Wallace (1976) reported above-chance performance at a delay of one second. Here too there do not appear to have been any studies with trial-unique stimuli.

Bird Song.   Another case of recognition memory that shows some of the qualities of explicit memory is that of species-specific song learning by some species of birds. Many birds learn songs that are unique for each individual, but share characteristics with other members of the species. Although this learning is not one-shot, in that it develops gradually over repeated exposures, nonetheless it is a form of recognition memory of arbitrary information and is limited to a specific time. Intraspecific learning of song has been found in every oscine species studied (Kroodsma, 1982). There are restrictions on what a species will learn. For example, swamp sparrows will not learn song sparrow songs (Marler & Peters, 1977). Song learning is restricted to particular critical periods (e.g., 20 to 30 days posthatching in the case of the swamp sparrow, Kroodsma, 1982; 15 to 35 days for the zebra finch, Marler, 1981). The brain structures responsible for this learning have been studied, but they do not include the hippocampus (Nottebohm, 1991).

Discrimination Reversals.   Hippocampally lesioned subjects usually have no problems learning simple sensory discriminations (e.g., responses to one stimulus are followed by reward, responses to another stimulus punished). These simple discriminations are learned gradually and are considered a form of implicit learning. However, N.J. Cohen and Eichenbaum (1993) have argued that one type of sensory discrimination task engages the explicit learning system. This is the reversal of a discrimination. A subject, having been trained to choose one stimulus out of a pair, now has to learn to choose the other stimulus. Though this is not one-shot learning, in that it takes many trials for successful performance to develop, nonetheless a successful subject has to pay attention to the particular reward relationships in place here and now, and not just average over all past experience. Even normal subjects find learning a reversed discrimination more difficult than learning a novel discrimination, but several studies have shown that subjects with lesions to the hippocampal formation have greater problems than do normal subjects. It appears that hippocampally lesioned subjects have difficulty attending to the particular pattern of reward and punishment in operation on any given trial. This has been demonstrated in rats (Eichenbaum, Fagan, P. Mathews, & N.J. Cohen, 1988; Stäubli, Ivy, & Lynch, 1984; Wible & Olton, 1988), monkeys (Malamut, Saunders, & Mishkin, 1984; Zola-Morgan & Squire, 1985).

Ingenious experiments have demonstrated that rabbits are capable of learning the reversal of a stimulus discrimination, and that this reversal performance is impaired by hippocampal lesions. Rabbits can be trained to blink to a stimulus that precedes a puff of air to the eye, or mild electric stimulation near the eye. In this way, Berger and Orr (1983) trained rabbits to respond with an eye blink to one tone, but not to a different tone. Such learning progresses gradually over many trials, and therefore it would not be considered explicit, and it is not surprising that hippocampal lesions had no effect on the learning of this discrimination. When Berger and Orr reversed the discrimination so that the previously positive (followed by an airpuff) stimulus was now negative (not followed by an airpuff) and vice versa, they found that hippocampal subjects needed over four times as long as normal subjects to learn this reversal.

Rich Representations in Spatial Learning and Memory

One set of problems that require very flexible representations for its solution concerns learning about spatial relationships. Even in a case as simple as training a rat to choose the left arm of a T- or Y-maze for food, the stimulus "left" is not really a simple elemental stimulus; rather it is a particular set of interrelationships between the local and distal cues available to the subject that together define the "left" arm of the apparatus. In more elaborate spatial learning tasks, such as pigeons finding their way back to a home loft, rats finding a hidden platform in a swimming tank, or chickadees finding caches of food in trees, the problems of interrelating discrete stimuli to find particular spatial locations are substantial. Human amnesiacs are impaired at learning about space (Aggleton, Nicol, Huston, & Fairbairn, 1988; Squire & Zola-Morgan, 1988), and the hippocampal formation has been implicated in many spatial learning tasks.

Spatial Learning in Rats.   Some of the earliest studies in comparative psychology involve rats in mazes (Small, 1901). These animals, being burrow dwellers, rapidly learn to perform in all sorts of mazes. Involvement of the hippocampus in spatial learning and memory in rats has been demonstrated in a wide range of spatial learning tasks. The evidence for hippocampal involvement in spatial learning is so overwhelming that some authors even have proposed the storage of a spatial "cognitive map" as the dominant function of the hippocampal formation (Nadel, 1991; O'Keefe & Nadel, 1978).

Two typical spatial learning tasks used with rats that show impairment after hippocampal lesions are the radial arm maze and the water maze. A radial arm maze is an arrangement of a number of arms (typically four or eight) radiating from a central area. The end of each arm is baited with food. The rat is placed in the central area and its task is to find the food at the end of each arm as quickly as possible. Either the animal is allowed to search as long as it likes until it finds all the food (and the number of reentries to an arm that no longer contains food is counted), or the subject is allowed to make only as many arm visits as there are arms to the maze (e.g., eight, in the case of the eight-arm maze), and the number of food items obtained is recorded. This task is highly sensitive to damage to the hippocampal formation. Rats with hippocampal lesions make more erroneous arm entries until they find all the food, or they find less of the food if they are restricted to a limited number of arm entries (Devenport, Hale, & Stidham, 1988).

The water maze is an interesting form of spatial task because it contains no internal cues. The "maze" is simply a tank of water, two meters in diameter, the surface of which has been made opaque with milk or coloring. Submerged under the surface of the water is an escape platform, and the rat's task is to swim to this platform. Of course, at first the subject swims around until finding the platform. But with training the amount of time the rat spends swimming in the tank decreases as it remembers the position of the escape platform from trial to trial. Damage to the hippocampal system has a very profound effect on this ability. Rats with hippocampal lesions fail to improve with practice, and every time they are put in the tank, they search exhaustively for the hidden platform (DiMattia & Kesner, 1988; Schenck & R.G.M. Morris, 1985; Sutherland, Wishaw, & Kolb, 1983).

Eichenbaum, Stewart, and R.G.M. Morris (1990) demonstrated that the problems hippocampally damaged rats have in the water maze are due to a problem in forming and interrogating flexible representations of the task. Rather than putting the rats into the water maze at different places on different trials (the usual procedure), Eichenbaum et al. trained a group that were always entered into the water at the same place. These subjects did not have the same need for flexibility and relationality of representations as did the subjects entered at different points on each trial. Eichenbaum et al. found that the subjects always entered at the same place in the maze were well able to swim to the platform despite hippocampal lesions. These subjects had learned simple inflexible routes that they could swim along to reach the escape platform.

Food-Caching Birds.   Many species of bird store food by hiding it in caches to which they return over periods of months (Sherry, 1989; Shettleworth, 1985; Vander Wall, 1990). For some species, such as Clark's nutcracker, local landmarks are more important than distant cues (Vander Wall, 1982). For others the opposite is true, and global cues are more important to successful cache recovery than local ones (e.g., black-capped chickadees; Sherry, 1992). Because the memorization of food caches is arbitrary and rapid, it qualifies as an explicit process. Consistent with this hypothesis, lesions of the hippocampus have been shown to disrupt this memorization, as would be expected of an explicit memory process. Sherry and Vaccarino (1989) gave black-capped chickadees the opportunity to cache seeds in a laboratory environment consisting of six "trees" made from natural tree branches. Each tree consisted of several branches and twigs and 12 predrilled holes as potential seed storage sites. Hippocampally lesioned birds stored just as many seeds as did controls, and they later searched for the stored seeds with equal vigor. However, the hippocampectomized subjects were significantly less successful in finding their stored seeds again.

Pigeons' Homing.   Another natural spatial learning task in birds is the homing of pigeons. Pigeons are capable of flying back to their home loft from sites they have never before visited. Bingman and colleagues have found that the hippocampal formation is important in several aspects of successful homing. Following lesions to the hippocampus, pigeons fail to recognize important stimuli for homing, such as their home loft (Bingman, Bagnoli, Ioalé, & Casini, 1984) and the release location (Bingman, Ioalé, Casini, & Bagnoli, 1987). With training, however, these lesioned pigeons can be taught to rerecognize their home loft (Bingman, Ioalé, Casini, & Bagnoli, 1985) and release site (Bingman, Ioalé, Casini, & Bagnoli, 1988b). Nonetheless, even after such postoperative retraining, hippocampally ablated pigeons show a lasting deficit in homing. These subjects appear to have a deficit in navigational ability (Bingman et al., 1988a). This deficit does not lie, however, in the ability to find a correct initial bearing for the homeward flight (Bingman et al., 1984, 1988a). Rather, the problems these subjects have appear to center on relating their correct direction to the landmarks available to them (Bingman, 1990; Bingman & Mench, 1990).

Summary.   The evidence for the ability to create flexible representations of space is widespread among vertebrates, including birds, as is the evidence that the hippocampal formation is crucial in these representations.

CONCLUSIONS

For many years after its inception, comparative psychology was dominated by the search for general-process theories of learning. These looked for commonalities in the learning abilities of disparate species. Then came the cognitive revolution. This led to a downgrading of the importance of comparative studies because commonalties were not expected—unique cognitive adaptations were to be the norm.

Nonetheless, some perverse psychologists have gone on studying animals and have amassed an interesting array of specimens, a subset of which we have considered here. These results show that explicit learning and memory are very widespread in the animal kingdom.

Several authors (Holyoak & Spellman, 1993; Reber, 1992; Rozin, 1976) have argued that the implicit learning and memory system is evolutionarily older than the explicit system. Certainly it is true that gradual forms of incremental learning without the concomitant ability to report on the material learned are very widespread in the animal kingdom. The gradual acquisition of an association between a response and reinforcement (operant conditioning), or between an initially neutral stimulus and reinforcement (classical conditioning), appears to be extremely common. Although the range of species assessed is still very incomplete, the evidence for implicit learning is very widespread compared with that for any other cognitive behavioral trait. Some fairly direct attempts have been made to assess the generality of this form of learning. Honeybees have been tested extensively (Couvillon & Bitterman, 1980, 1982, 1988, 1989). Marine mollusks (e.g., Carew, Hawkins, & Kandel, 1983), amphibia (Suboski, 1992), and even fruit flies (e.g., Holliday & Hirsch, 1986) and newts (Ellins, Cramer, & G.C. Martin, 1982) have all been trained successfully.

However, as this review has demonstrated, once we formulate definitions of explicit processing that could potentially apply to nonhumans, we find that this form of learning and memory is also very widespread. If at present the range of species in which explicit processing has been demonstrated is not as wide as that for implicit processing, then that is simply a function of the fact that fewer attempts have been made. There are few, if any, reports of failures to demonstrate explicit learning or memory where an attempt has been made.

As many authors have pointed out (e.g., Hodos & Campbell, 1967, 1990; Lewontin, 1990), the assessment of the distribution of a behavioral trait in extant species is a very weak instrument for assessing the evolutionary age of the trait. Nonetheless, the wide range of species in which some forms of explicit learning and memory have been found argues against the idea that this is an evolutionarily recent trait—certainly there is no reason to argue that it is more recent than implicit learning.

In order to argue that explicit learning and memory are evolutionarily more recent than implicit processing, explicit learning has been identified with consciousness in such a way that no experimental test could ever demonstrate the existence of explicit processing even in the human, never mind a nonhuman species. It is not considered necessary to experimentally demonstrate that humans have consciousness. Therefore the nonempirical nature of the claims being made about consciousness is not obvious. To then argue that nonhumans show no evidence of consciousness is equivocation—humans show no evidence of consciousness in this sense either.

Of course, it would be perverse to pretend there are no differences in the mental lives of different species. If this chapter has prompted those with an interest in these matters to ground their speculations in empirical studies of nonhuman species, then it will have succeeded in its purpose.

ACKNOWLEDGMENTS

I thank Kevin Durkin and Kim Kirsner for helpful comments on an earlier draft of this chapter. Research supported by the Australian Research Council.

III

APPLICATION

16

IMPLICIT CONTENT AND IMPLICIT PROCESSES IN MASS MEDIA USE

Kevin Durkin
University of Western Australia

In one of his celebrated stage performances, the hitherto publicly asexual megastar Michael Jackson grabbed his crotch and thrust his lower body forward in a distinctly carnal manner. He explained later on the Oprah Winfrey show that the incident was a *subliminal response* to the music. Some irresistible message lurking beneath the innocuous lyrics had evidently afflicted the singer's motor coordination and sense of propriety in a most unnerving manner, reducing him to a state of self-focused gonad groping.

The implications of this alarming demonstration of the potency of covert media content scarcely need spelling out. Jackson's recordings are heard by billions; if the subliminals prove contagious adolescents worldwide could find themselves manually compromised on an unprecedented scale. Worse, because the implicit surges are unpredictable and uncontrollable (after all, Jackson was beset while on stage, in front of the cameras), it is anybody's guess how many innocent bystanders who had missed the initial show could catch the clasp simply by inadvertent exposure to the first-generation video viewers' rudely copied compulsions. And then others could watch and learn from them. Readers with a statistical training will readily appreciate the exponential consequences.

It is disturbing prospects like these that have sustained a long-standing public interest in the relationship between implicit processes and mass media content. The matter rises above even pop stars' pudenda. Individuals living in free-enterprise societies are well aware of daily exposures to the commercial strategies of marketers and advertisers; citizens of totalitarian political systems can scarcely ignore the relentless propaganda extolling the virtues of the powers-that-be. Wherever we are, somebody is trying to persuade us of something, whether to purchase, to believe, to do. Although we like to think we are superior to the crass disseminations of the agents of capitalism and state control, we fear sometimes that this may reflect only our conscious reactions to explicit and easily detectable messages, such as television advertisements or political broadcasts. Dealing with covert media content is another matter. Perhaps what Michael Jackson's mishap reveals so tellingly is that we know very little of what is going on down below.

In this chapter, we look down below to consider the nature and impact of implicit messages in media content. We note first that implicit elements of the media are manifold: They may include subliminal or barely detectable imagery, but also expressions of attitudinal biases, social prejudices, and behavioral scripts that are in some respects overt (e.g., identifiable and quantifiable by researchers) yet not always consciously recognized by lay users of the media. We turn then to a summary of findings concerning lay beliefs about implicit content, and it is argued that these form an important component of contemporary orientations toward the media. Nevertheless, we see that it is difficult to ascertain exactly what or how much implicit content there is. Even if we beg this question, we still require an understanding of any effects. This topic is addressed in the subsequent section. To forewarn the reader of some possible disappointment, it has to be announced that the research evidence does not point consistently toward explanations as magical as those offered by Michael Jackson, and alternative accounts of his and other behavior attributed to subliminal effects are noted.

THE NATURE OF IMPLICIT MEDIA CONTENT
AND PROCESSING

It should be acknowledged at the outset that attempts to investigate implicit processes in relation to the mass media are beset by all of the usual definitional/conceptual challenges that dog research into implicit perception, and a few more. Media content can be *implicit* in the sense that someone (experimenter, broadcaster, advertiser) has placed something in the stimulus that is not consciously perceptible by the viewer/listener. Media content can also be *implicit* in the sense that the selection or organization of material reflects someone's priorities for attention or status. In this sense, what is left out may be as significant as what is included. Information or relationships can also be *implied*—motives, procedures, and time spans are often assumed in fictional media—otherwise, the entertainment would be as lengthy as the real-world activities it purports to represent.

Correspondingly, from the perspective of the media user, material may be *implicit* in the sense that she or he is not consciously aware of its presence or influence. Content may be *inferred* in the sense that real-world knowledge, our familiarity with routine media scripts, or formal features lead us to assume certain steps in a sequence without them being seen (e.g., as we try to work out who-did-it in a television crime mystery, or as we follow a flashback or other textual devices). Clearly, media processing demands a great deal of constructive activity by the user, though to what extent this is explicit, implicit, conscious, or automatic, and how processes at different levels interact, remains to be settled. Let us consider a few concrete examples.

Michael Jackson may indeed have found himself suffering from troubling sensations, but can we be sure that these were instigated by messages in the music? The problem is a general one. How frequently, for example, do advertisers exploit subliminal techniques to win our purchasing intentions? Regrettably, advertisers are reluctant to tell us and the fact that we buy their products might, or might not, be due to subconscious manipulations.

Take another dimension of implicit media content, the representation of social messages and values. The media may convey many subtle messages about human values. Possible themes include the relative status of different groups within a society (organized around criteria such as gender, ethnicity, social class, language), the relative priority of possible community goals (such as material affluence, individual attainment, democratic decision making, compliance), moral judgments of particular behaviors (such as crime, sexuality, drug use) or procedural schemes for dealing with aspects of social life (such as how to fall in love, get married, and live happily ever after). Some of these messages may be overt, but often they may be covert and detectable only by analyzing patterns of content across many instances.

For example, *explicit* announcements that old people are unattractive, incompetent, and uninteresting are not frequent in the media. But think about it: How often do we see *any* older people in the media? In fact, in the primary mass medium of television, older people are proportionately underrepresented, though when they do appear there is some tendency to cast them in negative stereotypes along the aforementioned lines (R.H. Davis & J.A. Davis, 1985; Gibson, 1993). Nobody actually gets on screen and *says* that all old people fall into these types, but it has been argued that the relative infrequency of the elderly in television, together with the caricatured natures of those individuals that do appear, help to perpetuate unfavorable beliefs and attitudes toward older people in real life (R.H. Davis & J.A. Davis, 1985; Gibson, 1993).

Similarly, women traditionally have appeared less frequently than men in most areas of media representation (Butler & Paisley, 1980; Durkin, 1985a). Some of the relevant data are not always attended to consciously, although they are striking when pointed out. Study after study has found that in television commercials, about 90% of the voiceovers are presented by men (Manstead & McCulloch, 1981; Mazzella, Durkin, Cerini, & Buralli, 1992). Study after study has found that, across the mass media, women tend to be depicted in a relatively restricted range of occupations, and men are more likely to be shown outside the home and "in charge" (Butler & Paisley, 1980; Durkin, 1985a). Broadcasters seem to share strong assumptions about gender roles and the social order. For many viewers/listeners, biases in the way men and women are represented may not always be obvious. C.H. Hansen and R.D. Hansen (1988) reported that few college-aged interviewees had noticed elements of gender role stereotyping in MTV videos (a medium in which assertive male stars predominate and scantily clad women serve decorative purposes). Nevertheless, others conclude that there are underlying, implicit messages about the relative status of the genders and it has been argued that the media's representations amount to a "symbolic annihilation" of women (Tuchman, 1978).

Analogous points have been made about the treatment of Black people in the U.S. media. At different times in recent history, members of this ethnic minority have been, variously, ignored altogether, portrayed as charming but simple servant folk, or depicted as malevolent antisocial threats (cf. Pierce, 1980). Pierce argued that in these ways television contributes to the "automatic, preconscious assumptions" of everyday life, and that it "promotes, sustains, and insists that these subtle rules of racism reign" (p. 250).

Finally, scripts for social behavior are legion in the mass media (Durkin, 1985b; Janis, 1980). We have already noted the "boy-meets-girl" script, but there are many more. Most of the fundamental preoccupations and decisions of our social lives (such as career, homebuilding, parenting, use of medical services, interpersonal problem solving) are modeled for us in television and other media scripts with implicit messages (Janis, 1980). Most of our experiences of law and order are provided by on-screen transactions involving bad guys and good guys and the ritual applications of justice that assure us that "crime doesn't pay" (Durkin, 1997; Low & Durkin, 1997; Sparks, 1992). Janis has proposed as a priority for television research "to ascertain when and among whom such implicit messages are internalized as personal scripts and thereafter acted upon" (p. 166).

In these respects, there is relatively good objective evidence (from rigorously conducted content analyses) that certain values, social categories, and behavioral schemata are "there," in the sense that they recur frequently or that they underlie the surface structures of media events. As indicated, even being implicitly "not there" (e.g., not appearing as often as other social groups, or not being allowed to take authoritative roles) may offer us some important information about where a particular social group or value system figures in relation to the status quo.

Unfortunately, this does not complete the story, because we have not yet addressed the rather more profound issue of how media users interpret and respond to these features. In fact, on this point there is much dispute. Advertisers will deny that there is any sexist bias (or subliminal content, or misleading claims) in their materials; television executives will assure us that they are not guilty of sexism, ageism, or racism. Once we shift our attention from the medium to the receiver, the problems of determining exactly what is implicit, and whether it has any impact, are multiplied. We return to this point, but to elaborate the difficulties of finding implicit content let us consider first the ostensibly more measurable issues of backward messages and embeds.

Backward Messages in Rock Music: Are They There?

Michael Jackson is not the only person to have suspected that there was something hidden in popular music. In the United States during the early 1980s, Pastor Gary Greenwald and other religious figures condemned this form of auditory stimulation on the grounds that frequently it contained backward messages encouraging young listeners to interests in Satanism or suicide (Vokey & Read, 1985). To alert the broader community to the problem, Pastor Greenwald held public meetings in which he played examples of this kind of implicit content.

Many members of the public were convinced and appalled, or vice versa. But experimental psychologists Vokey and Read (1985) set out to conduct a scientific evaluation. They accepted that Pastor Greenwald and his followers were able to hear messages in rock music when it was played backward. However, they questioned what might be the source of these messages. They noted that the Pastor normally forewarned sympathizers of what they were about to hear. Skeptics, aware of top–down cognitive processes, might suspect that this methodology increases the chances of message detection, and may even lead some to "hear" things that are not actually present (cf. Jacoby, Toth, Lindsay, & Debner, 1992; Thorne & Himelstein, 1984). In an imaginative study, Vokey and Read used two texts (readings from *Jabberwocky* and the *23rd Psalm*) played backward, and listened "creatively" for any sequences that could be interpreted as "sounding like something meaningful." Several phrases were found, including a hint of Satanism. With appropriate controls and counterbalancing, they then played the readings to subjects who were asked to listen specifically for the meaningful expressions first identified by the experimenters. Subjects agreed with the experimenters' diagnoses to well above chance levels, and also did not hear phrases for which they had been primed but that were not actually included in the stimulus materials.

These results indicate that people can hear intelligible phrases in backward speech, and that this is not simply a matter of suggestibility and expectation set. However, a further manipulation indicates that subjects can hear a message only when they have been prepared for it. Subjects were asked to listen several times to a backward passage, and then, prior to a final presentation, were advised of a particular phrase within it. A majority of subjects could hear the phrase on the final presentation, but most of these reported that this was the first time they had detected it.

Vokey and Read (1985) summarized other studies of their own that indicate that although people can discriminate among backwardly presented passages (e.g., differentiating gender of speaker, individual speakers, or language spoken) there is little evidence that they can detect much if any of the forward meaning. Subjects in one of their studies were unable to tell whether backward messages were nursery rhymes, advertisements, Satanic messages, Christian messages, or pornography. Similar conclusions are supported by Benoit and R.L. Thomas' (1992) findings of greater mood changes in subjects listening to music that they had been led to believe contained subliminal messages (compared with controls). All of this is consistent with the interpretation that people's detection of "hidden" messages is sometimes dependent on active attentional and constructive processes, rather than unconscious awareness (Jacoby, Toth, et al., 1992; Vokey & Read, 1985).

Sexual Embeds in Visual Media: Are They There?

Another means of implicit communication is to hide a potentially arousing image or word within a visual presentation. Examples include the use of sexual vocabulary or erotic photographs that are airbrushed into the main advertisement. This technique is known as *embedding*. In provocative analyses of the alleged hidden sexual content of mass media images, especially photographic advertisements, Key (1973, 1976, 1980) has outraged scientists in direct proportion to the extent he has entertained members of the general public. Much of his analysis is concerned with the detection of embeds, which he claimed are ubiquitous in advertising. In fact, Key held unequivocally that "Sex is alive and embedded in practically everything" (1973, p. 108). Although not readily visible, Key argued that sexual embeds are actually perceived subliminally by all exposed to the ad. Many interesting illustrations of these techniques are provided in Key's texts.

It remains controversial just how extensively subliminal messages and embeds are present in the mass media. Advertising executives tend to pour scorn on Key's claims that such manipulations are widespread—but then, they would, wouldn't they? Although the issue sounds like a straightforward empirical one, it proves difficult to address. The difficulty is that the significance of perceptible stimuli hinges on the ability of perceiving organisms to detect them.

Perception and Implicit Content

Part of the problem reflects definitional and procedural features of determining what is *subliminal*. The term means literally "below the threshold." It is not possible to identify an absolute threshold of stimulus intensity below which perception does not occur and above which it invariably does occur (Moore, 1982). There are both intra- and interindividual differences in this respect. Although there is continuing debate among experimentalists as to how to define and measure subliminal stimuli (cf. contributors to Bornstein & Pittman, 1992; Erdelyi, 1992; Greenwald, 1992; Holender, 1986; J. Miller, 1991), for practical research purposes an individual's perceptual threshold in a given task often is defined as the stimulus value that is detected 50% of the time (Moore, 1982).

At least two methodological problems arise here for experimental studies of subliminal perception in the mass media. First, even where the threshold has been identified accurately by the 50% correct criterion, then it remains the case that the subject may perceive the stimulus supraliminally on at least some trials and hence any "effects" cannot be attributed reliably to subconscious processing; on this argument there are risks of Type I errors. Second, there are good grounds for expecting threshold variability from trial to trial (reflecting practice effects, direction of attention, type of prior task, presence and content of accessory stimuli, internal metabolic state fluctuations, and other factors; see J. Miller, 1991); Miller showed that if the threshold is estimated at the lower end of the subject's actual threshold distribution, then there is risk of failing to detect effects that might actually occur (i.e., a risk of Type II errors). Miller pointed out that this is problematic because a real subliminal effect would be of theoretical interest even if it were quite small.

A real subliminal effect also would be of practical interest. Advertisers, for example, cannot aim to vary stimulus intensity to match the thresholds of individual media users. If they were prepared to use this technique on the public, then presumably thresholds would have to be set very low, perhaps too low for many (otherwise there is the uncomfortable prospect of conscious detection by the more sensitive members of the audience or the more vigilant consumers' associations). To the ruthless seeker of mass markets, this form of communication still would remain a tempting option, because even a small percentage increase in sales among such large populations as America or Europe would be gratifying. But to what extent the ruthless *are* pursuing subliminal strategies to this end, we do not know.

Summary

Defining and identifying implicit content in the mass media pose considerable challenges. There is no doubt that it is possible to disguise the presence of audiovisual images or messages by means of techniques such as subliminal exposure, embedding, and backward recording. There are also substantial bodies of evidence to support the view that subtle biases, values, and prejudices underlie the contents of much of our mass media fare. However, the extent to which implicit content, whether sensory or sociocultural, is influential in actual media experiences is difficult to appraise because it depends also on the processing capacities and preexisting beliefs of the receiver. Processing capacities may be invoked at different levels of consciousness, and there may well be individual differences in these respects.

BELIEF IN SUBLIMINAL MEDIA CONTENT

Despite these technical problems, Michael Jackson is not alone in attributing potency to subliminal messages. It is very likely that, during the commercial break, many members of the audience of the Oprah Winfrey show sat back and ruminated: "Perhaps there is an entirely separate cognitive system which feeds into emotional and unconscious mental processes and which is much more sensitive than the mechanisms we have considered so far" (Neisser, 1967, p. 130).

The idea is appealing. Surveys of randomly selected Americans, for example, have found consistently that about 75% to 80% of respondents have heard of subliminal advertising, and many of these believe that it is used widely and successfully in selling products (M.H. Block & Bergh, 1985; Rogers & K. Smith, 1993; Zanot, Pincus, & Lamp, 1983). Rogers and Smith found that more than 72% of respondents (drawn from Toledo, Ohio) who suspected subliminal advertisements were commonplace also perceived them as effective.

Some of the most notorious examples of alleged subliminal persuasion seem to inspire public fascination. These include a study conducted in 1957 on unwitting audiences of New Jersey cinemas, who were subjected to fleetingly presented suggestions that they "drink Coca Cola" and "eat popcorn." They include also the efforts of a Seattle radio station to subvert the dominance of a rival medium by broadcasting subaudible messages to advise listeners that "TV's a bore" (see Moore, 1982). The media themselves like to play around with the idea. Alternative comedy shows seem fond of the concept of subliminal stimulation, often flashing incongruous images briefly among regular scenes (viewers of the British series *The Young Ones* might recall this technique); because these flashes are actually discernible, this is not true subliminal presentation but its humor value rests in part on audience familiarity with the concept. Above all, Key's lively writings (1973, 1976, 1980; see earlier discussion) have alerted the public to the possibility that advertisers may exploit covert sexual imagery to enhance the appeal of their products.

On balance, consumers do not view this suspected state of affairs favorably. Researchers find a high degree of public antipathy to what is perceived as a devious means of obtaining commercial success and a potentially intrusive mode of communication that undermines the personal control of the individual media user (M.P. Block & Bergh, 1985). On the other hand, consumers do view this suspected state of affairs empathetically: that is, they can imagine the techniques working. Rogers and K.H. Smith (1993) found that people who believe that subliminal advertising works tend to believe that it also influences their own purchase decisions.

As already indicated, many people are prepared to believe, too, that there is an unpleasant underside to rock music. Vokey and Read (1985) reported that community outrage on revelations of backward devilry led politicians in the state of Arkansas to debate and eventually to pass a bill requiring the music industry to place warning labels on records and tapes, alerting purchasers to possible subliminal messages. Other states of a more litigious policy orientation began to give serious attention to establishing grounds on which consumers could sue record companies for any gratuitous contact with Satanism that they might suffer. Subsequently, the parents of two young men who committed suicide by shooting themselves did sue the rock band Judas Priest on the grounds that there were subliminal messages advocating self-destruction in one of their albums (Loftus & Klinger, 1992). Favoring explicit, preventive strategies, Pastor Greenwald organized mass record-smashing events wherever his public speaking engagements took him (Vokey & Read, 1985).

Not all subliminal content is feared as seditious. In some cases, lay belief in the efficacy of such materials is tapped directly by manufacturers of media purporting to contain implicit content. Numerous self-help audiotapes that promise to contribute to physical, social, and spiritual enhancement by means of subliminal techniques sell well on this basis.

It is instructive to trace possible arguments whereby people arrive at the conclusion that implicit content does have effects. Returning to the FM airways, for example, it may already have struck you that any attempts by radio stations to undermine the lure of television have not proven overwhelmingly successful to date. On the other hand, have you never reached the conclusion that TV *is* a bore? You may flatter yourself that this judgment is the outcome of the high-level application of your conscious and discerning viewing standards, but we cannot easily rule out sleeper effects—the impact of subliminal messages that you may have heard years ago, or could still be hearing. A lifetime of unwitting exposure to surreptitious intermedia slander may have persuaded you that TV is a bore. Similarly, perhaps you suffer occasionally from what you believe to be unintended and unrequited sexual thoughts? We have to ask: Do these occur shortly after listening to your Michael Jackson collection? Or after flicking through a magazine steeped in secret embeds? Still more tellingly, have you ever bought a Coke or a carton of popcorn at your cinema, or noticed other people doing so? Finally, as we see later, there is evidence that people using subliminal tapes sometimes do achieve the desired changes in their behavior. According to Key (1973), this is not surprising. He argued that: "subliminal stimuli, though invisible to conscious perception, are perceived instantly at the unconscious level by virtually everyone who perceives them even for an instant!" (p. 108). Although there are lots of *overt* means by which interest groups attempt to persuade us to make consumer/voter selections or change our behavior, the correlational evidence ensures the continuing popularity of the notion of subliminal persuasion.

Summary

The remarkable thing about subliminal content from the perspective of the layperson is that, by definition, it can never be seen or heard. This is the kind of brute limitation of the stimulus material that sustains a degree of skepticism in the empirical psychologist. Yet many members of the public seem readily to entertain the notion of hidden forces operating mysteriously on the consumer's subconscious. There is one sense in which implicit content undoubtedly does have impact on the audience, and that is that many people believe that it is there and that it is having some effect. Concern about covert forms of persuasion ranges through the suspected underhand techniques of advertisers to the ideological biases of mainstream television. Lay beliefs about the presence and effects of implicit content raise interesting issues about how members of the community perceive the nature and role of media in society, but they do not in themselves establish that any effects (other than belief in effects) actually occur. However, the facts that people do buy all sorts of advertised products, do have unprompted sexual thoughts, do buy Coke at the cinema, and do vote regularly for the most reprehensible of political candidates all support the suspicion that there must be something, somewhere influencing their behavior. Could it be the implicit contents of the mass media?

IMPLICIT CONTENTS: ARE THEY HAVING AN EFFECT?

There is extensive evidence from cognitive psychology that recognition, memory, and comprehension can be influenced (typically, enhanced) by prior exposure to subliminal visual or auditory images of which the subject retains no conscious awareness (Jacoby, Toth, et al., 1992; Kihlstrom, Barnhardt, & Tataryn, 1992; contributors to Lewandowsky, Dunn, & Kirsner, 1989; Loftus & Klinger, 1992; Marcel, 1983b; Reber, 1992; Roediger, 1990b). There is a growing body of evidence from social psychology that people's attitudes and impressions of others can be influenced by undetected information (Bargh, 1992a; Bornstein, Leone, & Galley, 1987; Erdley & D'Agostino, 1988; Lewicki et al., 1992; Niedenthal, 1990, 1992; see also Nesdale & Durkin, chap. 13 of this volume). Indeed, Lewicki et al. argued that our nonconscious information-processing system is able to process complex data and relationships more effectively and more swiftly than our conscious cognitions. Hill, Lewicki, Czewska, and Boss (1989) have demonstrated that covariations between quite subtle, arbitrary physical properties of individuals and the putative likability of those individuals can be acquired easily (but nonconsciously), and may then influence subsequent impression formation. As discussed previously, the mass media present many cues about covariations between say, social category and social status, and it is plausible that our nonconscious information-processing systems take note of these.

Research relating these themes to the study of mass media use is not extensive. Traditionally, it is well recognized that it is very difficult to measure the effects of the mass media on social attitudes and behavior (Durkin, 1985b; Howitt, 1982; Klapper, 1960). There are also substantial (though not insuperable) technical obstacles to implanting subliminal messages in the primary mass media of television and audio (cf. K.H. Smith & Rogers, 1994; Underwood, 1994; Urban, 1992). Furthermore, few studies in the area of media effects and use have distinguished implicit from explicit content—a distinction that is not always relevant to experimental work (where there is often a purposeful focus on some explicit message or enactment) and not manipulable in field investigations (where the distribution of implicit and explicit content in authentic media is typically beyond the control of the researcher).

However, there are some exceptions. A good example is an interesting experimental study by C.H. Hansen and R.D. Hansen (1988), which tested the hypothesis that recent exposure to mass media sex stereotypes can induce a transient increase in the cognitive accessibility of stereotypic schemata. Hansen and Hansen had subjects watch stereotypic or neutral rock videos, and then observe an interaction between a man and a woman in which the woman either reciprocated sexual advances from the man or did not reciprocate. Subjects' impressions of the actors indicated differences between conditions. When the subjects had viewed the stereotypic videos prior to observing the "real-life" interaction, the woman was rated as more skilled, competent, sexual, sensitive, and sympathetic when she reciprocated. Hansen and Hansen argued that the videos evoked a script for male–female interaction in which the male asserts his rights of domination and the female returns the complementary submissiveness and warmth; in their view, even though viewers are aware at a conscious level that media interactions are fantasies, once the traditional script is activated, it primes appraisal of subsequent social events.

This kind of research points to interesting directions for future research into media users' implicit and explicit responses to a wide range of implicit and explicit content. However, so far, the amount of such research is modest. Hence, for present purposes we focus on laboratory studies of more readily manipulated implicit stimuli, namely subliminal and embedded content.

Subliminal, Embedded, and Symbolic Content

It should be noted first that we set the parameters of "media" generously, to include various methods of stimulus presentation, and that "effects" can be assessed at different levels (traditionally, researchers distinguish among cognitive, affective, and conative). Can implicit content influence subjects' content knowledge, attitudes toward the content, and actual or intended behavior relating to the content? There are studies that do report some kind of effects due to subliminal stimuli, and others that do not; examples of each follow.

Studies That Do Report Effects of Implicit Media Content. An influential early study by Hawkins (1970) lent some preliminary support to the proposal that subliminal content may affect members of an audience. In the first of two experiments, Hawkins found that subjects presented subliminally with the stimulus word COKE subsequently rated their subjective thirst levels as higher than did subjects exposed in the same way to a nonsense letter string (NYTP). Unfortunately, the original article does not provide details of descriptive statistics for Experiment One and subsequent critics have pointed to the possibility of Type I errors (see Beatty & Hawkins, 1989; the data were analyzed in a series of pairwise nonparametric tests). Furthermore, corresponding effects were not obtained with the closely related but more exhortative DRINK COKE, which did not yield an effect on thirst ratings greater than exposure to the nonsense string.

Note that employing thirst as a dependent measure may actually work against the experimental hypothesis. *All* subjects were engaged in a laboratory task, having been instructed by experimenters and aware that they have to perform. Perhaps, like many experimental subjects, they wondered exactly what the experiment is all about. Although not necessarily a high-stress experience, this may be a sufficiently arousing task that perceived thirst levels could genuinely increase—and this should presumably be the case across all conditions. Readers who have participated in psychology experiments, and subsequently retreated to a cafeteria, may have relevant introspective evidence in this connection. Certainly, the task is different from watching a coke commercial at home or even at the movies. Hence, Hawkins' (1970) study is not conclusive, but it did at least provide a preliminary hint of influence.

One issue that has occasioned much discussion in this literature is the relative impact of subliminal content presented via different modalities (e.g., visual vs. auditory). Cuperfain and T.K. Clarke (1985) argued that we should expect greater evidence of effects due to subliminal exposures of visual stimuli rather than aural stimuli. Their main point is that right brain (graphical) perception is of greater importance in low-involvement conditions, such as typically prevail in television commercial viewing; left brain (language-based) perception might be more crucial in high-involvement conditions, where the media user is prepared to evaluate arguments for and against a product. They also suggested that subliminal presentations should be more effective for products already familiar in the marketplace than for novel products. The rationale is that it is easier to form a complete representation of a known product from a fleeting exposure than it is to become acquainted with an unfamiliar product on the same basis. (This argument is interesting because it suggests that implicit processing is facilitated by explicit knowledge.) The authors obtained preliminary evidence in support of this claim in a study that revealed slightly higher rankings of an already familiar brand than of a relatively unfamiliar brand when these were presented subliminally. Unfortunately, the experimenters did not report any details of the visual content of the slides used, and they acknowledge that their statistical analyses are limited.

Kilbourne, Painton, and Ridley (1985) conducted two experiments to investigate student subjects' responses to ads with sexual embeds. In both studies, two authentic, professionally produced ads taken from national U.S. magazines served as stimulus materials. One was a liquor ad (Chivas Regal) that contained an embed of a naked woman. The other was a cigarette ad (Marlboro) that contained an image of male genitals. Cognitive, affective, and sexual evaluations of the ads revealed no effects for embed in the Marlboro condition, but heightened evaluations of the embed ad in the Chivas Regal condition. In the second experiment, subjects' galvanic skin responses were slightly higher for the embedded versions (and this was true for both ads), although this was of only borderline statistical significance. The authors did not report figures for control ads, making it difficult to appraise the meaning of the differences obtained. The results were not strong, and many questions remain to be investigated, such as the possible relevance of subjects' sexual preferences (given both female and male erotic symbolism), preexisting alcohol usage, attitudes toward smoking—any of these might have contributed to reactions to the overt or covert stimuli.

Other researchers have investigated the related topic of the effects of symbolic imagery. Although visible, this imagery might not always receive conscious attention. Ruth and Mosatche (1985) presented student subjects with a series of liquor advertisements containing phallic and vaginal symbols. Shortly afterwards, the subjects completed a projective test. Responses to the projective test were scored for sexual imagery, sexual affect, and sexual symbolism. Results showed significantly higher scores on the first two measures for experimental subjects compared to controls, though there were no differences on the third measure. The authors interpreted the findings as indicating that subjects were sexually aroused by the symbolism of the ads, "even though they were not consciously aware of the presence of such stimuli" (p. 187). (In fact, the authors did not report a check on conscious awareness of the sexual symbolism. If you have ever seen a Cadbury's flake ad you may agree that sometimes the symbolism is difficult to miss.)

In a subsequent study, Ruth, Mosatche, and Kramer (1989) investigated student subjects' self-reported purchasing behavior as a function of exposure to symbolic and nonsymbolic ads for different brands of liquor. In a within-subjects design, purchasing tendencies were significantly greater for experimental (symbolic) ads, and this held for both male and female subjects. Unfortunately, it still remains uncertain whether conscious recognition of the symbolism may have played a part. For example, subjects were instructed to base their ratings on how "appealing" and how "alluring" the ads appeared to them; arguably, this may have alerted some subjects to appealing and alluring imagery. However, Ruth et al.'s study has the strengths that subjects acted as their own controls, and the content of the ads was controlled to the extent that no humans (i.e., potentially with overt sexual attractions) were present.

Mere Exposure, Affect, and Behavior.   The possible use of subliminal imagery to influence perceivers' attitudes toward some entity raises interesting issues in relation to the "mere exposure effect" (Zajonc, 1968). Zajonc and his colleagues have demonstrated that repetitive subliminal exposure to an object can enhance a person's attitude toward it (e.g., Kunst-Wilson & Zajonc, 1980). Zajonc's interpretation is that "familiarity breeds comfort," maintaining that affective orientations toward aspects of the environment can occur independently of conscious cognitive processing (see also Nesdale & Durkin, chap. 13 of this volume). This thesis has considerable interest in relation to uses of subliminal techniques in the media, where it might in principle be exploited to promote the appeal of commercial products or political candidates (Bornstein, 1989). There is evidence that repeated *conscious* exposure can eventually become counterproductive (as one becomes bored with the stimulus; Zajonc, Shaver, Tavris, & Van Kreveld, 1972), whereas subliminal exposure avoids this risk.

At present, there is relatively little research directed to this possibility using mass media stimuli, though there are some suggestive studies in neighboring areas of the literature. Krosnick, Betz, Jussim, and Lynn (1992), for example, argued that the subliminal presentation of paired associates offers a means of circumventing a problem that has dogged studies of classical conditioning of attitudes. They pointed out that many studies have influenced attitudes toward neutral stimuli by pairing presentations of those stimuli with presentations of stimuli that elicit affective responses. However, they noted that a major difficulty in interpreting these findings is that subjects may be aware of the pairing—and hence alert to the experimenter's requirements. These demand characteristics might be avoided if subjects were unaware that they were being exposed to the affect-eliciting stimuli, and this could be achieved by means of subliminal presentations. In two experiments with rigorous checks on subject awareness (which proved to be virtually nil), Krosnick et al. obtained evidence of a tendency to form an attitude toward a stimulus person in a direction consistent with the affective valence of preceding subliminal stimuli. Unfortunately, neither experiment included a control condition in which the stimulus person was rated without any subliminal associative pairings. Nevertheless, the studies are consistent with the hypothesis that unrecognized subliminal content might influence the direction of affect formed about a social stimulus.

One of the most striking demonstrations of the impact of mere exposure on subsequent cognitions and behavior was provided by Bornstein et al. (1987, Experiment 3). These experimenters found that prior subliminal exposure to a slide of an individual rendered subjects more likely to agree with that individual when they later observed him participating in a discussion (ostensibly part of a decision-making experiment).

Studies That Have Not Obtained an Effect.   Hawkins' (1970) report provided evidence that subliminal effects are not easy to obtain. In the second experiment described in that article, young males were exposed subliminally to the brand names of perfumes, one of which was superimposed over the seminude picture of a young woman. In this case, the results were disappointing. There was no evidence of a preference bias for the seductively associated product. But this outcome could be interpreted in various ways. Perhaps the merest mention of *any* perfume is enough to conjecture seminude or sensual imagery in the minds of some young males, thus undermining the benefits that it was hoped would accrue exclusively to subjects in the experimental condition; perhaps the seminude woman was not sufficiently arousing for the experimenters' purposes.

More problematically, Beatty and Hawkins (1989) reported an unsuccessful attempt at replication of the first experiment of the original Hawkins (1970) study (though dropping the DRINK COKE condition). In this case, fuller details are provided, including means. The results fail to support the original study. There were no significant differences among the three conditions (NYPT, subliminal COKE, supraliminal COKE). The authors concluded that the significant differences reported in Hawkins (1970) could indeed be due to Type I error.

Gable, Wilkens, Harris, and Feinberg (1987) had students indicate their preferences for different versions of pictorial advertisements paired so that one included embedded sexual stimuli and one (otherwise identical) did not. Using four product categories, they found that in two cases the nonembedded version was preferred, in one the embedded version, and in the fourth there was no preference. It could be argued that Gable et al. used a relatively insensitive dependent measure (dichotomous choice immediately on viewing), and did not investigate other possible variables (such as attentional biases, memory measures, purchase intentions). They did not report whether subjects were screened for possible conscious detection of the embeds. However, in a later study that employed a wider range of measures (including attention, attitude, and preferences) and did conduct a check for detection, D.L. Rosen and Singh (1992) also reported no effects associated with the presence of embeds.

K.H. Smith and Rogers (1994) had subjects watch TV commercials, forewarned that some of the ads would contain the hidden message "*choose this*." Subjects reported whether or not they believed they had detected the message in a given ad, and whether or not they intended to purchase or use the product advertised. Messages, varying in degrees of contrast to the visible background, were embedded in videotaped commercials. No differences were found among the responses of controls, those of subjects in trials where they did not detect the message and those of (the same) subjects in trials in which they did detect the message. That is, subliminal messages did not appear to influence purchase/use intention.

In a second experiment, K.H. Smith and Rogers (1994) attempted to heighten receptivity to the message by informing subjects that they could gain monetary reward for responding favorably to ads with the message (and lose points for false hits). Under these conditions, subjects' intention to purchase/use the message-detected product was increased (compared to their own responses in undetected trials and the responses of controls). That is, supraliminal messages had an effect when highly contrived support from the experimenters underwrote it, but the effect of nondetected, subliminal messages remained negligible.

The experimenters also reported the unexpected result that memory for the commercials with undetected messages was inferior to that of control and detectable ads. K.H. Smith and Rogers (1994) inferred that the subliminal message may have an unrecognized disruptive effect on the viewer's processing of the initial stimulus—the result being decidedly contrary to the goals of the subliminal advertiser. Underwood (1994) also obtained an outcome that suggests that where effects of subliminal content are achieved they might be contrary to the goals of those manipulating the medium. In a large-scale field experiment involving subliminal presentation of a smiling face "beneath" a visible, neutral expression, viewers in the experimental condition were more likely than controls to perceive the visible face as *sad*.

Other researchers have attempted to influence attitudes or beliefs by means of backward-recorded messages. Swart and Morgan (1992) exposed undergraduates to three wholesome messages (*Don't take drugs*, *Stay in school*, and *Clean up your room*) in this way, using a song by a rock group. Analyses of pre- and postexposure attitudes revealed no evidence of prosocial enhancement in subjects in the experimental conditions relative to peers who listened to nonpreaching recordings by the same artists. Russell, Rowe, and Smouse (1991) attempted to improve students' academic performance by having them listen to tapes including subliminal affirmations; again, no benefits of treatment were found. It appears to be very difficult to make undergraduates more wholesome or harder working using this technique. It is also difficult to get them to believe things. For example, Begg, Needham, and Bookbinder (1993) tested a more liberal prediction that might arise from the hypothesis of unconscious effects of backward masking. They noted that an argument could be made that, although hearers may not be induced to self-destruction by exposure to the hidden message, a possible outcome is to render forward versions of the messages more believable. They obtained evidence that subjects who had heard messages played backward could subsequently discriminate between these (old) messages and new ones, all played backward. But on measures of the *truth value* of the statements when they were presented forward in print, no effects were obtained; this contrasted with ratings for forward-presented messages that were rated as truer (consistent with the "familiarity enhances credibility" hypothesis). In short, subjects recognized some of the backward statements, but appeared impervious to their meanings.

Investigators have found significant changes in subjects using subliminal audiotapes to alter some aspect of their behavior, such as self-esteem, memory performance (Greenwald, Spangenberg, Pratkanis, & Eskenazi, 1991), and weight loss (P.M. Merikle & Skanes, 1992). However, these well-controlled experiments also reveal equivalent amounts of change in subjects in placebo conditions. In fact, Greenwald et al. found that self-esteem and memory could each be improved by listening to *either* self-esteem or memory tapes. Merikle and Skanes found that not only did experimental and placebo subjects lose weight during a course of subliminal self-help "treatment," but so did a group of subjects placed on a waiting list, who listened to no tapes at all.

Although these studies encourage caution in the interpretation of claims made by commercial proponents of subliminal audiotapes, they do not rule out the possibility that the techniques may be effective in some circumstances. In a careful review, Urban (1992) highlighted a range of technical, methodological, and metatheoretical issues bearing on the interpretation of the limited amount of experimental literature available to date. Technical difficulties include variation in the strategies and criteria employed by producers of subliminal audiotapes—inconsistencies in the stimulus materials may influence the quality and perceptibility of the messages in various ways. Methodological problems include questions of the optimal length of a treatment phase (some clinical studies reviewed by Urban achieved improvements in participants only after a long series of exposures). Metatheoretical issues include questions of the appropriate level of evidence demanded of clinical/therapeutic interventions. Urban argued that it is premature to dismiss the potential of subliminal audiotapes.

Summary

Various investigators have addressed questions relating to the possible effects of implicit content in the media. Contents studied include scripts for social behavior, subliminal images and messages, embeds, and backward recordings. Dependent measures range from attitudinal shifts to behavioral change. As is often the case as areas of psychological research expand, inconsistent findings emerge. Some studies report "effects," others do not. In several cases, limitations in design or strength of findings have been noted, though it should also be stressed that there are well-designed experiments yielding results on either side of the effects argument.

CONCLUSIONS

We must return to Michael Jackson to take note that, as Neisser (1967) forewarned, for many events in the natural environment that might be attributed to subliminal effects there is often a more mundane but more plausible explanation than recourse to the superdiscriminating subconscious. In the case of Jackson's crotch grabbing, two prime candidates are euphonious pulsation and Madonna. Naturalistic data might be drawn on to confirm the thesis that many young people are compelled to rotate and buck their pelvic regions on exposure to throbbing musical stimuli of sufficient intensity under conditions of reduced luminosity. It could be that Jackson's reactions were simply an extreme form of this arguably degenerate but scarcely mysterious phenomenon. More conventional psychological mechanisms could also be advanced to explain his behavior, such as prior associations with the sounds and normative influences within a peer culture. This is where Madonna comes in. She had been making a bigger name and a bigger income by doing much the same kind of thing. Of course, Madonna's behavior is explicit, and the axiom of theoretical parsimony dictates that we have no need of recourse to implicit (subliminal) processes when a simpler mechanism (such as observational learning) will do.

The upshot is that Jackson's interpretation of subliminal effects has to be viewed with some suspicion—as do the interpretations of anxious consumers in Toledo and as do the testimonials of satisfied customers of mail order subliminal audiotapes. Even those who scour heavy metal albums in the hope of evil ruminations should take heed of Begg, Needham, and Bockbinder's (1993) conclusion that people may attain higher than chance recognition of backward versions of phrases that were earlier presented in the same mode but, as a result, "would be no more likely to commit suicide than to worship bovine images" (p. 9). So far, research into backward recordings, lurid embedding and phallic symbols in advertisements has failed to provide strong evidence of effects on cognition, affect, or behavior.

Although skepticism is desirable and often well founded in respect of some of the more dramatic claims of implicit media effects, it should not blind us to the possibility of more subtle—and perhaps theoretically more interesting—processes (see Bornstein, 1989; Urban, 1992). Developments in cognitive and social psychology concerned with the nature of unconscious mental activities, together with continuing rapid progress in media technologies, provide exciting prospects of new advances. Like most uses of media, the potential for both negative and positive applications is wide ranging, but we will attain a fuller understanding of these only through systematic investigations in the field and the laboratory.

ACKNOWLEDGMENTS

I am grateful to Kim Kirsner, Angela O'Brien-Malone, and Craig Speelman for careful and constructive reviews of an earlier draft of this chapter.

17

DECISION SUPPORT AND BEHAVIORAL DECISION THEORY

Dan Milech
Melissa Finucane
University of Western Australia

With rare exceptions, human judgment and decision making have been found to be "suboptimal." Researchers have studied a wide variety of tasks and subjects of differing skills and expertise, and the general finding is that human intuitive judgment is far inferior to judgments that are based on the use of normative procedures or "formulas" (B. Kleinmuntz, 1990; Meehl, 1957).

Some find such results interesting because they indicate that the cognitive processes involved in human judgment and decision making are different from the processes represented by normative models. Many psychologists respond to such findings by developing theories that describe the cognitive processes involved in making a judgment or decision, where each of these decision theories accounts for some aspect of suboptimality (B. Kleinmuntz, 1990). As a group, such theories are termed "behavioral decision theories."

Others find such results disappointing because they indicate that poor decisions are being made, and the consequences of poor decision making can be profound. One response is to try to improve human decision making, and there are several ways this might be accomplished. In this chapter we consider one approach to improving the quality of decisions, and that is to provide on-the-job help or "decision support" to decision makers via a computer.

Computer-based decision support systems (DSSs) have been developed to provide help with a variety of tasks. Some of the earliest DSSs emerged in the areas of management decision making (see Sprague & Carlson, 1982) and in medical decision making such as MYCIN (Shortliffe, 1976), CADUCEUS (R.A. Miller, Pople, & Myers, 1982), or PIP (Barnett, Cimino, Hupp, & Hoffer, 1987; Pauker, Gorry, Kassirer, & W.B. Schwartz, 1976). More recently, DSSs have been used to help teams of experts make decisions about diverse policies such as evaluating the impact of catchment policies on water quality (J.R. Davis, Nanninga, Biggins, & Laut, 1991) or setting guidelines for child welfare and evaluating merit-pay decision making (e.g., POLICY PC; Milter & Rohrbaugh, 1988). DSSs have been used also in simulation models, such as the HOSTAGE CRISIS INTERFACE (Kraus, Wilkenfeld, Harris, & E. Blake, 1992).

In this chapter we briefly review research showing the need for such support and survey support systems that are currently available. We argue that many DSSs are inadequate because they are based on an analysis of what can be provided rather than an analysis of what decision makers need, and that a theoretical framework is needed to identify user needs. Behavioral decision theories must provide part of this framework. These theories, and some of the research findings addressed by these theories, are reviewed briefly. This is followed by a survey of decision support systems, which features a review of the applications of different behavioral decision theories to the design of DSSs. Finally, we argue that current theories are not comprehensive enough to serve as a basis for providing effective decision support. To assess user needs properly and provide adequate guidelines for the design of decision support systems, behavioral decision theories must expand to distinguish processes that are implicit from those that are explicit, or processes that are controlled from those that are automatic.

BEHAVIORAL DECISION THEORY

Behavioral decision theories describe how people reason when faced with judgments or decisions that involve uncertainty. Uncertainty may arise from several sources. For example, outcomes may be uncertain as in a gamble; the information on which a judgment is based may be unreliable as in clinical diagnosis; or the judgment itself might involve the formal estimation of "degree of uncertainty" as in probabilistic weather forecasts. There are behavioral decision theories describing human cognition for all of these tasks.

Most behavioral decision theories are pitched at the same level of explanation: They describe how information is transformed from the initial statement of a problem to a final judgment or decision. These theories usually do not address issues such as: how the human biological system performs these transformations or how these processes change over the life cycle. Nor do they distinguish between processes for which self-reports are accurate and processes for which reports are inaccurate; that is, they do not distinguish unreportable (implicit) from reportable (explicit) processes.

There are two salient facts that have emerged from studies of human judgment and decision making: (a) Intuitive judgment and decision making is suboptimal, far inferior to "normatively correct" procedures such as statistics, and (b) There are very large and consistent individual differences in the way people make judgments and decisions. Given in the next section is a brief and eclectic survey of research demonstrating that intuitive judgment is suboptimal and showing that there is a clear need for decision support. The fact that there are individual differences in judgment and decision making is commonly accepted; such differences are so large and so consistent that most researchers in this area do not perform analyses on aggregated data, for they believe that the patterns that are present in aggregated data are poor characterizations of any of the individuals who have been studied.

Theorists differ in their approach to explaining these two facts. Some believe that consistent individual differences and suboptimality are a result of differences in the use of a single process. Others believe that there are a number of judgment or decision making strategies that people use or elect to use. And finally, there is a small group of theorists who believe that individuals have stable, consistent cognitive styles (e.g., Ramamurthy, King, & Premkumar, 1992).

Suboptimality:
The Symptoms of the Inadequacy of Intuition

Researchers have consistently found that intuitive judgment and decision making is inferior to formal methods. This suboptimality has been demonstrated in a number of ways in a variety of experimental studies.

First, various studies have demonstrated that the information that people consider may be quite different from the information that is relevant. In particular, relevant information such as base-rates may be ignored (Bar-Hillel, 1980; Kahneman & Tversky, 1973) and irrelevant information may influence decisions. For example, people were asked: "Is the number X% an overestimate or an underestimate of the percentage of African countries in the UN? What is your best estimate?" It was found that "best estimates" were higher when X was large and smaller when X was small, even when X was observed to be generated randomly with a wheel of fortune (Tversky & Kahneman, 1974).

Second, the quality of judgments and decisions decrease as task complexity increases (Malhotra, 1982). Typically, quality of decision making is poor if the number of alternative choices is large (> 5) and if the number of factors that should be considered in evaluating a choice is large (> 10). In particular, the variability of responses and subjects' confidence in their judgments increase and the accuracy of decision making decreases (see Payne, 1982). Researchers have suggested that as complexity increases, people may vary their approach to making judgments and decisions, adopting strategies that are more likely to ease processing of complex information (Todd & Benbasat, 1991).

Third, people are inconsistent in their judgments and decisions. For example, it has been commonly observed that people are inconsistent in their evaluation of gambles, evaluating gamble A to be worth more than B but preferring B to A (Mellers, Ordonez, & Birnbaum, 1992; von Winterfeldt & W. Edwards, 1986).

And finally, people make judgments and decisions that violate the simplest of maxims for rational behavior. For example, in some circumstances people violate the principle of dominance when evaluating gambles, giving a higher evaluation to the gamble "win $96 with probability .95, otherwise win $0" than to the gamble "win $96 with probability .95, otherwise win $24" (Birnbaum & S.E. Sutton, 1992). In addition, research has shown that people violate the principle of transitivity when evaluating gambles: there are cases where gamble A is preferred to B, B to C, and C to A (Tversky, 1969).

The fact that human judgment and decision making is suboptimal is one of the primary motivations for developing behavioral decision theories that differ from culturally normative models such as statistics. In addition, these demonstrations of suboptimality clearly show that decision support is needed and, together with behavioral decision theory, give a general indication of where support needs to be provided.

Single-Process Theories:
Information Integration and Rule-Based Decision Making

There are two general types of single-process behavioral decision theories: information integration theories and rule-based decision theories. Both offer an account of how information is transformed from the initial statement of a problem to a final judgment or decision and, in addition, provide a technology for constructing a model of how an individual makes decisions. These explanations of and technologies for modeling individual differences give a general indication of how decision support might be tailored to an individual.

According to information integration theories, people make decisions by combining various sources of information in a balanced, compensatory manner. Each source is termed an attribute of the problem. Information integration theories generally describe or model the transformation of attributes into decisions with a continuous function, where the input to the function is the values of the attributes and the output of the function is the judgment itself (Hammond, G.H. McClelland, & Mumpower, 1980).

In practice, most theorists restrict their attention to simple continuous functions, usually a linear function. It is relatively straightforward to model the cognitive processes of an individual using simple functions. For example, a linear model of an individual is constructed by identifying the features or attributes of a problem $[X_i's]$; determining how important each attribute is to a particular individual, that is, the weight of each attribute in a linear equation $[w_i]$; and then writing the model of the individual as a linear equation [judgment = $w_1X_1 + w_2X_2 + \ldots$]. Simple models such as the linear model are popular because they give reasonably accurate predictions of an individual's judgments: In artificial tasks, correlations between model predictions and judgments range between 0.8 and 0.9, whereas for "real-world tasks", which are usually more complex, correlations range between 0.7 and 0.8 (Slovic & Lichtenstein, 1971). However, several studies show that there are small but statistically significant departures from linearity in the judgments of both experts and novices (e.g., N.H. Anderson, 1972; Goldberg, 1971), and so some theories have been expanded to incorporate more complex continuous functions with which to model information integration (e.g., Hammond, Hamm, Grassia, & Pearson, 1987). In addition, some theories have been expanded to incorporate a finer decomposition of problems (e.g., Keeney, 1982), representing the decision-making process in several stages.

According to this theory, suboptimality and individual differences in decision making are caused by differences in the way attributes are weighted. Thus, suboptimality will occur when important information is given too low a weight, when unimportant information is given too high a weight, or when weights change markedly depending on the nature of the task (e.g., Tversky, Sattah, & Slovic, 1988). Similarly, individual differences are explained by representing the attribute weights as unique to each individual.

The second group of single-process theories is "rule-based" decision theories. According to theories of this type, an individual has a set of rules that are applied, perhaps sequentially, until a conclusion is reached. Each rule has the form "if condition A pertains then do action B," where the action required in some situations is to find out more information. Note that this type of theory can represent information processing that is not balanced, where the value of one attribute can determine which if any additional attributes will be considered in reaching a conclusion as well as determining the conclusion itself. This type of information processing is termed a "rule-based" or "expert" system when represented and simulated on computers, but is better known in psychology as a "production system"; and such systems usually are depicted as a decision tree or as a collection of "sequential decision rules."

One of the major problems with this type of theory is in constructing a rule-based model of an individual. Two approaches to constructing models have been used. The first, efficient, and very popular approach is to interview each individual, in effect asking them what rules they are using; this approach has been called "process tracing" (Einhorn, D.N. Kleinmuntz, & B. Kleinmuntz, 1979; Larcker & Lessig, 1983). Such interviews are structured: An individual is presented with a number of cases, real or hypothetical, asked to make a decision on the basis of the information contained in each case description, and then asked to justify or rationalize their decisions. Thus, process tracing requires a subjective analysis on the part of the decision maker of the actual process by which they reach their final decision. The problem with this technique is that it presumes that valid descriptions of cognitive processes can be elicited from structured interviews, that is, that the processes under consideration are explicit. This is a very questionable presumption (see later discussion).

The second approach to developing individual models is to analyze a collection of judgments or decisions and infer the rules that will successfully model an individual's behavior. This is similar to using linear regression to construct a linear model of an individual judge, except that the technique used to construct a rule-based model is called recursive partitioning regression (RPR; Breiman, Friedman, Olshen, & Stone, 1984). In most cases the judgments or decisions that an individual makes can be described by a numerical value and represented in a multidimensional space, where each of the attributes of the task forms a dimension. If this representation is possible, RPR can be used to derive a rule-based model of the individual: RPR simply partitions the multidimensional space into distinct areas where the judgments or decisions are reasonably homogeneous. That is, for each of the partitions, the numerical values representing the judgments have a small variance. Such partitions can be represented easily as a rule-based system, where the rules discriminate the homogeneous areas in the space (e.g., IF the value of attribute X is large, THEN diagnose…). RPR has been very successful in constructing models of individuals in a variety of tasks requiring expertise, such as diagnosing the causes of acute chest pain in "accident and emergency" cases (Goldman et al., 1982) or diagnosing the locus and severity of brain damage (M.R. Diamond, 1983). However, one of the major problems with RPR is that it is too successful; almost any set of data can be described perfectly with a sufficiently large set of rules or a sufficiently fine partitioning. For example, we used a random number generator to obtain numerical values for the attributes of a case and analyzed a number of such cases using RPR; for all analyses, we found that RPR was very successful at constructing a rule-based partition of the space that explained all of the variance: It gave a complete analysis of "noise."

According to this theory, suboptimality and individual differences in decision making are caused by differences in the particular rules that are used. Thus, suboptimality results from the use of suboptimal rules and individual differences from the use of different rules by different individuals.

One important elaboration of rule-based theory is J.R. Anderson's ACT* model (1982, 1985, 1987). According to Anderson, all knowledge is rule based. Specifically, the performance of any task is governed by cognitive rules termed *productions*. However, experts and novices have different types of knowledge. A novice's knowledge is declarative or formal knowledge and is translated into action by general productions. Expert knowledge is developed with practice through the "proceduralization of declarative knowledge" whereby rules are compiled so that new productions are developed, and through the "composition of productions" whereby sequences of separate rules are collapsed into single, highly specific productions. Expert productions are highly discriminated, used to control perform-ance in the domain of expertise; strengthened, so that experts have fast access and processing times when performing tasks within that domain; and generalized, that is, used flexibly within that domain. Thus, Anderson's theory elaborates the types of rules that may exist in a rule-based system, an elaboration that distinguishes between strategic or explicit knowledge, which is declarative and characteristic of novice productions, and implicit knowledge, which embodies automatic processes and which is characteristic of expert productions (J.R. Anderson, 1992; see chap. 5 of this volume for an expanded description of Anderson's ACT* theory).

Strategies: Heuristics and Constructive Process Models

There are two general types of theory describing strategies: the heuristics model proposed by Tversky and Kahneman and the constructive process view proposed by Payne and other researchers. Theories of this type emphasize that people use relatively simple procedures when making judgments or decisions. Current theory holds that people simplify because they must, because our capacity for processing information is limited. These limitations in memory capacity and computational ability are referred to as "bounded rationality" (Newell & H.A. Simon, 1972). Given that rationality is bounded, simplification strategies are used because: (a) they are within capacity limitations and so easy to use, (b) they are applicable to a fairly wide variety of problems, and (c) they yield approximately correct solutions to many problems.

The simplification strategies described by Tversky and Kahneman (1974) are called *heuristics*. Heuristics were identified by discovering "cognitive illusions," problems for which a majority of subjects arrive at the same but mistaken conclusion, and then determining how subjects arrived at this nonveridical conclusion (for a review see Kahneman, Slovic, & Tversky, 1982). Three heuristics were identified from this research: representativeness, availability, and anchoring and adjustment. The first heuristic, representativeness, is applicable to a wide variety of tasks. This heuristic is simple: Match the current case under consideration with a general concept, and arrive at a solution by attributing all the properties of the concept to this case. Bigotry is one example of the representativeness heuristic in action and another is the gambler's fallacy. The second heuristic, availability, is more specialized; it is used when frequencies or probabilities must be estimated. Availability is the estima-tion of frequency from examples, in particular, the number of examples that can be retrieved from memory or that can be constructed, or the ease with which examples can be retrieved or constructed. "Illusory correlations" is one example of the availability heuristic in action: If it is easy to recall or construct examples where two things are associated, then subjects judge that there is a high correlation between these things. The final heuristic, anchoring and adjustment, is used in many situ-ations but is most useful when revising judgments or decisions. Again, the heuristic is simple: initial estimates are revised in the appropriate direction in the light of new information, but revised conservatively. That is, the initial estimate is an "anchor" and subsequent adjustments to this anchor are too small.

Suboptimality in human judgment and decision making is the basis for this theory: New heuristics would be identified as new patterns of suboptimality are observed. Individual differences are accounted for easily: Memory is unique to individuals and memory is the basis for the most important heuristics. However this theory, unlike other theories in this area, does not have an associated technology for constructing a model of the cognitive processes of an individual. Because of this, it is easier to apply other behavioral decision theories to the design of DSSs, particularly DSSs that are adaptive or tailored to the needs of individual users.

According to the constructive process view of judgment and decision making, people use a variety of decision-making strategies (Payne, Bettman, Coupey, & E.J. Johnson, 1992; Slovic, Griffin, & Tversky, 1990). This viewpoint suggests that when decision makers respond to a judgment or choice task, their preferences for objects are "constructed" rather than simply "revealed." The constructive nature of preferences has been attributed to an interaction between the bounded rationality of decision makers and task complexity (March, 1978). Decision makers are thought to determine their preferences by selecting one or more decision strategies from a repertoire of strategies during decision making. Lability or inconsistency of preferences occurs due to changes in the use of strategies. Changes in strategy use are thought to be related to a range of task and context factors that make different aspects of the decision problem salient, and evoke different strategies for combining information (Payne et al., 1992).

Constructive processes are likely to be used for complex or stressful decision problems where there is little prior knowledge of the decision task, because under such conditions it is probably too difficult for a decision maker to determine an overall strategy a priori. Constructive processes are unlikely to be used where there is considerable prior experience with a particular decision, because constructing new strategies when the decision task is well known would be inefficient (Payne et al., 1992).

Payne et al. (1992) proposed a theoretical framework that attempted to predict when a particular strategy would be used. Specifically, the use of several strategies was considered an adaptive response to an accuracy/effort trade-off for the task at hand, that is, achieving an accurate decision or preference, while limiting the cognitive effort used to make the decision. Payne and his colleagues argued that the cognitive effort required to use a particular strategy is reflected by the number and specific mix of elementary information processes (EIPs) needed to execute that strategy. EIPs include mental operations such as acquiring information in short-term memory, comparing values of two alternatives on an attribute to determine which is larger, multiplying a weight and attribute value, and so forth. Bettman, E.J. Johnson, and Payne (1990) demonstrated significant individual differences in the effort related to particular EIPs, suggesting that individuals may select different decision strategies partly because certain component EIPs may be relatively more or less effortful for different individuals.

Cognitive Style

The final approach to understanding suboptimality and individual differences in decision making has been an examination of specific decision-maker characteristics and their relation to decision processes or strategies. In particular, researchers have examined individual decision makers' cognitive styles. Their work has both theoretical importance in clarifying the individual differences in decision-making processes and the use of strategies, and practical importance in establishing the extent to which decision support needs to be tailored to individuals to maximize effectiveness.

H.A. Simon (1960) defined cognitive style as "the characteristic, self-consistent mode of functioning which individuals show in their perception and intellectual activities" (p. 72). Cognitive style focuses on specific cognitive activities, being most concerned with *how* an individual thinks, and under what circumstances the cognitive activities are evoked, maintained, and modified (Ramamurthy et al., 1992). A broad range of styles have been described. For example, people may differ in their preference or predisposition for: simple or complex integrative processes (Schroder, Driver, & Streufert, 1967), systematic versus heuristic-based processes (Huysman, 1970), perceptive-receptive and systematic-intuitive processes (McKenney & Keen, 1974), and evaluation—sensing/intuitive and thinking/feeling processes (Jung, 1962).

Although several researchers have examined the relationship between decision-maker characteristics and decision making (e.g., Einhorn, 1970; Onken, Hastie, & Revelle, 1985), empirical evidence of the relationship is inconclusive. Psychographic characterizations of cognitive style have provided little insight into the decision-making process, resulting in the lack of an integrated and theoretically relevant framework of decision-maker characteristics. Consequently, the nature of the influence of individual differences in cognitive style on decision processes and the use of strategies is largely unclear (see Punj & Stewart, 1983).

The lack of understanding of the relationship between cognitive style and decision making seems to have occurred for two main reasons. First, the inconclusiveness may be due to an inability to compare results across studies (Jarvenpaa, Dickson, & DeSanctis, 1985; Ramamurthy et al., 1992), for research in the area has been characterized by poor research design, and unresolved measurement problems. Second, few attempts have been made to separate individual decision-maker characteristics from one another, from task characteristics, and from decision processes or strategies.

DECISION SUPPORT SYSTEMS

Decision support systems provide a number of tools to aid decision makers, including tools for accessing information, analytical tools for processing information (e.g., an expert system), and tools for tinkering with models of the problem or solution alternatives under consideration. There have been several approaches to providing such decision support. After briefly outlining each approach and its limitations, we consider the issue of how decision support should be presented, arguing that a theoretical framework for designing information displays must be found in theories describing the different types of information processing that users might adopt.

The first approach to providing decision support is to ask "what *can* we provide the user?" DSSs developed from such a framework may be described as technology-driven, for what can be provided is generally delimited by technology. For computer-based systems, the trend has been to apply advances in microelectronics to supply decision makers with more information, more solution alternatives, and more opportunities to question fundamentals of the analytical models. Such technology-driven development has concentrated on providing the most "realistic" model of the problem or task, encouraging decision makers to explore their own "mental models" of the problem, and providing "user-friendly" interfaces that encourage novice computer users to interact readily with DSSs (Jones, 1991; L.D. Phillips, 1984). Although such an approach is interesting because it has created new options for decision makers, it is problematic because research on human judgment suggests that more complex representations of decision tasks and their analyses do not necessarily lead to improved decision making. In fact, more information may lead to more confusion (van der Colk, 1988).

A second approach to providing decision support is to ask "what are users' information needs?" DSSs developed from such a framework may be described as one-size-fits-all systems, for needs are assumed to be common to everyone. One type of one-size-fits-all DSS attempts to cure the symptoms of poor decision making. For example, systems have been developed to help users attend to relevant and ignore irrelevant information (e.g., Shortliffe, 1976). However, research suggests that effective decision support will not result from treating the symptoms, but from identifying and correcting the mechanisms by which the symptoms occur. The second type of one-size-fits-all DSS focuses on single-process behavioral decision theories, either information integration or rule-based theories, and has the advantage of providing a technology for modeling the cognitive processes of individual users. However, this technology is rarely used at more than a superficial level in constructing DSSs to constrain decision processes. Moreover, in applying information integration or rule-based decision theory to the design of DSSs, it may be erroneous to assume that decision-making responses are made according to particular processes such as the linear model or specific rules with the form "if condition A pertains then do action B" (Mellers et al., 1992).

A third approach to providing decision support is to ask "what are the information needs of this particular user?" DSSs developed from this framework may be described as tailored systems, for they try to accommodate individual differences in DSS users' stable cognitive styles or labile decision strategies. The cognitive style framework has yielded little stimulus for DSS development to date. Ramaprasad (1987) argued that the failure of cognitive style research to adequately inform DSS development may be due to researchers focusing on a "macro" level that explores general factors, and overlooks the specific influences of style on an individual's cognitive information processing. Thus, it may be more fruitful for researchers to examine a "micro" level, such as the components of decision strategies examined in Payne et al.'s (1992) constructive process view of decision making. Payne et al. outlined several strategies that decision makers may select or construct according to the demands of the decision task. This view makes specific suggestions as to what aspects of individual users' decision strategies can be targeted for decision support, encouraging individuals to use better or more accurate strategies, even if these strategies are not normative or optimal. However, few developers have applied the constructive process view of decision making to DSS system design.

TYPE OF KNOWLEDGE:
IMPLICATIONS FOR BEHAVIORAL DECISION THEORY
AND THE DESIGN OF DECISION SUPPORT SYSTEMS

The distinction between implicit and explicit knowledge or between automatic and controlled processes has not been a central issue for behavioral decision theory. This is unfortunate for several reasons. First, the distinction is easy to incorporate into most behavioral decisions theories: As we argue later, the question of whether information is processed strategically or automatically is in principle independent of the question of whether information is processed in a manner described by integration theory, rule-based decision theory, the heuristics model, or the constructive process view of decision making. Second, the generality of behavioral decision theories can be significantly enhanced by incorporating the distinction between types of information processing. In particular, distinguishing implicit from explicit processes may clarify some current debates and encourage the examination of new issues. And finally, the incorporation of process type distinctions into behavioral decision theories will significantly increase the contribution that these theories can make to the design of decision support systems. In particular, we argue that at present behavioral decision theory provides a framework for identifying a user's needs, but fails to provide a framework for determining how to provide information and support to a user to meet these needs.

Incorporating Process Type Distinctions
Into Behavioral Decision Theories

As the preceding review shows, most behavioral decision theories are concerned with a description of what happens to information, how it is transformed from the initial statement or attributes of a problem to a final judgment or decision. It should be clear that this concern is entirely independent of process type distinctions. For example, information integration theory suggests that people represent a problem as a set of attributes, and that these attributes are transformed into a final judgment or decision in a manner that can be described by an equation (usually linear). For this theory, what is important is what happens to the information, that it is integrated linearly, and not how this happens. This level of description of decision making is entirely independent of process type distinctions. For example, it might be the case that information is integrated linearly using an explicit or strategic process incorporating, perhaps, the classic external memory and information-processing aid: pencil and paper. Alternatively, it might be that people integrate information linearly using an "intuitive" (von Winterfeldt & W. Edwards, 1986) implicit or automatic process, such as those used by the sensory systems or by idiot savants. The essential elements of information integration theory will not be changed by incorporating process type distinctions into the theory, and this incorporation could add considerable weight to some of the explanations that this theory offers of suboptimality effects. For example, information integration theory explains inconsistencies in evaluations of and preferences for gambles by positing that people use different weights in these two situations. If it were further posited that people are using automatic processes in considering gambles, then the reason why different weights are used also would be explained: Automatic processes are highly specific and context dependent and different processes (different weights) should be expected when the context changes (from evaluation to choice).

The same argument applies to rule-based decision theory and to the heuristics model. For rule-based decision theory, a case has already been made by Anderson (see earlier discussion), who argued that what happens to the information, that it is processed with a set of rules, is independent of the type of process employed. In particular, he argued that either automatic processes (for experts) or strategic processes (for novices) could be employed but that these differences are independent of the rules that are used to transform information from an initial problem statement into a final judgment or decision. A similar argument applies to the heuristics model where, for example, it has been shown that there is little difference on traditional outcome measures between accounts that view the process of accessing concepts as strategic or automatic (cf. Kahneman & D. Miller, 1986).

The argument does not have to be made for the constructive process view of decision making, for there is already a debate as to the nature of simplification strategies. Most usually, authors describe simplification strategies as implicit or automatic processes, referring to them as rapid, nondeliberative, smooth processes that "require minimal cognitive processing and control" (T.R. Mitchell & Beach,

1990, p.14). People are thought to have low conscious awareness of their use of simplification strategies, to have high confidence in the judgments that result from using such strategies, but to have low confidence in describing the method that they used to reach such judgments (Hammond et al., 1987). For example, H.A. Simon (1987) claimed that "intuition and judgement...are simply analyses frozen into habit and into the capacity for rapid response through recognition" (p. 63). In contrast, others have argued that simplification strategies may be under conscious control (Payne et al., 1992; Payne, Bettman, & E.J. Johnson, 1993). Again, these differences in the account of type of process are independent of the particular simplification strategies that are thought to be used to transform information from an initial problem statement into a final judgment or decision.

The Effects of Incorporating Process Type Distinctions Into Behavioral Decision Theories

We believe that the benefits that will accrue from expanding behavioral decision theory to incorporate process type distinctions are considerable. The first and most obvious benefit is that it may clarify the debate concerning the degree of self-insight that judges have into their own cognitive processes. In general, studying self-insight requires a comparison of what people believe that they do with what they actually do. This comparison is usually difficult to make: Whereas it is easy to assess "what people believe they do" with interviews, it is difficult to assess "what people actually do." However, in the area of human judgment and reasoning, several theories offer technologies for modeling the cognitive processes of an individual and so self-insight is reasonably easy to study: Just compare a subject's self-report with a model of their cognitive processes, either a linear or rule-based model or a model of their strategies. For example, using a linear model of information integration, Pascoe (1986) selected subjects who appeared to have a high degree of self-insight: Preliminary tests were conducted and subjects who were regular in their judgments ($R^2 > .9$) and whose verbal and behavioral weights were in perfect agreement were selected for further study. These subjects, supposedly subjects with a high degree of self-insight, were taught a new method of making judgments. During the early phase of this training, subjects rarely used the new method—it required some practice to learn. However, all subjects reported that they were using the "new weights"—and so self-insight appeared to be low. By the end of training, virtually all subjects were using the new weights—and so self-insight appeared to be high. That is, subjects reported what they thought they ought to be doing, and if their behavior happened to match their intentions, they appeared to have a high degree of self-insight.

Although behavioral decision theories offer a technology for studying self-insight, experimental results have not been consistent. Some studies indicate that self-insight into the cognitive processes involved in judgment and decision making is high (e.g., Reilly & Doherty, 1989), at least for experts, but the majority of studies indicate that self-insight is low. In part, this conclusion is based on studies of calibration and confidence. People are said to be well calibrated if the confidence they show in their judgments matches the accuracy of those judgments, that is, if they have insight into the level of accuracy of their judgments. The general finding has been that people are overconfident in their judgments (D. Griffin & Tversky, 1992; Lichtenstein, Fischhoff, & L.D. Phillips, 1982), and this general trend has been documented in studies of calibration using a variety of tasks with a variety of subject populations: clinical psychologists (Oskamp, 1965), physicians (Lusted, 1977), and negotiators (Neale & Bazerman, 1990), among others. Furthermore, this overconfidence effect has been found to be relatively robust, invariant with respect to subjects' intelligence and expertise (Lichtenstein & Fischhoff, 1980).

The inconsistency in the results of experimental studies of self-insight might be resolved by expanding behavioral decision theories to incorporate process type distinctions. Expanded theories would address this issue directly by describing those conditions under which processing was implicit or automatic and those conditions under which processing was explicit or strategic. None of the studies described tried to address this issue directly (cf. Logan, 1992a), and it does not seem unreasonable to presume that incorporating process type distinctions formally into behavioral decision theories would resolve much of the inconsistency described previously. This resolution is extremely important for the study of human judgment and reasoning because many of the methodologies used to construct models of individual judges rests on the assumption that the self-insight of judges is high. For example, many of the process tracing methods used in constructing rule-based or strategy-based models of individual judges rely on the "self-reports," the "think-aloud protocols" or the "retrospective reevaluations" of individual judges, and at present these methodologies are used indiscriminately. The expansion of existing theory will serve to clarify under what circumstances what methodology is appropriate.

Another benefit to expanding current theory is that it may clarify ideas concerning the effects of stress and task complexity on the cognitive processes involved in judgment and decision making. It is generally accepted that as stress and task complexity increase, people tend to shift toward using simpler decision strategies. At the same time, their confidence in their judgments increases but their calibration and self-insight decrease. For example, proponents of the constructive process view of decision making have examined the effects of time pressure on decision-making strategy. They reported that time pressure clearly showed differential effects on different strategies. In particular, the elimination-by-aspects strategy was shown to be one of the most robust decision-making strategies across various task environments. The lexicographic strategy also seemed robust, although only when the complexity of the problem was relative low. In contrast, a strategy such as satisficing was much less robust, resulting in decreasing accuracy as time pressure increased. Payne and his colleagues explained their results in terms of the charac-

teristics of the strategies themselves: Those characterized by attribute-based processing and selectivity in processing were expected to be more effective under severe
time pressure. They speculated that as time pressure increases, less effortful
strategies will be used.

It should be clear that the introduction of process type distinctions into behavioral decision theory will help to inform and articulate this area of study. For
example, stress and task complexity are thought to be important in determining
whether an automatic or strategic process is used. Stress limits the capacity that can
be devoted to a task whereas complexity determines how much capacity must be
devoted to performing the task. Automatic processes are likely to be used when
stress and complexity are high and strategic processes when stress and complexity
are low. Thus the introduction of implicit/explicit and automatic/controlled distinctions into behavioral decision theory will deepen our understanding of the relative
robustness of simplification and other processing strategies depending on the
effects of a variety of stressors.

In addition to the aforementioned, there are a whole range of questions that could
become the focus of theory and research if process type distinctions were incorporated into behavioral decision theories. For example, researchers might study the
degree of control people have over the way they process information. It may be that
radical simplification strategies are only used by judges solving complex problems
in stressful environments when they attempt to control their cognitive processes.
As another example, researchers might study the degree of flexibility that people
evidence in their use of different problem-solving strategies. It may be that people
can use the same processes to solve different decision tasks when the tasks are
relatively simple and similar in structure (applying the same strategic process) or
when the tasks are relatively complex and similar in surface features (applying the
same automatic process). And, as a final example, researchers might study what
happens to decision makers as a function of practice. Although practice effects are
not central to most behavioral decision theories, such effects are addressed by some
theories (notably Anderson's; see chap. 5 of this volume) and are important in
determining how judgments might be improved through training. Thus, the introduction of process type distinctions into behavioral decision theories will expand
the phenomena that they address and possibly lead to the resolution of issues of
current theoretical and methodological importance.

The Application of Behavioral Decision Theory
to the Design of Decision Support Systems

In designing an effective decision support system, two things need to be considered.
The first is the identification of the information needs of individual users of the
system, and the second is the determination of what kind of support to provide to
meet these needs. Behavioral decision theory provides a theoretical framework for
identifying the needs of individual users. For example, information integration

theory could be used to design a DSS that supports the linear integration of information. The needs of a particular user can be identified by constructing an individual regression model of the user's cognitive processes. The support system then would aim at helping the user give appropriate weights to each attribute. However, behavioral decision theory does not provide a framework for determining the best way to provide support. It provides a clear framework for identifying needs, but no framework for determining how to meet the needs that have been identified.

Determining what kind of help or information displays to provide an individual user in a DSS is similar to the problem of determining what kind of information displays to provide in a computer-managed training system (Milech, Kirsner, Roy, & Waters, 1993). For both problems, this requires an identification of the capacities of the user: how the user is currently processing information and how they will process new information provided by the system. In particular, each user's mode of information processing must be identified: whether they are using an implicit or an explicit mode. For example, if a user is processing information explicitly, help could be provided in the form of a formal dialogue. This dialogue might provide access to statistical information, to explicit hints, or to analytical tools for processing information that replace "paper and pencil." The dialogue could also provide the user with feedback about their own judgments and decisions in the form of a formal model, similar to the cognitive feedback used in training (Balzer, Doherty, & R. O'Connor, 1989). However, if a user is processing information implicitly, help provided in the form of a formal dialogue is unlikely to be effective (see chap. 3 of this volume). For implicit processes, users might be supported with a case-based reasoning system that improves their discrimination of problem types and possible outcomes for the different problem types, or they might be provided with analytical tools that automatically integrate information supplied by the user (perhaps after it is properly regressed). There is virtually no research literature that addresses these issues, and these proposals must be treated as mere suggestions, unsupported by data.

It is reasonably straightforward to incorporate these suggestions into the architecture of decision support systems. As in training, diagnostic testing must be performed to identify the salient characteristics of the user: how information is being transformed and what mode of processing is being used. Procedures for identifying and representing these characteristics are currently being developed for computer-managed training systems (Milech, Waters, Noël, Roy, & Kirsner, 1993) and these procedures can be easily extended to decision support systems. In particular, a model of the user could be created and used to determine what type of help to provide to a particular user and the format in which the help is to be provided. The diagnostic tests that determine how a user is transforming information are specified by various behavioral decision theories: A sample of judgments should be collected from a user to construct a variety of models (linear regression, recursive partitioning regression, or other forms of modeling) and the best-fit model taken to represent how a user is transforming information. Similarly, the diagnostic tests that will determine a user's mode of information processing are specified by research concerning the distinction between implicit and explicit information processes. For example, task difficulty and the number of concurrent tasks that must be performed could be varied, and the pattern of deterioration in performance that occurs as difficulty increases will diagnose the mode of information transformation (cf. Milech, Waters et al., 1993).

Such testing is necessary to determine how to properly tailor a system to an individual: what needs to address and how to address them.

SUMMARY AND CONCLUSION

Research shows that people make suboptimal judgments and that there are large individual differences in the way in which people make judgments and decisions. One response to these findings is the development of a number of theories that describe the cognitive processes of individual decision makers: behavioral decision theories. Another response is the development of decision aids, and the newest approach to aiding decision makers is to provide them with computer-based support systems or DSSs. However, it is only recently that system designers have drawn on behavioral decision theories and associated research to formalize reasonable design principles for these systems. Behavioral decision theories have provided a technology for determining how a user is transforming information, and this technology can be used to construct a model of a user that identifies the user's information needs.

It was argued that these theories and their application to the design of DSSs could be improved by expanding the theories to incorporate processing type distinctions: the distinction between strategic and automatic and the distinction between implicit and explicit information processes. First, it is relatively straightforward to incorporate these distinctions into current theory and there are several benefits that would accrue if these distinctions were introduced: It will expand the phenomena that current theories address and possibly lead to the resolution of issues of current theoretical and methodological importance. Second, incorporating these distinctions into behavioral decision theories would improve the contribution these theories can make to the design of decision support systems. In particular, it was argued that the expanded theories could provide suggestions for how to design displays and support facilities to meet the needs that have been identified.

It is relatively straightforward to incorporate these ideas into the architecture of decision support systems. Tests can be introduced to determine how a user is transforming information and whether strategic or automatic process are being used. As in training systems, a module is simply added that contains a model of the relevant user characteristics, and this model is used to determine the type and form of help that the DSS provides. The only thing that is missing is the research that will determine what works.

18

MIXED PROCESSES
IN PROCESS CONTROL

David L. Morrison
University of Western Australia

Peter Lee
Murdoch University

This chapter identifies how implicit and explicit processes influence the performance of human operators in industrial process control. The primary focus is on
operators as diagnosticians of system failures because this is a major role that is
played by this class of personnel in this setting. Little has been written that
specifically deals with explicit and implicit processes and their development
outside of the laboratory. This may in part be due to the uncertainty that exists with
regard to the true nature of explicit and implicit processes (Seger, 1994) such that
conceptual clarification must precede application. Alternatively, it is possible that
most complex tasks have components that require the implementation of both
implicit and explicit knowledge (Berry & Dienes, 1993) and to study these
processes *in situ* is impossible and requires tight experimental control. Thus, rather
than providing a review of existing research that has directly addressed the role of
implicit and explicit processes in process control, this chapter explores the potential
applications of emergent knowledge with a view to understanding and, perhaps,
enhancing one aspect of human performance in this industrial setting namely, fault
diagnosis.

For the purposes of definition we treat implicit knowledge, procedural knowledge, and automatic processes as referring to a general class of information-processing activities that require little if any attentional control and cognitive resources.
The utility of the application of implicit knowledge is that it is time efficient and
minimum conscious intervention affords the opportunity of performing more than

one cognitive activity at once. The drawback is that the successful application of implicit knowledge is restricted to familiar and predictable events (e.g., Hayes & D.E. Broadbent, 1988). Explicit and declarative knowledge as well as controlled processing are considered to share the common characteristics with each other—that is, they are slow, effortful, and consume cognitive resources. The benefit of this form of processing is that although it is relatively slow and effortful, it is also applicable in novel or unpredictable situations. In other words, mental processing that can be controlled is also adaptive. We are not concerned with the debates surrounding the nature of the learning mechanisms underlying each form of knowledge. These have been described in detail elsewhere (Berry & Dienes, 1993; Seger, 1994). Our interest in the implicit/explicit distinction here is merely that there appear to be behavioral consistencies associated with each form of knowledge that have implications for human performance on complex tasks such as fault diagnosis.

The structure of the chapter is as follows: First, because many readers will be unfamiliar with the role of human operators as controllers and diagnosticians of system failures in process control, a brief overview of the process control domain is given. Second, the effect of operational conditions on the operators' cognitive capacity and hence diagnostic capability is considered. In the remaining sections of the chapter, ways in which human diagnosis performance may be improved are discussed. Natural preferences for particular modes of thinking, the development of implicit and explicit expertise, and the utilization of the characteristics of implicit and explicit modes of information processing as guides in interface development also are described.

CHARACTERISTICS OF INDUSTRIAL PROCESS CONTROL

Cummings and Blumberg (1987) divided manufacturing systems into two essential types: continuous and batch. Continuous systems or processes are most often thought of as being associated with power production or chemical and petroleum industries. However, mass production industries where discrete items such as cars or washing machines are manufactured may also use much of the same technology. A common feature of such industries is that they possess highly centralized command and control systems that are also used for monitoring and diagnosis of system failures.

Typically, manufacturing systems are controlled by operators who must interpret system data as presented from remote sensors. In many instances the process may never be observed directly, but instead, the state of the system must be inferred from a myriad of displays provided for the operator on one or a number of consoles. In continuous manufacturing environments, the display design philosophy of one sensor–one display, common in the 1950s, still prevails. Slowly this is being replaced by computerized displays where sometimes data are crammed on to several screens that can be called up as needed by the operator. It is quite usual to find that little improvement has been made by way of display design with this new technology. Indeed, many of the changes that have been observed with new technology have not been through the introduction of more innovative display designs, but by sophistication in control algorithms that frequently attempt further system automation. Computerized control means that the system can operate in a stand-alone fashion under the direct supervision of fewer workers. Where stand-alone systems are implemented, the operator will be less directly involved than before in the manufacturing process. Instead, he or she could be required to monitor equipment and make minor adjustments to equipment settings and possibly switch programs according to changes in batch production requirements (Morrison & Upton, 1994).

Although computerized process integration offers substantial cost savings, the increase in control comes at a price. The cost is in terms of the complexity of the software required to integrate and manage diverse operations. Consequently, the overall transparency of the total system can be reduced and hence, when failures do occur, the task of troubleshooting becomes ever more complex. There are two facets to the complexity of process control systems. One of these relates to psychological complexity (i.e., the difficulty operators have in comprehending system characteristics), described in detail later, and the other relates to the physical complexity of the working system.

By one definition, systems become complex when single components or processes can perform more than one function and perform in more than one subsystem in a larger superordinate system. In this sense such systems can be said to be interactively complex (Perrow, 1984). Examples of such systems are seen in the nuclear industry where steam generators drive turbines while at the same time helping to maintain temperature and pressure in the primary cooling system. This system is responsible for heat dissipation from the nuclear fuel. With such equipment there are many ways in which seemingly independent components may influence other parts of a working system. For instance, with just four components, twelve possible interactions can occur between them. This figure is multiplied many times as the number of components with common mode (dual-purpose) functions increases. As a consequence, many unforeseen interactions can occur for systems designed in this way. Thus, when failures arise it is possible that no procedures or manuals will exist to guide diagnosis because the designers cannot anticipate all possible failures. Examples of the bizarre and often highly improbable nature of failures in interactively complex systems have been described by Perrow (1984).

Process control systems are psychologically complex in that many system parameters can interact and affect the way that equipment behaves and ultimately influence product quality. The dual tasks of comprehension and control are made even more difficult by the fact that the sheer volume of information that is presented on the typical instrument console is beyond the conscious capacity of most operators. In addition to this, the sluggish nature of some systems is such that the effects of a trimming action implemented by one operator may not be directly observed until some time later, often after a change in operating personnel has occurred. Without adequate feedback, maintaining high levels of skill is difficult and, indeed, the most skilled operators use open loop control that does not require direct input from the environment. In this sense process control is anticipatory and clearly reliant on past experience. These conditions would seem to be ideal for the development and default adoption of implicit skill (Seger, 1994).

Diagnosing System Failures

Given the sluggish nature of many process control systems, it is difficult to imagine how operators could instantly develop internal models for the many potential unanticipated events that could occur in complex systems. Whereas implicit knowledge may be appropriate for normal monitoring and control conditions, this may not be true when things go wrong. Despite the advances made in automated control, humans are frequently given the job of dealing with the unexpected. The systems and the technology used to control them have become so complex that it is impossible for the system designers and engineers to specify, in advance, all possible failures. Ironically then, as technology-driven systems become more sophisticated (and complex) the role of humans has become increasingly important (L. Bainbridge, 1982). In assigning the task of dealing with unexpected failures to humans, there is a tacit recognition that they are capable of demonstrating high levels of creativity and flexibility and that these skills will be needed for diagnosis. For this reason alone, much of the human factors research literature has focused on the diagnostic process rather than that of system control which, due to advances in control theory, is largely technology driven. Paradoxically, improvements in engineering technology have meant that the very task human operators are required to perform is the one that they have the least opportunity to practice. Adding further to the irony is that there is an emerging literature in experimental psychology (e.g., Stanley et al., 1989) on the *control* of complex systems that has largely ignored diagnosis. The primary focus of interest in the control literature is the development of implicit expertise for control and its relationship with explicit forms of representation. As yet the dual roles of implicit and explicit knowledge in the diagnosis of system malfunction have been underresearched from this emergent perspective.

In reality the mental models required for normal and abnormal operation and control are likely to be very different. Under normal conditions much of the information that operators have at hand is redundant because many instrument readings are frequently correlated. Temperature and pressure in sealed reaction vessels will, for example, be positively and linearly related. Under abnormal conditions (e.g., a leaky valve) this relationship need not hold. Hence, the information search strategies appropriate to normal conditions may be deficient when things have gone wrong (Moray & Huey, 1981). Different search strategies should be applied under abnormal conditions, and possibly the way that data are interpreted should vary according to the immediate past history of the plant equipment. It is conceivable, therefore, that operators may hold a number of implicit mental models for different tasks that are sufficient under normal operations and for a limited set of known failures. The apparently effortless strategies of operational control could be selected from a limited repertoire for appropriate or normal conditions. These may, perhaps, be stored in a discrete form in a look-up table, as described by D.E. Broadbent et al. (1986), Hayes and D.E. Broadbent (1988), and Marescaux, Luc, and Karnas (1989), and only triggered at an unconscious level by a signal provided by the environment.

In addition to the abnormal–normal distinction that has just been made, the different tasks of monitoring and control have implications for the search strategies that are appropriate for each. Under normal conditions, for monitoring and control, operators typically focus on the forward flow of events: what causes what. For diagnosis, the chain of thought must be the reverse: Given a set of symptoms, what could have caused it. To give an illustrative example of what is meant by this, consider the following: Suppose that when I play football and receive the ball in the penalty area the probability I will score a goal is .75. The probability that when a goal is scored, it was scored by me is not .75 because there are 10 other players in the team. Thus the possibility that different patterns of play, other than those in which I was the last player to touch the ball in the penalty area, and resulted in the goal, must be considered. Diagnosis necessarily works backward from an event to its cause, whereas supervisory control is predictive and anticipatory in nature and in this sense similar to other forms of skill (Crossman & Cooke, 1974; Kragt & Landeweerd, 1974; McLeod, 1976; Moray, Lootsteen, & Pajak, 1988).

The distinction between novel and familiar events has implications for diagnosis as well as control. Failures that are unpredictable, or unusual, create at least three difficulties for experienced diagnosticians even with a large repertoire of well-tried solutions to novel problems: First, previous experience may be a hindrance rather than a help (Woods, O'Brien, & Hanes, 1987) in identifying the solution path. When novel failures are encountered, it is not unusual for operators to fail to recognize that they are dealing with something that they have not seen before. Indeed, a systematic analysis of the errors made by power plant operators (Woods et al., 1987) showed that they find it extremely difficult to deviate from pre-specified procedures appropriate for known events but that are not generally applicable in unforeseen abnormal conditions. One potential explanation for the difficulty that diagnosticians have in considering alternatives to "the most obvious" solution, is that they are unwittingly primed, like most humans, to respond to statistically predictable events (D.E. Broadbent, 1971; Einhorn & Hogarth, 1981; Kahneman & Tversky, 1982; C.R. Peterson & Beach, 1967).

Second, diagnosticians must be capable of uncoupling the automatic data collection routines, useful for familiar problems, in order that important diagnostic information, for unfamiliar events, is not overlooked (Rasmussen & Lind, 1981). A major obstacle to the uncoupling process is that the diagnosticians may be unaware of how they learned the expertise that they have developed. It is a characteristic of complex tasks that the process of skill development develops without the diagnostician being capable of describing what they have learned (Berry & D.E. Broadbent, 1984; D.E. Broadbent, 1977; D.E. Broadbent & Aston, 1978; Hayes & D.E. Broadbent, 1988; Stanley et al., 1989). Thus, without knowing what it is that triggers their responses, they may be blind to the fact that their behavior is suboptimal and/or incapable of thinking of what the appropriate response might be in the face of a novel event requiring a new and purposeful consideration.

The third explanation relies on the interplay between motivation, cognitive capacity, and the willingness to engage explicit processes. Dealing with unfamiliar events almost certainly requires application of explicit knowledge (e.g., active search through memory for rules followed by mental calculation) and by its very nature this is effortful. Those who are less motivated may well fail to deal with novel events because of an unwillingness to engage in effortful processing. Willingness to engage resources may, however, be contingent on the effort that is required, and this itself depends on the starting level of available resources. Given a task with a certain level of difficulty, those with the most cognitive resources will, of necessity, find the task easier if one supposes that there is an inverse relationship between required effort and spare capacity (see D.A. Norman & Bobrow, 1975).

From the discussion so far it might have appeared as though the modes of information processing that should be applied to diagnosis problems are contingent upon the binary categorization of problems as being familiar or novel. Such a rule is undoubtedly overly simplistic because the diagnosis of even the most unexpected failures probably will necessitate some utilization of familiar problem-solving routines. The skill in dealing with novel failures most likely will be related to the ability of the operator to break the task of diagnosis down into its subcomponents and recombine them in novel ways. In order to do this, it seems that a prerequisite is for the diagnostician to have some awareness of what those subcomponents might be. Some implicit skills are, however, learned implicitly (see Berry & Dienes, 1993; Seger, 1994). It is possible to hypothesize, therefore, that the development of implicit knowledge, via a process that is itself implicit, will not lead to the development of adaptable skills that can cope with the unexpected. Indeed, Berry (1991) and Marescaux et al. (1989) have shown that, for control tasks, subjects who have undergone an implicit learning regime "do not perform well when presented with *new random* situations" (Berry & Dienes, 1993, p. 25, italics added).

So far then, there are three aspects to the successful diagnosis of system failures: (a) the classification of the fault as novel or familiar plus the correct selection of the form of expertise to be applied, (b) the willingness to engage in explicit processing if necessary, and (c) the capability to develop a novel response using existing knowledge and the mental capacity to recombine complex sequences of simple mental routines. The first of these is arguably dependent on an adequate search of the available problem cues prior to making a decision, whereas the latter two may be influenced by the mental resources that are free at the time a diagnosis is required.

Apart from level of expertise and natural capacity limitations, research in cognitive psychology has shown that the conditions under which the mental activity is required influence both environmental sampling behavior (e.g., Bacon. 1974; Baddeley, 1972; D.E. Broadbent & Gregory, 1965; Hockey, 1970) as well as resource availability (e.g., Kahneman, 1973; Moray, 1967; Navon & Gopher, 1979; Wickens, 1991). In the next section, the operational conditions under which diagnoses must be made are reviewed for the purpose of highlighting how these may adversely impact on the application of explicit expertise in particular.

DIAGNOSIS UNDER STRESS

Stress may have an important effect on the operator's ability to diagnose failures because there is evidence that, when stressed, information-processing resource availability and information-processing efficiency are compromised (Hockey, 1984, 1986). As a consequence, the ability of operators to engage in explicit information-processing activities, so important for the diagnosis of novel failures, is significantly reduced. In highly reliable systems, such as continuous process control, the operators' job has been described as 95% boredom and 5% sheer panic (Sheridan, 1981). There are two effects that this can have on performance. First, during the extended quiet period, operators may become bored and less sensitive to small changes in machine performance. Such oversights may later prove to be costly (Parasuraman, 1986). As boredom sets in, operators may be unaware of the changes in their behavior that occur over time. A second cost is that with highly reliable systems, operators have little opportunity to practice their unique skills (L. Bainbridge, 1982). Over time, the skills learned in training inevitably will become "rusty" unless they are given sufficient practice. The increase in "rustiness" will be manifest in the greater cognitive effort that is required in order to maintain performance at its previous level. Things that may be automatic to practiced personnel become less so as the level of skill deteriorates. Thus, even routine failures may become more difficult to deal with if the time between events is sufficiently large for skills to significantly deteriorate. In one study (E.C. Marshall, Scanlon, Shepard, & Duncan, 1981), for example, experienced operators were found to correctly diagnose plant failures at an astonishingly low 33%.

The effects of lack of practice will be exaggerated when operators are expected to perform under stressful conditions (Welford, 1976). Cognitive resource theory (e.g., Kahneman, 1973) suggests that exposure to stress reduces cognitive efficiency most notably for resource-demanding tasks. According to theories of arousal (e.g., Easterbrook, 1959, Kahneman, 1973; Yerkes & Dodson, 1908) exposure to excessive stress has negative consequences for information-processing efficiency and capacity. Empirically, albeit with simple laboratory tasks, it has been shown that both attention (Hockey, 1986) and memory systems are affected (see M.W. Eysenck, 1982). Among the changes in performance that occur with excessive arousal are: increases in speed of reaction often at the expense of errors, more superficial processing of stimuli, a narrowing of attention and a reduction in short-term memory capacity. More contemporary accounts (e.g., A. Smith, 1989) of changes in performance as a function of exposure to stress focus on changes in strategy, from one relying on explicit knowledge to one that depends on implicit processes, rather than levels of arousal. Thus, reported biases in the diagnostic behavior of industrial machine operators (Morrison & Upton, 1994) may well be the result of attempts to reduce excessive cognitive load to manageable proportions by strategy adjustment. Such effects are not always detrimental. Speeded responses may be highly adaptive under some circumstances, especially those that are familiar. However, changes in behavior that result from exposure to stress may be thought of as attempts to compensate for the reduced availability of resources that is a consequence of exposure to stress.

By implication, tasks that can be performed competently under normal circumstances become more difficult when the human subject is stressed. In process control, unexpected events may place substantial demands on operators, not only because of the elevated levels of arousal that often accompany time-pressured decision making, but also the need to actively process large amounts of incoming data as displayed on the instrument console. Under such conditions, operators have been known to make errors of judgment by fixating on the most salient rather than the most appropriate symptoms of the problem. In this context salience may be a function of equipment performance in the recent past or the result of extended experience in dealing with a series of known failures. At Three Mile Island (TMI; see Perrow, 1984; Rubinstein & Mason, 1979; Torrey, 1979a, 1979b), for example, operators formulated an incorrect hypothesis and failed to revise their solution in the face of strong evidence that they were wrong. Instead, they continued to sample the data from the environment in a way that supported a decision about the failure that had been made earlier. Perhaps because the operators were inexperienced at dealing with any but proceduralized problem solutions, they were unwilling or unable to step back and evaluate the incoming data on its merits and generate a novel solution to a novel event (Woods et al., 1987). The strategies used under these conditions have been successful in the past and, unless operators realize that they are inappropriate, then there is no reason to abandon them. Unfortunately, as at TMI (see Rubinstien & Mason, 1979) and other well-documented industrial accidents (e.g., Chernobyl; see Medvedev, 1990), operators may be forced to face their error only when the situation has become critical and when they must reconsider their position.

In summary, the operational conditions under which diagnoses must be made appear frequently to be prejudicial to the application of resource-dependent explicit processing. The combination of a sampling bias implicitly induced by the statistical properties of the environment (discussed previously), plus anxiety or overarousal (created by such variables as time pressure or fear), and lack of practice in dealing with novel events (demand for conscious processing resources), may all serve to bias diagnostic behavior in favor of implicit processing and consequent errors when applied to novel problems. The manifestation of such misjudgments might be found in a variety of different errors. Included among these would be those due to diagnosticians having insufficient mental resources to cope with the complexity of the task to hand (i.e., operators persist with their attempts to deal with a problem by the application of explicit knowledge and have insufficient capacity to cope). Other forms of error, similarly resulting from a lack of resources, but manifest in a different way, are those where the troubleshooter implements a routine effective for familiar failures, but inappropriate for those that are novel (i.e., the application of implicit knowledge). Thus, in the first example, the complexity of the data manipulation aspect of diagnosis exceeds capacity, whereas in the second, errors result from inadequate data input induced by strategies deployed to cope with complexity.

Although the points just made may seem to be rather abstract in nature, they are frequently supported by the anecdotal reports of operators who have been confronted with the need to troubleshoot a failure under difficult circumstances. Indeed, interviews of the operators present at the time of the Chernobyl accident provide a real-life example of the points raised earlier as the following extract illustrates:

> The chaps who were there that night said that Lenya Tuptonov couldn't cope with shifting from automatic controls and let the power fall. There are so many instruments there, that he could have failed to see what was happening…the more so because he was probably nervous. It was the first time this situation had occurred, that the power had to be reduced. After all, he had only worked as a senior engineer of the reactor control for four months and in that time the power of the reactor had never been reduced. (taken from Shcherbak, 1988; quoted in Medvedev, 1990, p. 37)

The preceding paragraphs have outlined the problems faced by diagnosticians of system failures in complex systems. It is apparent that environmental and personal parameters influence the behavior of operators. Sometimes diagnosticians will be aware of these influences and sometimes they will not. For the most part it might be argued that operators seek to optimize their utilization of available cognitive resources by opting to use the strategies at which they are most skilled (Vicente & Rasmussen, 1992). When conditions are normal, the application of search heuristics that avoid "redundant" visual sampling of the instrument console is one example of this. When conditions change and operators are required to apply a different mental model (i.e., one that is appropriate for novel system disturbances), then it is important that the appropriate model is selected. The principle of least effort would suggest that operators should prefer to apply mental procedures that do not incur a large cost in terms of mental effort. Familiar failures afford this luxury but those that are novel do not. The solution to a novel problem may, however, be costly in terms of mental effort. First, the operator must consider whether the problem has been seen before. This will entail a thorough sampling of system symptoms. Many problems, both novel and familiar, could share some of the same characteristics but not all. If a problem cannot be classified, then more data must be gathered and perhaps the problem considered from first principles. Simply providing trainees with practice in diagnosis and system control may not be sufficient and, for complex tasks, implicit expertise typically is developed under such conditions (Seger, 1994). As we have said already, such skills are unlikely to be flexible enough to cope with novelty (Berry & Dienes, 1993). For novel failures, diagnosticians need to avoid the trap of only pursuing the default implicit option. They must be able to decompose the process and response into component parts. If the job of most operators is to deal with familiar and unfamiliar tasks, then it seems only sensible that they are able to switch freely between both implicit and explicit processing. Although to our knowledge few, if any, training programs have expressly tackled this issue, the heuristics training described by Shepherd and Duncan (1977), discussed here in a later section, may have been successful precisely because it retarded the application of implicit knowledge until the problem at hand had been classified as familiar or novel. Whether all operators are able to switch between modes of processing as required is an empirical question of some importance especially in view of the suggestion of Hayes and D.E. Broadbent (1988) that individuals show preferences for deploying different forms of cognitive skill, no matter what the situation requires.

IMPLICATIONS OF IMPLICIT AND EXPLICIT PROCESSES FOR ENABLING EFFECTIVE PERFORMANCE

From what has been described so far, diagnostic performance is dependent on the complex interplay of different levels of cognitive control, mental resources, and a correct classification of the problem at hand. The task for system designers who seek to optimize the performance of process control operators is to ensure that the operators are able to identify the circumstances under which implicit and explicit processes should be deployed. There are three broad strategies that could be applied:

1. Train operators to recognize novel from familiar situations, perhaps by the judicious sampling of data, rule selection, and signal response.
2. Select operators who have relatively more processing capacity and hence the potential for dealing with more resource-demanding and complex tasks which will arise under novel circumstances. Another approach that similarly

relies on targeted selection is to identify operators who are able to quickly develop and retain implicit skills, thereby freeing up controlled cognitive resources that may be applied to cognitively demanding tasks.

3. Develop interface designs that support explicit processes by making use of well-established perceptual skills that rely on implicit processes.

Each of these now are considered in turn.

Selection

Most of the work on individual differences in fault-finding behavior has sought to establish a relationship between level of fault-finding skill and measures of general intelligence. This approach has been remarkably unsuccessful. General measures of cognitive ability have proven to be unreliable predictors of diagnostic skill (Dale, 1958; Elliot, 1965, 1967; Henneman & Rouse, 1984). This state of affairs may exist for a number of conceptual and methodological reasons including: (a) the range of intellectual capability within the sample under study being unduly narrow thus attenuating the magnitude of correlation coefficients, (b) the extent of prior experience, and (c) the characteristics of the criterion task. In the present context the last two of these would seem to be particularly important. Experience and the opportunity to practice could influence the extent to which skills are developed (i.e., resource independence established) and hence the measures that they are predicted by. Similarly, task characteristics are important in that they govern the type or mode of processing that should be applied to the problem at hand. The novel versus familiar distinction is relevant here yet again. Familiar problems may be dealt with by highly practiced problem-solving procedures, whereas novel failures must be dealt with by recourse to first principles and, therefore, controlled processing resources.

The preceding comments notwithstanding, part of the failure to find consistent relationships between psychometric measures and fault diagnosis performance is that test selection never appears to have been guided by a theory of cognitive skill. The lack of reliable results may be attributed to both subject and task characteristics that were not controlled by previous researchers. Building on contemporary cognitive learning theories (e.g., J.R. Anderson, 1986, 1989; Shiffrin & Schneider, 1977), Ackerman (1989) has been among those who have attempted to deliberately link cognitive resources and cognitive abilities. It is argued that the performance-resource function originally described by D.A. Norman and Bobrow (1975) can be translated into a performance-ability function where those with higher intellectual ability demonstrate greater attentional resources and mental capacity. At the heart of Ackerman's thinking is the extent to which the cognitive components of task performance have become automated. He argued that performance on cognitive tasks should be predictable when both subject and task characteristics are carefully analyzed.

Ackerman's (1989) theory undoubtedly has been influenced by Shiffrin and Schneider (1977) and J.R. Anderson (1986). Common to both are hypotheses that: (a) Practice results in some form of restructuring of component processes in a way that converts a verbal causal description of task performance into a nonverbal and implicit form of representation that (b) reduces the load on working memory. Ackerman described how different levels of cognitive skill will be predicted by different forms of psychometric test at different stages of practice:

> For novel tasks, initial (that is, absence of pre-treatment practice) individual differences will be determined by the general ability, as well as by task-appropriate broad content abilities....The overall magnitude of association between these abilities and performance will depend on task complexity, but also on the adequacy of instruction and of course the population under study. With practice as production systems are formulated to accomplish the *consistent* components of the task, the influence of general and content abilities will diminish. (p. 190)

As novelty and complexity diminish, signal and action come to rely less on the intervention of cognitive control whereupon measures of perceptual speed and motor control are hypothesized to predict performance.

The conditions that control the rate of transition from explicit control to implicit control are task complexity and mental capacity. Thus, one might expect that those with the highest level of intellectual capacity will be advantaged over individuals who are not similarly blessed in that they will learn faster and be better able, in theory at least, to deal with novelty. Given sufficient time one would expect that those who are less able will be capable of showing similar levels of expertise on predictable tasks. Thus, for experienced personnel, measures of intelligence would not be expected to distinguish between the diagnostic performance of those with different levels of intellectual capacity. It is only for unfamiliar tasks that psychometric tests of general ability will be indicators of performance. As plausible as these suggestions may be, they are awaiting empirical verification.

Training

Training of diagnosticians to solve novel and familiar problems has proved as problematic as has selection. Various methods, such as training in theory (Shepherd & Duncan, 1977; D.L. Williams & Whitmore, 1959), the provision of verbal and visual feedback (Brooke, Cook, & Duncan, 1983; Rouse, 1978), and training operators to use heuristics (rules of thumb) (E.C. Marshall et al., 1981; Shepherd & Duncan, 1977), have been explored and all have been found inadequate in one way or another for enabling personnel to deal with novel failures. Initially, Duncan's work, just cited, seemed to hold the most promise in training fault diagnosticians to deal with unexpected failures. His technique was to teach operators problem-solving heuristics that were to be applied when faults occurred. In teaching operators heuristics, they learned to explore all relevant sources of data from a control panel. Such a technique may have been beneficial insofar as trainees were enabled to avoid attentional biases that may have induced cognitive tunnel vision (Sheridan, 1981), especially when under stress. The effects, however, were short-lived (E.C. Marshall et al., 1981) and have proved difficult to replicate (Patrick & Haines, 1988). Exactly why the beneficial effects disappeared has never been answered satisfactorily. One explanation is that the operators simply forgot what they had learned. Another is, however, that once they had returned to the plant the operators' implicit model of plant operations developed to the point that it became the default option. Once implicitly represented, the explicit mental model of the system may have to be relearned. Or at least, the act of explicitly representing complexity might have to be relearned.

The studies that have attempted to train diagnostic skills might have been more successful had the special requirements of novel failure diagnosis been considered with the implicit/explicit distinction in mind. The maxim that practice makes perfect might be true only if the practice is of a particular kind. A major problem in training operators to cope with novelty is how to prevent implicit representations developing to a point where they are beyond verbal recall.

From research on the development of skills for controlling complex systems, it seems that simply providing trainees with exposure to tasks (simulated or otherwise) is unlikely to engender the skills necessary for dealing with novelty. Under such conditions learning appears to be unselective as the trainee tracks the task in order to arrive at an acceptable level of performance. According to Berry and Dienes (1993),"the person will retain a large number of condition action links that will secure effective performance. It may well be hard to report so many links, however, or have confidence in any one of them. Use of this unselective or implicit mode is therefore unlikely to be associated with accurate verbalisable knowledge" (p. 27). Perhaps learning through a verbal declarative route will allow the skill subcomponents to be unpacked and recombined in novel ways for unfamiliar problems. As mentioned earlier, one way of doing this might be, as Duncan and his associates (e.g., Duncan & Shepherd, 1977) did by teaching a small number of explicit rules. Specifically, in the implicit learning domain, Stanley et al. (1989) found that using rule-based instruction, providing simple heuristics, and/or studying expert transcripts all facilitated verbal knowledge on a complex control task. Unfortunately, it was unclear from this study whether subjects were better able to cope with novelty as a result of using this technique. Berry and D.E. Broadbent (1990) have shown, however, that the requirement to verbalize following instruction does facilitate performance on a transfer diagnostic task. In this study, however, subjects were required to complete only four trials. Thus the effects of extended practice and subsequent transfer are unknown.

The suggestion that the best way to improve performance on novel tasks is to prevent implicit skill development, may run the risk of throwing the "baby away with the bath water" because only a small proportion of the operator/diagnostician's task will be to cope with novelty. Ideally, operators will be capable of handling both and most failures are, hopefully, predictable. It would seem desirable, therefore, that a combination of implicit and explicit skill is what the most effective operator should possess. Exactly how this might be achieved is again not clear, especially in light of a further comment by Berry and Dienes (1993) that "it is safest to conclude that verbal instruction will not necessarily lead to improved performance, particularly where the tasks have a relatively complex or non-obvious underlying structure" (p. 131).

The preceding quotation is a pessimistic view; there are few experiments that have attempted to develop both implicit and explicit skill with the specific aim of assessing the extent and form of skill transfer. The studies that come closest in this regard are those described by Hayes and D.E. Broadbent (1988) but unfortunately the results have proved hard to replicate (Green & Shanks, 1993; Sanderson, 1989).

How then is the ability to diagnose novel failures to be engendered? One way of doing this may be to revert to the old part task training methods (Naylor, 1962) that were used to train physical skill. Subcomponents of the diagnostic skill may be trained to a level that no longer requires conscious mental effort whereupon their application to a whole task is developed in a way that maintains the linkages at a verbal descriptive level. Ackerman (1992) has been successful in applying what he called the *theory of ability determinants of skill acquisition* to the development of air traffic control skills, but as yet little has been done for the cognitive skills necessary in process control environments. Little is known about how much practice is required before the components of complex cognitive skills become resource independent. Also, little is known about the size of the cognitive chunks that can be automated and how sequences of individual routines might be strung together, or prevented from being chained. Finally, we have virtually no information about how long established automatic information-processing routines will last without practice. The heuristics trained by Duncan and his colleagues (see, in particular, E.C. Marshall et al., 1981) may also have failed to show a performance advantage on delayed retest because the working environment was such that the cognitive links established during training were not reinforced back on the job. Although it is not advisable that operators be given a remit that allows them to conduct personal experiments on complex systems, one of the benefits of cheap computer memory is that realistic real-time simulations of process control systems may be located in the control rooms of many plants. It could become a requirement of operator certification that a certain number of hours in any given time period must be spent maintaining declarative cognitive skill.

In this and the previous section, we have attempted to explain why it is that current selection and training methods have failed to identify or enable individuals to become expert diagnosticians. Common to each section is the idea that expertise in the diagnosis of industrial process control systems is difficult to define and difficult to train because of the many interacting variables that act to influence operator performance. The selection and training solution to the problem may be viewed as an extension of the old-fashioned "fit the person to the task" mentality of a bygone era in ergonomics. The developments in learning and cognitive theory that have been described here may lead to new forms of selection and training but in addition may also suggest ways in which the task might be altered to fit the person. One way in which the task might be made a better fit to the person is to simplify the complex systems themselves (see Perrow, 1984). Another might be to design interfaces that present information in a way that is compatible with how humans assimilate and process data from the environment. Such displays would take advantage of the "naturally" occurring information-processing abilities, perceptual skills and learning capacities that are held by many individuals. If this could be done, then some of the training and selection issues described previously may become less problematic. In the next section, some recent developments in interface design methodology that may facilitate the development of implicit knowledge and support explicit knowledge are described.

Display Design

Until around the 1940s, process control was implemented using pneumatic (air-signal driven) controllers, and the operator was informed via wall panels of analog meters, dials, and alarm-tiles located in close proximity to the process equipment. With the advent of inexpensive computer hardware and software, and the development of sophisticated control algorithms, process control has been taken over by computerized (digital) controllers with VDU information displays situated in centralized control rooms remote from the plant.

Convention shows that in both continuous process and batch manufacture, the designers of computerized information displays clearly have been tempted to simply transfer what was already displayed on the control panels to the screen of a VDU. Conventional operator interfaces typically comprise topological equipment diagrams, alphanumeric variable displays, presentation of control loop set-point values, measured values and signal values, and trend displays of plant history. This type of information display delivers limited information in a spatially detached form, with little visible correlation to what's happening in the plant, and with little consideration of the types of decisions to be made. As discussed previously, the effect on the operator is to further isolate them from the process, dulling their understanding of the physical mechanisms and denying them opportunities to make informed decisions based on fundamental knowledge. The operator ends up relying on patterns of previously experienced symptoms to identify failures—as we have said repeatedly throughout this chapter, this may create a situation with possibly disastrous consequences, when something out-of-the-ordinary takes place. There are few firm guidelines, other than rules of thumb, that might be used by man-machine interface designers to overcome these problems.

In looking for alternative forms to the one-sensor–one-display format, the operators' perception and mental processing of the system needs to be understood, and the spectrum of tasks, from routine to the unfamiliar and unanticipated catered for. One of the major challenges is to develop an interface design that encourages operators to sample the process information efficiently and to develop appropriate and robust mental models or representations.

Display design should promote implicit processing during the monitoring and fault detection stages, but still contain rich enough information to support explicit fault diagnosis and problem solving when necessary. There are two separate features of the display that impact on the operators' ability to perceive and process the system information: the *information content* and the *visual format* ("what to show?" and "how to show it?"). The natures of explicit and implicit processing make the consideration of these two questions central to the achievement of the design objective.

The formation and updating of an operator's internal representation of a complex system depends on the representation offered of the underlying process by the operator interface. The choice of variables displayed thus influences the way the mental model evolves. Under the one-sensor–one-display philosophy, the raw measured plant data is displayed on a mimic diagram. The higher order, more abstract, and integrated information used by the control system remains hidden. The raw data in no way reflect the underlying mechanisms by which the process operates nor, perhaps, as we see later, the different ways in which human operator might represent the system.

Examination of the problem-solving trajectories of experts (Vicente & Rasmussen, 1992) have revealed that they usually follow a method that can be mapped in terms of system *abstraction* and system *decomposition*. Experts typically monitor and detect problems at a high level of abstraction and aggregation, that is, watch the "big picture" for changes. When a problem is discovered, the diagnosis begins with a search for more detailed (decomposed) information about subsystems (less abstract). As the diagnosis proceeds the problem is further decomposed and physical subsystems examined, to the point where the specific faulty component is located and the problem rectified. Thus it appears that process monitoring and supervision entail a mixture of implicit and explicit expertise. Ideally, the operator's mental model for control and diagnosis should guide him or her along this problem-solving route. The display designer, therefore, should analyze the system in terms of these orthogonal dimensions, and represent it in a way that enables and encourages implicit detection, and perhaps diagnosis of familiar faults as well as explicit diagnosis of faults. Ideally, then, the interface should display information in a way that complements both the conscious and unconscious data-processing capabilities of the human cognitive system. To date the best attempt at describing what such a system would look like has been articulated by Rasmussen (1986; Rasmussen & Vicente, 1992).

Rasmussen has identified three levels of cognitive control essential to the detection and diagnosis of system failures. When activated each handles incoming information in different ways. The levels of cognitive control have been labeled as knowledge-based processing, rule-based processing, and skill-based processing. According to Vicente and Rasmussen (1992), "the three levels of cognitive control can be grouped together into two general categories. KBB [knowledge-based behavior] is concerned with analytical problem solving based on symbolic representation, whereas RBB and SBB [rule-based behavior and skill based behavior] are concerned with perception and action" (p. 594).

In general, rule- and skill-based behavior represent what might be thought of as relying on well-learned cognitive processes and hence much information processing is undertaken implicitly at a subconscious level. Skill-based behavior appears to be largely driven by discrete signals from the environment in much the same way that the reflex arc responds to a tap on the knee. No additional conscious processing of the data is required beyond the response that the signal activates. Simple examples of this phenomenon are readily found in the environment. For example, rain on the windscreen of a car signals that the wipers should be turned on. Over time, this response becomes so automated that when one drives an unfamiliar car and the switch for the wipers is on the opposite side of the steering column from "normal" the indicator may be activated. Rule-based behavior, on the other hand, is said to be more complex in that a complex set of rules may be used to define a set of conditions that trigger a preset action routine. Once the preconditions for rule selection have been satisfied, the subsequent action sequence may be initiated in a fashion that does not require extensive monitoring as each activity component serves as the signal for the next action. Rule-based behavior is also largely driven by automatic processes and the initial action initiators (signs in Rasmussen's, 1986, terms) may be obscured from consciousness as a consequence of the complex nature of the task domains. Before an action sequence or rule is activated the rule that should be applied might need to be selected from one of many possibilities. A key characteristic of both skill- and rule-based behavior is that they are utilized with little or no conscious control and in this sense the mental activities involved in their execution may be implicit. At the rule selection stage at least two forms of errors can occur during fault diagnosis: (a) the wrong rule is applied to a familiar situation, and (b) an action sequence appropriate for a familiar problem is applied when the task is novel and when a different mode of cognitive control, knowledge-based control, should have been applied.

Knowledge-based behavior is qualitatively different from either skill- or rule-based behavior. At this level conscious cognitive resources are marshalled and used to solve problems from first principles. Control at this level does not exist in isolation because cognitive processing here might be undertaken with a view to classifying a new task into one that has familiar subcomponents, which may then be referred for execution at the other levels. Although the subcomponents themselves may be automated, the sequence in which they are put together may be novel and require substantial monitoring until the new sequence becomes automated and then a conditional rule developed for its application.

As alluded to previously, when faults are identified as familiar, the predominant modes of control are at the skill- and rule-based levels. Some knowledge-based activity must also play a part in diagnosis especially during the problem classification phase. Exactly how much influence knowledge-based processing has on subsequent diagnostic behavior may be task and situation dependent. Tasks that are quickly identified as familiar may only fleetingly engage explicit knowledge-based processing as competing alternatives are rapidly recalled and selected or rejected. On the other hand, those that are more puzzling may require the investment of more cognitive effort. The problem, as we have said repeatedly in this chapter, is how to enable the would-be diagnostician to select the correct mode of cognitive operation. The opportunity for misclassification may be made more likely if a novel problem has a number of common surface characteristics.

The question is, how should information be displayed on an instrument console to facilitate both the selection and execution of the appropriate level of cognitive control? In answering such a question, Duncan and Praetorius (1992) identified three problems of diagnosis that well-designed displays should strive to eliminate: (a) confusability, (b) symptom referral, and (c) "cognitive lockup." The first and last of this list are directly relevant here. The reduction of confusability between problems is vital for the implementation of the correct level of cognitive control (knowledge- vs. rule-based problem-solving behavior). The cognitive lock-up phenomenon is a well-known problem and seems to be more likely when human decision makers are stressed (cf. Rubinstein & Mason's, 1979, description of the accident at Three Mile Island). As described earlier in the chapter, one explanation for this phenomenon is the lack of spare mental-processing resources that could be used for considering either new data or potential alternative solutions to the problem. It is arguably the case, therefore, that one way to avoid lock-up is to present display interfaces in a way that avoids, where possible, unnecessary burdens on the human information-processing system.

It would seem that two principles for display design might be devised. The first is that the display should facilitate the processes of problem identification, perhaps making it easier for diagnosticians to recognize patterns in the data presented on the console. The use of flow charts (Brooke & Duncan, 1980) and task displays that reduce "visual clutter" (Brooke & Duncan, 1981, 1983; Morrison & Duncan, 1988) have all been found to facilitate fault location. Given the human propensity for perceptual organization (Brunswick, 1956), information should be presented in a highly configured form that allows it to be represented in meaningful ways such that useful properties can emerge (Buttigieg & Sanderson, 1991). Here, ideas are borrowed from Gestalt psychology in which the sum of the information found in a display is greater than each of the individual parts viewed in isolation. To borrow an example used by Buttigieg and Sanderson, four straight lines can be arranged to produce a shape, which has closure, area, and symmetry. Each of these emergent features can be varied and used to describe a system state. Configural displays with emergent features have been found helpful in fault detection (Buttigieg & Sanderson, 1991) where the operator is aided in the recognition of abnormal behavior by changes in the patterns and shapes of the display elements. In so doing, the display assists the diagnostician by reducing clutter and allowing the diagnostician to impose some top–down organization on bottom–up data.

A second, and related principle for display design is that the information should be easily aggregated and decomposed. The configural displays referred to earlier may be useful for this purpose because the features that combine to produce the configural display could each be separated. It is possible, however, that different levels of information granularity are best presented to operators by means of hierarchical displays. By representing information in this way both abstract and local information may be provided on demand as diagnosticians zoom up and down an information hierarchy (see Goodstein, 1982; Lind, 1982; Rasmussen & Lind, 1981). In so doing the information requirements of each form of knowledge may implicitly, or explicitly, be satisfied.

SUMMARY

In this chapter we have attempted to illustrate how implicit and explicit modes of processing influence human performance on an important task in the context of industrial process control. Our position is that they are both a benefit and a hindrance to effective performance tasks of this sort. Implicit processes are clearly advantageous when the industrial process is either running effectively or, when failures do occur, they are correctly recognized as having been seen previously. The seduction of the implicit mode is probably its drawback when novel events must be contended with. The temptation for humans to apply the principle of least effort, inappropriately, is clearly there when mental resources are at a premium and time is of the essence. In a sense, the default option for the human information-processing system in the context of complex industrial process control has, for a large number of people, been wrongly configured. This statement is true if the primary role of the human operator in such systems is to deal with novel problems. Ironically, the more the process has been automated, the more likely it is that the diagnostic role is of this type. If explicit processing is mandatory for unexpected events, for those problems that are routine they are cumbersome both in time and effort required.

The enablement of effective personnel as diagnosticians has been hampered by the failure of previous research to take account of the dual-processing modes, and their implications, when selecting, training, or designing system interfaces. Ongoing research in our laboratories is attempting to address these deficiencies. At the present time research is being undertaken that is examining the cognitive predictors of novel failure diagnosis for tasks of different levels of task difficulty and novelty at different stages of practice. Preliminary results (Morrison & LeMap, 1996) reveal that diagnosis performance is highly predictable when the right variables are taken into account. A second line of research is examining the methods by which elements of the fault-finding skill are trained. Essentially, the hypothesis that expertise developed via a serial verbal descriptive route is better placed to cope with novelty when compared to when the skill is learned under implicit conditions. Finally, the interface designs shown in the last section of the chapter are currently being trialed, and compared against the performance of operators using a more traditional interface design. Though these lines of investigation may prove fruitful in under-standing how personnel might be enabled to deal with novel failures when they are recognized, they do not address the important first step, which is to enable diagnosticians to distinguish the new from the old. In our view it is only when this problem has been satisfactorily resolved that significant enhancements in the reliability with which humans operate in complex systems will be realized.

19

IMPLICIT PROCESSES
IN MEDICAL DIAGNOSIS

Timothy Griffin
Centre for Developmental Disability Studies
The University of Sydney

Steven Schwartz
Murdoch University

Katherine Sofronoff
University of Queensland

Anyone who must categorize people or objects on the basis of a set of signs is engaging in a diagnostic process. For example, motor mechanics diagnose car faults, systems analysts find the flaws in computing systems, and football coaches are forever trying to find the weaknesses in their team's defenses (especially after a loss).

In medicine today, diagnosis is widely and correctly seen as one of the doctor's main tasks, an important aspect of patient management. However, it is not commonly known that accurate diagnosis became an important goal of medicine only in the middle of the last century. Prior to this, medicine was pretty much a hit-and-miss affair (L. Thomas, 1979). Weird theories (tuberculosis is caused by the night air) and even stranger treatments (cupping, purging, bleeding) were accepted as if they were scientifically proven. Because all patients received the same treatments, diagnosis was not considered important.

Diagnosis is made difficult by the probabilistic nature of the relationship among symptoms, signs, and diseases. (Symptoms are patients' presenting complaints—what they report; the doctor interprets symptoms as signs which, in turn, lead to diagnoses.) If a particular sign is always present in one disease and never present in any other disease, diagnosis would be simply a matter of learning which sign goes with which disease. Such "pathognomic" signs exist (e.g., high intraocular pressure is always a sign of glaucoma). Unfortunately, more often the relationship between a sign and a disease is probabilistic. That is, certain signs are related to specific diseases but they are not always present and they may also be present in other diseases. For example, a headache is usually, but not always, present with meningitis, and headaches also are associated with many other conditions. Doctors must learn to associate an uncertain sign (or set of signs) with a specific disease.

As well as the inherent uncertainty in the relationship between signs and diseases, uncertainty occurs at every other stage of the diagnostic and patient management process. S. Schwartz and T. Griffin (1986) described these sources of uncertainty, which include the probabilistic relationship between symptoms and signs (patients do not always report their symptoms accurately and doctors sometimes misunderstand patients' complaints), the uncertainty inherent in the information doctors gather to help them make diagnoses (laboratory tests, physical examinations, etc.); and the selection, evaluation, and combination of this information. Moreover, once a diagnosis has been made, the treatment prescribed usually has only some probability of success.

Nevertheless, expert doctors are acknowledged as such because they have managed to learn to diagnose diseases and prescribe treatments with a high degree of accuracy (S. Schwartz & T. Griffin, 1986). Somehow, they learn to assess and integrate uncertain information.

It is reasonably easy to identify expert doctors, computer analysts, and football coaches but difficult to characterize how they became better than the rest. This is not a new problem. Socrates was reputed to have quizzed Euthyphro, a religious prophet and self-proclaimed expert at recognizing piety, about pious characteristics that could be used as a standard by which to judge peoples' actions. Instead of giving guidelines or rules, Euthyphro could only give examples of situations in which people and gods had acted piously, not how they had become so (H.L. Dreyfus & S.E. Dreyfus, 1984).

Presumably, Euthyphro once knew the rules by which he judged piety; how else could he have learned? But, over a long period of judging piety, these rules may have, somehow, changed form or been forgotten. The example of Euthyphro illustrates a now well-researched characteristic of experts in many fields, including medical diagnosis: They cannot always articulate the rules that they use to make judgments. However, cognitive psychologists are not entirely convinced that the judgment rules that are so hard to recall are necessarily forgotten; perhaps they were never known. Euthyphro's ability to recognize piety may have been acquired unconsciously; he may never have been able to articulate them. This possibility is the subject of this chapter, using the example of acquiring expertise in medical diagnosis.

A useful distinction to make in reviewing implicit processes in learning is between "implicit learning" and "implicit expertise." In chapter 3 of this book, implicit learning has been defined as the acquisition of complex rule-governed knowledge largely independent of awareness. Implicit expertise, on the other hand, was defined as skill or knowledge closed to verbal report. This distinction, although often clouded in the literature, is useful because it separates knowledge from its manner of acquisition (Hayes & D.E. Broadbent, 1988). The paradigms used to study each differ too. Implicit learning is studied by examining the learning of artificial grammars and by observing how subjects control interactive tasks. Implicit expertise, in contrast, is studied by examining skilled performance after extended naturalistic practice.

In practice, however, the distinction between implicit learning and expertise is difficult to maintain. Studying the knowledge already resident in experts leaves open questions about the acquisition of that expertise. Expertise is best understood by studying its development. Only then can we understand how knowledge changes as expertise grows. In this chapter we consider the nature of expertise in medical diagnosis *through* studies of implicit learning. A sensible start can be made with a reference to another Ancient Greek, Hippocrates of Kos.

IS BASIC SCIENCE NECESSARY FOR DIAGNOSIS?

Hippocrates of Kos was a Greek physician who lived around the same time as Socrates (460–377 B.C.) Although often referred to as the "father of modern medicine," little is actually known about Hippocrates' life. One thing seems certain, many of the writings attributed to him actually were produced by others (B. Simon, 1978). Nevertheless, the Hippocratic writings share a certain unity of approach. The authors consistently favored naturalistic observation and logic over speculation and, despite respectful references to the gods, they clearly considered the ancient doctrine of demonology (illness is caused by demonic possession) to be absurd. In its place, they developed a systematic theory of human disease that attributed ill health to aberrations in physiology (Weckowicz & Liebel-Weckowicz, 1990).

Hippocratic physiology was based around the four classic elements: water, air, fire, and earth. These elements, in turn, were the basic building blocks of the four types of body fluids, the humors. Phlegm was the equivalent of water, blood equated to air, yellow bile was equal to fire, and black bile was the equivalent of the earth. In a healthy body, the humors are in a state of equilibrium. Ill health results from disharmony—too much of one humor, too little of another.

The Greeks were good at many things, but physiology was not one of them. (Aristotle believed that the function of the brain is to cool the blood.) Nevertheless, misguided as it was, the humoral theory was an improvement over demonology. Faulty physiology was blamed for illness, not demons. Over the centuries, knowledge about physiology and anatomy grew. In the 16th century alone, Eustachius identified the connections between the ears and the throat, Fallopius clarified female reproductive anatomy, and Harvey showed how blood circulated through the body.

By the beginning of the 20th century, it became generally accepted that patient management decisions—ordering tests, instituting procedures, prescribing drugs—should be guided by the underlying pathophysiology (Flexner, 1910). Today, all doctors are taught to apply knowledge gained from the "basic sciences" (not only anatomy and physiology but also microbiology, genetics, and psychology) to clinical problems. Yet, cognitive psychologists who study medical expertise are not entirely convinced that scientific facts play a crucial role in everyday clinical decision making. Their scepticism comes from studies of expertise.

BASIC SCIENCE INFORMATION: IMPLICIT OR INERT?

Recently, cognitive psychologists have become increasingly interested in the nature of expertise in general and medical expertise in particular (Ericsson & J. Smith, 1991; S. Schwartz & T. Griffin, 1986; G. Wright & Bolger, 1992). As already noted, psychological studies of medical experts have accepted that expertise (e.g., in making diagnoses) depends on a thorough knowledge of the underlying pathophysiology and sign-disease relationships (Kuipers & Kassirer, 1984; Lesgold, 1984). Yet, the research findings are far from clear.

Schmidt, Boshuizen, and Hobus (1988), for example, asked medical students and experienced doctors to think aloud while making a difficult diagnosis. They found that the students were *more likely* to refer to basic science findings than were expert doctors. In a series of experiments, Patel and Groen reported similar findings (see Patel & Groen, 1991, for a review). Studies of expert radiologists also have found that increasing expertise is accompanied by decreasing attention to the relevant anatomy (Hillard, Myles-Worsley, Johnston, & Baxter, 1985).

Boshuizen and H.G. Schmidt (1992) offered three possible explanations for this apparent paradox (i.e., basic science is considered to be crucial, yet experts do not seem to use it as much as beginners). The first possibility is that basic science knowledge is only important for beginners. As expertise develops, clinical acumen replaces biomedical knowledge in medical decision making. The second possibility is that experts do not forget biomedical knowledge, they just do not use it in diagnostic decision making. In Boshuizen and Schmidt's terminology, basic science knowledge becomes "inert." The third possibility is that, with increasing expertise, basic science knowledge becomes implicit and is used automatically. Because it is implicit, expert clinicians are not aware that they are using this knowledge and, therefore, they do not verbalize it.[1]

---

[1]Boshuizen and H.G. Schmidt (1992) separated basic science knowledge from clinical knowledge such as signs and symptoms. In this chapter, we classify both types of knowledge as *explicit* provided the relevant knowledge can be verbalized. Explicit knowledge is also known as *declarative* knowledge, which typically is contrasted with *implicit* or *procedural* knowledge. Each of the various terms has theoretical implications. We have opted to use the terms *explicit* and *implicit* in this chapter without implying any specific theory of how the two types of knowledge are acquired or used.

On the basis of a small-scale study, Boshuizen and H.G. Schmidt (1992) concluded that the third possibility is the most likely one. Diagnostic expertise, they claimed, passes through three stages: the acquisition of basic domain knowledge, a period of practical experience applying this knowledge to patients, and finally, automatization of biomedical knowledge. This sequence is similar to the more general theory of skill acquisition developed by J.R. Anderson (1983, 1987). In Anderson's theory, increasing competence involves a move away from "declarative" (explicit, verbalizable) knowledge toward highly automatized "procedural" (implicit, nonverbalizable) knowledge. With sufficient practice, cognitive procedures become "autonomous." Experts are unaware of using them and cannot describe them in words.

A similar model of the development of expertise has been proposed by H.L. Dreyfus and S.E. Dreyfus (1984, 1986). In their model, the practitioner progresses from novice to expert in a series of graded steps: novice, advanced beginner, competent, proficient, and finally, expert. Like Anderson's theory, beginners rely on concrete rules and examples whereas experts are characterized by "intuitive" judgments, which embody only vague rules.

Anderson's and Dreyfus and Dreyfus' general theories, and the more specific clinical model developed by Boshuizen and Schmidt, all rely on two important assumptions: First, they assume that there are two types of knowledge, declarative (explicit) and procedural (implicit), and second, they assume that increasing expertise is largely a matter of transforming (*compiling* is Anderson's term) explicit, verbalizable knowledge into implicit, automatic, procedures. These assumptions are addressed next.

THE RELATIONSHIP BETWEEN
EXPLICIT AND IMPLICIT KNOWLEDGE

As noted elsewhere in this book, there are several lines of evidence supporting the first assumption, that implicit and explicit knowledge are two different things. Studies of amnesic patients, for example, have shown a fairly clear dissociation between memory for new information (and events) and the ability to acquire new skills (Warrington & Weiskrantz, 1968a). Experimental manipulations can produce similar dissociations even among nonamnesic people (Roediger, 1990b). Dissociations between implicit and explicit knowledge also have been demonstrated in learning studies.

The Dissociation Between Explicit and Implicit Learning

The dissociation between performance based on implicit procedural knowledge and the possession of explicit declarative knowledge is hardly a new observation;

we see it every day. People learn to speak grammatically without being able to express a single rule of grammar. Similarly, professional golfers are (usually) unable to express the physical laws governing the trajectories of struck balls while still scoring under par. This dissociation, which shows that good performance does not require declarative knowledge, is "one-directional" and is not, by itself, sufficient evidence for asserting that there are two types of knowledge. To support this conclusion, it is necessary to show a "bidirectional" dissociation. That is, we must also be able to show that a high level of explicit knowledge does not guarantee good performance. (To maintain the golfing analogy, an example would be a physicist who knows all the laws governing struck balls but cannot strike one with any precision.) This is exactly what Berry and D.E. Broadbent (1984) set out to achieve.

They used two computer simulation tasks in their research. The first simulation was a sugar production task in which subjects were required to take on the role of the manager of a sugar factory. As managers, their aim was to maintain certain levels of sugar production by varying the number of workers employed in the factory. The second task required subjects to interact with a "computer person" by entering "behaviors" from a keyboard. There were 12 behaviors ranging from "very rude" through "indifferent" to "loving." The behaviors were represented in the computer program by numbers from 1 to 12. Each change in a subject's behavior produced a change in the computer person's behavior. The subjects were asked to elicit a "friendly" response from the computer and maintain the computer at this friendly level. Thus, in both the sugar production and the computer person tasks, the subjects were required to reach and maintain a specified target level on an output variable by varying a single input variable. In both tasks, the rule governing the relationship between the independent and dependent variables was mathematically identical.

Berry and D.E. Broadbent (1984) found that practice resulted in improved performance on the tasks but had no effect on their subjects' ability to answer written questions about the relationship between the independent and dependent variables. This is a one-directional dissociation—good performance but poor explicit knowledge. When subjects were provided with verbal instructions on how to reach and maintain a specific target value, their ability to answer the written questions improved dramatically yet their control task performance was unaffected. There was even a small negative correlation between control task performance and question answering: Subjects who were able to answer the written questions accurately were actually poorer at reaching their targets than those who could not answer the questions. In other words, a high level of explicit knowledge did not guarantee a high level of control task performance and a high level of performance did not guarantee that the subjects had verbalizable explicit knowledge of the task. This bidirectional dissociation is strong evidence for Broadbent's view that there are two types of knowledge—explicit and implicit.

IMPLICIT ACQUISITION OF SKILL

The evidence for the second assumption, that expertise involves a sequence of stages in which explicit knowledge is gradually automatized, is not as clear as for the first assumption that the two types of knowledge exist. Most of the supporting evidence comes from Anderson's work. For example, Neves and J.R. Anderson (1981) found that students learning to prove geometric theorems began with verbalizable knowledge that later became implicit. Benner (1984) found that the development of clinical nursing expertise matched well with H.L. Dreyfus and S.E. Dreyfus' (1984, 1986) five stages of expertise. In contrast, other researchers, using a wide variety of paradigms, have found that knowledge can be acquired implicitly, without first going through an explicit stage.

Explicit learning involves learning from instruction: learning to play chess from a book of rules and tactics, for example. The product of explicit learning is a database (rules, facts, strategies), the contents of which can be described verbally (D.E. Broadbent et al., 1986). Implicit learning, in contrast, is mainly a function of observation and discovery. It involves the unconscious induction of concepts and rules from observed examples rather than learning from overt instruction. The product of implicit learning is a set of exemplars and rules that can be used to assign objects to categories or to perform complex tasks but that are not expressible in words. Because the knowledge gained through implicit learning cannot be verbalized, it is referred to as "tacit" (Reber, 1989a). Current interest in implicit learning owes its origins to problems encountered in the field of artificial intelligence, especially the construction of "expert systems." "Knowledge engineers" have found that experts often have difficulty putting all of their knowledge into words (because much of it is tacit). In fact, the major impediment to the development of expert systems is extracting rules from experts, a process known in the field as "knowledge elicitation" (Berry, 1987).

Research Paradigms

There are two main research paradigms used in implicit learning research: the learning of artificial grammars and, as already mentioned, the control of complicated computer simulations. (Other, less frequently used paradigms were described by Lewicki et al., 1988, and by Nissen & Bullemer, 1987.) The artificial grammar paradigm has been used most extensively by Reber and his colleagues (Reber, 1967, 1976, 1989a, 1989b; Reber & Allen, 1978; Reber et al., 1980; Reber & S. Lewis, 1977). The typical procedure involves asking people to memorize strings of letters. These letter strings appear random but, in reality, their sequence is determined by a set of rules known as an artificial grammar. Following the initial memorization phase, the subjects are told that the letter sequences are determined by rules. They then are shown new sequences and asked to categorize them as "grammatical" or "nongrammatical." Numerous experiments have shown that subjects can make these "grammaticality" judgments even though they are unable to verbalize the grammatical rules used to generate the letter strings. Reber concluded that the grammatical rules must have been unconsciously inducted from the examples. These unconsciously inducted rules constituted the tacit knowledge that subjects used to make their grammaticality judgments. In other words, implicit knowledge was acquired directly rather than by "compiling" explicit knowledge.

Reber's research has not entirely escaped criticism. Brody (1989), for example, claimed that more subtle testing methods would reveal that the subjects were at least vaguely aware of the grammatical rules. Along the same lines, Perruchet and Pacteau (1990, 1991) have shown that fragmentary (but conscious) knowledge of which pairs of letters go together could account for grammaticality judgments without assuming the unconscious induction of rules. The debate about whether or not subjects in Reber's experiments are at least partly aware of the underlying rules is still active with no clear consensus in sight.

The second common implicit learning paradigm, the control of complex systems, has been used mainly by Broadbent and his colleagues (Berry, 1987; Berry & D.E. Broadbent, 1984, 1987a, 1987b, 1988; D.E. Broadbent, 1977; D.E. Broadbent & Aston, 1978; D.E. Broadbent et al., 1986; Hayes & D.E. Broadbent, 1988). The typical task requires subjects to control the value of one or more dependent variables by deciding on the value of one or more independent variables. For example, in one of his earliest studies on implicit learning, D.E. Broadbent (1977) required subjects to control the transport system of a computer-simulated "city." Two independent variables were within the subjects' control: the time interval between buses entering the city and the amount charged for use of the city's car parks. Manipulating these independent variables affected two dependent variables: the number of passengers carried by the buses and the number of empty spaces remaining in the car parks. Subjects were allocated targets to achieve on the dependent variables (e.g., a specific number of bus passengers). As they altered the independent variables, subjects observed the effect on the dependent variables.

Broadbent found that, with practice, subjects could attain their targets, but they were unable to explain how they did so. Subjects could not verbalize the relationship between the independent and dependent variables. Because subjects were unable to explain how the system worked, but were still able to control it, Broadbent concluded that their mode of learning was implicit.

Taken as a whole, it is fair to conclude that the first of the two assumptions underlying Anderson's and Boshuizen and Schmidt's theories is correct—there are two independent types of knowledge, explicit and implicit. Their second assumption, however, is not supported by most of the psychological research. In the laboratory at least, it does not appear that knowledge is first acquired explicitly and then "compiled"; under certain conditions, explicit and implicit knowledge can be acquired independently. If the laboratory findings are generalizable to the real world of the clinic, then it is possible that the ability to verbalize explicit biomedical facts about a specific medical problem and the ability to make accurate diagnoses may rely on largely separate types of knowledge. The remainder of this chapter summarizes some recent work the authors have conducted in relation to the two main points covered thus far: (a) A dissociation between implicit and explicit knowledge can be demonstrated using medical diagnostic tasks, and (b) the acquisition of both types of knowledge can occur independently. Our work has been primarily concerned with training medical students to diagnose acute abdominal pain.

IMPLICIT PROCESSES IN MEDICAL DIAGNOSIS

Like learning an artificial grammar or learning to control a computer simulation, medical diagnosis requires a person to learn the relationships among numerous interacting variables. The input to the doctor is a set of symptoms and signs (which include test results). Sometimes these signs have a direct relationship to a specific disease. For example, malaria can be definitively diagnosed by the presence of the malaria parasite in the blood. In most cases, however, the relationship between signs and the disease are only probabilistic, they indicate the possibility of a disease but the presence of any one sign is not definitive. Consider, for example, the diagnosis of acute abdominal pain. The underlying cause of acute abdominal pain is notoriously difficult to diagnose because the signs and symptoms are common to a range of diseases and disorders (perforated ulcer, appendicitis, bowel obstruction, dyspepsia, diverticular disease, cholecystitis, nonspecific abdominal pain, pancreatitis, or renal colic). All of these conditions share the same set of fifty or more signs and symptoms, although to different degrees and in different patterns. Doctors must learn to recognize the complex patterns of signs and symptoms that best characterize each condition. Not unexpectedly, these patterns are quite difficult to learn. This is why around 20% to 30% of appendectomies result in the removal of a healthy appendix (Lau, Fan, Yui, Chu, & Wong, 1984). This high false–positive rate reflects a combination of the difficulty of diagnosis and the serious consequences of failing to operate on an infected appendix, that is, the possible death of the patient. Clearly, any method of reducing diagnostic errors is of considerable practical value.

The typical approach to training doctors to diagnose acute abdominal pain is to teach them a set of rules. For example, they are taught that pain that migrates from the central abdomen to the lower right quadrant *probably* indicates appendicitis. In the present terminology, the typical learning mode is clearly explicit. One reason for this is the understandable importance placed on being able to justify one's diagnostic judgments.

The dependence on explicit learning is further emphasized by traditional university examinations that require students to demonstrate their knowledge in words. Because students are tested mainly on their ability to express their knowledge in words, it is not clear whether they are reaching their optimum diagnostic performance, which may, as we have seen, rely on implicit knowledge that is not expressible in words.

As many of the tasks faced by doctors require the analysis of complex stimuli with many interacting variables and numerous possible hypotheses, they seem to be ideal tasks for implicit learning. Indeed, as an alternative to explicit teaching, students can be taught implicitly. They can be exposed to real or simulated patients in all their complexity and then given feedback about the correct diagnosis. As Reber found when studying artificial grammars, this procedure should allow students to learn to recognize the different diagnoses even though they may perform poorly on traditional verbal examinations.

Our own work is beginning to show this predicted dissociation between diagnostic performance and verbalizable knowledge (T. Griffin, 1991; S. Schwartz & T. Griffin, 1993). In one study, in which we compared implicit and explicit learning modes in the domain of acute abdominal pain, one group of students learned diagnostic rules and domain knowledge whereas another group received practice in diagnosing only simulated cases of acute abdominal pain. On a posttest of diagnostic skill and explicit knowledge, we found that medical students who were given explicit training in the rules relating to the diagnosis of the acute abdomen were able to verbalize their knowledge and answer questions about acute abdominal pain but were poor at applying their knowledge to diagnosing cases. On the other hand, subjects who were trained by repeated exposure to simulated cases followed by various forms of diagnostic feedback showed great improvement in their ability to diagnose cases but not in their ability to verbalize their knowledge. Like Broadbent and Reber, we concluded that there is a dissociation between verbalizable knowledge (explicit learning) and skilled performance (implicit learning) on a complex task and that transfer from one to the other cannot be taken for granted. The dissociation, however, was not apparent when we reduced the number of diagnostic signs and the number of possible diagnoses. This is consistent with Hayes and D.E. Broadbent's (1988) finding that explicit mode learning is more likely to occur when a small number of variables are involved. Reducing the number of signs makes the disease-sign relationships "salient," allowing students to acquire both explicit and implicit knowledge.

In other studies, we are investigating the possibility of inducing both explicit and implicit learning using the same diagnostic training task. (For example, Hayes and D.E. Broadbent, 1988, used two rather different training tasks to induce explicit and implicit learning. In one task the rules were salient and allowed subjects to learn via the explicit mode, whereas in the second task the rules were not salient thereby compelling the subjects to use implicit mode learning.) For example, we expose medical students to complex simulated patients with acute abdominal pain, ask them to make a diagnoses and then provide case-by-case feedback about their performance. Depending on the nature of this feedback, it is possible to induce implicit or explicit learning or some combination of the two. Students who are provided only with feedback about the correct diagnosis must use a global strategy and learn implicitly. In contrast, students who receive explicit rule-based feedback after each case (e.g., "decreased movement or rigidity is a sign of perforated ulcer") learn explicitly. The latter students do better on tests of explicit knowledge; the former are poorer on tests of explicit knowledge but show equal or better diagnostic performance.

We have used the aforementioned approach to investigate the implicit acquisition of diagnostic skill. Rather than rely on studying well-formed expertise, we were interested in the development of diagnostic skill and, in particular, whether explicit knowledge changes in line with the predictions of Anderson's and Boshuizen and Schmidt's theories. If expertise involves the gradual automatization of explicit knowledge, then students taught explicit rules should gradually become better at making diagnoses and, at the same time, less able to verbalize rules. On the other hand, if explicit and implicit knowledge are acquired independently, then students taught traditionally should not lose their explicit knowledge as they become more expert. Students who are taught implicitly (who learn by inducing rules on the basis of repeated feedback) should become expert at diagnosing patients without ever acquiring any explicit verbalizable rules. By using these two different teaching methods, it was possible to demonstrate a dissociation between the *acquisition* of verbalizable knowledge and skilled performance in medical diagnosis. The dissociation was apparent as we tracked not only the acquisition of implicit diagnostic skill but also explicit knowledge of diagnostic rules as students learned to diagnose acute abdominal pain. We found that both types of knowledge were acquired separately. Although diagnostic performance was similar for the two groups, students who learned with explicit rules acquired those rules that did not show signs of tailing off as performance increased.

The preceding studies aim to observe the acquisition of implicit and explicit knowledge directly, as it is reflected in diagnostic performance and verbalizable diagnostic rules. However, it is also possible that the differences between the two types of knowledge are reflected, indirectly, in confidence ratings. This possibility is discussed next.

Confidence and Clinical Decisions

Numerous studies in clinical psychology and medicine have shown that, with increased experience, clinicians become more confident in their opinions and diagnoses. This would seem self-evident, and reasonable, if it were not for the fact that this increase in confidence is not necessarily accompanied by an increase in accuracy (Fischhoff, Slovic, & Lichtenstein, 1977; Koriat, Lichtenstein, & Fischhoff, 1980; Lichtenstein & Fischhoff, 1980; Lichtenstein, Fischhoff, & D.L. Phillips, 1977; Oskamp, 1962). Clinicians seem to be more confident than their performance would warrant. As pointed out by Sharp, Cutler, and Penrod (1988), such misplaced confidence has been demonstrated in a variety of subject populations using a variety of tasks.

The general conclusion from these studies is that judges are poorly "calibrated." That is, they over- or underestimate probabilities. The most common deviation from perfect calibration is "overconfidence." In the context of our investigations, this translates to students having higher confidence that their diagnoses are correct than their performance actually justifies.

Lichtenstein and Fischhoff (1977) looked at the factors that influence calibration; more specifically, they were interested in whether the amount of knowledge a subject had about the area being assessed would affect calibration. They found an inverse relationship between knowledge and overconfidence. Those who knew more about a domain underestimated their ability whereas those who knew much less overestimated their ability. Lichtenstein and Fischhoff concluded that experts who know more are not necessarily aware of how much they know.

In practice, it is possible that overconfident clinicians, who place too much faith in their probability estimates, will make incautious decisions. They either may prematurely foreclose when gathering diagnostic data or may be less likely to revise their opinion when their diagnoses are incorrect. For this reason, researchers have examined whether calibration can be improved by training. Koriat et al. (1980), for example, found that providing subjects with feedback about how well they were performing reduced overconfidence and improved calibration.

In our own work, we have found overconfidence to be related to learning mode (T. Griffin, 1991). When subjects were asked to rate how confident they were in the accuracy of their diagnoses of acute abdominal pain, subjects in the explicit learning condition were more confident than those in the implicit learning condition. As previously reported, this increase in confidence was not accompanied by a commensurate increase in accuracy; both groups showed approximately the same level of diagnostic accuracy. We hypothesise that, because explicit learning provides a verbalizable rationale for their diagnostic judgments, subjects who learn explicitly become more confident in their performance than implicit mode subjects who cannot provide an explicit rationale for their judgments.

The possibility that a metacognitive measure (confidence) is systematically related to learning mode is being further researched (also see Haist, Shimamura, & Squire, 1992). Confidence may well be positively related to accuracy when learning is explicit but, when learning is implicit, confidence and accuracy could be unrelated because subjects who learn implicitly do not know what they know.

CONCLUSIONS

The theoretical significance of the work reviewed in this chapter is that diagnostic expertise can be learned directly; it is not dependent on first learning explicitly. There is also a practical significance. Because explicit knowledge and diagnostic performance appear to be unrelated, traditional paper-and-pencil examinations may not be adequate ways to assess diagnostic knowledge. Students also should be tested using simulated patients in order to directly assess their implicit knowledge (as reflected in their diagnostic performance). Indeed, teaching also should involve both the explicit and implicit modes.

Finally, knowledge engineers seeking to develop computerized expert systems and educators wishing to revise the medical curriculum should be aware that much diagnostic expertise is implicit and not verbalizable. It cannot be elicited verbally; at best it can only be observed in performance. Knowledge engineers and educators will need to modify their current knowledge acquisition practices (asking experts to think aloud as they make a diagnosis) if they wish to understand how clinicians really work.

ACKNOWLEDGMENTS

Some of the research described in this chapter was supported by grants from the Australian Research Council.

20

INTELLECTUAL DISABILITIES

Janet Fletcher
University of Western Australia

Clare Roberts
Curtin University of Technology

Intellectual disability (or mental retardation) is defined by the American Association on Mental Retardation as:

> substantial limitations in present functioning. It is characterized by significantly subaverage intellectual functioning, existing concurrently with related limitations in two or more of the following applicable adaptive skill areas: communication, self-care, home-living, social skills, community use, self-direction, health and safety, functional academics, leisure and work. Mental retardation manifests before age 18. (Luckasson et al., 1992, p. 1)

This definition is used in many countries as a basis for diagnosis and determination of eligibility for service provision. Though providing a description of the disorder and suggesting assessment methods, this definition does not provide an understanding of the nature of the cognitive impairment in intellectual disability or the deficits associated with the disorder. Neither does it provide a basis for intervention by practitioners who seek to educate or train people with an intellectual disability.

Before trying to educate or train (i.e., change) behavior, it is important to know as much as possible about the cognitive structures and processes that underlie that behavior. Thus, as noted by P.H. Brooks and McCauley (1984), a good model of cognitive functioning "is an essential prerequisite" for those attempting "efficient focussed interventions" (p. 479).

Over the past four decades there has been extensive research aimed at providing the basis for such a model. At a general level researchers have sought to answer the question of whether people with an intellectual disability differ qualitatively or simply quantitatively from those who are not disabled in this way (Wishart & L. Duffy, 1990; Zigler & Balla, 1982). At the more detailed level attempts have been made to understand specific cognitive structures and functions. In this chapter we examine an important direction this research has taken in noting the distinction between explicit and implicit processing and the apparent differences in the degrees to which these types of processing are impaired for individuals with intellectual disabilities. Our focus is on implicit processing and its implications for intervention. It should be pointed out at the outset, however, that, in the absence of a fully developed model of cognitive functioning, interventions have proceeded based on partial models, practitioners' intuitions, or the pragmatics of behavior modification.

To set the scene for this chapter we introduce key concepts and distinctions. We then go on to provide a brief outline of research into explicit processing in people with an intellectual disability, some of which took place prior to the more recent awareness of the part implicit processing plays when attempting to gain a complete picture of intellectual disability. The next section of the chapter details relevant recent research into implicit functioning. Finally, we consider the implications of this research for education and training procedures employed with people who have intellectual disabilities.

DEFINITIONS AND DISTINCTIONS

Throughout this chapter we have used the term explicit processing to mean effortful processing. It is effortful in that it requires selective attention, is under voluntary control, and requires a conscious intention to be performed (Ellis, Woodley-Zanthos, Dulaney, & Palmer, 1989). It is, therefore, likely to be negatively affected by stress and competing task requirements (D. Goldstein et al., 1983). By contrast, we have used the term *implicit processing* to mean automatic processing. Automatic processes occur without the direct intention or awareness of the individual, do not require attentional resources, and hence are not disrupted by stress or competing processing demands (Hasher & Zacks, 1979; Shiffrin & Schneider, 1977).

It has been suggested within the literature that there may be two distinct sources of this automaticity. First, it has been suggested that some automatic processes may be biologically determined, prewired, mature at a relatively young age, and remain invariant as the child develops (M. Anderson, 1992b; Hasher & Zacks, 1979). Certain primitive processes of evolutionary value such as encoding of frequency, spatial location, and temporal order are often considered to be of this nature (Ellis et al., 1989; Hasher & Zacks, 1984). Second, automaticity may come about through extensive practice. This phenomenon is well documented in the experimental literature (e.g., C.M. MacLeod & Dunbar, 1988; Schneider & Shiffrin, 1977;

Shiffrin & Schneider, 1977). Processes that may initially proceed under conscious control can, with extended practice, become involuntary and nonconscious and can function independently of capacity constraints, thereby freeing up attentional resources for explicit processing. Facets of many activities (e.g., driving a car, reading) can be considered automatic under normal conditions when performed by experts (see chap. 5 of this volume).

Within this dichotomy of implicit and explicit processing, there is another distinction that requires clarification, that between learning and memory. This distinction should be kept in mind as past research is reviewed, because frequently researchers reach conclusions about success or failure to learn on the basis of tasks that require retrieval of previously learned information from memory. In this context, it is thus possible that they have attempted to examine implicit learning by means that require explicit memory. This is clearly a matter for concern as competence in learning that takes place without effort or intention may be being masked by performance difficulties in retrieving information through effortful memory search.

EXPLICIT PROCESSING IN PEOPLE
WITH AN INTELLECTUAL DISABILITY

Research into information processing in people with an intellectual disability has a long history. (For more detail than provided in this section, see Borkowski & Day, 1987; P.H. Brooks, Sperber, & McCauley, 1984; Matson & Mulick, 1991.) The information-processing paradigm has been seen as useful in decomposing performance into smaller component processes, from stimulus registration through to behavioural response, in an effort to identify factors underlying performance deficits in people with an intellectual disability. Although much of this research has been carried out before the explicit/implicit processing dichotomy was raised as an issue, it is of interest to look at this research anew in the light of the dichotomy.

In this section of the chapter we provide a brief outline of several studies that, we suggest, meet the criteria for explicit processing, in order to create a context for, and useful contrasts with, research on implicit processing.

If we start at the input stage of an information-processing model, with attention, we find evidence that people with intellectual disabilities are more likely to show attentional deficiencies associated with voluntary processes, such as focusing, than involuntary responses related to arousal (Nettelbeck & Brewer, 1981). For example Krupski (1975) examined deceleration in heart rate in a simple reaction time task involving university students and a similar aged group of young people with intellectual disabilities. Her research showed that, when a reaction signal is preceded by a warning signal at a fixed interval, heart rate drops immediately following the warning signal then rises and then drops again just prior to the onset of the expected stimulation. In this study the adolescents with mild intellectual disabilities not only showed slower reaction times but also much less marked deceleration in heart rate immediately prior to the onset of the reaction stimulus than did the university students. By comparison, there was no significant difference between groups in heart rate response to the warning stimulus. Krupski took this to indicate that signals were effectively registered by both groups but only the university students made the preparatory attentional response requisite for fast reaction time. In a subsequent study of attention using a similar reaction time task, Krupski (1977) found that subjects with an intellectual disability were not only slower in reaction time to an anticipated stimulus, but also glanced away from the stimulus object during the preparatory interval to a far greater extent than their normally functioning counterparts.

Deficiencies in consciously distributing attention across competing tasks have also been found in individuals with intellectual disabilities (Carr, 1984). Many researchers have suggested that these and other attentional difficulties impact on later stages of information processing and are responsible for a variety of performance deficits (P.H. Brooks & McCauley, 1984; Carr, 1984; Nettelbeck & Brewer, 1981).

Encoding is another aspect of information processing that has been examined in groups of people with intellectual disabilities. Merrill and Mar (1987) studied speed of processing auditorily presented sentences in a series of studies in which they compared adolescents with intellectual disabilities with mental-age-matched primary-school children. In their first study they presented a series of short prose passages at six different speech rates ranging from 150 to 400 words per minute. Following each version of a given passage, subjects were asked comprehension questions that could be answered with a yes/no response. As expected they found that, for all subjects, there was a decrease in the mean number of correct responses with increases in speech rate. Of interest was the group by rate interaction, which indicated that the rate of decline in comprehension as speech rate increased was greater for the group with intellectual disabilities.

The second study was similar in design but did not require semantic analysis of the material heard prior to response. Instead, subjects were simply required to answer yes/no to indicate whether a particular probe word had occurred in the sentence they had heard. In other words the comparison was phonological rather than semantic. On this task there was no evidence of a group effect. Merrill and Mar (1987) attributed the differences in results between the studies to be due to the semantic-analytic component of coding speed requiring "more active processes" than the phonological component.

There has been extensive research on the relationship between short-term memory and individual differences in intelligence (e.g., Belmont & Butterfield, 1969; Butterfield, Wambold, & Belmont, 1973; Ellis & Wooldridge, 1985). In the majority of these studies memory has been assessed by means of conscious recognition or recall of material that has been previously presented, usually with explicit instructions designed to encourage learning. The study by Ellis and Wooldridge is outlined as an example.

Ellis and Wooldridge (1985) compared a group of university undergraduate students with a group of young adults (mean chronological age of 19.75 years) with intellectual disabilities on two short-term memory tasks. The tasks required subjects to remember the names of three objects after being shown either drawings of the objects or the written names of the objects. Recall was requested after delays of 0, 10, 20, or 30 seconds. Where there was delayed recall the time was filled with a number-naming distractor task. Subjects were told in all conditions that it was important to remember the pictures (or words). For both groups there was a drop in retention rate with increased time intervals, with the greatest change occurring between 0 and 10 seconds. Subjects with intellectual disabilities forgot more rapidly over the initial 10 seconds than the university students. The students recalled both the pictures and words better than the subjects with intellectual disabilities, but whereas there was no difference between recall of pictures and words for the students, the subjects with intellectual disabilities performed significantly better at recall of pictures than recall of words. Ellis and Wooldridge did not attribute this to reading difficulties on the part of the group with disabilities as these subjects had previously been assessed to ensure that they could read all the stimulus words. They interpreted their findings as reflecting a structural memory deficit on the part of people with intellectual disabilities. In terms of our current analysis this study serves to illustrate the common finding that individuals with intellectual disabilities perform more poorly than peers on tasks involving explicit recall of intentionally learned material, but that this decrement is more marked for some types of stimulus materials than others.

Transfer of information from short-term to longer term memory is usually considered to occur through the application of processes such as grouping, labeling, imagining, and rehearsal. These processes are frequently learned as explicitly taught strategies, but there is evidence that in normally developing people they become overlearned and then are applied quite automatically. There is evidence that people with intellectual disabilities can be trained to use strategies such as rehearsal and labeling (A.L. Brown & Barclay, 1976; Ellis, 1970). Some research has suggested that the benefits of training are short-lived, as people with intellectual disabilities do not seem to retain the strategies in their repertoire, or generalize their use (Campione & A.L. Brown, 1977). Yet other research has suggested that generalization can be improved through active strategy-inducing procedures (Wanschura & Borkowski, 1975), modifications to the instructional approach (Butterfield & Ferretti, 1984), and extensive systematic instruction in both retention and retrieval strategies (Butterfield et al., 1973). These studies suggest that strategies can be explicitly learned by people with intellectual disabilities, though they may not be automatically applied.

Underlying much of the research on memory processes is the question of whether performance deficits in subjects with intellectual disabilities are due to the fact that the relevant information is not stored in memory or to difficulties in retrieving such information from memory. A.L. Brown (1974, in Hale & Bork-owski, 1991) has suggested that people with an intellectual disability fail to store information in memory in a way that can be readily accessed. Other researchers have provided evidence that these subjects may well have information categorized in a way that should allow retrieval but for some reason they are less capable of explicitly accessing it (D. Davies, Sperber, & McCauley, 1981; Sperber, Ragain, & McCauley, 1976).

IMPLICATIONS OF RESEARCH INTO
EXPLICIT PROCESSING OF INFORMATION

A number of conclusions can be drawn from this thumbnail sketch of research into information processing concerned with explicitly learned and/or recalled material in people with an intellectual disability. First, there appears to be substantial evidence that people with intellectual disabilities show deficits in consciously controlling selective attention (Krupski, 1975, 1977). They also show deficits in explicit learning when this is assessed by explicit recall (Ellis & Wooldridge, 1985). It is not clear from the literature outlined to this point whether this is due to deficiencies in explicit learning or explicit memory or some combination of the two. However, it is evident that the level of performance deficit on tasks requiring explicit learning depended on the nature of the stimulus material. For example, the learning of pictorially presented material appears to be less impaired in subjects with intellectual disabilities than is written material.

These deficits in explicit information processing appear potentially to be respon-sible either individually or cumulatively for a variety of behaviors in people with intellectual disabilities that are commonly reported by parents, teachers, and clinicians. Behaviors frequently noted include: failure to display observational learning, poor maintenance of new skills and knowledge over time, slow learning of new material, and failure to generalize learning to new stimuli (Hale & Bork-owski, 1991). Yet the research also raises many questions. In the context of this chapter, the important questions are: What is the relative contribution of learning and memory to the performance decrements shown by people with intellectual disabilities? Can the two be methodologically disambiguated so that we can ascertain what aspects of learning and memory may be intact in people with intellectual disabilities?

IMPLICIT PROCESSING IN PEOPLE
WITH INTELLECTUAL DISABILITIES

By comparison with research on explicit processing in people with intellectual disability, research on implicit processing has a comparatively short history, and it would be fair to say that it is one of which the majority of practitioners are ignorant. Yet if the claim of Reber et al. (1991) that implicit learning should be intact in people with intellectual disabilities, is correct, there would be important implications for those involved with the education and training of these people.

In their 1991 article, Reber and his colleagues stated that implicit systems (a) should be "robust in the face of various psychiatric or neurological insults," (b) ought to "display tighter distributions in the population when compared with explicit systems," and (c) should operate "largely independently of standard measures of cognitive capability such as intelligence" (p. 888). How well do these expectations hold up? Reber and his colleagues considered that there is good evidence for item (a) (Abrams & Reber, 1988; Reber et al., 1991). They also considered that research reported in their 1991 article provides support for items (b) and (c) in that performance on an implicit grammar-learning task did not correlate with IQ, whereas performance by the same subjects on a similar, but explicit, series solution task did correlate with IQ. However, it should be noted that the subjects in their study were all college students with mean IQ of 110, and although the range of IQ was greater than might be expected in a sample of college students (73 to 150), nevertheless, it is probable that none of them would be classed as "intellectually disabled" given our definition.

There have been studies to test Reber's hypothesis using subjects with genuine intellectual disabilities. Before attempting to examine these, however, it is necessary to look more carefully at the necessary characteristics of implicit systems and the tasks that have been used to tap their functioning.

Implicit processes, by our definition, operate automatically, without conscious awareness. As previously noted, it has been suggested that there may be two distinct sources of this automaticity. The majority of studies on implicit processing in people with intellectual disabilities have looked at automatic processing of the biologically determined, "prewired" kind. We look at some examples.

Ellis, Katz, and J.E. Williams (1987) compared adolescents with IQ in the 50 to 75 range with unimpaired children and adults on a location recall task. Subjects were shown pictures, in sets of four, arranged in quadrants in a book. Half of each group of subjects were instructed to name the pictures and to study them so that they could recall them after they had looked through the book. The other half were told to name each picture and tell what it was used for. This group was not informed of the subsequent memory test. This manipulation was intended to serve the dual function of minimizing the use of location as a cue to remembering items, and also of ensuring "better encoding of individual pictures" (p. 407). After completing this section of the task, all subjects were then asked to recall the names of the pictures for 2 minutes. They were then given the pictures one at a time and asked to place each in the quadrant in which it had been located. Although there were significant differences between groups on the picture recall task, with the disabled group performing similarly to the sixth-grade and elderly groups but more poorly than the college students, there were no significant differences between groups on location recall, which was performed at a better than chance level. Both picture recall and location recall involved intentional search of memory, yet location recall was not impaired in the subjects with intellectual disability. Ellis and his colleagues concluded that location information must have been implicitly learned and suggested that "encoding of location is a primitive process in the evolution of cognition, maturing early and functioning optimally throughout the lifespan in the normally healthy organism" (p. 411). Overall the semantic encoding instructions were shown to facilitate memory for both picture name and location to a small but significant degree. An examination of the different groups indicates that this trend was true for all except the elderly on the picture recall task and the second graders on the location recall task.

In 1988, Ellis and Allison looked at memory for frequency of occurrence in college students and a group of slightly younger adolescents with a mean IQ of 67. Subjects from each group were randomly assigned to one of four stimulus conditions: word, line drawing, photograph, or photograph with semantic encoding instructions. In the first three conditions subjects were told to look at each item, name it aloud, and try to remember it for a later test. In the fourth condition subjects had to not only name the item and try to remember it, but say what it was used for. Items were shown to the subjects by means of slide projection. Items could appear one, two, three, or four times and no item appeared more than once in any five-item block. After being shown the slides subjects were given three minutes in which to free recall as many items as possible. This provided a measure, dependent on explicit memory, of explicit learning, as subjects had been instructed to remember the names of the objects that had been represented in each condition. Each subject was then shown the original slides together with some new slides that had not been shown previously and asked to say how many times (0, 1, 2, 3, 4) the item had been seen in the previous phase of the task. As attention had not been drawn to this aspect of the stimuli by means of instructions, it was assumed that acquisition of this type of information had been through implicit learning.

On the recall task college students performed significantly better than the group with intellectual disabilities, and within the latter group, subjects exposed to words performed significantly worse than those exposed to pictures. On the frequency estimate (implicit learning) task, both groups were most accurate in estimating frequency of semantically encoded photographs and least accurate in estimating word frequency. On the latter task the two groups were of comparable accuracy, however the college group were significantly more accurate in the other three stimulus conditions due to a tendency by the group with disabilities to overestimate frequency. Graphing of individual cases suggested that poorer performance by the group with disabilities was due, in part at least, to outliers. However, Ellis and Allison (1988) interpreted these data as indication of an encoding deficiency in people with an intellectual disability "which does not allow them to take full advantage of distinctive sensory information which, if encoded, would facilitate retrieval" (p. 72). Retrieval of past occurrences by the cue was therefore less efficient. In other words, the subjects with intellectual disabilities were inferior in estimating frequency in three of the four stimulus conditions not because of inferior implicit learning of the attribute, frequency, but because of inferior encoding of the "event"—the stimulus object.

Now let us look at a study in which subjects with and without intellectual disabilities were compared on a task involving automatic processing of the over-learned variety, namely reading. Ellis et al. (1989) compared young adults with intellectual disabilities with college students in a series of experiments using a modified Stroop color-word interference test. In the Stroop task (Stroop, 1935) color names are printed in an ink color other than the name. Subjects are asked to ignore the word itself and name the color in which the word has been printed. Subjects typically find this more difficult than either color naming of nonwords or reading of color names presented in monochrome, and this difficulty results in slower color-naming latencies (i.e., the Stroop effect). In the first of these experiments, the subjects with intellectual disability experienced more Stroop effect than did the college students. Ellis and his colleagues interpreted this finding in terms of inability by the subjects with intellectual disability to use effortful explicit processing effectively, in order to suppress overlearned and hence, automatic, reading responses.

In their second experiment, Ellis et al. (1989) looked at the development of automatization of a suppression response to the Stroop effect with extended practice. They compared the rate and accuracy with which their subject groups read the *words* on a Stroop task before and after 4 days of practice with the standard Stroop task (i.e., naming the color in which the words were printed). They found that the practice led to slower reading of the Stroop words for both groups, but this effect was extreme for the group with intellectual disabilities. With extensive postpractice at the original reading task, these subjects improved markedly but their reading rate did not return to prepractice rate.

In their final experiment, Ellis et al. (1989) sought to find whether the suppression response was specific to words or if subjects "developed an automatic attentional response to colour, thus attending less to other stimulus features" (p. 418). Procedures in this study were similar to those in Experiment 2; only half the subjects in each group practiced naming the color of Stroop words, whereas the other half practiced naming the color of Xs. Color naming Xs had no effect on the postpractice Stroop word-reading rate of either group. Color naming Stroop words led to performance decrements on the subsequent word-reading version of the task, similar to those noted in Study 2. Ellis and his colleagues concluded that the automatization of a cognitive response has differing consequences for people with intellectual disability than for college students in that it persists in a situation in which it is no longer adaptive. Ellis et al. coined the term *cognitive inertia* to refer to this phenomenon.

What then can we conclude from studies of this type? First, it would appear that people with intellectual disabilities do display implicit learning on a variety of tasks. With some stimulus materials this learning is equivalent to that in nonimpaired subjects. However, the efficiency of implicit learning in people with and without intellectual disabilities may be differentially affected by properties of the stimulus. Ellis and Allison's (1988) study suggests that although frequency estimates in subjects with intellectual disabilities were more accurate for pictorial materials than for words, they did not benefit from these "enriched" stimuli to the same extent as did their nonimpaired counterparts and hence were less accurate in frequency recall. As a consequence, deficits in explicit processing of the stimuli led to nonequivalent registration of the automatically registered stimulus attribute, frequency. This interpretation is in keeping with Hasher and Zacks' theory (1979, 1984), which proposes that memory for the frequency of the occurrence of events is affected by the memorability of the events.

Extent of retrieval of implicitly learned information also depends on how the stimulus was initially encoded. Deep processing of the stimulus results in better recall of the implicitly learned attributes of the stimulus (e.g., Ellis et al., 1987; Schultz, 1983). Research on strategy use by people with intellectual disabilities (e.g., A.L. Brown & Barclay, 1976) suggests that they may need to be directed to encode in this way. Both these areas of research thus suggest that deficiencies in explicit processing may impact on use of an intact implicit processing system.

Performance deficits on cognitive tasks may also come about because processing that has become automatic in people with intellectual disabilities is not as easily suppressed by effortful processing and may persist when it is no longer advantageous—the cognitive inertia problem.

There are, however, several common features requiring comment in the studies just noted. First, these studies typically employed tasks that required subjects to retrieve by complex and explicit processes what they had learned, even though this learning itself may have occurred implicitly. Hence explicit memory difficulties may be obscuring information that could be accessed through other means. Schultz's (1983) study suggests that this is reasonable conjecture. His study, with 12 students with intellectual disabilities and a mental-age-matched control group, required subjects to look at words shown individually on a screen and then to answer a question that related to either its position, sound properties, or meaning, features considered to require increasing depth of processing. They were then shown each of the words together with two equally common distractor words and asked to indicate which of the words they had seen before. That is, the task required the less complex retrieval operation of recognition rather than recall. The two subject groups showed equal recognition accuracy even though the subjects with intellectual disabilities were significantly slower at making decisions and this difference in speed of response increased with the depth of processing required.

To gain a clear picture of the effectiveness of implicit processes in people with intellectual disability, what is really needed is a study that manipulates not only implicit and explicit learning, but also implicit and explicit memory. This remains to be done. A study by Sperber et al. (1976) does, however, give some insight into the relative difficulty that people with an intellectual disability have in explicit retrieval from memory compared with implicit retrieval. These researchers used a semantic priming task to investigate category knowledge. The priming effect of a stimulus relies on implicitly retrieved associations between it and a target stimulus facilitating response to that target. In this instance pairs of pictures of common objects were shown to the subjects whose IQ range on a Wechsler scale was 41 to 74. Half of the pictures belonged to the same category (e.g., both fruit), whereas half were unrelated. The first picture was the priming picture and the second the target picture. Time taken to name each picture was recorded. Target pictures that had been primed by a picture in the same category were named faster than those that had been preceded by an unrelated picture. This facilitation effect was unrelated to the intellectual ability of subjects. Yet when the same subjects were administered two category usage tasks "designed to test the recognition and verbalisation of categorical relationships" (p. 227), there was a significant relationship between performance and intelligence. It is not clear from this study whether the categories had at some stage been explicitly taught to the subjects or whether they had been implicitly acquired. Nevertheless, this study suggests that the category knowledge was available to these subjects and could be implicitly retrieved by them, but that they had difficulty either in explicitly retrieving it or in articulating it.

A similar conclusion was reached by McFarland and Sandy (1982), following their study comparing the performance of subjects with and without intellectual disabilities on a picture-word interference task designed to tap automatic processing. In their study, subjects were asked to name pictures as quickly as possible. In the control condition, pictures alone were shown. In the experimental conditions, the pictures were labeled, with either the name of the picture, the name of an object from the same semantic category as the picture (e.g., the label, *truck*, on a picture of a car), a word that rhymed with the name of the object, or an unrelated label. Any interference or facilitation produced by the label on the picture-naming latency was assumed to be due to the automatic processing of the words "without conscious attention" (p. 30). Both groups of subjects showed minor nonsignificant facilitation for a label of the name of the picture, and significant decrements for all other labels, with a label of the same semantic category causing maximal interference. Although the subjects with intellectual disabilities were slower and made more errors in all conditions, the extent of the slowing of responses in these conditions compared with the no-label control condition was similar for both subject groups, and both showed identical patterns of response. The subjects with intellectual disabilities thus appeared to be implicitly accessing information that they typically find difficult or impossible to explicitly retrieve and articulate.

There is clearly a possibility that difficulties in explicit retrieval have affected the performance of subjects with intellectual disabilities in the majority of studies involving implicit learning but explicit memory retrieval.

A second feature of these studies that warrants comment is that they have all used subjects in the mild intellectual disability range. Most theorists who have written about automatic processing of the biologically determined, prewired variety, suggest that there is either an age or stage of development at which this type of processing comes into play. Studies that have looked at developmental differences in frequency estimation (Ellis et al., 1988; D. Goldstein et al., 1983; Lund, Hall, K.P. Wilson, & M.S. Humphreys, 1983) suggest that there may be a minimal age (estimates range from "preschool" to "7 or 8" years of age) at which automatic encoding of event frequency comes into play. If some minimal developmental level is required for automatic processing, then it is likely that some subjects, with more severe disabilities than the majority of those used in studies to date, will show evidence of impaired automatic processing or may even show absence of automatic processing. (It is possible that the "outliers" in the Ellis & Allison, 1988, article fell into this category.) Alternatively, if chronological age is of more importance, then automatic processing should be evidenced even in people with moderate to severe impairments, unless there is brain damage. The difficulties inherent in testing these hypotheses are obvious. Nevertheless, answers to them would help us gain a clearer understanding both of automatic processing itself, and the nature of intellectual disabilities.

IMPLICATIONS OF IMPLICIT PROCESSING THEORY AND RESEARCH

To date implicit processing theory and research have not reached the awareness of many practitioners working in the field of intellectual disability. It is useful to ask why this might be the case. One possible answer lies in the type of learning that has been the focus of the two groups. Practitioners, concerned with the practicalities of helping people with intellectual disabilities learn to live as independently as possible in the community, have frequently focused on the acquisition of skills (i.e., learning of the "learning how" variety). It is common knowledge to parents and educators that children with an intellectual disability do not "pick up" or incidentally acquire skills such as cleaning teeth and brushing hair. Learning that has been the focus of interest for many researchers into implicit processing, has been more often of the "learning that" variety, such as recognizing that something has appeared in the same location before. The usefulness of this type of learning is not so immediately apparent, especially when it appears that effortful processing deficiencies may reduce the extent of implicit learning or have a negative impact on the individual's ability to retrieve at will implicitly learned information.

Nevertheless, even from the practitioner viewpoint, there appears to be enough promise in the attempts to apply implicit processing theory to the field of intellectual disability to warrant further research, and in some instances applications are already suggested. Let us look first at areas requiring further research.

It appears important to ascertain the extent to which implicit learning is preserved in people with intellectual disabilities. What is the range of types of information that can be acquired in this way and who can acquire it? Here it is important to determine whether skills can be implicitly learned by people with intellectual disabilities if they are attending to the stimulus, or whether implicit learning is restricted to the "learning that" variety. It is also important to ask whether there is a cut-off point in terms of developmental level or life experience below which this type of learning will not occur. As noted previously, studies by Ellis et al. (1988), D. Goldstein et al. (1983), and Lund et al. (1983) all suggest there is a base developmental or chronological level necessary for prewired automatic learning. Is this also the case for overlearned automatic learning? As developmental age and chronological age are not closely aligned in people with intellectual disabilities, it is important to examine the relative importance of each of these variables for the maturation of automatic processing ability.

There is also a need for further research to investigate how people with intellectual disabilities may gain maximal benefit from intact implicit processing. If capacity to learn about location, frequency, and categories is intact, how can we enable people with intellectual disabilities to capitalize on such knowledge in order to facilitate future learning and enhance self-efficacy and positive attributions about learning? One direction suggested by past research is to modify the retrieval requirements of the task (Schultz, 1983); other directions remain to be explored. Research on explicit and implicit processing in people with intellectual disability needs to go hand in hand so that we gain a better understanding of how effortful processing deficits may interfere with the use of intact implicit processing, and how these deficits, or at least their interfering effects, can be minimized.

Despite the unanswered questions, there have been research findings that should inform practitioners and affect educational and training practices. Research by Ellis and his colleagues (1988, 1989) has shown that overlearning can be as much a problem for people with intellectual disabilities as underlearning. Their studies on cognitive inertia give insight into the development of inappropriate automatic habits such as repetitive conversational phrases and inappropriate affectionate behavior. Difficulty in changing behavior once it has become automatic means that learning objectives need to be carefully structured so as to avoid building habits that will interfere with the future learning of adaptive behavior.

Research into prewired automatic processing suggests that people with intellectual disabilities do have an intact learning system that could be used to build up a history of successful learning experiences so that they will develop more positive attributions and some of the motivational barriers to learning will be reduced.

It is only in relatively recent years that serious attempts have been made to look at the implications of implicit processing theory for the area of intellectual disability. Much more research remains to be carried out before we will have a clear idea of the role of implicit processing in the total picture of the cognitive functioning of the person with an intellectual disability. In the meantime each study edges us closer to that "good model of cognitive processes" that P.H. Brooks and McCauley (1984, p. 479) saw as "an essential prerequisite for educators and others charged with developing efficient, focussed interventions."

21

IMPLICIT AND EXPLICIT PROCESSES IN READING ACQUISITION

William E. Tunmer
James W. Chapman
Massey University

How do children learn to read? Two general views have emerged in the literature. One view places almost exclusive emphasis on the role of implicit processes, whereas the second view proposes a two-stage conceptualization of beginning reading in which implicit processes are associated with the first stage and explicit processes with the second. The chapter is divided into three sections. The first section describes these two views and briefly summarizes the theoretical arguments and empirical evidence in support of each. The second section discusses the key distinguishing feature of the second view, the development of explicit awareness and knowledge of the systematic correspondences between graphemes and phonemes, an ability referred to as *phonological recoding skill*. The third section summarizes research on the two cognitive prerequisite skills that are thought to be necessary for acquiring phonological recoding skill, phonological awareness, and syntactic awareness, both of which involve explicit processes.

TWO VIEWS OF READING ACQUISITION

According to the first view, the ability to read evolves naturally and spontaneously out of children's prereading experiences in much the same way that their oral language develops (K.S. Goodman & Y.M. Goodman, 1979; Y.M. Goodman &

Altwerger, 1981; Harste, C. Burke, & Woodward, 1982). As children are exposed to print in their environment, they acquire print-meaning associations for environmental labels and signs, which in turn provide the basis for learning about the graphic system. Initially, children are unable to read the words in labels and signs. They can only point to the location where it says "milk" or "stop." However, after repeated exposure to these labels and signs, children eventually learn to recognize the words from the graphic cues alone.

This view of early reading is consistent with an overall model of reading acquisition proposed by K.S. Goodman (1967) and F. Smith (1978). According to this model, skilled reading is primarily an activity of (implicitly) using the syntactic and semantic redundancies of language to generate hypotheses about the text yet to be encountered. Efficient readers are thought to pay little attention to the bulk of the words of text because the flow of language follows a predictable pattern. Instead, they use the fewest cues possible to make a prediction and test their guess against their developing meaning.

The major conclusion derived from these claims was that unlike fluent readers, poor and beginning readers are less able to make use of contextual redundancy in ongoing sentence processing. Reading instruction should therefore place little emphasis on using visual information to identify individual words and more on using context to guess words. A major assumption of this conceptualization of reading is that learning to read is a natural process not unlike the acquisition of spoken language. Reading failure is thought to result from methods of reading instruction that conflict with the natural course of events.

According to the first view, then, all that is needed is for children to learn a few sight words and focus on the meaning of text; the rest will take care of itself. In short, children "learn to read by reading." K.S. Goodman (1986), a leading proponent of the "whole language" approach to literacy learning and instruction, argued that teachers make learning to read difficult "by breaking whole (natural) language into bite-size, abstract little pieces" (p. 7). The use of word analysis activities such as phonemic segmentation training provides little or no benefit to beginning readers because language is not kept "whole." Word study activities should emphasize the process of "making meaning," not the mechanics of reading words in isolation or translating written words into sounds. If children are immersed in a print-rich environment in which the focus is on the meaning of print, they will readily acquire reading skills, according to this view.

In opposition to this view is Gough and Hillinger's (1980) two-stage model of beginning reading development (see also Gough & Juel, 1991; Gough, Juel & Griffith, 1992). The first stage of the model involves primarily implicit processes, whereas the second stage involves primarily explicit processes. According to the model beginning readers quickly learn to recognize dozens of words through the natural strategy of selective association, the pairing of a partial stimulus cue to a response. As Gough and Juel pointed out:

> Any cue which will distinguish the word will suffice. It might be a character, or a matching pair of characters, or even the font in which the characters appear; if the child knows the names of some letters, it might be the name of one of them (cf. Ehri & Wilce, 1985). Or it might be a property of the whole word; it might be its colour, or its length, or even the resemblance of the whole to some familiar object. Whatever the child might notice, the child will associate the word with that cue, and with that cue only. The child will select that cue, and so his association will be selective. (p. 49)

Beginning readers who continue to learn in this way, however, will face two serious problems (Gough et al., 1992). First, although the hypothesis of selective association predicts that the beginning reader will easily acquire a few visually distinct sight words, it also predicts that the child's natural strategy of associating a familiar spoken word with some feature or attribute of the word's printed form will eventually break down. Each new word will become increasingly harder to acquire because of the difficulty of finding a unique cue to distinguish it from those that have already been learned. Beginning readers will make an ever increasing number of errors, and become confused and frustrated, unless they discover or are led to discover an alternative strategy for establishing the relationship between the written and spoken forms of the language.

Second, the strategy of selective association based on distinctive visual cues is not generative; that is, it provides no way of recognizing unfamiliar words. This is an important consideration because most of the words that the beginning reader encounters in print are novel. Beginning reading materials typically employ upwards of 1,500 words, each of which must be encountered a first time. Moreover, when a new word does appear in print it does not suddenly begin appearing with great frequency. Approximately 35% to 40% of the words used in beginning reading materials appear only once (Jorm & Share, 1983). Thus beginning readers are continually encountering words that they have not seen before and may not set eyes on again for some time. Sentence context will be of little help because research has demonstrated that the average predictability of content words in running text is about 0.10, as compared to about 0.40 for function words (e.g., *on*, *the*, *to*), which are typically short, high-frequency sight words that the child can already recognize (Gough, 1983). In other words, unless the child is reading a very low level text with repeated sentence structures, a high degree of predictability, and a large amount of picture support, he or she will have a one in ten chance of guessing the correct word.

Gough and colleagues argued that normal progress in learning to read can occur only if the child makes the transition to the next stage of acquisition, the *cipher* stage. Entering this stage requires that the child becomes conceptually aware of the interrelatedness of the visual patterns and sounds shared by different words. Gough and Juel (1991) referred to this awareness as *cryptanalytic intent*. The child "must grasp that there is a system of correspondences to be mastered" (p. 51). Unlike the first stage, where the child naturally (and subconsciously) associates a spoken word with some particularly salient visual cue in the corresponding written word, the cipher stage is not natural. Rather, it is characterized by fully analytic processing that requires an explicit and conscious awareness of the relationship that exists between alphabetic shapes and phonological segments. According to this view, then, reading skill is not picked up simply through exposure to print but almost always requires extensive adult intervention to promote the development of analytic processing. A basic discontinuity in the acquisition of word recognition skill is therefore proposed.

Recent research has supported Gough and Hillinger's (1980) two-stage conceptualization of beginning reading. B. Byrne (1991, 1992) reported the results of a series of experiments demonstrating that prereaders are largely ignorant of phonological segments, adopting instead a nonanalytic strategy in which new words are learned by associating some distinguishing feature of the printed word with its spoken counterpart as a whole. Preschool children with no knowledge of reading or the sounds of individual letters could be taught to discriminate FAT from BAT but this did not enable them to discriminate FUN from BUN at a level above chance. Byrne concluded that the failure of prereaders to develop analytic links between print and speech results from the extension of the more natural nonanalytic strategy, a strategy that can, however, be altered by explicit instruction in phonemic segmentation and letter-phoneme relations (B. Byrne & Fielding-Barnsley, 1989).

Gough et al. (1992) described several studies providing further evidence of a visual cue reading stage in early reading acquisition. In one study, a group of prereaders were asked to learn to read four words presented on flashcards to a criterion of two successive trials. For each child, one of the four flashcards was deliberately marred by a thumbprint in the corner. During the test phase, when the children were shown a clean card bearing the word that had been accompanied by the thumbprint, less than half the children could identify the word. However, when shown a card bearing only the thumbprint, almost all the children produced the word that had accompanied the thumbprint during training. As a further test, the children were shown a thumbprinted card containing a word different from the one that had originally accompanied the thumbprint. Almost all children produced the word that accompanied the thumbprint during training, a finding consistent with the claim that children initially rely on salient visual cues to acquire print-meaning associations.

A study by Masonheimer, Drum, and Ehri (1984) indicated that, in contrast to the views of Goodman and others, environmental print experiences alone do not enable children to advance to the cipher stage of beginning reading; that is, later stages of beginning reading are not *continuous extensions* of the kind of spontaneous word learning that results from exposure to environmental print. Masonheimer and colleagues selected 102 preschoolers 3 to 5 years old who were environmental print "experts." These were children who could identify at least 8 out of 10 photographs of commonly occurring environmental labels (Pepsi label on a bottle, McDonald's sign on a restaurant, etc.). The children were then given a reading test containing high-frequency beginning-level words. The researchers reasoned that "if environmental print experiences lead to gradual decontextualisation of graphic cues, then the scores of our 'experts' on the word-reading task ought to be distributed normally" (Ehri, 1991, p. 61). However, in contrast to this prediction, a bimodal distribution was observed. Most of the children ($n = 96$) could read few if any words, whereas a few children ($n = 6$) could read most or all of the words. Masonheimer and colleagues also found that the 96 prereaders could correctly identify the environmental labels only when they were accompanied by contexts and logos, not when presented in isolation. Moreover, the prereaders were unable to detect spelling errors in environmental print (e.g., Pepsi misspelled Xepsi), even when they were asked whether there was something wrong or strange about the print. In contrast, the six readers encountered no difficulty in reading the labels with or without contexts, and spontaneously noticed letter alterations in labels. These children were reading the print, as opposed to "reading the environment." On the basis of their findings, Masonheimer and colleagues concluded that learning to read is not a "natural" process that occurs simply through exposure to print.

PHONOLOGICAL RECODING SKILL

To advance to the cipher stage of early reading acquisition, the child must come to realize that there are systematic correspondences between the 26 letters of the English alphabet and the 44 phonemes of the English phonological system. Cipher knowledge, or phonological recoding skill, may be defined as the ability to translate letters and letter patterns into phonological forms. When confronted with an unfamiliar word, beginning readers who possess such knowledge are able to convert the graphemic representation of the word (which is a coding of its sequence of letters) into a phonological representation (which is a coding of its corresponding string of phonemes based on the word's sequence of letters) that is then used to gain access to the meaning of the word as represented in the appropriate entry in the mental lexicon (which has already been organized by phonological codes through the process of language acquisition). The process of converting a graphemic representation of a word into its corresponding phonological representation may involve sequentially converting graphemic units into phonemes (a process that may be subject to position-specific constraints and "marker" letters), analogizing to known words that are stored in lexical memory (a process that may involve the subsyllabic units of onset and rime, which are easier to segment than phonemic units), or, most likely, some combination of these two processes (Ehri & Robbins, 1992).

As noted earlier, although beginning readers quickly learn to recognize dozens of words through selective association, this natural strategy eventually breaks down because it becomes increasingly difficult to find a unique cue that distinguishes each new word. Beginning readers of alphabetic writing systems must eventually engage in the explicit use of the systematic correspondences between elements of written and spoken language to be able to identify unfamiliar words (including irregularly spelled ones) and to gain the practice required for developing speed and automaticity in recognizing familiar words in text (Adams, 1990; Gough & Hillinger, 1980; Jorm & Share, 1983). The development of automatic (i.e., implicit) word recognition processes (possibly by means of a connectionist system; Seidenberg, 1992) in turn frees up cognitive resources for allocation to higher order cognitive functions, such as comprehension monitoring and determining the meanings of unknown words.

Research indicates that children who continue to rely on selective association and contextual cues at the expense of phonological information will encounter severe difficulties in learning to read (Snowling, 1987). The reason that the ability to use phonological information is so critical is that sublexical analyses involving phonological information result in positive learning trials (i.e., correct word identifications), which in turn lead to the amalgamation of orthographic and phonological representations in semantic memory (Ehri, 1992). These amalgamated representations provide the basis for rapid and efficient access to the mental lexicon. Children who use ineffective or inappropriate word identification strategies (such as relying on sentence context and initial letters to guess words) will experience progressive deterioration in the rate of reading development as they grow older (Bruck, 1992; B. Byrne, Freebody, & Gates, 1992). Because there is little interaction between orthographic and phonological codes in the word processing of poor readers who rely on compensatory strategies, the development of awareness of individual phonemes and knowledge of correspondences between graphemes and phonemes is not promoted. Consequently, the word recognition skills of these children remain relatively weak because they do not develop links between orthographic and phonological representations in semantic memory.

Gough and Juel (1991) noted that although we do not know the exact mechanism by which the cipher operates, "we do know how to measure it: the child's mastery of the cipher is directly reflected in his ability to pronounce pseudowords" (p. 51). Pseudowords are synthetic words that conform to the rules of English orthography (e.g., *toin*, *sark*, *nep*). Because pseudowords have not been seen before, it would be impossible to pronounce pseudowords without knowledge of the connections between graphemes in spellings and phonemes in pronunciations. Adams (1990) claimed that "the best differentiator between good and poor readers is…their knowledge of spelling patterns and their proficiency with spelling-sound translations" (p. 290). In support of this claim is research indicating that naming pseudowords is one of the tasks that most clearly differentiates good from poor comprehenders of text, especially in the beginning stages of learning to read (Hoover & Gough, 1990; Juel, 1988; Juel, Griffith, & Gough, 1986; Stanovich, Cunningham, & Feeman, 1984; Tunmer, 1989; Tunmer, Herriman, & Nesdale,

1988; Tunmer & Nesdale, 1985; Vellutino & Scanlon, 1987; Vellutino, Scanlon, Small, & Tanzman, 1991; Vellutino, Scanlon, & Tanzman, 1991).

A common response to the suggestion that beginning readers must acquire phonological recoding skill is that written English contains so many irregularities that such an effort would not only waste valuable time but possibly even confuse children and impede progress (e.g., F. Smith, 1978). But what is the evidence? Gough and Hillinger (1980) argued that because no word in English is spelled completely arbitrarily, even irregular words provide some accurate phonological cues to the word's identity. One can easily imagine how difficult it would be to learn to read if spoken words like *stomach* were represented as random sequences of letters (e.g., *xbquvnt*) rather than as irregular spellings. When beginning readers with knowledge of grapheme–phoneme correspondences apply their knowledge to unfamiliar irregular words, the result will often be close enough to the correct phonological form that the word can be correctly identified (provided, of course, that the word is in the child's *listening* vocabulary).

A recent study by Gough and Walsh (1991) provides support for the claim that knowledge of grapheme–phoneme correspondences is essential for acquiring word-specific knowledge. They found the standard positive correlation between pseudoword naming and exception word naming in beginning readers ($r = .66$), but on closer examination of their data they discovered that this relationship was of a particular nature. A scatterplot revealed that there were many children who performed reasonably well on the pseudoword-naming test but recognized few exception words. However, there were no children who performed poorly on the pseudoword-naming test and well on the exception word-naming test. These results suggest that phonological recoding ability (as measured by pseudoword naming) is necessary but not sufficient for the development of word-specific knowledge. Consistent with this interpretation, Gough and Walsh also found that beginning readers with higher levels of phonological recoding skill required fewer trials to learn unfamiliar exception words than did children with lower levels of phonological recoding ability. Gough and Walsh concluded from these results that "word-specific information does not reside in a mechanism separate and apart from the cipher, but instead is accumulated on top of the cipher, and cannot be otherwise acquired" (p. 15).

Gough and Hillinger (1980) also suggested that beginning readers may combine knowledge of the constraints of sentence context with the available grapho-phonemic information to identify unfamiliar irregular words and thus increase their word-specific knowledge. In the next section we argue that the use of such a strategy requires explicit processes. To test this hypothesis we recently carried out two experiments (Tunmer & J. Chapman, 1993). In the first experiment, which involved a listening-only task, beginning readers were introduced to a hand-held puppet named Peter. The children were told that when Peter tried to say a word, he said it the "wrong way." The child's task was to attempt to figure out what word Peter was trying to say. The "words" presented to the children were all formed from the regular pronunciations of irregular words. For example, the word *stomach* was pronounced by Peter as *stow-match*. The children were presented with 80 regularized pronunciations (derived from words of varying frequency) and managed to figure out many of them (about 25% on average). More important, when these same mispronounced words were presented in context in another test session, the children performed much better (about 75% on average). For example, when Peter said, "The football hit him in the *stow-match*," most children immediately said that Peter was trying to say the word *stomach*. Note that the context we used in the task was deliberately underdetermining. When presented as an oral cloze task to a separate sample of children, very few of the children said that the missing word was *stomach*. The experiment clearly demonstrates that the graphophonemic information contained in irregularly spelled words can be very useful, especially when it is combined with sentence context cues.

In the second experiment, beginning readers were asked to read aloud 80 irregular words, first in isolation and then, on another occasion, in context (the words and contexts were the same as those used in the first experiment). For example, words like *stomach* were first presented in a list of words. In a second session, *stomach* was presented again, but this time it appeared in context: *The football hit him in the stomach*. The children were asked to read along silently as the experimenter read aloud the prior sentence context. When the target word was reached, the experimenter pointed to the word and asked the child to read it aloud. As in the previous experiment, all contexts were underdetermining (which linguistic research indicates is the more naturally occurring situation; as noted earlier, the average predictability of content words in running text is about 0.10). To assess their phonological recoding ability, the children were also given a pseudoword-naming test.

For each child, a "context facilitation" score was computed by subtracting the number of words read in isolation from the number of words read in context. Overall, the results indicated that the accuracy of recognizing irregular words improved with context, a finding consistent with earlier studies (Adams & Huggins, 1985). A more interesting finding, however, was obtained when we divided the children into three groups according to their performance on the pseudoword-naming test: poor recoders, emerging recoders, and good recoders. The isolated words scores and context facilitation scores of the poor recoders were very low, suggesting that if beginning readers are unable to take advantage of the graphophonemic information provided in irregular words, context will be of little or no benefit to them. The context facilitation scores of the good recoders were also low, but this was because their ability to read words in isolation was so high. Consistent with this finding is an enormous amount of research reported during the past 20 years indicating that better readers rely less on context to identify difficult words because of their superior word recognition skills (Stanovich, 1986).

Interestingly, the children classified as having moderate or emerging phonological recoding skills had the highest context facilitation scores. The ability of these children to take advantage of the available graphophonemic cues in irregular words was not sufficiently advanced that they could identify many of the words in isolation. However, when the words appeared in context the performance of these children improved considerably. These results suggest that beginning readers of moderate phonological recoding ability can combine knowledge of the constraints of sentence context with incomplete graphophonemic information to identify unfamiliar words, and thus increase both their word-specific knowledge and their knowledge of grapheme–phoneme correspondences. Increased knowledge of the latter would help beginning readers to become even more proficient in identifying unfamiliar words.

To explore this issue further, we identified a subgroup of children who performed poorly on a common subset of the irregular words when the words were presented in isolation (not surprisingly, these were more difficult words of lower frequency). We then divided these children into two groups (high vs. low) according to their performance on the pseudoword-naming test and compared their performance on the same subset of irregular words when the words were presented in context. As predicted, the children of higher phonological recoding ability outperformed the children of lower phonological recoding ability. In summary, language prediction skills may be useful in acquiring word recognition ability, but only if they are applied to the problem of breaking the orthographic code. Exclusive reliance on contextual guessing to identify unfamiliar words will not result in progress (Tunmer & Hoover, 1992).

Consistent with these findings are the results of a study by M. Evans and Carr (1985) that compared the effects of two instructional approaches (decoding oriented vs. language experience oriented) on beginning reading development. They found that the use of context to make predictions was positively correlated with reading achievement but only in the group that had received instruction in decoding skills. Evans and Carr concluded from their findings that "a focus on predictive context utilisation 'worked' in the [decoding-oriented] classrooms because it was combined with print-specific skills taught through word analysis activities, but did not work in the [language experience-oriented] classrooms because the children had few resources for dealing with unfamiliar words" (pp. 343–344).

METALINGUISTIC OPERATIONS

According to the model proposed by Gough and Hillinger (1980), learning to read requires the development of explicit awareness and knowledge of the systematic correspondences between graphemes and phonemes. The question that can now be asked is what cognitive prerequisite skills are necessary to acquire phonological recoding skills. We hypothesize that the development of phonological recoding ability depends crucially on two types of *metalinguistic ability*, where metalinguistic ability (or awareness) is defined as the ability to reflect on and manipulate the structural features of spoken language (Tunmer & Hoover, 1992, in press). To discover correspondences between graphemes and phonemes requires the ability to decompose spoken words into their constituent phonemic elements (called *phonological awareness*), and to use sentence context cues as a backup mechanism to confirm hypotheses about what the word might be (and thus increase knowledge of grapheme-phoneme correspondences) requires sensitivity to the semantic and syntactic constraints of sentence context (called *syntactic awareness*). We further propose that both skills require explicit processes not unlike those required for the development of cryptanalytic intent as proposed in the Gough and Hillinger (1980) model.

Metalinguistic operations differ from normal language operations in the type of cognitive processing that is required. Normal language processing is modular in nature, involving component operations that are fast, automatic, and largely sealed off from conscious inspection. In contrast, metalinguistic operations require controlled (i.e., explicit) processing, which entails an element of choice in whether or not the operations are performed, as well as relative slowness and deliberateness in the application of such operations. When comprehending or producing an utterance, language users are normally unaware of the individual phonemes and words comprising the utterance and the grouping relationships among the utterance's constituent words unless they deliberately reflect on the structural features of the utterance.

The relationship between normal language processing and metalinguistic operations can be expressed in terms of a model of sentence comprehension that specifies a set of interacting processors in which the output of each becomes the input to the next (Tunmer & Hoover, 1992, in press). This model provides the basis for a definition of metalinguistic operations in information-processing terms as the use of controlled processing to perform mental operations on the products (i.e., the phonemes, words, sentences, and sets of interrelated propositions) of the modular subsystems involved in sentence comprehension. The model also provides the basis for classifying the various manifestations of metalinguistic awareness into four broad categories: phonological, word, syntactic, and pragmatic (or discourse) awareness. Thus, *phonological awareness* refers to the ability to perform mental operations on the output of the speech perception mechanism, and *syntactic awareness* refers to the ability to perform mental operations on the output of the mechanism responsible for assigning intrasentential structural representations to groups of words.

Research indicates that metalinguistic ability is a distinct kind of linguistic functioning that develops separately from and later than basic speaking and listening skills; the ability to perform metalinguistic operations does not come free with the acquisition of language. Rather, metalinguistic ability begins to emerge somewhat later, when children are around 4 to 6 years of age (see Tunmer, Pratt, &

Herriman, 1984, for reviews of research on the development of metalinguistic abilities in children). Research further indicates that metalinguistic development is related to a more general change in information-processing capability that occurs during the early stages of middle childhood, namely, the development of metacognitive control over the information-processing system. The results of several studies suggest that during this period children become increasingly aware of how they can control their intellectual processes in a wide range of situations and tasks, including those requiring metalinguistic operations.

This linkage of metalinguistic development to metacognitive development provides an explanation for what at first seems rather puzzling; namely, that many 5- and 6-year-old children who appear to possess normal language comprehension and speaking abilities are nevertheless unable to perform simple metalinguistic operations such as segmenting familiar spoken words into their constituent phonemes, or correcting word-order violations in simple sentence structures. The important distinction is that *using* (implicit) knowledge of the grammatical rules of spoken language to construct and comprehend meaningful utterances, which is done intuitively and at a subconscious level, is not the same as the *metalinguistic* act of deliberately performing mental operations *on* the products of the mental operations involved in comprehending and producing utterances.

Phonological Awareness

Beginning readers must be able to analyze the internal structure of spoken words to discover how phonemes are related to graphemes. However, many school-age children find it extraordinarily difficult to reflect on and manipulate the phonemic segments of speech. This may seem surprising because even very young children are capable of discriminating between speech sounds and using phonemic contrasts to signal meaning differences. The important distinction, however, is that using a phonemic contrast to signal a meaning difference involves *implicit* processes, whereas the (metalinguistic) act of realizing that the relevant difference is a phonemic difference requires *explicit* processes. Consciously reflecting on phonemic segments is much more difficult for children because there is no simple physical basis for recognizing phonemes in speech. It is not possible to segment a speech signal such that each segment corresponds to one and only one phoneme (A.M. Liberman, F.S. Cooper, Shankweiler, & Studdert-Kennedy, 1967). Rather, the information necessary for identifying a particular phoneme often overlaps with that of another phoneme.

The research on speech perception may help explain why many beginning readers fail to benefit from either letter-name knowledge or letter-sound knowledge in learning to recognize words. Because there is no one-to-one correspondence between phonemes and segments of the acoustic signal, it is not possible to pronounce in isolation the sound corresponding to most phonemes. Consequently, the strategy of simply "sounding out" a word like *drag* will result in *duh-ruh-ah-*

guh, a nonsense word comprising four syllables (I. Liberman & Shankweiler, 1985). Letter sounds and letter names are only imprecise physical analogues of the phonemes in spoken words. Whether children learn to associate the sound "duh" or the name "dee" or both with the letter *d*, they must still be able to segment the sound or name to make the connection between the letter *d* and the phoneme /d/. In short, beginning readers must acquire phonemic segmentation ability.

On logical grounds alone it would appear that at least some minimal level of explicit phonological awareness is necessary for children to be able to discover the systematic correspondences between graphemes and phonemes. Several studies provide support for the claim that phonological awareness is required to break the orthographic code. This research shows (a) that measures of children's phonological awareness taken before they begin formal reading instruction predict their later reading achievement even when those showing any preschool reading ability are excluded, (b) that phonological awareness influences reading comprehension indirectly through phonological recoding ability, (c) that the more successful readers in strictly whole-word reading programs are the children who score higher on tests of phonological awareness, and (d) that training in phonological awareness during or before reading instruction produces significant experimental group advantages in reading achievement (see Tunmer & Rohl, 1991, for a review of research).

Evidence that some minimal level of explicit phonological awareness is necessary for acquiring knowledge of grapheme–phoneme correspondences comes from studies that have generated scatterplots of the relationship between phonological awareness and pseudoword naming (Juel et al., 1986; Tunmer, 1989; Tunmer & Nesdale, 1985). The scatterplots have shown that, although many children performed well on phoneme segmentation and poorly on pseudoword naming, no children performed poorly on phoneme segmentation and well on pseudoword naming. Explicit phonological awareness appears to be necessary but not sufficient for acquiring phonological recoding skill.

Syntactic Awareness

When confronted with an unfamiliar word, syntactically aware children who are in the process of acquiring phonological recoding skill are able to combine knowledge of the constraints of sentence context with incomplete graphophonemic information to identify the word, and thus increase their knowledge of grapheme–phoneme correspondences. The ability to reflect on the structural features, both semantic and syntactic, of sentences may also help beginning readers discover *homographic* spelling patterns (letter sequences that have different pronunciations in different words; e.g., *ough*, as in *cough*, *rough*, and *dough*). When attempting to identify an unfamiliar word containing a homographic spelling pattern, beginning readers who have acquired knowledge of such patterns can generate alternative pronunciations until one matches a word in their listening vocabulary. Children who have yet to acquire this knowledge and are poor at using sentence-context cues to discover polyphonic letter sequences may be restricted to pronouncing *flown* like *clown* or *clear* like *bear* and obtain misleading learning trials as a result.

In support of these claims are several studies reporting positive correlations between syntactic awareness (or grammatical sensitivity) and context-free word recognition and/or phonological recoding (see Tunmer & Hoover, in press, for a review of research). Research further indicates that syntactic awareness typically correlates more strongly with context-free word recognition than with reading comprehension. And when measures of both word recognition and phonological recoding are included in a study, syntactic awareness usually correlates more highly with phonological recoding. Siegel and Ryan (1988), for example, found that each of three measures of syntactic awareness correlated more strongly with phonological recoding (as measured by pseudoword naming) than with real-word recognition.

Although syntactic awareness is clearly related to phonological recoding skill, it must be demonstrated that syntactic awareness makes an *independent* contribution to phonological recoding skill when phonological awareness is included in the analysis. It is possible that syntactic awareness is related to phonological recoding simply because syntactic awareness, like phonological awareness, is a metalinguistic ability and therefore shares in common with phonological awareness many of the same component skills (invoking control processing, performing mental operations on the structural features of language, etc.). However, if syntactic awareness facilitates the development of phonological recoding skill by enabling children to use context to identify unfamiliar words which, in turn, increases their knowledge of grapheme–phoneme correspondences and homographic spelling patterns, then syntactic awareness should make a contribution to the development of phonological recoding skill that is distinct from that made by phonological awareness. A further hypothesis is that syntactic awareness, unlike phonological awareness, also influences the development of comprehension skills by facilitating the development of comprehension monitoring. Syntactically aware children may be better able to check that their responses to the words of the text conform to the surrounding grammatical context, and to make intelligent guesses about the meanings of unfamiliar words in written or spoken discourse.

Support for these claims comes from path analytic studies showing that phonological and syntactic awareness in beginning readers each makes an independent and approximately equal contribution to phonological recoding, that both influence reading comprehension indirectly through phonological recoding, and that syntactic awareness also makes an independent contribution to the development of listening comprehension (Tunmer, 1989; Tunmer et al., 1988). Research further indicates that syntactic awareness is necessary but not sufficient for acquiring phonological recoding skills; that syntactic awareness predicts later reading achievement even when the effects of verbal intelligence, general cognitive ability, and phonological awareness are controlled; and that training in syntactic awareness transfers positively to reading achievement (see Tunmer & Hoover, 1992, in press).

CONCLUDING REMARKS

In this chapter we examined implicit and explicit processes in reading acquisition. We began the chapter by describing two general views of how children learn to read. According to the first view, implicit processes are primarily involved. Reading ability is thought to evolve naturally and spontaneously in much the same way that oral language develops (K.S. Goodman & Y.M. Goodman, 1979). According to the second view, children move through two stages in acquiring reading skills (Gough & Hillinger, 1980). The first stage involves primarily implicit processes, whereas the second involves primarily explicit processes. It is claimed that during the first stage children naturally (and subconsciously) associate a spoken word with some particularly salient visual cue in the corresponding written word. However, movement into the next stage requires explicit and conscious awareness of the relationship that exists between alphabetic shapes and phonological segments. Arguments and evidence were presented in support of this two-stage conceptualization of beginning reading.

This led to a discussion of phonological recoding skill, which we defined as the ability to translate letters and letter patterns into phonological forms. It was argued that beginning readers must acquire phonological recoding skill to be able to identify unfamiliar words and to gain the practice required for developing speed and automaticity in recognising words in text. We then presented evidence indicating that phonological recoding skill is essential for acquiring word-specific knowledge, and that the ability to use sentence context cues may also be useful in acquiring word recognition ability, but only when combined with phonological recoding skills. In the final section of the chapter we described research indicating that the development of phonological recoding skill depends crucially on two types of metalinguistic ability, phonological awareness and syntactic awareness, both of which require explicit processes.

IV

SYNTHESIS

22

IMPLICIT LEARNING AND MEMORY: SCIENCE, FICTION, AND A PROSPECTUS

Stephan Lewandowsky
University of Western Australia

During the 1950s, when technology was uncritically accepted by most to be the guarantor of unlimited future economic growth, the experts' predictions about the success of nuclear power were particularly enthusiastic. It was said that energy was going to be so abundant and its generation so easy, efficient, and cheap, that consumers would, at worst, be charged a flat fee to cover the cost of the infrastructure necessary to transmit power from the plant to the home (D.A. Norman, 1993).

This chapter, too, attempts to speculate about the future, in this case of research in several areas of implicit cognition. Unlike forecasts by early nuclear aficionados, the predictions here are stated not in the belief that they will turn out to be accurate, but in the hope of stimulating some debate about which approach the field should follow. Toward this end, the chapter first selectively reviews the field to assess its viability, followed by an examination of the circumstances that are likely to shape future research. A synthesis of these examinations is attempted in two final sections that provide prolegomena to a theory of implicit cognition and foreshadow a new paradigm for theorizing and experimentation.

THE VIABILITY OF IMPLICIT COGNITION

Failed Paradigms: The Verbal Learning Precedent

Ideas and paradigms sometimes fail so thoroughly that they virtually cease to exist. In psychology, one memorable case concerns the doctrine of behaviorism, whose attempts to explain human performance and language collapsed under its own emptiness without leaving much of a discernible trace.

The cognitive branch of behaviorism, the verbal learning paradigm, started out as a well-ordered empirical domain in which simple but elegant experiments established functions and transfer surfaces describing human learning and interference. The empirical cohesion was paralleled in the theoretical domain by the straightforward simplicity and sufficiency of interference theory. This period culminated in a landmark article by Postman (1961) that revealed—and revelled in—a rare harmony between data and theory (see Crowder, 1976, p. 261, for a brief review). Alas, a mere 15 years later, verbal learning was characterized by a large but confused empirical database that was no longer interpretable within the impoverished interference framework. This terminal stage was reflected in a chapter by Postman (1976), in which he noted that "one cannot help wonder why after so many years of patient experimental effort interference theory today finds itself entangled in so many empirical inconsistencies and theoretical complications" (p. 179).

In line with Kuhn's (1962) now widely accepted view of scientific paradigm shifts, these inconsistencies were resolved not within the verbal learning paradigm but required the emergence of a revolutionary new paradigm, in this case the contemporary cognitive approach. To cite two specific examples, the absence of any interaction between lists learned in the laboratory and previous natural-language "habits" is now easily accommodated by the distinction between episodic and semantic memory (Tulving, 1983). Second, the dramatically reduced extent of interference when memory is tested by recognition is now easily explained by cue-dependent forgetting models (e.g., SAM; Raaijmakers & Shiffrin, 1981).

Critically, on Kuhn's (1962) view, competing paradigms have their own unique ways of organizing questions and reporting data. In consequence, they are incommensurable and the competing practitioners cannot productively communicate with each other. Accordingly, adherents of verbal learning could only note the difficulties for the current paradigm (Postman, 1976), but their resolution had to come from elsewhere. It follows that speculations about the future of implicit cognition must involve two stages: First, the prevailing paradigm and its "theory" must be identified and its current state assessed. The second, far more speculative stage, involves the attempt to foreshadow the future, either by extrapolating within the current paradigm or by attempting to anticipate what that future, as yet invisible, paradigm might look like.

The State of the Prevailing Paradigm

The Prevailing Paradigm

By definition, implicit cognition stands in contrast to explicit forms of processing. The "prevailing paradigm" is therefore necessarily built on a network of consistent empirical dissociations between implicit and explicit cognition. Relevant theories acknowledge and explain two fundamentally different manifestations of cognition, one of which entails the lack of awareness, on the part of the subject, that performance is affected by exposure to the critical stimulus.

The contributions to this volume illustrate the extent and scope of the implicit cognition paradigm, which has grown far too large for analysis in a single chapter. In consequence, the present discussion excludes topics such as subliminal activation and selective attention (e.g., Greenwald, 1992), which do not involve a memorial component between stimulus and response. Instead, discussion focuses on the memorial aspects of implicit cognition, schematically shown in Fig. 22.1, with primary emphasis on the classic implicit learning and implicit memory domains. Thus, the presumed state of "awareness" in the figure refers not to conscious registration of the *presence* of the stimulus, but rather conscious analysis of its functional role as something to be learned or to be recollected. These putative states of awareness are supported by a set of dissociations between implicit and explicit manifestations of learning and memory that, at first glance, appear robust and convincing.

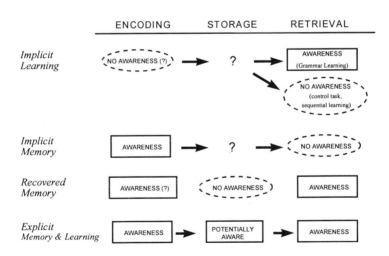

FIG. 22.1. Simplified overview of the principal domains of implicit cognition. Awareness refers to a "traditional" view of subject's conscious understanding of the functional role of the stimulus which, in the case of implicit learning, may no longer be valid. See text for further explanation.

For implicit memory, a long-standing characteristic attribute has been its apparent resistance to levels of processing manipulations (e.g., Jacoby & Dallas, 1981) combined with its sensitivity to changes in the surface characteristics of the stimulus (e.g., Kirsner et al., 1983). For implicit learning, one defining characteristic has been that task performance increases in the absence of verbalizable knowledge and, often, lack of awareness of what is learned (for a review see, Reber, 1989a). The opposite holds true for the explicit counterpart of both paradigms: Memory is typically more a function of levels of processing than of surface features, and learning is typically almost synonymous with verbalizable knowledge.

Hence, serious difficulties for the prevailing paradigm would arise in any way that waters down the distinction between implicit cognition and other forms of processing. Most troubling would be experiments in which variables previously thought to dissociate implicit and explicit phenomena were eventually found to have comparable effects on both measures: Implicit cognition would simply cease to exist if it were no longer convincingly different from traditional explicit processing. Less noticeable but more insidious trouble would arise if existing logic and methodology were to be called in question: After all, empirical dissociations can only be informative if their interpretation is beyond dispute. Finally, difficulties would also arise if implicit cognition were found to be empirically incoherent or fragmented: A paradigm that escapes summary by elegant theories may enter a period of Kuhnian crisis even though its basic premise—that it differs from explicit cognition—might still be supported. These potential sources of difficulty are now taken up in turn.

Troubling Empirical Inconsistencies

There is no reason to expect that *all* possible variables would dissociate implicit and explicit modes of cognition. Indeed, variables with parallel effects on implicit and explicit cognition have been catalogued previously (e.g., Lewandowsky & J.V. Bainbridge, 1994) without imperiling the paradigm. That said, the impact of parallel effects would be more serious if they involved experimental variables previously thought to dissociate implicit and explicit performance. Such troubling parallelisms have recently emerged: In implicit memory, there is growing evidence of a sensitivity toward levels-of-processing manipulations, and in implicit learning performance has been repeatedly shown to be correlated with verbal knowledge.

Parallelisms in Implicit Learning.   Sanderson (1989) conducted a particularly thorough examination of the conditions under which task performance is associated with verbalizable knowledge. She found that when given enough training, subjects were able to extract a correct verbal mental model in an implicit learning situation, provided that the task was sufficiently difficult to discourage trial-and-error strategies (Sanderson, 1989, Experiment 1). This verbal knowledge emerged in the absence of verbal training and without subjects verbalizing during task performance, previously thought necessary to associate implicit and explicit performance (Berry & D.E. Broadbent, 1984). Sanderson furthermore showed how subjects' explicit mental model changed during the course of training, from a collection of preconceived notions about the experimental task (a simulation of a simplified public transport system) to an abstraction of the relationship between the simulation variables. Putting Sanderson's results into the context of Fig. 22.1, it appeared that subjects can be aware of what it is they are learning throughout training and testing.

Several more recent articles have expanded on the theme in Sanderson's (1989) work. Berry and D.E. Broadbent (1995), after thorough examination of empirical dissociations, concluded that recent studies "...provide evidence suggesting that the dissociation may not be as great as was originally thought" (p. 132). This revised view was mandated by two replicable findings: First, even without any explicit instructions about a task, people often develop verbalizable knowledge after sufficient exposure, similar to Sanderson's (1989) results. These findings extend to serial response paradigms where improved performance for detection of serially presented four-choice stimuli had often been taken to be a particularly pure measure of implicit learning. A reevaluation of this task by Perruchet and Amorim (1992; Perruchet & Gallego, 1993) revealed the presence of explicit knowledge whenever performance was found to improve.

Second, Berry and D.E. Broadbent (1995) concluded that secondary tasks often affect both modes of learning, contrary to the initial claim by Hayes and D.E. Broadbent (1988) that only explicit learning suffers from a reduction in cognitive resources. This is particularly relevant because the Hayes and Broadbent study has been cited as one of the few, if not the only, instance in which a variable was found to have opposing effects on implicit and explicit learning (Shanks & St. John, 1994).

Taken together, these recent studies thus go a long way toward supporting earlier doubts about implicit learning (e.g., Dulany, Carlson, & Dewey, 1984, 1985). The magnitude of that trend can be conveyed by a statistical survey of the 93 entries on implicit learning recorded in *Psychological Abstracts* since 1984. Among those, only 15 can be unambiguously classified as reporting novel differences between implicit and explicit learning, whereas 10 can be classified as reporting parallel effects. The remaining nearly 70 articles, to the extent that they can be classified on the basis of the abstract alone, presuppose the existence of implicit learning. The fact that the number of articles is nearly evenly divided between those maintaining and those denying the unique status of implicit learning, is supportive of the conclusions offered by Shanks and St. John (1994) after their particularly thorough examination of the field: On the one hand, whatever it is that has been called implicit learning is in fact unlikely to entail an absence of awareness, and is particularly unlikely to involve the abstract knowledge originally thought to be acquired by subjects (e.g., Reber, 1989a). On the other hand, it remains beyond dispute that the learning shown by subjects under implicit task conditions differs interestingly from performance under explicit instructions. In particular, it appears as though the former may be based on the retrieval from memory of previously encountered relevant precedents (Dienes & Fahey, 1995), whereas the latter may involve testing of tentative hypotheses about the task (E.E. Smith, Langston, & Nisbett, 1992). Emerging models that capture this distinction in processing are discussed later.

Parallelisms in Implicit Memory.   Turning from learning to memory, a re-evaluation of the implicit/explicit dichotomy seems to be underway there as well. Perhaps most important is a continuing reassessment of the effects of level of processing at study. Hamann (1990) was among the first to show that implicit memory can be measurably better following "deep" semantic encoding than following "shallow" encoding. Since then, two meta-analyses have supported and extended Hamann's results. Challis and Brodbeck (1992), in addition to reporting four experiments of their own, summarized results from 35 previous studies. All but 2 of those experiments reported a small and typically nonsignificant, but nonetheless consistently positive effect of semantic encoding in a variety of implicit memory tests. In another meta-analysis, A.S. Brown and D.B. Mitchell (1994) reviewed 166 outcomes from some 40 articles and found that in about 80% of all cases, implicit priming was greater following semantic than nonsemantic encoding. Although only a small set of these differences were significant when considered on their own, the overall pattern suggests that semantic processing can enhance priming, albeit minimally, in most varieties of implicit tests.

Similarly, there is now increasing evidence that self-generation of stimuli (e.g., generating an item in response to the cue "HOT-C____") can improve performance on implicit tests (e.g., Masson & C.M. MacLeod, 1992). This is again in contrast to earlier results showing that self-generation, at best, does not benefit performance on implicit tests (e.g., Jacoby, 1983). Other results that have arguably narrowed the gap between implicit and explicit memory include serial position effects in implicit stem completion (Gershberg & Shimamura, 1994; however, see B.M. Brooks, 1994), unanticipated effects of perceptual overlap between study and test items in explicit recognition (Snodgrass & Hirshman, 1994), and effects of massed repetitions on some implicit tests (Challis & Sidhu, 1993).

Overall, are these results as damaging to implicit memory as the earlier, more pessimistic conclusion concerning implicit learning? This issue can again be addressed by statistical argument. A survey of *Psychological Abstracts* reveals that some 400 articles and monographs have been published on implicit memory since 1984. It can be assumed, on the basis of previous literature reviews, that the majority of those studies reported *differences* between implicit and explicit processing. Assessed against that background, the relatively small number (ignoring the pervasive but tiny levels of processing effect) of troubling results discussed here are perhaps best interpreted as extreme samples from two truly different underlying distributions. Specifically, suppose that implicit and explicit memory differ from each other, each having associated with it a distribution of possible behavioral manifestations arising from manipulation of an experimental variable. If we furthermore suppose that experimental outcomes represent samples from those distributions, then it is a simple statistical fact that, as the total number of studies increases, extreme results, including those showing *no difference* between implicit and explicit memory, will become more likely (e.g., Paulos, 1988). Hence, the more research is being conducted on implicit memory, the more likely it is that studies will uncover previously unsuspected implicit/explicit parallelisms even if the two forms of memory are truly different. On balance, therefore, contrary to implicit learning, recent parallelisms between implicit and explicit memory represent too small a fraction of the total database to imperil the status of implicit memory as a distinct phenomenon worthy of continued study.

Logic and Methodologies

Over the years, several techniques have been introduced to differentiate implicit from explicit processing. Emphasis has been variously on stochastic independence between tasks (e.g., Tulving et al., 1982), functional dissociation (e.g., Warrington & Weiskrantz, 1974), reversed association (Dunn & Kirsner, 1988), and, more recently, process dissociation (e.g., Jacoby, 1991). Of those techniques, only functional dissociation has been applied to implicit learning, whereas the remainder have been confined to applications involving implicit memory.

The first three techniques have relied on comparing performance across two tasks, assumed to selectively involve implicit and explicit processing, with little reference to the subject's intentions and conscious strategies. This entails the risk of "contamination" of the ostensibly implicit task by unwanted explicit recollection. This fundamental risk seems to override other criticisms that have been leveled against the techniques (e.g., whether stochastic independence might be artifactual; Hintzman & Hartry, 1990; Shimamura, 1985; whether functional dissociation might arise from a single underlying process; Dunn & Kirsner, 1988; for a recent summary of criticisms see Ratcliff & McKoon, 1995). As a case in point, Schacter et al. (1989) showed that stem completion in the presence of contextual retrieval cues, previously thought to reflect implicit new associations, were in fact largely governed by explicit recollection. Only those subjects who reported awareness of the repetition of test items showed associative priming. In general, there can be no assurance for any experiment involving the standard independence or functional dissociation techniques that implicit retrieval might not be contaminated by explicit recollection. Likewise, explicit tasks may include an unanticipated implicit processing component. Together, these possible cross-contaminations cast the shadow of a doubt on much of the existing literature.[1]

Jacoby's (1991; Jacoby, Lindsay, & Toth, 1992) process dissociation procedure, in contrast, presumes the existence of contamination and relies on explicit memory retrieval to help identify implicit processing components. The technique combines

---

[1] Schacter et al. (1989) offered a retrieval intentionality criterion to deal with possible contaminations. The criterion states that implicit and explicit processes should be compared across tasks that use the exact same stimuli and retrieval cues and vary only retrieval instructions (e.g., Graf & G. Mandler, 1984). Reingold and Toth (in press) showed that this is insufficient to rule out contamination.

results from a condition in which explicit recall acts in concert with implicit retrieval and another condition in which explicit and implicit retrieval are put in opposition. In both conditions, subjects perform a test on which implicit memory may be manifest, but in the opposition condition responses must be eliminated from consideration when they are explicitly recognized as being from an initial study list, whereas in the in-concert condition, recalled items are to be included as valid retrievals. Thus, if the item "window" comes to mind when completing the stem "win___," and the subject is aware that "window" was previously studied, then the item is to be rejected in one condition but to be used as a completion in the other. Comparison of performance across the two conditions allows assessment of the net contribution of explicit recollection, defined as "...the difference between performance when one is trying to as compared with trying not to engage in some act" (Jacoby et al., 1993, p. 141). From that estimate of recollection, implicit retrieval components can be derived by simple algebra and without worry of contamination (e.g., Jacoby et al., 1993, p. 141). By implication, implicit memory retrieval in the absence of awareness (see the earlier Fig. 22.1) can be investigated with renewed confidence.

The attractiveness and intuitive appeal of the process dissociation method is obvious; in the present context, it is tempting to speculate that application of the method might identify explicit "contamination" as the cause of the small but persistent levels of processing effects in implicit memory discussed earlier (cf. A.S. Brown & Mitchell, 1994; Challis & Brodbeck, 1992). Indeed, Toth et al. (1994) showed that the implicit processing component in a stem completion task, as estimated by the process dissociation procedure, was not affected by a levels-of-processing manipulation. The recent literature contains numerous additional instances in which implicit task components were estimated by the process dissociation methodology (for a brief review, see Ratcliff, van Zandt, & McKoon, 1995).

However, contrary to its apparent simplicity, the methodology is not a theory-free tool that can reliably unravel the contributions of implicit and explicit retrieval. Instead, process dissociation relies on several strong assumptions (Jacoby, 1991), all of which have attracted much recent criticism: To cite but one example, process dissociation assumes that task performance reflects a mixture of implicit and explicit processing components that are assumed to be stochastically independent. Joordens and P.M. Merikle (1993) suggested it would be equally plausible to assume that there is redundancy between implicit and explicit task components, such that any explicit recollection necessarily subsumes operation of an implicit process. Joordens and Merikle showed that the two assumptions give rise to very different estimates of performance components for a given set of data (see also Curran & Hintzman, 1995).

Overall, there is sufficient evidence to suggest that the method should be used with some caution and should not be considered the panacea for implicit memory research (e.g., Buchner, Erdfelder, & Vaterrodt-Plünnecke, 1995; Graf & Komatsu, 1994; Komatsu, Graf, & Uttl, 1995; Ratcliff et al., 1995; Richardson-Klavehn & Gardiner, 1995; Richardson-Klavehn, Gardiner, & Java, 1994). Reingold and Toth (in press) pointed toward a more model-aware and circumspect use of process dissociation.

It thus appears that all existing techniques for differentiating between implicit and explicit cognition are subject to criticism: A pessimistic summary would state that functional dissociation, stochastic independence, and reversed association suffer from the overriding problem of contamination, and process dissociation is based on assumptions of questionable generality. The problems associated with the existing inductive techniques have contributed to the recent recognition that "...progress in this domain can best occur through the articulation of specific, falsifiable models" (McKoon & Ratcliff, 1995, p. 777).

The Status of Theories

Arguments in favor of computational models of cognition have been made repeatedly (e.g., Hintzman, 1991; Lewandowsky, 1993). Most relevant here is the fact that models permit a quantitative level of description, which stands in contrast to the prevailing lack of precision in theoretical and empirical discourse surrounding implicit cognition. For example, is a tiny level of processing effect in implicit memory tolerable or does it impugn the integrity of existing views? Why does a new dissociation mandate a new memory system? Or does it not?

Implicit Memory: Division Not Computation.   The field of implicit memory represents a case study of the adverse consequences resulting from the absence of computational theories.[2] The pair of traditional theoretical views, multiple memory systems and transfer appropriate processing, that has been dominating the field almost since its inception cannot be expected to guide us toward a more rigorous theoretical future.

Consider first the transfer-appropriate-procedures (TAP) view (e.g., Roediger, 1990b; Roediger & McDermott, 1993), which holds that implicit memory is the result of a reinstatement of the same type of cognitive processes that were used during encoding. Thus, because most traditional implicit memory tasks are primarily data-driven (e.g., perceptual identification, fragment completion), they are disrupted by changes in surface form but do not benefit from additional "deep" processing at study. Conversely, because most explicit tasks are primarily conceptually driven (e.g., free recall), they benefit from "deep" processing at study but are not affected by changes in surface form. Based on those assumptions, TAP predicts that tasks should be dissociated along the type-of-processing dimension (data-

---

[2]Existing computational models should not be ignored, but they are either too new (Phaf, Mul, & Wolters, 1994; Ratcliff & McKoon, 1996), too limited in scope (Rueckl, 1990), or too limited in application (Humphreys, Bain, & Burt, 1989; Humphreys, Bain, & Pike, 1989; Wiles & Humphreys, 1993) to have had much impact on the field.

driven vs. conceptual) rather than necessarily along the implicit/explicit dimension. That prediction has been repeatedly confirmed (e.g., Blaxton, 1989; Roediger, Srinivas, & Weldon, 1989; for a review see Roediger & McDermott, 1993). In addition, TAP handles many of the remaining dissociations between implicit and explicit memory tests (e.g., Roediger, 1990b, p. 1052; Rajaram & Roediger, 1993).

Paradoxically, those successes may in the long run do more damage to the paradigm than the failures of TAP: The idea of transfer appropriate processing was first postulated as an alternative explanation for the full range of (explicit) levels-of-processing phenomena (C.D. Morris, Bransford, & Franks, 1977). Thus, rather than being a view of implicit memory, TAP is best considered to be a transcendental framework for explaining storage and retrieval of *all* manifestations of memory (Crowder, 1993). It follows that implicit memory, as an independent paradigm, might actually thrive on the failures of TAP. Most consequential among those is TAP's inability to handle the selective effects of amnesia on explicit memory, in particular the fact that priming on conceptually driven implicit tasks remains preserved in most forms of amnesia (Roediger, 1990b).

The selective deficits observed in most forms of amnesia are naturally accommodated by the rival multiple-memory systems view (e.g., Schacter & Tulving, 1994). The view also handles the dissociations observed in normal subjects—indeed, it may accommodate those dissociations somewhat too easily: Critics have argued that the multiple systems view has failed to specify the characteristics of the relevant memory systems a priori, thus limiting its testability (Hintzman, 1984; McKoon, Ratcliff, & Dell, 1986). As a case in point, even proponents of the view sometimes resort to exclusion to describe a memory system: "Procedural memory refers to a system, or systems, concerned with learning and memory functions other than those supported by the other four major systems" (Schacter & Tulving, 1994, p. 27).

Given such loose definitions, it is indeed difficult to discern what the multiple memory systems view would predict, other than that some variables sometimes dissociate some memory measures. Moreover, again owing to the lack of a principled specification of their properties, the number of memory systems is potentially unlimited. Roediger (1990a) enumerated some 20 systems that had been identified to date and warned that any and all future empirical dissociations could be accommodated by the addition, if needed, of yet another memory system. Although more specific criteria for the postulation of a new memory system have since been proposed (Schacter & Tulving, 1994), the predictive power of an approach that emphasizes classification over testing (Tulving, 1986) must remain limited.

On balance, the continued attraction of the systems view derives mainly from its ability to accommodate elegantly the amnesic data, and the continued promise that the relevant neural substrates may eventually be identified. Toward this end, Schacter (1992b) proposed a new approach to understanding implicit memory that relies on an integration of cognitive and neuroscientific techniques. Specifically,

Schacter called for what he labeled cross-domain hypothesis generation and cross-domain hypothesis testing to constrain the interpretations of results from cognitive experiments. Thus, an empirical dissociation would suggest the presence of another memory system only if there is additional independent evidence, for example in the form of positron emission tomography (PET) scans or evidence from brain-damaged patients (Schacter, 1992b).

This approach is best illustrated by considering implicit memory for novel visual objects (e.g., L.A. Cooper, Schacter, Ballesteros, & C. Moore, 1992). Subjects study line drawings of fictitious three-dimensional objects and memory is later assessed either through a recognition test or an implicit object-verification test, in which subjects must decide, without explicit reference to the prior study, whether a briefly presented drawing is structurally possible and could exist in three-dimensional space. Previously presented items yield priming only if the stimulus is structurally possible—no priming is observed for structurally impossible objects, even in situations in which explicit recognition is particularly high.

Schacter (1992b) suggested that a separate perceptual subsystem—unable to encode structurally impossible objects and insulated from semantic processing—underlies the observed object priming. Most relevant in the present context is that this conclusion was suggested by several converging pieces of neuroscientific evidence (beyond the now routine observation that priming was preserved in amnesic patients; Schacter et al., 1991): First, single-cell recordings in subhuman species have identified the inferior temporal cortex (ITC) as playing a significant role in identifying the structure of objects; second, ITC response is known to be unaffected by changes in retinal size, just like object priming but unlike explicit recognition; third, mirror reversals are known not to affect ITC, again like object priming; and fourth, specific deficits of object processing can be identified (Schacter, 1992b; Schacter & L.A. Cooper, 1995). However, Schacter's interpretation has been subject to considerable empirical and theoretical challenge (e.g., McKoon & Ratcliff, 1995; Ratcliff & McKoon, 1995, in press), and an alternative interpretation has been offered that ascribes object priming to a bias to call *all* previously seen objects possible. On this view, priming is not observed for impossible objects because, for them, explicit memory counteracts the response bias (Ratcliff & McKoon, 1995).

How can that alternative explanation be reconciled with the neuropsychological results that seemed so supportive of Schacter's (1992b) memory systems interpretation in the first place? Ratcliff and McKoon (1995,[3] in press) point to the danger of circularity inherent in the use of amnesic data, stating that:

---

[3]Ratcliff and McKoon (1995) also suggested that the data concerning preserved priming in amnesia are more equivocal than commonly believed, a point elaborated by Ostergaard and Jernigan (1993). Concerning the apparent independence of priming and retinal size, Kosslyn and Intriligator (1992) discussed a possible alternative interpretation of another set of results originally thought to mandate a nonretinocentric structure or process.

Implicit memory is what is spared in amnesia; what is spared in amnesia is shown by performance on implicit tasks, and implicit tasks are those that tap implicit memory....If the relevant implicit system is preserved under amnesia, then the patients should perform as well as normal subjects. When the patients do not perform as well as normal subjects, it is said to be because the normal subjects used conscious recollection. Ironically, as the problems outlined here show, it is to avoid the circularity of explaining the data from amnesic patients that an account of the mechanisms of performance in implicit tasks is most urgently needed. (Ratcliff & McKoon, in press)

The issue of circularity is no doubt crucial, and it must give rise to concern about the state of theorizing present and future that the problem escaped mention in at least one recent article on neuropsychological methodology (Shimamura, 1993). It must also give rise to concern that circular appeals to explicit memory to explain superior priming in control subjects have been made quite casually and without mention of the issue (e.g., Moscovitch, Goshen-Gottstein, & Vriezen, 1994). A full discussion of the proper role of neuroscience is beyond the scope of this chapter; however, it is clear that Schacter's (1992b) proposed integration of cognitive and neuroscientific approaches is a step in the right direction. But, by itself, it is insufficient to eliminate concerns about circularity. To eliminate those fears additionally requires the use of computational models whose predictions are subject to rigorous test (cf. Kosslyn & Intriligator, 1992).

Briefly, computational models eliminate circularity by specifying precisely and a priori the conditions that give rise to a prediction, thus constraining reinterpretations upon availability of the data. This benefit of computational modeling is quite general and extends beyond the problematic use of cognitive neuroscience reasoning. To illustrate, consider a hypothetical computational model of transfer appropriate processing. By virtue of being computationally formalized, the model would necessarily specify the cognitive processes involved at study and whether or not they are being reinstated at test. Thus, for a given experimental condition, it would be unambiguously known which experimental outcome would support the model and which would not. By contrast, a verbally stated TAP view could simultaneously accommodate several mutually exclusive outcomes: An observed reduction in priming after some change in surface form, say, would be taken to indicate a mismatch of processing operations between study and test, as typically expected by TAP. However, persistence of priming under identical conditions could also be explained by assuming that the manipulation did not affect a feature relevant to processing (Schacter, 1992b).[4]

---

[4]In light of the earlier analysis by Ratcliff and McKoon (in press), it is interesting that Schacter (1992a) pointed to this apparent circularity in TAP to motivate and support his preferred cross-domain approach. In fairness to the TAP approach, it must be noted that operational definitions to control circularity were proposed by Roediger, Weldon, and Challis (1989).

Implicit Learning: Computational Models.   Unlike implicit memory re-search, which has benefited from a vigorous exchange with neuroscience, theorizing in implicit learning has been largely based on standard behavioral-cognitive data (however, see Berry & Dienes, 1993; Cleeremans, 1993; Grafton, Hazeltine, & Ivry, 1995; Knowlton & Squire, 1996). Accordingly, theorists have sought constraints not through cognitive deficits or other neurological results, but by formulating computa-tional models, thus giving rise to a very different set of strengths and weaknesses.

One of the first computational models of implicit learning was proposed by Servan-Schreiber and J.R. Anderson (1990) for the artificial grammar-learning task. The model, called *competitive chunking* (CC), was based on the assumption that people, when confronted with long, seemingly meaningless strings, will break them up into a hierarchical set of clusters. Owing to the redundancy built into a set of grammatical strings, chunks formed for grammatical strings will overlap and differ from those formed for nongrammatical strings. When simulating a decision process based on how much a test item could be chunked (with grammatical items yielding more compact percepts than nongrammatical strings), the model was found to capture close to 90% of the variance in the implicit learning performance of human subjects. A related model, developed by R.C. Mathews (e.g., 1991) relied on a series of condition-action pairs, called classifiers, that accumulate partial information in a message list, functionally akin to a working memory, on which a decision is based. The model successfully predicted performance in a grammar-learning task by original subjects who actively engaged in the task, as well as by other, yoked, participants who were only periodically instructed by the original subjects (R.C. Mathews et al., 1989).

A second approach to modeling formalizes the "look-up table" idea originally proposed by D.E. Broadbent et al. (1986). Models of that type (e.g., Dienes & Fahey, 1995) are based on the idea that people use previously encountered and successfully managed instances as the basis for their current actions. In support, Dienes and Fahey showed that a version of Logan's (1988b) instance theory of skill acquisition could quantitatively describe behavior in a simulated control task (e.g., the person interaction task of Hayes & Broadbent, 1988), in particular when there was no obvious rule to be induced.

The third class of models embraces the connectionist approach (e.g., Cleere-mans, 1993; Cleeremans & J.L. McClelland, 1991; Dienes, 1992) and has provided accounts of a variety of implicit learning tasks. Dienes compared several instance models against variants of connectionist networks and found that a suitable network provided the best quantitative account of performance in a grammar-learning task. Cleeremans and colleagues (Cleeremans, 1993; Cleeremans & J.L. McClelland, 1991) have focused primarily on sequential pattern acquisition, where subjects learn to anticipate the next stimulus in a complex and seemingly random sequence of choice reaction time trials.

Overall, it is clear that implicit learning enjoys a theoretically more advanced state than implicit memory. Models that account for 90% of the variance among subjects (Servan-Schreiber & J.R. Anderson, 1990) or predict the rank ordering of difficulty among individual items (Dienes, 1992) must be preferable to loose theorizing about putative memory systems, however attractive their potential neural correlates may appear. Moreover, these models also deal with vexing questions about how *implicit* implicit learning truly is. Earlier, the available data were interpreted as providing insufficient evidence that implicit learning takes place without awareness: The models replace the question of awareness with questions—and indeed some answers—concerning what exactly is learned and how it is acquired.

THE FUTURE OF IMPLICIT LEARNING AND MEMORY

Restating the conclusions concerning implicit learning within a Kuhnian framework, it appears that its defining feature—learning without awareness—has been eroded to the point where a completely new way of thinking about implicit learning may be imminent. For implicit memory, by contrast, the differentiation between implicit and explicit forms of retrieval does not (yet) appear to be threatened by empirical erosion. However, the popular methodologies are all troubled by some form of logical or diagnostic ambiguity, and there is a disquieting lack of cohesion among experimental findings.

Thus, the current state of implicit learning and memory suggests that predictions about the future should be pursued along two lines; one that extrapolates current research within the prevailing paradigm and one that attempts to anticipate the new postcrisis paradigm.

Between Science and Fiction:
Projections Within the Paradigm

Methodologies

Starting with foreseeable trends concerning implicit memory research, use of the process dissociation methodology will continue to spread because its appealing resolution of the contamination problem will outweigh the criticisms mounted against it. In consequence, because the technique enshrines the unaware status of implicit recollection, it will be the primary agent in extending the life span of the implicit memory paradigm.

Reverse association, proposed by Dunn and Kirsner (1988, 1989), will also receive the increased attention it deserves. Although widely cited, most authors have so far parenthetically referred to the technique without systematically applying it to the body of existing findings. As the creation of new empirical factoids becomes less attractive, attention will increasingly turn to meta-analyses, to the benefit of reverse association.

Another burgeoning line of research will extend the experiential approach (e.g., Gardiner & Java, 1993), which relies on subjects classifying their memory retrievals into those clearly recollected and those "known" to have been presented previously. The former judgments often correlate with explicit recollective processes, as inferred by traditional experimental means, whereas the latter often correspond to implicit retrievals. Experimental variables, such as study intentionality (Gardiner & Java, 1993) or picture superiority (Rajaram, 1996), often affect "remember" responses without altering "know" judgments, thus producing dissociations similar to those between explicit and implicit tasks. The principal difficulty of this approach, that it relies on subjective judgments that are critically dependent on instructions, also constitutes its greatest strength: Empirical and theoretical examination of subjective states of awareness must be a principal goal of cognitive science.

Turning to implicit learning, research there will produce few, if any, new dissociations. For a while, the field will focus on tasks that are maximally "implicit" in order to preserve the original dichotomy. Eventually, however, to bridge the conceptual gap between what used to be called implicit and what always has been explicit learning, emphasis will necessarily shift to the detailed nature and effects of experimental instructions. What do subjects extract from instructions? How does that in turn determine what is learned? It turns out that questions of this type have long been of interest to applied psychologists.

Applications and Real-World Constraints.   Much traditional research in implicit learning parallels long-standing activity in human engineering that explores operator behavior in supervisory industrial control. A common finding in the engineering literature is that operators who are given virtually no prior training sometimes reach levels of performance comparable to those achieved by explicitly trained subjects (N.M. Morris & Rouse, 1985). The parallel to implicit learning is obvious. In addition, when comparing levels of performance across modes of explicit training, it is often found that operators can handle even novel faults in a simulated industrial plant better after rule-based instruction than after theory-driven training (e.g., N.M. Morris & Rouse, 1985; Shepherd et al., 1977).

Although the extensive engineering literature has so far almost completely escaped citation by basic researchers, exceptions are beginning to appear. For example, Kirsner and Speelman (Kirsner & Speelman, 1996; Kirsner, Speelman, & Schofield, 1993) recently extended the power law of practice, a standard human engineering tool to describe skill acquisition, to examine and explain repetition-priming effects. Conversely, Sanderson (1989), a human factors psychologist, has a continuing interest in basic issues surrounding implicit cognition.

In an era of increasing cost-consciousness and emphasis on scientific accountability, further links between basic and applied research can be expected to emerge. Of particular interest will be specification of the exact factors determining when (explicit) verbal knowledge is associated with (potentially implicit) task performance and when it is not (e.g., Sanderson, 1989). Knowledge of these factors could help explain why the performance of experts is sometimes consistent with their verbal expertise, whereas on other occasions performance fails even though verbally stated expertise would dictate otherwise (e.g., Lewandowsky, Dunn, Kirsner, Randell, & W. Smith, 1995).

In implicit memory, one hotly debated question that can be expected to gain some currency in the intermediate future involves the recovery of previously repressed memories for traumatic events, most often sexual abuse (e.g., Loftus & Ketcham, 1994). Regardless of one's position on that issue, it is clear that no manifestation of human memory has ever captured the public's attention as much as the recent spate of recoveries of previously repressed memories of childhood sexual abuse. At present, there is no clear empirical connection between implicit memory and the recovery of repressed memories; however, the fact that lack of recollective awareness at some stage during a memorial process is common to both phenomena, as shown earlier in Fig. 22.1, invites the exploration of a theoretical link.

Prolegomenon to a Future Theory of Implicit Cognition.   Newell (1990) observed that it takes some 30 years for a psychological paradigm to mature from its infancy to its high point, with a recognizable unified theory being available by the end of that period. By that metric, arbitrarily choosing the articles by Warrington and Weiskrantz (1974) or Reber (1967) as the starting gate, implicit cognition is at most 8 years away from its high point, and in dire need of a recognizable unified theory. What might that theory look like?

A relevant precedent can be identified that, though limited in scope, may provide a pointer to the desired type of theory: J.L. McClelland, McNaughton, and O'Reilly (1995) presented a connectionist account of memory that integrated experimental and neuroscientific approaches within a computational framework. The model incorporated two anatomically separate structures: a hippocampal system dedicated to fast and immediate encoding and a neocortical system dedicated to permanent storage but restricted to very gradual and incremental learning. Information was seen to be gradually transferred from the hippocampal to the neocortical system by repeated reinstantiation, thus allowing the neocortical neural network to adjust its weights slowly, without new information creating undue interference.

The focus of J.L. McClelland et al.'s (1995) theory was on providing an account for various aspects of amnesia following hippocampal lesions, in particular the apparent extended consolidation period after encoding that is observed with delayed hippocampal lesions. Although limited in application and data fitting, McClelland et al.'s work anticipated the type of theory that is needed for implicit cognition in several ways: First, anatomical substrates were identified and linked to manifestations of neurological deficits, in particular amnesia. Second, empirical regularities in human memory, including the dissociation between implicit and explicit forms of remembering, were ascribed to those two putative memory systems. Third, and perhaps most important, the mathematical properties of connectionist networks were analyzed and independently used to justify the existence of two memory systems. Fourth, a computer simulation was used to verify, at a quantitative level, that the observed nuances of amnesia could indeed be the consequence of those two, now anatomically identifiable and computationally tractable, memory structures.

The work of J.L. McClelland et al. (1995) illustrates how several diverse approaches can be successfully integrated under a single umbrella. Their work provides a flavor of the type of theories we must be seeking. I predict that we will attain them by the end of the millennium, as the crowning achievement of the current paradigm. Immediately on their creation, those theories will be absorbed by the new paradigm.

Fiction: The New Paradigm

The new paradigm will encompass two principal components: First, it will do away with the dichotomy between implicit and explicit cognition that has been the hallmark of our current thinking. Second, it will reemphasize that the ultimate goal of cognitive science is to understand the human mind. Currently, this pursuit entails the use of statistical techniques that ignore individual minds in favor of an aggregate and somehow statistically "significant" construct. This will no longer be deemed acceptable in the forthcoming communication age with its plethora of individual choices and personalized service. The new paradigm in cognitive science will therefore focus on *individuals* rather than groups.

Models of Individuals. The study of individual cases has been a continuing theme throughout the history of psychology. However, what has been missing to date is a comprehensive prolonged examination of individuals in order to allow continued and precise predictions of each person's cognitive behavior across several novel situations. To achieve this, computational models of individuals must be constructed that are based on the set of common principles and criteria identified by the current paradigm—neurologically plausible computational models of implicit learning and memory among them—but that under the new paradigm will be adapted to accommodate each individual person.

The new paradigm therefore resembles the single-case approach to cognitive neuropsychology (e.g., Caramazza & McCloskey, 1988), which has been subject to extensive debate and criticism (e.g., L.C. Robertson, Knight, Rafal, & Shimamura, 1993), as well as rebuttal—to the extent of engendering an article whose title includes the somewhat unlikely but certainly exhaustive: "A reply to a rebuttal to an answer to a response to the case against..." (Caramazza & Badecker, 1991, p. 11). However, unlike the present instantiation of single-case research in cognitive neuropsychology, the new paradigm, important to note, will not come into existence until *after* availability of a more comprehensive theory along the lines foreshadowed earlier. In consequence, the new research will be conducted along better theoretical constraints. Moreover, the new approach does not intend to generalize from a single patient to an entire population: Instead, the approach seeks to refine theories of normal cognitive functioning by adapting them to specific individuals, thus maximally exploiting the richness of our database in preference to considering it full of annoying noise.

Turning to (at least partial) precedents for the new approach, the work of Patricia Carpenter, Marcel Just, and colleagues is particularly informative. Carpenter, Just, and Shell (1990) provided a detailed analysis of cognitive processing in the Raven Progressive Matrices test, and the relationship between performance on that test and the Tower of Hanoi task. Two computational models were developed that captured, respectively, performance of the median and the best students in the sample. Similarly, Just and Carpenter (1992) presented an examination of discourse processing that predicted the comprehension score of individuals from their memory span. Again, individual differences were captured by a computational model, thus pointing the way toward an approach that captures individuals' performance across tasks.

The projected new approach goes beyond those precedents in several ways: First, performance will be integrated and modeled across more than a few tasks. Experimentation under the new paradigm will involve the recruitment of a very small number of volunteers who will be exposed to a barrage of cognitive tests. For example, a volunteer might be given several memory tests, followed by problem-solving tasks, stem completion, picture recognition, and so on. To mention a partial precedent, the desire to arrive at a more complete and all-encompassing description of performance is shared by some recent European research on complex problem solving, for example the microworlds containing up to 2,000 interconnected variables pioneered by Dörner and colleagues (e.g., Dörner, Kreuzig, Reither, & Stäudel, 1983).

Second, building on knowledge gathered under the current paradigm, an individual's model will be constructed to provide an integrated account of performance across the elemental experimental tasks. Subsequent experimental tests will ensure validation or refinement of that model. This, of course, is no different than the task currently facing the field; however, by focusing on a few individuals throughout, relations between tasks will arguably be easier to detect. One implication of the new paradigm is that publications will report the performance of a few individuals across many studies, in contrast to the current approach of reporting one or two studies involving many subjects. And whereas we currently make aggregate predictions with little coherence across task boundaries, under the new paradigm we will state with some confidence how exactly a given person will approach the next problem-solving task or memory test.

Third, the new approach will provide a better account of subjective states of awareness. Whereas current methodologies dichotomize recollective awareness on isolated tasks into remembering and knowing (e.g., Gardiner & Java, 1993), the new paradigm will need to develop enriched instruments that provide detailed inventories of awareness applicable in a variety of situations.

Fourth, unlike current research, the new paradigm will acknowledge the experiences and personal cognitive history of subjects prior to entering the laboratory. Although autobiographical memory has been a topic for research (e.g., Conway & Bekerian, 1987), there has been little effort to relate prior autobiographical experience to memory performance in general (however, see Bellezza & Buck, 1988; Kuyken & Brewin, 1995). Clearly, any attempt to explain in detail the performance of an individual must begin by acknowledging that individual's set of prior cognitive experiences. Maybery and O'Brien-Malone's (chap. 9, this volume) developmental analysis of implicit and automatic processing points in that direction. In this context, the similarity between the projected new paradigm and the existing microgenetic approach used by developmental psychologists (e.g., Siegler, 1995) must be pointed out. The microgenetic approach involves prolonged and detailed observations of individual children undergoing cognitive change; its success in that arena suggests that a similar approach to cognition in general may also be fruitful.

Finally, the most likely outcome is that none of this will actually happen.

ACKNOWLEDGMENTS

Electronic mail may be sent to lewan@psy.uwa.edu.au. Personal home page at URL: http://www.psy.uwa.edu.au/user/lewan/. I wish to thank Kim Kirsner, Murray Maybery, and Bruce Whittlesea for many helpful comments on earlier versions of this chapter. Thanks are also due to Jim Neely for pointing out some relevant literature. Preparation of this chapter was facilitated by Large Research Grant No. A79600016 from the Australian Research Council to the author.

REFERENCES

Aboud, F. E. (1988). *Children and prejudice*. Oxford, England: Blackwell.

Abrams, M., & Reber, A. S. (1988). Implicit learning: Robustness in the face of psychiatric disorders. *Journal of Psycholinguistic Research, 17*, 425–439.

Ackerman, P. L. (1988). Determinants of individual differences during skill acquisition: Cognitive abilities and information processing. *Journal of Experimental Psychology: General, 117*, 288–318.

Ackerman P. L. (1989). Within-task intercorrelations of skilled performance: Implications for predicting individual differences? (A comment on Henry & Hulin, 1987), *Journal of Applied Psychology, 74*, 360–364.

Ackerman P. L. (1992). Predicting individual differences in complex skill acquisition: Dynamics of ability determinants, *Journal of Applied Psychology, 77*, 598–614.

Acredelo, L. P., Pick, H. L., & Olsen, M. G. (1975). Environmental differentiation and familiarity as determinants of children's memory for spatial location. *Developmental Psychology, 11*, 495–501.

Adair, J. G. (1973). *The human subject: The social psychology of the psychological experiment*. Boston: Little, Brown.

Adams, M. J. (1990). *Beginning to read: Learning and thinking about print*. Cambridge, MA: MIT Press.

Adams, M. J., & Huggins, A. (1985). The growth of children's sight vocabulary: A quick test with educational and theoretical implications. *Reading Research Quarterly, 20*, 262–281.

Aggleton, J. P. (1985). One-trial object recognition by rats. *Quarterly Journal of Experimental Psychology: Comparative & Physiological Psychology, 37B*, 279–294.

Aggleton, J. P., Nicol, R. M., Huston, A. E., & Fairbairn, A.F. (1988). The performance of amnesic subjects on tests of experimental amnesia in animals: Delayed matching-to-sample and concurrent learning. *Neuropsychologia, 26*, 265–272.

Allard, F., & Starkes, J. L. (1991). Motor-skill experts in sports, dance, and other domains. In K. A. Ericsson & J. Smith (Eds.), *Toward a general theory of expertise* (pp. 126–152). Cambridge, England: Cambridge University Press.

Allen, R., & Reber, A. S. (1980). Very long term memory for tacit knowledge. *Cognition, 8*, 175–185.

Allison, J. (1963). Cognitive structure and receptivity to low intensity stimulation. *Journal of Abnormal Social Psychology, 67*, 132–138.

Allport, D. A. (1977). On knowing the meaning of words we are unable to report: The effects of visual masking. In S. Dornic (Ed.), *Attention and performance* (pp. 56–73). New York: Lawrence Erlbaum Associates.

Allport, G. W. (1954). *The nature of prejudice*. Cambridge, England: Addison-Wesley.

Altmann, G. (1987). Modularity and interaction in sentence processing. In J. L. Garfield (Ed.), *Modularity in knowledge representation and natural-language understanding* (pp. 249–257). Cambridge, MA: Bradford Books.

Altmann, G., & Steedman, M. (1988). Interaction with context during human sentence processing. *Cognition, 30*, 191–238.

Amir, N., McNally, R. J., Riemann, B. C., & Clements, C. (1996). Implicit memory bias for threat in panic disorder: Application of the "white noise" paradigm, *Behaviour Research & Therapy, 2,* 156–162.

Anderson, J. R. (1982). Acquisition of cognitive skill. *Psychological Review, 89,* 369–406.

Anderson, J. R. (1983). *The architecture of cognition.* Cambridge, MA: Harvard University Press.

Anderson, J. R. (1985). *Cognitive psychology and its implications* (2nd ed.). New York: Freeman.

Anderson, J. R. (1986). Category learning: Things aren't so black and white. *Behavioural & Brain Sciences, 9,* 651.

Anderson, J. R. (1987). Skill acquisition: Compilation of weak-method problem solutions. *Psychological Review, 94,* 192–210.

Anderson, J. R. (1989). Practice, working memory, and the ACT* theory of skill acquisition: A comment on Carlson, Sullivan, and Schneider (1989). *Journal of Experimental Psychology: Learning, Memory, and Cognition, 15,* 527–530.

Anderson, J. R. (1992). Automaticity and the ACT* theory. *American Journal of Psychology, 105,* 165–180.

Anderson, J. R. (1993). *Rules of the mind.* Hillsdale, NJ: Lawrence Erlbaum Associates.

Anderson, J. R., & Bower, G. (1973). *Human associative memory.* Washington, DC: Winston.

Anderson, M. (1992a). Intelligence. In A. P. Smith & D. M. Jones (Eds.), *Handbook of human performance* (Vol. 3, pp. 1–24). London: Academic Press.

Anderson, M. (1992b). *Intelligence and development: A cognitive theory.* Oxford, England: Blackwell.

Anderson, M., O'Connor, N., & Hermelin, B. (in press). A specific calculating ability. *Intelligence.*

Anderson, N. H. (1972). Looking for configurality in clinical judgment. *Psychological Bulletin, 78,* 93–102.

Andrade, J. (1995). Learning during anaesthesis: A review. *British Journal of Psychology, 86,* 479–506.

Annett, J. (1986). On knowing how to do things. In H. Heuer & C. Fromm (Eds.), *Generation and modulation of action patterns* (pp. 187–200). Berlin: Springer-Verlag.

Antell, S. E., & Keating, D. P. (1983). Perception of numerical invariance in neonates. *Child Development, 54,* 695–701.

Argote, L., & Epple, D. (1990). Learning curves in manufacturing. *Science, 247,* 920–924.

Ashmore, R., & Del Boca, F. K. (1981). Conceptual approaches to stereotypes and stereotyping. In D. L. Hamilton (Ed.), *Cognitive processes in stereotyping and intergroup behaviour* (pp. 1–35). Hillsdale, NJ: Lawrence Erlbaum Associates.

Ashmore, R. D., Del Boca, F. K., & Wohler, A. J. (1986). Gender stereotypes. In R. D. Ashmore, & F. K. Del Boca (Eds.), *The social psychology of female-male relations: A critical analysis of central concepts* (pp. 69–119). Orlando, FL: Academic Press.

Atkinson, J. E. (1978). Correlation analysis of the physiological factor's controlling fundamental voice frequency. *Journal of the Acoustical Society of America, 63,* 211–222.

Atkinson, R. C., & Juola, J. F. (1973). Factors influencing speed and accuracy of word recognition. In S. Kornblum (Ed.), *Attention and performance IV.* New York: Academic Press.

Atkinson, R. C. & Shiffrin, R. M. (1968). Human memory: A proposed system and its control processes. In K. W. Spence & J. T. Spence (Eds.), *Advances in the psychology of learning and motivation* (Vol. 2, pp. 89–195). New York: Academic Press.

Baars, B. J. (1992). Is consciousness recent? *Consciousness and Cognition, 1,* 139–142.

Bacon, S. J. (1974). Arousal and the range of cue utilization. *Journal of Experimental Psychology, 102,* 81–87.

Baddeley, A. (1972). Selective attention and performance in dangerous environments. *British Journal of Psychology, 63,* 537–546.

Bagozzi, R. P. (1978). The construct validity of the affective, behavioural, and cognitive components of attitude by analysis of covariance structures. *Multivariate Behavioural Research, 13,* 9–31.

Baillargeon, R., & Graber, M. (1987). Where's the rabbit? 5.5-month-old infants' representation of the height of a hidden object. *Cognitive Development, 2,* 375–392.

Bainbridge, J. V., Lewandowsky, S., & Kirsner, K. (1993). Context effects in repetition priming are sense effects. *Memory & Cognition, 21*(5)*,* 619–626.

Bainbridge, L. (1977).Verbal reports as evidence of the process operator's knowledge. *International Journal of Man-Machine Studies, 11,* 411–436.

Bainbridge, L. (1982). Ironies of automation. In G. Johannsen & J. E. Rijnsdorp (Eds.), Proceedings of the IFAC/IFLIP/IFORS/IEA Conference, Baden Baden, Federal Republic of Germany, 27–29 September 1982. Oxford: Pergamon Press. (pp. 129–136).

Baker, L. E. (1937). The influence of subliminal stimuli upon verbal behaviour. *Journal of Experimental Psychology, 20*, 84–100.

Balzer, W. K., Doherty, M. E., & O'Connor, R., Jr. (1989). Effects of cognitive feedback on performance. *Psychological Bulletin, 106*, 410–433.

Banaji, M. R., Hardin, C., & Rothman, A. J. (in press). Implicit stereotyping in person judgement. *Journal of Personality and Social Psychology.*

Bargh, J. A. (1982). Attention and automaticity in the processing of self-referent information. *Journal of Personality and Social Psychology, 43*, 425–436.

Bargh, J. A. (1989). Conditional automaticity: Varieties of automatic influence in social perception and cognition. In J.S. Uleman & J.A. Bargh (Eds.), *Unintended thought* (pp. 3–51). New York: Guilford.

Bargh, J. A. (1992a). Does subliminality matter to social psychology? Awareness of the stimulus versus awareness of its influence. In R. F. Bornstein & T. S. Pittman (Eds.), *Perception without awareness. Cognitive, clinical, and social perspectives* (pp. 236–255). New York: Guilford.

Bargh, J. A. (1992b). The ecology of automaticity: Toward establishing the conditions needed to produce automatic processing effects. *American Journal of Psychology, 105*, 181–199.

Bargh, J. A., & Pietromonaco, P. (1982). Automatic information processing and social perception: The influence of trait information presented outside of conscious awareness on impression formation. *Journal of Personality and Social Psychology, 43*, 437–449.

Bar-Hillel, M. (1980). The base-rate fallacy in probability judgments. *Acta Psychologica, 44*, 211–233.

Barnard, P. J., & Teasdale, J. D. (1991). Interacting cognitive subsystems: A systemic approach to cognitive-affective interaction and change. *Cognition & Emotion, 5,* 1–39.

Barnett, G. O., Cimino, J. J., Hupp, J. A., & Hoffer, E. P. (1987). CX-plain: An evolving diagnostic decision-support system. *Journal of the American Medical Association, 258*, 67–74.

Baron-Cohen, S., Leslie, A. M. & Frith, U. (1985). Does the autistic child have a theory of mind? *Cognition, 21*, 37–46.

Bartlett, F. (1932). *Remembering.* Cambridge, England: Cambridge University Press.

Beatty, S. E., & Hawkins, D. I. (1989). Subliminal stimulation: Some new data and interpretation. *Journal of Advertising, 18*, 4–8.

Beck, A. T. (1967). *Depression.* New York: Hober Medical.

Beck, A. T. (1976). *Cognitive therapy and the emotional disorders.* New York: International Universities Press.

Beck, A. T., & Clark, D. A. (1988). Anxiety and depression: An information processing perspective. *Anxiety Research, 1*, 23–36.

Beck, A. T., Emery, G., & Greenberg, R. (1986). *Anxiety disorders and phobias: A cognitive perspective.* New York: Basic Books.

Beck, A. T., Laude, R., & Bohnert, M. (1974). Ideational components of anxiety neurosis. *Archives of General Psychiatry, 31*, 319–325.

Begg, I. M., Needham, D. R., & Bookbinder, M. (1993). Do backward messages unconsciously affect listeners? No. *Canadian Journal of Psychology, 47,* 1– 4.

Bellezza, F. S., & Buck, D. K. (1988). Expert knowledge as mnemonic cues. *Applied Cognitive Psychology, 2,* 147–162.

Belmont, J. M. & Butterfield, E. C. (1969). The relations of short-term memory to development and intelligence. In L. P. Lipsett & H. W. Reese (Eds), *Advances in child development and behavior* (Vol. 4, pp. 29–82). New York: Academic Press.

Belmont, J. M. & Mitchell, D. W. (1987). The general strategic hypothesis as applied to cognitive theory in mental retardation. *Intelligence, 11,* 91–105.

Benner, P. (1984). *From novice to expert: Excellence and power in clinical nursing practice.* Reading, MA: Addison-Wesley.

Bennett, H. L., Davis, H. S., & Giannini, A. J. (1985). Non-verbal response to introoperative conversation. *British Journal of Anaesthesia, 57*, 174–179.

Benoit, S. C., & Thomas, R. L. (1992). The influence of expectancy in subliminal perception experiments. *Journal of General Psychology, 119*, 335–341.

Berger, T. W., & Orr, W. B. (1983). Hippocampectomy selectively disrupts discrimination reversal conditioning of the rabbit nictitating membrane response. *Behavioural Brain Research, 8*, 49–68.

Berry, D. C. (1987). The problem of implicit knowledge. *Expert Systems, 4*, 144–151.

Berry, D. C. (1991). The role of action in implicit learning. *Quarterly Journal of Experimental Psychology, 43A*, 881–906.

Berry, D. (1993). Implicit learning: Reflections and prospects. In A. Baddeley & L. Weiskrantz (Eds.), *Attention: Selection, awareness and control* (pp. 246–259). Oxford, England: Clarendon.

Berry, D. C., & Broadbent, D. E. (1984). On the relationship between task performance and associated verbalizable knowledge. *Quarterly Journal of Experimental Psychology, 36A*, 209–231.

Berry, D. C., & Broadbent, D. E. (1987a). The combination of explicit and implicit learning processes in task control. *Psychological Research, 49*, 7–15.

Berry, D. C., & Broadbent, D. E. (1987b). Explanation and verbalization in a computer-assisted search task. *The Quarterly Journal of Experimental Psychology, 39A* , 585–609.

Berry, D. C., & Broadbent, D. E. (1988). Interactive tasks and the implicit-explicit distinction. *British Journal of Psychology, 79*, 251–272.

Berry, D. C., & Broadbent, D. E. (1990). The role of instruction and verbalization in improving performance on complex search tasks. *Behaviour and Information Technology, 9*, 175–190.

Berry, D. C., & Broadbent, D. E. (1995). Implicit learning in the control of complex systems. In P. A. Frensch & J. Funke (Eds.), *Complex problem solving: The European perspective* (pp. 131–150). Hillsdale, NJ: Lawrence Erlbaum Associates.

Berry, D. C., & Dienes, Z. (1993). *Implicit learning: Theoretical and empirical issues.* Hove, England: Lawrence Erlbaum Associates.

Bettman, J. R., Johnson, E. J., & Payne, J. W. (1990). A componential analysis of cognitive effort in choice. *Organizational Behavior and Human Decision Processes, 45*, 111–139.

Biernat, M. (1990). Stereotypes on campus: How contact and liking influences perceptions of group distinctiveness, *Journal of Applied Social Psychology, 20*, 1485–1513.

Billig, M. (1985). Prejudice, categorisation, and particularisation: From a perceptual to a rhetorical approach. *European Journal of Social Psychology, 15*, 79–103.

Bingman, V. P. (1990). Spatial navigation in birds. In R. P. Kesner, & D. S. Olton (Eds.), *Neurobiology of comparative cognition* (pp. 423–447). Hillsdale, NJ: Lawrence Erlbaum Associates.

Bingman, V. P., Bagnoli, P., Ioalé, P., & Casini, G. (1984). Homing behavior of pigeons after telencephalic ablations. *Brain Behavior and Evolution, 24*, 94–108.

Bingman, V.P., Ioalé, P., Casini, G., & Bagnoli, P. (1985). Dorsomedial forebrain ablations and home loft association behavior in homing pigeons. *Brain and Behavioral Evolution, 26*, 1–9.

Bingman, V. P, Ioalé, P., Casini, G. & Bagnoli, P. (1987). Impaired retention of preoperatively acquired spatial reference memory in homing pigeons following hippocampal ablation. *Behavioural Brain Research, 24*, 147–156.

Bingman, V. P., Ioalé, P., Casini, G., & Bagnoli, P. (1988a). Hippocampal ablated homing pigeons show a persistent impairment in the time taken to return home. *Journal of Comparative Physiology, 163A*, 559–563.

Bingman, V. P., Ioalé, P., Casini, G., & Bagnoli, P. (1988b). Unimpaired acquisition of spatial reference memory, but impaired homing performance in hippocampal-ablated pigeons. *Behavioural Brain Research, 27*, 179–187.

Bingman V. P., & Mench, J. A. (1990). Homing behavior of hippocampus and parahippocampus lesioned pigeons following short-distance releases. *Behavioural Brain Research, 40*, 227–385.

Birnbaum, M. H., & Sutton, S. E. (1992). Scale convergence and utility measurement. *Organizational Behavior and Human Decision Processes, 52*, 183–215.

Bjorklund, D. F., & Bjorklund, B. R. (1985). Organization versus item effects of an elaborated knowledge base on children's memory. *Developmental Psychology, 21*, 1120–1131.

Blake, R., & Dennis, W. (1943). Development of stereotypes concerning the negro. *Journal of Abnormal and Social Psychology, 38,* 525–531.

Blaney, P. H. (1986). Affect and memory: A review. *Psychological Bulletin, 99*, 229–246.

Blaxton, T. A. (1989). Investigating dissociations among memory measures: Support for a transfer-appropriate processing framework. *Journal of Experimental Psychology: Learning, Memory, and Cognition, 15*, 657–668.

Block, M. P., & Bergh, B. G. V. (1985). Can you sell subliminal messages to consumers? *Journal of Advertising, 14,* 59–62.

Block, N. (1995). On a confusion about a function of consciousness. *The Behavioural and Brain Sciences, 18,* 227–287.

Block, R. I., Ghoneim, M. M., Sum Ping, S. T., & Ali, M. A. (1991). Human learning during general anaesthesia and surgery. *British Journal of Anaesthesia, 66,* 170–178.

Bolinger, D. (1978). Intonation across languages. In J. Greenberg (Ed.), *Universals of human language: Phonology* (pp. 471–524). Stanford, CA: Stanford University Press.

Bonanno, G. A., & Stillings, N. A. (1986). Preference, familiarity, and recognition after repeated brief exposures to random geometric shapes. *American Journal of Psychology, 99,* 403–415.

Bootzin, R. R., & Stephens, M. W. (1967). Individual differences and perceptual defence in the absence of response bias. *Journal of Personality & Social Psychology, 6,* 408–412.

Borkowski, J. G., & Day, J. D. (1987). *Cognition in special children: Comparative approaches to retardation, learning difficulties and giftedness.* Norwood, NJ: Ablex.

Bornstein, R. F. (1987). Subliminal mere exposure effects and conscious cognition: A study of attitude change in response to stimuli perceived without awareness. *Dissertation Abstracts International, 47,* 3841.

Bornstein, R. F. (1989). Subliminal techniques as propaganda tools: Review and critique. *Journal of Mind & Behaviour, 10,* 231–262.

Bornstein, R. F., & D'Agostino, P. A. (1992). Stimulus recognition and the mere exposure effect. *Journal of Personality and Social Psychology, 63,* 545–552.

Bornstein, R. F., Leone, D. R., & Galley, D. J. (1987). The generalizability of subliminal mere exposure effects: Influence of stimuli perceived without awareness on social behavior. *Journal of Personality and Social Psychology, 53,* 1070–1079.

Bornstein, R. F., & Pittman, T. S. (Eds.). (1992). *Perception without awareness: Cognitive, clinical and social perspectives.* New York: Guilford.

Boshuizen, H. P. A., & Schmidt, H. G. (1992). On the role of biomedical knowledge in clinical reasoning by experts, intermediates and novices. *Cognitive Science, 16,* 153–184.

Boss, B. (1984). Dysphasia, dyspraxia, and dysarthria: Distinguishing features, Part 1. *Journal of Neurosurgical Nursing, 16,*151–160.

Bouchard, T. J., Lykken, D. T., McGue, M., Segal, N. L., & Tellegen, A. (1990). Sources of human psychological differences: The Minnesota study of twins reared apart. *Science, 250,* 223–250.

Bower, G. H. (1981). Mood and memory. *American Psychologist, 36,* 129–148.

Bower, G. H. (1983). Affect and cognition. *Philosophical Transactions of the Royal Society London, B302,* 387–402.

Bower, G. H., & Cohen, P. R. (1982). Emotional influences on memory and thinking: Data and theory. In S. Fiske & M. Clark (Eds.), *Affect and cognition* (pp. 47–63). Hillsdale, NJ: Lawrence Erlbaum Associates.

Bowers, J., & Schacter, D. L. (1993). Priming of novel information in amnesic patients: Issues and data. In P. Graf & M. E. J. Masson (Eds.), *Implicit memory: New directions in cognition, development, and neuropsychology* (pp. 303–326). Hillsdale, NJ: Lawrence Erlbaum Associates.

Bradley, B., & Mathews, A. (1983). Negative self-schemata in clinical depression. *British Journal of Clinical Psychology, 22,* 173–182.

Bradley, B., & Mathews, A. (1988). Memory bias in recovered clinical depressives. *Cognition & Emotion, 2,* 235–246.

Bradley, B., Mogg, K., Galbraith, M., & Perrett, A. (1993). Negative recall bias and neuroticism: State vs trait effects. *Behaviour Research & Therapy, 31,* 125–127.

Bradley, B. P., Mogg, K., Millar, N., & White, J. (1995). Selective processing of negative information: Effects of clinical anxiety, concurrent depression, and awareness. *Journal of Abnormal Psychology, 104,* 532–536.

Bradshaw, J. L. (1974). Peripherally presented and unreportable words may bias the perceived meaning of a centrally fixated homograph. *Journal of Experimental Psychology, 103,* 1200–1202.

Braine, M. (1963). On learning the grammatical order of words. *Psychological Review, 70,* 323–348.

Bransford, J. D., Franks, J. J., Vye, N. J. & Sherwood, R. D. (1989). New approaches to instruction: Because wisdom can't be told. In S. Vosniadou & A. Ortony (Eds.), *Similarity and analogical reasoning* (pp. 470–497). Cambridge, England: Cambridge University Press.

Breckler, S. J. (1984). Empirical validation of affect, behavior, and cognition as distinct components of attitude. *Journal of Personality and Social Psychology, 47,* 1191–1205.

Breiman, L., Friedman, J. H., Olshen, R. A., & Stone, C. J. (1984). *Classification and regression trees.* Belmont, CA: Wadsworth.

Bressler, J. (1931). Illusion in the case of subliminal visual stimulation. *Journal of General Psychology, 5,* 244–251.

Brewer, M. B. (1989). A dual process model of impression formation. In R. S. Wyer & T. K. Srull (Eds.), *Advances in social cognition* (Vol. 1, pp. 1–36). Hillsdale N.J.: Lawrence Erlbaum Associates.

Brigham, J. C. (1974). Views of black and white children concerning the distribution of personality characteristics. *Journal of Personality and Social Psychology, 42,* 145–158.

Britt, M. A., Perfetti, C. A., Garrod, S., & Rayner, K. (1992). Parsing in discourse: Context effects and their limits. *Journal of Memory and Language, 31,* 293–314.

Broadbent, D. E. (1958). *Perception and communication.* Oxford, England: Pergamon.

Broadbent, D. E. (1971). *Decision and stress.* New York: Academic Press.

Broadbent, D. E. (1977). Levels, hierarchies, and the locus of control. *Quarterly Journal of Experimental Psychology, 29,* 181–201.

Broadbent, D. E. (1989). Lasting representations and temporary processes. In H. L. Roediger III & F. I. M. Craik (Eds.), *Varieties of memory and consciousness* (pp. 211–227). Hillsdale, NJ: Lawrence Erlbaum Associates.

Broadbent, D. E., & Aston, B. (1978). Human control of a simulated economic system. *Ergonomics, 21,* 1035–1043.

Broadbent, D. E., & Broadbent, M. (1988). Anxiety and attentional bias: State and trait. *Cognition & Emotion, 2,* 165–183.

Broadbent, D. E., FitzGerald, P., & Broadbent, M. H. P. (1986). Implicit and explicit knowledge in the control of complex systems. *British Journal of Psychology, 77,* 33–50.

Broadbent, D. E., & Gregory, M. (1965). Effects of noise and of signal rate upon vigilance analysed by means of decision theory. *Human Factors, 7,* 155–162.

Broadbent, D. E., & Gregory, M. (1967). Perception of emotionally toned words. *Nature, 215,* 581–584.

Brody, N. (1989). Unconscious learning of rules: Comment on Reber's analysis of implicit learning. *Journal of Experimental Psychology: General, 118,* 236–238.

Brooke, J. B., Cook, J. F., & Duncan, K. D. (1983). Effects of computer-aiding and pre-training on fault location. *Ergonomics, 26,* 669–686.

Brooke, J. B. & Duncan, K. D. (1980). An experimental study of flowcharts as an aid to indentification of procedural faults. *Ergonomics, 23,* 387–399.

Brooke, J. B., & Duncan, K. D. (1981). Effects of system display format on performance in a fault diagnosis task. *Ergonomics, 24,* 175–189.

Brooke, J. B., & Duncan, K. D. (1983). A comparison of hierarchically paged and scrolling displays for fault-finding. *Ergonomics, 26,* 465–477.

Brooks, B. M. (1994). A comparison of serial position effects in implicit and explicit word stem completion. *Psychonomic Bulletin and Review, 1*(2), 264–268.

Brooks, D. N., & Baddeley, A. D. (1976). What can amnesic patients learn? *Neuropsychologia, 14,* 111–122.

Brooks, L. (1978). Nonanalytic concept formation and memory for instances. In E. Rosch & B. Lloyd (Eds.), *Cognition and categorization* (pp. 169–211). Hillsdale, NJ: Lawrence Erlbaum Associates.

Brooks, L. (1984). Decentralized control of categorization: The role of prior processing episodes. In U. Neisser (Ed.), *Categories reconsidered: The ecological and intellectual basis of categories* (pp. 141–174). Cambridge, England: Cambridge University Press.

Brooks, P. H., & McCauley, C. (1984). Cognitive research in mental retardation. *American Journal of Mental Deficiency, 88,* 479–486.

Brooks, P. H., Sperber, R., & McCauley, C. (1984). *Learning and cognition in the mentally retarded.* Hillsdale, NJ: Lawrence Erlbaum Associates.

Brown, A. L. (1974). The role of strategic behavior in retardate memory. In N. R. Ellis (Ed.), *International review of research in mental retardation* (Vol. 7, pp. 55–111). New York: Academic Press.

Brown, A. L., & Barclay, C. R. (1976). The effect of training specific mnemonics on the metamnemonic efficiency of retarded children. *Child Development, 47,* 71–80.

Brown, A. S., & Mitchell, D. B. (1994). A reevaluation of semantic versus nonsemantic processing in implicit memory. *Memory & Cognition, 22,* 533–541.

Bruck, M. (1992). Persistence of dyslexics' phonological awareness deficits. *Developmental Psychology, 28,* 874–886.

Bruner, J. S., & Postman, L. (1947). Emotional selectivity in perception and reaction. *Journal of Personality, 15,* 300–308.

Brunswick, E. (1956). *Perception and representative design of experiments* (2nd ed.). Berkeley: University of California Press.

Bryan, K. (1989). Language prosody and the right hemisphere. *Aphasiology, 3*(4), 285–299.

Buchner, A., Erdfelder, E., & Vaterrodt-Plünnecke, B. (1995). Toward unbiased measurement of conscious and unconscious memory processes within the process dissociation framework. *Journal of Experimental Psychology: General, 124,* 137–160.

Bullock, T. H., Orkand, R., & Grinnell, A. (1977). *Introduction to nervous systems.* San Francisco: Freeman.

Burgess, I. S., Jones, L. N., Robertson, S. A., Radcliffe, W. N., Emerson, E., Lawler, P., & Crow, T. J. (1981). The degree of control exerted by phobic and non-phobic verbal stimuli over the recognition behaviour of phobic and non-phobic subjects. *Behaviour Research & Therapy, 19,* 223–234.

Burke, M., & Mathews, A. (1992). Autobiographical memory and clinical anxiety. *Cognition & Emotion, 6,* 23–35.

Butler, M., & Paisley, W. (1980). *Women and the mass media: Sourcebook of research and action.* New York: Human Sciences Press.

Butterfield, E. C. & Ferretti, R. R. (1984). Some extension of the instructional approach to the study of cognitive development and a sufficient condition for transfer of training. In P. H. Brooks, R. Sperber, & C. McCauley (Eds.) *Learning and cognition in the mentally retarded* (pp. 311–332). Hillsdale, NJ: Lawrence Erlbaum Associates.

Butterfield, E. C., Wambold, C., & Belmont, J. M. (1973). On the theory and practice of improving short-term memory. *American Journal of Mental Deficiency, 77,* 654–669.

Butters, N., Heindel, W. C., & Salmon, D. P. (1990). Dissociation of implicit memory in dementia: Neurological implications. *Bulletin of the Psychonomic Society, 28,* 359–366.

Buttigieg, M. A., & Sanderson, P. M. (1991). Emergent features in visual display design for two types of failure detection tasks. *Human Factors, 33,* 631–651.

Byrne, A., & Eysenck, M. W. (1995). Trait anxiety, anxious mood and threat detection. *Cognition & Emotion, 9,* 549–569.

Byrne, B. (1991). Experimental analysis of the child's discovery of the alphabetic principle. In L. Rieben, & C. Perfetti (Eds.), *Learning to read: Basic research and its implications* (pp. 75–84). Hillsdale, NJ: Lawrence Erlbaum Associates.

Byrne, B. (1992). Studies in the acquisition procedure for reading: Rationale, hypotheses, and data. In P. B. Gough, L. Ehri, & R. Treiman (Eds.), *Reading acquisition,* (pp. 1–34). Hillsdale, NJ: Lawrence Erlbaum Associates.

Byrne, B., & Fielding-Barnsley, R. (1989). Phonemic awareness and letter knowledge in the child's acquisition of the alphabetic principle. *Journal of Educational Psychology, 81,* 313–321.

Byrne, B., Freebody, P. & Gates, A. (1992). Longitudinal data on the relations of word-reading strategies to comprehension, reading time, and phonemic awareness. *Reading Research Quarterly, 27,* 141–151.

Camerer, C. F., & Johnson, E. J. (1991). The process-performance paradox in expert judgment. In K. A. Ericsson & J. Smith (Eds.), *Toward a general theory of expertise* (pp. 195–217). Cambridge, England: Cambridge University Press.

Campion, J., Latto, R., & Smith, Y. (1983). Is blinksight an effect of scattered light, spared cortex, and near-threshold vision? *The Behavioral and Brain Sciences, 6,* 423–486.

Campione, J. C. & Brown, A. L. (1977). Memory and metamemory development in educable retarded children. In R. V. Kail & J. W. Hagen (Eds.), *Perspectives on the development of memory and cognition* (pp. 367–406). Hillsdale, NJ: Lawrence Erlbaum Associates.

Campione, J. C., Brown, A. L., & Ferrara, R. A. (1982) Mental retardation and intelligence. In R. J. Sternberg (Ed.), *Handbook of human intelligence* (pp. 392–490). Cambridge, England: Cambridge University Press.

Caramazza, A. (1984). The logic of neuropsychological research and the problem of patient classification in aphasia. *Brain and Language, 21*(1), 9–20.

Caramazza, A., & Badecker, W. (1991). Clinical syndromes are not God's gift to cognitive neuropsychology: A reply to a rebuttal to an answer to a response to the case against syndrome-based research. *Brain and Cognition, 16*, 211–227.

Caramazza, A., & McCloskey, M. (1988). The case for single-patient studies. *Cognitive Neuropsychology, 5*, 517–528.

Card, S. K., English, W. K., & Burr, B. (1978). Evaluation of mouse, rate controlled isometric joystick, step keys, and text keys for text selection on a CRT. *Ergonomics, 21*, 601–613.

Carew, T. J., Hawkins, R. D. & Kandel, E. R. (1983). Differential classical conditioning of a defensive withdrawal reflex in *Aplysia californica*. *Science, 219*, 397–400.

Carlson, R. A., Sullivan, M. A., & Schneider, W. (1989). Practice and working memory effects in building procedural skill. *Journal of Experimental Psychology: Learning, Memory, and Cognition, 15*, 517–526.

Carpenter, P. A., & Just, M. A. (1989). The role of working memory in language comprehension. In D. Klahr & K. Kotovsky (Eds.), *Complex information processing* (pp. 31–68). Hillsdale, NJ: Lawrence Erlbaum Associates.

Carpenter, P. A., Just, M. A., & Shell, P. (1990). What one intelligence test measures: A theoretical account of the processing in the Raven Progressive Matrices test. *Psychological Review, 97*, 404–431.

Carr, T. H. (1984). Attention, skill and intelligence: some speculations on extreme individual differences in human performance. In P. H. Brooks, R. Sperber, & C. McCauley (Eds.), *Learning and cognition in the mentally retarded* (pp. 189–215). Hillsdale, NJ: Lawrence Erlbaum Associates.

Carroll, M., Byrne, B., & Kirsner, K. (1985). Autobiographical memory and perceptual learning: A developmental study using picture recognition, naming latency, and perceptual identification. *Memory and Cognition, 13,* 273–279.

Case, R. (1985). *Intellectual development: Birth to adulthood*. New York: Academic Press.

Case, R. (Ed.). (1992). *The mind's staircase: Exploring the conceptual underpinnings of children's thought and knowledge*. Hillsdale, NJ: Lawrence Erlbaum Associates.

Case, R. (1995). Capacity-based explanations of working memory growth: A brief history and reevaluation. In F. E. Weinert & W. Schneider (Eds), *Memory performance and competencies: Issues in growth and development* (pp. 23–44). Hillsdale, NJ: Lawrence Erlbaum Associates.

Case, R., Kurland, M., & Goldberg, J. (1982). Operational efficiency and the growth of short-term memory span. *Journal of Experimental Child Psychology, 33*, 386–404.

Caseley-Rondi, G., Merikle, P. M., & Bowers, K. S. (1994). Unconscious cognition in the context of general anesthesia. *Consciousness & Cognition: An International Journal, 3*, 166–195.

Cassiday, K. L., McNally, R. J., & Zeitlin, S. B. (1992). Cognitive processing of trauma cues in rape victims with post-traumatic stress disorder. *Cognitive Therapy & Research, 16*, 283–295.

Cattell, R. B. (1963). Theory of fluid and crystallised intelligence: A critical experiment. *Journal of Educational Psychology, 54*, 1–22.

Ceci, S. J. (1990). *On intelligence...more or less. A bioecological treatise on intellectual development*. Englewood Cliffs, NJ: Prentice-Hall.

Cerella, J., & Hale, S. (1994). The rise and fall of information-processing rates over the life span. *Acta Psychologica, 86*, 109–197.

Cermak, L. S., Blackford, S. P., O'Connor, M., & Bleich, R. P. (1988). The implicit memory ability of a patient with amnesia due to encephalitis. *Brain and Cognition, 7*, 145–156.

Cermak, L. S., Talbot, N., Chandler, K., & Wolbarst, L. R. (1985). The perceptual priming phenomenon in amnesia. *Neuropsychologia, 23,* 615–622.

Challis, B. H., & Brodbeck, D. R. (1992). Level of processing affects priming in word fragment completion. *Journal of Experimental Psychology: Learning, Memory, and Cognition, 18*, 595–607.

Challis, B. H., & Krane, R. V. (1988). Mood induction and the priming of semantic memory in a lexical decision task: Asymmetric effects of elation and depression. *Bulletin of the Psychonomic Society, 26*, 309–312.

Challis, B. H., & Sidhu, R. (1993). Dissociative effect of massed repetition on implicit and explicit measures of memory. *Journal of Experimental Psychology: Learning, Memory, and Cognition, 19*, 115–127.

Chapman, M., & Lindenberger, U. (1989). Concrete operations and attentional capacity. *Journal of Experimental Child Psychology, 47*, 236–258.

Charness, N. (1979). Components of skill in bridge. *Canadian Journal of Psychology, 33*, 1–6.

Charness, N. (1989). Expertise in chess and bridge. In D. Klahr & K. Kotovsky (Eds.), *Complex information processing* (pp. 183–208). Hillsdale, NJ: Lawrence Erlbaum Associates.

Charness, N. (1991). Expertise in chess: The balance between knowledge and search. In K. A. Ericsson & J. Smith (Eds.), *Towards a general theory of expertise* (pp. 39–63). Cambridge, England: Cambridge University Press.

Chase, W. G., & Ericsson, K. A. (1982). Skill and working memory. In G. Bower (Ed.), *The psychology of learning and motivation* (Vol. 16, pp. 1–58). New York: Academic Press.

Chase, W. G. & Simon, H. A. (1973). The mind's eye in chess. In W. G. Chase (Ed.), *Visual information processing* (pp. 215–281). New York: Academic Press.

Cherry, E. C. (1953). Some experiments on the recognition of speech with one and two ears. *Journal of the Acoustical Society of America, 25*, 975–979.

Chi, M. T. H., Feltovich, P., & Glaser, R. (1981). Categorization and representation of physics problems by experts and novices. *Cognitive Science, 5*, 121–152.

Chiesi, H. L., Spilich, G. J., & Voss, J. F. (1979). Acquisition of domain-related information in relation to high and low domain knowledge. *Journal of Verbal Learning and Verbal Behavior, 18*, 257–273.

Chomsky, N. (1959). Review of Skinner's "verbal behaviour." *Language, 35*, 26–58.

Chomsky, N. (1980) *Rules and representations.* Oxford, England: Blackwell.

Chomsky, N. (1986). *Knowledge of language: Its nature, origin and use.* New York: Praeger.

Clark, D. A., & Teasdale, J. D. (1982). Diurnal variations in clinical depression and accessibility of memories of positive and negative experiences. *Journal of Abnormal Psychology, 52*, 1090–1097.

Clark, D. M., Teasdale, J. D., Broadbent, D. E., & Martin, M. (1983). Effects of mood on lexical decisions. *Bulletin of the Psychonomic Society, 48*, 1598–1608.

Clark, H. H., & Haviland, S. E. (1977). Comprehension and the given-new contract. In R. O. Freedle (Ed.), *Discourse production and comprehension* (pp. 1–40). Norwood, NJ: Ablex.

Clarke, R., & Morton, J. (1983). Cross-modality facilitation in tachistoscopic word recognition. *Quarterly Journal of Experimental Psychology, 35A*, 79–96.

Cleeremans, A. (1993). *Mechanisms of implicit learning: Connectionist models of sequence processing.* Cambridge, MA: MIT Press.

Cleeremans, A., & McClelland, J. L. (1991). Learning the structure of event sequences. *Journal of Experimental Psychology: General, 120*, 235–253.

Clifton, C., & Ferreira, F. (1987). Modularity in sentence comprehension. In J. L. Garfield (Ed.), *Modularity in knowledge representation and natural-language understanding* (pp. 277–290). Cambridge, MA: Bradford Books.

Cohen, A., Collier, R., & 't Hart, J. (1982). Declination: construct or intrinsic feature of speech pitch? *Phonetica, 39*, 254–273.

Cohen, A., Ivry, R. I., & Keele, S. W. (1990). Attention and structure in sequence learning. *Journal of Experimental Psychology: Learning, Memory, and Cognition, 16*, 17–30.

Cohen, N. J. (1984). Preserved learning capacity in amnesia: Evidence for multiple memory systems. In L. R. Squire & N. Butters (Eds.), *Neuropsychology of memory* (pp. 83–103). New York: Guilford.

Cohen, N. J., & Eichenbaum, H. (1993). *Memory, amnesia and the hippocampal system.* Cambridge, MA: MIT Press.

Cohen, N. J., Eichenbaum, H., Deacedo, B. S., & Corkin, S. (1985). Different memory systems underlying acquisition of procedural and declarative knowledge. In D. S. Olton, E. Gamzu, & S.

Corkin (Eds.), *Memory dysfunction: An integration of animal and human research from preclinical and clinical perspectives* (pp. 54–71). New York: New York Academy of Sciences.

Cohen, N. J., & Squire, L. R. (1980). Preserved learning and retention of a pattern-analyzing skill in amnesia: Dissociation of knowing how and knowing that. *Science, 210*, 207–210.

Collier, R. (1990). On the perceptual analysis of intonation. *Speech & Communication, 9*, 443 – 451.

Collins, A. M., & Loftus, E. F. (1975). A spreading activation theory of semantic processing. *Psychological Review, 39*, 593–597.

Collins, A. M., & Quillian, M. R. (1969). Retrieval time from semantic memory. *Journal of Verbal Learning & Verbal Behaviour, 82*, 407–428.

Compton, B. J., & Logan, G. D. (1991). The transition from algorithm to retrieval in memory-based theories of automaticity. *Memory and Cognition, 19* (2) 151–158.

Conway, M. A., & Bekerian, D. A. (1987). Organization in autobiographical memory. *Memory & Cognition, 15*, 119–132.

Cook, S. W., & Selltiz, C. (1964). A multiple indicator approach to attitude measurement. *Psychological Bulletin, 62*, 36–55.

Cooper, L. A., Schacter, D. L., Ballesteros, S., & Moore, C. (1992). Priming and recognition of transformed three-dimensional objects: Effects of size and reflection. *Journal of Experimental Psychology: Learning, Memory, and Cognition, 18*, 43–57.

Coover, J. E. (1917). *Experiments in psychical research at Leland Stanford Junior University, California*. Stanford, CA: Stanford University Press.

Cork, R. C., Kihlstrom, J. F., & Schacter, D. L. (1993). Implicit and explicit memory with isoflurane compared to sufentanil/nitrous oxide. In P. S. Sebel, B.Bonke, & E. Winegrad (Eds.), *Memory and awareness in anesthesia* (pp. 74–80). Englewood Cliffs, NJ: Prentice-Hall.

Corkin, S. (1968). Acquisition of a motor skill after bilateral medial temporal lobe excision. *Neuropsychologia, 6*, 225– 265.

Corteen, R. S., & Dunn, D. (1974). Shock-associated words in a nonattended message: A test for momentary awareness. *Journal of Experimental Psychology, 102*, 1143–1144.

Corteen, R. S., & Wood, B. (1972). Autonomic responses to shock-associated words in an unattended channel. *Journal of Experimental Psychology, 94*, 308–313.

Couvillon, P. A., & Bitterman, M. E. (1980). Some phenomena of associative learning in honeybees. *Journal of Comparative and Physiological Psychology, 94*, 878–885.

Couvillon, P. A., & Bitterman, M. E. (1982). Compound conditioning in honeybees. *Journal of Comparative and Physiological Psychology, 96*, 192– 199.

Couvillon, P. A. & Bitterman, M. E. (1988). Compound-component and conditional discrimination of colors and odors by honeybees: Further tests of a continuity model. *Animal Learning & Behavior, 16*, 67–74.

Couvillon, P. A., & Bitterman, M. E. (1989). Reciprocal overshadowing in the discrimination of color-odor compounds by honeybees: Further tests of a continuity model. *Animal Learning & Behavior, 17*, 213–222.

Cowey, A., & Stoerig, P. (1992). The neurobiology of blindsight. *Trends in Neuroscience, 29*, 65–80.

Cowley, J. J., Johnson, A. L., & Brooksbanck, B. W. L. (1977). The effects of two odorous compounds on performance in an assessment-of-people text. *Psychoneuroendocrinology, 2*, 159–172.

Craik, F. I. M., & Lockhart, R. S. (1972). Levels of processing: A framework for memory research. *Journal of Verbal Learning and Verbal Behavior, 11*, 671–684.

Crain, S., & Steedman, M. (1985). On not being led up the garden-path: The use of context by the psychological syntax parser. In D. R. Dowty, L. Karttunen, & A. M. Zwicky (Eds.), *Natural language parsing: Psychological, computational, and theoretical perspectives* (pp. 320–354). Cambridge, England: Cambridge University Press.

Cristoffanini, P. M., Kirsner, K., & Milech, D. (1986). Bilingual lexical representation: The status of Spanish-English cognates. *Quarterly Journal of Experimental Psychology, 38A*, 367–393.

Crossman, E. R. (1953). Entropy and choice-time: The effect of frequency on balance on choice response. *Journal of Experimental Psychology, 5*, 41–51.

Crossman, E. R. (1959). A theory of the acquisition of speed-skill. *Ergonomics, 2*, 153–166.

Crossman, E. R. F. & Cooke, J. E. (1974). Manual control of slow response systems. In E. Edwards & F. Lees (Eds.), *The human operator in process control*(pp. 51–66). London: Taylor & Francis.

Crowder, R. G. (1976). *Principles of learning and memory*. Hillsdale, NJ: Lawrence Erlbaum Associates.

Crowder, R. G. (1993). Systems and principles in memory theory: Another critique of pure memory. In A. F. Collins, S. E. Gathercole, M. A. Conway, & P. E. Morris (Eds.), *Theories of memory* (pp. 139–161). Hove, England: Lawrence Erlbaum Associates.

Cummings, T. & Blumberg, M. (1987). Advanced manufacturing technology and work design. In T. D. Wall, C. W. Clegg, & N. J. Kemp (Eds.), *The human side of advanced manufacturing technologies* (pp. 36–60). Chichester, England: John Wiley.

Cuperfain, R., & Clarke, T. K. (1985). A new perspective of subliminal perception. *Journal of Advertising, 14*, 36–41.

Curran, T., & Hintzman, D. L. (1995). Violations of the independence assumption in process dissociation. *Journal of Experimental Psychology: Learning, Memory, and Cognition, 21*, 531–547.

Curran, T., & Keele, S. W. (1993). Attentional and nonattentional forms of sequence learning. *Journal of Experimental Psychology: Learning, Memory, and Cognition, 19*, 189–202.

Cutler, A. (1982). The reliability of speech error data. In A. Cutler (Ed.), *Slips of the tongue* (pp. 79–92). Berlin: Mouton.

Cutting, J. (1978). A cognitive approach to Korsakoff's syndrome. *Cortex, 14*, 485–495.

Czerwinski, M., Lightfoot, N., & Shiffrin, R. M. (1992). Automatization and training in visual search. *American Journal of Psychology, 105*, 271–315.

Dagenbach, D., Carr, T. H., & Wilhelmsen, A. L. (1989). Task-induced strategies and near-threshold priming: Conscious influences on unconscious perception. *Journal of Memory and Language, 28*, 412–443.

Dale, H. C. A. (1958). Fault-finding in electronic equipment. *Ergonomics, 1*, 356–358.

Dalgleish, T. (1994). The relationship between anxiety and memory biases for material that has been selectively processed in a prior task. *Behaviour Research & Therapy, 32*, 227–231.

Daneman, M. & Carpenter, P. A. (1980). Individual differences in working memory and reading. *Journal of Verbal Learning and Verbal Behavior, 19*, 450–466.

Darley, F., Aronson A., & Brown, J. (1975). *Motor Speech Disorders*. Philadelphia: Saunders.

Davies, D., Sperber, R. D., & McCauley, C. (1981). Intelligence-related differences in semantic processing speed. *Journal of Experimental Child Psychology, 31*, 387–402.

Davis, J. R., Nanninga, P. M., Biggins, J., & Laut, P. (1991). Prototype decision support system for analyzing impact of catchment policies. *Journal of Water Resources Planning and Management, 117*, 399–414.

Davis, R. H. & Davis, J. A. (1985). *TV's image of the elderly: A practical guide for change*. Lexington, MA: Lexington Books.

Deaux, K., & Kite, M. E. (1985). Gender stereotypes: Some thoughts on the cognitive organization of gender-related information. *Academic Psychology Bulletin, 7*, 123–144.

Debner, J. A., & Jacoby, L. (1994). Unconscious perception: Attention, awareness and control. *Journal of Experimental Psychology: Learning, Memory, and Cognition, 20*, 304–317.

De Boysson-Bardies, B., Sagart, L., & Durand, C. (1984). Discernible differences in the babbling of infants according to target language. *Journal of Child Language, 11*, 1–15.

de Groot, A. (1966). Perception and memory versus thought: Some old ideas and recent findings. In B. Kleinmuntz (Ed.), *Problem solving* (pp. 19–49). New York: Wiley.

de Groot, A. (1978). *Thought and choice in chess*. The Hague, Netherlands: Mouton.

de Groot, A. M. B & Nas, G. L. J. (1991). Lexical representation of cognates and noncognates in compound bilinguals. *Journal of Memory and Language, 30*, 90–123.

de Kleer, J., & Brown, J. S. (1983). Assumptions and ambiguities in mechanistic mental models. In D. Gentner & A. L. Stevens (Eds.), *Mental models* (pp. 155–190). London: Lawrence Erlbaum Associates.

Dell, G. S., McKoon, G., & Ratcliff, R. (1983). The activation of antecedent information during the processing of anaphoric reference in reading. *Journal of Verbal Learning and Verbal Behaviour, 22*, 121–132.

Dempster, F. N. (1992). The rise and fall of the inhibitory mechanism: Toward a unified theory of cognitive development and aging. *Developmental Review, 12*, 45–75.

Dennett, D. C. (1983) Styles of mental representation. *Proceedings of the Aristotelian Society, May,* 213–226.

Dennett, D. C. (1991). *Consciousness explained.* Boston: Little, Brown.

Denny, E. B., & Hunt, R. R. (1992). Affective valence and memory in depression: Dissociation of recall and fragment completion. *Journal of Abnormal Psychology, 101,* 575–580.

Derry, P. A., & Kuiper, N. A. (1981). Schematic processing and self-reference in clinical depression. *Journal of Abnormal Psychology, 90,* 286–297.

Deutsch, J. A., & Deutsch, D. (1963). Attention: Some theoretical considerations. *Psychological Review, 70,* 80–90.

Devenport, L. D., Hale, R. L., & Stidham, J. A. (1988). Sampling behavior in the radial maze and operant chamber: Role of the hippocampus and prefrontal area. *Behavioral Neuroscience, 102,* 489–498.

Devine, P. G. (1989). Stereotypes and prejudice: Their automatic and controlled components. *Journal of Personality and Social Psychology, 56*(1), 5–18.

Diamond, M. R. (1983). *A comparison of objectively derived linear and decision-tree models of judgement.* Unpublished master's thesis, University of Western Australia, Perth.

Diamond, R., & Rozin, P. (1984). Activation of existing memories in anterograde amnesia. *Journal of Abnormal Psychology, 93,* 98–105.

Dienes, Z. (1992) Connectionist and memory-array models of artificial grammar learning. *Cognitive Science, 16,* 41–79.

Dienes, Z., Broadbent, D., & Berry, D. (1991). Implicit and explicit knowledge bases in artificial grammar learning. *Journal of Experimental Psychology: Learning, Memory, and Cognition, 17,* 875–887.

Dienes, Z., & Fahey, R. (1995). Role of specific instances in controlling a dynamic system. *Journal of Experimental Psychology: Learning, Memory, and Cognition, 21*(4), 848–862.

DiMattia, B. V., Kesner, R. P. (1988). Spatial cognitive maps: Differential role of parietal cortex and hippocampal formation. *Behavioral Neuroscience, 102,* 471–480.

Dixon, N. F. (1968). Perception without awareness. A reply to K. M. Banreti-Fuchs. *Acta Psychologica, 28,* 171–180.

Dixon, N. F. (1971). *Subliminal perception.* London: McGraw-Hill.

Dixon, N. F. (1981). *Preconscious processing.* Chichester, England: John.

Dobson, K. S., & Shaw, B. F. (1987). Specificity and stability of self-referent encoding in clinical depression. *Journal of Abnormal Psychology, 10,* 13–29.

Dörner, D., Kreuzig, H. W., Reither, F., & Sträudel, T. (Eds.). (1983). *Lohhausen. Vom Umgang mit Unbestimmtheit und Komplexität* [Lohhausen: Dealing with uncertainty and complexity]. Bern, Switzerland: Hans Huber.

Dovidio, J. F. (1990). *Evaluative responses to racial primes: Automatic activation.* Unpublished manuscript, Colgate University, Hamilton, NY.

Dovidio, J. F., Evans, N., & Tyler, R. B. (1986). Racial stereotypes: The contents of their cognitive representations. *Journal of Experimental Social Psychology, 22,* 22–37.

Dovidio, J. F., Evans, N., & Tyler, R. B. (1988). *Cognitive and evaluative responses to racial primes: Extending the range.* Unpublished manuscript, Colgate University, Hamilton, NY.

Dovidio, J. F., & Gaertner, S. L. (1993). Stereotypes and evaluative intergroup bias. In D. M. Mackie & D. L. Hamilton (Eds.), *Affect, cognition, and stereotyping: Interactive processes in group perception* (pp. 167–193). San Diego: Academic Press.

Downie, R., Milech, D. & Kirsner, K. (1985). Unit definition in the mental lexicon. *Australian Journal of Psychology, 37*(2), 141–155.

Dreyfus, H. L., & Dreyfus, S. E. (1984, November / December). Mindless machines. *The Sciences,* pp. 18–22.

Dreyfus, H. L., & Dreyfus, S. E. (1986). *Mind over machine: The power of human intuition and expertise in the era of the computer.* New York: The Free Press.

Duffy, S. A., Morris, R.K., & Rayner, K. (1988). Lexical ambiguity and fixation times in reading. *Journal of Memory & Language, 27,* 429–446.

Dulany, D. E., Carlson, R. A., & Dewey, G. I. (1984). A case of syntactical learning and judgement: How conscious and how abstract? *Journal of Experimental Psychology: General, 113,* 541–555.

Dulany, D. E., Carlson, R. A., & Dewey, G. I. (1985). On consciousness in syntactical learning and judgment: A reply to Reber, Allen, & Regan. *Journal of Experimental Psychology: General, 114*, 25–32.

Duncan, K. D., & Praetorius, N. (1992). Verbal reports in psychological investigations: A logical and psychological analysis. *Psyke & Logos, 7*, 259–287.

Duncan, K. D., & Shepherd, A. (1977). A simulator and training technique for diagnosing plant failures from control panels. *Ergonomics, 18*, 626–641.

Dunlap, K. (1900). The influence of past experience upon perception of properties. *American Journal of Psychology, 7*, 435–453.

Dunn, J. C., & Kirsner, K. (1988). Discovering functionally independent mental processes: The principle of reversed association. *Psychological Review, 95*(1), 91–101.

Dunn, J. C., & Kirsner, K. (1989). Implicit memory: Task or process? In S. Lewandowsky, J. C. Dunn, & K. Kirsner (Eds.), *Implicit memory: Theoretical issues* (pp. 17–31). Hillsdale, NJ: Lawrence Erlbaum Associates.

Durkin, K. (1985a). Television and sex role acquisition 1: Content. *British Journal of Social Psychology, 24*, 101–113.

Durkin, K. (1985b). *Television, sex roles and children. A developmental social psychological account.* Milton Keynes: Open University Press.

Durkin, K. (1987). Social cognition and social context in the construction of sex differences in human performance. In M. A. Baker (Ed.), *Sex differences in human performance* (pp. 141–170). London: Wiley.

Durkin, K. (1997). *The death of a human bean: Children's understanding of crime and legal processes on television.* Manuscript in preparation.

Eagly, A. H., & Mladinic, A. (1989). Gender stereotypes and attitudes toward women and men. *Personality and Social Psychology Bulletin, 15*, 543–558.

Easterbrook, J. A. (1959). The effect of emotion on cue utilisation and the organisation of behaviour. *Psychological Review, 66*, 183–201.

Eaves, G., & Rush, A. J. (1984). Cognitive patterns in symptomatic and remitted unipolar major depression. *Journal of Abnormal Psychology, 93*, 31–40.

Edwards, A. L. (1957). *Techniques of attitude scale construction.* New York: Appleton–Century–Crofts.

Egan, D. E., & Schwartz, B. J. (1979). Chunking in recall of symbolic drawings. *Memory & Cognition, 7*, 149–158.

Ehlers, A., Margraf, J., Davies, S., & Roth, W. T. (1988). Selective processing of threat cues in subjects with panic attacks. *Cognition & Emotion, 2*, 201–220.

Ehri, L. (1991). Learning to read and spell words. In L. Reiben & C. Perfetti (Eds.), *Learning to read: Basic research and its implications* (pp. 57–73). Hillsdale, NJ: Lawrence Erlbaum Associates.

Ehri, L. (1992). Reconceptualizing the development of sight word reading and its relationship to recoding. In P. Gough, L. Ehri, & R. Treiman (Eds.), *Reading acquisition* (pp. 107–143). Hillsdale, NJ: Lawrence Erlbaum Associates.

Ehri, L. C., & Robbins, C. (1992). Beginners need some decoding skill to read by analogy. *Reading Research Quarterly, 27*, 13–26.

Ehri, L., & Wilce, L. (1985). Movement into reading: Is the first stage of printed word learning visual or phonetic? *Reading Research Quarterly, 20*, 163–179.

Ehrlich, H. J. (1973). *The social psychology of prejudice.* New York: Wiley.

Eichenbaum, H., Fagan, A., Mathews, P., & Cohen, N. J. (1988). Hippocampal system dysfunction and odor discrimination learning in rats: Impairment of facilitation depending on representational demands. *Behavioral Neuroscience, 102*, 331–339.

Eichenbaum, H., Stewart, C., & Morris, R. G. M. (1990). Hippocampal representation in spatial learning. *Journal of Neuroscience, 10*, 331–339.

Einhorn, H. J. (1970). The use of nonlinear, noncompensatory models in decision making. *Psychological Bulletin, 73*, 171–192.

Einhorn, H. J., & Hogarth, R. M. (1981). Behaviour decision theory. *Annual Review of Psychology, 85*, 395–416.

Einhorn, H. J., Kleinmuntz, D. N., & Kleinmuntz, B. (1979). Linear regression and process-tracing models of judgement. *Psychological Review, 86*, 465–485.

Ellins, S. R., Cramer, R. E., & Martin, G. C. (1982). Discrimination reversal learning in newts. *Animal Learning and Behavior, 10*, 301– 304.

Elliot, T. K. (1965). *Effect of format and detail of job performance aids in performing simulated trouble-shooting tasks* (Tech. Rep. No. ARML-TR-65-154). Valencia, PA: Applied Science Association.

Elliot, T. K. (1967). *The effect of electronic aptitude on performance of proceduralised troubleshooting tasks* (Tech. Rep. No. AMRL-TR-67-154). Valencia, PA: Applied Science Association.

Ellis, N. R. (1970). Memory processes in retardates and normals. In N. R. Ellis (Ed.), *International review of research in mental retardation* (Vol. 4, pp. 1–32). New York: Academic Press.

Ellis, N. R., & Allison, P. (1988). Memory for frequency of occurrence in retarded and nonretarded persons. *Intelligence, 12*, 61–75.

Ellis, N. R., Katz, E. & Williams, J. E. (1987). Developmental aspects of memory for spatial location. *Journal of Experimental Child Psychology, 44*, 401–412.

Ellis, N. R., Meador, D. M., & Bodfish, J. W. (1985). Differences in intelligence and automatic memory processes. *Intelligence, 9*, 265–273.

Ellis, N. R., Palmer, R. L., & Reeves, C. L. (1988). Developmental and intellectual differences in frequency processing. *Developmental Psychology, 24*, 38–45.

Ellis, N. R., Woodley-Zanthos, P., Dulaney, C. & Palmer, R. L. (1989). Automatic-effortful processing and cognitive inertia in persons with mental retardation. *American Journal of Mental Retardation, 93*, 412–423.

Ellis, N. R., & Wooldridge, P. W. (1985). Short-term memory for pictures and words by mentally retarded and non-retarded persons. *American Journal of Mental Deficiency, 89*, 622–626.

Erdelyi, M. H. (1984). The recovery of unconscious (inaccessible) memories: Laboratory studies of hypermnesia. In G. Bower (Ed.), *The psychology of learning and motivation* (pp. 95–127). New York: Academic Press.

Erdelyi, M. H. (1992). Psychodynamics and the unconscious. *American Psychologist, 47*, 784–787.

Erdley, C. A., & D'Agostino, P. R. (1988). Cognitive and affective components of automatic priming effects. *Journal of Personality and Social Psychology, 54*, 741–747.

Ericcson, K. A., Krampe, R., & Tesch-Römer, C. (1993). The role of deliberate practice in the acquisition of expert performance. *Psychological Review, 100*, 363–406.

Ericsson, K. A., & Polson, P. G. (1988). A cognitive analysis of exceptional memory for restaurant orders. In M. T. H. Chi, R. Glaser, & M. J. Farr (Eds.), *The nature of expertise* (pp. 23–70). Hillsdale, NJ: Lawrence Erlbaum Associates.

Ericsson, K. A., & Smith, J. (1991). *Towards a general theory of expertise: Prospects and limits.* Cambridge, England: Cambridge University Press.

Ericsson, K. A. & Staszewski, J. J. (1989). Skilled memory and expertise: Mechanisms of exceptional performance. In D. Klahr & K. Kotovsky (Eds.), *Complex information processing* (pp. 235–267). Hillsdale, NJ: Lawrence Erlbaum Associates.

Eriksen, C. W. (1963). Perception and personality. In N. J. Wepman & R. W. Heine (Eds.), *Concepts of personality* (pp. 34–55). Chicago: Aldine.

Eriksen, C. W., & Collins, J. F. (1964). Backward masking in vision. *Psychonomic Science, 1*, 101–102.

Eriksen, C. W., & Collins, J. F. (1965). Reinterpretation of one form of backward and forward masking in visual masking. *Journal of Experimental Psychology, 70*, 343–351.

Evans, M., & Carr, T. (1985). Cognitive abilities, conditions of learning and the early development of reading skill. *Reading Research Quarterly, 20*, 327–350.

Eysenck, H. J. (1988). The concept of "intelligence": Useful or useless? *Intelligence, 12*, 1–16.

Eysenck, M. W. (1982). *Attention and Arousal*. New York: Springer-Verlag.

Fagan, J. F. (1990). The paired-comparison paradigm and infant intelligence. In A. Diamond (Ed.), *Annals of the New York Academy of Sciences: Vol. 608. The development and neural bases of higher cognitive functions* (pp. 337–364). New York: New York Academy of Sciences.

Farah, M. J. (1994). Visual perception and visual awareness after braindamage: A tutorial overview. In C. Umilta & M. Moscovitch (Eds.), *Attention and performance XV: Conscious and nonconscious information processing* (pp. 37–76). Cambridge, MA: Bradford Press.

Farnetani, E., Torsello, C. T., & Cosi, P. (1988). English compound versus non-compound noun phrases in discourse: An acoustic perceptual study. *Language and Speech, 31*(2), 157–180.

Ferreira, F., & Clifton, C. (1986). The independence of syntactic processing. *Journal of Memory and Language, 25*, 348–368.

Fink, E. L., Monahan, J. L., & Kaplowitz, S. A. (1989). A spatial model of the mere exposure effect. *Communication Research, 16*, 746–769.

Fischhoff, B., Slovic, P., & Lichtenstein, S. (1977). Knowing with certainty: The appropriateness of extreme confidence. *Journal of Experimental Psychology: Human Perception and Performance, 3*, 552–564.

Fishbein, M., & Ajzen, I. (1975). *Belief, attitude, intention, and behaviour: An introduction to theory and research.* Reading, MA: Addison-Wesley.

Fisher, C. (1960). Subliminal and supraliminal influences on dreams. *American Journal of Psychology, 116*, 1009–1017.

Fiske, S. T. (1981). Social cognition and affect. In J. Harvey (Ed.), *Cognition, social behaviour and the environment* (pp. 227–264). Hillsdale, NJ: Lawrence Erlbaum Associates.

Fiske, S. T. (1982). Schema-triggered affect: Applications to social perception. In M. S. Clarke & S. T. Fiske (Eds.), *Affect and cognition: The 17th Annual Carnegie Symposium on Cognition* (pp. 55–78). Hillsdale, NJ: Lawrence Erlbaum Associates.

Fiske, S. T. (1992). Stereotypes work...but only sometimes: Comment on how to motivate the "unfinished mind." *Psychological Inquiry, 3*, 161–2.

Fiske, S. T., & Neuberg, S. L. (1990). A continuum model of impression formation, from category-based to individuating processes: Influences of information and motivation on attention and interpretation. In M. P. Zanna (Ed.), *Advances in experimental social psychology* (Vol. 23, pp. 1–74). San Diego: Academic Press.

Fiske, S. T., & Pavelchak, M. A. (1986). Category-based versus piecemeal-based affective responses: Developments in schema-triggered affect. In R. M. Sorrentino & E. T. Higgins (Eds.), *Handbook of motivation and cognition: Foundations of social behaviour* (pp. 167–203). New York: Guilford.

Fiske, S. T., & Taylor, S. E. (1991). *Social cognition* (2nd ed.). New York: McGraw-Hill.

Fitts, P. M. (1964). Perceptual-motor skill learning. In A. W. Melton (Ed.), *Categories of human learning* (pp. 243 – 285). New York: Academic Press.

Flexner, A. (1910). *Medical education in the United States and Canada: A report to the Carnegie Foundation for the Advancement of Teaching.* New York: Carnegie Foundation for the Advancement of Teaching.

Foa, E. B., & McNally, R. J. (1986). Sensitivity to feared stimuli in obsessive-compulsives: A dichotic listening analysis. *Cognitive Therapy & Research, 10*, 477–486.

Foa, E. B., McNally, R., & Murdock, T. B. (1989). Anxious mood and memory. *Behaviour Research & Therapy, 27*, 141–147.

Fodor, J. A. (1983). *The modularity of mind.* Cambridge, MA: MIT Press.

Fodor, J. A. (1986). Information and Association. In M. Brand & R. M. Harnish (Eds.), *The representation of knowledge and belief* (pp. 80–100). Tucson: University of Arizona Press.

Fodor, J. A., & Pylyshyn, Z. W. (1988). Connectionism and cognitive architecture: A critical analysis. *Cognition, 28*, 3–71.

Forbach, G. B., Stanners, R. F., & Hochhaus, L. (1974). Repetition and practice effects in a lexical decision task. *Memory & Cognition, 2*, 337–339.

Forestell, P. H., & Herman, L. M. (1988). Delayed matching of visual materials by a bottlenosed dolphin aided by auditory symbols. *Animal Learning & Behavior, 15*, 137–146.

Forster, K., Booker, J., Schacter, D. L., & Davis, C. (1990). Masked repetition priming: Lexical activation or novel memory trace? *Bulletin of the Psychonomic Society, 28*, 341–345.

Forster, K. I., & Davis, C. (1984). Repetition priming and frequency attenuation in lexical access. *Journal of Experimental Psychology: Learning, Memory, and Cognition, 10*, 680–698.

Forster, P. M., & Govier, E. (1978). Discrimination without awareness? *Quarterly Journal of Experimental Psychology, 30*, 289–295.

Foss, D. J., & Ross, J. R. (1983). Great expectations: Context effects during sentence processing. In G. Flores D'Arcais & R. J. Jarvella (Eds.), *The process of language understanding* (pp. 169–191). Chichester, England: Wiley.

Foss, D. J., & Speer, S. R. (1991). Global and local context effects in sentence processing. In R. R. Hoffman & D. S. Palermo (Eds.), *Cognition and the symbolic processes* (pp. 115–139). Hillsdale, NJ: Lawrence Erlbaum Associates.

Fowler, C. A. (1989). Differential shortening of repeated content words produced in various communicative contexts. *Language and Speech, 31,* 307–319

Fowler, C. A., & Housum, J. (1987). Talkers' signalling of "new" and "old" words in speech and listeners' perception and use of the distinction. *Journal of Verbal Learning and Verbal Behaviour, 26,* 489–504.

Fowler, C. A., Wolford, G., Slade, R., & Tassinary, L. (1981). Lexical access with and without awareness. *Journal of Experimental Psychology: General, 110,* 115–125.

Franchina, J. J. (1991). Mere exposure to telereceptive cues facilitates intake of a novel flavor in chickens (*Gallus domesticus*). *Behavioural & Neural Biology, 56,* 108–112.

Frazier, L. (1987). Theories of sentence processing. In J. L. Garfield (Ed.), *Modularity in knowledge representation and natural-language understanding* (pp. 291–307). Cambridge, MA: Bradford Books.

Freud, S. (1912). In J. Strachey (Ed. and Trans.), *The standard edition of the complete psychological works of Sigmund Freud* (Vol. 12). London: Hogarth.

Frick, R. W. (1985). Communicating emotion: The role of prosodic features. *Psychological Bulletin, 97*(3), 412 – 429.

Gable, M., Wilkens, H. T., Harris, L., & Feinberg, R. (1987). An evaluation of subliminally embedded sexual stimuli in graphics. *Journal of Advertising, 16,* 26–40.

Gabrieli, J. D. E., Cohen, N. J., & Corkin, S. (1988). The impaired learning of semantic knowledge following bilateral medial temporal-lobe resection. *Brain and Cognition, 7,* 157–177.

Gabrieli, J. D. E., Milberg, W., Keane, M. M., & Corkin, S. (1990). Intact priming of patterns despite impaired memory. *Neuropsychologia, 28,* 417–427.

Gaertner, S. L., & McLaughlin, J. P. (1983). Racial stereotypes: Associations and ascriptions of positive and negative characteristics. *Social Psychology Quarterly, 46,* 23–30.

Gaffan, D. (1972). Loss of recognition memory in rats with lesions of the fornix. *Neuropsychologia, 10,* 327–341.

Gallistel, C. R., Brown, A. L., Carey, S., Gelman, R., & Keil, F. C. (1991). Lessons from animal learning for the study of cognitive development. In S. Carey & R. Gelman (Eds.), *The epigenesis of mind: Essay on biology and cognition* (pp. 3–36). Hillsdale, NJ: Lawrence Erlbaum Associates.

Gammack, J., & Young, R. (1985). Psychological techniques for eliciting expert knowledge. In M. Bramer (Ed.), *Research and development in expert systems* (pp. 105–112). Cambridge, England: Cambridge University Press.

Gardiner, J. M., & Java, R. I. (1993). Recognising and remembering. In A. F. Collins, S. E Gathercole, M. A. Conway, & P. E. Morris (Eds.), *Theories of memory* (pp. 163–188). Hove, England: Lawrence Erlbaum Associates.

Gardner, H. (1983). *Frames of mind: The theory of multiple intelligences.* London: Heinemann.

Gardner, R. C. (1973). Ethnic stereotypes: The traditional approach, a new look. *The Canadian Psychologist, 14*(2), 133–148.

Gardner, R. C., Taylor, D. M., & Feenstra, H. J. (1970). Ethnic stereotypes: Attitudes or beliefs? *Canadian Journal of Psychology, 24,* 321–334.

Gardner, R. C., Wonnacott, E. J., & Taylor, D. M. (1968). Ethnic stereotypes: A factor analytic investigation. *Canadian Journal of Psychology, 22,* 35–44.

Garfield, J. L. (Ed.)(1987). *Modularity in knowledge representation and natural-language understanding.* Cambridge, MA: Bradford Books.

Garrod, S. C., & Sanford, A. J. (1977). Interpreting anaphoric relations: The integration of semantic information while reading. *Journal of Verbal Learning and Verbal Behavior, 16,* 77–90.

Gazzaniga, M. (1989). Organisation of the human brain. *Science, 245,* 947–952.

Gazzaniga, M. S., Fendrich, R., & Wessinger, C. M. (1994). Blindsight reconsidered. *Current Directions in Psychological Science, 3,* 93–96.

Gee, J. P., & Grosjean, F. (1983). Performance structure: A psycholinguistic and linguistic appraisal. *Cognitive Psychology, 15,* 411–458.

Gellatly, A. R. H. (1980). Perception of an illusory triangle with masked inducing figure. *Perception, 9,* 599–602.

Gentner, D., & Stevens, A. L. (Eds.). (1983). *Mental models.* Hillsdale, NJ: Lawrence Erlbaum Associates.

Gerken, L., Jusczyk, P., & Mandel, D. (1994). When prosody fails to cue syntactic structure: 9-month-olds' sensitivity to phonological versus syntactic phrases. *Cognition, 51,* 237–265.

Gershberg, F. B., & Shimamura, A. P. (1994). Serial position effects in implicit and explicit tests of memory. *Journal of Experimental Psychology: Learning, Memory, and Cognition, 20,* 1370–1378.

Gibson, H. R. (1993). Emotional and social adjustment in later life. In S. Asher & M. Evandrou (Eds.), *Ageing, independence and the life course* (pp. 75–84). London: Jessica Kingsley.

Gilbert, D. T., & Hixon, J. G. (1991). The trouble of thinking: Activation and application of stereotypic beliefs. *Journal of Personality and Social Psychology, 60,* 509–517.

Glisky, E. L., & Schacter, D. L. (1988). Long-term retention of computer learning by patients with memory disorders. *Neuropsychologia, 26,* 173–178.

Glucksberg, S., & Cohen, G. N. J. (1970). Memory for nonattended auditory material. *Cognitive Psychology, 1,* 149–156.

Goldberg, L. R. (1971). Five models of clinical judgment: An empirical comparison between linear and nonlinear representations of the human inference process. *Organizational Behavior and Human Performance, 6,* 458–479.

Goldman, L., Weinberg, M., Weisberg, M., Olshen, R., Cook, E. F., Sargent, R. K., Lamas, G. A., Dennis, C., Wilson, C., Deckelbaum, L., Fineberg, H., Stiratelli, R., & the Medical House Staffs at Yale-New Haven Hospital and Brigham and Women's Hospital. (1982). A computer-derived protocol to aid in the diagnosis of emergency room patients with acute chest pain. *The New England Journal of Medicine, 307,* 588–596.

Goldmann, L. (1986). *Awareness under general anaesthesia.* Unpublished doctoral dissertation, Cambridge University, Cambridge, England.

Goldmann, L., Shah, M. V., & Helden, M. W. (1987). Memory of cardiac anaesthesia: Psychological sequelae in cardiac patients of introoperative suggestion and operating room conversation. *Anaesthesia, 42,* 596–603.

Goldstein, D., Hasher, L., & Stein, D. K. (1983). Processing of occurrence-rate and item information by children of different age and abilities. *American Journal of Psychology, 96,* 229–241.

Goldstein, M. J., & Barthol, R. P. (1960). Fantasy responses to subliminal stimuli. *Journal of Abnormal Social Psychology, 68,* 22–26.

Goodman, K. S. (1967). Reading: A psycholinguistic guessing game. *Journal of the Reading Specialist, 6,* 126–135.

Goodman, K. S. (1986). *What's whole in whole language: A parent-teacher guide.* Portsmouth, NH: Heinemann.

Goodman, K. S., & Goodman, Y. M. (1979). Learning to read is natural. In L. B. Resnick & P. A. Weaver (Eds.), *Theory and practice of early reading* (Vol. 1, pp. 137–154). Hillsdale, NJ: Lawrence Erlbaum Associates.

Goodman, Y. M., & Altwerger, B. (1981). Print awareness in preschool children: A working paper. In *A study of the development of literacy in preschool children* (Occasional Papers No. 4). Tucson, University of Arizona: Program in Language and Literacy.

Goodstein, L. P. (1982). An integrated display set for process operators. In *IFAC analysis, design and evaluation of man-machine systems* (pp. 63–70) Oxford: Pergamon Press.

Gordon, B. (1988). Preserved learning of novel information in amnesia: Evidence for multiple memory systems. *Brain and Cognition, 7,* 257–282.

Gordon, G. (1967) *Semantic determination by subliminal verbal stimuli: A qualitative approach.* Unpublished doctoral dissertation, University of London, London.

Gotlib, I. H., & McCann, C. D. (1984). Construct accessibility and depression: An examination of cognitive and affective factors. *Journal of Personality & Social Psychology, 47,* 427–439.

Gotlib, I. H., McLachlan, A. L., & Katz, A. N. (1988). Biases in visual attention in depressed and nondepressed individuals. *Cognition & Emotion, 2,* 185–200.

Gough, P. (1983). Context, form and interaction. In K. Rayner (Ed.), *Eye movements in reading: Perceptual and language processes* (pp. 203–211). San Diego: Academic Press.

Gough, P., & Hillinger, M. (1980). Learning to read: An unnatural act. *Bulletin of the Orton Society, 30,* 179–196.

Gough, P., & Juel, C. (1991). The first stages of word recognition. In L. Rieben & C. Perfetti (Eds.), *Learning to read: Basic research and its implications* (pp. 47–56). Hillsdale, NJ: Lawrence Erlbaum Associates.

Gough, P., Juel, C., & Griffith, P. (1992). Reading, spelling, and the orthographic cipher. In P. Gough, L. Ehri, & R. Treiman (Eds.), *Reading acquisition* (pp. 35–48). Hillsdale, NJ: Lawrence Erlbaum Associates.

Gough, P. B., & Walsh, M. (1991). Chinese, Phoenicians, and the orthographic cipher of English. In S. Brady & D. Shankweiler (Eds.), *Phonological processes in literacy* (pp. 199–209). Hillsdale, NJ: Lawrence Erlbaum Associates.

Govier, E., & Pitts, M. (1982). The contextual disambiguation of a polysemous word in an unattended message. *British Journal of Psychology, 73,* 537–545.

Gracco, V. (1990). Characteristics of speech as a motor control system. In G. E. Hammond (Ed.), *Cerebral control of speech and limb movements* (pp. 3–28). North Holland: Elsevier Science Publishers.

Graf, P. (1990). Life-span changes in implicit and explicit memory. *Bulletin of the Psychonomic Society, 28,* 353–358.

Graf, P., & Gallie, K. A. (1992). A transfer-appropriate processing account for memory and amnesia. In L. R. Squire & N. Butters (Eds), *Neuropsychology of memory* (pp. 241–248). New York: Guilford.

Graf, P., & Komatsu, S.-I. (1994). Process dissociation procedure: Handle with caution! *European Journal of Cognitive Psychology, 6,* 113–129.

Graf, P., & Mandler, G. (1984). Activation makes words more accessible but not necessarily more retrievable. *Journal of Verbal Learning & Verbal Behaviour, 23,* 553–568.

Graf, P., & Masson, M. E. J. (Eds.) (1993). *Implicit memory: New directions in cognition, development, and neuropsychology.* Hillsdale, NJ: Lawrence Erlbaum Associates.

Graf, P., & Ryan, L. (1990). Transfer-appropriate processing for implicit and explicit memory. *Journal of Experimental Psychology: Learning, Memory, and Cognition, 16,* 978–992.

Graf, P., & Schacter, D. (1985). Implicit and explicit memory for new associations in normal and amnesic subjects. *Journal of Experimental Psychology: Learning, Memory, and Cognition, 11,* 501–518.

Grafton, S. T., Hazeltine, E., & Ivry, R. (1995). Functional mapping of sequence learning in normal humans. *Journal of Cognitive Neuroscience, 7,* 497–510.

Grant, D. S. (1976). Effect of sample presentation time on long-delay matching in the pigeon. *Learning and Motivation, 7,* 580–590.

Green, R. E. A., & Shanks, D. R. (1993). On the existence of independent explicit and implicit learning systems: An examination of some evidence. *Memory & Cognition, 21,* 304–317.

Greenbaum, J. L., & Graf, P. (1989). Preschool period development of implicit and explicit remembering. *Bulletin of the Psychonomic Society, 27,* 417–420.

Greene, J. O., & Cappelli, J. N. (1986). Cognition and talk: The relationship of semantic units to temporal patterns of fluency in spontaneous speech. *Language & Speech, 29,* 141–157.

Greene, R. L. (1984). Incidental learning of event frequency. *Memory & Cognition, 12,* 90–95.

Greene, S. B., McKoon, G., & Ratcliff, R. (1992). Pronoun resolution and discourse models. *Journal of Experimental Psychology: Learning, Memory, and Cognition, 18,* 266–283.

Greeno, J. G. (1989). Situations, mental models, and generative knowledge. In D. Klahr & K. Kotovsky (Eds.), *Complex information processing* (pp. 295–318). Hillsdale, NJ: Lawrence Erlbaum Associates.

Greenwald, A.G. (1992). New look 3: Unconscious cognition reclaimed. *American Psychologist, 47,* 766–779.

Greenwald, A. G., & Banaji, M. R. (1993). *Implicit social cognition: Attitudes, self-esteem, and stereotypes.* Unpublished manuscript.

Greenwald, A. G., Klinger, M. R., & Liu, T. J. (1989). Unconscious processing of dichoptically masked words. *Memory & Cognition, 17,* 35–47.

Greenwald, A. G., Spangenberg, E. R., Pratkanis, A. R., & Eskenazi, J. (1991). Double-bind tests of subliminal self-help audiotapes. *Psychological Science, 2,* 119–122.

Griffin, D., & Tversky, A. (1992). The weighing of evidence and the determinants of confidence. *Cognitive Psychology, 24,* 411–435.

Griffin, T. (1991). *Learning to make diagnostic judgements with Bayesian, rule-based, and outcome feedback: An alternative approach to multiple-cue probability learning.* Unpublished doctoral dissertation, University of Queensland, Australia.

Haist, F., Musen, G., & Squire, L. R. (1991). Intact priming of words and nonwords in amnesia. *Psychobiology, 19,* 275–285.

Haist, F., Shimamura, A. P., & Squire, L. R. (1992). On the relationship between recall and recognition memory. *Journal of Experimental Psychology: Learning, Memory, and Cognition, 18,* 691–702.

Hale, C. A. & Borkowski, J. G. (1991). Attention, memory and cognition. In J. L. Matson & J. A. Mulick (Eds.), *Handbook of mental retardation* (2nd ed., pp. 505–528). New York: Pergamon.

Halford, G. S. (1982). *The development of thought.* Hillsdale, NJ: Lawrence Erlbaum Associates.

Halford, G. S. (1993). *Children's understanding: the development of mental models.* Hillsdale, NJ: Lawrence Erlbaum Associates.

Halford, G. S., Maybery, M. T., O'Hare, A. W., & Grant, P. (1994). The development of memory and processing capacity. *Child Development, 65,* 1338–1356.

Halliday, M. (1967). *Intonation and grammar in British English.* The Hague, Netherlands: Mouton.

Hamann, S. B. (1990). Level-of-processing effects in conceptually driven implicit tasks. *Journal of Experimental Psychology: Learning, Memory, and Cognition, 16,* 970–977.

Hamilton, D. L. (1981). Stereotyping and intergroup behaviour: Some thoughts on the cognitive approach. In D. L. Hamilton (Ed.), *Cognitive processes in stereotyping and intergroup behaviour* (pp. 333–353). Hillsdale, NJ: Lawrence Erlbaum Associates.

Hamilton, D. L., & Sherman, J. W (1993). Stereotypes. In R. S. Wyer & T. K. Srull (Eds.), *Handbook of social cognition* (2nd ed., pp. 1–68). Hillsdale NJ: Lawrence Erlbaum Associates.

Hammond, K. R., Hamm, R. M., Grassia, J., & Pearson, T. (1987). Direct comparison of the efficacy of intuitive and analytic cognition in expert judgments. *IEEE Transactions on Systems, Man, and Cybernetics, SMC-17,* 753–770.

Hammond, K. R., McClelland, G. H., & Mumpower, J. (1980). *Human judgment and decision making: Theories, methods and procedures.* New York: Praeger.

Hansen, C. H., & Hansen, R. D. (1988). How rock music videos can change what is seen when boy meets girl: Priming stereotypic appraisal of social interactions. *Sex Roles, 19,* 287–316.

Harste, J., Burke, C., & Woodward, V. (1982). Children's language and world: Initial encounters with print. In J. Langer & M. Smith-Burke (Eds.), *Bridging the gap: Reader meets author* (pp. 105–131). Newark, DE: International Reading Association.

Hartman, M., Knopman, D. S., & Nissen, M. J. (1989). Implicit learning of new verbal associations. *Journal of Experimental Psychology: Learning, Memory, and Cognition, 15,* 1070–1082.

Hasher, L., & Chromiak, W. (1977). The processing of frequency information: An automatic mechanism? *Journal of Verbal Learning and Verbal Behaviour, 16,* 173–184.

Hasher, L., & Zacks, R. T. (1979). Automatic and effortful processes in memory. *Journal of Experimental Psychology: General, 108,* 356–388.

Hasher, L., & Zacks, R. T. (1984). Automatic processing of fundamental information. The case of frequency of occurrence. *American Psychologist, 39,* 1372–1388.

Hatano, G. (1988). Social and motivational bases for mathematical understanding. In G. B. Saxe & M. Gearhart (Eds.), *Children's mathematics: New directions for child development* (Vol. 41, pp. 55–70). San Francisco: Jossey-Bass.

Hatano, G. & Inagaki, K. (1986). Two courses of expertise. In H. Stevenson, H. Azuma & K. Hakuta (Eds.), *Child development and education in Japan* (pp. 262–272). San Francisco: Freeman.

Hauser, M. D., & Fowler, C. (1992). Fundamental frequency declination is not unique to human speech. Evidence from nonhuman primates. *Journal of the Acoustical Society of America, 91*(1), 363–369.

Hawkins, D. (1970). The effects of subliminal stimulation on drive level and brand preference. *Journal of Marketing Research, 7,* 322–326.

Hayes, N. A., & Broadbent, D. E. (1988). Two modes of learning for interactive tasks. *Cognition, 28,* 249–276.

Heindel, W. C., Butters, N., & Salmon, D. P. (1988). Impaired learning of a motor skill in patients with Huntington's disease. *Behavioral Neuroscience, 102,* 141–147.

Henley, S. H. A. (1975). Cross-modal effects of subliminal verbal stimuli. *Scandanavian Journal of Psychology, 16,* 30–36.

Henley, S. H. A., & Dixon, N. F. (1974). Laterality differences in the effects of incidental stimuli upon evoked imagery. *British Journal of Psychology, 65*, 529–536.

Henneman, R. L., & Rouse, W. B. (1984). Measures of human problem solving performance in fault diagnosis tasks. *IEEE Transactions on Systems, Man and Cybernetics, SMC-14*, 112–120.

Herman, L. M., Hovancik, J. R., Gory, J. D. & Bradshaw, G. L. (1989). Generalization of visual matching by a bottlenosed dolphin (*Tursips truncatus*): Evidence for invariance of cognitive performance with visual and auditory materials. *Journal of Experimental Psychology: Animal Behavior Processes, 15*, 124–136.

Hermelin, B., & O'Connor, N. (1986). Idiot savant calendrical calculators: rules and regularities. *Psychological Medicine, 16*, 885–893.

Hermelin, B., & O'Connor, N. (1990). Factors and primes: A specific numerical ability. *Psychological Medicine, 20*, 163–169.

Hermelin, B., O'Connor, N., Lee, S., & Treffert, D. (1989). Intelligence and musical improvisation. *Psychological Medicine, 19*, 447–457.

Hibbert, G. A. (1984). Ideational components of anxiety: Their origin and content. *British Journal of Psychiatry, 144*, 618–624.

Hick, W. G. (1952). On the rate of gain of information. *Quarterly Journal of Experimental Psychology, 4*, 11–26.

Hickey, T., Hickey, L., & Kalish, R. A. (1968). Children's perceptions of the elderly. *Journal of Genetic Psychology, 112*, 227–235.

Higgins, E. T., Kuiper, N. A., & Olson, J. M. (1981). Social cognition: A need to get personal. In D. L. Hamilton (Ed.), *Cognitive processes in stereotyping and intergroup behaviour* (pp. 298–332). Hillsdale, NJ: Lawrence Erlbaum Associates.

Hill, T., Lewicki, P., Czyzewska, M., & Boss, A. (1989). Self-perpetuating development of encoding biases in person perception. *Journal of Personality and Social Psychology, 57*, 373 – 387.

Hillard, A., Myles-Worsley, M., Johnston, W., & Baxter, B. (1985). The development of radiologic schema through training and experience: A preliminary communication. *Investigative Radiology, 18*, 422–425.

Hines, D., Czerwinski, M., Sawyers, P. K., & Dwyer, M. (1986). Automatic priming effects: Effect of category levels and word association level. *Journal of Experimental Psychology: Human Perception and Performance, 12* (1), 370–379.

Hintzman, D. L. (1984). Episodic versus semantic memory: A distinction whose time has come—and gone? Commentary on Tulving, E., Precis of *Elements of episodic memory. Behavioral and Brain Sciences, 7*, 240–241.

Hintzman, D. L. (1986). "Schema abstraction" in a multiple-trace memory model. *Psychological Review, 93*, 411–428.

Hintzman, D. L. (1991). Why are formal models useful in psychology? In W. E. Hockley & S. Lewandowsky (Eds.), *Relating theory and data: Essays in honor of Bennet B. Murdock* (pp. 39–56). Hillsdale, NJ: Lawrence Erlbaum Associates.

Hintzman, D. L., & Hartry, A. L. (1990). Item effects in recognition and fragment completion: Contingency relations vary for different subsets of words. *Journal of Experimental Psychology: Learning, Memory, and Cognition, 16*, 955–969.

Hird, K., & Kirsner, K. (1993). Dysprosody following acquired neurogenic impairment. *Brain and Language, 45*, 46–60.

Hirsh-Pasek, K., Kemler Nelson, D., Jusczyk, P., Wright Cassidy, K., Druss, B., & Kennedy, L. (1987). Clauses are perceptual units for prelinguistic infants. *Cognition, 26*, 269–286.

Hockey, G. R. J. (1970). Effect of loud noise on attentional selectivity. *Quarterly Journal of Experimental Psychology, 22*, 28–36.

Hockey, G. R. J. (1984). Varieties of attentional state: The effect of the environment. In R. S. Parasuraman and D. R. Davies (Eds.), *Varieties of attention* (pp. 469–479). Orlando, FL: Academic Press.

Hockey, G. R. J. (1986). Changes in operator efficiency as a function of environmental stress, fatigue, and circadian rhythms. In K. R. Boff, L. Kaufman, & J. P. Thomas (Eds.), *Handbook of perception and human performance* (Vol. 2, pp. 1–49) New York: Wiley.

Hodos, W., & Campbell, C. B. G. (1967). Scalae naturae: Why there is no theory in comparative psychology. *Psychological Review, 76,* 337–350.

Hodos, W. & Campbell, C. B. G. (1990). Evolutionary scales and comparative studies of animal cognition. In R. P. Kesner, & D. S. Olton (Eds.), *Neurobiology of comparative cognition* (pp. 1–20). Hillsdale, NJ: Lawrence Erlbaum Associates.

Holender, D. (1986). Semantic activation without conscious identification in dichotic listening, parafoveal vision, and visual masking: A survey and appraisal. *The Behavioral and Brain Sciences, 9,* 1–66.

Holliday, M., & Hirsch, J. (1986). Excitatory conditioning of individual *Drosophila melanogaster. Journal of Experimental Psychology: Animal Behavior Processes, 12,* 131–142.

Holyoak, K. J. (1991). Symbolic connectionism: Toward third-generation theories of expertise. In K. A. Ericsson & J. Smith (Eds.), *Toward a general theory of expertise: Prospects and limits* (pp. 301–335). Cambridge, England: Cambridge University Press.

Holyoak, K. J., & Spellman, B. A. (1993). Thinking. *Annual Review of Psychology, 44,* 265–315.

Hoover, W., & Gough, P. (1990). The simple view of reading. *Reading and Writing: An Interdisciplinary Journal, 2,* 127–160.

Hope, D. A., Rapee, R. M., Heimberg, R. C., & Dombeck, M. J. (1990). Representations of the self in social phobia: Vulnerability to social threat. *Cognitive Therapy & Research, 14,* 177–189.

Horowitz, W. A., Kestenbaum, C., Person, E. & Jarvik, L. (1965). Identical twin—"idiots savants"—calender calculators. *American Journal of Psychiatry, 121,* 1075–1079.

House, A., Rowe, D., & Standen, P. J. (1987). Affective prosody in the reading voice of stroke patients. *Journal of Neurology, Neurosurgery, and Psychiatry, 50,* 910–912.

Howard, D. V., & Howard, J. H., Jr. (1989). Age differences in learning serial patterns: Direct versus indirect measures. *Psychology and Aging, 4,* 357–364.

Howard, D. V., & Howard, J. H., Jr. (1992). Adult age differences in the rate of learning serial patterns: Evidence from direct and indirect tests. *Psychology and Aging, 7,* 232–241.

Howe, M. J. A. (1990). *The origins of exceptional abilities.* Oxford, England: Blackwell.

Howe, M. J. A., & Smith, J. (1988). Calendrical calculating in "idiots savants": How do they do it? *British Journal of Psychology, 79,* 371–386.

Howes, D. H. (1954). A statistical theory of the phenomenon of subception. *Psychological Review, 61,* 98–110.

Howie, D. (1952). Perceptual defence. *Psychological Review, 59,* 308–315.

Howitt, D. (1982). *Mass media and social problems.* Oxford, England: Pergamon.

Huey, E. G. (1968). *The psychology and pedagogy of reading.* Cambridge, MA: MIT Press. (Original work published 1908)

Humphreys, G. W., & Riddoch, M. J. (1987). Routes to object constancy: implications from neurological impairments of object constancy. *Quarterly Journal of Experimental Psychology, 36A,* 385–415.

Humphreys, M. S., Bain, J. D., & Burt, J. S. (1989). Episodically unique and generalized memories: Applications to human and animal amnesics. In S. Lewandowsky, J. C. Dunn, & K. Kirsner (Eds.), *Implicit memory: Theoretical issues* (pp. 139–156). Hillsdale, NJ: Lawrence Erlbaum Associates.

Humphreys, M. S., Bain, J. D., & Pike, R. (1989). Different ways to cue a coherent memory system: A theory for episodic, semantic, and procedural tasks. *Psychological Review, 96,* 208–233.

Hunt, E. (1980). Intelligence as an information processing concept. *British Journal of Psychology, 71,* 449–474.

Hunt, E., Lenneborg, C., & Lewis, J. (1975). What does it mean to be high verbal? *Cognitive Psychology, 7,* 194–227.

Huysman, J. H. B. M. (1970). The effectiveness of cognitive style constraint in implementing operations research proposals. *Management Science, 17,* 92–104.

Hyman, R. (1953). Stimulus information as a determinant of reaction time. *Journal of Experimental Psychology, 45,* 188–196.

Jackson, J. H. (1879). On affectations of speech from disease of the brain. *Brain, 2,* 203–222.

Jackson, L. A., & Sullivan, L.A. (1988). Cognition and affect in evaluations of stereotyped group members. *The Journal of Social Psychology, 129*(5), 659–672.

Jacoby, L. L. (1983). Remembering the data: Analyzing interactive processes in reading. *Journal of Verbal Learning and Verbal Behavior, 22,* 485–508.

Jacoby, L. L. (1991). A process dissociation framework: Separating automatic from intentional uses of memory. *Journal of Memory & Language, 30*(5), 513–541.

Jacoby, L. L., Allan, L. G., Collins, J. C., & Larwill, L. K. (1988). Memory influences subjective experience: Noise judgments. *Journal of Experimental Psychology: Learning, Memory, and Cognition, 14*(2), 240–247.

Jacoby, L. L., & Dallas, M. (1981). On the relationship between autobiographical memory and perceptual learning. *Journal of Experimental Psychology, 110*, 306–340.

Jacoby, L. L., & Kelley, C. M. (1992). A process-dissociation framework for investigating unconscious influences: Freudian slips, projective tests, subliminal perception and signal detection theory. *Current Directions in Psychological Science, 1*(6), 175–179.

Jacoby, L. L., Lindsay, S. D., & Toth, J. P. (1992). Unconscious influences revealed: Attention, awareness, and control. *American Psychologist, 47*, 802–809.

Jacoby, L. L., Toth, J. P., Lindsay, D. S., & Debner, J. A. (1992). Lectures for a layperson: Methods for revealing unconscious processes. In R. F. Bornstein & T. S. Pittman (Eds.), *Perception without awareness. Cognitive, clinical, and social perspectives* (pp. 81–120). New York: Guilford.

Jacoby, L. L., Toth, J. P., & Yonelinas, A. P. (1993). Separating conscious and unconscious influences of memory: Measuring recollection. *Journal of Experimental Psychology: General, 122*(2), 139-154.

Jacoby, L. L., Toth, J. P., Yonelinas, A. P. & Debner, J. A. (1994). The relationship between conscious and unconscious influences: Independency or redundancy? *Journal of Experimental Psychology: General, 123*(2), 218-219.

Jacoby, L. L., & Whitehouse, K. (1989). An illusion of memory: Recognition influenced by unconscious perception. *Journal of Experimental Psychology: General, 118*, 126-135.

Jacoby, L. L., Woloshyn, V. & Kelley, C. M. (1989). Becoming famous without being recognized: Unconscious influences of memory produced by dividing attention. *Journal of Experimental Psychology: General, 118*, 115-125.

James, W. (1890). *Principles of psychology*. New York: Holt.

Janis, I. (1980). The influence of television on personal decision-making. In S. B. Withey & R. P. Abeles (Eds.), *Television and social behavior: Beyond violence and children* (pp. 161 – 189). Hillsdale, NJ: Lawrence Erlbaum Associates.

Jarvenpaa, S. L., Dickson, G. W., & DeSanctis, G. (1985). Methodological issues in experimental IS research: Experiences and recommendations. *MIS Quarterly, 9*, 141–156.

Jelicic, M., de Roode, A., Bovile, J. G., & Bonke, B. (1992). Unconscious learning during anaesthesia. *Anaesthesia, 47*, 835–837.

Jenkinson, J. C. (1983). Is speed of information processing related to fluid or to crystallized intelligence? *Intelligence, 7*, 91–106.

Jensen, A. R. (1980). Chronometric analysis of mental ability. *Journal of Social and Biological Structures, 3*, 181–224.

Jensen, A. R. (1982). The chronometry of intelligence. In R. J. Sternberg (Ed.), *Advances in the psychology of human intelligence* (Vol. 1, pp. 255–310). Hillsdale, NJ: Lawrence Erlbaum Associates.

Jensen, A. R. (1984). Test validity: g versus the specificity doctrine. *Journal of Social and Biological Structures, 7*, 93–118.

Jensen, A. R., & Munro, E. (1979). Reaction time, movement time and intelligence. *Intelligence, 3*, 121–126.

Jensen, A. R. & Weng, L. (1994). What is good *g*? *Intelligence, 18*, 231–258.

Johnson, A. K., & Multhaup, K. S. (1992). Emotion and MEM. In S.A. Christianson (Ed.), *Handbook of emotion and memory* (pp. 33–66). Hillsdale, NJ: Lawrence Erlbaum Associates.

Johnson, M. H., & Magaro, P. A., (1987). Effects of mood and severity on memory processes in depression and mania. *Psychological Bulletin, 101*, 28–40.

Johnson, M. K., Raye, C., Hasher, L., & Chromiak, C. (1979). Are there developmental differences in reality monitoring. *Journal of Experimental Child Psychology, 27*, 120–128.

Johnson, P. E. (1983). What kind of expert should a system be? *The Journal of Medicine and Philosophy, 8*, 77–97.

Johnson-Laird, P. N. (1983). *Mental models*. Cambridge, England: Cambridge University Press.

Johnston, W. A., Dark, V. J., & Jacoby, L. L. (1985). Perceptual fluency and recognition judgments. *Journal of Experimental Psychology: Learning, Memory and Cognition, 11*(1), 3–11.

Jones, M. R. (1991). Interactive modelling in decision support systems. *Interacting with Computers, 3,* 167–186.

Joordens, S., & Merikle, P. M. (1993). Independence or redundancy? Two models of conscious and unconscious influences. *Journal of Experimental Psychology: General, 122*(4), 462–467.

Jorm, A., & Share, D. (1983). Phonological recoding and reading acquisition. *Applied Psycholinguistics, 4,* 103–147.

Juel, C. (1988). Learning to read and write: A longitudinal study of 54 children from first through fourth grades. *Journal of Educational Psychology, 80,* 437–447.

Juel, C., Griffith, P., & Gough, P. (1986). Acquisition of literacy: A longitudinal study of children in first and second grade. *Journal of Educational Psychology, 78,* 243–255.

Jung, C.G. (1916). *Wandlungen und Symbole der Libido* [Psychology of the unconscious: A study of the transformations and symbolisms of the libido: A contribution to the history of the evolution of thought. Authorized translation, with introduction by Beatrice M. Hinkle.] New York: Moffat, Yard and Co.

Jung, C. G. (1962). *Collected works: Six psychological types* (W. McGuire, Ed.). Princeton, NJ: Princeton University Press.

Jusczyk, P., Cutler, A., & Redanz, L. (1993). The infants preference for the predominant stress patterns of English words. *Child Development, 64*(3), 675–687.

Just, M. A., & Carpenter, P. A. (1992). A capacity theory of comprehension: Individual differences in working memory. *Psychological Review, 99,* 122–149.

Kahneman, D. (1973). *Attention and effort.* Englewood Cliffs, NJ: Prentice-Hall.

Kahneman, D., & Chajczyk, D. (1983). Tests of the automaticity of reading: Dilution of Stroop effects by color-irrelevant stimuli. *Journal of Experimental Psychology: Human Perception and Performance, 9,* 497–509.

Kahneman, D., & Miller, D. (1986). Norm theory: Comparing reality to its alternatives. *Psychological Review, 93*(2), 136–153.

Kahneman, D., Slovic, P., & Tversky, A. (Eds.). (1982). *Judgment under uncertainty: Heuristics and biases.* New York: Cambridge University Press.

Kahneman, D., & Tversky, A. (1973). On the psychology of prediction. *Psychological Review, 80,* 237–251.

Kahneman, D., & Tversky, A. (1982). The simulation heuristic. In D. Kahneman, P. Slovic, & A. Tversky (Eds.), *Judgement under uncertainty: Heuristics and biases* (pp. 201–210). London: Cambridge University Press.

Kail, R. (1993). The role of a global mechanism in developmental change in speed of processing. In M. L. Howe & R. Pasnak (Eds.), *Emerging themes in cognitive development: Vol. 1. Foundations* (pp. 97–119). New York: Springer-Verlag.

Kail, R. V., & Siegal, A. W. (1977). The development of mnemonic encoding in children: From perception to abstraction. In R. V. Kail & J.W. Hagen (Eds.), *Perspectives on the development of memory and cognition* (pp. 61–88). Hillsdale, NJ: Lawrence Erlbaum Associates.

Karmiloff-Smith, A. (1986). Stage/structure versus phase/process in modelling linguistic and cognitive development. In I. Levin (Ed.), *Stage and structure: Reopening the debate* (pp. 164–190). Norwood, NJ: Ablex.

Karmiloff-Smith, A. (1992). *Beyond modularity: A developmental perspective on cognitive science.* Cambridge, MA: MIT Press.

Karmiloff-Smith, A. (1994). Precis of Beyond modularity: A developmental perspective on cognitive science. *Behavioral and Brain Sciences, 17,* 693–707.

Karmiloff-Smith, A., & Inhelder, B. (1974). If you want to get ahead get a theory. *Cognition, 3,* 195–212.

Katz, D., & Stotland, E. (1959). A preliminary statement to a theory of attitude structure and change. In S. Koch (Ed.), *Psychology: A study of a science* (Vol. 3, pp. 423–475). New York: McGraw-Hill.

Keane, M. M., Gabrieli, J. D. E., Fennema, A. C., Growdon, J. H., & Corkin, S. (1991). Evidence for a dissociation between perceptual and conceptual priming in Alzheimer's disease. *Behavioral Neuroscience, 105,* 326–342.

Keeney, R. L. (1982). Decision analysis: An overview. *Operations Research, 30,* 803–838.

Kellogg, R. T., & Bourne, L. E. (1989). Nonanalytic-automatic abstraction of concepts. In J. B. Sidowski (Ed.), *Conditioning, cognition and methodology: Contemporary issues in experimental psychology* (pp. 89–111). Lanham, MD: University Press of America.

Kemp-Wheeler, S. M., & Hill, A. B. (1987). Anxiety responses to subliminal experiences of mild stress. *British Journal of Psychology, 78*, 365–374.

Kemp-Wheeler, S. M., & Hill, A. B. (1988). Semantic priming without awareness: Some methodological considerations and replications. *Quarterly Journal of Experimental Psychology, 40*, 671–692.

Kent, R., & Rosenbeck, J. (1982). Prosodic disturbance and neurologic lesion. *Brain and Language, 15*, 259–291.

Key, W. B. (1973). *Subliminal seduction*. New York: Signet Books.

Key, W. B. (1976). *Media sexploitation*. Englewood Cliffs, NJ: Princeton.

Key, W. B. (1980). *The Clam-Plate Orgy and other subliminal techniques for manipulating your behavior*. New York: Prentice-Hall.

Kihlstrom, J. F. (1987). The cognitive unconscious. *Science, 237*, 1445–1452.

Kihlstrom, J. F. (1993). The continuum of consciousness. *Consciousness & Cognition: An International Journal, 2*, 334–354.

Kihlstrom, J. F., Barnhardt, T. M., & Tataryn, D. J. (1992). Implicit perception. In R. F. Bornstein & T. S. Pittman (Eds.), *Perception without awareness. Cognitive, clinical, and social perspectives* (pp. 17–54). New York: Guilford.

Kihlstrom, J. F., Schacter, D. L., Cork, R. C., Hurt, C. A., & Behr, S. E. (1990). Implicit and explicit memory following surgical anaesthesia. *Psychological Science, 1*, 303–306.

Kilbourne, W. E., Painton, S., & Ridley, D. (1985). The effect of sexual embedding on responses to magazine advertisements. *Journal of Advertising, 14*, 48–56.

Kinsbourne, M., & Wood, F. (1975). Short-term memory processes and the amnesic syndrome. In D. Deutsch & J. A. Deutsch (Eds.), *Short-term memory* (pp. 258–291). New York: Academic Press.

Kintsch, W., & Mross, E. F. (1985). Context effects in word recognition. *Journal of Memory and Language, 24*, 336–349.

Kirby, D. M., & Gardner, R. C. (1973). Ethnic stereotypes: Determinants in Children and their parents. *Canadian Journal of Psychology, 27*, 127–143.

Kirk-Smith, M., Booth, D. A., Carroll, D., & Davies, P. (1978). Human social attitudes affected by androstenol. *Research on Community, Psychological and Psychiatric Behaviour, 3*, 379–384.

Kirsner, K., & Dunn, J. C. (1985). The perceptual record: A common factor in repetition priming and attribute retention. In M. I. Posner & O. S. M. Marin (Eds.), *Mechanisms of attention: Attention and performance XI* (pp. 547–565). Hillsdale, NJ: Lawrence Erlbaum Associates.

Kirsner, K., Milech, D., & Standen, P. (1983). Common and modality-specific processes in the mental lexicon. *Memory & Cognition, 11*, 621–630.

Kirsner, K., Milech, D., & Stumpfel, V. (1986). Word and picture recognition: Is representational parsimony possible? *Memory & Cognition, 14*(5), 398–408.

Kirsner, K., & Pratley, D. (1996). *Are transfer effects in skill acquisition modality-specific?* Manuscript in preparation.

Kirsner, K., & Smith, M. C. (1974). Modality effects in word identification. *Memory & Cognition, 2*, 637–640.

Kirsner, K. & Speelman, C. P. (1993). Is lexical processing just an "ACT"? In A. F. Collins, S. E. Gathercole, M. A. Conway, & P. E. Morris (Eds.), *Theories of memory* (pp. 303–326). Hove, England: Lawrence Erlbaum Associates.

Kirsner, K., & Speelman, C. (1996). Skill acquisition and repetition priming: One principle, many processes. *Journal of Experimental Psychology: Learning, Memory, and Cognition, 22*(3), 563–575.

Kirsner, K., Speelman, C., & Schofield, P. (1993). Implicit memory and skill acquisition: Is synthesis possible? In P. Graf & M. E. J. Masson (Eds.), *Implicit memory: New directions in cognition, development, and neuropsychology* (pp. 119–139). Hillsdale, NJ: Lawrence Erlbaum Associates.

Klapp, S. T., & Lee, P. (1974). Time-of-occurrence cues for "unattended" auditory material. *Journal of Experimental Psychology, 102*, 176–177.

Klapper, J. T. (1960). *The effects of mass communication*. New York: The Free Press.

Kleinmuntz, B. (1990). Why we still use our heads instead of formulas: Toward an integrative approach. *Psychological Bulletin, 107*, 296–310.

Klinger, M. R., & Greenwald, A. G. (1995). Unconscious priming of association judgements. *Journal of Experimental Psychology: Learning, Memory, and Cognition, 21*(1), 569–581.

Knopman, D. (1991). Unaware learning versus preserved learning in pharmacologic amnesia: Similarities and differences. *Journal of Experimental Psychology: Learning, Memory, and Cognition, 17*, 1017–1029.

Knopman, D. S., & Nissen, M. J. (1987). Implicit learning in patients with probable Alzheimer's disease. *Neurology, 37*, 784–788.

Knowlton, B. J., Ramus, S. J., & Squire, L. R. (1992). Intact artificial grammar learning in amnesia: Dissociation of classification learning and explicit memory for specific instances. *Psychological Science, 3*, 172–179.

Knowlton, B. J., & Squire, L. R. (1994). The information acquired during artificial grammar learning. *Journal of Experimental Psychology: Learning, Memory, and Cognition, 20*, 79–91.

Knowlton, B. J., & Squire, L. R. (1996). Artificial grammar learning depends on implicit acquisition of both abstract and exemplar-specific information. *Journal of Experimental Psychology: Learning, Memory, and Cognition, 22*, 169–181.

Kolers, P. A. (1975). Memorial consequences of automatised encoding. *Journal of Experimental Psychology: Human Learning and Memory, 1*(6), 689–701.

Kolers, P. A., & Roediger, H. L. (1984). Procedures of mind. *Journal of Verbal Learning and Verbal Behavior, 23*, 425–449.

Komatsu, S.-I., Graf, P., & Uttl, B. (1995). Process dissociation procedure: Core assumptions fail, sometimes. *European Journal of Cognitive Psychology, 7*, 19–40.

Koriat, A., Lichtenstein, S., & Fischhoff, B. (1980). Reasons for confidence. *Journal of Experimental Psychology: Human Learning and Memory, 6*, 107–118.

Korsakoff, S. S. (1955). Psychic disorder in conjunction with multiple neuritis. *Neurology, 5*, 396–406.

Kosslyn, S. M., & Intriligator, J. M. (1992). Is cognitive neuropsychology plausible? The perils of sitting on a one-legged stool. *Journal of Cognitive Neuroscience, 4*, 96–106.

Kothandapani, V. (1971). Validation of feeling, belief, and intention to act as three components of attitude and their contribution to prediction of contraceptive behaviour. *Journal of Personality and Social Psychology, 19*, 321–333.

Kragt, H., & Landeweerd, J. A. (1974). Mental skills in process control. In E. Edwards & F. P. Lees (Eds.), *The human operator in process control* (pp. 135–145). London: Taylor & Francis.

Kranzler, J. H., & Jensen, A. R. (1989). Inspection time and intelligence: A meta-analysis. *Intelligence, 13*, 329–348.

Kraus, S., Wilkenfeld, J., Harris, M. A., & Blake, E. (1992). The HOSTAGE CRISIS SIMULATION. *Simulation and Gaming, 23*, 398–416.

Krech, D., & Crutchfield, R. S. (1948). *Theory and problems of social psychology.* New York: McGraw-Hill.

Kroodsma, D. E. (1982). Song repertoires: Problems in their definition and use. In D. E. Kroodsma & E. H. Miller (Eds.), *Acoustic communication in birds* (Vol. 2, pp. 1–23). New York: Academic Press.

Krosnick, J. A., Betz, A. L., Jussim, L. J., & Lynn, A. R. (1992). Subliminal conditioning of attitudes. *Personality and Social Psychology Bulletin, 18*, 152–162.

Krupski, A. (1975). Heart rate changes during a fixed reaction time task in normal and retarded adult males. *Psychophysiology, 12*, 262–267.

Krupski, A. (1977). Role of attention in the reaction-time performance of mentally retarded adolescents. *American Journal of Mental Deficiency, 82*, 79–83.

Kucera, H., & Francis, W. N. (1967). *Computational analysis of present-day American English.* Providence, RI: Brown University Press.

Kuhn, T. S. (1962). *The structure of scientific revolutions.* Chicago: University of Chicago Press.

Kuipers, B. J., & Kassirer, J. P. (1984). Causal reasoning in medicine: Analysis of a protocol. *Cognitive Science, 8*, 363–385.

Kunst-Wilson, W. R., & Zajonc, R. B. (1980). Affective discrimination of stimuli that cannot be recognized. *Science, 207*, 557–558.

Kushner, M., Cleeremans, A., & Reber, A. (1991, August) *Implicit detection of event interdependencies and a PDP model of the process.* Paper presented at the Thirteenth annual meeting of the Cognitive Science Society, Chicago.

Kuyken, W, & Brewin, C. R. (1995). Autobiographical memory functioning in depression and reports of early abuse. *Journal of Abnormal Psychology, 104*, 585–591.

Ladd, D. (1983). Peak features and overall slope. In A. Cutler & D. Ladd (Eds.), *Prosody: Models and measurements* (pp. 39–52). New York: Springer-Verlag.

Ladd, D. (1988). Declination "reset" and the hierarchical organisation of utterances. *Journal of the Acoustic Society of America, 84* (2), 530–544.

Ladd, D., & Cutler, A. (1983). Introduction. Models and measurements in the study of prosody. In A. Cutler & D. Ladd (Eds.), *Prosody: Models and measurements* (pp. 1–10). New York: Springer-Verlag.

Ladd, D. R., Silverman, K., Tolkmitt, F., Bergmann, G. M. & Scherer, K. R. (1985). Evidence for the independent function of intonation contour type, voice quality, and Fo range in signalling speaker affect. *Journal of the Acoustic Society of America, 78*, 435 – 444.

Lane, D. M., & Robertson, L. (1979). The generality of levels of processing hypothesis: An application to memory for chess positions. *Memory & Cognition, 7*, 253–256.

Larcker, D. F., & Lessig, V. P. (1983). An examination of linear and retrospective process tracing approaches to judgement modelling. *The Accounting Review, 58*, 58–77.

Larkin, J. H., McDermott, J., Simon, D. P., & Simon, H. A. (1980). Models of competence in solving physics problems. *Cognitive Science, 4*, 317–345.

Lau, W., Fan, S., Yiu, T., Chu, K., & Wong, S. (1984). Negative findings at laparotomy. *American Journal of Surgery, 148*, 375–378.

Lavy, E. H., van Oppen, P., & van den Hout, M. A. (1994). Selective processing of emotional information in obsessive compulsive disorder. *Behaviour Research & Therapy, 32*, 243–246.

Lesgold, A. M. (1984). Acquiring expertise. In J. R. Anderson & S. M. Kosslyn (Eds.), *Tutorials in learning and memory: Essays in honor of Gordon Bower* (pp. 31–60). New York: Freeman.

Lesgold, A. M. (1988). Problem solving. In R. J. Sternberg and E. E. Smith (Eds.), *The psychology of human thought* (pp. 188–213). Cambridge, England: Cambridge University Press.

Lesgold, A., Glaser, R., Rubinson, H., Klopfer, D., Feltovich, P. & Wang, Y. (1988). Expertise in a complex skill: Diagnosing X-ray pictures. In M. T. H. Chi, R. Glaser, & M. J. Farr (Eds.), *The nature of expertise* (pp. 311–342). Hillsdale, NJ: Lawrence Erlbaum Associates.

Leslie, A. M. (1986). Getting development off the ground: Modularity and the infant's perception of causality. In P. van Geert (Ed.), *Theory building in developmental psychology* (pp. 405–437). New York: Elsevier North Holland.

Leslie, A. M. (1987). Pretense and representation: The origins of "theory of mind." *Psychological Review, 94*, 412–426.

Leslie, A. M. (1991). The theory of mind impairment in autism: Evidence for a modular mechanism of development? In A. Whiten (Ed.), *Natural theories of mind* (pp. 63–78). Oxford, England: Blackwell.

Levelt, W. J. (1989). *Speaking: From intention to articulation*. Cambridge, MA: MIT Press.

Levy, B. A., & Kirsner, K. (1989). Re-processing text: Indirect measures of word and message level processes. *Journal of Experimental Psychology: Learning, Memory, and Cognition, 15*, 407–417.

Levy, L. H. (1958). Perceptual defence in tactual perception. *Journal of Personality, 26*, 467–478.

Lewandowsky, S. (1993). The rewards and hazards of computer simulations. *Psychological Science, 4*, 236–243.

Lewandowsky, S., & Bainbridge, J. V. (1994). Implicit memory. In V. S. Ramachandran (Ed.), *Encyclopedia of human behavior* (pp. 589–600). San Diego: Academic Press.

Lewandowsky, S., Dunn, J. C., & Kirsner, K. (Eds.). (1989). *Implicit memory: Theoretical issues*. New York: Lawrence Erlbaum Associates.

Lewandowsky, S., Dunn, J. C., Kirsner, K., Randell, M., & Smith, W. (1995, November). *Mental models and decision making in bush fire fighting*. Paper presented at the 36th annual meeting of the Psychonomics Society, Los Angeles.

Lewicki, P. (1986). *Nonconscious social information processing*. Orlando, FL: Academic Press.

Lewicki, P., Czyzewska, M., & Hoffman, H. (1987). Unconscious acquisition of complex procedural knowledge. *Journal of Experimental Psychology: Learning, Memory, and Cognition, 13*, 523–530.

Lewicki, P., Hill, T., & Bizot, E. (1988). Acquisition of procedural knowledge about a pattern of stimuli that cannot be articulated. *Cognitive Psychology, 20*, 24–37.

Lewicki, P., Hill, T., & Czyzewska, M. (1992). Nonconscious acquisition of information. *American Psychologist, 47,* 796–801.

Lewis, J. L. (1970). Semantic processing of unattended messages using dichotic listening. *Journal of Experimental Psychology, 85,* 225–228.

Lewontin, R. C. (1990). The evolution of cognition. In *Thinking: An invitation to cognitive science* (Vol. 3, pp. 229–246). Cambridge, MA: MIT Press.

Liberman, A. M., Cooper, F. S., Shankweiler, D., & Studdert-Kennedy, M. (1967). Perception of the speech code. *Psychological Review, 74,* 431–461.

Liberman, I., & Shankweiler, D. (1985). Phonology and the problem of learning to read and write. *Remedial and Special Education, 6,* 8–17.

Lichtenstein, S., & Fischhoff, B. (1977). Do those who know more also know more about how much they know? *Organizational Behavior and Human Performance, 20,* 159–183.

Lichtenstein, S., & Fischhoff, B. (1980). Training for calibration. *Organizational Behavior and Human Performance, 26,* 149–171.

Lichtenstein, S., Fischhoff, B., & Phillips, L. D. (1977). Calibration of probabilities: The state of the art. In H. Jungermann & G. de Zeeuw (Eds.). *Decision making and change in human affairs* (pp. 275–324). Dordrecht, Netherlands: Reidel.

Lichtenstein, S., Fischhoff, B., & Phillips, L. D. (1982). Calibration of probabilities: The state of the art to 1980. In D. Kahneman, P. Slovic, & A. Tversky (Eds.), *Judgment under uncertainty: Heuristics and biases* (pp. 306–334). Cambridge, England: Cambridge University Press.

Lieberman, P. (1967). Intonation, perception and language. *Research Monographs, 38.* Cambridge, MA: MIT Press.

Lieberman, P., Katz, W., Jongman, A., Zimmerman, R., & Miller, M. (1985), Measures of the sentence intonation of read and spontaneous speech in American English. *Journal of the Acoustic Society of America, 77*(2), 649–657.

Light, L. L., & La Voie, D. (1993). Direct and indirect measures of memory in old age. In P. Graf & M. E. J. Masson (Eds.), *Implicit memory: New directions in cognition, development, and neuropsychology* (pp. 207–230). Hillsdale, NJ: Lawrence Erlbaum Associates.

Lind, M. (1982). *Multilevel flow modelling of process plant for diagnosis and control.* Unpublished paper presented at the International Meeting on Thermal Nuclear Research Safety, Chicago. (also available as Report No. M2357, Risö National Laboratory. Roskilde, Denmark)

Locke, V., MacLeod, C., & Walker, I. (1994). Automatic and controlled activation of stereotypes: Individual differences associated with prejudice. *British Journal of Social Psychology, 33,* 29–46

Loftus, E. F., & Ketcham, K. (1994). *The myth of repressed memory: False memories and allegations of sexual abuse.* New York: St. Martin's Press.

Loftus, E. F., & Klinger, M. R. (1992). Is the unconscious smart or dumb? *American Psychologist, 47,* 761–765.

Logan, G. D. (1988a). Automaticity, resources, and memory: Theoretical controversies and practical implications. *Human Factors, 30,* 583–598.

Logan, G. D. (1988b). Toward an instance theory of automatization. *Psychological Review, 95,* 492–527.

Logan, G. D. (1990). Repetition priming and automaticity: Common underlying mechanisms. *Cognitive Psychology, 22,* 1–35.

Logan, G. D. (1992a). Attention and preattention in theories of automaticity. *The American Journal of Psychology, 105,* 317–339.

Logan, G. D. (1992b). Shapes of reaction-time distributions and shapes of learning curves: A test of the instance theory of automaticity. *Journal of Experimental Psychology: Learning, Memory, and Cognition, 18,* 883–914.

Logan, G. D., & Cowan, W. B. (1984). On the ability to inhibit thought and action: A theory of an act of control. *Psychological Review, 91,* 295–327.

Longstreth, L. E. (1984). Jensen's reaction time investigations of intelligence: A critique. *Intelligence, 8,* 139–160.

Longstreth, L. E. (1986). The real and the unreal: A reply to Jensen and Vernon. *Intelligence, 10,* 181–191.

Low, J., & Durkin, K. (in press). Children's understanding of events and criminal justice processes in police programs. *Journal of Applied Developmental Psychology.*

Luckasson, R., Coulter, D. L., Polloway, E., Reiss, S., Schalock, R. L., Snell, M. E., Spitalnick, D. M., & Stark, J. A. (1992). AAMR Board approves new MR definition. *AAMR News and Notes, 5*, 1, & 6.

Lund, A. M., Hall, J. W., Wilson, K. P., & Humphreys, M.S. (1983). Frequency judgement accuracy as a function of age and school achievement (learning disabled vs. non-learning-disabled) patterns. *Journal of Experimental Child Psychology, 35*, 236–247.

Lundh, L. G., & Ost, L. G. (1996). Stroop interference, self focus and perfectionism in social phobics. *Behaviour Research & Therapy, 20,* 725–731.

Luria, A, (1973). *The working brain: an introduction to neuropsychology.* Harmondsworth, England: Penguin Books.

Lusted, L. B. (1977). *A study of the efficacy of diagnostic radiologic procedures: Final report on diagnostic efficacy.* Chicago: Efficacy Study Committee of the American College of Radiology.

MacKay, D. G. (1973). Aspects of a theory of comprehension, memory and attention. *Quarterly Journal of Psychology, 25*, 22–40.

MacKay, D. G. (1982). The problems of flexibility, fluency and speed-accuracy trade-off in skilled behaviour. *Psychological Review, 89*, 483–506.

MacLeod, C. (1990). Mood disorders and cognition. In M. W. Eysenck (Ed.), *Cognitive psychology* (pp. 9–56). Chichester, England: Wiley.

MacLeod, C. (1991). Clinical anxiety and the selective encoding of threatening information. *International Review of Psychiatry, 3*, 279–292.

MacLeod, C. (1993). Cognition in clinical psychology: Measures, methods or models? *Behaviour Change, 10*, 169–195.

MacLeod, C., & Hagan, R. (1992). Individual differences in the selective processing of threatening information, and emotional responses to a stressful life event. *Behaviour Research & Therapy, 30*, 151–161.

MacLeod, C., & Mathews, A. (1988). Anxiety and the allocation of attention to threat. *Quarterly Journal of Experimental Psychology: Human Experimental Psychology, 38*, 659–670.

MacLeod, C., & Mathews, A. (1991). Cognitive-experimental approaches to the emotional disorders. In P.R. Martin (Ed.), *Handbook of behaviour therapy and psychological science: Human experimental psychology* (pp. 116–150). New York: Pergamon.

MacLeod, C., Mathews, A., & Tata, P. (1986). Attentional bias in emotional disorders. *Journal of Abnormal Psychology, 95*, 15–20.

MacLeod, C., & McLaughlin, K. (1995). Implicit and explicit memory bias in anxiety: A conceptual replication. *Behaviour Research & Therapy, 33*, 1–14.

MacLeod, C., & Ng, V. (1997). *Prediction of anxiety reactions to subsequent migration in overseas students using a colour naming interference index of selective threat processing.* Manuscript in preparation.

MacLeod, C., & Rutherford, E. M. (1992). Anxiety and the selective processing of emotional information: Mediating roles of awareness, trait and state variables, and personal relevance of stimulus materials. *Behaviour Research & Therapy, 30*, 479–491.

MacLeod, C., Tata, P., & Mathews, A. (1987). Perception of emotionally valenced information in depression. *British Journal of Psychology, 26*, 67–68.

MacLeod, C. M., & Dunbar, K. (1988). Training and Stroop-like interference: Evidence for a continuum of automaticity. *Journal of Experimental Psychology: Learning, Memory, and Cognition, 14*, 126–135.

Malamut, B. L., Saunders, R. C., & Mishkin, M. (1984). Monkeys with combined amygdalo-hippocampal lesions succeed in object discrimination learning despite 24-hour intertrial intervals. *Behavioral Neuroscience, 98*, 759–769.

Malhotra, N. K. (1982). Reflections on the overload paradigm in consumer decision making. *Journal of Consumer Research, 8,* 419–430.

Mandler, G. (1975). Consciousness: Respectable, useful, and probably necessary. In R. L. Solso (Ed.), *Information processing and cognition: The Loyola symposium* (pp. 229–254). Hillsdale, NJ: Erlbaum.

Mandler, J. M. (1984). Representation and recall in infancy. In M. Moscovitch (Ed.), *Infant memory: Its relation to normal and pathological memory in humans and other animals* (pp. 75–101). New York: Plenum.

Mandler, J. M. (1988). How to build a baby: On the development of an accessible representational system. *Cognitive Development, 3,* 113–136.

Mandler, J. M., Seegmiller, D., & Day, J. (1977). On the coding of spatial information. *Memory & Cognition, 5,* 10–16.

Manstead, A. S. R., & McCulloch, C. (1981). Sex-role stereotyping in British television advertisements. *British Journal of Social Psychology, 20,* 171 – 180.

Marcel, A. J. (1978). Unconscious reading: Experiments on people who do not know that they are reading. *Visible Language, 12,* 391–404.

Marcel, A. J. (1980). Conscious and preconscious recognition of polysemous words: Locating the selective effect of prior verbal context. In R. S. Nickerson (Eds.), *Attention and performance* (pp. 92–112). Hillsdale, NJ: Lawrence Erlbaum Associates.

Marcel, A. J. (1982). *Is cortical blindness a problem of visual function or of visual consciousness?* Paper presented at the fifth International Neuropsychology Society European conference, Deauville, France.

Marcel, A. J. (1983a). Conscious and unconscious perception: An approach to the relations between phenomenal experience and perceptual awareness. *Cognitive Psychology, 15,* 283–300.

Marcel, A. J. (1983b). Conscious and unconscious perception: Experiments on visual masking and word recognition. *Cognitive Psychology, 15,* 197–237.

Marcel, A. J., Katz, L., & Smith, M. (1974). Laterality and reading proficiency. *Neuropsychologia, 12,* 131–139.

March, J. G. (1978). Bounded rationality, ambiguity, and the engineering of choice. *Bell Journal of Economics, 9,* 587–608.

Marescaux, P. J., Luc, F., & Karnas, G. (1989). Modes d'apprentissage electif et non-selectif et connaissances acquises x au controle d'un processus: evaluation d'un modele simule. [Modes of selective and non-selective learning and acquired knowledge in x the control of a process: Evaluation of a simulated model]. *Cahiers de Psychologie Cognitive, 9,* 239–264.

Marler, P. (1981). Birdsong: the acquisition of a learned motor skill. *Trends in Neurosciences, 4,* 88–94.

Marler, P. R., & Peters, S. (1977). Selective vocal learning in a sparrow. *Science, 198,* 519– 521.

Marr, D. (1982). *Vision.* New York: Freeman.

Marshall, E. C., Scanlon, K. E., Shepherd, A., & Duncan, K. D. (1981, February). Panel diagnosis training for major-hazard, continuous-process installations. *Chemical Engineer,* pp. 66–70.

Marshall, J. C., & Newcombe, F. (1966). Syntactic and semantic errors in paralexia. *Neuropsychologia, 4,* 169–176.

Martin, D. G., Hawryluk, G. A., & Guse, L. L. (1974). Experimental study of unconscious influences: Ultrasound as a stimulus. *Journal of Abnormal Psychology, 83,* 589–608.

Masonheimer, P., Drum, P., & Ehri, L. (1984). Does environmental print identification lead children into word reading? *Journal of Reading Behaviour, 16,* 257–271.

Massaro, D. W. (1989). Multiple book review of Speech perception by ear and eye: A paradigm for psychological enquiry. *Behavioral and Brain Sciences, 12,* 741–794.

Masson, M. E. J., & Freedman, L. (1990). Fluent identification of repeated words. *Journal of Experimental Psychology: Learning, Memory, and Cognition, 16,* 355–373.

Masson, M. E. J., & MacLeod, C. M. (1992). Reenacting the route to interpretation: Enhanced perceptual identification without prior perception. *Journal of Experimental Psychology: General, 121,* 145–176.

Mathews, A., & Bradley, B. (1983). Mood and the self-reference bias in recall. *Behaviour Research & Therapy, 21,* 233–239.

Mathews, A., & MacLeod, C. (1985). Selective processing of threat cues in anxiety states. *Behaviour Research & Therapy, 23,* 563–569.

Mathews, A., & MacLeod, C. (1986). Discrimination of threat cues without awareness in anxiety states. *Journal of Abnormal Psychology, 95,* 131–136.

Mathews, A., & MacLeod, C. (1994). Cognitive approaches to emotion and emotional disorders. *Annual Review of Psychology, 45,* 25–50.

Mathews, A., Mogg, K., Kentish, J., & Eysenck, M. (1995). Effect of psychological treatment on cognitive bias in generalized anxiety disorder. *Behaviour Research & Therapy, 33*, 293–303.

Mathews, A., Mogg, K., May, J., & Eysenck, M. W. (1989). Implicit and explicit memory bias in anxiety. *Journal of Abnormal Psychology, 98*, 236–240.

Mathews, M. E., & Fozard, J. L. (1970). Age differences in judgements of recency for short sequences of pictures. *Developmental Psychology, 3*, 208–217.

Mathews, R. C. (1991). The forgetting algorithm: How fragmentary knowledge of exemplars can abstract knowledge. *Journal of Experimental Psychology: General, 120*, 117–119.

Mathews, R. C., Buss, R. R., Stanley, W. B., Blanchard-Fields, F., Cho, J. R., & Druhan, B. (1989). Role of implicit and explicit processes in learning from examples: A synergistic effect. *Journal of Experimental Psychology: Learning, Memory, and Cognition, 15*, 1083–1100.

Matson, J. L., & Mulick, J. A. (Eds.). (1991). *Handbook of mental retardation* (2nd ed.). New York: Pergamon.

Maybery, M. T., & O'Brien-Malone, A. (1996). *Implicit learning and verbal knowledge of an interactive task: Testing alternative models by manipulating available attentional resources.* Manuscript in preparation.

Maybery, M. T., Taylor, M., & O'Brien-Malone, A. (1995). Implicit learning: Sensitive to age but not IQ. *Australian Journal of Psychology, 47*(1), 8–17.

Mazzella, C., Durkin, K., Cerini, E., & Buralli, P. (1992). Sex role stereotypes in Australian television advertisements. *Sex Roles, 26*, 243 – 259.

McAndrews, M. P., Glisky, E. L., & Schacter, D. L. (1987). When priming persists: Long-lasting implicit memory for a single episode in amnesic patients. *Neuropsychologia, 25*, 497–506.

McCabe, S. B., & Gotlib, I. H. (1995). Selective attention and clinical depression: Performance on a deployment-of-attention task. *Journal of Abnormal Psychology, 104*, 241–245.

McClelland, J. L., McNaughton, B. L., & O'Reilly, R. C. (1995). Why there are complementary learning systems in the hippocampus and neocortex: Insights from the success and failures of connectionist models of learning and memory. *Psychological Review, 102*, 419–457.

McClelland, J. L., Rumelhart, D. E., & Hinton, G. E. (1986) The appeal of parallel distributed processing. In D. E. Rumelhart, J. L. McClelland, and the PDP Research Group (Eds.), *Parallel distributed processing* (pp. 3–44). Cambridge, MA: Bradford.

McDowell, J. (1984). Recall of pleasant and unpleasant words in depressed subjects. *Journal of Abnormal Psychology, 93*, 401–407.

McFarland, C. E., & Sandy, J. T. (1982). Automatic and conscious processing in retarded and nonretarded adolescents. *Journal of Experimental Child Psychology, 33*, 20–38.

McGuire, W. J. (1968). The nature of attitudes and attitude change. In G. Lindzey & E. Aronson, (Eds.), *The handbook of social psychology* (2nd ed., Vol. 3, pp. 136–314). Reading MA: Addison-Wesley.

McKee, R. D., & Squire, L. R. (1993). On the development of declarative memory. *Journal of Experimental Psychology: Learning, Memory, and Cognition, 19*, 397–404.

McKeithen, K. B., Reitman, J. S., Rueter, H. H., & Hirtle, S. C. (1981). Knowledge organisation and skill differences in computer programmers. *Cognitive Psychology, 13*, 307–325.

McKenney, J. L., & Keen, P. G. W. (1974, May-June). How managers' minds work. *Harvard Business Review*, pp. 79–90.

McKoon, G., & Ratcliff, R. (1992). Inference during reading. *Psychological Review, 99*, 440–466.

McKoon, G., & Ratcliff, R. (1995). How should implicit memory phenomena be modeled. *Journal of Experimental Psychology: Learning, Memory, and Cognition, 21*, 777–784.

McKoon, G., Ratcliff, R., & Dell, G. S. (1986). A critical evaluation of the semantic-episodic distinction. *Journal of Experimental Psychology: Learning, Memory, and Cognition, 12*, 295–306.

McLeod, P. (1976). Control strategies of novice and experienced controllers with a slow response system (a zero-energy nuclear reactor). In T. B. Sheridan & G. Johannsen (Eds.), *Monitoring behaviour and supervisory control* (pp. 351–358). New York: Plenum.

McNally, R. J., Lasko, N. B., Macklin, M. L., & Pitman, R. K. (1995). Autobiographical memory disturbance in combat-related posttraumatic stress disorder. *Behaviour Research & Therapy, 3*, 619–630.

McNally, R. J., Litz, B. T., Prassas, A., Shin, L. M., & Weathers, F. W. (1994). Emotional priming of autobiographical memory in post-traumatic stress disorder. *Cognition & Emotion, 8*, 351–367.

McNally, R. J., Riemann, B. C., & Kim, E. (1990). Selective processing of threat cues in panic disorder. *Behaviour Research & Therapy, 28,* 407–412.

Medvedev, Z. A. (1990). *The legacy of Chernobyl.* Oxford, England: Basil Blackwell.

Meehl, P. E. (1957). When shall we use our heads instead of the formula? *Journal of Counselling Psychology, 4,* 268–273.

Mehler, J., Jusczyk, P., Lambertz, G., Halstead, N., Bertoncini, J., & Amiel-Tison, C. (1988). A precursor of language acquisition in young infants. *Cognition, 29,* 143–178.

Meichenbaum, D. H. (1995). Cognitive-behavioural therapy in historical perspective. In B. M. Bongar & L. E. Beutler (Eds.), *Comprehensive textbook of psychotherapy: Theory and practice* (pp. 140–158). New York: Oxford University Press.

Mellers, B. A., Ordonez, L. D., & Birnbaum, M. H. (1992). A change-of-process theory for contextual effects and preference reversals in risky decision making. *Organizational Behavior and Human Decision Processes, 52,* 331–369.

Menn, L., & Boyce, S. (1982). Fundamental frequency and discourse structure. *Language and Speech, 24*(4), 341 – 383.

Menzel, R. (1990). Learning, memory, and "cognition" in honey bees. In R. P. Kesner & D. S. Olton (Eds.), *The neurobiology of comparative cognition* (pp. 237–292). Hillsdale, NJ: Lawrence Erlbaum Associates.

Merikle, P. A. (1982). Unconscious perception revisited. *Perception and Psychophysics, 31,* 298–301.

Merikle, P. M., & Reingold, E. M. (1990). Recognition and lexical decision without detection: Unconscious perception. *Journal of Experimental Psychology: Human Perception & Performance, 16,* 574–583.

Merikle, P. M., & Reingold, E. M. (1992). Measuring unconscious perceptual processes. In R. F. Borstein & T. S. Pittman (Eds.), *Perception without awareness: Cognitive, clinical, and social issues* (pp. 55–80). New York: Guildford.

Merikle, P. M., & Skanes, H. E. (1992). Subliminal self-help audiotapes: A search for placebo effects. *Journal of Applied Psychology, 77,* 772 – 776.

Merrill, E. C., & Mar, H. H. (1987). Differences between mentally retarded and nonretarded persons' efficiency of auditory sentence processing. *American Journal of Mental Deficiency, 91,* 406–414.

Meyer, D. E., Schvaneveldt, R. W., & Ruddy, M. G. (1972). *Activation of lexical memory.* Paper presented at the meeting of the Psychonomic Society, St. Louis, MO.

Milech, D., Kirsner, K., Roy, G., & Waters, B. (1993). Applications of psychology to computer based tutoring systems. *International Journal of Human-Computer Interaction, 5,* 1-23.

Milech, D., Waters, B., Noël, S., Roy, G., & Kirsner, K. (1993). Student modelling in hybrid training systems. In G. Salvendy & M. J. Smith (Eds.), *Human-computer interaction: Software and hardware interfaces* (pp. 754–759). Amsterdam: Elsevier.

Millar, K., & Watkinson, N. (1983). Recognition of words presented during general anaesthesia. *Ergonomics, 26,* 585–594.

Miller, G. A. (1956). The magic number seven, plus or minus two: Some limits on our capacity for processing information. *Psychological Review, 63,* 81–93.

Miller, G. A., Galanter, E., & Pribram, K. H. (1960). *Plans and the structure of behavior.* New York: Holt, Rinehart & Winston.

Miller, J. (1991). Threshold variability in subliminal perception experiments: Fixed threshold estimates reduce power to detect subliminal effects. *Journal of Experimental Psychology: Human Perception and Performance, 17,* 841–851.

Miller, J. G. (1939). Discrimination without awareness. *American Journal of Psychology, 52,* 562–578.

Miller, R.A., Pope, H.E., & Myers, J.D. (1982). INTERNIST–I, an experimental computer-based diagnostic consultant for general internal medicine. *New England Journal of Medicine, 307,* 468–476.

Milner, D. A. (1992). Disorders of perceptual awareness: Commentary. In D. A. Milner & M. D. Rugg (Eds.), *The neuropsychology of consciousness* (pp. 139–158). London: Academic Press.

Milter, R. G., & Rohrbaugh, J. (1988). Judgment analysis and decision conferencing for administrative review: A case study of innovative policy making in government. *Advances in Information Processing in Organizations, 3,* 245–262.

Minard, J. G. (1965). Response-bias interpretation of perceptual defense. *Psychological Bulletin, 72,* 74–88.

Mitchell, D. B. (1993). Implicit and explicit memory for pictures: Multiple views across the lifespan. In P. Graf & M. E. J. Masson (Eds.), *Implicit memory: New directions in cognition, development, and neuropsychology* (pp. 171–190). Hillsdale, NJ: Lawrence Erlbaum Associates.

Mitchell, T. R., & Beach, L. R. (1990). "...Do I love thee? Let me count..." Toward an understanding of intuitive and automatic decision making. *Organizational Behavior and Human Decision Processes, 47,* 1–20.

Mogg, K., Bradley, B. P., Millar, N., & White, J. (1995). A follow-up study of cognitive bias in generalized anxiety disorder. *Behaviour Research & Therapy, 33,* 927–935.

Mogg, K., Bradley, B. P., Williams, R., & Mathews, A. (1993). Subliminal processing of emotional information in anxiety and depression. *Journal of Abnormal Psychology, 102,* 304–311.

Mogg, K., Mathews, A., & Eysenck, M. (1992). Attentional bias to threat in clinical anxiety states. *Cognition & Emotion, 6,* 149–159.

Mogg, K., Mathews, A., & Weinman, J. (1987). Memory bias in clinical anxiety. *Journal of Abnormal Psychology, 96,* 94–98.

Mogg, K., Mathews, A., & Weinman, J. (1989). Selective processing of threat cues in anxiety states: a replication. *Behaviour Research & Therapy, 27,* 317–323.

Monrad-Krohn, G. (1947). Dysprosody or altered "melody of language". *Brain, 70,* 405–423.

Moore, T. E. (1982). Subliminal advertising: What you see is what you get? *Journal of Marketing, 46,* 38–47.

Moray, N. (1959). Attention in dichotic listening: Affective cues and the influence of instructions. *Quarterly Journal of Experimental Psychology, 11,* 56–60.

Moray, N. (1967). Where is attention limited? A survey and a model. *Acta Pscyhologica, 27,* 83–92.

Moray, N. (1981). The role of attention in the detection of errors and the diagnosis of errors in man-machine systems. In J. Rasmussen & W. Rouse (Eds.), *Human detection and diagnosis of system failures* (pp.185–198). New York: Plenum.

Moray, N., Lootsteen, P., & Pajak, J. (1988). Acquisition of process control skills. *IEEE Transactions on Systems, Man, & Cybernetics, 16,* 497–504.

Morris, C. D., Bransford, J. D., & Franks, J. J. (1977). Levels of processing versus transfer appropriate processing. *Journal of Verbal Learning and Verbal Behavior, 16,* 519–533.

Morris, N. M., & Rouse, W. B. (1985). The effects of type of knowledge upon human problem solving in a process control task. *IEEE Transactions on Systems, Man, and Cybernetics, SMC-15,* 698–707.

Morris, P. E., Tweedy, M. & Gruneberg, M. M. (1985). Interest, knowledge and the memorisation of soccer scores. *British Journal of Psychology, 76,* 415–425.

Morrison, D. L., & Duncan, K. D. (1988). The effect of scrolling, hierarchically paged displays and ability on fault diagnosis performance. *Ergonomics, 31,* 889–904.

Morrison, D. L., & LeMap, A. (1996). Individual differences in fault finding skill can be reliably predicted after all. In S. A. Robertson (Ed.) *Contemporary ergonomics* (pp. 234–239). London: Taylor & Francis.

Morrison, D. L., Lewis, G., & LeMap, A. (in press). Predictors of fault finding skill. *Australian Psychologist.*

Morrison, D. L., & Upton, D. (1994). Fault diagnosis and computer integrated manufacturing systems. *IEEE Transactions on Engineering Management, 41,* 69–83.

Morrow, D. G. (1985). Prominent characters and events organize narrative understanding. *Journal of Memory and Language, 24,* 304–319.

Morrow, D. G., Leirer, V. O., & Altieri, P. A. (1992). Aging, expertise, and narrative processing. *Psychology and Aging, 7,* 376–388.

Morton, D., & Broadbent, D. E. (1967). Passive versus active recognition models or Is your homunculus really necessary? In W. Wathen-Dunn (Ed.), *Models for the perception of speech and visual form* (pp. 103–110). Cambridge, MA: MIT Press.

Morton, J. (1969). Interaction of information in word recognition. *Psychological Review, 76,* 165–178.

Morton, J. (1979). Facilitation in word recognition: Experiments causing change in the logogen model. In P. A. Kolers, M. E. Wrolstad, & H. Bouma, *The processing of visible language* (pp. 259–268). New York: Plenum.

Morton, J. (1980). The logogen and orthographic structure. In U. Frith (Ed.), *Cognitive processes in spelling* (pp. 117–133). London: Academic Press.

Morton, J., & Patterson, K. (1980). A new attempt at an interpretation or an attempt at a new interpretation. In M. Coltheart, K. E. Patterson, & J. C. Marshall (Eds.), *Deep dyslexia* (pp. 91–118). London: Routledge & Kegan Paul.

Moscovitch, M. (1992a). Memory and working-with-memory: A component process model based on modules and central systems. *Journal of Cognitive Neuroscience, 4,* 257–267.

Moscovitch, M. (1992b). A neuropsychological model of memory and consciousness. In L. R. Squire & N. Butters (Eds.), *Neuropsychology of memory* (pp. 5–22). New York: Guilford.

Moscovitch, M., Goshen-Gottstein, Y., & Vriezen, E. (1994). Memory without conscious recollection: A tutorial review from a neuropsychological perspective. In C. Umilta & M. Moscovitch (Eds.), *Attention and performance XV: Conscious and nonconscious information processing* (pp. 619–660). Cambridge, MA: MIT Press.

Moscovitch, M., Winocur, G., & McLachlan, D. (1986). Memory as assessed by recognition and reading time in normal and memory impaired people with Alzheimer's disease and other neurological disorders. *Journal of Experimental Psychology: General, 115*(4), 331–347.

Mumby, D. G., Pinel, J. P., & Wood, E. R. (1990). Nonrecurring-items delayed nonmatching-to-sample in rats: A new paradigm for testing nonspatial working memory. *Psychobiology, 18,* 321–326.

Murrell, G. A., & Morton, J. (1974). Word recognition and morphemic structure. *Journal of Experimental Psychology, 102,* 963–968.

Musen, G., & Squire, L. R. (1991). Normal acquisition of novel verbal information in amnesia. *Journal of Experimental Psychology: Learning, Memory and Cognition, 17,* 1095–1104.

Myers, C., & Conner, M. (1992). Age differences in skill acquisition and transfer in an implicit learning paradigm. *Applied Cognitive Psychology, 6,* 429–442.

Mykel, N., & Daves, W. F. (1979). Emergence of unreported stimuli into imagery as a function of laterality of presentation: A replication and extension of research by Henley and Dixon. *British Journal of Psychology, 70,* 253–258.

Myles-Worsley, M., Johnston, W. A., & Simons, M. A. (1988). The influence of expertise on X-ray image processing. *Journal of Experimental Psychology: Learning, Memory, and Cognition, 14,* 553–557.

Nadel, L. (1991). The hippocampus and space revisited. *Hippocampus, 1,* 221–229.

Naito, M. (1990). Repetition priming in children and adults: Age-related dissociation between implicit and explicit memory. *Journal of Experimental Child Psychology, 50,* 462–484.

Naito, M., & Komatsu, S. (1993). Processes involved in childhood development of implicit memory. In P. Graf & M. E. J. Masson (Eds.), *Implicit memory: New directions in cognition, development, and neuropsychology* (pp. 231–260). Hillsdale, NJ: Lawrence Erlbaum Associates.

Natsoulas, T. (1978). Consciousness. *American Psychologist, 33,* 906–914.

Naveh-Benjamin, M. (1987). Coding of spatial-location information: An automatic process? *Journal of Experimental Psychology: Learning, Memory, and Cognition, 13,* 595–605.

Naveh-Benjamin, M. (1990). Coding of temporal order information: An automatic process? *Journal of Experimental Psychology: Learning, Memory, and Cognition, 16,* 117–126.

Naveh-Benjamin, M., & Jonides, J. (1986). On the automaticity of frequency coding: Effects of competing task load, encoding strategy, and intention. *Journal of Experimental Psychology: Learning, Memory, and Cognition, 12,* 378–386.

Navon, D., & Gopher, D. (1979). On the economy of the human information processing systems. *Psychological Review, 86,* 254-255.

Naylor, J. (1962). *Parameters affecting the relative effectiveness of part and whole training methods: A review of the literature.* New York: U.S. Naval Training Devices Center Report No. 950-1.85.

Neale, M. A., & Bazerman, M. H. (1990). *Cognition and rationality in negotiation.* New York: The Free Press.

Neisser, U. (1963). The multiplicity of thought. *British Journal of Psychology, 54,* 1–14.

Neisser, U. (1967). *Cognitive psychology.* New York: Appleton–Century–Crofts.

Neisser, U., Novick, R., & Lazar, R. (1963). Searching for ten targets simultaneously. *Perceptual and Motor Skills, 17,* 955–961.

Nelson, D. L. (1994). Implicit memory. In P. Morris & M. Gruneberg (Eds.), *Theoretical aspects of memory* (pp. 130–167). London: Routledge.

Nesdale, A. R. (1987). *Ethnic stereotypes and children* (Multicultural Australia Papers No. 57), Melbourne: Clearing House on Migration Issues.

Nesdale, A. R., & McLaughlin, K. (1987). Effects of sex stereotypes on young children's memories, predictions and liking. *British Journal of Developmental Psychology, 5*, 231–241.

Nettelbeck, T. (1982). Inspection time: An index for intelligence? *Quarterly Journal of Experimental Psychology, 34A*, 299–312.

Nettelbeck, T. (1987). Inspection time and intelligence. In P. A. Vernon (Ed.), *Speed of information processing and intelligence* (pp. 295–346). New York: Ablex.

Nettelbeck, T. (1990). Intelligence does exist: A rejoinder to M. J. A. Howe. *The Psychologist: Bulletin of the British Psychological Society, 3*, 494–497.

Nettelbeck, T., & Brewer, N. (1981). Studies of mild mental retardation and timed performance. In N. R. Ellis (Ed.), *International review of research in mental retardation* (Vol. 10, pp. 61–106). New York: Academic Press.

Nettelbeck, T., & Lally, M. (1976), Inspection time and measured intelligence. *British Journal of Psychology, 67*, 17–22.

Neves, D. M., & Anderson, J. R. (1981). Knowledge compilation: Mechanisms for the automatization of cognitive skills. In J. R. Anderson (Ed.), *Cognitive skills and their acquisition* (pp. 57–84). Hillsdale, N.J.: Lawrence Erlbaum Associates.

Newcombe, F. & Young, A. W. (1989). Prosopagnosia and object agnosia without covert recognition. *Neuropsychologia, 27*, 179–191.

Newell, A. (1989). Putting it all together. In D. Klahr & K. Kotovsky (Eds.), *Complex information processing* (pp. 399–440). Hillsdale, NJ: Lawrence Erlbaum Associates.

Newell, A. (1990). *Unified theories of cognition.* Cambridge, MA: Harvard University Press.

Newell, A., & Rosenbloom, P. S. (1981). Mechanisms of skill acquisition and the law of practice. In J. R. Anderson (Ed.), *Cognitive skills and their acquisition* (pp. 1–55). Hillsdale, NJ: Lawrence Erlbaum Associates.

Newell, A., & Simon, H. A. (1972). *Human problem solving.* Englewood Cliffs, NJ: Prentice-Hall.

Newstead, S. E., & Dennis, I. (1979). Lexical and grammatical processing of unshadowed messages: A reexamination of the MacKay effect. *Quarterly Journal of Experimental Psychology, 31*, 477–488.

Niedenthal, P. M. (1990). Implicit perception of affective information. *Journal of Experimental Social Psychology, 26*, 505–527.

Niedenthal, P. M. (1992). Affect and social perception: On the psychological validity of rose-colored glasses. In R. F. Bornstein & T. S. Pittman (Eds.), *Perception without awareness: Cognitive, clinical, and social perspectives* (pp. 211–235). New York: Guilford.

Nisbett, R. E., & Wilson, T. D. (1977). Telling more than we can know: Verbal reports on mental processes. *Psychological Review, 84*, 231–259.

Nissen, M. J. (1992). Procedural and declarative learning: Distinctions and interactions. In L. R. Squire & N. Butters (Eds), *Neuropsychology of memory* (pp. 203–210). New York: Guilford.

Nissen, M. J., & Bullemer, P. (1987). Attentional requirements of learning: Evidence from performance measures. *Cognitive Psychology, 19*, 1–32.

Nissen, M. J., Knopman, D. S., & Schacter, D. L. (1987). Neurochemical dissociation of memory systems. *Neurology, 37*, 789–794.

Nissen, M. J., Willingham, D., & Hartman, M. (1989). Explicit and implicit remembering: When is learning preserved in amnesia? *Neuropsychologia, 27*, 341–352.

Norman, D. A. (1987). Some observations on mental models. In R. M. Baecker & W. A. S. Buxton (Eds.), *Readings in human-computer interaction* (pp. 241–244). Los Altos, CA: Morgan Kaufman.

Norman, D. A. (1993). *Things that make us smart: Defending human attributes in the age of the machine.* Reading, MA: Addison-Wesley.

Norman, D. A., & Bobrow, D. G. (1975). On data-limited and resource-limited processes. *Cognitive Psychology, 7*, 44–64.

Norman, R. (1975). Affective-cognitive consistency, attitudes, conformity, and behaviour. *Journal of Personality and Social Psychology, 32*, 83–91.

Norris, D. (1990). How to build a connectionist idiot (savant). *Cognition, 35*, 277–291.

Nottebohm, F. (1991). Reassessing the mechanisms and origins of vocal learning in birds. *Trends in Neurosciences, 14*, 206–211.

Nugent, K., & Mineka, S. (1994). The effect of high and low trait anxiety on implicit and explicit memory tasks. *Cognition & Emotion, 8*, 147–163.

Nunn, J. D., Stevenson, R., & Whalan, G. (1984). Selective memory effects in agoraphobic patients. *British Journal of Clinical Psychology, 23*, 195–201.

Oakhill, J., Garnham, A., & Vonk, W. (1989). The on-line construction of discourse models. *Language and Cognitive Processes, 4*, 263–286.

Oatley, K., & Johnson-Laird, P. N. (1987). Towards a cognitive theory of emotions. *Cognition & Emotion, 1*, 29–50.

O'Brien-Malone, A., & Maybery, M. T. (1994, April). *Implicit learning under incidental exposure conditions?* Paper presented at the 21st Annual Australian Experimental Psychology Conference, Sydney.

O'Connor, N., & Hermelin, B. (1984). Idiot savant calendrical calculators: Maths or memory? *Psychological Medicine, 14*, 801–806.

O'Connor, N., & Hermelin, B. (1990). The recognition failure and graphic success of idiot savant atristis. *Journal of Child Psychology and Psychiatry, 31*, 203–215.

O'Connor, N., & Hermelin, B. (1991). A specific linguistic ability. *American Journal on Mental Retardation, 95*, 673–680.

Ohlsson, S. (1992). The learning curve for writing books: Evidence from Professor Asimov. *Psychological Science, 3*, 380–382.

O'Keefe, J., & Nadel, L. (1978). *The hippocampus as a cognitive map.* Oxford, England: Oxford University Press.

Olton, D. S., Becker, J. T., & Handleman, G. E. (1979). Hippocampus, space, and memory. *Behavioral and Brain Sciences, 2*, 313–365.

Onken, J., Hastie, R., & Revelle, W. (1985). Individual differences in the use of simplification strategies in a complex decision-making task. *Journal of Experimental Psychology: Human Perception and Performance, 11*, 14–27.

Orne, M. R. (1962). On the social psychology of the psychological experiment: With particular reference to demand characteristics and their implications. *American Psychologist, 17*, 776–783.

Oskamp, S. (1962). The relationship of clinical experience and training methods to several criteria of clinical prediction. *Psychological Monographs, 76*(28, Whole No. 547).

Oskamp, S. (1965). Overconfidence in case-study judgments. *The Journal of Consulting Psychology, 29*, 261–265.

Ostergaard, A. L., & Jernigan, T. L. (1993). Are word priming and explicit memory mediated by different brain structures? In P. Graf & M. E. J. Masson (Eds.), *Implicit memory: New directions in cognition, development, and neuropsychology* (pp. 327–349). Hillsdale, NJ: Lawrence Erlbaum Associates.

Otto, T., & Eichenbaum, H. (1992). Complementary roles of the orbital prefrontal cortex and the perirhinal-entorhinal cortices in an odor-guided delayed-nonmatching-to-sample task. *Behavioral Neuroscience, 106*, 762–775.

Owens, R. (1992). *Language development. An introduction* (3rd ed.). New York: Macmillan.

Paillard, J., Michel, F., & Stelmach, C. E. (1983). Localization without content: A tactile analogue of "blindsight." *Archives of Neurology, 40*, 548–551.

Parasuraman, R. (1986). Vigilance, monitoring and search. In K. R. Boff, L. Kaufman, & J. P. Thomas (Eds.), *Handbook of perception and human performance* (pp. 1–39). New York: Wiley.

Parkin, A. J. (1979). Specifying levels of processing. *Quarterly Journal of Experimental Psychology, 31*, 179–195.

Parkin, A. J. (1982). Residual learning capability in organic amnesia. *Cortex, 18*, 417–440.

Parkin, A. J. (1988). *Memory and amnesia.* Oxford, England: Blackwell.

Parkin, A. J. (1992). The functional significance of etiological factors in human amnesia. In L. R. Squire & N. Butters (Eds.), *Neuropsychology of memory* (pp. 122–129). New York: Guilford.

Parkin, A. J. (1993). Implicit memory across the lifespan. In P. Graf & M. E. J. Masson (Eds.), *Implicit memory: New directions in cognition, development, and neuropsychology* (pp. 191–206). Hillsdale, NJ: Lawrence Erlbaum Associates.

Parkin, A. J., Dunn, J. C., Lee, C., O'Hara, P. F., & Nussbaum, L. (1993). Neuropsychological sequelae of Wernicke's Encephalopathy in a 20 year-old woman: Selective impairment of a frontal memory system. *Brain and Cognition, 21,* 1–19.

Parkin, A. J., & Leng, N. R. C. (1993). *Neuropsychology of the amnesic syndrome.* Hove, England: Lawrence Erlbaum Associates.

Parkin, A. J., & Streete, S. (1988). Implicit and explicit memory in young children and adults. *British Journal of Psychology, 79,* 361–369.

Parkinson, L., & Rachman, S. (1981). Speed of recovery from an uncontrived stress. *Advances in Behaviour Research & Therapy, 3,* 119–123.

Pascoe, E. (1986). *Awareness of cue-weighting policies in two prediction tasks.* Unpublished Honours Thesis, University of Western Australia, Perth.

Patel, V. L., & Groen, G. J. (1991). The general and specific nature of medical expertise: a critical look. In K. A. Ericsson & J. Smith (Eds.), *Toward a general theory of expertise: Prospects and limits* (pp. 93–125). Cambridge, England: Cambridge University Press.

Patrick, J., & Haines, B. (1988). Training and transfer of fault-finding skill. *Ergonomics, 31,* 193–210.

Pauker, S. G., Gorry, G. A., Kassirer, J. P., & Schwartz, W. B. (1976). Towards the simulation of clinical cognition: Taking the present illness by computer. *American Journal of Medicine, 60,* 981–996.

Paulos, J. A. (1988). *Innumeracy: Mathematical illiteracy and its consequences.* New York: Hill & Wang.

Payne, J. W. (1982). Contingent decision behavior. *Psychological Bulletin, 92,* 382–402.

Payne, J. W., Bettman, J. R., Coupey, E., & Johnson, E. J. (1992). A constructive process view of decision making: Multiple strategies in judgment and choice. *Acta Psychologica, 80,* 107–141.

Payne, J. W., Bettman, J. R., & Johnson, E. J. (1993). *The adaptive decision maker.* Cambridge, England: Cambridge University Press.

Pellegrino, J. W., & Kail, R. (1982). Process analyses of spatial aptitude. In, R. J. Sternberg (Ed.), *Advances in the psychology of human intelligence* (Vol 1, pp. 311–365). Hillsdale, NJ: Lawrence Erlbaum Associates.

Pepperberg, I. M. (1981). Functional vocalisations of an African gray parrot (*Psittacus erithacus*). *Zeitschrift für Tierpsychologie, 55,* 139–151.

Pepperberg, I. M. (1983). Cognition in the African grey parrot: Preliminary evidence for auditory/vocal comprehension of the class concept. *Animal Learning & Behavior, 11,* 179–185.

Pepperberg, I. M. (1990). Cognition in an African gray parrot (*Psittacus erithacus*): Further evidence for comprehension of categories and labels. *Journal of Comparative Psychology, 104,* 41–52.

Perdue, C. W., Dovidio, J. F., Gurtman, M. B., & Tyler, R. B. (1990). Us and them: Social categorisation and the process of intergroup bias. *Journal of Personality and Social Psychology, 59,* 475–486.

Perdue, C. W., & Gurtman, M. B. (1990). Evidence for the automaticity of ageism. *Journal of Experimental Social Psychology, 26,* 199–216.

Perecman, E. (1984). Spontaneous translation and language mixing in polyglotaphasia. *Brain & Language, 23,* 46–53.

Perfetti, C. A., Beverly, S., Bell, L., Rodgers, K. & Faux, R. (1987). Comprehending newspaper headlines. *Journal of Memory and Language, 26,* 692–713.

Perrow, C. (1984). *Normal accidents: Living with high risk technology.* New York: Basic Books.

Perruchet, P., & Amorim, M. A. (1992). Conscious knowledge and changes in performance in sequence learning: Evidence against dissociation. *Journal of Experimental Psychology: Learning, Memory, and Cognition, 18,* 785–800.

Perruchet, P., & Gallego, J. (1993). Association between conscious knowledge and performance in normal subjects: Reply to Cohen and Curran (1993) and Willingham, Greeley, and Bardone (1993). *Journal of Experimental Psychology: Learning, Memory, and Cognition, 19,* 1438–1444.

Perruchet, P., Gallego, J., & Savy, I. (1990). A critical reappraisal of the evidence for unconscious abstraction of deterministic rules in complex experimental situations. *Cognitive Psychology, 22,* 493–516.

Perruchet, P., & Pacteau, C. (1990). Synthetic grammar learning: Implicit rule abstraction or explicit fragmentary knowledge? *Journal of Experimental Psychology: General, 119,* 264–275.

Perruchet, P., & Pacteau, C. (1991). Implicit acquisition of abstract knowledge about artificial grammar: Some methodological and conceptual issues. *Journal of Experimental Psychology: General, 120,* 112–116.

Peterson, C. R., & Beach, L. R. (1967). Man as an intuitive statistician. *Psychological Bulletin, 68,* 29–46.

Petty, R. E., & Caccioppo, J. T. (1986). The elaboration likelihood model of persuasion. In I. Berkowitz (Ed.), *Advances in experimental social psychology* (Vol. 19, pp. 123–205). New York: Academic Press.

Phaf, R. H., Mul, N. M., & Wolters, G. (1994). A connectionist view on dissociations. In C. Umilta & M. Moscovitch (Eds.), *Attention and performance XV: Conscious and nonconscious information processing* (pp. 725–751). Cambridge, MA: MIT Press.

Phillips, J. G. & Hughes, B. G. (1988). Internal consistency of the concept of automaticity. In A. M. Colley & J. R. Beech (Eds.), *Cognition and action in skilled behaviour* (pp. 317–331). New York: Elsevier North Holland.

Phillips, L. D. (1984). A theory of requisite decision models. *Acta Psychologica, 56,* 29–48.

Phillips, R. J. (1978). Recognition, recall and imagery of faces. In M. M. Gruneberg, P. E. Morris, & R. N. Sykes (Eds.), *Practical aspects of memory* (pp. 270–277). London: Academic Press.

Phillips, R. R., & Mishkin, M. (1984). Further evidence of a severe impairment in associative memory following combined amygdalo-hippocampal lesions in monkeys. *Society for Neuroscience Abstracts, 10,* 136.

Philpott, A., & Wilding, J. (1979). Semantic interference from subliminal stimuli in a dichotic viewing situation. *British Journal of Psychology, 70,* 559–563.

Piaget, J. (1950). *The psychology of intelligence.* London: Routledge & Kegan Paul.

Piaget, J. (1976). *The grasp of consciousness.* Cambridge, MA: Harvard University Press.

Piaget, J., & Inhelder, B. (1973). *Memory and intelligence.* (A. J. Pomerans, Trans.). London: Routledge & Kegan Paul. (Original work published in 1968)

Pickles, A. J., & van den Broek, M. D. (1988). Failure to replicate evidence for phobic schemata in agoraphobic patients. *British Journal of Clinical Psychology, 27,* 271–272.

Pierce, C. M. (1980). Social trace contaminants: Subtle indicators of racism in TV. In S. B. Withey & R. P. Abeles (Eds.), *Television and social behavior: Beyond violence and children* (pp. 249–257). Hillsdale, NJ: Lawrence Erlbaum Associates.

Pierrehumbert, J. (1979). The perception of fundamental frequency declination. *Journal of the Acoustical Society of America, 66*(2), 363–369.

Poppel, E., Held, R., & Frost, D. (1973). Residual function of brain wounds involving the central visual pathways in man. *Nature, 243,* 295–296.

Posner, M. I., & Snyder, C. R. R. (1975). Attention and cognitive control. In R. L. Solso (Ed.), *Information processing and cognition: The Loyola symposium* (pp. 55–85). Hillsdale, NJ: Lawrence Erlbaum Associates.

Postman, L. (1961). The present status of interference theory. In C. N. Cofer (Ed.), *Verbal learning and verbal behavior* (pp. 152–179). New York: McGraw-Hill.

Postman, L. (1976). Interference theory revisited. In J. Brown (Ed.), *Recall and recognition* (pp. 157–181). London: Wiley.

Punj, G. N., & Stewart, D. W. (1983). An interaction framework of consumer decision making. *Journal of Consumer Research, 10,* 181–196.

Raaijmakers, J. G. W., & Shiffrin, R. M. (1981). Search of associative memory. *Psychological Review, 88,* 93–134.

Rabbitt, P. M. A. (1985). Oh *g* Dr. Jensen! or, *g*-ing up cognitive psychology? Open peer commentary, *Behavioral and Brain Sciences, 8,* 238–239.

Rafaelle, K. C., & Olton, D. S. (1988). Hippocampal and amygdaloid involvement in working memory for nonspatial stimuli. *Behavioral Neuroscience, 102,* 349–355.

Rajaram, S. (1996). Perceptual effects on remembering: Recollective processes in picture recognition memory. *Journal of Experimental Psychology:Learning, Memory, and Cognition, 22,* 365–377.

Rajaram, S., & Roediger, H. L., III (1993). Direct comparison of four implicit memory tests. *Journal of Experimental Psychology: Learning, Memory, and Cognition, 19,* 765–776.

Ramamurthy, K., King, W. R., & Premkumar, G. (1992). User characteristics—DSS effectiveness linkage: an empirical assessment. *International Journal of Man-Machine Studies, 36,* 469–505.

Ramaprasad, A. (1987). Cognitive process as a basis for MIS and DSS design. *Management Science, 33,* 139–148.

Rapee, R. M., McCallum, S. L., Melville, L. F., Ravenscroft, H., & Rodney, J. M. (1994). Memory bias in social phobia. *Behaviour Research & Therapy, 32,* 89–99.

Rasmussen, J. (1986). *Information processing and human-machine interaction,* Amsterdam: North Holland.

Rasmussen, J., & Lind, M. (1981). Coping with complexity. Roskilde, Denmark. Risö Laboratory Report No. M-2293.

Rasmussen, J., & Vicente, K. J. (1992). Coping with human errors through system design: implications for ecological interface design. *International Journal of Man-Machine Studies, 31,* 517–534.

Ratcliff, R., & McKoon, G. (1995). Bias in the priming of object decisions. *Journal of Experimental Psychology: Learning, Memory, and Cognition, 21,* 754–767.

Ratcliff, R., & McKoon, G. (1996). *A counter model for implicit priming in perceptual word identification.* Manuscript submitted for publication.

Ratcliff, R., & McKoon, G. (in press). Bias effects in implicit memory tasks. *Journal of Experimental Psychology: General.*

Ratcliff, R., van Zandt, T., & McKoon, G. (1995). Process dissociation, single-process theories, and recognition memory. *Journal of Experimental Psychology: General, 124,* 352–374.

Raven, J. C, Court, J. H., & Raven, J. (1987). *A manual for Raven's Progressive Matrices and Vocabulary Tests.* London: H. K. Lewis.

Rayner, K., Carlson, M., & Frazier, L. (1983). The interaction of syntax and semantics during sentence processing: Eye movements in the analysis of semantically biased sentences. *Journal of Verbal Learning and Verbal Behavior, 22,* 358–374.

Rayner, K., Garrod, S., & Perfetti, C. A. (1992). Discourse influences during parsing are delayed. *Cognition, 45,* 109–139.

Reber, A. S. (1967). Implicit learning of artificial grammars. *Journal of Verbal Learning and Verbal Behavior, 6,* 855–863.

Reber, A. S. (1969). Transfer of syntactic structure in synthetic languages. *Journal of Experimental Psychology, 81,* 115–119.

Reber, A. S. (1976). Implicit learning of synthetic languages: The role of instructional set. *Journal of Experimental Psychology: Human Learning and Memory, 2,* 88–94.

Reber, A. S. (1989a). Implicit learning and tacit knowledge. *Journal of Experimental Psychology: General, 118,* 219–235.

Reber, A. S. (1989b). More thoughts on the unconscious: Reply to Brody and to Lewicki and Hill. *Journal of Experimental Psychology: General, 118,* 242–244.

Reber, A. S. (1992). The cognitive unconscious: An evolutionary perspective. *Consciousness and Cognition, 1,* 93–133.

Reber, A. S., & Allen, R. (1978). Analogic and abstraction strategies in synthetic grammar learning: A functionalist interpretation. *Cognition, 6,* 189–221.

Reber, A. S., Allen, R., & Regan, S. (1985). Syntactical learning and judgement, still unconscious and still abstract: Comment on Dulany, Carlson, and Dewey. *Journal of Experimental Psychology: General, 114,* 17–24.

Reber, A. S., Kassin, S. M., Lewis, S., & Cantor, G. (1980). On the relationship between implicit and explicit modes in the learning of a complex rule structure. *Journal of Experimental Psychology: Human Learning and Memory, 6,* 492–502.

Reber, A. S., & Lewis, S. (1977). Implicit learning: An analysis of the form and structure of a body of tacit knowledge. *Cognition, 5,* 333–361.

Reber, A. S., Walkenfeld, F. F., & Hernstadt, R. (1991). Implicit and explicit learning: Individual differences and IQ. *Journal of Experimental Psychology: Learning, Memory, and Cognition, 17,* 888–896.

Reilly, B., & Doherty, M. E. (1989). A note on the assessment of self-insight in judgment research. *Organizational Behavior and Human Decision Processes, 44,* 123–131.

Reingold, E. M., & Merikle, P. M. (1988). Using direct and indirect measures to study perception without awareness. *Perception and Psychophysics, 44,* 563–574.

Reingold, E. M., & Merikle, P. M. (1990). On the inter-relatedness of theory and measurement in the study of unconscious processes. *Mind and Language, 5,* 9–28.

Reingold, E. M., & Toth, J. P. (in press). Process dissociations versus task dissociations: A controversy in progress. In G. Underwood (Ed.), *Implicit cognition*. New York: Oxford University Press.

Reitman, J. (1976). Skilled perception in go: Deducing memory structures from inter-response times. *Cognitive Psychology, 8*, 336–356.

Richards, A., & French, C. C. (1991). Effects of encoding and anxiety on implicit and explicit memory performance. *Personality & Individual Differences, 12*, 131–139.

Richards, A., French, C. C., Johnson, W., Naparstek, J., & Williams, J. (1992). Effects of mood manipulation and anxiety on performance of an emotional Stroop task. *British Journal of Psychology, 83*, 479–491.

Richardson-Klavehn, A., & Bjork, R. A. (1988). Measures of memory. *Annual Review of Psychology, 39*, 475–543.

Richardson-Klavehn, A., & Gardiner, J. M. (1995). Retrieval volition and memorial awareness in stem completion: An empirical analysis. *Psychological Research, 57*, 166–178.

Richardson-Klavehn, A., Gardiner, J. M., & Java, R. I. (1994). Involuntary conscious memory and the method of opposition. *Memory, 2*, 1–29.

Roberts, P. L., & MacLeod, C. (1995a). Two data structures in cognition. In P. Slezak, T. Caelli, & R. Clark (Eds.), *Perspectives on cognitive science* (pp. 157–166). Norwood NJ: Ablex.

Roberts, P. L., & MacLeod, C. (1995b) Representational consequences of two modes of learning. *The Quarterly Journal of Experimental Psychology, 48A*, 296–319.

Roberts, P. L., & MacLeod, C. (submitted) *Automatic and strategic retrieval of structure knowledge following two modes of learning.*

Roberts, P. L., & MacLeod, C. (submitted) *Implicit learning and the transfer of relational knowledge.*

Robertson, C., & Kirsner, K. (1996). *Word repetition patterns and given/new marking in normal subjects and amnesics.* Manuscript under review.

Robertson, L. C., Knight, R. T., Rafal, R., & Shimamura, A. P. (1993). Cognitive neuropsychology is more than single-case studies. *Journal of Experimental Psychology:Learning, Memory, and Cognition, 19*, 710–717.

Robin, D., Tranel, D., & Damasio, H. (1990). Auditory perception of temporal and spectral events in patients with focal left and right cerebral lesions. *Brain and Language, 39*, 539–555.

Roediger, H. L. (1990a). Implicit memory: A commentary. *Bulletin of the Psychonomic Society, 28*, 373–380.

Roediger, H. L. (1990b). Implicit memory: Retention without remembering. *American Psychologist, 45*, 1043–1056.

Roediger, H. L., III., & McDermott, K. B. (1993). Implicit memory in normal human subjects. In H. Spinnler & F. Boller (Eds.), *Handbook of neuropsychology* (pp. 63–131). Amsterdam: Elsevier.

Roediger, H. L., Rajaram, S., & Srinivas, K. (1990). Specifying criteria for postulating memory systems. In A. Diamond (Ed.), *The development and neural bases of higher cognitive functions*, (Annals of the New York Academy of Sciences, No. 608, pp. 572–595). New York: New York Academy of Sciences.

Roediger, H. L., Srinivas, K., & Weldon, M. S. (1989). Dissociations between implicit measures of retention. In S. Lewandowsky, J. C. Dunn, & K. Kirsner (Eds.), *Implicit memory: Theoretical issues* (pp. 67–84). Hillsdale, NJ: Lawrence Erlbaum Associates.

Roediger, H. L., Weldon, M. S., & Challis, B. H. (1989). Explaining dissociations between implicit and explicit measures of retention: A processing account. In H. L. Roediger & F. I. M. Craik (Eds.), *Varieties of memory and consciousness: Essays in honour of Endel Tulving* (pp. 3–41). Hillsdale, NJ: Lawrence Erlbaum Associates.

Rogers, M., & Smith, K. H. (1993, March/April). Public perceptions of subliminal advertising: Why practitioners shouldn't ignore this issue. *Journal of Advertising Research*, pp. 10–18.

Roitblat, H. L. (1993). Representations and processes in working memory. In T. R. Zentall (Ed.), *Animal cognition: A tribute to Donald A. Riley* (pp. 175–192). Hillsdale, NJ: Lawrence Erlbaum Associates.

Roitblat, H. L., Penner, R. H., & Nachtigall, P. E. (1990). Matching-to-sample by an echolocating dolphin (*Tursiops truncatus*). *Journal of Experimental Psychology: Animal Behavior Processes, 16*, 85–95.

Roorda-Hrdlickova, V., Wolters, G., Bonke, B., & Phaf, R. H. (1990). Unconscious perception during general anaesthesia, demonstrated by an implicit memory task. In B. Bonke, W. Fitch, & K. Millar (Eds.), *Memory and awareness in anaesthesia* (pp. 511–531). London: Balliere.

Rosch, E. H. (1978) Principles of categorisation. In E. Rosch & B. B. Lloyd (Eds), *Cognition and categorisation* (pp. 27–48). Hillsdale NJ: Lawrence Erlbaum Associates.

Rosen, A. M. (1981). Adult calendrical calculators in a psychiatric OPD: A report of two cases and a comparative analysis of ability. *Journal of Autisim and Developmental Disorders, 11*, 285–292.

Rosen, D. L., & Singh, S. R. (1992). An investigation of subliminal embed effect on multiple measures of advertising effectiveness. *Psychology & Marketing, 9*, 157–173.

Rosenberg, M. J. (1956). Cognitive structure and attitudinal affect. *Journal of Abnormal and Social Psychology, 53*, 367–372.

Ross, E. (1981). The aprosodias. Functional-anatomic organization of the affective components of language in the right hemisphere. *Archives of neurology, 38*, 561–569.

Ross, E., Edmondson, J., Seibert, G., & Homan, R. (1988). Acoustic analysis of affective prosody during right sided Wada Test: A within-subjects verification of the right hemisphere's role in language. *Brain and Language, 33*, 128–145.

Rothblat, L. A., & Kromer, L. F. (1991). Object recognition memory in the rat: The role of the hippocampus. *Behavioural Brain Research, 42*, 25–32.

Rouse, W. B. (1978). Human problem solving performance in a fault diagnosis task. *IEEE Transactions on Systems, Man, and Cybernetics, SMC-8*, 258–271.

Rouse, W. B., & Morris, N. M. (1986). On looking into the black box: Prospects and limits in the search for mental models. *Psychological Bulletin, 100*, 349–363.

Rozin, P. (1976). The evolution of intelligence and access to the cognitive unconscious. *Progress in Psychology and Physiological Psychology, 6*, 245–280.

Rubinstein, T., & Mason, A. F. (1979). The accident that shouldn't have happened: An analysis of Three Mile Island. *IEEE Spectrum*, 33–57.

Ruddock, K. H., & Waterfield, V. A. (1978). Selective loss of function associated with a central visual field defect. *Neuroscience Letters, 8*, 93–98.

Rueckl, J. G. (1990). Similarity effects in word and pseudoword repetition priming. *Journal of Experimental Psychology: Learning, Memory, and Cognition, 16*, 374–391.

Rumelhart, D. E., Hinton, G. E., & McClelland, J. L. (1986) A general framework for parallel distributed processing. In D. E. Rumelhart, J. L. McClelland, and the PDP Research Group (Eds.), *Parallel distributed processing*. Cambridge, MA: Bradford.

Russell, T. G., Rowe, W., & Smouse, A. D. (1991). Subliminal self-help tapes and academic achievement: An evaluation. *Journal of Counselling and Development, 69*, 359–362.

Rusted, J. M., & Dighton, K. (1991). Selective processing of threat-related material by spider phobics in a prose recall task. *Cognition & Emotion, 5*, 123–132.

Ruth, W. J., & Mostache, H. S. (1985). A projective assessment of the effects of Freudian sexual symbolism in liquor advertisements. *Psychological Reports, 56*, 183–188.

Ruth, W. J., Mostache, H. S., & Kramer, A. (1989). Freudian sexual symbolism: Theoretical considerations and an empirical test in advertising. *Psychological Reports, 64*, 1131–1139.

Ryalls, J., & Behrens, S. (1988). An overview of changes in fundamental frequency associated with cortical insult. *Aphasiology, 2*, 107–115.

Sackeim, H. A., Packer, I. K., & Gur, R. C. (1977). Hemisphericity, cognitive set and susceptibility to subliminal perception. *Journal of Abnormal Psychology, 86*, 624–630.

Sahgal, A. (1984). Hippocampal lesions disrupt recognition memory in pigeons, *Behavioural Brain Research, 11*, 47–58.

Salasoo, A., Shiffrin, R. M., & Feustel, T. C. (1985). Building permanent codes: Codification and repetition effects in word identification. *Journal of Experimental Psychology: General, 114*, 50–77.

Sales, B. D., & Haber, R. N. (1968). A different look at perceptual defence for taboo words. *Perception & Psychophysics, 3*, 156–160.

Salmon, D. P., Shimamura, A. P., Butters, N., & Smith, S. (1988). Lexical and semantic priming deficits in patients with Alzheimer's disease. *Journal of Clinical and Experimental Neuropsychology, 10*, 477–494.

Salthouse, T. A. (1991). Expertise as the circumvention of human processing limitations. In K. A. Ericsson & J. Smith (Eds.), *Toward a general theory of expertise* (pp. 286–300). Cambridge, England: Cambridge University Press.

Sanders, M. D., Warrington, E. K., Marshall, J., & Weiskrantz, L. (1974, April 20). "Blindsight": Vision in a field defect. *Lancet*, pp. 707–708.

Sanders, R. E., Gonzalez, E. G., Murphy, M. D., Liddle, C. L., & Vitina, J. R. (1987). Frequency of occurrence and the criteria for automatic processing. *Journal of Experimental Psychology: Learning, Memory, and Cognition, 13*, 241–250.

Sanders, R. E., Wise, J. L., Liddle, C. L., & Murphy, M. D. (1990). Adult age comparisons in the processing of event frequency information. *Psychology and Aging, 5*, 172–177.

Sanders, R. E., Zembar, M. J., Liddle, C. L., Gonzalez, E. G., & Wise, J. L. (1989). Developmental effects in the processing of event frequency. *Journal of Experimental Child Psychology, 47*, 142–159.

Sanderson, P. M. (1989). Verbalizable knowledge and skilled task performance: Association, dissociation, and mental models. *Journal of Experimental Psychology: Learning, Memory, and Cognition, 15*, 729–747.

Sanz, J. (1996). Memory biases in social anxiety and depression. *Cognition & Emotion, 10*, 87–105.

Saxe, G. B., & Gearhart, M. (1990). A developmental analysis of everyday topology in unschooled straw weavers. *British Journal of Developmental Psychology, 8*, 251–258.

Scarborough, D. L., Cortese, C, & Scarborough, H. S. (1977). Frequency and repetition effects in lexical memory. *Journal of Experimental Psychology: Human Perception and Performance, 3*, 1–17.

Scarborough, D. L., Gerard, L. & Cortese, C. (1979). Accessing lexical memory: The transfer of word repetition effects across task and modality. *Memory & Cognition, 7*, 3–12.

Schacter, D. L. (1987). Implicit memory: History and current status. *Journal of Experimental Psychology: Language, Memory, and Cognition, 13*(3), 501–518.

Schacter, D. L. (1989). On the relation between memory and consciousness: Dissociable interactions and conscious experience. In H. L. Roediger III & F. I. M. Craik (Eds.), *Varieties of memory and consciousness: Essays in honour of Endel Tulving* (pp. 355–389). Hillsdale, NJ: Lawrence Erlbaum Associates.

Schacter, D. L. (1990). Perceptual representation systems In A. Diamond (Ed.), *The development and neural bases of higher cognitive functions*, (Annals of the New York Academy of Sciences, No. 608, pp. 572–595). New York: New York Academy of Sciences.

Schacter, D. L. (1992a). Priming and multiple memory systems: Perceptual mechanisms of implicit memory. *Journal of Cognitive Neuroscience, 4*, 244–256.

Schacter, D. L. (1992b). Understanding implicit memory: A cognitive neuroscience approach. *American Psychologist, 47*, 559–569.

Schacter, D. L. (1993). Implicit memory: A selective review. *Annual Review of Neurosciences, 16*, 159–182.

Schacter, D. L., Bowers, J., & Booker, J. (1989). Intention, awareness, and implicit memory: The retrieval intentionality criterion. In S. Lewandowsky, J. C. Dunn, & K. Kirsner (Eds.), *Implicit memory: Theoretical issues* (pp. 47–65). Hillsdale, NJ: Lawrence Erlbaum Associates.

Schacter, D. L., Chiu, C. Y. P., & Ochsner, K. N. (1993). Implicit memory: A selective review. *Annual Review of Neuroscience, 16*, 159–182.

Schacter, D. L., Church, B., & Treadwell, J. (1994). Implicit memory in amnesic patients: Evidence for spared auditory priming. *Psychological Science, 5*, 20–25.

Schacter, D. L., & Cooper, L. A. (1995). Bias in the priming of object decisions: Logic, assumption, data. *Journal of Experimental Psychology:Learning, Memory, and Cognition, 21*, 768–776.

Schacter, D. L., Cooper, L. A., Delaney, S. M., Peterson, M. A. & Thiran, M. (1991). Implicit memory for possible and impossible objects: constraints on the construction of structural descriptions. *Journal of Experimental Psychology: Language, Memory, and Cognition, 17*(1), 3–19.

Schacter, D. L., Cooper, L. A., Tharan, M., & Rubens, A. B. (1991). Preserved priming of novel objects in patients with memory disorders. *Journal of Cognitive Neuroscience, 3*, 118–131.

Schacter, D. L., Cooper, L. A., & Treadwell, J. (1993). Preserved priming of novel objects across size transformation in amnesic patients. *Psychological Science, 4*, 331–335.

Schacter, D. L., & Graf, P. (1986). Preserved learning in amnesic patients: Perspectives from research on direct priming. *Journal of Clinical and Experimental Neuropsychology, 8,* 727–743.

Schacter, D. L., & Graf, P. (1989). Modality specificity of implicit memory for new associations. *Journal of Experimental Psychology: Learning, Memory and Cognition, 15,* 3–12.

Schacter, D. L., McAndrews, M. P., & Moscovitch, M. (1988). Access to consciousness: Dissociations between implicit and explicit knowledge in neuropsychological syndromes. In L. Weiskrantz, (Ed.), *Thought without language* (pp. 242–278). Oxford, England: Clarendon.

Schacter, D. L., & Moscovitch, M. (1984). Infants, amnesics, and dissociable memory systems. In M. Moscovitch (Ed.), *Infant memory: Its relation to normal and pathological memory in humans and other animals* (pp. 172–216). New York: Plenum.

Schacter, D. L., & Tulving, E. (1982). Memory, amnesia, and the episodic/semantic distinction. In R. L. Isaacson & N. E. Spear (Eds.), *Expression of knowledge* (pp. 33–65). New York: Plenum.

Schacter, D. L., & Tulving, E. (1994). What are the memory systems of 1994? In D. L. Schacter & E. Tulving (Eds.), *Memory systems 1994* (pp. 1–38). Cambridge, MA: MIT Press.

Schenck, F., & Morris, R. G. M. (1985), Dissociation between components of spatial memory in rats after recovery from the effects of retrohippocampal lesions. *Experimental Brain Research, 58,* 11–28.

Scherer, K. R. (1986). Vocal affect expression: A review and a model for future research. *Psychological Bulletin, 99*(2), 143–165.

Scherer, K. R., Ladd, D. R., & Silverman, K. E. A. (1984). Vocal cues to speaker affect: Testing two models. *Journal of the Acoustical Society of America, 76,* 1346–1356.

Schmidt, H. G., Boshuizen, H. P. A., & Hobus, P. P. M. (1988). Transitory stages in the development of medical expertise: The "intermediate effect" in clinical case presentation studies. In *Proceedings of the 10th Annual Conference of the Cognitive Science Society* (pp. 139–145). Hillsdale, NJ: Lawrence Erlbaum Associates.

Schneider, W., Dumais, S. T., & Shiffrin, R. M. (1984). Automatic and control processing and attention. In R. Parasuraman & D. R. Davies (Eds.), *Varieties of attention* (pp. 1–27). New York: Academic Press.

Schneider, W., & Fisk, A. D. (1982). Degree of consistent training: Improvements in search performance and automatic process development. *Perception & Psychophysics, 31,* 160–168.

Schneider, W., & Shriffrin, R. M. (1977). Controlled and automatic human information processing: I. Detection, search and attention. *Psychological Review, 84,* 1–66.

Schoenfeld, A. H., & Herrmann, D. J. (1982). Problem perception and knowledge structure in expert and novice mathematical problem solvers. *Journal of Experimental Psychology: Learning, Memory, and Cognition, 8,* 484–494.

Schroder, H. M., Driver, M. J., & Streufert, S. (1967). *Human information processing.* New York: Holt, Rinehart & Winston.

Schulman, A. I. (1973). Recognition memory and the recall of location. *Memory & Cognition, 1,* 256–260.

Schultz, E. E. (1983). Depth of processing by mentally retarded and MA-matched nonretarded individuals. *American Journal of Mental Deficiency, 88,* 307–313.

Schvaneveldt, R. W., & Meyer, D. E. (1973). Retrieval and comparison processes in semantic memory. In S. Kornblum (Ed.), *Attention and performance* (pp. 13–39). New York: Academic Press.

Schwartz, B. L., & Hashtroudi, S. (1991). Priming is independent of skill learning. *Journal of Experimental Psychology: Learning, Memory, and Cognition, 17*(6), 1177–1187.

Schwartz, S., & Griffin, T. (1986). *Medical thinking: The psychology of medical judgment and decision making.* New York: Springer-Verlag.

Schwartz, S., & Griffin, T. (1993). Comparing different types of performance feedback and computer-based instruction in teaching medical students how to diagnose acute abdominal pain. *Academic Medicine, 68,* 862–864.

Seamon, J. G., Brody, N., & Kauff, D. M. (1983). Affective discrimination of stimuli that are not recognized: II. Effect of delay between study and test. *Bulletin of the Psychonomic Society, 21,* 187–189

Secord, P. F., & Backman, C. W. (1974). *Social psychology.* New York: McGraw-Hill.

Seger, C. A. (1994). Implicit learning. *Psychological Bulletin, 115,* 163–196.

Seidenberg, M. (1992). Dyslexia in a computational model of word recognition in reading. In P. Gough, L. Ehri & R. Treiman (Eds.), *Reading acquisition* (pp. 243–273). Hillsdale, NJ: Lawrence Erlbaum Associates.

Seidenberg, M. S., Tanenhaus, M. K., Leiman, J. M., & Bienkowski, M. (1982). Automatic access of the meanings of ambiguous words in context: Some limitations of knowledge-based processing. *Cognitive Psychology, 14*, 489–537.

Servan-Schreiber, E., & Anderson, J. R. (1990). Learning artificial grammars with competitive chunking. *Journal of Experimental Psychology: Learning, Memory, and Cognition, 16*, 592–608.

Shallice, T. (1988). *From neuropsychology to mental structure*. Cambridge, England: Cambridge University Press.

Shanks, D. R., & St. John, M. F. (1994). Characteristics of dissociable human memory systems. *Behavioral and Brain Sciences, 17*, 367–447.

Shapiro, G., & Danly, M. (1985). The role of the right hemisphere in the control of speech prosody in propositional and affective contexts. *Brain and Language, 25*, 19–36.

Sharp, G. L., Cutler, B. L., & Penrod, S. D. (1988). Performance feedback improves the resolution of confidence judgments. *Organizational Behavior and Human Decision Processes, 42*, 271–283.

Shepherd, A., & Duncan, K. D. (1977). A simulator training technique for diagnosing plant failures from control panels. *Ergonomics, 18*, 627–641.

Shepherd, A., Marshall, E. C., Turner, A., & Duncan, K. D. (1977). Diagnosis of plant failures from a control panel: A comparison of three training methods. *Ergonomics, 20*, 347–361.

Sheridan, T. B. (1981). Understanding human error and aiding human diagnostic behaviour in nuclear power plants. In J. Rasmussen & W. B. Rouse (Eds.), *Human detection and diagnosis of system failures* (pp. 19–36). New York: Plenum.

Sherry, D. F. (1989). Food storing in the Paradae. *Wilson Bulletin, 101*, 289–304.

Sherry, D. F. (1992). Landmarks, the hippocampus, and spatial search in food-storing birds. Cognitive aspects of stimulus control. In W. K. Honig & J. G. Fetterman (Eds.), *Cognitive aspects of stimulus control* (pp. 185–201). Hillsdale, NJ: Lawrence Erlbaum Associates.

Sherry, D. F., & Schacter, D. L. (1987). The evolution of multiple memory systems. *Psychological Review, 94*, 439–454.

Sherry, D. F., & Vaccarino, A. L. (1989). Hippocampus and memory for food caches in black-capped chickadees. *Behavioral Neuroscience, 103*, 308–318.

Shettleworth, S. J. (1985). Questions about foraging. *Behavioral & Brain Sciences, 8*, 347–348.

Shevrin, H., & Dickman, S. (1980). The psychological unconscious: Necessary assumption for all psychological theory? *American Psychologist, 35*, 421–434.

Shiffrin, R. M., & Schneider, W. (1977). Controlled and automatic human information processing: II. Perceptual learning, automatic attending, and a general theory. *Psychological Review, 84*, 127–190.

Shimamura, A. P. (1985). Problems with the finding of stochastic independence as evidence for multiple memory systems. *Bulletin of the Psychonomic Society, 23*, 506–508.

Shimamura, A. P. (1986). Priming effects in amnesia: Evidence for a dissociable memory function. *Quarterly Journal of Experimental Psychology, 38A*, 619–644.

Shimamura, A. P. (1993). Neuropsychological analyses of implicit memory: History, methodology, and theoretical interpretations. In P. Graf & M. E. J. Masson (Eds.), *Implicit memory: New directions in cognition, development, and neuropsychology* (pp. 265–285). Hillsdale, NJ: Lawrence Erlbaum Associates.

Shimp, C. P. (1981). The local organization of behavior: Discrimination of and memory for simple behavioral patterns. *Journal of the Experimental Analysis of Behavior, 36*, 303–315.

Shimp, C. P. (1982). On metaknowledge in the pigeon: An organism's knowledge about its own behavior. *Animal Learning and Behavior, 10*, 358–364.

Shortliffe, E. (1976). *Computer-based medical consultations: MYCIN*. New York: American Elsevier.

Sidis, B. (1898). *The psychology of suggestion*. New York: Appleton.

Sidman, M., Stoddard, L. T., & Mohr, J. P. (1968). Some additional quantitative observations of immediate memory in a patient with bilateral hippocampal lesions. *Neuropsychologia, 6*, 245–254.

Sidtis, J. J., & Volpe, B. T. (1988). Selective loss of complex—Pitch or speech discrimination after unilateral lesion. *Brain and Language, 34*, 235–245.

Siegel, L., & Ryan, E. (1988). Development of grammatical-sensitivity, phonological, and short-term memory skills in normally achieving and learning disabled children. *Developmental Psychology, 24*, 28–37.

Siegler, R. S. (1987). The perils of averaging data over strategies: An example from children's addition. *Journal of Experimental Psychology: General, 116*(3), 250–264.

Siegler, R. S. (1988). Strategy choice procedures and the development of multiplication skill. *Journal of Experimental Psychology: General, 117*, 258–275.

Siegler, R. S. (1989). How domain-general and domain-specific knowledge interact to produce strategy choices. *Merrill–Palmer Quarterly, 35*(1), 1–26.

Siegler, R. S. (1991). *Children's thinking* (2nd ed.). Englewood Cliffs, NJ: Prentice-Hall.

Siegler, R. S. (1995). Children's thinking: How does change occur. In F. E. Weinert & W. Schneider (Eds.), *Memory performance and competencies: Issues in growth and development* (pp. 404–430). Hove, England: Lawrence Erlbaum Associates.

Siegler, R. S., & Jenkins, E. (1989). *How children discover new strategies.* Hillsdale, NJ: Lawrence Erlbaum Associates.

Siegler, R. S., & Shipley, C. (1995). Variation, selection, and cognitive change. In T. J. Simon & G. S. Halford (Eds.), *Developing cognitive competence: New approaches to process modeling* (pp. 31–76). Hillsdale, NJ: Lawrence Erlbaum Associates.

Siegler, R. S., & Shrager, J. (1984). Strategy choices in addition and subtraction: How do children know what to do? In C. Sophian (Ed.), *Origins of cognitive skills* (pp. 229–293). Hillsdale, NJ: Lawrence Erlbaum Associates.

Sigelman, C. K., Carr, M. B., & Begley, N. L. (1986). Developmental changes in the influence of sex-role stereotypes on person perception. *Child Study Journal, 16*, 191–205.

Simon, B. (1978). *Mind and madness in ancient Greece.* Ithaca, NY: Cornell University Press.

Simon, H. A. (1960). *The new science of management decision.* New York: Harper & Row.

Simon, H. A. (1987, February). Making management decisions: The role of intuition and emotion. *Academy of Management Executive*, pp. 57–64.

Singley, M. K., & Anderson, J. R. (1989). *The transfer of cognitive skill.* Cambridge, MA: Harvard University Press.

Slife, B. D., Miura, S., Thompson, L. W., Shapiro, J. L., & Gallagher, D. (1984). Differential recall as a fuction of mood disorder in clinically depressed patients: Between- and within-subject differences. *Journal of Abnormal Psychology, 9*, 391–400.

Sloboda, J. (1991). Musical expertise. In K. A. Ericsson & J. Smith (Eds.), *Toward a general theory of expertise* (pp. 153–171). Cambridge, England: Cambridge University Press.

Sloboda, J. A., Heremelin, B. & O'Connor, N. (1985). An exceptional musical memory. *Music Perception, 3*, 155–170.

Slovic, P., Griffin, D., & Tversky, A. (1990). Compatibility effects in judgment and choice. In R. M. Hogarth (Ed.), *Insights in decision making: A tribute to Hillel J. Einhorn* (pp. 5–27). Chicago: University of Chicago Press.

Slovic, P., & Lichtenstein, S. (1971). Comparison of Bayesian and regression approaches to the study of information processing in judgment. *Organizational Behavior and Human Performance, 6*, 649–744.

Small, W. S. (1901). An experimental study of the mental processes of the white rat. II. *American Journal of Psychology, 12*, 206–239.

Smith, A. (1989). Diurnal variations in performance, In A. M. Colley & J. R. Beech (Eds.), *Acquisition and performance of cognitive skills* (pp. 301–326). Chichester, England: Wiley.

Smith, E. E., Langston, C., & Nisbett, R. E. (1992). The case for rules in reasoning. *Cognitive Science, 16*, 1–40.

Smith, F. (1978). *Understanding reading.* New York: Holt, Rinehart & Winston.

Smith, G. A. & Stanley, G. (1983). Clocking *g*: Relating intelligence and measures of timed performance. *Intelligence, 7*, 353–368.

Smith, G. J. W., Spence, D. P., & Klein, G. S. (1959). Subliminal effects of verbal stimuli. *Journal of Abnormal Social Psychology, 59*, 167–176.

Smith, K. H., & Rogers, M. (1994). Effectiveness of subliminal messages in television commercials: Two experiments. *Journal of Applied Psychology, 79*, 866–874.

Smith, M. C., Theodor, L. & Franklin, P.E. (1983). The relationship between contextual facilitation and depth of processing. *Journal of Experimental Psychology: Learning, Memory, and Cognition, 9*, 697–712.

Snoddy, G. S. (1926). Learning and stability. *Journal of Applied Psychology, 10*, 1–36.

Snodgrass, J. G. (1989). Sources of learning in the picture fragment completion task. In S. Lewandowsky, J. C. Dunn, & K. Kirsner (Eds.), *Implicit memory: theoretical issues* (pp. 259–282). New York: Lawrence Erlbaum Associates.

Snodgrass, J. G., & Hirshman, E. (1994). Dissociations among implicit and explicit memory tasks: The role of stimulus similarity. *Journal of Experimental Psychology: Learning, Memory, and Cognition, 20*, 150–160.

Snowling, M. (1987). *Dyslexia: A cognitive developmental perspective.* Oxford, England: Basil Blackwell.

Snyder, F. W., & Pronko, H. H. (1952). *Vision with spatial inversion.* Wichita, KS: University of Wichita Press.

Somekh, D. E., & Wilding, J. M. (1973). Perception without awareness in a dichoptic viewing situation. *British Journal of Psychology, 64*, 339–349.

Sparks, R. (1992). *Television and the drama of crime. Moral tales and the place of crime in public life.* Philadelphia: Open University Press.

Spearman, C. (1904). "General intelligence," objectively determined and measured. *American Journal of Psychology, 15*, 201–293.

Spearman, C. (1927). *The abilities of man.* London: Macmillan.

Speelman, C. P., & Kirsner, K. (1990). The representation of text-based and situation-based information in discourse comprehension. *Journal of Memory and Language, 29*, 119–132.

Speelman, C. P., & Kirsner, K. (1996). Predicting transfer from training performance. Manuscript in preparation.

Speer, S., Crowder, R., & Thomas, L. (1993). Prosodic structure and sentence recognition. *Journal of Memory and Language, 32*, 336–358.

Spelke, E. S. (1987). Where perceiving ends and thinking begins: the apprehension of objects in infancy. In A. Yonas (Ed.), *Perceptual development in infancy. Minnesota Symposia on child psychology* (pp. 197–234). Hillsdale, NJ: Lawrence Erlbaum Associates.

Sperber, R. D., Ragain, R. D., & McCauley, C. (1976). Reassessment of category knowledge in retarded individuals. *American Journal of Mental Deficiency, 81*, 227–234.

Spitz, H. H. (1982). Intellectual extremes, mental age, and the nature of human intelligence. *Merrill–Palmer Quarterly, 28*, 167–192.

Spitz, H. H. (1986). *The raising of intelligence.* Hillsdale, NJ: Laurence Erlbaum Associates.

Spitz, H. H. (1994). Lewis Carroll's formula for calendrical calculating. *American Journal of Mental Retardation, 98*, 601–606.

Sprague, R. H., & Carlson, E. D. (1982). *Building effective decision support systems.* Englewood Cliffs, NJ: Prentice-Hall.

Squire, L. R. (1992). Declarative and nondeclarative memory: Multiple brain systems supporting learning and memory. *Journal of Cognitive Neuroscience, 4*, 232–243.

Squire, L. R., & Frambach, M. (1990). Cognitive skill learning in amnesia. *Psychobiology, 18*, 109–117.

Squire, L. R., & Zola-Morgan, S. (1988). Memory: Brain systems and behavior [Special Issue]. *Trends in Neurosciences, 11*, 170–175.

Stadler, M. A. (1989). On learning complex procedural knowledge. *Journal of Experimental Psychology: Learning, Memory, and Cognition, 15*, 1061–1069.

Standen, P. (1988). *Surface form in auditory and visual word recognition.* Unpublished doctoral thesis, University of Western Australia, Perth.

Stanley, W. B., Mathews, R. C., Buss, R. R., & Kotler-Cope, S. (1989). Insight without awareness: On the interaction of verbalization, instruction and practice in a simulated process control task. *The Quarterly Journal of Experimental Psychology, 41A*, 553–577.

Stanovich, K. E. (1986). Matthew effects in reading: Some consequences of individual differences in the acquisition of literacy. *Reading Research Quarterly, 21*, 360–406.

Stanovich, K. E., Cunningham, A. E., & Feeman, D. J. (1984). Intelligence, cognitive skills and early reading progress. *Reading Research Quarterly, 19*, 278–303.

Starkey, P., & Cooper, R. G. (1980). Perception of numbers by human infants. *Science, 210*, 1033–1035.

Staszewski, J. J. (1988). Skilled memory and expert mental calculation. In M. T. H. Chi, R. Glaser, & M. J. Farr (Eds.), *The nature of expertise* (pp. 71–128). Hillsdale, NJ: Lawrence Erlbaum Associates.

Stäubli, U., Ivy, G., & Lynch, G. (1984). Hippocampal denervation causes rapid forgetting of olfactory information in rats. *Proceedings of the National Academy of Science, U.S.A., 81*, 5885–5887.

Steinert, P., Fallon, D., & Wallace, J. (1976). Matching to sample in Goldfish (*Carassuius auratus*), *Bulletin of the Psychonomic Society, 8*, 265.

Sternberg, R. J. (1983). Components of human intelligence. *Cognition, 15*, 1–48.

Sternberg, R. J. (1984). Toward a triarchic theory of human intelligence. *Behavioral and Brain Sciences, 7*, 269–315.

Sternberg, R. J. (1988). Explaining away intelligence: A reply to Howe. *British Journal of Psychology, 79*, 527–533.

Sterrer, W. (1992). Prometheus and Proteus: The creative, unpredictable individual in evolution. *Evolution & Cognition, 1*, 101–129.

Stroh, N., Shaw, A. M., & Washbourn, M. F. (1908). A study in guessing. *American Journal of Psychology, 21*, 243–245.

Stroop, J. R. (1935). Studies of interference in serial verbal reactions. *Journal of Experimental Psychology, 18*, 643–662.

Stroop, J. R. (1938). Factors affecting speed in serial verbal reactions. *Psychological Monographs, 50*, 38–48.

Suboski, M. D. (1992). Releaser-induced recognition learning by amphibians and reptiles. *Animal Learning & Behavior, 20*, 63–82.

Sutherland, R. J., Wishaw, I. Q., & Kolb, B. (1983). A behavioral analysis of spatial localization following electrolytic, kainate- or colchicine-induced damage to the hippocampal formation in the rat. *Behavioral Brain Research, 7*, 133–153.

Sutton, L. J., Teasdale, J. D., & Broadbent, D. E. (1988). Negative self-schema: The effects of induced depressed mood. *British Journal of Clinical Psychology, 27*(2), 188–190.

Swart, L. C., & Morgan, C. L. (1992). Effects of subliminal backward-recorded messages on attitudes. *Perceptual and motor skills, 75*, 1107–1113.

Swinney, D. A. (1979). Lexical access during sentence comprehension: (Re)consideration of context effects. *Journal of Verbal Learning and Verbal Behavior, 18*, 645–659.

Swinney, D. A., Onifer, W., Prather, P., & Hirschkowitz, M. (1979). Semantic facilitation across sensory modalities in the processing of individual words and sentences. *Memory & Cognition, 7*, 159–165.

Tabossi, P. (1988a). Accessing lexical ambiguity in different types of sentential contexts. *Journal of Memory and Language, 27*, 324–340.

Tabossi, P. (1988b). Effects of context on the immediate interpretation of unambiguous nouns. *Journal of Experimental Psychology: Learning, Memory, and Cognition, 14*, 153–162.

Tajfel, H., & Forgas, J. P. (1981). Social categorization: Cognitions, values and groups. In J. P. Forgas (Ed.), *Social cognition: Perspectives on everyday understanding* (pp. 113–135). London: Academic Press.

Tata, P., Leibowitz, J., Prunty, M. J., Cameron, M., & Pickering, A.D. (1996). Attentional bias in obsessional disorder. *Behaviour Research & Therapy, 34*, 53–60.

Taylor, D. M., & Lalonde, R. N. (1987). Ethnic stereotypes: A psychological analysis. In L. Driedger (Ed.), *Ethnic Canada: Identities and inequalities* (pp. 347–373). Toronto: Copp Clark Pitman.

Taylor, S. E. (1981). On the interface of cognitive and social psychology. In J. Harvey (Ed.), *Cognition, social behaviour, and the environment* (pp. 241–276). Hillsdale, NJ: Lawrence Erlbaum Associates.

Taylor, S. E., & Falcone, H. (1982). Cognitive bases of stereotyping: The relationship between categorization and prejudice. *Personality and Social Psychology Bulletin, 8*(3), 426–432.

Teasdale, J. D., & Dent, J. (1987). Cognitive vulnerability to depression: An investigation of two hypotheses. *British Journal of Clinical Psychology, 26*, 113–126.

Teasdale, J. D., & Russell, M. L. (1983). Differential effects of induced mood on the recall of positive negative and neutral words. *British Journal of Clinical Psychology, 22*, 163–172.

Terrace, H. S., Petitto, L. A., Sanders, R. J., & Bever, T. G. (1979). Can an ape create a sentence? *Science, 200*, 891–902.

't Hart, J., & Cohen, R. (1973). Intonation by rule: A perceptual quest. *Journal of Phonetics, 1*, 309–327.

Thomas, G. J. & Gash, D. M. (1988). Differential effects of hippocampal ablations on dispositional and representational memory in the rat. *Behavioral Neuroscience, 102*, 635–642.

Thomas, L. (1979). Medical lessons from history. In L. Thomas (Ed.), *The medusa and the snail* (pp. 131–144). New York: Viking.

Thorndike, E. L. (1911). *Animal intelligence: experimental studies.* New York: Macmillan.

Thorne, S. B., & Himelstein, P. (1984). The role of suggestion in the perception of Satanic messages on rock-and-roll recordings. *Journal of Psychology, 116*, 245–248.

Thorsen, N. (1983). Two issues in the prosody of standard Danish. In A. Cutler & D. Ladd (Eds.), *Prosody: Models and measurements* (pp. 27–38). New York: Springer-Verlag.

Thurstone, L. L. (1931). The measurement of attitudes. *Journal of Abnormal and Social Psychology, 26*, 249–269.

Thurstone, L. L. (1938). *Primary Mental Abilities.* Chicago: University of Chicago Press.

Titchener, A. B., & Pyle, W. H. (1907). The effect of imperceptual shadows on the judgement of distance. *Practical American Philosophical Society, 46*, 94–109.

Todd, P., & Benbasat, I. (1991). An experimental investigation of the impact of computer based decision aids on decision making strategies. *Information Systems Research, 2*, 87–115.

Tompkins, C., & Mateer, C. (1985). Right hemisphere appreciation of prosodic and linguistic indications of implicit attitude. *Brain and Language, 24*, 185–203.

Torrey, L. (1979a, November 8). The accident at Three Mile Island. *New Scientist*, pp. 424–428.

Torrey, L. (1979b, April 19). The week they almost lost Pennsylvania. *New Scientist*, pp. 174–178.

Toth, J. P., Reingold, E. M., & Jacoby, L. L. (1994). Toward a redefinition of implicit memory: Process dissociations following elaborative processing and self-generation. *Journal of Experimental Psychology: Learning, Memory, and Cognition, 20*(2), 290–303.

Treisman, A. M. (1960). Contextual cues in selective listening. *Quarterly Journal of Experimental Psychology, 12*, 242–248.

Treisman, A. (1988). Features and objects: The fourteenth Bartlett memorial lecture. *Quarterly Journal of Experimental Psychology, 40A*(2), 201–237.

Treisman, A., Squire, R., & Green, J. (1974). Semantic processing in dichotic listening? A replication. *Memory & Cognition, 2*, 641–646.

Trimble, R., & Eriksen, C. W. (1966). Subliminal cues in the Muller-type illusion. *Perception & Psychophyics, 1*, 401–404.

Tuchman, G. (1978). The symbolic annihilation of women by the mass media. In G. Tuchman, A. Daniels & J. Benet (Eds.), *Hearth and home: Images of women in the mass media* (pp. 108–121). New York: Oxford University Press.

Tulving, E. (1983). *Elements of episodic memory.* New York: Oxford University Press.

Tulving, E. (1985). Multiple learning and memory systems. In K. Lagerspetz & P. Niemi (Eds.), *Psychology in the 1990's.* Amsterdam: North-Holland.

Tulving, E. (1986). What kind of a hypothesis is the distinction between episodic and semantic memory. *Journal of Experimental Psychology: Learning, Memory, and Cognition, 12*, 307–311.

Tulving, E., Hayman, C. A. G., & Macdonald, C. A. (1991). Long-lasting perceptual priming and semantic learning in amnesia: A case experiment. *Journal of Experimental Psychology: Learning, Memory, and Cognition, 17*, 595–611.

Tulving, E., & Schacter, D. L. (1990). Priming and human memory systems. *Science, 247*, 301–306.

Tulving, E., Schacter, D. L., & Stark, H. A. (1982). Priming effects in word-fragment completion are independent of recognition memory. *Journal of Experimental Psychology, Learning, Memory, and Cognition, 8*(4), 336–342.

Tunmer, W. (1989). The role of language-related factors in reading disability. In D. Shankweiler & I. Liberman (Eds.), *Phonology and reading disability: Solving the reading puzzle* (pp. 91–131). Ann Arbor: University of Michigan Press.

Tunmer, W., & Chapman, J. (1993). To guess or not to guess, that is the question: Metacognitive strategy training, phonological recoding skill, and beginning reading. *Reading Forum New Zealand, 8*, 3–14.

Tunmer, W. E., Herriman, M. L., & Nesdale, A. R. (1988). Metalinguistic abilities and beginning reading. *Reading Research Quarterly, 23*, 134–158.

Tunmer, W., & Hoover, W. (1992). Cognitive and linguistic factors in learning to read. In P. Gough, L. Ehri, & R. Treiman (Eds.), *Reading acquisition* (pp. 175–214). Hillsdale, NJ: Lawrence Erlbaum Associates.

Tunmer, W., & Hoover, W. (in press). Components of variance models of language-related factors in reading disability: A conceptual overview. In M. Joshi & C. K. Leong (Eds.), *Reading disabilities: Diagnosis and component process*. Dordrecht, Netherlands: Kluwer Academic Publishers.

Tunmer, W. E., & Nesdale, A. R. (1985). Phonemic segmentation skill and beginning reading. *Journal of Educational Psychology, 77*, 417–427.

Tunmer, W., Pratt, C., & Herriman, M. (1984). *Metalinguistic awareness in children: Theory, research and implications*. New York: Springer-Verlag.

Tunmer, W., & Rohl, M. (1991). Phonological awareness and reading acquisition. In D. Sawyer & B. Fox (Eds.), *Phonological awareness in reading: The evolution of current perspectives* (pp. 1–30). New York: Springer-Verlag.

Turvey, M. T. (1973). On peripheral and central processes in vision: Inferences from an information-processing analysis of masking with patterned stimuli. *Psychological Review, 80*, 1–52.

Tversky, A. (1969). Intransitivity of preferences. *Psychological Review, 76*, 31–48.

Tversky, A., & Kahneman, D. (1974). Judgment under uncertainty: Heuristics and biases. *Science, 185*, 1124–1131.

Tversky, A., Sattah, S., & Slovic, P. (1988). Contingent weighting in judgment and choice. *Psychological Review, 95*, 371–384.

Umeda, N. (1981). The influence of segmental factors on fundamental frequency in fluent speech. *Journal of the Acoustic Society of America, 70*, 350–355.

Underwood, G. (1976). Semantic interference from unattended printed words. *British Journal of Psychology, 67*, 327–328.

Underwood, G. (1994). Subliminal perception on TV. *Nature, 370*, 103.

Underwood, G., Whitefield, A., & Winfield, J. (1982). Effects of contextual constraints and non-fixated words in a simple reading task. *Journal of Research in Reading, 5*, 89–99.

Urban, M. J. (1992). Auditory subliminal stimulation: A re-examination. *Perceptual and Motor Skills, 74*, 515–541.

Vaissiere, J. (1983). Language—Independent prosodic features. In A. Cutler & D. Ladd (Eds.), *Prosody: Models and measurements* (pp. 53–66). New York: Springer-Verlag.

van der Colk, H. (1988). Risky behaviour resulting from bounded rationality. *Ergonomics, 31*, 485–490.

Vander Wall, S. B. (1982). An experimental analysis of cache recovery in Clark's nutcracker. *Animal Behaviour, 30*, 84–94.

Vander Wall, S. B. (1990). *Food hoarding in animals*. Chicago: University of Chicago Press.

Van Heusden, A. R. (1980). Human prediction of third-order autoregressive time series. *IEEE Transactions on Systems, Man, and Cybernetics, SMC-10*, 38–43.

van Lancker, D., & Sidtis, J. (1992). The identification of affective-prosodic stimuli by left and right hemisphere damaged subjects: All errors are not created equal. *Journal of Speech and Hearing Research, 35*, 963–970.

van Wijk, C. (1987). The psy behind phi: A Psycholinguistic model for performance structures. *Journal of Psycholinguistic Research, 16*(2), 185–199.

Vellutino, F., & Scanlon, D. (1987). Phonological coding, phonological awareness and reading ability: Evidence from a longitudinal and experimental study. *Merrill–Palmer Quarterly, 33*, 321–363.

Vellutino, F., Scanlon, D., Small, S., & Tanzman, M. (1991). The linguistic bases of reading ability: Converting written to oral language. *Text, 11*, 99–133.

Vellutino, F., Scanlon, D., & Tanzman, M. (1991). Bridging the gap between cognitive and neuropsychological conceptualizations of reading disability. *Learning and Individual Differences, 3*, 181–203.

Vicente, K. J. (1992). Memory recall in a process control system: A measure of expertise and display effectiveness. *Memory & Cognition, 20*, 356–373.

Vicente, K. J., & Rasmussen, J. (1992). Ecological interface design: Theoretical foundations. *IEEE Transactions on Systems, Man, and Cybernetics, 22*, 589–606.

Villemure, C., Plourde, G., Lussier, I., & Normandin, N. (1993). Auditory processing during isoflurane anesthesia: A study with an implicit memory task and auditory evoked potentials. In P. S. Sebel, B.

Bonke, & E. Winegrad (Eds.), *Memory and awareness in anesthesia* (pp. 99–106). Englewood Cliffs, NJ: Prentice-Hall.

Vokey, J. R., & Brooks, L. R. (1992). Salience of item knowledge in learning artificial grammars. *Journal of Experimental Psychology: Learning, Memory, and Cognition, 18,* 328–344.

Vokey, J. R., & Read, J. D. (1985). Subliminal messages. Between the devil and the media. *American Psychologist, 40,* 1231–1239.

von Frisch, K. R. (1967). *The dance language and orientation of bees.* London: Oxford University Press.

von Winterfeldt, D., & Edwards, W. (1986). *Decision analysis and behavioral research.* Cambridge, England: Cambridge University Press.

von Wright, J. M. (1973). Judgement of relative recency: Developmental trends. *The Journal of Psychology, 84,* 3–12.

von Wright, J. N., Anderson, K., & Stenman, U. (1975). Generalisation of conditioned GSRs in dichotic listening. In P. M. A. Rabbitt & S. Dornic (Eds), *Attention and performance IV* (pp. 109–127). New York: Academic Press.

Walker, P., & Myer, R. R. (1978). The subliminal perception of movement and the course of autokinesis. *British Journal of Psychology, 69,* 225–231.

Wallman, J. (1992). *Aping language.* Cambridge, England: Cambridge University Press.

Wanschura, P. B., & Borkowski, J. G. (1975). Long-term transfer of a mediational strategy by moderately retarded children. *American Journal of Mental Deficiency, 80,* 323–333.

Warrington, E. K., & Weiskrantz, L. (1968a). Amnesic syndrome: Consolidation or retrieval? *Nature, 218,* 629–630.

Warrington, E. K., & Weiskrantz, L. (1968b). New method for testing long-term retention with special reference to amnesic patients. *Nature, 217,* 972–974.

Warrington, E. K., & Weiskrantz, L. (1974). The effect of prior learning on subsequent retention in amnesic patients. *Neuropsychologia, 12,* 419–428.

Watkins, P. C., Mathews, A., Williamson, D. A., & Fuller, R. D. (1992). Mood-congruent memory in depression: Emotional priming or elaboration? *Journal of Abnormal Psychology, 101,* 581–586.

Watson, J. B. (1914). *Behavior: An introduction to comparative psychology.* New York: Holt, Rinehart & Winston.

Watson, J. B. (1924). *Behaviorism.* Chicago: University of Chicago Press.

Watts, F. N., Trezise, L., & Sharrock, R. (1986). Processing of phobic stimuli. *British Journal of Clinical Psychology, 25 ,* 253–261.

Weckowicz, T. E., & Liebel-Weckowicz, H. P. (1990). *A history of great ideas in abnormal psychology.* Amsterdam: North Holland.

Weiskrantz, L. (1993). Search for the unseen. In A. Baddeley & L. Weiskrantz (Eds.), *Attention: Selection, awareness, and control. A tribute to Donald Broadbent* (pp. 235–245). Oxford, England: Oxford University Press.

Weismer, S., & Hesketh, L. (1993). The influence of prosodic and gestural cues on novel word acquisition by children with specific language impairment. *Journal of Speech and Hearing Research, 36,* 1013–1025.

Welford, A. T. (1976). *Skilled performance.* Glenview, IL: Scott Foresman.

Wertheimer, M. (1961). Psychomotor coordination of auditory-visual space at birth. *Science, 134,* 1692.

Whitfield, D., & Jackson, A. (1982). The air traffic controller's "picture" as an example of a mental model. In G. Johannsen & J. E. Rijnsdorp (Eds.), *Analysis, design, and evaluation of man-machine systems* (pp. 45–52). London: Pergamon.

Whittlesea, B. W. A. (1989). Selective attention, variable processing and distributed representation: Preserving particular experiences of general structures. In R. G. M. Morris (Ed.), *Parallel distributed processing: Implications for psychology and neurobiology* (pp. 76–101). Oxford, England: Clarendon.

Whittlesea, B. W. A., & Dorken, M. D. (1993). Incidentally, things in general are particularly determined: An episodic-processing account of implicit learning. *Journal of Experimental Psychology: General, 122,* 227–248.

Whittlesea, B. W. A., Jacoby, L. L., & Girard, K. (1990). Illusions of immediate memory: Evidence of an attributional basis for feelings of familiarity and perceptual quality. *Journal of Memory and Language, 29,* 716–732.

Whyte, L. L. (1978). *The unconscious before Freud*. London: Longwood.

Wible, C. G., & Olton, D. S. (1988). Effect of fimbria-fornix, hippocampal, and hippocampal-amygdala lesions on performance of 8-pair concurrent object discrimination, object reversal, and T-maze alternation in rats. *Society for Neuroscience Abstracts, 14*, 232.

Wickens, C. D. (1984). *Engineering psychology and human performance*. Columbus, OH: Merrill.

Wickens, C. D. (1991). Processing resources and attention. In D. Damos (Ed.), *Multiple task performance* (pp. 3–34). London: Taylor & Francis.

Wiles, J., & Humphreys, M. S. (1993). Using artificial neural nets to model implicit and explicit test performance. In P. Graf & M. E. J. Masson (Eds.), *Implicit memory: New directions in cognition, development, and neuropsychology* (pp. 141–165). Hillsdale, NJ: Lawrence Erlbaum Associates.

Williams, A. (1938). Perception of subliminal visual stimuli. *Journal of Psychology, 6*, 187–199.

Williams, J. M. G., & Broadbent, K. (1986). Distraction by emotional stimuli: Use of a Stroop task with suicide attempters. *British Journal of Clinical Psychology, 25*, 101–110.

Williams, J. M. G., Watts, F. N., MacLeod, C., & Mathews, A. (1988). *Cognitive psychology and the emotional disorders*. Chichester, England: John Wiley.

Williams, W. L., & Whitmore, P. G. (1959). *The development and use a performance test as a basis for comparing technicians with and without experience: the Nike Ajax maintenance technicians* (Tech. Rep. No. 52). Washington, DC: George Washington University, Human Resources Research Office.

Willingham, D. B., Nissen, M. J., & Bullemer, P. (1989). On the development of procedural knowledge. *Journal of Experimental Psychology: Learning, Memory, and Cognition, 15*, 1047–1060.

Wilson, J. R., & Rutherford, A. (1989). Mental models: Theory and application in human factors. *Human Factors, 31*, 617–634.

Wingfield, A., Lombardi, L., & Sokol, S. (1984). Prosodic features and the intelligibility of accelerated speech: Syntactic versus periodic segmentation. *Journal of Speech and Hearing Research, 27*, 128–134.

Winnick, W. A., & Daniel, S. A. (1970). Two kinds of response priming in tachistoscopic recognition. *Journal of Experimental Psychology, 84*, 74–81.

Wishart, J. G., & Duffy, L. (1990). Instability of performance on cognitive tests in infants and young children with Down's syndrome. *British Journal of Educational Psychology, 60*, 10–22.

Wittengenstein, L. (1958). *Philosophical investigations*. Oxford, England: Blackwell.

Woods, D. D., O'Brien, J. F., & Hanes, L. F. (1987). Human factors challenges in process control: The case of nuclear power plants. In G. Salvendy (Ed.), *Handbook of human factors* (pp. 1724–1770). New York: Wiley.

Wright, A. A., Cook, R. G., Rivera, J. J., Sands, S. F., & Delius, J. J. (1988). Concept learning by pigeons: Matching-to-sample with trial-unique video picture stimuli. *Animal Learning & Behavior. 16*, 436–444.

Wright, G., & Bolger, F. (1992). *Expertise and decision support*. New York: Plenum.

Wrightsman, L. S., & Deaux, K. (1981). *Social psychology in the 80s* (3rd ed.). Monterey, CA: Brooks/Cole.

Wuketitis, F. M. (1986). Evolution and cognition: Paradigms, perspectives, problems. *Evolution & Cognition, 1*, 1 – 29.

Wundt, W. (1888). Selbstbeobachting und innere warnehmung [Observation of the self and inner perception] *Philosphische Studiene, 4*, 292–309.

Yates, J. (1985). The content of awareness is a model of the world. *Psychological Review, 92*, 249–284.

Yekovich, F. R., Walker, C. H., Ogle, L. T., & Thompson, M. A. (1990). The influence of domain knowledge on inferencing in low-aptitude individuals. *The Psychology of Learning and Motivation, 25*, 259–278.

Yerkes, R. M., & Dodson, J. D. (1908). The relationship of strength of stimulus to rapidity of habit formation. *Journal of Comparative Neurological Psychology, 18*, 459–482.

Young, R. L., & Nettelbeck, T. (1994). The "intelligence" of calendrical calculators. *American Journal of Mental Retardation, 99*, 186–200.

Young, S. (1990). Use of dialogue, pragmatics and semantics to enhance speech recognition. *Speech Communication, 9*(5–6), 551–564.

Zajonc, R. B. (1968). Attitudinal effects of mere exposure. *Journal of Personality and Social Psychology Monograph Supplement, 9* (2, Pt. 2), 1–27.

Zajonc, R. B. (1980). Feeling and thinking. *American Psychologist, 35,* 151–175.

Zajonc, R. B. (1984). On the primacy of affect. *American Psychologist, 39,* 117–123.

Zajonc, R. B., Shaver, P., Tavris, C., & Van Kreveld, D. (1972). Exposure, satiation, and stimulus discriminability. *Journal of Personality and Social Psychology, 21,* 270–280.

Zanna, M. P., & Rempel, J. K. (1988). Attitudes: A new look at an old concept. In D. Bar-Tal & A.W. Kruglanski (Eds.), *The social psychology of knowledge* (pp. 315–334). Cambridge, England: Cambridge University Press.

Zanot, E. J., Pincus, J. D., & Lamp, E. J. (1983). Public perceptions of subliminal advertising. *Journal of Advertising, 12,* 39–45.

Zigler, E., & Balla, D. (1982). Motivational and personality factors in the performance of the retarded. In E. Zigler & D. Balla (Eds), *Mental retardation: The developmental-difference hypothesis* (pp. 9–26). Hillsdale, NJ: Lawrence Erlbaum Associates.

Zihl, J., & Werth, R. (1984). Contributions to the study of "blindsight": I. Can stray light account for saccadic localization in patients with postgeniculate field defects? *Neuropsychologia, 22*(1), 1–11.

Zola-Morgan, S., & Squire, L. R. (1985). Medial temporal lesions in monkeys impair memory on a variety of tasks sensitive to human amnesia. Behavioral *Neuroscience, 99,* 22–34.

Zola-Morgan, S., Squire, L. R., & Mishkin, M. (1982). The neuroanatomy of amnesia: Amygdala-hippocampus vs. temporal stem. *Science, 218,* 1337–1339.

AUTHOR INDEX

SUBJECT INDEX

E